ABUSE OF EU LAW AND REGULATION OF THE INTERNAL MARKET

How can the concept of abuse of European Union law—which can be defined as an undesirable choice of law artificially made by a private citizen—generate so much disagreement among equally intelligent individuals? Seeking to transcend the classical debate between its supporters and adversaries, the present study submits that the concept of abuse of EU law is located on three major fault-lines of EU law, which accounts for the well-established controversies in the field.

The first fault-line, which is common to all legal orders, opposes legal congruence (the tendency to yield equitable legal outcomes) to legal certainty (the tendency to yield predictable legal outcomes). Partisans of legal congruence tend to advocate the prohibition of abuses of law, whereas partisans of legal certainty tend to oppose it.

The second fault-line is specific to EU law and divides two conceptions of the regulation of the internal market. If economic integration is conceived as the promotion of cross-border competition among private businesses (the paradigm of 'regulatory neutrality'), choices of law must be proscribed as abusive, for they distort business competition. But if economic integration is intended to promote competition among Member States (the paradigm of 'regulatory competition'), choices of law by EU citizens represent a desirable process of arbitrage among national laws.

The third and final fault-line corresponds to the tension between two orientations of the economic constitution of the European Union, namely the fear of private power and the fear of public power. Those who fear private power more than public power tend to endorse the prohibition of abuses of law, whereas those who fear public power more than private power tend to reject it.

Seen in this way, the concept of abuse of EU law offers a forum in which fundamental questions about the nature and function of EU law can be confronted and examined in a new light.

In May 2013, the thesis that this book was based on won the First Edition of the European Law Faculties Association Award for Outstanding Doctoral Thesis.

Abuse of EU Law and Regulation of the Internal Market

Alexandre Saydé

·HART·
PUBLISHING
OXFORD AND PORTLAND, OREGON
2016

Published in the United Kingdom by Hart Publishing Ltd
16C Worcester Place, Oxford, OX1 2JW
Telephone: +44 (0)1865 517530
Fax: +44 (0)1865 510710
E-mail: mail@hartpub.co.uk
Website: http://www.hartpub.co.uk

Published in North America (US and Canada) by
Hart Publishing
c/o International Specialized Book Services
920 NE 58th Avenue, Suite 300
Portland, OR 97213-3786
USA
Tel: +1 503 287 3093 or toll-free: (1) 800 944 6190
Fax: +1 503 280 8832
E-mail: orders@isbs.com
Website: http://www.isbs.com

First published in hardback 2014
Paperback edition, 2016

Hart Publishing is an imprint of Bloomsbury Publishing plc.

British Library Cataloguing in Publication Data
Data Available

ISBN: HB: 978-1-84946-528-1
PB: 978-1-50990-740-3

Typeset by Compuscript Ltd, Shannon
Printed and bound in Great Britain by
Lightning Source UK Ltd

'Ten Thousand Laws more cannot reach so far, but Malice goes beyond'.[1]

Samuel Daniel, English poet and historian (1562–1619)

[1] S Daniel, 'Epistle to Sir Thomas Egerton' in S Daniel (ed), *Poetical Works*, vol II (London, R Gosling et al, 1718) 345.

To all the victims of these pages,

Friends and relatives, all too often neglected for a few more lines,

Bruno de Witte, who patiently commented on their ever-evolving content,

Susanna Greijer-Saydé, who graciously lived with them

and the author of these lines.

Foreword

Anyone who reads the first chapter with concentration and looks at the table of contents can immediately see that this is an original book which is worth reading. Although its focus is European Union law, some of the analysis is also relevant to purely national law questions. I think it outstandingly well done.

'Abuse of law', 'abuse of rights', just plain 'abuse' or 'sham' or 'artificial construction' are phrases which spring to mind in cases where someone, to use the English phrase, is being 'too clever by half' and whom the Germans would describe as 'neunmalklug' or nine times clever. He produces a result which seems to get round a law. The careful judge, who feels that this cannot be allowed, will try and formulate in legal terms exactly why. Different judges, whose instincts as to the just result are the same, will employ analyses which differ from one another. Some simply forego any profound analysis. These concepts have intrigued me over the years and I always had it in mind to try and write something. I never did and I am delighted that Saydé has. There are things which a fine academic mind can do better than a judge writing a judgment. He identifies different types of analysis which the Court has adopted over the years and makes a useful attempt to pull the learning together.

I recollect a prosecution under English domestic law 40 years ago for selling a writing desk on a Sunday—which at that stage was illegal in England. One was allowed to sell carrots but not furniture. The seller had a showroom full of furniture and also a supply of carrots. He offered carrots for sale at a price of, I think, two hundred pounds each. By way of an inducement he offered buyers a gift of a bed or a desk with each carrot which they bought. A number of people bought these very expensive carrots and gratefully received the gift of furniture. The first instance court acquitted him of selling the writing desk but on appeal he was convicted. At the time, while I was at ease with the result, I felt that the Court's analysis lacked profundity. On arrival at the CJEU I found myself rapporteur in *Levob*,[1] which Saydé cites under a heading 'Informal doctrine of abuse', where the Court was faced with a similar artificial splitting of a transaction and had a similar lack of tolerance towards it.

It is common for an experienced judge to look at a set of papers, to understand the broad nature of the dispute before him, to have an intuitive reaction as to how it should be resolved and yet initially to be unclear in his own mind as to the best legal path which enables him to arrive at the conclusion which seems to him to be appropriate. Finding that path is often a matter of seeking to identify

[1] Case C-41/04 *Levob* [2005] ECR I-9433.

questions of fact and of law and then setting out the answers to those questions and the steps which have caused him to arrive at those answers. Sometimes in the course of writing a judgment one will reformulate the questions, sometimes reformulate the answers and occasionally one will come to the conviction that one's intuitive reaction does not stand up to scrutiny.

I had the privilege, when a judge of the Court of Justice of the EU, of having Alexandre Saydé as one of my legal secretaries who aided me in this process, challenging in discussion my intuitive reaction or my choice of path to the conclusion. Anyone who reads this book will immediately see why I think myself privileged to have had his assistance. He has a rare capacity for unravelling a tangled skein of thought and laying out the strands so that they can be examined and tested.

Sir Konrad Schiemann
Judge at the Court of Justice of the EU from 2004 to 2012

Table of Contents

Foreword vii
Lists of Tables and Figures xiii
Table of Cases xv
Table of Legislation xxix

General Introduction: The Topicality of the Concept of Abuse of Union Law 1

PART I: THE PHENOMENON OF ABUSE OF UNION LAW

Introduction: A Dynamic Perspective on Abuses of Union Law 9

1. Identification of the Phenomenon of Abuse of Union Law 11
- I. Abuses Committed by Public Authorities 16
- II. Abuses Committed by Private Individuals 19
  - A. Abuses Private-Private (including Abuses of Rights) 19
  - B. Abuses Private-Public (including Abuses of Law) 23
- III. Abuses of Law and Abuses of Rights under Union Law 27
- IV. The Universality of the Prohibition of Abuses 32

2. The Formal Doctrine of Abuse of Union Law 44
- I. At the Legislative Origins of the Formal Doctrine of Abuse of Union Law 44
- II. Applications of the Formal Doctrine of Abuse in the Field of Export Refunds 49
  - A. *Emsland-Stärke* (2000) 50
    - i. Facts 50
    - ii. Decision of the Court 50
  - B. *Vonk Dairy Products* (2007) 52
    - i. Facts 52
    - ii. Decision of the Court 52
- III. Applications of the Formal Doctrine of Abuse in the Field of VAT 53
  - A. *Halifax* (2006) 55
    - i. Facts 55
    - ii. Decision of the Court 58
  - B. *Part Service* (2008) 60
    - i. Facts 60
    - ii. Decision of the Court 62

IV. Applications of the Formal Doctrine of Abuse in the Field of Direct Taxation 63
A. *Cadbury Schweppes* (2006) 64
i. Facts 64
ii. Decision of the Court 66
B. *Thin Cap Group Litigation* (2007) 69
i. Facts 69
ii. Decision of the Court 70
V. Other Applications of the Formal Doctrine of Abuse in the Field of Free Movement 72
A. *Agip Petroli* (2006) 72
i. Facts 72
ii. Decision of the Court 73
B. *ING. AUER* (2007) 74
i. Facts 74
ii. Decision of the Court 76

3. Definition of the Concept of Abuse of Union Law 78
I. The Basics: Abuse of Law as Gain-Seeking Choice of Law 79
II. The Artificiality Requirement: Abuse of Law as Naked Choice of Law 83
A. Artificiality as Economic Irrationality 84
B. The Fallacy of Economic Reality 89
III. The Teleological Assessment: Abuse of Law as Undesirable Choice of Law 93
IV. The Sanction: Denying the Choice of Law 98

4. Typology of Union Law Reactions to Artificial Practices 102
I. Informal Doctrines of Abuse of Law 104
II. Suspect Periods 114
III. Centres of Gravity 120
A. Centre of Gravity Approaches for Legal Persons (Real Seat Theory) 121
i. Applications of the 'Real Seat Theory' in Union Law 122
ii. 'Output' versus 'Input' Centre of Gravity 131
B. Centre of Gravity Approaches for Natural Persons (Habitual Residence and Genuine Integration Requirements) 137
i. 'Habitual Residence' Requirements 138
ii. The 'Genuine Integration' Requirement 141
IV. Incidental Prevention of Artificial Practices 149
V. Free Choice of Law 154

5. Abuse of Union Law and Legal Certainty 167
I. The Trade-off between Legal Certainty and Legal Congruence 167
A. The Universality of the Trade-off between Legal Certainty and Legal Congruence 168

B. The Trade-off between Legal Certainty and Legal Congruence in Union Law 175
II. Legal Certainty as Source of Abusive Practices....183
A. Abuses of Rigid Union Laws 183
B. The Congruence Gap as Room for Abusive Practices 189
III. The Fight against Abusive Practices as Source of Legal Congruence....192
A. The Legal Uncertainty Inherent to the Doctrine of Abuse 193
B. Fighting Abusive Practices by Enacting Flexible Legal Norms....202

Conclusion: The Certainty of Abuse and the Illusion of Legal Certainty....211

PART II: ABUSES OF UNION LAW AND ECONOMIC INTEGRATION

Introduction: The Ambivalent Notion of Free 'Movement' 221

6. The Competing Paradigms of Economic Integration.... 227
I. The Function of Local Laws in a Process of Economic Integration 229
II. The Paradigm of Regulatory Neutrality: Economic Integration as Business Competition....235
III. The Paradigm of Regulatory Competition: Economic Integration as State Competition 242

7. Dilemmas in the Regulation of the Internal Market.... 249
I. Protectionism....250
II. Multiple Regulation....254
III. The Eventuality of Positive Harmonisation....259
IV. The Negative Harmonisation Conundrum 264
A. Home Regulation and Host Regulation 264
B. The Negative Harmonisation Conundrum....272
C. Addressing the Negative Harmonisation Conundrum....276
V. The Regulatory Mobility Dilemma 279
A. Regulatory Immobility under Multiple Regulation and Union Regulation....280
B. Regulatory Mobility under Home Regulation and Host Regulation 283
C. Addressing the Regulatory Mobility Dilemma 286
VI. Synthesis: The Trade-off between Regulatory Neutrality and Regulatory Competition 291

8. Reviewing Practical Issues of Free Movement Law.... 296
I. The Ambivalent Status of Differentials of Regulation 296
II. The Acceptance of Reverse Discriminations....301
III. The Inconsistent Prohibition of Abuses of Union Law....304
IV. The Ambiguity Towards Social Dumping....309

9. State Aids and Economic Integration **315**
I. The State Aids Regime between Regulatory Neutrality and Regulatory Competition 315
II. Reviewing the Classical Definition of 'State Aid' under Union Law 321
III. The Functional Parallelism between Prohibition of Abuses of Law and Prohibition of State Aids 331

10. Abuse of Union Law and the Economic Constitution of the European Union **340**
I. The Notion of Economic Constitution of the European Union 341
II. Historical Conditions of the Emergence of the Phenomenon of Abuse of Union Law 348
III. The Rise of a New Form of Private Power Originating in Mobility 354
IV. Dealing with Private Mobility-Power 360

Conclusion: One (Internal Market) Law, Two Competitions **365**

General Conclusion: The Concept of Abuse of Union Law as a Privileged Forum for Thinking about Union Law **370**

Annex 378

Bibliography 406

Index 459

Lists of Tables and Figures

List of Tables

Table 1 – Union Official Documents Mentioning the Term 'Abuse' (1954–2009): Data 12
Table 2 – Evolution of the 'Abuse Distribution' (1954–2009): Data 14
Table 3 – Treatment of Abuses of Rights and Abuses of Law in Selected EU Countries 41
Table 4 – Judgments Applying the Doctrine of Abuse, Sorted by Chronological Order 47
Table 5 – *Halifax*: Detail of the Transactional Structure 56
Table 6 – Distinguishing the Abuse of Union Law 79
Table 7 – Abuse of Law as Election of a Pleasing Legal Cloak 81
Table 8 – The Trade-off between Legal Certainty and Legal Congruence 170
Table 9 – Rigid Wording versus Flexible Wording of Legal Norms 171
Table 10 – Abuse of Union Law and the Illusion of Legal Certainty 215
Table 11 – Regulatory Mobility versus Socioeconomic Mobility 222
Table 12 – Five Issues in the Regulation of the Internal Market 291
Table 13 – Regulatory Modes of the Internal Market 293
Table 14 – Parallel Case Studies of Abuse of Law and State Aid 339
Table 15 – One (Internal Market) Law, Two Competitions 367
Table 16 – Case Study: a Holistic Approach to Union Company Law 376

List of Figures

Figure 1 – Union Official Documents Mentioning the Term 'Abuse' (1954–2009): Chart 11
Figure 2 – Evolution of the 'Abuse Distribution' (1954–2009): Chart 15
Figure 3 – *Halifax*: Detail of the VAT Flows 57
Figure 4 – *Part Service*: Detail of VAT Flows 61
Figure 5 – Structure of the Cadbury Schweppes Group 66
Figure 6 – ING. AUER: Transactional Structure 75
Figure 7 – The Congruence Gap 190

Figure 8 – *Emsland-Stärke* between Legal Certainty and Legal Congruence.....199
Figure 9 – Artificial Practices, Legal Congruence and Legal Certainty..............204
Figure 10 – *Agip Petroli* and the Function of Local Laws in a Process of Economic Integration 232
Figure 11 – Negative Harmonisation Conundrum and Regulatory Mobility Dilemma...283
Figure 12 – State Aids and Paradigms of Economic Integration........................319
Figure 13 – A Conceptual Timeline of the Regulation of the Internal Market 350
Figure 14 – An Analytical Matrix for Thinking about Union Law.....................373

Table of Cases*

Court of Justice of the European Union

Joined Cases 7/56 and 3/57 to 7/57 Algera v ECSC Common Assembly [1957] ECR 39 .... 17, 18
Case 1/58 Stork v ECSC High Authority [1958] ECR 43 18
Case 9/61 Netherlands v ECSC High Authority [1962] ECR 413 21
Case 26/62 van Gend and Loos [1963] ECR 3 .... 181, 346
Case 6/64 Costa v ENEL [1964] ECR 1141 .... 181, 252
Joined Cases 56 and 58/64 Établissements Consten [1966] ECR 429 .... 19, 241
Case 17/68 Reinarz [1969] ECR 61 17
Case 24/68 Commission v Italy ('Statistical Levy') [1969] ECR 193 252
Case 45/69 Boehringer Mannheim v Commission [1970] ECR 769 18
Case 48/69 ICI v Commission (Dyestuffs) [1972] ECR 619 111–12
Case 35/70 Manpower [1970] ECR 1251 275
Case 78/70 Deutsche Grammophon [1971] ECR 487 .... 238, 347
Case 46/72 De Greef v Commission [1973] ECR 543 18
Case 13/73 Angenieux [1973] ECR 935 140
Case 173/73 Italy v Commission [1974] ECR 709 17
Case 2/74 Reyners [1974] ECR 631 .... 67, 252
Case 8/74 Dassonville [1974] ECR 837 241
Case 33/74 Van Binsbergen [1974] ECR 1299 .... 16, 49, 120–21, 371
Case 39/75 Coenen [1975] ECR 1547 .... 121, 195
Case 43/75 Defrenne II [1976] ECR 455 .... 298–99, 300, 368
Case 125/75 Eierkontor I [1976] ECR 771 .... 49, 153–54
Case 28/76 Milac GmbH Groß- und Außenhandel [1976] ECR 1639 18
Case 44/76 Eierkontor II [1977] ECR 393 49
Case 76/76 Di Paolo [1977] ECR 315 .... 160, 195
Case 85/76 Hoffmann-La Roche [1979] ECR 461 19
Case 125/76 Cremer [1977] ECR 1593 .... 51, 53, 58, 73
Case 13/77 GB-INNO-BM v Association des Détaillants en Tabac (ATAB) [1977] ECR 2115 316
Case 82/77 Van Tiggele [1978] ECR 25 .... 297–98, 301, 312, 328, 368
Case 102/77 Hoffmann-La Roche [1978] ECR 1139 19
Case 1/78 Kenny [1978] ECR 1489 274
Case 35/78 Schouten [1978] ECR 2543 18
Case 115/78 Knoors [1979] ECR 399 .... 66, 88, 106, 118, 281
Case 120/78 Rewe-Zentral ('Cassis de Dijon') [1979] ECR 649 .... 105, 176, 235, 246, 254, 258, 264–65, 270–71, 273, 303, 350, 351, 361

* Any case listed within the Annex that does not appear in the text is not referenced in these tables.

Case 128/78 Commission v United Kingdom [1979] ECR 419 21
Case 136/78 Auer [1979] ECR 437 ....257, 273
Case 159/78 Commission v Italy [1979] ECR 3247 ....238, 347
Case 175/78 Saunders [1979] ECR 1129 268
Case 243/78 Simmenthal v Commission [1980] ECR 593 ....21, 27
Case 250/78 DEKA [1983] ECR 421 31
Case 730/79 Philip Morris Holland [1980] ECR I-2671 327
Case 246/80 Broekmeulen [1981] ECR 2311 303
Case 250/80 Töpfer [1981] ECR 2465 ....153, 154
Case 268/80 Guglielmi v European Parliament [1981] ECR 2295 18
Case 272/80 Frans-Nederlandse Maatschappij voor Biologische Producten [1981] ECR 3277 270
Case 15/81 Schul [1982] ECR 1409 ....238, 347
Case 53/81 Levin [1982] ECR 1035 ....157, 158, 194, 286
Case 249/81 Commission v Ireland (Buy Irish) [1982] ECR I-4005 326
Case 283/81 CILFIT [1982] ECR 3415 181
Case C-203/82 Commission v Italy [1983] ECR 2525 337
Case 126/83 STS v Commission [1984] ECR 2769 18
Joined Cases 140, 146, 221 and 226/82 Walzstahl-Vereinigung v Commission [1984] ECR 951 18
Case 338/82 Albertini and Montagnani [1984] ECR 2123 21
Case 346/82 Pierre Favre v Commission [1984] ECR 2269 17
Case 8/83 Officine Fratelli Bertoli v Commission [1984] ECR 1649 18
Case 35/83 BAT Cigaretten-Fabriken [1985] ECR 363 23
Joined Cases 187 and 190/83 Nordbutter [1984] ECR 2553 24
Case 191/83 Salzano [1984] ECR 3741 159
Case 207/83 Commission v United Kingdom ('Original Marking') [1985] ECR 1201 ....238, 347
Case 229/83 Leclerc [1985] ECR 1 ....105, 297
Case 249/83 Hoeckx [1985] ECR 973 114
Case 18/84 Commission v France [1985] ECR 1339 316
Case 21/84 Commission v France ('Postal franking machine') [1985] ECR 1355 252
Case 41/84 Pinna [1986] ECR 1 159
Case 44/84 Hurd [1986] ECR 29 301
Case 54/84 Michael Paul [1985] ECR 915 26
Case 103/84 Commission v Italy [1986] ECR 1759 316
Case 122/84 Scrivner [1985] ECR 1027 114
Case 168/84 Berkholz [1985] ECR 2251 ....129, 130
Case 188/84 Commission v France ('Woodworking Machines') [1986] ECR 419 270
Case 197/84 Steinhauser [1985] ECR 1819 252
Case 234/84 Belgium v Commission [1986] ECR 2263 323
Case 1/85 Miethe [1986] ECR 1837 160
Case 9/85 Nordbutter II [1986] ECR 2831 24
Case 66/85 Lawrie-Blum [1986] ECR 2121 ....157–58, 286
Case 79/85 Segers [1986] ECR 2375 ....26, 222, 267, 304
Joined Cases C-89/85, C-104/85, C-114/85, C-116/85, C-117/85 and C-125/85 to C-129/85 Ahlström Osakeyhtiö and Others v Commission (Woodpulp) [1993] ECR I-1307 ....133–34, 135, 137

Case 139/85 Kempf [1986] ECR 1741 .... 156, 157, 158, 286
Joined Cases 277/85 and 300/85 Canon v Council [1988] ECR 5731 18
Case 314/85 Foto-Frost [1987] ECR 4199 18
Case 316/85 Lebon [1987] ECR 2811 .... 114, 268
Case 39/86 Lair [1988] ECR 3161 .... 26, 106, 114, 146
Case 46/86 Romkes [1987] ECR 2671 .... 165, 166
Case 98/86 Mathot [1987] ECR 809 301
Case 197/86 Brown [1988] ECR 3205 157
Case 223/86 Pesca Valentia [1988] ECR 83 165
Case 292/86 Gullung [1988] ECR 111 150–51
Case C-3/87 Agegate [1989] ECR 4459 165
Case 81/87 Daily Mail [1988] ECR 5483 .... 16, 103, 149
Case C-216/87 Jaderow [1989] ECR 4509 165–66
Case 236/87 Bergemann [1988] ECR 5125 160
Case 284/87 Schäflein [1988] ECR 4475 141
Case C-333/87 France v Commission [1989] ECR 3773 24
Case 341/87 EMI Electrola [1989] ECR 79 23
Case 382/87 Buet [1989] ECR 1235 20
Case 130/88 van de Bijl [1989] ECR 3039 118
Case 145/88 B & Q (Sunday Trading) [1989] ECR 3851 254
Case C-2/89 Kits van Heijningen [1990] ECR I-1755 159
Case C-61/89 Bouchoucha [1990] ECR I-3551 .... 66, 106, 150, 154, 257, 258, 280–81
Case C-93/89 Commission v Ireland [1991] ECR I-4569 .... 26, 165
Case C-113/89 Rush Portuguesa [1990] ECR I-1417 .... 127, 268, 275, 311, 338
Case C-213/89 Factortame I [1990] ECR I-2433 165
Case C-216/89 Reibold [1990] ECR I-4163 195
Case C-221/89 Factortame II [1991] ECR I-3905 .... 67, 127, 128, 165, 166, 201, 333
Case C-235/89 Commission v Italy [1992] ECR I-777 23
Case C-246/89 Commission v United Kingdom [1991] ECR I-4585 .... 67, 127, 165
Order of the President in Case C-246/89 R Commission v United Kingdom [1989] ECR 3125 165
Case C-279/89 Commission v United Kingdom [1992] ECR I-5785 165
Case C-288/89 Gouda [1991] ECR I-4007 255
Case C-292/89 Antonissen [1991] ECR I-745 156
Case C-297/89 Ryborg [1991] ECR I-1943 138
Case C-340/89 Vlassopoulou [1991] ECR I-2357 269
Case C-357/89 Raulin [1992] ECR I-1027 .... 146, 157, 158, 286
Joined Cases C-19/90 and C-20/90 Karella and Karellas [1991] ECR I-2691 22
Case C-286/90 Poulsen [1992] ECR I-6019 .... 163, 163–64, 333, 334, 339, 371
Case C-369/90 Micheletti [1992] ECR I-4239 162
Case C-370/90 Singh [1992] ECR I-4265 .... 26, 106, 160
Joined Cases C-72/91 and C-73/91 Sloman Neptun [1993] ECR I-887 328
Case C-89/91 Shearson Lehman Hutton [1993] ECR I-139 328
Case C-102/91 Knoch [1992] ECR I-4341 .... 160, 195

Joined Cases C-134/91 and C-135/91 Kerafina-Keramische and Vioktimatiki [1992] ECR I-5699 22
Case C-148/91 Veronica Omroep Organisatie [1993] ECR I-487 ....124–26, 132
Joined Cases C-267/91 and C-268/91 Keck and Mithouard [1993] ECR I-6097 272
Case C-317/91 Deutsche Renault [1993] ECR I-6227 18
Case C-326/91 P Henri de Compte v European Parliament [1994] ECR I-2091 18
Case C-8/92 General Milk Products [1993] ECR I-779 ....51, 58, 73, 195
Case C-19/92 Dieter Kraus [1993] ECR I-1663 ....106, 117, 281, 361
Joined Cases C-278/92, C-279/92 and C-280/92 Spain v Commission [1994] ECR I-4103 324
Case C-292/92 Hünermund [1993] ECR I-6787 272
Case C-379/92 Peralta [1994] ECR I-3453 ....275, 301, 302, 304
Case C-23/93 TV10 [1994] ECR I-4795 .... 124, 125, 126, 131, 132, 363
Case C-43/93 Vander Elst [1994] ECR I-3803 276
Joined Cases C-46/93 and C-48/93 Brasserie du Pêcheur and Factortame ('Factortame III') [1996] ECR I-1029 18
Case C-76/93 P Scaramuzza v Commission [1994] ECR I-5173 17
Case C-347/93 Boterlux [1994] ECR I-3933 ....28, 49, 50, 154, 195
Case C-384/93 Alpine Investments [1995] ECR I-1141 20
Case C-452/93 P Magdalena Fernández [1994] ECR I-4295 141
Case C-4/94 BLP [1995] ECR I-983 ....59, 194
Case C-13/94 P v S [1996] ECR I-2143 149
Joined Cases C-29/94 to C-35/94 Aubertin [1995] ECR I-301 ....301, 303, 304, 368
Case C-55/94 Gebhard [1995] ECR I-4165 67
Case C-177/94 Perfili [1996] ECR I-161 ....275, 302–03, 304
Case C-198/94 Italy v Commission [1996] ECR I-2797 17
Case C-206/94 Paletta II [1996] ECR I-2357 ....25, 87
Case C-222/94 Commission v United Kingdom [1996] ECR I-4025 ....26, 124–25, 132
Case C-231/94 Faaborg-Gelting Linien [1996] ECR I-2395 111
Joined Cases C-283/94, C-291/94 and C-292/94 Denkavit International [1996] ECR I-5063 119
Case C-293/94 Brandsma [1996] ECR 1-3159 270
Case C-27/95 Bakers of Nailsea [1997] ECR I-1847 19
Case C-28/95 Leur-Bloem [1997] ECR I-4161 ....106, 109, 119
Joined Cases C-34/95 to C-36/95 De Agostini [1997] ECR I-3843 ....151–52, 154
Case C-54/95 Germany v Commission [1999] ECR I-35 49
Case C-124/95 Centro-Com [1997] ECR I-81 24
Case C-166/95 P Commission v Daffix [1997] ECR I-983 17
Case C-260/95 DFDS [1997] ECR I-1005 ....110–11, 129–30, 132, 287
Case C-296/95 EMU Tabac [1998] ECR I-1605 111
Case C-184/96 Commission v France (Foie Gras) [1998] ECR I-6197 272
Case C-264/96 ICI [1996] ECR I-4695 ....67, 71, 106
Case C-238/96 Ireland v Commission [1998] ECR I-5801 28
Case C-349/96 CPP [1999] ECR I-973 ....55, 62, 110
Case C-367/96 Kefalas [1998] ECR I-2843 ....22, 29, 31
Joined Cases C-369/96 and C-376/96 Arblade and Others [1999] ECR I-8453 ....127, 268, 311, 338

Case C-400/96 Harpegnies [1998] ECR 1-1512 270
Joined Cases C-52 to C-54/97 Epifanio Viscido [1998] ECR 1-2629 ....328, 330, 337
Case C-75/97 Belgium v Commission (Maribel) [1999] ECR I-3671 ....337, 339
Case C-90/97 Swaddling [1999] ECR I-1075 ....140, 195
Case C-178/97 Barry Banks and Others [2000] ECR I-2005 ....139–40, 338
Case C-202/97 Fitzwilliam [2000] ECR I-883 .... 26, 103, 126, 205, 275, 338
Case C-212/97 Centros [1999] ECR I-1459 ....2, 26, 40, 66, 86, 93, 97– 98, 105, 128, 133, 154–56, 165, 210, 221–22, 225, 245, 248, 267, 281, 284, 289, 294, 296, 303, 304–05, 307–08, 341, 349, 352, 355, 360–61, 365, 368, 371, 373
Case C-273/97 Sirdar [1999] ECR I-7403 18
Case C-337/97 Meeusen [1999] ECR I-3289 ....146–47, 157
Case C-373/97 Diamantis [2000] ECR I-1705 ....22, 27, 29, 31
Case C-378/97 Wijsenbeek [1999] ECR I-6207 18
Case C-433/97 P IPK-München [1999] ECR I-6795 18
Case C-6/98 ARD [1999] ECR I-7599 20
Joined Cases C-49/98, C-50/98, C-52/98 to C-54/98 and C-68/98 to C-71/98 Finalarte and Others [2001] ECR I-7831 ....127, 311, 338
Joined Cases C-110/98 to C-147/98 Gabalfrisa and Others [2000] ECR I-1577 195
Case C-396/98 Schloßstraße [2000] ECR I-4279 ....54, 60
Case C-400/98 Breitsohl [2000] ECR I-4321 ....24, 60, 195
Case C-404/98 Plum [2000] ECR I-9379 ....126, 205, 275, 337–38
Case C-454/98 Schmeink & Cofreth [2000] ECR I-6973 24
Case C-30/99 Commission v Ireland ('Precious Metals') [2001] ECR I-4619 270
Case C-63/99 Gloszczuk [2001] ECR I-6369 25
Case C-108/99 Cantor Fitzgerald International [2001] ECR I-7257 59
Case C-110/99 Emsland-Stärke [2000] ECR I-11569 .... 25, 26, 46–47, 49, 50–51, 53, 58–60, 79, 87, 94, 99, 184–85, 195, 205
Case C-114/99 Roquette Frères [2000] ECR I-8823 ....49, 87, 88, 89
Case C-143/99 Adria-Wien Pipeline [2001] ECR I-8365 325
Case C-153/99 P Commission v Giannini [2000] ECR I-2891 17
Case C-164/99 Portugaia Construções [2002] ECR I-787 268
Case C-173/99 BETCU [2001] ECR I-4881 21
Case C-187/99 Eru Portuguesa [2001] ECR I-1429 26
Case C-235/99 Kondova [2001] ECR I-6427 25
Case C-248/99 P France v Monsanto and Commission [2002] ECR I-1 18
Case C-262/99 Louloudakis [2001] ECR I-5547 138
Case C-310/99 Italy v Commission [2002] ECR I-2289 ....17, 327
Case C-326/99 Goed Wonen [2001] ECR I-6831 54
Joined Cases C-393/99 and C-394/99 Hervein II [2002] ECR I-2829 275
Case C-453/99 Courage [2001] ECR I-6297 20
Case C-3/00 Denmark v Commission [2003] ECR I-2643 17
Case C-12/00 Commission v Spain ('Chocolate') [2003] ECR I-459 270
Case C-41/00 P Interporc [2003] ECR I-2125 18
Case C-115/00 Andreas Hoves [2002] ECR I-6077 156

Case C-137/00 Milk Marque [2003] ECR I-7975 105
Case C-208/00 Überseering [2002] ECR I-9919 ....122, 154, 248, 267, 284, 285, 304
Case C-280/00 Altmark [2003] ECR I-7747 ....322, 323
Order of the President of the Court of First Instance in Case T-302/00
R Goldstein v Commission [2001] ECR II-1127 ....21, 27
Case C-324/00 Lankhorst-Hohorst [2002] ECR I-11779 ....67, 70–71, 88–89, 106
Case C-336/00 Huber [2002] ECR I-7699 195
Case C-436/00 X and Y [2002] ECR I-10829 106
Case C-442/00 Rodríguez Caballero [2002] ECR I-11915 25
Case C-82/01 P Aéroports de Paris [2002] ECR I-9297 19
Case C-109/01 Akrich [2003] ECR I-9607 ....26, 86, 103, 160–61, 194, 207, 360
Case C-117/01 KB [2004] ECR I-541 149
Case C-167/01 Inspire Art [2003] ECR I-10155 ....26, 66, 133, 154, 222, 248, 267, 284, 304
Case C-224/01 Köbler [2003] ECR I-10239 18
Case C-245/01 RTL Television [2003] ECR I-12489 20
Case C-322/01 Deutscher Apothekerverband [2003] ECR I-14887 26
Case C-364/01 Barbier [2003] ECR I-15013 66
Case C-387/01 Weigel [2004] ECR I-4981 275
Case C-413/01 Ninni-Orasche [2003] ECR I-13187 ....26, 106, 114, 146, 157, 158, 286
Joined Cases C-487/01 and C-7/02 Gemeente Leusden and
Holin Groep [2004] ECR I-5337 ....54, 59, 195
Case C-9/02 de Lasteyrie du Saillant [2004] ECR I-2409 ....67, 106
Case C-66/02 Italy v Commission [2005] ECR I-10901 327
Case C-138/02 Collins [2004] ECR I-2703 ....26, 116, 157, 268
Case C-148/02 Garcia Avello [2003] ECR I-11613 162
Case C-159/02 Turner [2004] ECR I-3565 195
Case C-200/02 Zhu and Chen [2004] ECR I-9925 ....26, 86, 162, 210, 371
Case C-255/02 Halifax [2006] ECR I-1609 ....4, 9, 24, 25, 26, 28–31, 35, 38, 40, 46, 47, 48, 53, 55–60, 62, 63, 64, 73, 74, 76, 78, 80, 82, 84, 86, 87, 90, 91, 92, 94, 98, 99, 104, 108, 110, 113, 152, 183, 189, 194, 196, 197, 201, 203, 204, 205, 212, 226, 282, 370, 371
Case C-295/02 Gerken [2004] ECR I-6369 46
Case C-365/02 Lindfors [2004] ECR I-7183 275
Case C-372/02 Adanez-Vega [2004] ECR I-10761 160
Case C-376/02 Goed Wonen II [2005] ECR I-3445 54
Case C-394/02 Commission v Greece [2005] ECR I-4713 ....15, 21
Case C-419/02 BUPA Hospitals [2006] ECR I-1685 ....16, 28, 152, 153
Case C-456/02 Trojani [2004] ECR I-7573 ....115, 157
Case C-464/02 Commission v Denmark [2005] ECR I-7929 ....106, 139, 157
Case C-32/03 Fini H [2005] ECR I-1599 ....24, 60, 87, 270
Case C-88/03 Portugal v Commission (Azores Tax Regime) [2006] ECR I-7115 324
Case C-147/03 Commission v Austria [2005] ECR I-5969 26

Case C-176/03 Commission v Council [2005] ECR I-7879 17
Joined Cases C-182/03 and C-217/03 Belgium and Forum 187 v Commission ('Coordination Centres') [2006] ECR I-5479 ....322, 335
Case C-209/03 Bidar [2005] ECR I-2119.... 104, 114–15, 195, 285, 370
Case C-223/03 University of Huddersfield [2006] ECR I-1751....35, 54
Case C-284/03 Temco Europe [2004] ECR I-11237....152, 153
Joined Cases C-354/03, C-355/03 and C-484/03 Optigen [2006] ECR I-483....58, 194
Case C-399/03 Commission v Council [2006] ECR I-5629 16
Case C-403/03 Schempp [2005] ECR I-6421 275
Case C-411/03 SEVIC Systems [2005] ECR I-10805 127
Case C-432/03 Commission v Portugal [2005] ECR I-9665 270
Case C-445/03 Commission v Luxembourg [2004] ECR I-10191 ....26, 276
Case C-446/03 Marks & Spencer [2005] ECR I-10837 ....3, 67, 71, 80, 82, 95, 106, 108, 281, 304, 352–53, 355
Case C-452/03 RAL [2005] ECR I-3947 .... 16, 28, 103, 152, 153
Case C-515/03 Eichsfelder Schlachtbetrieb [2005] ECR I-7355.... 26, 49, 59, 74, 87–88, 195
Case C-520/03 Olaso Valero [2004] ECR I-12065....25
Case C-1/04 Staubitz-Schreiber [2006] ECR I-701 131
Case C-41/04 Levob [2005] ECR I-9433.... 16, 55, 62, 110
Case C-63/04 Centralan [2005] ECR I-11087 ....16, 103, 152–53
Case C-144/04 Mangold [2005] ECR I-9981....21
Joined Cases C-151/04 and C-152/04 Nadin [2005] ECR I-11203 139
Case C-196/04 Cadbury Schweppes [2006] ECR I-7995 ....2, 3, 4, 9, 25–26, 28, 29, 31, 38, 40, 42, 46, 47, 48, 53, 63, 64–69, 71, 80, 82, 84, 86, 89–90, 92, 93, 96, 98, 100, 107, 109, 127, 128, 132, 153, 195, 197, 204–05, 210, 212, 221, 222–23, 225, 287, 294, 296, 299–301, 304, 305, 307, 334–35, 339, 341, 349, 352, 355–56, 358, 360, 361–62, 363, 368, 371
Case C-244/04 Commission v Germany [2006] ECR I-885 ....311, 366
Case C-258/04 Ioannidis [2005] ECR I-8275 116
Case C-313/04 Franz Egenberger [2006] ECR I-6331....18
Case C-341/04 Eurofood IFSC [2006] ECR I-3813....68, 122, 131
Case C-347/04 Rewe Zentralfinanz [2007] ECR I-2647 ....109, 305, 308
Case C-391/04 Georgakis [2007] ECR I-3741 20
Case C-409/04 Teleos [2007] ECR I-7797 ....194, 195
Case C-423/04 Richards [2006] ECR I-3585 149
Joined Cases C-439/04 and C-440/04 Kittel [2006] ECR I-6161....194, 195
Case C-452/04 Fidium Finanz [2006] ECR I-9521 ....16, 150
Case C-456/04 Agip Petroli [2006] ECR I-3395 ....72–74, 80, 86, 87, 95, 100, 197, 232–33, 287
Case C-494/04 Heintz van Landewijck [2006] ECR I-5381 24
Case C-513/04 Kerckhaert and Morres [2006] ECR I-10967 257

Case C-524/04 Thin Cap Group Litigation [2007] ECR I-2107..........4, 9, 38, 46, 47, 48, 64, 69–72, 80, 82, 84, 88–90, 91, 95–96, 100, 107, 109, 197, 205, 304, 355, 360
Case C-1/05 Jia [2007] ECR I-1 161
Case C-81/05 Cordero Alonso [2006] ECR I-7569 25
Case C-94/05 Emsland-Stärke II [2006] ECR I-2619..........46
Case C-110/05 Commission v Italy ('Motorcycle Trailer') [2009] ECR I-519..........270
Case C-142/05 Mickelsson [2009] ECR I-4273 270
Case C-146/05 Collée [2007] ECR I-7861 195
Order in Case C-177/05 Guerrero Pecino [2005] ECR I-10887..........25
Case C-178/05 Commission v Greece [2007] ECR I-4185 ....26, 48, 109
Case C-192/05 Tas-Hagen [2006] ECR I-10451..........142
Order in Case C-201/05 CFC and Dividend Group Litigation [2008] ECR I-2875..........26
Case C-212/05 Hartmann [2007] ECR I-6303..........145
Case C-213/05 Geven [2007] ECR I-6347..........145, 157, 159
Case C-231/05 Oy AA [2007] ECR I-6373 .... 46, 84, 89, 95, 107–09, 153, 304–05, 307, 352, 355
Case C-240/05 Eurodental [2006] ECR I-11479 282–83
Case C-279/05 Vonk Dairy Products [2007] ECR I-239..........4, 9, 26, 46, 47, 48, 49, 52–53, 80, 84, 153, 154, 195, 287
Case C-287/05 Hendrix [2007] ECR I-6909.......... 144–45
Case C-291/05 Eind [2007] ECR I-10719..........161
Case C-298/05 Columbus [2007] ECR I-10451 .... 103, 153, 200, 300, 335, 368
Case C-321/05 Kofoed [2007] ECR I-5795..........106, 109, 153, 195
Case C-328/05 P SGL Carbon [2007] ECR I-3921..........18
Case C-341/05 Laval [2007] ECR I-11767.......... 83, 112, 126–27, 225, 234, 275, 276, 294, 296, 299, 303, 311–14, 338, 339, 353, 365–66, 368, 370
Case C-363/05 JP Morgan [2007] ECR I-5517..........188, 239
Case C-392/05 Alevizos [2007] ECR I-3505..........138, 275
Case C-424/05 P Commission v Hosman-Chevalier [2007] ECR I-5027..........141
Case C-428/05 Laub [2007] ECR I-5069 195
Case C-433/05 Sandström [2010] ECR I-2885..........270
Case C-438/05 Viking [2007] ECR I-10779.......... 127, 166, 313, 333, 353
Case C-10/06 P De Bustamente Tello [2007] ECR I-10381 141
Case C-73/06 Planzer [2007] ECR I-5655 ....16, 110–11, 122, 129–30
Case C-133/06 Parliament v Council [2008] ECR I-3189 16
Case C-194/06 Orange European Smallcap Fund [2008] ECR I-3747 257
Case C-210/06 Cartesio [2008] ECR I-9641.......... 149, 154, 155, 248, 267, 284, 289, 304, 307
Case C-246/06 Velasco Navarro [2008] ECR I-105 25
Case C-251/06 ING AUER [2007] ECR I-9689 ....4, 9, 26, 47, 48, 64, 72, 74–77, 80, 84, 87, 89, 100, 109, 197, 280
Case C-268/06 Impact [2008] ECR I-2483..........21

Case C-271/06 Netto Supermarkt [2008] ECR I-771 195
Case C-286/06 Commission v Spain [2008] ECR I-8025 ....26, 119, 303
Case C-311/06 Cavallera [2009] ECR I-415 ....16, 88, 89, 118–19, 287–88
Case C-314/06 Société Pipeline Méditerranée et Rhône [2007] ECR I-12273 83
Case C-319/06 Commission v Luxembourg [2008] ECR I-4323 126
Joined Cases C-329/06 and C-343/06 Wiedemann [2008] ECR I-4635 .... 138, 151, 202, 281
Joined Cases C-334/06 to C-336/06 Zerche [2008] ECR I-4691 ....138, 151
Case C-346/06 Rüffert [2008] ECR I-1989 .... 126, 298–99, 301, 303, 312–13, 338, 368
Case C-374/06 BATIG [2007] ECR I-11271 24
Case C-414/06 Lidl Belgium [2008] ECR I-3601 ....95, 109, 304, 355
Case C-425/06 Part Service [2008] ECR I-897 ....4, 23, 26, 47, 48, 55, 60–63, 80, 86, 91–92, 95, 110
Joined Cases C-428/06 to C-434/06 UGT-Rioja [2008] ECR I-6747 324
Case C-498/06 Robledillo Núñez [2008] ECR I-921 25
Case C-499/06 Nerkowska [2008] ECR I-3993 ....142, 143
Joined Cases C-501/06 P, C-513/06 P, C-515/06 P and C-519/06 P GlaxoSmithKline [2009] ECR I-9291 ....15, 21
Case C-1/07 Weber [2008] ECR I-8571 ....138, 151, 154, 202
Case C-42/07 Bwin [2009] ECR I-7633 ....150, 257, 280
Joined Cases C-95/07 and C-96/07 Ecotrade [2008] ECR I-3457 195
Case C-105/07 Lammers & Van Cleef [2008] ECR I-173 89
Case C-151/07 Chatzithanasis [2008] ECR I-9013 ....26, 119
Case C-158/07 Förster [2008] ECR I-8507 .... 104, 114, 115, 117, 146, 206, 207, 210, 268, 285
Case C-161/07 Commission v Austria [2008] ECR I-10671 25
Case C-162/07 Ampliscientifica [2008] ECR I-4019 ....119, 120
Case C-169/07 Hartlauer [2009] ECR I-1721 ....21, 112
Case C-208/07 von Chamier [2009] ECR I-6095 ....157, 275
Case C-269/07 Commission v Germany [2009] ECR I-7811 268
Joined Cases C-316/07, C-358/07 to C-360/07, C-409/07 and C-410/07 Markus Stoß [2010] ECR I-8069 ....150, 176, 257, 280
Case C-319/07 P 3F [2010] ECR I-5963 334
Case C-330/07 Jobra [2008] ECR I-9099 89
Case C-339/07 Seagon [2009] ECR I-767 131
Joined Cases C-378/07 to C-380/07 Angelidaki [2009] ECR I-3071 21
Case C-385/07 P Der Grüne Punkt [2009] ECR I-6155 19
Case C-397/07 Commission v Spain [2009] ECR I-6029 ....26, 48, 89, 109
Joined Cases C-402/07 and C-432/07 Sturgeon and others [2009] ECR I-10923 ....176, 178–80
Case C-418/07 Papillon [2008] ECR I-8947 ....82, 352
Case C-523/07 A [2009] ECR I-2805 141
Case C-531/07 LIBRO [2009] ECR I-3717 297
Case C-46/08 Carmen Media Group [2010] ECR I-8149 ....132, 150, 280, 336
Case C-47/08 Commission v Belgium (Notaries) [2011] ECR I-4105 252
Case C-66/08 Kozłowski [2008] ECR I-6041 117
Case C-67/08 Block [2009] ECR I-883 ....257, 275
Case C-103/08 Gottwald [2009] ECR I-9117 143

Case C-123/08 Wolzenburg [2009] ECR I-9621 ... 117
Case C-127/08 Metock [2008] ECR I-6241 ... 106, 161, 301
Case C-128/08 Damseaux [2009] ECR I-6823 ... 176, 257, 258
Case C-158/08 Pometon [2009] ECR I-4695 ... 46
Case C-168/08 Hadadi [2009] ECR I-6871 ... 26
Case C-201/08 Plantanol [2009] ECR I-8343 ... 176
Case C-311/08 SGI [2010] ECR I-487 ... 26, 108, 352
Case C-337/08 X Holding [2010] ECR I-1215 ... 109
Case C-352/08 Modehuis A Zwijnenburg [2010] ECR I-4303 ... 109
Case C-364/08 Vandermeir [2008] ECR I-8087 ... 139
Case C-406/08 Uniplex [2010] ECR I-817 ... 195
Case C-425/08 Enviro Tech v Etat belge [2009] ECR I-10035 ... 17
Order in Case C-445/08 Wierer [2009] ECR I-119 ... 151
Case C-461/08 Don Bosco [2009] ECR I-11079 ... 110
Case C-569/08 Internetportal und Marketing [2010] ECR I-4871 ... 195
Joined Cases C-585/08 and C-144/09 Pammer and Hotel Alpenhof [2010] ECR I-12527 ... 135
Case C-14/09 Hava Genc [2010] ECR I-931 ... 157
Case C-16/09 Schwemmer [2010] ECR I-9717 ... 160
Case C-34/09 Zambrano [2011] ECR I-1177 ... 161
Case C-52/09 TeliaSonera [2011] ECR I-527 ... 241
Case C-84/09 X [2010] ECR I-11645 ... 277
Case C-103/09 Weald Leasing [2010] ECR-13589 ... 97, 98
Joined Cases C-106/09 P and C-107/09 P Commission and Spain v Gibraltar and United Kingdom [2011] ECR I-0000 ... 336
Case C-118/09 Koller [2010] ECR I-13627 ... 119
Case C-140/09 Fallimento Traghetti del Mediterraneo [2010] ECR I-5243 ... 322
Case C-221/09 AJD Tuna [2011] ECR I-1655 ... 164
Joined Cases C-230/09 and C-231/09 Etling [2011] ECR I-3097 ... 48
Case C-277/09 RBS Deutschland Holdings [2010] ECR I-13805 ... 91–92
Case C-324/09 L'Oréal [2011] ECR I-6011 ... 135–36, 137
Case C-347/09 Dickinger [2011] ECR I-8185 ... 150, 257, 280
Case C-380/09 P Melli Bank [2012] ECR I-0000 ... 112
Case C-396/09 Interedil [2011] ECR I-9915 ... 130–31
Case C-424/09 Toki [2011] ECR I-2587 ... 117–18
Case C-462/09 Stichting de Thuiskopie [2011] ECR I-5331 ... 135–37
Case C-489/09 Vandoorne [2011] ECR I-225 ... 24
Case C-503/09 Lucy Stewart [2011] ECR I-6497 ... 142
Case C-542/09 Commission v Netherlands [2012] ECR I-0000 ... 115, 144, 147
Case C-29/10 Koelzsch [2011] ECR I-1595 ... 130
Case C-124/10 P Commission v EDF [2012] ECR I-0000 ... 323
Case C-126/10 Foggia [2011] ECR I-10923 ... 64, 109
Case C-184/10 Grasser [2011] ECR I-4057 ... 138, 151, 281
Case C-240/10 Schulz [2011] ECR I-8531 ... 275
Joined Cases C-244/10 and C-245/10 Mesopotamia Broadcast [2011] ECR I-8777 ... 152
Case C-371/10 National Grid Indus [2011] ECR I-12273 ... 269, 276
Case C-378/10 VALE Építési [2012] ECR I-0000 ... 66, 128, 156, 269

Case C-417/10 3M Italia [2012] ECR I-0000....23, 324
Case C-504/10 Tanoarch [2011] ECR I-10853....48, 54
Case C-577/10 Commission v Belgium ('Limosa') [2012] ECR I-0000....310
Joined Cases C-581/10 and C-629/10 Nelson and Others [2012]
ECR I-0000....175–76, 178, 179
Case C-5/11 Donner [2012] ECR I-0000.... 136–37
Case C-33/11 A Oy [2012] ECR I-0000....188, 239
Case C-128/11 UsedSoft v Oracle [2012] ECR I-0000....113, 283
Case C-174/11 Zimmermann [2012] ECR I-0000....188
Case C-190/11 Mühlleitner [2012] ECR I-0000....135
Case C-256/11 Dereci [2011] ECR I-11315....162
Joined Cases C-523/11 and C-585/11 Prinz and Seeberger [2013]
ECR I-0000....142, 143, 145, 146
Case C646/11 P 3F [2013] ECR I-0000....334
Case C-628/11 International Jet Management [2014] ECR I-0000....177, 252
Case C-20/12 Giersch and Others [2013] ECR I-0000....115–16, 144, 147
Case C-137/12 Commission v Council [2013] ECR I-0000....282
Case C-218/12 Emrek [2013] ECR I-0000.... 134–35
Case C-456/12 O [2014] ECR I-0000....162
Case C-457/12 S[2014] ECR I-0000....162

Opinions of Advocates General of the Court of Justice of the European Union

AG Lagrange, Case 30/59 Mines du Limbourg [1961] ECR 3....316
AG Capotorti, Case 730/79 Philip Morris Holland [1980] ECR I-2671....327
AG Capotorti, Case 249/81 Commission v Ireland (Buy Irish) [1982] ECR I-4005....325
AG Darmon, Case 191/83 Salzano [1984] ECR 3741....159
AG Lenz, Case 234/84 Belgium v Commission [1986] ECR 2263....323
AG Darmon, Case 79/85 Segers [1986] ECR 2375....222
AG Slynn, Case 39/86 Lair [1988] ECR 3161....114
AG Darmon, Case 81/87 Daily Mail [1988] ECR 5483....127, 132, 348
AG Van Gerven, Case 145/88 B & Q (Sunday Trading) [1989] ECR 3851....254, 256
AG Mischo, Case C-221/89 Factortame II [1991] ECR I-3905....163
AG Tesauro, Case C-300/89 Commission v Council ('Titanium Dioxide') [1991]
ECR I-2867....237
AG Darmon, Joined Cases C-72/91 and C-73/91 Sloman Neptun [1993]
ECR I-887....328–29, 334
AG Jacobs, Case C-168/91 Konstantinidis [1993] ECR I-1191....303
AG Lenz, Case C-222/94 Commission v United Kingdom [1996] ECR I-4025....125, 132
AG Jacobs, Case C-241/94 France v Commission [1996] ECR I-4551....330
AG Tesauro, Case C-367/96 Kefalas [1998] ECR I-2843....43, 202
AG Jacobs, Joined Cases C-52 to C-54/97 Epifanio Viscido [1998] ECR I-2629....330
AG La Pergola, Case C-212/97 Centros [1999] ECR I-1459.... 3, 98, 194, 206, 209,
222, 248, 307–08, 363
AG Mischo, Joined Cases C-49/98, C-50/98, C-52/98 to C-54/98 and
C-68/98 to C-71/98 Finalarte and Others [2001] ECR I-7831....314
AG Fennelly, Case C-190/98 Graf [2000] ECR I-493....268

AG Jacobs, Case C-379/98 PreussenElektra [2001] ECR I-2099 329–30
AG Alber, Case C-110/99 Emsland-Stärke [2000] ECR I-11569 .... 185, 192, 216
AG Léger, Case C-280/00 Altmark [2003] ECR I-7747 323
AG Geelhoed, Case C-109/01 Akrich [2003] ECR I-9607 .... 194, 207, 222
AG Tizzano, Case C-200/02 Zhu and Chen [2004] ECR I-9925 216
AG Maduro, Case C-255/02 Halifax [2006] ECR I-1609 .... 3, 56, 84. 87, 94, 97, 191, 192, 196, 198, 199, 211, 216–17
AG Maduro, Case C-419/02 BUPA Hospitals [2006] ECR I-1685 .... 103, 152
AG Geelhoed, Case C-456/02 Trojani [2004] ECR I-7573 115
AG Léger, Case C-152/03 Ritter-Coulais [2006] ECR I-1711 301
AG Maduro, Case C-446/03 Marks & Spencer [2005] ECR I-10837 305–06
AG Maduro, Case C-452/03 RAL [2005] ECR I-3947 .... 103, 152
AG Kokott, Case C-63/04 Centralan [2005] ECR I-11087 .... 103, 152
AG Léger, Case C-196/04 Cadbury Schweppes [2006] ECR I-7995 .... 132, 148, 194, 196, 223, 349
AG Colomer, Case C-207/04 Vergani [2005] ECR I-7453 309
AG Geelhoed, Case C-244/04 Commission v Germany [2006] ECR I-885 366
AG Maduro, Case C-347/04 Rewe Zentralfinanz [2007] ECR I-2647 .... 108, 305
AG Stix-Hackl, Case C-452/04 Fidium Finanz [2006] ECR I-9521 .... 16, 150
AG Mengozzi, Case C-341/05 Laval [2007] ECR I-11767 366
AG Maduro, Case C-438/05 Viking [2007] ECR I-10779 347
AG Maduro, Case C-210/06 Cartesio [2008] ECR I-9641 365
AG Maduro, Case C-311/06 Cavallera [2009] ECR I-415 .... 3, 88, 103, 148, 223
AG Bot, Case C-346/06 Rüffert [2008] ECR I-1989 311
AG Mazák, Case C-158/07 Förster [2008] ECR I-8507 207
AG Sharpston, Joined Cases C-402/07 and C-432/07 Sturgeon and others [2009] ECR I-10923 180
AG Mengozzi, Case C-46/08 Carmen Media Group [2010] ECR I-8149 280
AG Sharpston, Case C-200/08 Commission v France ('Snowboarders'), removed 303
AG Kokott, Case C-480/08 Teixeira [2010] ECR I-1107 148
AG Jääskinen, Joined Cases C-106/09 P and C-107/09 P Commission and Spain v Gibraltar and United Kingdom [2011] ECR I-11113 336
AG Cruz Villalón, Case C-318/10 SIAT [2012] ECR I-0000 108
AG Jääskinen, Case C-5/11 Donner [2012] ECR I-0000 137
AG Sharpston, Joined Cases C-523/11 and C-585/11 Prinz and Seeberger [2013] ECR I-0000 .... 178, 208
AG Bot, Case C-628/11 International Jet Management [2014] ECR I-0000 .... 177, 253
AG Cruz Villalón, Case C-218/12 Emrek [2013] ECR I-0000 135

National and International Case Law

Badoit v André (1856) 2 DP 199 (Cour d'Appel de Lyon) 39
Doerr v Keller (1856) 2 DP 9 (Cour d'Appel de Colmar) 39
Ibbotson v Peat (1865) 3 HC 644 (HL) 36
Prince de Wagram v Marais (1873) 2 DP 185 (Cour d'Appel de Paris) 36
Princesse de Bauffremont (1876) 78 S I-193 (Cour de Cassation française) 40
Riggs v Palmer (1889) 115 NY 506 (Court of Appeals of New York) 173

Christie v Davey (1893) 1 Ch 316 (HL)........ 35–37
Bradford Corporation v Pickles (1895) Appeal Cases 587 (HL)........35–37, 55
Allen v Flood (1898) Appeal Cases 1 (HL)........35
Quinn v Leathem (1901) Appeal Cases 495 (HL)........35
South Wales Miners' Federation v Glamorgan Coal Co Ltd (1905)
Appeal Cases 239 (HL)........35
Coquerel v Clément-Bayard (1917) 1 DP 79 (Cour d'Appel d'Amiens)........39
Coquerel v Clément-Bayard (1920) S 300 (Cour de Cassation française)........39
Hollywood Silver Fox Farm Ltd v Emmett (1936) 2 KB 468 (HL)........36, 37
Nottebohm (Liechtenstein v Guatemala) [1955] ICJ Rep 5........ 162–63
N Pac Ry v United States (1958) 356 US 1 (USSC)........342
S/S Employment v ASLEF (no 2) (1972) 2 ALL ER 949 (HL)........36
United States v Topco Associates (1972) 405 US 596 (USSC)........342
James Buchanan & Co Ltd v Babco Forwarding & Shipping (UK) Ltd (1977)
2 WLR 107 (HL)........181
Boston Stock Exchange v State Tax Commission (1977) 429 US 318 (USSC)........317
Stephens v Anglian Water Authority (1987) 1 WLR 1381 (HL)........35
Earle and Earle v East Riding (1999) RVR 200 (LT)........35
Cuno v DaimlerChrysler 386 F 3d 738 (6th Cir 2004)........ 320–21
Janfin (2006) Leb 410 (Conseil d'État français)........40
Bank of Scotland (2006) Leb 578 (Conseil d'État français)........40
DaimlerChrysler v Cuno (2006) 547 US 332 (USSC)........320
Secretary of State for Communities and Local Government v
Welwyn Hatfield BC (2010) EWCA Civ 26........173

Table of Legislation[*]

European Union Legislation

Decisions

Framework Dec 2002/584/JHA on the European Arrest Warrant and the surrender procedures between Member States [2002] OJ L190/1
Art 4(6) 117
Dec 2011/853/EU on the signing, on behalf of the Union, of the European Convention on the legal protection of services based on, or consisting of, conditional access [2011] OJ L336/1 282

Directives

Dir 64/427/EEC laying down detailed provisions concerning transitional measures in respect of activities of self-employed persons in manufacturing and processing industries falling within ISI Major Groups 23–40 (Industry and small craft industries) [1964] OJ L117/1863
Art 3 118
Dir 67/227/EEC on the harmonisation of legislation of Member States concerning turnover taxes [1967] OJ L71/1301
Preamble 188
Dir 69/335/EEC concerning indirect taxes on the raising of capital [1969] OJ L249/25 .....47, 72, 74–77
Art 3(1) 76
Art 3(2) 76
Art 4(1) 75, 76
Art 4(1)(g) 76
Art 4(3) 75, 76
Dir 73/79/EEC amending Directive 69/335/EEC concerning indirect taxes on the raising of capital [1973] OJ L103/13 74
Dir 73/80/EEC fixing common rates of capital duty [1973] OJ L103/15 74
Dir 75/442/EEC on waste (Waste Framework Directive) [1975] OJ L194/39 182
Dir 77/91/EEC on coordination of safeguards which, for the protection of the interests of members and others, are required by Member States of companies within the meaning of the second paragraph of Article 58 of the Treaty, in respect of the formation of public limited liability companies and the maintenance and alteration of their capital, with a view to making such safeguards equivalent [1976] OJ L26/1
Art 25(1) 22

[*] Any legislation listed within the Annex that does not appear in the text is not referenced in these tables.

Dir 77/249/EEC to facilitate the effective exercise by lawyers of freedom to provide services [1977] OJ L78/17 151
Dir 77/388/EEC on the harmonisation of the laws of the Member States relating to turnover taxes—Common system of value-added tax: uniform basis of assessment [1977] OJ L145/1
Art 13C 54
Dir 79/1072/EEC on the harmonization of the laws of the Member States relating to turnover taxes—Arrangements for the refund of value added tax to taxable persons not established in the territory of the country [1979] OJ L331/11
Rec 3 238
Dir 80/987/EEC on the approximation of the laws of the Member States relating to the protection of employees in the event of the insolvency of their employer [1980] OJ L283/23 25
Dir 83/182/EEC on tax exemptions within the Community for certain means of transport temporarily imported into one Member State from another [1983] OJ L105/59
Art 7(1) 138–39
Dir 85/303/EEC amending Directive 69/335/EEC concerning indirect taxes on the raising of capital [1985] OJ L156/23 74
Rec 2–3 74
Dir 86/560/EEC on the harmonization of the laws of the Member States relating to turnover taxes—Arrangements for the refund of value added tax to taxable persons not established in Community territory (Thirteenth VAT Directive) [1986] OJ L326/40 122
Dir 88/378/EEC on the approximation of the laws of the Member States concerning the safety of toys [1988] OJ L187/1
Rec 1 237
Dir 89/48/EEC on a general system for the recognition of higher-education diplomas awarded on completion of professional education and training of at least three years' duration [1989] OJ L19/16 ....88, 118
Art 1(a) 118
Art 3(1)(b) 117
Dir 89/104/EEC to approximate the laws of the Member States relating to trade marks [1988] OJ L40/1
Art 3(2)(d) 195
Dir 89/552/EEC on the coordination of certain provisions laid down by Law, Regulation or Administrative Action in Member States concerning the pursuit of television broadcasting activities (Audiovisual Media Services Directive) [1989] OJ L298/23 ....125, 151
Art 2 124
Dir 90/434/EEC on the common system of taxation applicable to mergers, divisions, transfers of assets and exchanges of shares concerning companies of different Member States [1990] OJ L225/1
Art 11(a) 109, 203
Dir 90/435/EEC on the common system of taxation applicable in the case of parent companies and subsidiaries of different Member States [1990] OJ L225/6 69
Art 1(2) 109, 203
Art 3(2) 119

Dir 91/439/EEC on driving licences [1991] OJ L237/1 .... 138, 151, 202, 203, 267
Art 2(1) 267
Art 9 138
Dir 92/12/EEC on the general arrangements for products subject to excise duty and on the holding, movement and monitoring of such products [1992] OJ L76/1
Art 14(1) 83
Art 14(3) 109
Art 39(3) 109
Dir 92/59/EEC on general product safety [1992] OJ L228/24
Rec 2 238
Dir 93/13/EEC on unfair terms in consumer contracts [1993] OJ L95/29 20
Rec 9 20
Dir 93/42/EEC on medical devices [1993] OJ L169/1
Rec 2 238
Dir 93/89/EEC on taxes on vehicles used for the carriage of goods by road and tolls and charges for the use of certain infrastructures [1993] OJ L279/32 156
Dir 93/104/EC concerning certain aspects of the organization of working time [1993] OJ L307/18
Art 7(1) 21
Dir 94/5/EC supplementing the common system of value added tax and amending Directive 77/388/EEC—Special arrangements applicable to second-hand goods, works of art, collectors' items and antiques [1994] OJ L60/16
Rec 2 234
Dir 94/25/EC on the approximation of the laws, regulations and administrative provisions of the Member States relating to recreational craft [1994] OJ L164/15
Rec 2 238
Dir 94/47/EC on the protection of purchasers in respect of certain aspects of contracts relating to the purchase of the right to use immovable properties on a timeshare basis [1994] OJ L280/83
Rec 1 237–38
Dir 96/71/EC concerning the posting of workers in the framework of the provision of services [1996] OJ L18/1 .... 127, 311, 313, 338, 366
Art 3(1) 127, 276, 311–13, 338
Rec 5 366
Rec 12 366
Rec 13 366
Rec 17 366
Dir 97/36/EC amending Council Directive 89/552/EEC on the coordination of certain provisions laid down by law, regulation or administrative action in Member States concerning the pursuit of television broadcasting activities [1997] OJ L202/60 125
Rec 10–11 126
Dir 98/84/EC on the legal protection of services based on, or consisting of, conditional access [1998] OJ L320/54 282
Dir 1999/44/EC on certain aspects of the sale of consumer goods and associated guarantees [1999] OJ L171/12 20
Dir 1999/70/EC concerning the framework agreement on fixed-term work concluded by ETUC, UNICE and CEEP [1999] OJ L175/43 21

Dir 2000/13/EC on the approximation of the laws of the Member States relating to the labelling, presentation and advertising of foodstuffs [2000] OJ L109/29
Rec 2 237
Dir 2001/17/EC on the reorganisation and winding-up of insurance undertakings [2001] OJ L110/28 267
Dir 2001/24/EC on the reorganisation and winding up of credit institutions [2001] OJ L125/15
Rec 6 .... 247, 266–67
Dir 2001/84/EC on the resale right for the benefit of the author of an original work of art [2001] OJ L272/32
Rec 9–10 263
Dir 2001/95/EC on general product safety [2001] OJ L11/4
Dir 2002/83/EC concerning life assurance [2002] OJ L345/1
Arts 1(e), 4 and 6(3) 123
Dir 2003/6/EC on insider dealing and market manipulation (market abuse) [2003] OJ L96/16 20
Rec 12 20
Dir 2003/48/EC on taxation of savings income in the form of interest payments [2003] OJ L157/38 288
Rec 5–6 288
Dir 2003/49/EC on a common system of taxation applicable to interest and royalty payments made between associated companies of different Member States [2003] OJ L157/49
Art 5 .... 109, 203
Dir 2004/17/EC coordinating the procurement procedures of entities operating in the water, energy, transport and postal services sectors [2004] OJ L134/1
Art 17(2) 113
Dir 2004/18/EC on the coordination of procedures for the award of public works contracts, public supply contracts and public service contracts [2004] OJ L134/114
Art 7 112
Art 9(3) 112
Dir 2004/39/EC on markets in financial instruments amending Council Directives 85/611/EEC and 93/6/EEC and Directive 2000/12/EC of the European Parliament and of the Council and repealing Council Directive 93/22/EEC [2004] OJ L145/1
Art 5(4) 123
Dir 2004/38/EC on the right of citizens of the Union and their family members to move and reside freely within the territory of the Member States amending Regulation (EEC) No 1612/68 and repealing Directives 64/221/EEC, 68/360/EEC, 72/194/EEC, 73/148/EEC, 75/34/EEC, 75/35/EEC, 90/364/EEC, 90/365/EEC and 93/96/EEC [2004] OJ L229/35 .... 116, 285
Art 6 .... 116, 286
Art 7 .... 116, 286
Art 16 .... 116, 286
Art 16(1) 115
Art 24(1) 115
Art 24(2) 115
Art 35 .... 106, 148

Dir 2004/48/EC on the enforcement of intellectual property rights [2004] OJ L157/45
Rec 8 237
Art 3 23
Art 3(2) 23, 28
Dir 2004/83/EC on minimum standards for the qualification and status of third country nationals or stateless persons as refugees or as persons who otherwise need international protection and the content of the protection granted [2004] OJ L304/2
Art 29 17
Dir 2005/29/EC concerning unfair business-to-consumer commercial practices in the internal market and amending
Council Directive 84/450/EEC, Directives 97/7/EC, 98/27/EC and 2002/65/EC of the European Parliament and of the Council and Regulation (EC) No 2006/2004 of the European Parliament and of the Council (Unfair Commercial Practices Directive) [2005] OJ L149/22 20
Art 9(b) 20
Dir 2005/36/EC on the recognition of professional qualifications [2005] OJ L255/22 269–70
Art 14 269
Dir 2006/112/EC on the common system of value added tax [2006] OJ L347/1 109
Rec 7 187
Art 1(2) 188
Art 9 56
Art 43 129
Art 135 ....57, 187
Art 137 54
Art 168 ....56, 187
Art 173 56
Art 174 57
Dir 2007/65/EC amending Council Directive 89/552/EEC on the coordination of certain provisions laid down by law, regulation or administrative action in Member States concerning the pursuit of television broadcasting activities [2007] OJ L332/27 125–26
Rec 32–33 126
Dir 2008/94/EC on the protection of employees in the event of the insolvency of their employer [2008] OJ L283/36 25
Dir 2008/118/EC concerning the general arrangements for excise duty and repealing Directive 92/12/EEC [2008] OJ L9/12
Arts 14(3) 109
Art 39(3) 109
Dir 2009/24/EC on the legal protection of computer programs [2009] OJ L111/16 113
Art 4(2) 113, 283
Dir 2009/65/EC on the coordination of laws, regulations and administrative provisions relating to undertakings for collective investment in transferable securities (UCITS) [2009] OJ L302/32
Art 7(1)(d) 123

Dir 2009/133/EC on the common system of taxation applicable to mergers, divisions, partial divisions, transfers of assets and exchanges of shares concerning companies of different Member States and to the transfer of the registered office of an SE or SCE between Member States [2009] OJ L310/34
Art 15(1)(a) 109, 203
Dir 2009/138/EC on the taking-up and pursuit if the business of Insurance and Reinsurance (Solvency II) [2009] OJ L335/1
Art 20 123
Dir 2010/13/EU on the coordination of certain provisions laid down by law, regulation or administrative action in Member States concerning the provision of audiovisual media services (Audiovisual Media Services Directive) [2010] OJ L95/1
Rec 40–43 126
Art 2 .... 125, 151
Art 4 .... 126, 132, 151

Regulations
Reg 17: First Regulation implementing Articles 85 and 86 of the Treaty [1962] OJ 13/204
Art 1 20
Reg 1612/68 on freedom of movement for workers within the Community [1968] OJ L257/2 160
Rec 4 146
Art 7 .... 144, 268, 273
Art 7(2) 146, 156, 158
Reg 1408/71 on the application of social security schemes to employed persons and their families moving within the Community [1971] OJ L149/2 127
Art 2(1) 158
Art 3 .... 268, 273
Art 10(a) 140
Art 13 156
Art 14(1)(a) 126, 139, 275, 305
Art 71(1) 160
Art 76 .... 159, 294
Art 76(1) 159–60
Art 76(2) 160
Reg 574/72 fixing the procedure for implementing Regulation (EEC) No 1408/71 on the application of social security schemes to employed persons and their families moving within the Community [1972] OJ L74/1
Art 10 .... 159, 294
Reg 101/76 laying down a common structural policy for the fishing industry [1976] OJ L20/19 .... 164, 201
Art 4 164
Reg 2730/79 laying down common detailed rules for the application of the system of export refunds on agricultural products [1979] OJ L317/1 .... 50–51, 183–87, 198
Art 9(1) 50, 51

Art 10...186
Art 10(1)...50, 184, 185, 198
Art 10(1)(a)...50
Art 10(1)(b)...50
Art 20(2)...50
Reg 170/83 establishing a Community system for the conservation and management of fishery resources [1983] OJ L24/1...164, 201
Art 3...164
Art 4...164
Art 4(1)...166
Art 5(2)...164
Reg 2287/83 laying down provisions for the implementation of Article 127 of Regulation 918/83 setting up a Community system of reliefs from customs duty [1983] OJ L220/12
Rec 3...288
Reg 3821/85 on recording equipment in road transport [1985] OJ L370/8...21
Reg 3094/86 laying down certain technical measures for the conservation of fishery resources [1986] OJ L288/1...164
Reg 4028/86 on Community measures to improve and adapt structures in the fisheries and aquaculture sector [1986] OJ L376/7... 163–64
Reg 3665/87 laying down common detailed rules for the application of the system of export refunds on agricultural products [1987] OJ L351/1...52
Arts 4...52
Arts 5(1)(a)...52
Art 17(3)...52
Art 18...52
Art 18(2)...52
Reg 859/89 laying down detailed rules for the application of intervention measures in the beef and veal sector [1989] OJ L91/5...28
Reg 3427/89 amending Regulation 1408/71 on the application of social security schemes to employed persons, to self-employed persons and to members of their families moving within the Community and Regulation 574/72 laying down the procedure for implementing Regulation [1989] OJ L331/1
Art 76(1)...159
Reg 2913/92 establishing the Community Customs Code [1992] OJ L302/1
Art 24...104, 186
Reg 3577/92 applying the principle of freedom to provide services to maritime transport within Member States (maritime cabotage) [1992] OJ L364/7...47, 72–73
Arts 1...72
Art 3...72
Art 3(1)...72
Art 3(2)...72, 73, 95
Art 3(3)...72, 73, 95
Reg 793/93 on the evaluation and control of the risks of existing substances [1993] OJ L84/1
Rec 1...238

Reg 3118/93 laying down the conditions under which non-resident carriers may operate national road haulage services within a Member State [1993] OJ L279/1 156
Art 6 156
Reg 40/94 on the Community trade mark [1993] OJ L11/1 120
Art 8 119
Art 51(1)(b) 195
Reg 2988/95 on the protection of the European Communities financial interests [1995] OJ L312/1 44–47
Art 1 46
Art 1(2) 45
Art 4(3) 46–47, 103
Reg 384/96 on protection against dumped imports from countries not members of the European Community [1995] OJ L56/1 288
Reg 800/1999 laying down common detailed rules for the application of the system of export refunds on agricultural products [1999] OJ 102/11 185
Reg 1346/2000 on Insolvency Proceedings [2000] OJ L160/1 130
Rec 4 130
Art 3 ....206, 208
Art 4 206
Reg 44/2001 on jurisdiction and the recognition and enforcement of judgments in civil and commercial matters (Brussels I) [2001] OJ L12/1
Art 15(1)(c) 134
Reg 2201/2003 concerning jurisdiction and the recognition and enforcement of judgments in matrimonial matters and the matters of parental responsibility, repealing Regulation 1347/2000 (Brussels II) [2003] OJ L338/1
Art 3(1) 141
Art 8(1) 141
Reg 139/2004 on the control of concentrations between undertakings (EC Merger Regulation) [2004] OJ L24/1 347
Rec 4 347
Rec 5 347
Art 2(3) 347
Reg 261/2004 establishing common rules on compensation and assistance to passengers in the event of denied boarding and of cancellation or long delay of flights, and repealing Regulation 295/91 [2004] OJ L46/1 178–79
Art 7 178–79
Reg 1236/2005 concerning trade in goods which could be used for capital punishment, torture or other cruel, inhuman or degrading treatment or punishment [2005] OJ L200/1
Rec 10 17
Reg 1889/2006 on establishing a financing instrument for the promotion of democracy and human rights worldwide [2006] OJ L386/1
Art 1(2) 17
Reg 423/2007 concerning restrictive measures against Iran [2007] OJ L103/1 112
Art 7(2) 112
Reg 1370/2007 on public passenger transport services by rail and by road and repealing Council Regulations 1191/69 and 1107/70 [2007] OJ L315/1 113
Rec 23 113

Reg 207/2009 on the Community trade mark [2009] OJ L78/1..120
Reg 169/2009 applying rules of competition and transport by rail, road and inland waterway [2009] OJ L61/1
Art 1...20
Reg 612/2009 on laying down common detailed rules for the application of the system of export refunds on agricultural products (recast) [2009] OJ L186/1..185
Rec 23–30 186
Rec 25 288
Rec 35 186
Re 43 186
Art 27...186, 199, 203
Art 27(4)(c) 104
Reg 1225/2009 on protection against dumped imports from countries not members of the European Community [2009] OJ L343/51
Art 1(2)..309

Other
Rules of Procedure of the Court of Justice [2010] OJ C177/1
Art 139...21, 28, 31

International Conventions

European Convention on the legal protection of services based on, or consisting of, conditional access (adopted 24 January 2001, entered into force 1 July 2003) 2246 UNTS 29...282
Geneva Convention on the high seas (adopted 29 April 1958, entered into force 30 September 1962) 450 UNTS 11
Art 5(1)..163, 165, 201
Montego Bay Convention on the law of the sea (adopted 10 December 1982, entered into force 16 November 1994) 1834 UNTS 3..164
Reykjavik Convention for the conservation of salmon in the North Atlantic Ocean (adopted 2 March 1982, entered into force 1 October 1983) 1338 UNTS 33...164

General Introduction: The Topicality of the Concept of Abuse of Union Law

THE RELOCATION OF businesses for regulatory motives, namely cross-border movements spurred not by the prospect of a better economic environment but by the prospect of more hospitable laws, constitutes one of the most salient economic and political phenomena of this early-twenty-first century. Not a day goes by without stories of relocation or threats of relocation being related in the press, together with the correlative obligation of States to remain 'competitive'. Aggressive tax planning or tax avoidance, a kindred phenomenon by which private persons (chiefly multinational corporations) structure their activities not to improve their efficiency but to elect a hospitable tax jurisdiction, has raised sufficiently ample concern to attract official reactions from the G8,[1] the US Congress,[2] the OECD,[3] the European Parliament,[4] the European Commission,[5] the European Council,[6] the Council[7] and the European Economic and Social Committee.[8]

[1] G8 Summit, 'Lough Erne Declaration', 18 June 2013.

[2] JG Gravelle, 'Tax Havens: International Tax Avoidance and Evasion' (CRS Report for US Congress), 23 January 2013.

[3] OECD, *Action Plan on Base Erosion and Profit Shifting* (Paris, OECD Publishing, 2013).

[4] Parliament (EC), 'Fight against Tax Fraud, Tax Evasion and Tax Havens' (Report) A7-0162/2013, 2 May 2013.

[5] Commission (EC), 'Concrete ways to reinforce the fight against tax fraud and tax evasion including in relation to third countries' (Communication) COM (2012) 351 final, 27 June 2012; Commission (EC), 'Impact Assessment accompanying inter alia Commission Recommendation on aggressive tax planning' (Staff Working Document) SWD (2012) 403 final, 6 December 2012; Commission (EC), 'An Action Plan to strengthen the fight against tax fraud and tax evasion' (Communication) COM (2012) 722 final, 6 December 2012; Commission (EC), 'Measures intended to encourage third countries to apply minimum standards of good governance in tax matters' (Recommendation) C (2012) 8805 final, 6 December 2012; Commission (EC), 'Aggressive tax planning' (Recommendation) C (2012) 8806 final, 6 December 2012.

[6] European Council (EC), 'Conclusions' EUCO 75/1/13, 22 May 2013.

[7] Council (EC), 'Council conclusions on tax evasion and tax fraud' 9549/13, 14 May 2013.

[8] European Economic and Social Committee (EC), 'Tax and financial havens: a threat to the EU's internal market' (Own-Initiative Opinion) C229/02, 24 May 2012.

These phenomena of relocation and aggressive tax planning are manifestations of a general tendency of private mobility to become a systemic constraint upon public action. Admittedly, private mobility has always been a sporadic thorn in the side of public power. Voltaire, for instance, is well known for having acquired in 1759 a castle erected on the border between the kingdom of France and the republic of Geneva, in a town nowadays called Ferney-Voltaire. From that moment onwards, Voltaire would alternatively slip into exile in France or Geneva, allegedly by moving to the appropriate wing of his castle, in reaction to public action taken in either country. Thus, when French authorities planned to requisition all golden and silver crockery on French territory in order to melt it into coins, Voltaire claimed that his crockery was a product of Geneva.[9]

Nevertheless, it can hardly be disputed that the impact of private mobility upon public power has taken on a systemic dimension in the last decades, as illustrated by the exponential growth of the phenomena of relocation and aggressive tax planning, under the combined influence of socioeconomic and legal factors. On the one hand, new communication technologies and modern transportation means have provoked an explosion of private mobility. On the other hand, the European process of integration has reached a specific moment in which territorial unity is secured (through the enforcement of the freedoms of movement) but regulatory diversity preserved (no Union harmonisation). This legal environment structurally opens a space for cross-border movements designed to elect a more hospitable jurisdiction, which new communication technologies and modern transportation means enable private individuals to exploit.

Within the Union legal order, the concept of abuse of Union law has progressively become the main forum in which the effects of private mobility upon public action are apprehended. Abuses of Union law can be defined as undesirable choices of law artificially made by private individuals. In a cross-border context, abuses of Union law are best described as an unequal cat-and-mouse game, in which the public cat is confined to a national territory, whereas the private mice may run across the Union territory. Put more formally, abusive practices are attempts by Union citizens to exploit the discrepancy between the national scope of public action undertaken by Member States and the Union-wide scope of private action guaranteed by the freedoms of movement. In cases such as *Centros* or *Cadbury Schweppes*, corporations sought to escape public action in the State of origin (Danish company law in *Centros*, UK direct taxation in *Cadbury Schweppes*) and place themselves under the public action of a hospitable jurisdiction (UK company law in *Centros*, Irish direct taxation in *Cadbury Schweppes*).[10]

[9] See L Choudin et al, *Voltaire à Ferney 1759–2009* (Ferney, Fondation Voltaire à Ferney, 2009) 12. Many such anecdotes are recounted in the diaries of Voltaire's life in Ferney, published by the Fondation Voltaire à Ferney and available at http://voltaire-a-ferney.org/13.html.

[10] Case C-212/97 *Centros* [1999] ECR I-1459; Case C-196/04 *Cadbury Schweppes* [2006] ECR I-7995.

By outlawing artificial choices of law, the prohibition of abusive practices allows the public cat to catch runaway mice.

The study of the concept of abuse of Union law is, however, complicated by the fundamental ambivalence of Union law towards artificial choices of law. In some cases, artificial choices of law are ratified as the legitimate exercise of the freedoms of movement (*Centros*), whereas they are prohibited as abusive in other cases (*Cadbury Schweppes*). More generally, few concepts of Union law have proved as controversial as that of 'abuse of Union law', both in the case law of the Court of Justice of the European Union (the Court) and in the vast literature on the subject, which are thoroughly examined in the course of this study.[11]

The central question addressed by the present study is, accordingly, the following: how can the apparently simple concept of abuse of Union law generate so much disagreement among equally intelligent individuals? Seeking to transcend the classical debate between its supporters and adversaries, the present study submits that the concept of abuse of Union law straddles three major fault-lines of Union law, which accounts for the amount of controversy it creates.

The *first fault-line*, which is common to all legal orders, opposes legal congruence (the tendency to yield equitable legal outcomes) to legal certainty (the tendency to yield predictable legal outcomes). Partisans of legal congruence tend to advocate the prohibition of abuses of law, whereas partisans of legal certainty tend to oppose it.

The *second fault-line* is specific to Union law and divides two conceptions of the regulation of the internal market. If economic integration is conceived as the promotion of cross-border competition among private businesses (the paradigm of 'regulatory neutrality'), choices of law must be proscribed as abusive, for they distort business competition. But if economic integration is intended to promote competition among Member States (the paradigm of 'regulatory competition'), choices of law by Union citizens represent a desirable process of arbitrage among national laws.

The *third and final fault-line* corresponds to the tension between two orientations of the economic constitution of the European Union, namely the fear of private power and the fear of public power. Those who are more fearful of private power tend to endorse the prohibition of abuses of law, whereas those who are more fearful of public power tend to reject it.

Seen in this way, the concept of abuse of Union law offers a forum in which fundamental questions about the nature and function of Union law can be confronted and examined in a new light.

The content of this study can be outlined as follows. Part one proceeds to the deconstruction of the phenomenon of abuse of Union law.

[11] By way of preliminary illustration, the concept of abuse of Union law was rejected by AG La Pergola but adopted by AG Maduro: see AG La Pergola, Case C-212/97 *Centros* [1999] ECR I-1459; Case C-446/03 *Marks & Spencer* [2005] ECR I-10837; AG Maduro, Case C-255/02 *Halifax* [2006] ECR I-1609; AG Maduro, Case C-311/06 *Cavallera* [2009] ECR I-415.

Chapter one proposes a negative definition of abuse of law, by differentiating it from other phenomena commonly coined as 'abusive' under Union law. Chiefly, abuses of law are committed by private individuals and must accordingly be distinguished from abuses committed by public authorities. Moreover, if abuses of rights are committed by private individuals, they constitute undesirable exercises of an existing right, whereas abuses of law form undesirable acquisitions of a new right.

Chapter two is devoted to the formal doctrine of abuse enounced by the Court in *Emsland-Stärke*. A particular emphasis will be put on the legislative origins of the doctrine and on eight seminal judgments in which the Court applied the formal doctrine of abuse: *Emsland-Stärke*, *Halifax*, *Agip Petroli*, *Cadbury Schweppes*, *Vonk Dairy Products*, *Thin Cap Group Litigation*, *ING. AUER* and *Part Service*. Three steps can be identified in the evolution of the formal doctrine of abuse: its first enunciation in the field of export refunds, in *Emsland-Stärke* (December 2000); the extension of its scope to all 'internal' abuses of law, in *Halifax* (February 2006); and the extension of its scope to 'cross-border' abuses of law, in *Cadbury Schweppes* (September 2006).

Chapter three proposes a positive definition of the concept of abuse of Union law. In essence, abuses of Union law will be defined as undesirable choices of law artificially made by private individuals. This definition can be decomposed into three elements: the presence of a gain-seeking choice of law, the artificiality requirement and the teleological assessment. The last section of this chapter describes the sanction of abusive practices, which consists in denying the undesirable choice of law attempted without questioning the validity of the economic transactions carried out.

Chapter four explores the alternative reactions of Union law, next to the formal doctrine of abuse, to artificial choices of law made by private individuals. Such strategies are indeed commonly addressed without having recourse to the formal doctrine of abuse, which can be shown through an extensive survey of Union case law and legislation. These alternative reactions include informal doctrines of abuse, suspect periods, centre of gravity tests, free choice of law approaches and other legal grounds unrelated to the issue of abuse. This survey should incidentally demonstrate that the phenomenon of abuse of Union law is much broader than often assumed, and is by no means limited to cases in which the Court applied the formal doctrine of abuse.

Chapter five investigates the first fault-line on which is located the concept of abuse of Union law, namely the trade-off between legal certainty and legal congruence. Without disputing that the prohibition of abusive practices is a source of legal uncertainty, this chapter argues that such criticism is simplistic as it ignores another fundamental value of any legal order, designated as legal congruence. Every legal order is characterised by a well-established trade-off between legal certainty and legal congruence: the more predictable are legal norms, the less equitable they can be in particular cases. Accordingly, the concept of abuse of Union law must be appraised in light of this trade-off between legal certainty and legal congruence; in particular, the prohibition of abusive practices amounts to a decision to reinstate legal congruence at the expense of legal certainty in particular cases.

Part two undertakes a reconstruction of the phenomenon of abuse of Union law in light of the process of economic integration initiated by the Treaty of Paris establishing the European Coal and Steel Community (ECSC) in 1951.

Chapter six identifies the existence of two paradigms of economic integration designated as the paradigms of 'regulatory neutrality' and 'regulatory competition'. The regulatory neutrality paradigm seeks to avoid competition among private businesses being distorted by national regulations, therefore aiming at the creation of a 'level playing field', an idealised situation in which all businesses competing throughout the internal market are subject to identical regulatory conditions. The regulatory competition paradigm seeks to ensure the proper functioning of the process of competition among Member States, and accordingly aims at maximising the opportunities for regulatory arbitrage, a process by which citizens elect the national law best suited to their preferences. As a result, the regulatory neutrality paradigm promotes 'socioeconomic' mobility, whereas the regulatory competition paradigm promotes 'regulatory' mobility (choice of law).

Chapter seven enquires into the contradictory influence of the paradigms of regulatory neutrality and regulatory competition upon the law of the internal market. The trade-off between those two paradigms of economic integration materialises in three central 'nodes' of internal market law: positive harmonisation (Union regulation or not), negative harmonisation (home or host regulation) and regulatory mobility (restricted or free choice of law). In other words, while mostly ignored, the conflicting influences of the regulatory neutrality and regulatory competition paradigms account to a considerable extent for the inconsistency of the free movement jurisprudence.

Chapter eight corroborates the existence of a causal link between the coexistence of two paradigms of economic integration, on the one hand, and the contradictions of internal market law, on the other, by re-examining a few practical issues of free movement law: the ambivalent status of differentials of regulation, the acceptance of reverse discriminations, the inconsistent prohibition of abuses of law and the ambiguity towards social dumping. Indeed, the solutions advocated to these practical issues depend on the adoption, most often unconscious, of either regulatory neutrality or regulatory competition as a paradigm of economic integration. Therefore, the trade-off between regulatory neutrality and regulatory competition constitutes a second fault-line of Union law accounting for the controversies surrounding the concept of abuse of Union law.

Chapter nine proposes an alternative reading of the State aid regime, based on the established trade-off between the paradigms of regulatory neutrality and regulatory competition. Indeed, the very principle of a prohibition of State aids can only be accounted for by the regulatory neutrality paradigm; on the other hand, restrictions to the scope of that prohibition (through the criteria of selectivity and transfer of State resources) are best understood in light of the regulatory competition paradigm. Incidentally, this alternative reading has the advantage of providing a common framework of analysis for the freedoms of movement and the State aid regime.

Chapter ten adopts a broader perspective and interprets the emergence of the concept of abuse of Union law as an evolution of the economic constitution of the European Union, by which public power seeks to reaffirm its capacity to control private power within the internal market. The combination of low moving costs, high regulatory diversity and high territorial unity has led to the emergence of a new form of private power originating in mobility, enabling private individuals to escape the deployment of public power. The practical effect of the prohibition of abusive practices is to restrict this new private power originating in mobility, to the benefit of public power. In that context, the ambivalence towards abusive practices can be usefully reconstructed in light of the tension between fear of private power and fear of public power, which forms the third fault-line on which the concept of abuse of Union is located: those who are more fearful of private power tend to advocate the prohibition of abusive practices, whereas those who are more fearful of public power tend to reject it.

Part I

The Phenomenon of Abuse of Union Law

Introduction: A Dynamic Perspective on Abuses of Union Law

THE STUDY OF the phenomenon of abuse of Union law is characterised by a lack of clarity at the terminological, conceptual and practical levels. First, the terminology surrounding the abuse of law is notoriously versatile: on the one hand, the term 'abuse' and its derivatives are regularly used to aim at a broad range of phenomena going well beyond abuses of law; on the other hand, abuses of law are often addressed without having recourse to the term 'abuse' or its derivatives. Secondly, the definition of the concept of abuse of law has proved controversial, particularly in relation to the eventual use of subjective criteria and the distinction between abuse of law and abuse of rights. Thirdly and lastly, the treatment applied in practice to abuses of law is still heavily debated, both with regard to the technique (autonomous doctrine of abuse or statutory construction) and the outcome (proscribed or ratified).

The objective assigned to this part one is the deconstruction of the phenomenon of abuse of Union law with a view to clarifying the terms of the controversies present in this vast field of study. To that end, chapter one proceeds to a preliminary identification of the phenomenon of abuse of law, starting with a statistical analysis of the numerous official acts of Union law mentioning the term 'abuse'. Two central distinctions will be drawn from this statistical analysis: the distinction between abuses committed by public authorities and by private individuals, on the one hand, and between abuses of law and abuse of rights, on the other.

Following the identification of the phenomenon of abuse of Union law, chapter two is devoted to the formal doctrine of abuse enounced by the Court in *Emsland-Stärke*. A particular emphasis will be put on the legislative origins of the doctrine and on eight seminal judgments in which the Court applied the formal doctrine of abuse: *Emsland-Stärke*, *Halifax*, *Agip Petroli*, *Cadbury Schweppes*, *Vonk Dairy Products*, *Thin Cap Group Litigation*, *ING. AUER* and *PartService*.

Building on the knowledge gained from the identification of the abuse of Union law and the study of the formal doctrine of abuse, chapter three proposes a definition of the concept of abuse of law. In essence, abuses of Union law will be defined as undesirable choices of law artificially made by private individuals. This definition can be decomposed in three elements: the presence of a gain-seeking choice of law attempted by a Union citizen; the artificiality requirement, which aims at identifying 'naked' choices of law that cannot be explained but for the regulatory benefit sought; and the teleological assessment, which seeks to determine whether such choices of law are desirable in the context of the legal regime affected. The last section describes the sanction of abusive practices, which consists in denying the undesirable choice of law attempted without questioning the validity of the economic transactions carried out.

On the basis of the definition of abuse of law established in the previous chapter, chapter four seeks to identify and treat a critical mass of Union legal acts in which abuses of Union law are addressed by means of alternative legal grounds, namely without having recourse to the formal doctrine of abuse. Common Union law reactions to artificial practices include informal doctrines of abuse, suspect periods, centre of gravity tests, free choice of law approaches or other legal grounds unrelated to the issue of abuse of law. This survey should incidentally demonstrate that the prohibition of abusive practices is a much broader phenomenon than is often contended, by no means limited to the cases in which the Court applied the formal doctrine of abuse.

Lastly, chapter five is devoted to the long-standing debate on the room for legal uncertainty entailed by the prohibition of abuses of Union law. Without disputing that the prohibition of abusive practices is a source of legal uncertainty, this chapter argues that such criticism is simplistic as it ignores another fundamental value of any legal order, designated as legal congruence. Every legal order is characterised by a well-established trade-off between legal certainty and legal congruence: the more predictable are legal norms, the less equitable they can be in particular cases. The concept of abuse of law must be appraised in light of this trade-off between legal certainty and legal congruence. On the one hand, artificial practices are manifestations of a lack of legal congruence of Union law; in that sense, legal certainty can be viewed as a source of artificial practices. On the other hand, the fight against artificial practices amounts to a decision to reinstate legal congruence at the expense of legal certainty in particular cases.

Overall, this part one should hopefully provide a dynamic perspective on the phenomenon of abuse of Union law. Abuses of Union law form part of an endless cycle of public action and private reaction. Abuses of law are reactions of Union citizens to the adoption of Union laws; by contrast with other 'abusive' phenomena, they are characterised by the private nature of their author and the public nature of the victim (abuse private-public: chapter one). Indeed, Union laws are likely to be abused by Union citizens whenever they leave room for artificial choices of law (definition of abuse of Union law: chapter three). This private reception of Union laws provokes a renewal of public action at Union level: indeed, Union law reacts to artificial practices in specific ways explored in chapters two (formal doctrine of abuse) and four (alternative reactions). Yet these reactions of Union law are contradictory, as artificial practices can be either proscribed or ratified. As explained in the General Introduction, understanding this contradiction in the reactions of Union law to artificial practices is the fundamental purpose assigned to this study. A first explanation is sketched in chapter five, which submits that the concept of abuse of Union law cuts across an unsolvable trade-off present in every legal order and which opposes legal certainty to legal congruence.

1

Identification of the Phenomenon of Abuse of Union Law

THIS FIRST CHAPTER seeks to introduce and identify the phenomenon of abuse of Union law, by contrasting it with other phenomena of 'abuse', chiefly the abuse of rights. The use of the term 'abuse' and of its derivatives is indeed extremely common in the legal vocabulary of the European Union. A simple search executed on the official website of the European Union (*EUR-Lex*) is edifying on the near-frivolity with which the abuse terminology is invoked:[1] during the period 1954–2009, 5785 official documents mentioned the term 'abuse' or one of its derivatives. Within the European Treaties, which form the primary law of the European Union, the term 'abuse' appears in the three following contexts: first, in competition law, which prohibits *abuses of a dominant position* (Articles 102 and 104 TFEU, former Articles 82 and 84 EC); secondly, in the chapter on the protection of public health, in relation to the *abuse of alcohol* (Article 168 TFEU; the former Article 152 EC did not explicitly emphasise that objective); and finally, in Article 54 of the Charter of Fundamental Rights, which prohibits *abuses of rights* (replicating Article 17 of the European Convention on Human Rights).

The growing presence of the abuse terminology in Court's rulings, regulations, directives and, overall, in the whole of European Union official documents is striking, as shown in Table 1 and Figure 1.

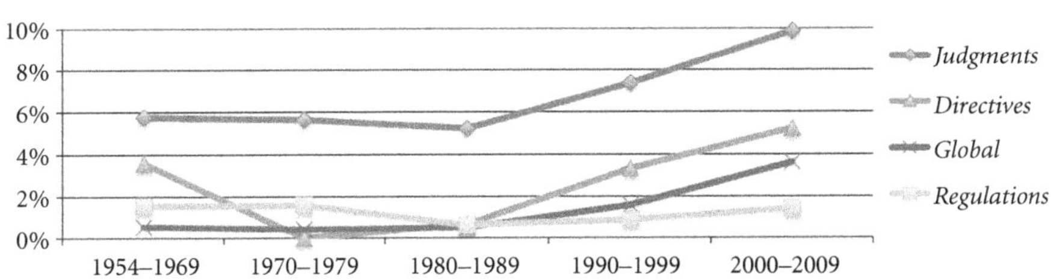

Figure 1 – Union Official Documents Mentioning the Term 'Abuse' (1954–2009): Chart

[1] The methodology applied to retrieve the data exploited in this chapter is described in the Annex.

Table 1 – Union Official Documents Mentioning the Term 'Abuse' (1954–2009): Data

	Judgments			**Regulations**			**Directives**			**Global**		
	Total	*Abuse*	*Ratio*	*Total*	*Abuse*	*Ratio*	*Total*	*Abuse*	*Ratio*	*Total*	*Abuse*	*Ratio*
1954–69	294	17	5.8%	65	1	1.5%	28	1	3.6%	8297	44	0.5%
1970–79	833	47	5.6%	321	5	1.6%	175	0	0.0%	33240	138	0.4%
1980–89	1779	93	5.2%	657	4	0.6%	295	2	0.7%	73600	379	0.5%
1990–99	2093	155	7.4%	2039	18	0.9%	512	17	3.3%	106428	1688	1.6%
2000–09	3433	339	9.9%	5425	76	1.4%	979	52	5.3%	97584	3536	3.6%
Total	**8432**	**651**	**7.7%**	**8507**	**104**	**1.2%**	**1989**	**72**	**3.6%**	**319149**	**5785**	**1.8%**

Both in absolute and relative terms, the evolution of the number of Union official documents mentioning the term 'abuse' is impressive. In relative terms, their number has been growing steadily since 1980 in all four types of documents, the most impressive growths concerning directives (from 0.7 per cent to 5.3 per cent of abuse presence) and the global set of official documents (from 0.6 per cent to 3.6 per cent). For the period 2000–09 alone, 339 Court rulings, 76 regulations, 52 directives and overall 3536 European Union official documents mentioned the term 'abuse' or a derivative (contrast with 17, 1, 1 and 44 for the period 1954–69). The evolution is particularly marked for the activity of the Court: if the Court used the term 'abuse' (or a derivative) once in every 19 decisions during the period 1980–89, it did so once in every 10 judgments during the period 2000–09.[2] Still more impressively, the Advocates General had recourse to the abuse terminology once in every 22 Opinions during the period 1980–89, and nearly once in every five Opinions during the period 2000–09.[3]

In short, *abuse is everywhere* in Union law. To explain this omnipresence of the abuse terminology, one could evoke both the adaptability and the high illustrative force of the word 'abuse', which is capable of spelling out striking ideas in very different contexts. However, this omnipresence of the abuse terminology creates a serious methodological pitfall to studies on any phenomenon of abuse: the identification of the right phenomenon among the plethoric set of utilisations of the abuse terminology.[4]

In order to identify the phenomenon of abuse of Union law within this vast set of occurrences, it is convenient to work on a reduced and yet representative sample of occurrences. In that regard, a search restricted to Court rulings, regulations and directives still generates a list of 827 occurrences of the word 'abuse' (or a derivative): 651 Court rulings, 104 regulations and 72 directives. Among those 827 occurrences, 81 can be discarded as irrelevant (mostly Court rulings merely quoting a legal provision mentioning the term 'abuse'), which leaves the conscientious reader with 746 relevant mentions of abuse. When one strives to sort those 746 mentions by the public or private nature of the parties involved, the following picture progressively emerges from the abuse limbo (as shown in Table 2 and Figure 2), in which behaviours qualified as 'abusive' in Union law can be classified in four categories: public-public (I), public-private (II), private-private (III), private-public (IV).

[2] Those statistics only concern judgments issued by the Court, which excludes: orders of the Court, judgments and orders of the General Court and the Civil Service Tribunal AG Opinions.

[3] Rate of 18.6% for the period 2000-09 (416 Opinions out of 2242); of 11.5% for the period 1990–99 (241 Opinions out of 2098); and of 4.6% for the period 1980-89 (79 Opinions out of 1714).

[4] See eg M Gestri, *Abuso del Diritto e Frode alla Legge nell'Ordinamento Comunitario* (Milan, Giuffrè, 2003) 4–13; A Kjellgren, 'On the Border of Abuse—The Jurisprudence of the European Court of Justice on Circumvention, Fraud and Other Misuses of Community Law' (2000) 11 *European Business Law Review* 179, 179–80; D Triantafyllou, 'L'interdiction des abus de droit en tant que principe général du droit communautaire' (2002) 38 *Cahiers de Droit Européen* 611, 612–13.

Table 2 – Evolution of the 'Abuse Distribution' (1954–2009): Data

	Abuse I				Abuse II				Abuse III				Abuse IV				Irrelevant				
	ECJ	*Reg*	*Dir*	*Total*	*ECJ*	*Reg*	*Dir*	*Total*	*ECJ*	*Reg*	*Dir*	*Total*	*ECJ*	*Reg*	*Dir*	*Total*	*ECJ*	*Reg*	*Dir*	*Total*	*Total*
1954–69	3	0	0	3	5	0	0	5	4	1	0	5	5	0	1	6	0	0	0	0	**19**
1970–79	1	0	0	1	5	0	0	5	28	2	0	30	13	3	0	16	0	0	0	0	**52**
1980–89	1	0	0	1	8	0	1	9	52	2	0	54	31	2	0	33	1	0	1	2	**99**
1990–99	1	0	0	1	11	1	0	12	83	2	10	95	46	15	7	68	14	0	0	14	**190**
2000–09	9	1	0	10	9	5	1	15	123	33	33	189	133	37	18	188	65	0	0	65	**467**
Total	**15**	**1**	**0**	**16**	**38**	**6**	**2**	**46**	**290**	**40**	**43**	**373**	**228**	**57**	**26**	**311**	**80**	**0**	**1**	**81**	**827**

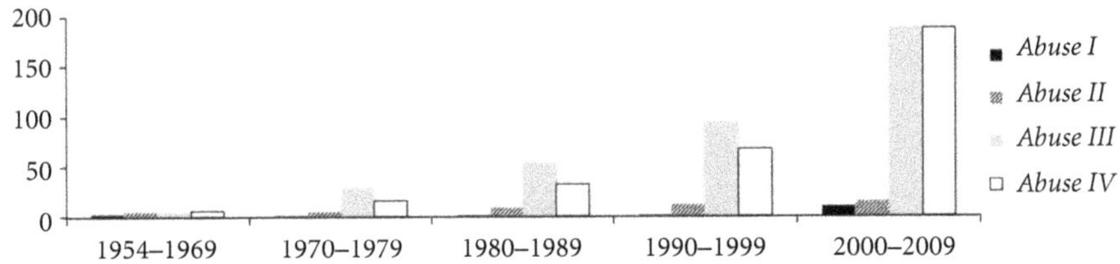

Figure 2 – Evolution of the 'Abuse Distribution' (1954–2009): Chart

This distinction between abuses committed by public authorities and by private individuals is routinely made in the literature on abuse of Union law: for instance, Lyons distinguishes between abuses committed by economic operators and by institutions; similarly, Triantafyllou opposes abuses committed by Union institutions and Member States to abuses committed by private individuals.[5] In this typology, public authorities act in their public capacity when they exercise a prerogative of public power, chiefly the power of adopting binding laws. By contrast, public authorities act in a private capacity whenever they are themselves subject to binding laws, and not authors of binding laws.[6] Thus, abuse by a public authority of the right to initiate judicial proceedings is classified in the category private-private, since it does not involve prerogatives of public power (type III).[7] By contrast, the abusive adoption of a regulation involves the exercise of public power, and must accordingly be classified in the category public-public (type I) or public-private (type II).

As shall be explained below, abuses of Union law are committed by private individuals at the expense of communities of individuals (abuses private-public, type IV). The growing concern generated by abuses of law over the last 30 years is statistically demonstrated by the evolution of the distribution of 'abuse' references among all four categories of abuse. Indeed, as shown in Figure 2, the share of abuses of type IV among the mentions of abuse has been growing steadily since the period 1980–89, and ended up equalling the importance of abuses of type III during the period 2000–09.[8] In addition, those statistics do not include the numerous cases in which Union institutions addressed abuses of law without

[5] T Lyons, 'State Aid, Taxation and Abuse of Law' in R de la Feria and S Vogenauer (eds), *Prohibition of Abuse of Law: a New General Principle of EU Law?* (Oxford, Hart Publishing, 2011) 494–500; Triantafyllou, 'L'interdiction des abus de droit en tant que principe général du droit communautaire' (n 4) 612. See also Gestri, *Abuso del Diritto e Frode alla Legge nell'Ordinamento Comunitario* (n 4) 6–8; A Noblet, *La lutte contre le contournement des droits nationaux en droit communautaire* (Lille, ANRT, 2004) 13.

[6] A classical instance of abuse of law (abuse private-public) committed by public authorities is specifically prohibited by the public procurement directives: see ch 4 nn 47–48 and accompanying text.

[7] See eg Joined Cases C-501/06 P, C-513/06 P, C-515/06 P and C-519/06 P *GlaxoSmithKline* [2009] ECR I-9291, para 31; Case C-394/02 *Commission v Greece* [2005] ECR I-4713, paras 25–28.

[8] When considered globally (proportion of abuses of type IV within all European Union documents), this growth is even higher since the proportion of Union documents mentioning the term 'abuse' has itself steadily grown over the least 30 years.

ever mentioning the term 'abuse;'[9] if those occurrences were included, the growth of abuses of type IV would be even higher.

I. Abuses Committed by Public Authorities

A small share of the 746 mentions of 'abuse' aim at behaviours adopted by public authorities at the expense of either other public authorities (abuses of type I, public-public: 1.9 per cent of total occurrences) or private individuals (abuses of type II, public-private: 5.6 per cent of total occurrences). If the Treaties do not explicitly aim at 'abuses of power' committed by public authorities, Article 263 TFEU grants jurisdiction to the Court to review the legality of Union acts intended to produce legal effects vis-à-vis third parties, in actions 'brought by a Member State, the European Parliament, the Council or the Commission on grounds of … misuse of powers'. The category of '*détournement de pouvoir*' or misuse of power is a classical concept aiming at abuses of public power.[10] By virtue of Article 263 TFEU (and its predecessors), the Court has thus addressed pleas of 'misuse of power' without ever mentioning the word 'abuse',[11] so that those cases were not indexed in the count previously exposed.

Still, a handful of the Court's rulings referring to the concept of 'abuse' concern disputes among public authorities (abuses public-public, type I). For instance, 'abuse' has been argued to contest the competence of the Council to adopt certain provisions of Council Directive 2005/85/EC (provisions annulled)[12] or a decision authorising a State aid (decision annulled).[13] In that context, the argument of abuse is used to qualify actions allegedly outside the sphere of competence of

[9] See, among many others, Case C-311/06 *Cavallera* [2009] ECR I-415; Case C-73/06 *Planzer* [2007] ECR I-5655; Case C-419/02 *BUPA Hospitals* [2006] ECR I-1685; Case C-63/04 *Centralan* [2005] ECR I-11087; Case C-41/04 *Levob* [2005] ECR I-9433; Case C-452/03 *RAL* [2005] ECR I-3947; Case 81/87 *Daily Mail* [1988] ECR 5483; Case 33/74 *Van Binsbergen* [1974] ECR 1299; AG Stix-Hackl, Case C-452/04 *Fidium Finanz* [2006] ECR I-9521, para 96. Many scholars have underlined the Court's terminological inconsistency, which indifferently refers to abuse, abusive practice, avoidance, evasion, circumvention, fraud, sham or wholly artificial arrangement: see S Vogenauer, 'The Prohibition of Abuse of Law: an Emerging General Principle of EU Law' in de la Feria and Vogenauer, *Prohibition of Abuse of Law* (n 5) 524–25; R de la Feria, 'Prohibition of Abuse of (Community) Law: the Creation of a New General Principle of EC Law through Tax' (2008) 45 *Common Market Law Review* 395, 396; P Schammo, 'Arbitrage and Abuse of Rights in the EC Legal System' (2008) 14 *European Law Journal* 351, 358; L Cerioni, 'The "Abuse of Rights" in EU Company Law and EU Tax Law: A Re-reading of the ECJ Case Law and the Quest for a Unitary Notion' (2010) 21 *European Business Law Review* 783, 783.

[10] See Gestri (n 4) 6–7.

[11] See eg Case C-285/94 *Italy v Commission* [1997] ECR I-3519, para 52; Case C-84/94 *United Kingdom v Council* [1996] ECR I-5755, para 69; Case C-156/93 *Parliament v Commission* [1995] ECR I-2019, para 31.

[12] Case C-133/06 *Parliament v Council* [2008] ECR I-3189, para 30.

[13] Case C-399/03 *Commission v Council* [2006] ECR I-5629, para 15.

their author, an institution of the European Union. For the same motives, the Commission accused the Council of 'abuse of process' for having adopted, without having recourse to the Community method, Council Framework Decision 2003/80/JHA of 27 January 2003 on the protection of the environment through criminal law (framework decision annulled).[14] More frequently, the Commission itself is accused of 'abusing' its power by Member States; for instance, in a seminal State aid case, the Italian Government argued that 'by encroaching upon a field reserved by the Treaty to the sovereignty of Member States—that of the levying of internal taxation—the [Commission's decision was] vitiated by reason of abuse of powers'.[15] Other such examples include the Commission's assessments regarding the dangerousness of added nitrites and nitrates used in foodstuffs (decision annulled),[16] the definition of the category of 'young persons' (decision upheld)[17] or the liability of the Italian State following its failure to check the quality of canned meat delivered to the people of the Soviet Union (decision upheld).[18]

A second group of European Union documents mentioning the term 'abuse' can be classified as abuses public-private (type II), in which public bodies abuse their prerogatives of public power at the expense of private individuals. Human rights 'abuses' form the worst form of abuses committed by States against private individuals, and are mentioned as such in several instruments of secondary legislation.[19] But public institutions are liable to commit milder forms of abuse of power. As a matter of fact, the very first Court decision mentioning the term 'abuse' was *Algera* (1957), in which it was alleged that the Common Assembly of the ECSC had abusively withdrawn decisions regarding the grade and seniority of certain staff members.[20] Later, abuse of power has been argued against the Commission in relation to the management of its staff;[21] the classification of dangerous substances (in execution of Council Directive 67/548)[22] or of veterinary medicinal products in foodstuffs of animal origin (in execution

[14] Case C-176/03 *Commission v Council* [2005] ECR I-7879, para 24.

[15] Case 173/73 *Italy v Commission* [1973] ECR 709, para 12.

[16] Case C-3/00 *Denmark v Commission* [2003] ECR I-2643, para 104.

[17] Case C-310/99 *Italy v Commission* [2002] ECR I-2289, paras 56–57.

[18] Case C-198/94 *Italy v Commission* [1996] ECR I-2797, para 29.

[19] See, inter alia, Regulation (EC) 1889/2006 of the European Parliament and of the Council of 20 December 2006 on establishing a financing instrument for the promotion of democracy and human rights worldwide [2006] OJ L386/1 art 1(2); Council Regulation (EC) 1236/2005 of 27 June 2005 concerning trade in certain goods which could be used for capital punishment, torture or other cruel, inhuman or degrading treatment or punishment [2005] OJ L200/1 rec 10; Council Directive 2004/83/EC of 29 April 2004 on minimum standards for the qualification and status of third country nationals or stateless persons as refugees or as persons who otherwise need international protection and the content of the protection granted [2004] OJ L304/2 art 29.

[20] Joined Cases 7/56 and 3/57 to 7/57 *Algera v ECSC Common Assembly* [1957] ECR 39, 56.

[21] Case C-153/99 P *Commission v Giannini* [2000] ECR I-2891, para 5; Case C-188/96 P *Commission v V* [1997] ECR I-6561, para 11; Case C-166/95 P *Commission v Daffix* [1997] ECR I-983, para 9; Case C-76/93 P *Scaramuzza v Commission* [1994] ECR I-5173, para 8; Case 346/82 *Pierre Favre v Commission* [1984] ECR 2269, para 31; Case 17/68 *Reinarz v Commission* [1969] ECR 61, para 10.

[22] Case C-425/08 *Enviro Tech v Etat belge* [2009] ECR I-10035, paras 65 and 71.

of Council Regulation 2377/90);[23] the imposition of sanctions in competition law;[24] access to documents;[25] the organisation of the common market for coal;[26] the organisation of the common agricultural policy;[27] the recovery of import duties;[28] the grant of subsidies (to support ecological tourism in Europe);[29] or public tenders.[30] Likewise, the Council and the Parliament have been accused of abusing their power: the Council in relation to health requirements for fresh meat (Council Directive 64/433/EEC)[31] and the imposition of anti-dumping duties;[32] the Parliament in relation to the management of its staff.[33]

Behaviour of Member States vis-à-vis private individuals was also qualified as 'abusive' in certain judgments of the Court. In *Brasserie du Pêcheur*, when examining the issue of State liability for breach of Union law, the Court referred to the eventuality of 'abuse of power' on the part of a national legislature.[34] The *Köbler* case concerned State liability for breach of Union law committed by a national judge: in that regard, the Commission submitted that the 'existence of a sufficiently serious breach of Community law should be recognised only where the national court is manifestly abusing its power or discernibly disregarding the meaning and scope of Community law'.[35] Furthermore, the Court has been asked to ascertain whether Member States had not 'abusively' restricted the freedom of movement of persons (requirement to produce a valid passport or identity card at internal frontiers)[36] or goods (justification on grounds of the protection of industrial and commercial property),[37] or the equal treatment for men and women (refusal to employ a woman as a chef in the Royal Marines).[38]

[23] Case C-248/99 P *France v Monsanto and Commission* [2002] ECR I-1, para 90.

[24] Case C-328/05 P *SGL Carbon* [2007] ECR I-3921, para 108; Case C-298/98 P *Metsä-Serla Sales* [2000] ECR I-10157, para 84; Case C-248/98 P *NV Koninklijke KNP BT* [2000] ECR I-9641, para 84; Case 45/69 *Boehringer Mannheim v Commission* [1970] ECR 769, para 52.

[25] Case C-41/00 P *Interporc* [2003] ECR I-2125, para 3 (quoting Case T-50/96 *Interporc* [1998] ECR II-3773, para 20) and 74 (quoting Case T-50/96 *Interporc* [1998] ECR II-3773, para 74).

[26] Case 8/83 *Officine Fratelli Bertoli v Commission* [1984] ECR 1649, para 24; Joined Cases 140, 146, 221 and 226/82 *Walzstahl-Vereinigung v Commission* [1984] ECR 951, para 15; Case 1/58 *Stork v ECSC High Authority* [1958] ECR 43, 31.

[27] Case C-313/04 *Franz Egenberger* [2006] ECR I-6331, para 36; Case 35/78 *Schouten* [1978] ECR 2543, para 3; Case 28/76 *Milac GmbH Groß- und Außenhandel* [1976] ECR 1639, para 9.

[28] Case 314/85 *Foto-Frost* [1987] ECR 4199, paras 9 and 29.

[29] Case C-433/97 P *IPK-München* [1999] ECR I-6795, paras 11 and 14.

[30] Case 126/83 *STS v Commission* [1984] ECR 2769, para 5.

[31] Case C-27/95 *Bakers of Nailsea* [1997] ECR I-1847, para 36.

[32] Joined Cases 277/85 and 300/85 *Canon v Council* [1988] ECR 5731, para 17.

[33] Case C-326/91 P *Henri de Compte v European Parliament* [1994] ECR I-2091, para 201; Case 268/80 *Guglielmi v European Parliament* [1981] ECR 2295, para 9; Case 46/72 *De Greef v Commission* [1973] ECR 543, para 46; Joined Cases 7/56 and 3/57 to 7/57 *Algera v ECSC Common Assembly* [1957] ECR 39, 56.

[34] Joined Cases C-46/93 and C-48/93 *Brasserie du Pêcheur and Factortame ('Factortame III')* [1996] ECR I-1029, para 73.

[35] Case C-224/01 *Köbler* [2003] ECR I-10239, para 19.

[36] Case C-378/97 *Wijsenbeek* [1999] ECR I-6207, para 36.

[37] Case C-317/91 *Deutsche Renault* [1993] ECR I-6227, para 19.

[38] Case C-273/97 *Sirdar* [1999] ECR I-7403, para 31.

II. Abuses Committed by Private Individuals

If public authorities do commit 'abuses' of power, the large majority of the 746 relevant allegations of 'abuse' have been argued against private individuals, in their relations either with other private individuals (abuses of type III, private-private: 45.1 per cent of total occurrences) or with public authorities (abuses of type IV, private-public: 37.6 per cent of total occurrences).

The crucial distinction investigated below concerns abuses of rights and abuses of law: if abuses of rights are committed at the expense of isolated citizens (abuse private-private, type III), abuses of law affect entire communities of citizens (abuse private-public, type IV).

A. Abuses Private-Private (including Abuses of Rights)

Abuses occurring between private individuals (abuses private-private, type III) are classically further decomposed into two subcategories, on the basis of their relationship with their legal environment.[39] On the one hand, abuses of rights occur within the framework of a specific right held by the abuser, such as the right to initiate judicial proceedings or intellectual property rights. On the other hand, abuses of factual situations are committed by individuals who do not act within the framework of well-identified rights, although their behaviour is shaped by their legal environment. In short, abuses of rights constitute abuses of a specific legal position, whereas abuses of factual situations merely occur within the general legal environment.

The main types of abuses of factual situations are abuses of a dominant position, market abuses, abuses against consumers and abuses against workers. Predictably, competition law is the field in which the term 'abuse' is the most quoted in a private-private setting; more precisely, the Court evoked abuses of a dominant position in 176 cases during the period 1954–2009, from *Établissements Consten*[40] in 1966 to *Der Grüne Punkt*[41] in 2009. Abuses of a dominant position consist in the exploitation by one or more undertakings of a situation of economic power[42] to the detriment of competitors and/or consumers. Abuses of a

[39] See A Metzger, 'Abuse of Law in EU Private Law: A (Re-)Construction from Fragments' in de la Feria and Vogenauer (n 5) 239 ('legal position'), 247 ('factual position') and 249 ('factual position'); VS Karayannis, 'L'abus des droits découlant de l'ordre juridique communautaire à propos de l'arrêt C-367/96 Kefalas' (1999) 35 *Cahiers de Droit Européen* 521, 526; Gestri (n 4) 10; Noblet, *La lutte contre le contournement des droits nationaux en droit communautaire* (n 5) 16 and 413; Triantafyllou (n 4) 612.

[40] Joined Cases 56 and 58/64 *Établissements Consten* [1966] ECR 429.

[41] Case C-385/07 P *Der Grüne Punkt* [2009] ECR I-6155.

[42] See eg Case C-82/01 P *Aéroports de Paris* [2002] ECR I-9297, para 107: 'ADP wields economic power which enables it to prevent effective competition from being maintained in the relevant market by giving it the opportunity to act independently'. Similar references to 'economic power' or 'strength' can be found in the following seminal cases: Case 85/76 *Hoffmann-La Roche* [1979] ECR 461, para 38; Case 102/77 *Hoffmann-La Roche* [1978] ECR 1139, para 91; Case 27/76 *United Brands Company (Chiquita)* [1978] ECR 207, para 10.

dominant position are explicitly prohibited by the Treaty (Article 102 TFEU) and by many instruments of secondary legislation.[43] In the same context, undertakings finding themselves in a position of economic weakness, and forced into an agreement restricting competition, are entitled to claim damages for loss caused by performance of that agreement (*Courage*).[44]

A second type of abuse occurring among economic actors is addressed by Directive 2003/6/EC of the European Parliament and of the Council of 28 January 2003 on insider dealing and market manipulation, practices designated as 'market abuses'[45] and committed at the expense of other investors.[46]

The term 'abuse' is often used as well in relation to two archetypal figures of weak contractual party: workers and consumers. The prevention of abuses against consumers is the objective of several instruments of secondary legislation, such as Directive 2005/29/EC,[47] Directive 1999/44/EC[48] and Directive 1993/13/EEC.[49] This objective is explicitly stated by Recital 9 in the Preamble to Directive 1993/13: 'acquirers of goods and services should be protected against the abuse of power by the seller or supplier, in particular against one-sided standard contracts and the unfair exclusion of essential rights in contracts'. The term 'abuse' also appears at Article 9(b) of Directive 2005/29.[50] Irrespective of those instruments of secondary legislation, the Court has acknowledged several times the need to protect consumers against '*abuses*' of marketing techniques such as advertising,[51] cold calling[52] or canvassing.[53]

[43] Among many others, see Council Regulation (EC) 169/2009 of 26 February 2009 applying rules of competition to transport by rail, road and inland waterway (codified version) [2009] OJ L61/1 art 1; EEC Council Regulation 17: First Regulation implementing Articles 85 and 86 of the Treaty [1962] OJ 13/204 art 1.

[44] Case C-453/99 *Courage* [2001] ECR I-6297, paras 32–36.

[45] See Directive 2003/6/EC of the European Parliament and of the Council of 28 January 2003 on insider dealing and market manipulation (market abuse) [2003] OJ L96/16 rec 12; see also Case C-45/08 *Spector Photo Group* [2009] ECR I- and Case C-391/04 *Georgakis* [2007] ECR I-3741.

[46] T Tridimas, 'Abuse of Rights in EU Law: Some Reflections with Particular Reference to Financial Law' in de la Feria and Vogenauer (n 5) 189: 'In general, manipulation refers to practices which are intended to mislead investors by artificially affecting market activity, such as matched orders or wash sales'.

[47] Directive 2005/29/EC of the European Parliament and of the Council of 11 May 2005 concerning unfair business-to-consumer commercial practices in the internal market and amending Council Directive 84/450/EEC, Directives 97/7/EC, 98/27/EC and 2002/65/EC of the European Parliament and of the Council and Regulation (EC) 2006/2004 of the European Parliament and of the Council (Unfair Commercial Practices Directive) [2005] OJ L149/220.

[48] Directive 1999/44/EC of the European Parliament and of the Council of 25 May 1999 on certain aspects of the sale of consumer goods and associated guarantees [1999] OJ L171/12.

[49] Council Directive 93/13/EEC of 5 April 1993 on unfair terms in consumer contracts [1993] OJ L95/29.

[50] Under art 9(b), in determining whether a commercial practice uses harassment, coercion, including the use of physical force, or undue influence, account shall be taken of the 'use of threatening or abusive language or behaviour'.

[51] Case C-245/01 *RTL Television* [2003] ECR I-12489, para 71; Case C-6/98 *ARD* [1999] ECR I-7599, para 50.

[52] Case C-384/93 *Alpine Investments* [1995] ECR I-1141, para 54.

[53] Case 382/87 *Buet* [1989] ECR 1235, para 13.

Lastly, abuses against workers have historically been prevented through the adoption of labour and social legislations. This objective was explicitly stated in Council Directive 1999/70/EC whose main purpose is 'to prevent abuse arising from the use of successive fixed-term employment contracts or relationships'.[54] In the same vein, secondary legislation has been adopted 'to eliminate certain abuses to which [lorry drivers] are subject and which in addition involve a threat to road safety',[55] by introducing recording equipment (tachographs) in road transport.[56] The Court has evoked the possibility of abuses against workers in many judgments. In *BETCU*, for instance, it acknowledged that national rules subjecting the right to paid annual leave to a minimum period of 13 weeks' uninterrupted employment with the same employer 'are liable to give rise to abuse',[57] in the form of a frequent resort by employers to short-term employment relationships to evade their obligation to pay annual leave.

Abuses of rights form the other significant subcategory of abuses private-private. By contrast with the former category, abuses of rights occur within the explicit framework of a specific right held by the abuser. For instance, an abuse of process (or procedure) consists in a misuse of the right to initiate judicial proceedings.[58] Abuse of process is often argued before the Court,[59] and the principle is even codified in the Rules of Procedure in relation to the costs of procedure;[60] yet the Court has rarely welcomed such claims.[61]

[54] Council Directive 1999/70/EC of 28 June 1999 concerning the framework agreement on fixed-term work concluded by ETUC, UNICE and CEEP [1999] OJ L175/43, cls 1(b) and 5 of the Framework Agreement. On the interpretation of the Framework Agreement, see among others Joined Cases C-378/07 to C-380/07 *Angelidaki* [2009] ECR I-3071; Case C-268/06 *Impact* [2008] ECR I-2483; Case C-144/04 *Mangold* [2005] ECR I-9981.

[55] See Case 128/78 *Commission v United Kingdom* [1979] ECR 419, para 9.

[56] Council Regulation (EEC) 3821/85 of 20 December 1985 on recording equipment in road transport [1985] OJ L370/8.

[57] Case C-173/99 *BETCU* [2001] ECR I-4881, para 51. The Court held that those rules contravened art 7(1) of Council Directive 93/104/EC of 23 November 1993 concerning certain aspects of the organization of working time [1993] OJ L307/18.

[58] Abuses of process attributed to public actors are classified under the heading 'Abuses Private-Private' for initiating judicial proceedings does not involve the exercise of prerogatives of public power: see eg Joined Cases C-501/06 P, C-513/06 P, C-515/06 P and C-519/06 P *GlaxoSmithKline* [2009] ECR I-9291, para 31; Case C-394/02 *Commission v Greece* [2005] ECR I-4713, paras 25–28.

[59] Abuse of process was argued for the first time in Case 9/61 *Netherlands v ECSC High Authority* [1962] ECR 413, 233.

[60] See Rules of Procedure of the Court of Justice [2010] OJ C177/1 art 139, which enables the Court to order a party to pay costs in case of unreasonable or vexatious procedure; applied in Case 338/82 *Albertini and Montagnani* [1984] ECR 2123, paras 51–52; Order of the President of the Court of First Instance in Case T-302/00 R *Goldstein v Commission* [2001] ECR II-1127, paras 40–41.

[61] See eg Case 243/78 *Simmenthal v Commission* [1980] ECR 593, paras 10–11; Order of the President of the Court of First Instance in Case T-302/00 R *Goldstein v Commission* [2001] ECR II-1127, paras 40–41. See also D Simon and A Rigaux, 'La technique de consécration d'un nouveau principe général de droit communautaire: l'exemple de l'abus de droit' in M Blanquet (ed), *Mélanges en hommage à Guy Isaac: 50 ans de droit communautaire* (Toulouse, Presses de l'Université des sciences sociales de Toulouse, 2004) 571–72. A specific type of abuse of process at the European level consists in artificially establishing a cross-border element, in order to make a preliminary ruling admissible: Case C-169/07 *Hartlauer* [2009] ECR I-1721, para 23.

The existence of an abuse of rights has also been claimed in a series of preliminary references involving Greek undertakings in financial difficulties. A governmental body (the OAE) had rescued several Greek undertakings in serious financial difficulties through various refinancing and restructuring measures, decided without convening the general meeting of shareholders. Following the adoption of those measures, shareholders of several Greek companies contested the alterations in the capital of their companies, on the ground that they had not been decided by the general meeting, as required by Article 25(1) of the Second Council Directive 77/91/EEC.[62] The Greek Government submitted that such a claim amounted to an abuse of rights, on the following grounds: they were minority shareholders; they had benefited from the reorganisation of the company; they had not exercised their right of pre-emption; they had requested the OAE's intervention; and/or they had allowed a period of five years to elapse before bringing their action. However, the Court systematically dismissed the argument of abuse of rights, except where shareholders relying on Article 25(1) sought 'a remedy that will cause such serious damage to the legitimate interests of others that it appears manifestly disproportionate'.[63] As noted by Vogenauer, those rulings fit the figure of abuse of rights (*abus de droit* or *Rechtsmissbrauch*), committed by an individual in a horizontal relationship with another private person.[64]

Entitled '*Prohibition of Abuses of Rights*', Article 54 of the Charter of Fundamental Rights of the European Union explicitly prohibits abuses of fundamental rights, which reads as follows:

> Nothing in this Charter shall be interpreted as implying any right to engage in any activity or to perform any act aimed at the destruction of any of the rights and freedoms recognised in this Charter or at their limitation to a greater extent than is provided for herein.

Article 17 of the European Convention on Human Rights, whose wording is similar, has been interpreted as preventing uses of the fundamental rights guaranteed by the Convention to anti-democratic ends, such as the use of the freedom of expression to spread national-socialist propaganda, in conformity with the motto 'no freedom for the enemies of freedom'.[65]

[62] Second Council Directive 77/91/EEC of 13 December 1976 on coordination of safeguards required by Member States of companies in respect of the formation of public limited liability companies and the maintenance and alteration of their capital, with a view to making such safeguards equivalent [1976] OJ L26/1.

[63] Case C-373/97 *Diamantis* [2000] ECR I-1705, para 43. See also Case C-367/96 *Kefalas* [1998] ECR I-2843, para 29; Case C-441/93 *Pafitis* [1996] ECR I-1347, para 70; Joined Cases C-134/91 and C-135/91 *Kerafina* [1992] ECR I-5699; Joined Cases C-19/90 and C-20/90 *Karella and Karellas* [1991] ECR I-2691.

[64] Vogenauer, 'The Prohibition of Abuse of Law: an Emerging General Principle of EU Law' (n 9) 556.

[65] See A Sajó, *Abuse: the Dark Side of Fundamental Rights*, Issues in Constitutional Law 3 (Utrecht, Eleven International Publishing, 2006); Y Lécuyer, *Les droits politiques dans la jurisprudence de la Cour européenne des droits de l'homme* (Paris, Dalloz, 2009) 334 ff; F Sudre, *Les grands arrêts de la Cour européenne des droits de l'homme*, 5th edn (Paris, PUF, 2009) 59 ff; A Spielmann and D Spielmann, 'The Concept of Abuse of Rights and the European Convention for the Protection of Human Rights

Lastly, intellectual property rights can be abused as well, as explicitly acknowledged by Article 3(2) of Directive 2004/48 on the enforcement of intellectual property rights,[66] when their holders create illegitimate barriers to trade.[67]

B. Abuses Private-Public (including Abuses of Law)

The fourth and last category of 'abuse' identified in Union official documents consists of abuses committed in a private-public setting. Those abuses are committed by private individuals at the expense of public actors in the exercise of their prerogatives of public power, more precisely their regulatory capacity. In *3M Italia* and *Safilo*, the Court indirectly acknowledged the fact that abuses of law are strategies designed by private individuals, and not by public authorities:

> [A]s regards the principle of the prohibition of abuse of rights …, it must be observed to begin with that the dispute in the main proceedings is not one in which taxpayers rely or are liable to rely on a provision of European Union law for fraudulent or abusive ends. Consequently, the judgments in Halifax and Others and Part Service, cases concerning value added tax which the referring court mentions in connection with its uncertainty as to whether the principle of the prohibition of abuse of rights defined in those judgments extends to the field of non-harmonised taxes, are not relevant in the present case.[68]

Furthermore, if abuses private-private (chiefly abuses of rights) are committed at the expense of isolated private individuals, abuses private-public (chiefly abuses of law) affect communities of individuals as a whole. As observed by Ziegler:

> [The concept of abuse in EU law] is not used to restrict one individual right vis-a-vis another individual right at the same level, which is its main application in national legal systems and in international law. Instead, it operates in a vertical dimension between individuals, the EU and the Member States.[69]

and Fundamental Freedoms' in Council of Europe (ed), *Abuse of Rights and Equivalent Concepts: the Principle and its Present Day Application* (Strasbourg, Council of Europe, Publishing and Documentation Service, 1990) 66 ff.

[66] Art 3 of Directive 2004/48/EC of the European Parliament and of the Council of 29 April 2004 on the Enforcement of Intellectual Property Rights [2004] OJ L157/45 provides:

1. Member States shall provide for the measures, procedures and remedies necessary to ensure the enforcement of the intellectual property rights covered by this Directive. …
2. Those measures, procedures and remedies shall also be effective, proportionate and dissuasive and shall be applied in such a manner as to avoid the creation of barriers to legitimate trade and to provide for safeguards against their abuse.

[67] See, in relation to patents, Case C-235/89 *Commission v Italy* [1992] ECR I-777, para 27; in relation to trade marks, Case 35/83 *BAT Cigaretten-Fabriken* [1985] ECR 363, para 35; in relation to copyright, Case 341/87 *EMI Electrola* [1989] ECR 79, paras 8 ff. More generally, see Metzger, 'Abuse of Law in EU Private Law' (n 39) 240–43.

[68] Case C-470/10 *3M Italia* [2012] ECR I-0000, para 30; see also Order in Case C-529/10 *Safilo* [2012] ECR I-0000, para 21.

[69] KS Ziegler, '"Abuse of Law" in the Context of the Free Movement of Workers' in de la Feria and Vogenauer (n 5) 296. In the same sense, see C Amand, 'Prohibition of Abusive Practices in European VAT: Court Aid to National Legislations Bugs?' (2008) 36 *Intertax* 189, 189, who distinguishes between

In more detail, the term 'abuse' is used to designate two different strategies designed by individuals and affecting entire communities: frauds and abuses of law. If both frauds and abuses of law aim at wrongfully obtaining a benefit from the legal system, frauds involve misrepresentation, whereas abuses of law rely on circumvention. A claim of fraud disputes the veracity of facts presented to the authorities, but not the applicable legal norm (as in *Paletta*). Conversely, a claim of abuse of law questions the applicability of a legal norm to a given set of facts, the latter being undisputed (as in *Halifax*). As better explained by Vogenauer:

> Abuse of law concerns the question of whether a rule is or is not applied to a given set of facts. Fraud is concerned with the issue of whether the facts to which the rule is subsequently applied correspond to reality.[70]

A fraud consists in concealing the fact that the conditions of application of a legal rule are not fulfilled (misrepresentation), in order to wrongfully obtain a regulatory benefit. Under Union law, numerous instances of fraud have been coined as 'abuses'. Within the Common Commercial Policy, for instance, the term 'abuse' has been invoked to qualify the 'mis-description of goods and unreliability of the documents issued, or apparently issued, by the [Sanctions Committee for the export of goods to Serbia and Montenegro]'.[71] Within the Common Agricultural Policy, another risk of 'abuse-fraud' regarded the possibility that skimmed milk be purchased under favourable conditions intended to encourage its use as feed for animals other than young calves, and then be used to feed young calves.[72] In the field of VAT, abuse-fraud has been invoked against individuals who had mentioned VAT as a separate entry on an invoice while knowing that they had no right to do so;[73] who faked their intention to engage in economic activities;[74] or who concealed the end of their economic activities.[75] In the area of excise duties, the same risk of abuse-fraud was highlighted to refuse refunds in case of alleged loss of excise stamps[76] or tax markings.[77]

abuses among private individuals (abuse of rights) and in the relationship with public authorities (abuses of law).

[70] Vogenauer (n 9) 560; see also C Costello, 'Citizenship of the Union: Above Abuse?' in de la Feria and Vogenauer (n 5) 323; Amand, 'Prohibition of Abusive Practices in European VAT' (n 69) 191; Gestri (n 4) 184–85; Triantafyllou (n 4) 612; KE Sørensen, 'Abuse of Rights in Community Law: a Principle of Substance or Merely Rhetoric?' (2006) 43 *Common Market Law Review* 423, 431; D Waelbroeck, 'La notion d'abus de droit dans l'ordre juridique communautaire' in J-V Louis et al (eds), *Mélanges en hommage à Jean-Victor Louis* (Brussels, Éditions de l'université de Bruxelles, 2003) 595.

[71] Case C-124/95 *Centro-Com* [1997] ECR I-81, para 15.

[72] Case C-333/87 *France v Commission* [1989] ECR 3773, para 22; Case 9/85 *Nordbutter II* [1986] ECR 2831, para 15; Joined Cases 187 and 190/83 *Nordbutter* [1984] ECR 2553, para 6.

[73] Case C-454/98 *Schmeink and Cofreth* [2000] ECR I-6973, paras 35, 41, 46.

[74] Case C-400/98 *Breitsohl* [2000] ECR I-4321, paras 38–39.

[75] Case C-32/03 *Fini H* [2005] ECR I-1599, paras 31–32.

[76] Case C-494/04 *Heintz van Landewijck* [2006] ECR I-5381, paras 43–45.

[77] Case C-374/06 *BATIG* [2007] ECR I-11271, paras 39–41 and 46; Case C-489/09 *Vandoorne* [2011] ECR I-225, paras 28 and 43.

Within the scope of the freedoms of movement, the term 'abuse' has also been used in relation to the issuance of allegedly fake medical certificates in Italy, in order to obtain payment of wages in Germany during the sickness period (*Paletta*).[78] It was also used to qualify the creation of partnerships or companies in 'old' Member States, in order to conceal the existence of an employment relationship, and thereby circumvent the transitional restrictions affecting workers coming from 'new' Member States (following the 2003 Accession).[79] With regard to immigration matters, abuse-fraud was invoked as well in two twin cases, when discussing the legal implications of false representations made to the immigration authorities in order to be admitted to a Member State.[80]

Lastly, a series of preliminary references concerned the obligation imposed upon Member States to guarantee the payment of remuneration in the event of the employer's insolvency, under Directive 80/987.[81] The competent Spanish public body (FOGASA) contended that certain elements of remuneration determined by conciliation between employer and employee had to be excluded from its liability, owing to the risk of 'abuse' consisting in fraudulently increasing the failed employer's liability, at the expense of public monies. Overall, the Court dismissed the possibility of abuse-fraud in judicial conciliations, owing to the supervision exerted by a judge,[82] but accepted that the risk of abuse-fraud could justify the exclusion of amounts established in extra-judicial conciliations.[83]

If abuses of Union law and frauds share the same objective (obtaining undue benefits from the legal system), abuses of law do not involve misrepresentation but rather circumvention. In such cases, all conditions of application of a legal rule are indeed fulfilled (no misrepresentation), but one or more conditions are fulfilled *artificially*. Since the phenomenon of abuse of law will be analysed in great detail in the remainder of this study, this section will be limited to an introductory description of the mechanisms at play. The Court had recourse to the formal doctrine of abuse of law in a few seminal cases, such as in *Emsland-Stärke*,[84] *Halifax*[85] and *Cadbury Schweppes*.[86] *Emsland-Stärke*, a German undertaking, tried to artificially obtain an export refund (ie a subsidy granted upon export

[78] Case C-206/94 *Paletta II* [1996] ECR I-2357, paras 10–13, 23–28.

[79] Case C-161/07 *Commission v Austria* [2008] ECR I-10671, paras 17 and 33.

[80] Case C-63/99 *Gloszczuk* [2001] ECR I-6369, paras 74–75; Case C-235/99 *Kondova* [2001] ECR I-6427 paras 79–80.

[81] Council Directive 80/987/EEC of 20 October 1980 on the approximation of the laws of the Member States relating to the protection of employees in the event of the insolvency of their employer [1980] OJ L283/23; replaced by Directive 2008/94/EC of the European Parliament and of the Council of 22 October 2008 on the protection of employees in the event of the insolvency of their employer (codified version) [2008] OJ L283/36.

[82] Case C-246/06 *Velasco Navarro* [2008] ECR I-105; Case C-81/05 *Cordero Alonso* [2006] ECR I-7569; Order in Case C-177/05 *Guerrero Pecino* [2005] ECR I-10887; Case C-520/03 *Olaso Valero* [2004] ECR I-12065; Case C-442/00 *Rodríguez Caballero* [2002] ECR I-11915, paras 35–38.

[83] Case C-498/06 *Robledillo Núñez* [2008] ECR I-921, paras 33–44.

[84] Case C-110/99 *Emsland-Stärke* [2000] ECR I-11569.

[85] Case C-255/02 *Halifax* [2006] ECR I-1609.

[86] Case C-196/04 *Cadbury Schweppes* [2006] ECR I-7995.

of agricultural goods outside the Union), by exporting several consignments of goods to Switzerland before re-importing them immediately into the Union. *Halifax*, a British financial institution with a limited right to deduct VAT, sought to artificially increase its right to deduct input VAT on the construction of four call centres, by outsourcing their construction to a subsidiary enjoying a full right to deduction. *Cadbury Schweppes*, another British company, incorporated two subsidiaries in Ireland in order to benefit from the favourable rate of income tax applicable in the International Financial Services Centre (IFSC) of Dublin (10 per cent at the material time).

As shall be described at length in the remainder of this study, all three disputed arrangements consisted in artificial choices of law, namely attempts to elect a specific legal regime through artificial means. Under that meaning, the term 'abuse' has been used in the most various areas of Union law, in instances that will be analysed in the remainder of this study: common agricultural policy,[87] customs duties,[88] direct taxation,[89] capital duties,[90] VAT[91] and other indirect taxes,[92] fishing quotas,[93] company law,[94] posting of workers,[95] forum shopping,[96] professional requirements,[97] broadcasting,[98] re-importations of goods to circumvent national regulations,[99] social benefits,[100] immigration of third country nationals[101] and so forth.

[87] Case C-279/05 *Vonk Dairy Products* [2007] ECR I-239, paras 31–34; Case C-515/03 *Eichsfelder Schlachtbetrieb* [2005] ECR I-7355, paras 29 ff; Case C-110/99 *Emsland-Stärke* [2000] ECR I-11569, paras 36–39 and 50–59.

[88] Case C-7/08 *Har Vaessen* [2009] ECR I-5581, paras 39–46; Case C-187/99 *Eru Portuguesa* [2001] ECR I-1429, paras 25–26; Case C-103/96 *Eridania* [1997] ECR I-1453, paras 25–31.

[89] Case C-311/08 *SGI* [2010] ECR I-487, para 57; Order in Case C-201/05 *CFC and Dividend Group Litigation* [2008] ECR I-2875, paras 77 ff; Case C-196/04 *Cadbury Schweppes* [2006] ECR I-7995, paras 34, 37, 55 ff.

[90] Case C-397/07 *Commission v Spain* [2009] ECR I-6029, para 29; Case C-251/06 *ING. AUER* [2007] ECR I-9689, paras 41 and 47; Case C-178/05 *Commission v Greece* [2007] ECR I-4185, para 32.

[91] Case C-162/07 *Ampliscientifica* [2008] ECR I-4019, paras 27–30; Case C-425/06 *Part Service* [2008] ECR I-897, paras 41 ff; Case C-255/02 *Halifax* [2006] ECR I-1609, paras 68 ff.

[92] Case 54/84 *Michael Paul* [1985] ECR 915, paras 16–19.

[93] Case C-93/89 *Commission v Ireland* [1991] ECR I-4569, para 12.

[94] Case C-167/01 *Inspire Art* [2003] ECR I-10155, paras 87, 91, 96, 105, 115 ff; Case C-212/97 *Centros* [1999] ECR I-1459, para 23-29; Case 79/85 *Segers* [1986] ECR 2375, paras 10 and 17.

[95] Case C-445/03 *Commission v Luxembourg* [2004] ECR I-10191, paras 18 and 28; Case C-202/97 *FTS* [2000] ECR I-883, paras 35 and 38.

[96] Case C-168/08 *Hadadi* [2009] ECR I-6871, paras 45 and 57.

[97] Case C-151/07 *Chatzithanasis* [2008] ECR I-9013, para 32; Case C-286/06 *Commission v Spain* [2008] ECR I-8025, paras 68–72; Case C-147/03 *Commission v Austria* [2005] ECR I-5969, paras 54–55 and 67–70.

[98] Case C-222/94 *Commission v United Kingdom* [1996] ECR I-4025, paras 59–61.

[99] Case C-322/01 *Deutscher Apothekerverband* [2003] ECR I-14887, paras 126–30.

[100] Case C-138/02 *Collins* [2004] ECR I-2703, para 50; Case C-413/01 *Ninni-Orasche* [2003] ECR I-13187, paras 16, 31, 36; Case 39/86 *Lair* [1988] ECR 3161, para 43.

[101] Case C-200/02 *Zhu and Chen* [2004] ECR I-9925, para 34; Case C-109/01 *Akrich* [2003] ECR I-9607, paras 41–42 and 55–58; Case C-370/90 *Singh* [1992] ECR I-4265, para 24.

III. Abuses of Law and Abuses of Rights under Union Law

The previous section offered a general overview of the various phenomena labelled as 'abusive' under Union law, by proposing a typology based on the public or private nature of the parties involved. Abuses of law and abuses of rights were described as unlawful strategies committed by private individuals; however, abuses of law are committed at the expense of a whole community (abuses private-public, type IV), whereas abuses of rights are committed at the expense of well-identified private individuals (abuses private-private, type III). The present section proceeds to a more detailed analysis of the distinction between abuse of law and abuse of rights.

In the previous section, abuses of rights were classified under the heading 'abuses private-private'.[102] They were described as occurring within the explicit framework of a well-identified right held by the abuser, such as the right to initiate judicial proceedings or intellectual property rights. In more detail, in the particular context of Union law, the following phenomena were identified as abuses of rights: abuses of process, abuses of tendering procedure, abuses of intellectual property rights, abuses of shareholder's voting rights (Greek saga) and abuses of fundamental rights.

The distinction between abuses of law and abuses of rights is rarely articulated in Union law: most often, they are jointly and indistinctly examined.[103] As a matter of fact, abuses of law and abuses of rights are often confused because they share a remarkable feature when proscribed by an autonomous doctrine of abuse: their formal lawfulness. Indeed, when judges have recourse to a doctrine of abuse, both types of behaviours occur without any visible infringement of a formal legal requirement.[104] Thus, abuses of process, one of the oldest and most common forms of abuse of rights,[105] are committed by litigants abiding by all procedural requirements imposed to initiate judicial proceedings,[106] as acknowledged by the Court in *Diamantis* (Greek saga).[107] Similarly, abuses of law are condemned while all formal requirements imposed by the relevant legislation are fulfilled, as

[102] See section II.A.

[103] See eg de la Feria, 'Prohibition of Abuse of (Community) Law' (n 9); Triantafyllou (n 4).

[104] See DJ Devine, 'Some Comparative Aspects of the Doctrine of Abuse of Rights' (1964) 1964 *Acta Juridica* 148, 148: 'Where there is an "abuse of right" the exercise of that right is prima facie lawful and within the bounds or limits which the law sets for the exercise of the right'.

[105] Abuses of legal proceedings were already proscribed in Roman law through the *actio calumniae*; furthermore, they are prohibited in literally every legal order: see Devine, 'Some Comparative Aspects of the Doctrine of Abuse of Rights' (n 104) 152 and 182; A Berger, 'Encyclopedic Dictionary of Roman Law' (1953) 43 *Transactions of the American Philosophical Society* 333, Verbo 'Iudicium Calumniae'.

[106] See eg Case 243/78 *Simmenthal v Commission* [1980] ECR 593, para 11; Order of the President of the Court of First Instance in Case T-302/00 R *Goldstein v Commission* [2001] ECR II-1127, paras 40–41.

[107] Case C-373/97 *Diamantis* [2000] ECR I-1705, para 43.

explicitly acknowledged by the Court in *Emsland-Stärke* (paras 46–49 and 52), *Halifax* (para 74) or *Cadbury Schweppes* (para 64).[108]

However, this joint treatment of abuses of law and abuses of rights originates in a confusion between the phenomena of abuse and the techniques used to prevent them.[109] Indeed, both abuses of rights and abuses of law (*phenomena*) can be proscribed through an autonomous doctrine of abuse or by mere interpretation of a legal norm's conditions of application (*techniques*): in the latter case, abuses of rights and abuses of law cannot be regarded as formally lawful, for they breach at least one explicit legal requirement. For instance, the following abuses of rights are explicitly proscribed by written legal norms of Union law: the abuse of process in relation to the costs of procedure before the Court,[110] the abuse of tendering procedure in the beef and veal sector,[111] or the abuse of intellectual property rights.[112] Similarly, abuses of law are frequently impeded through statutory construction of requirements imposed by the relevant legal norms.[113]

Therefore, despite its striking nature, the quality of formal lawfulness is merely contingent to both phenomena of abuse. If 'one should more properly differentiate between abusing of a right and abusing of a law',[114] how can we actually distinguish those two phenomena, irrespective of their contingent prima facie lawfulness? Arguably, the main criterion of distinction of those two phenomena resides in their relation to the legal environment: abuses of law are essentially undesirable choices of law, whereas abuses of rights are undesirable exercises of rights. Indeed, from the perspective of their impact on individual rights, abuses of law constitute improper *acquisitions* of rights, and abuses of rights illegitimate *exercises* of existing rights. This distinction largely coincides with the distinction classically made under French law between '*fraude à la loi*' and '*abus de droit*', which has however been ignored by the Court.[115] This distinction has been abundantly highlighted in the literature:

> [T]he doctrine of the 'abuse of rights' is used to control the exercise of ascertained and delineated individual rights, whereas most examples of 'fraud on the law' do not concern

[108] See ch 3 section II.A.

[109] See ch 4.

[110] See Rules of Procedure of the Court of Justice art 139 (n 60 and case law cited).

[111] On the anti-abuse provisions of Commission Regulation (EEC) 859/89 of 29 March 1989 laying down detailed rules for the application of intervention measures in the beef and veal sector [1989] OJ L91/5, see Case C-233/96 *Denmark v Commission* [1998] ECR I-5759, paras 22–25; Case C-238/96 *Ireland v Commission* [1998] ECR I-5801, paras 68–71.

[112] See Directive 2004/48/EC of the European Parliament and of the Council of 29 April 2004 on the Enforcement of Intellectual Property Rights [2004] OJ L157/45 art 3(2):

> 2. [The measures, procedures and remedies adopted by the Member States to ensure the enforcement of intellectual property rights] ... shall be applied in such a manner as to avoid the creation of barriers to legitimate trade and to provide for safeguards against their abuse.

[113] See eg Case C-347/93 *Boterlux* [1994] ECR I-3933, paras 31 ff; Case C-419/02 *BUPA Hospitals* [2006] ECR I-1685, paras 44–51; Case C-452/03 *RAL* [2005] ECR I-3947, paras 30–34. See ch 4 and ch 5 section III.B.

[114] Confédération Fiscale Européenne, 'The Concept of Abuse in European Law, based on the Judgments of the European Court of Justice Delivered in the Field of Tax Law' (Opinion Statement of the CFE ECJ Task Force), November 2007, available at www.cfe-eutax.org/node/87, no 25.

[115] See section IV of this chapter; Schammo, 'Arbitrage and Abuse of Rights in the EC Legal System' (n 9) 355.

the exercise of a right, but rather the 'diversion of a legal rule so as to acquire a right which one would not otherwise do'.[116]

> There is an abuse of law when persons seek the improper application of a statute to atypical situations, ie situations other than those which the lawmaker intended to regulate … By contrast, an abuse of right generally indicates the use of such right for an improper purpose, such as harming someone else's right.[117]

In that sense, the concept of abuse of law is concerned with the conditions of application of a legal norm; the norm's legal effect, by contrast, is not disputed. Thus, it was not disputed that the legal effect of the legal norms at stake in *Emsland-Stärke*, *Halifax* or *Cadbury Schweppes* was respectively the grant of an export refund, a higher VAT deduction and the payment of lower income taxes. Rather, the legal issue was whether the conditions of application of the applicable norms could be considered as fulfilled when they were done so through artificial means; that is, whether the rights sought by *Emsland-Stärke*, *Halifax* and *Cadbury Schweppes* existed at all.

Conversely, the concept of abuse of rights is concerned with the legal effect of legal norms, whereas the fulfilment of their conditions of application—and accordingly the existence of the right at stake—is not disputed. In the Greek saga, for instance, the Greek authorities did not dispute the existence of the shareholders' right to decide an increase in the capital of a company (Article 25(1) of the Second Council Directive), but rather sought to assess whether this right '[was] being exercised abusively'.[118] Similarly, the prohibition of abuses of *procedure*, *intellectual property rights* and *human rights* does not question the existence of the underlying rights, but rather the legitimacy of certain practices adopted on behalf of those rights. To take the most obvious example, preventing the use of fundamental rights to anti-democratic ends (such as the use of the freedom of expression to spread national-socialist propaganda[119]) does not amount to questioning the existence of those fundamental rights, for they can be readily declared inextinguishable.

[116] S Whittaker, 'Comments on "Abuse of Law" in European Private Law' in de la Feria and Vogenauer (n 5) 259.

[117] P Pistone, 'Abuse of Law in the Context of Indirect Taxation: From (Before) Emsland-Stärke 1 to Halifax (and Beyond)' in de la Feria and Vogenauer (n 5) 381; see also Tridimas, 'Abuse of Rights in EU Law' (n 46) 169; Gestri (n 4) 185–86; Confédération Fiscale Européenne, 'The Concept of Abuse in European Law' (n 114) points 25–26; Amand (n 69) 189.

[118] Case C-441/93 *Pafitis* [1996] ECR I-1347, para 68; see also Case C-373/97 *Diamantis* [2000] ECR I-1705, paras 32–43; Case C-367/96 *Kefalas* [1998] ECR I-2843, paras 22–29. More precisely, the legal issue in those three cases was whether this right—whose existence was undisputed—included the possibility to request the revocation of alterations in the capital, where the shareholders had clearly benefited from the reorganisation of the company, requested the OAE's intervention or allowed a period of five years to elapse before bringing their action.

[119] See art 54 of the Charter of Fundamental Rights of the European Union and art 17 of the European Convention on Human Rights; Sajó, *Abuse* (n 65); A Spielmann and D Spielmann, 'The Concept of Abuse of Rights' (n 65).

In sum, abuses of law are strategies of *appropriation* of a new legal position (right or duty), whereas abuses of rights are strategies of *exploitation* of an existing legal position. Abuses of law question the conditions of application (or 'hypothesis'[120]) of legal norms, and provoke a legal debate on the very existence of a right in the hands of the alleged abuser. Abuses of rights, by contrast, seek to magnify the legal effect (or 'consequence') of legal norms, so that the legal debate concerns the precise extent of an existing right held by the alleged abuser.

A second criterion of distinction is the relational context in which abuses of law and abuses of rights occur, which justified their classification under two different categories of abuse in the previous section (private-private and private-public). As highlighted by Amand,

> A first fundamental distinction derives from the context in which such abuse occurs. In the relations between individuals, abuse of rights means using a right in order to cause damage. In the Clement Bayard case, the French Court of Cassation decided in 1915 that the owner of a piece of land who had built a 16-metre high fence with iron rods was abusing his ownership right. In the relations with the authorities, abuse of rights aims at obtaining advantages, by only formally complying with the conditions for obtaining such advantages but without accepting the costs thereof.[121]

If abuses of rights are committed 'horizontally', at the expense of isolated citizens (abuse private-private), abuses of law occur 'vertically', affecting communities of citizens (abuse private-public). Abuses of law committed in the tax field have been said to harm the Treasury as a whole.[122] This distinction also justifies the very appellation 'abuse of law', for abuses of law affect an entire legal community (the 'law'), whereas abuses of rights only have an impact on isolated citizens.[123]

A third difference regards the criteria on which judges rely when assessing abuses of law and abuses of rights, as already noted by Josserand in his pioneer work on both phenomena.[124] As shall be exposed in great detail below, the formal doctrine of abuse of law developed by the Court in *Emsland-Stärke*, *Halifax* and *Cadbury Schweppes* consists of two main elements: the artificiality requirement and the teleological assessment.[125] The doctrine of abuse of law seeks to determine whether the legal norm's conditions of applications have been fulfilled artificially, and whether such artifice is compatible with the purpose of the legal regime affected. By contrast, doctrines of abuse of rights do not refer to artificiality, but

[120] See R von Jhering, O de Meulenaere (trans), *L'Esprit du Droit Romain*, 3rd edn, vol 1 (Paris, Librairie A Marescq, 1886) 52, free translation: 'Every legal rule attaches to a given hypothesis ("if someone has done this or that") a given consequence ("in such case, this or that will happen")'.

[121] Amand (n 69) 189.

[122] L de Broe, *International Tax Planning and Prevention of Abuse* (Amsterdam, IBFD, 2008) 159.

[123] Tridimas and Pistone similarly differentiate between abuse of right and abuse of law (statute): Tridimas (n 46) 169; Pistone, 'Abuse of Law in the Context of Indirect Taxation' (n 117) 381.

[124] L Josserand, *De l'esprit des droits et de leur relativité: théorie dite de l'abus des droits*, 2nd edn (Paris, LGDJ, 1939) no 268 and 274.

[125] See ch 3.

rather to harmful intent or general criteria of proportionality or reasonableness.[126] For instance, the Court evoked the eventuality that shareholders exert the right conferred by Article 25(1) of the Second Directive 'for the purpose of deriving, to the detriment of the company, an improper advantage, manifestly contrary to the objective of that provision'.[127] Abuses of process occur when a judicial action is introduced 'unreasonably or vexatiously';[128] moreover, a judge may set aside 'certain acts of a debtor committed to the detriment of the interests of creditors and, in particular, those which are of a fraudulent nature vis-à-vis creditors'.[129] An abuse of right can also be committed by a litigant who has chosen a remedy 'that will cause such serious damage to the legitimate interests of others that it appears manifestly disproportionate'.[130]

A fourth and last difference between abuse of law and abuse or right resides in the sanction of such behaviours. As will be explained below, the sanction of abuse of law consists in denying the choice of law attempted, without questioning the validity of the underlying economic transaction. For instance, the sanction applied in *Emsland-Stärke* consisted in denying the choice of law attempted through a re-import strategy, by imposing an obligation to repay the export refunds received. In other words, the Court did not question the validity of the sale of agricultural products, or even prohibit Emsland-Stärke from setting up re-import strategies; rather, it merely ruled that such practices should not benefit from export refunds, owing to their abusive nature. Abuses of rights, by contrast, are usually prohibited as such owing to their harmful nature. Thus, abuses of proceedings, abuses of intellectual property rights and abuses of fundamental rights (article 54 of the Charter) are proscribed as outright undesirable courses of behaviour.

To sum up, abuses of law form undesirable acquisitions of a right (choices of law), whereas abuses of rights constitute undesirable exercises of an existing right. Indeed, abuses of rights occur within the stable legal regime of specific rights (eg the right to initiate proceedings, intellectual property rights or shareholder's voting rights), which abusers try to stretch in their favour. By contrast, the purpose of abuses of law is to make a choice of law, by artificially meeting the conditions of application of the relevant legal norm. Abuses of law aim at the substitution of the applicable legal regime: *Emsland-Stärke* attempted to 'move' into the export subsidy scheme; *Halifax* into the (full) VAT deduction scheme; and *Cadbury Schweppes* into the Irish taxation scheme.

[126] J Gordley, 'The Abuse of Rights in the Civil Law Tradition' in de la Feria and Vogenauer (n 5) 34; Schammo (n 9) 356; Confédération Fiscale Européenne (n 114) points 25–26; Gestri (n 4) 228–30; Karayannis, 'L'abus des droits' (n 39) 525; L Neville Brown, 'Is there a General Principle of Abuse of Rights in European Community Law?' in D Curtin, et al (eds), *Institutional Dynamics of European Integration—Essays in Honour of Henry G. Schermers*, vol II (Dordrecht, M Nijhoff, 1994) 515.

[127] Case C-373/97 *Diamantis* [2000] ECR I-1705, paras 33 and 38; Case C-367/96 *Kefalas* [1998] ECR I-2843, para 28.

[128] See Rules of Procedure of the Court of Justice art 139 (n 60 and case law cited).

[129] Case 250/78 *DEKA* [1983] ECR 421, para 15.

[130] Case C-373/97 *Diamantis* [2000] ECR I-1705, para 43.

IV. The Universality of the Prohibition of Abuses

The Union law scholarship on the doctrine of abuse commonly states that abuses of law are not prohibited in all national legal orders; more precisely, the United Kingdom and the other countries following the common law approach (former British colonies, Nordic countries) would reject the principle of a prohibition of abuses of law.[131] If a thorough investigation of the treatment of abuses of law at the national level would largely exceed the scope of this study, this section will nevertheless strive to show that every legal order prohibits abuses of law, the only real difference being in the techniques deployed. As rightly pointed out by A Lenaerts,

> It is true that in the Common Law systems and in the Nordic countries, there is no general recognition of the principle of the prohibition of abuse of rights. Nevertheless, in these legal systems, pragmatic solutions are found through the use of concepts that, in concrete situations, will lead to a similar result as the prohibition of abuse of rights would do.[132]

The central difficulty of this comparative undertaking resides in the conceptual diversity characterising the treatment of abuses of law across legal orders. Indeed, depending on the legal order, artificial choices of law can be prohibited as 'abuse of law', 'abuse of rights', 'fraus legis' or without any consistent reference to a unique concept.[133] In other words, one cannot expect the conceptual distinction proposed in the previous section (abuse of law *versus* abuse of rights) to be consistently observed across legal orders.

Nevertheless, one must underline the strong resemblance between the concept of abuse of law under Union law and the concept of fraus legis or *fraude à la loi* developed by the French scholarship in the field of private international law.[134] The fraus legis (*fraude à la loi*, *frode alla legge*, *fraude a la ley*, *fraude à lei*) is indeed classically defined as a 'manoeuvre intended to escape the scope of application of a given law in order to integrate the scope of application of another law regarded

[131] See, inter alia, Kjellgren, 'On the Border of Abuse' (n 4) 179: 'Principles of abuse of rights—or practical equivalents—do exist in several of the Member States but far from all'; de la Feria, 'Prohibition of Abuse of (Community) Law: the Creation of a New General Principle of EC Law through Tax' (n 9) 395.

[132] A Lenaerts, 'The General Principle of the Prohibition of Abuse of Rights: A Critical Position on Its Role in a Codified European Contract Law' (2010) 18 *European Review of Private Law* 1121, 1125. See also Neville Brown, 'Is there a General Principle of Abuse of Rights' (n 126) 515.

[133] See also A Zalasinski, 'Some Basic Aspects of the Concept of Abuse in the Tax Case Law of the European Court of Justice' (2008) 36 *Intertax* 156, 156.

[134] See A Ligeropoulo, *Le problème de la fraude à la loi* (Paris, Librairie du Recueil Sirey, 1928); J Vidal, *Essai d'une théorie générale de la fraude en droit français* (Paris, Dalloz, 1957); B Audit, *La fraude à la loi* (Paris, Dalloz, 1974).

as more favourable'.[135] In other words, both the prohibition of abuses of law under Union law and the prohibition of fraudes legis seek to preclude artificial choices of law. Despite the clear preference of the Court of Justice for the 'abuse' terminology, this functional similitude between the concept of fraus legis in private international law, on the one hand, and that of *abuse of law* in Union law, on the other, has been underlined in various occasions,[136] to the extent that their resemblance has been described as 'blinding'.[137] As a matter of fact, the expression *fraude à la loi*—and its linguistic variants—is often used by scholars of Latin languages to designate the phenomenon of abuse of law under Union law.[138]

Going back to roots of civil law systems, it is often stated that Roman law did not punish abuses of law, on the basis of a few maxims of the *Digesta*[139] allegedly

[135] P de Vareilles-Sommières, 'Fraude à la loi' in *Répertoire International Dalloz* (Paris, Dalloz, 1998) 2. See also M Fallon, 'La délocalisation comme instrument de fraude lié à la circulation des biens et des personnes' in J Verhoeven (ed), *La loyauté: mélanges offerts à Etienne Cerexhe* (Brussels, Larcier, 1997) 165, free translation:

> Fraus legis under private international law is characterized by a deliberate action, from private individuals, on one element of location of the situation, with the sole intention of avoiding the application of the national law normally applicable in absence of such manipulation.

[136] See inter alia Vogenauer (n 9) 555: '[T]he prohibition of abuse of law ... is much more akin to domestic doctrines such as fraude à la loi and Gesetzesumgebung than to the typical 'abuse of rights' scenario'; Fallon, 'La délocalisation comme instrument de fraude lié à la circulation des biens et des personnes' (n 135) 189, free translation: 'Both private international law and Community law have various instruments at their disposal to fight such loopholes ... The most traditional is that of fraude à la loi'; H Gaudemet-Tallon, 'Le pluralisme en droit international privé: richesses et faiblesses (Le funambule et l'arc-en-ciel)' (2005) 312 *Recueil des Cours de l'Académie de Droit International* 9, 258, free translation: 'It is indisputable that, somehow, Community law punishes fraud: both fraud to the domestic law of a Member State and fraud to Community law as a whole'; de Broe, *International Tax Planning and Prevention of Abuse* (n 122) 752: 'Many of [the European cases of abuse] resemble the cases of «fraus legis» (*«abuse of law»/«wetsontduiking»/«fraude à la loi»*) in matters of international private law'.

[137] O Fouquet, 'Fraude à la loi et abus de droit' (2006) 47 *Droit fiscal* 65, no 23–24, free translation: 'the parallelism between the motives of the *Halifax* case and those of the *Janfin* ruling is blinding'. In *Janfin*, the French Conseil d'Etat applied the theory of *«fraude à la loi»* in tax matters: *Janfin* (2006) Leb 410 (Conseil d'État français); see n 190 and accompanying text.

[138] See eg L Driguez, 'Reconnaissance mutuelle des diplômes' (2008) 12 *Europe* 412; L Idot, 'Cabotage et contournement de la loi de l'État d'accueil' (2006) 6 *Europe* 196; Fouquet, 'Fraude à la loi et abus de droit' (n 137) no 18; Gestri (n 4); C Doutrelepont, 'Le secteur audiovisuel et la libre prestation des services dans l'Union européenne' in C Doutrelepont and M Waelbroeck (ed), *Questions de droit de l'audiovisuel européen* (Brussels, Bruylant, 1997) 163.

[139] The *Digesta* regrouped all legal principles and rules applicable to the relations among individuals at the time of Justinian, product of the centuries-long writing of the classical Roman jurists (such as Gaius, Paulus, Ulpianus, Modestinus, or Pomponius). It was granted the status of law on 31 December 533. Latin version in T Mommsen et al, *Corpus iuris civilis* (Berolini, Apud Weidmannos, 1912); English translation by SP Scott, *The Civil Law, including the Twelve Tables, the Institutes of Gaius, the Rules of Ulpian, the Opinions of Paulus, the Enactments of Justinian, and the Constitutions of Leo* (Cincinnati, Central Trust Co, 1932); both available at http://web.upmf-grenoble.fr/Haiti/Cours/Ak/

demonstrating the 'absolutist' character[140] of Roman law.[141] However, it can hardly be denied that Roman law proscribed certain forms of abuses of rights[142] and fraudes legis.[143] For example, abuses of the right to bring legal proceedings were punished through the *actio calumniae*;[144] similarly, the *ius vitae necisque* (right of life and death) of the *pater familias* over his slaves[145] and family[146] has been incrementally restricted. Furthermore, Rotondi relates the oldest documented case of fraus legis, mentioned by Titus-Livius in his *History of Rome*: Licinius Stolo sought to circumvent the *Lex Licinia Searfia*, which he had himself promulgated to impose quantitative restrictions on the ownership of agricultural land (a maximum of 500 'iugera' of 'ager publicus' per person), by emancipating his son in order for them to jointly own 1000 'iugera'.[147] The prohibition of fraudes legis is also attested by other maxims reported in the *Digesta*.[148] Nevertheless, it

[140] Ulpianus, *Digesta* 39.2.24.12:

There was no reason to believe that I caused you damage through any defect of my work, where I was only making use of a right to which I was entitled (*Neque enim existimari operis mei vitio damnum tibi dari in ea re, in qua iure meo usus sum*);

Gaius, *Digesta* 50.17.55:

No one is considered to commit a fraud when exercising his right (*Nullus videtur dolo facere, qui suo iure utitur*);

Paulus, *Digesta* 50.17.151:

No one commits a wrong against another unless he does something which he has no right to do (*Nemo damnum facit, nisi qui id fecit, quod facere ius non habet*).

[141] See eg HC Gutteridge, 'Abuse of Rights' (1933-35) 5 *Cambridge Law Journal* 22, 32: '[Roman law] was in essence absolutist'; D Johnston, *Roman Law in Context* (Cambridge, Cambridge University Press, 2004) 30 and 55: 'Paternal power (patria potestas) … was power of an extraordinary degree, and for those subject to it represented impotence of an extraordinary degree; [t]he owner in Roman law was fairly uninhibited in the use of his property'.

[142] On the treatment of abuses of rights in Roman law, see U Elsener, *Les racines romanistes de l'interdiction de l'abus de droit* (Brussels, Bruylant, 2004); Devine (n 104) 150–53.

[143] On the treatment of *fraudes legis* in Roman law, see M Rotondi, *Gli atti in frode alla legge nella dottrina romana e nella sua evoluzione posteriore* (Turin, L'Erma di Bretschneider, 1911); Vidal, *Essai d'une théorie générale de la fraude en droit français* (n 134) 13–33.

[144] See Devine (n 104) 152 and 182; Berger, 'Encyclopedic Dictionary of Roman Law' (n 105).

[145] See A Watson, 'Roman Slave Law and Romanist Ideology' (1983) 37 *Phoenix* 53.

[146] The question of whether the *pater familias* did hold such a power over his wife and children is disputed: see S Thompson, 'Was Ancient Rome A Dead Wives Society? What Did The Roman Paterfamilias Get Away With?' (2006) 31 *Journal Of Family History* 3.

[147] See Rotondi, *Gli atti in frode alla legge nella dottrina romana e nella sua evoluzione posteriore* (n 143); Vidal (n 134) 13, who refers to Titus-Livius, D Spillan (trans), *The History of Rome*, vol I (New York, Harper & Brothers, 1871) book VII ch 16 no 9:

The same year Caius Licinius Stolo was condemned in a fine of 10,000 *asses*, on his own law, by Marcus Popilius Laenas, because he possessed, in conjunction with his son, a thousand acres of land, and because he had attempted to evade the law by emancipating his son (*Eodem anno C. Licinius Stolo a M. Popilio laenate sua loge decem milibus aeris est damnatus, quod mille iugerum agri cum filio possideret emancipandoque filium fraudem legi fecisset*).

[148] Paulus, *Digesta* 1.3.29:

To do what the law prohibits violates the law, and anyone who evades the meaning of the law without disobeying its words, is guilty of fraud against it (*Contra legem facit, qui id facit quod lex prohibet, in fraudem vero, qui salvis verbis legis sententiam eius circumvenit*).

Ulpianus, *Digesta* 1.3.30:

Fraud is committed against the law when something is done which the law did not wish to be done, but did not absolutely prohibit (*Fraus enim legi fit, ubi quod fieri noluit, fieri autem non vetuit, id fit*).

is true that those scattered prohibitions were never elaborated into general prohibitions of abuse of rights or fraudes legis in Roman law.[149]

Under English law, the *Bradford v Pickles* case[150] is classically regarded as founding the formal rejection of the prohibition of abuses.[151] In the city of Bradford,[152] water supply had been a recurrent problem for decades, until the Many Wells Spring was located and exploited.[153] However, the water sheet feeding the Many Wells Spring was located under Mr Pickles' estate; in the early 1890s, Mr Pickles communicated to the Bradford Corporation (the public company exploiting Many Wells Spring) his intention to mine for flagstones on his estate, which required the draining of the water sheet inundating its underground—namely the Many Wells Spring. It is not disputed that Mr Pickles' intention was to sell his estate at a price inflated by the value of a 'water right'. Mr Pickles and the Bradford Corporation were unable to reach an agreement, the latter refusing to cede to what it viewed as blackmail. The dispute went all the way up to the House of the Lords, which ruled in favour of Mr Pickles; according to Lord Halsbury's famous statement:

> But although it does deprive them of water which they would otherwise get, it is necessary for the plaintiffs to establish that they have a right to the flow of water, and that the defendant had no right to do what he is doing. I am of opinion that neither of those propositions can be established. …
>
> If it was a lawful act, however ill the motive might be, he had a right to do it. If it was an unlawful act, however good his motive might be, he would have no right to do it. Motives and intentions in such question as is now before your Lordships seem to me absolutely irrelevant.[154]

In sum, *Bradford v Pickles* seemed to establish the 'general irrelevancy of evil motive'[155] under English law. However, in two subsequent cases of nuisance, the House of Lords explicitly relied on the presence of a harmful intent (*animus nocendi*) to qualify a behaviour as unlawful. In *Christie v Davey*,[156] it found that the actions taken by Mr Davey (banging on the party-wall, beating on trays, shouting,

[149] See however Elsener, *Les racines romanistes* (n 142) 188–95, arguing in favour of the existence of a general prohibition of abuses of rights in Roman law.

[150] *Bradford Corporation v Pickles* (1895) Appeal Cases 587 (HL).

[151] See eg Gutteridge, 'Abuse of Rights' (n 141) 22.

[152] Bradford is surprisingly located barely 10 and 15 miles away from Halifax and Huddersfield. The rulings of the European Court of Justice in Case C-255/02 *Halifax* [2006] ECR I-1609 and Case C-223/03 *University of Huddersfield* [2006] ECR I-1751 have greatly contributed to the development of a doctrine of abuse in Union law.

[153] M Taggart, *Private Property and the Abuse of Rights in Victorian England: The Story of Edward Pickles and Bradford Water Supply* (Oxford, Oxford University Press, 2002) 7 ff.

[154] *Bradford Corporation v Pickles* (1895) Appeal Cases 587 (HL), 600.

[155] WVH Rogers, PH Winfield and JA Jolowicz, *Winfield and Jolowicz on Tort*, 17th edn (London, Sweet and Maxwell, 2006) 79. *Bradford* was confirmed in *Earle and Earle v East Riding* (1999) RVR 200 (LT); *Stephens v Anglian Water Authority* (1987) 1 WLR 1381 (HL); *Quinn v Leathem* (1901) Appeal Cases 495 (HL); *South Wales Miners' Federation v Glamorgan Coal Co Ltd* (1905) Appeal Cases 239 (HL); *Allen v Flood* (1898) Appeal Cases 1 (HL).

[156] *Christie v Davey* (1893) 1 Ch 316 (HL).

shrieking and whistling) in retaliation to the music played by his neighbours, the Christie family, were unlawful. According to Lord North,

> [The noises made by Mr Davey] were made deliberately and maliciously for the purpose of annoying the [Christie's]. If what has taken place had occurred between two sets of persons both perfectly innocent, I should have taken an entirely different view of the case. But I am persuaded that what was done by [Mr. Davey] was done only for the purpose of annoyance, and in my opinion it was not a legitimate use of [Mr. Davey]'s house to use it for the purpose of vexing and annoying neighbours.[157]

In *Hollywood Silver Fox Farm v Emmett*,[158] Mr Emmett sought to discourage the exploitation of a silver fox farm bordering his estate by asking his son to discharge bird-scaring guns nearby the breeding pens, which led some vixens to stop breeding and others to cannibalism. Explicitly referring to Mr Emmett's malice, Lord Macnaghten granted an injunction and damages to the *Hollywood Silver Fox Farm*: firing guns on one's property was a priori reasonable and thus lawful, except when gunshots were motivated by an *animus nocendi.*[159]

If all three cases concerned deliberately harmful behaviours, how can we reconcile their contrasted outcomes (allowed in *Bradford v Pickles*; disallowed in *Christie v Davey* and *Hollywood Silver Fox Farm v Emmett*)? If some have argued that *Bradford v Pickles* was simply wrong,[160] the most widely accepted explanation is that Mr Pickles' behaviour did not match the definition of 'nuisance'—or any other tort. Indeed, to be actionable under English law, a wrong must fit into a category of tort; since the tort of nuisance supposes an 'emanation' (eg of noise, liquid, odour), the prevention of an emanation (of water) by Mr Pickles was not actionable.[161] Therefore, the meaning of *Bradford v Pickles* is not that motives are altogether irrelevant under English law,[162] as illustrated by *Christie v Davey* and *Hollywood Silver Fox Farm*, but rather that English law does not comprise a general doctrine prohibiting deliberately harmful behaviours.[163] In sum,

157 *Christie v Davey* (1893) 1 Ch 316 (HL).

158 *Hollywood Silver Fox Farm Ltd v Emmett* (1936) 2 KB 468 (HL).

159 For another case of malicious noise nuisance, intended to scare away the game on a neighbour's land, see *Ibbotson v Peat* (1865) 3 HC 644 (HL). Similar facts were treated in the same way in a French case: see *Prince de Wagram v Marais* (1873) 2 DP 185 (Cour d'Appel de Paris).

160 H Foster, 'Abuse of Rights—Civil Law—Legal Reasoning: Bradford v Pickles Revisited' (1973) 8 *University of British Columbia Law Review* 343, 351; Gutteridge (n 141) 44.

161 See Taggart, *Private Property and the Abuse of Rights in Victorian England* (n 153) 189; M Lunney and K Oliphant, *Tort Law: Text and Materials*, 3rd edn (Oxford, Oxford University Press, 2008) 645; J Wightman, 'Nuisance: the Environmental Tort? Hunter v Canary Wharf in the House of Lords' (1998) 61 *The Modern Law Review* 870, 873: '[The] confinement of nuisance to emanations from land implicitly excludes any weighing of malice where there is no emanation. Only if something can count as a nuisance at all can malice be relevant'.

162 See also Lord Denning's statement in *S/S Employment v ASLEF (no 2)* (1972) 2 All ER 949 (HL), 967: 'There are many branches of our law when an act which would otherwise be lawful is rendered unlawful by the motive or object with which it is done'.

163 Nevertheless, both Ames and Holmes sought to construct general theories of tort respectively based on motive and foreseeable consequences: JB Ames, 'How Far an Act May be a Tort because of the Wrongful Motive of the Actor' (1905) 18 *Harvard Law Review* 411, 412; OW Holmes, Jr, 'Privilege, Malice, and Intent' (1894) 8 *Harvard Law Review* 1.

'[t]here is no remedy for abuse of property right, unless it can be fitted within an existing tort'.[164]

As a matter of fact, it has been repeatedly demonstrated that English law proscribes most abuses of rights (namely spiteful or unreasonable exercises of rights) proscribed in civil law jurisdictions. In relation to the right of property, it has been observed that the tort of nuisance—object of the three judgments evoked above—'extend[s] over much of the same ground as that which is covered by the continental theories of abuse'.[165] Likewise, English law routinely condemns abuses of legal procedures, through the torts of malicious prosecution and abuse of process.[166] It has also been argued that the principles of equity perform the same function as a doctrine of abuse of rights, namely the 'relativisation' of rights in order to prevent their abusive exercise.[167]

Overall, despite differences in the methods used (formal rejection of a general doctrine of abuse), it is widely acknowledged that the solutions adopted under English law are roughly similar to those adopted by civil law systems—with a few notable exceptions, such as *Bradford v Pickles*.[168] The law of the United States went even further by overriding most of those exceptions, to the extent that Perillo advocated the formal recognition of a general doctrine of abuse of rights in US law.[169] One argument put forward to explain the difference of approach to abuse of rights between civil law and common law lies in their difference of approach to rights themselves:

> Comparativists tend to explain approaches to abuse of rights in light of the diverse approaches to rights themselves. 'Abuse of rights' emerges as a judicial construct where codified rights are rigid and exhaustive. In civilian systems, the abuse doctrine emerges in the context of exhaustive codes of abstract principles. In contrast, part of the explanation of the lack of abuse on common law relates to the specificity of legislation, and

[164] Taggart (n 153) 191; see also 'Allen v Flood' (1898) 11 *Harvard Law Review* 405, 406:

> [A]n act which is not in itself unlawful apart from the motive of the person doing it, as falling within some of the ancient and tolerably well-defined classes of wrongful acts, cannot render a man liable to an action at law, however bad the motives on which he may have acted, and however serious the loss he may succeed in inflicting upon others.

[165] Gutteridge (n 141) 30; see also Devine (n 104) 165; P Catala and JA Weir, 'Delict and Torts: A Study in Parallel—Part II' (1964) 38 *Tulane Law Review* 221, 243 ff

[166] Catala and Weir, 'Delict and Torts' (n 165) 252–53; Devine (n 104) 167–69; Rogers, Winfield and Jolowicz, *Winfield and Jolowicz on Tort* (n 155) 861–71.

[167] D Anderson, 'Abuse of Rights' (2006) 11 *Judicial Review* 348, 350; Foster, 'Abuse of Rights' (n 160) 349–50. More generally, see JH Baker, *An Introduction to English Legal History*, 3rd edn (London, Butterworths, 1990); S Worthington, *Equity* (Oxford, Clarendon Press, 2003).

[168] Catala and Weir (n 165) 237; Devine (n 104) 172; Gutteridge (n 141) 44: 'A considerable portion of the area ascribed to the theory of abuse by continental law is already covered in English law either by the Common Law rules of tort or by statute'. With regard to the tort of nuisance, it is now undisputed that '*Christie v Davey* and the *Hollywood Silver Fox Farm* case represent the normal rule, most rights of enjoyment and use of land being relative, and *Bradford v Pickles* turns on the peculiarity of the law governing percolating water': see Rogers, Winfield and Jolowicz (n 155) 659.

[169] JM Perillo, 'Abuse of Rights: a Pervasive Legal Concept' (1995) 27 *Pacific Law Journal* 37; see also A di Robilant, 'Abuse of Rights: the Continental Drug and the Common Law' (2010) 61 *Hastings Law Journal* 687.

> the tendency to codify limits and exceptions along with specified rights. Where a code is rigid, it is important to allow judges discretion to adjudicate problematic cases going beyond the letter of the code.[170]

Closer to the concept of abuse of law, Graveson, Fawcett or Tetley have shown that fraudes legis—which they translate by 'evasions of the law'—are commonly sanctioned under English private international law, despite the absence of a general doctrine similar to the French doctrine of *fraude à la loi*.[171] For instance, English courts refused to recognise the validity of 'evasive' marriages and divorces between English nationals, contracted abroad in order to evade the stricter English law.

Tax avoidance is another form of abuse of law[172] commonly fought at the national level. The tax law applied throughout the United Kingdom is no exception, as attested by the Court's rulings in *Cadbury Schweppes* and *Thin Cap Group Litigation*: in both cases, the Court assessed the validity of UK anti-avoidance rules.[173] Therefore, as for abuses of rights and fraudes legis, the question is not whether UK law proscribes tax avoidance, but whether UK law comprises a *general doctrine* potentially applicable to every type of tax avoidance (commonly designated as GAAR or 'General Anti-Avoidance Rule', in opposition to TAARs or 'Targeted Anti-Avoidance Rules'). Although the answer to that question is marked by contradictory judicial decisions, it seems that the recent case law flirts with the judicial recognition of a GAAR under UK tax law.[174] Furthermore, the adoption

[170] Costello, 'Citizenship of the Union' (n 70) 328.

[171] R Graveson, 'The Doctrine of Evasion of the Law in England and America' (1937) 19 *Journal of Comparative Legislation and International Law* 21; W Tetley, 'Evasion/Fraude à la Loi and Avoidance of the Law' (1994) 39 *McGill Law Journal* 303; JJ Fawcett, 'Evasion of Law and Mandatory Rules in Private International Law' (1990) 49 *Cambridge Law Journal* 44, 44:

> It has often been asserted that English private international law has no doctrine of evasion of the law. It is true that English law has never developed a general doctrine, like the French one of fraude a la loi, to deal with cases of evasion. Nonetheless, evasion of the law has been recognised as a problem in at least some areas of private international law, and an increasing number of specific anti-evasion measures have been introduced in to this.

[172] The fact that tax avoidance is a form of abuse of law is evidenced by the Court's application of the doctrine of abuse to tax avoidance schemes in Case C-255/02 *Halifax* [2006] ECR I-1609, Case C-196/04 *Cadbury Schweppes* [2006] ECR I-7995 or Case C-524/04 *Thin Cap Group Litigation* [2007] ECR I-2107. See ch 2 section IV. More generally, see GJ Airs et al, 'Abuse of Tax Law across Europe—Part One' (2010) 19 *EC Tax Review* 85; GJ Airs et al, 'Abuse of Tax Law across Europe—Part Two' (2010) 19 *EC Tax Review* 123; de Broe (n 122) 799 ff; de la Feria (n 9); Zalasinski, 'Some Basic Aspects of the Concept of Abuse' (n 133); A Zalasinski, 'Proportionality of Anti-Avoidance and Anti-Abuse Measures in the ECJ's Direct Tax Case Law' (2007) 35 *Intertax* 310; F Vanistendael, 'Halifax and Cadbury Schweppes: One Single European Theory of Abuse in Tax Law?' (2006) 15 *EC Tax Review* 192; V Ruiz Almendral, 'Tax Avoidance and the European Court of Justice: What is at Stake for European General Anti-Avoidance Rules?' (2005) 33 *Intertax* 562; P Pistone, *Abuso del Diritto ed Elusione Fiscale* (Padua, CEDAM, 1995).

[173] Case C-196/04 *Cadbury Schweppes* [2006] ECR I-7995; Case C-524/04 *Thin Cap Group Litigation* [2007] ECR I-2107.

[174] T Bowler, *Countering Tax Avoidance in the UK: Which Way Forward?*, TLRC Discussion Paper no 7 (London, The Institute For Fiscal Studies, 2009); J Freedman, 'Converging Tracks? Recent Developments in Canadian and UK Approaches to Tax Avoidance' (2005) 53 *Canadian Tax Journal* 1038; G Virgo, 'The Tax Avoidance Rollercoaster: Yet Another New Approach' (2001) 60 *Cambridge Law Journal* 259; A Shipwright, 'L'esperienza britannica' in A Di Pietro (ed), *L'Elusione Fiscale nell'Esperienza Europea* (Milan, Giuffrè, 1999).

of a statutory GAAR has been the object of a recurrent debate in the United Kingdom since the 1990s.[175]

In many—if not all—aspects, the French approach to abuses of rights and abuses of law is opposite to the approach adopted under English law and UK tax law. If English law and UK tax law, as they currently stand, counter abuses of rights, fraudes legis and tax avoidance through fragmented sets of *particular measures*, French law is characterised by *general doctrines* intended to cover every instance of those phenomena. First of all, it is well known that the French scholarship and jurisprudence have developed a general doctrine of abuse of rights, whose official advent occurred through a trilogy of leading cases: *Doerr v Keller*,[176] *Badoit v André*[177] and *Coquerel v Clément-Bayard*.[178] Josserand famously grounded the prohibition of abuse of rights in the theory of the 'relativity of rights', according to which all rights are conferred by the community upon individuals for achieving a certain social purpose. In his own words, 'the abusive act is the act contrary to the purpose of the institution, its spirit and finality'.[179] Gordley commented:

> The French proponents of this doctrine claimed to be leading an attack on the school of legal thought that had dominated the nineteenth century. The members of this school, they said, had regarded legal rights as 'absolute' and so misunderstood the nature of legal rights. The exercise of a right should be limited by the purpose that led the law to recognise such a right. A person abused a right when he exercised it in a way that did not serve this purpose.[180]

In practice, the French courts repositioned the debate on abuses of rights within the 'more reassuring framework of civil liability':[181] the exercise of a right becomes

[175] I Griffiths, 'No Levy on Non-Doms—but Budget Raises Threat of Sweeping Anti-avoidance Measures', *The Guardian*, 22 June 2010.

[176] *Doerr v Keller* (1856) 2 DP 9 (Cour d'Appel de Colmar). A landowner had elevated a dummy chimney on his land for the only purpose of preventing his neighbour's home from enjoying daylight.

[177] *Badoit v André* (1856) 2 DP 199 (Cour d'Appel de Lyon). The famous Saint Galmier mineral water was accessible from several springs located on estates owned by different landlords. One of them decided to install a powerful pump on his spring to improve water extraction, which greatly increased the water extraction on his spring (important quantities of water ended up wasted into a nearby river) and reduced the flow of water on the plaintiff's adjoining spring by two-thirds.

[178] *Coquerel v Clément-Bayard* (1917) 1 DP 79 (Cour d'Appel d'Amiens); *Coquerel v Clément-Bayard* (1920) S 300 (Cour de Cassation française). Clément-Bayard experimented with airships on behalf of the French Government. The speculator Mr Coquerel purchased a piece of land adjoining the airfield, with the intention of selling it to Clément-Bayard at an inflated price. To make his case stronger, Mr Coquerel built up two wooden fences 10 metres high, on top of which he installed four steel spikes three metres high in order to complicate the launching and landing of airships, especially in case of strong wind. As a matter of fact, a steel spike pierced one of Clément-Bayard's airships.

[179] Josserand, *De l'esprit des droits et de leur relativité* (n 124) no 292, free translation.

[180] Gordley, 'The Abuse of Rights in the Civil Law Tradition' (n 126) 36.

[181] A Pirovano, 'L'abus de droit dans la doctrine et la jurisprudence françaises' in M Rotondi (ed), *L'abus de droit* (Padua, CEDAM, 1979) 351.

abusive when it constitutes a 'fault', the usual operative tests being harmful intent or disproportionate hardship suffered by the abused.[182]

The French theory of *fraude à la loi* originates in a leading case of the Cour de Cassation, *Princesse de Bauffremont*.[183] The Princesse de Bauffremont had acquired German nationality in order to obtain her divorce under German law, at a time when divorces were not allowed under French law. The theory of *fraude à la loi* now extends to the most varied phenomena, such as 'evasive' divorces, marriages or changes of name, as well as forum and law shopping in international litigations[184] Moreover, the French real seat doctrine, whose ambit has been severely curtailed by the *Centros*-line of case law, is viewed as an application of the *fraude à la loi* doctrine.[185]

French tax law also includes statutory provisions prohibiting tax avoidance, namely Articles L. 64 and L. 64A of the Livre des Procédures Fiscales (LPF), which explicitly rely on the concept of *abus de droit*. In addition, in *Janfin*[186] and *Bank and Scotland*,[187] the Conseil d'Etat approved the recourse by the tax administration to the theory of *fraude à la loi* to proscribe tax avoidance schemes that escaped the ambit of Article L. 64 LPF. This case law has led the French legislature to broaden the ambit of Article L. 64 LPF,[188] in order to make it coincide with the concept of *fraude à la loi* applied in *Janfin* and *Bank of Scotland*,[189] which corresponds to the concept of 'abuse of law' developed by the European Court of Justice in *Halifax* and *Cadbury Schweppes*.[190]

182 See R Saleilles, *Étude sur la théorie génerale de l'obligation*, 3rd edn (Paris, LGDJ, 1925) no 310 ff; R Demogue, *Traité des obligations en général*, vol IV (Paris, Rousseau, 1923-33) no 634 ff; H H Mazeaud et al, *Obligations: Théorie Générale*, 8th edn, Leçons de droit civil tome 2/1 (Paris, Montchrestien, 1991) 469–70; H Mazeaud, L Mazeaud and A Tunc, *Traité théorique et pratique de la responsabilité civile délictuelle et contractuelle*, 6th edn, vol I (Paris, Montchrestien, 1965) no 647 ff; G Ripert, 'Abus et relativité des droits' (1929) 49 *Revue Critique de Législation et Jurisprudence* 33; G Ripert, *La règle morale dans les obligations civiles* (Paris, LGDJ, 1949); M Planiol, *Traité élémentaire de droit civil*, 4th edn, vol 2 (Paris, LGDJ, 1951) no 871.

183 *Princesse de Bauffremont* (1876) 78 S I-193 (Cour de Cassation française).

184 *JurisClasseur Civil Code*, art 309, Fascicule 20, no 88–91; *JurisClasseur Notarial Répertoire*, V° Nom, Fascicule 60, no 136; *JurisClasseur Procédure civile*, Fascicule 124-7, no 98–100. See also E Cornut, 'Forum shopping et abus du choix de for en droit international privé' (2007) 134 *Journal de Droit International* 27; E Cornut, Théorie critique de la fraude à la loi (Paris, Defrénois, 2006); de Vareilles-Sommières, 'Fraude à la loi' (n 135); Audit, *La fraude à la loi* (n 134); Vidal (n 134); Ligeropoulo, *Le problème de la fraude à la loi* (n 134).

185 Schammo (n 9) 356. See ch 4 section III.A

186 *Janfin* (2006) Leb 410 (Conseil d'État français).

187 *Bank of Scotland* (2006) Leb 578 (Conseil d'État français).

188 See Direction Générale des Finances Publiques Française, 'Procédure de l'Abus de Droit Fiscal: Article 35 de la Loi de Finances Rectificative pour 2008' (Instruction 13 L-9-1), 9 Septembre 2010, Bulletin Officiel des Impôts no 84 du 20/09/2010.

189 P Fernoux, 'Abus de droit: revisitons le passé à l'aune de la nouvelle définition' (2010) 49 *Droit fiscal* 584, no 3

190 P Fumenier, 'Délocalisations: difficultés posées par l'arrêt de la fabrication en France des produits d'un groupe étranger' (2010) 49 *La Semaine Juridique Entreprise et Affaires* 2095, no 3; Fouquet (n 137) no 23–24, free translation: 'the parallelism between the motives of the *Halifax* case and those of the *Janfin* ruling is blinding'.

To sum up, the only relevant question when exploring the treatment of abuses of rights and abuses of law (fraus legis and tax avoidance) at the national level is not *whether* they are proscribed at all, but rather *how* they are proscribed: through particular legal rules and/or rules of general application. In that connection, all national legal orders can be located on a spectrum defined by those two poles: the particular measures adopted under English law and UK tax law, and the general doctrines developed under French law. For that purpose, one can usefully refer to comparative studies investigating the treatment of abuses of rights[191] and tax avoidance[192] in national legal orders. By contrast, the treatment of fraudes legis at the national level is rarely the object of comprehensive reviews;[193] such a review is complicated by the fact that certain legal orders tend to proscribe fraudes legis through the prohibition of abuse of rights.[194] By way of illustration, Table 3 is composed of EU countries for which all three categories of information are provided by existing comparative studies.

Table 3 – Treatment of Abuses of Rights and Abuses of Law in Selected EU Countries

Country	Abuse of Rights	Fraus Legis	Tax Avoidance
Austria	General	General	General
Belgium	General	General	General
France	General	General	General
Germany	General	General	General
Greece	General	General	Particular
Italy	Particular	General	General
Netherlands	General	General	General
Portugal	General	General	General
Spain	General	General	General
United Kingdom	Particular	Particular	Particular

[191] Gestri (n 4) 24–52; M Byers, 'Abuse of Rights: An Old Principle, A New Age' (2002) 47 *McGill Law Journal* 389; E Reid, 'Abuse of Rights in Scots Law' (1998) 2 *Edinburgh Law Review* 129; J Voyame, B Cottier and B Rocha, 'Abuse of Rights in Comparative Law' in Council of Europe (n 65); Rotondi, *L'abus de droit* (n 181); Devine (n 104).

[192] Airs, 'Abuse of Tax Law across Europe—Part One' (n 172); Airs, 'Abuse of Tax Law across Europe—Part Two' (n 172); J Freedman (ed), *Beyond Boundaries: Developing Approaches to Tax Avoidance and Tax Risk Management* (Oxford, Oxford University Centre for Business Taxation, 2008); Di Pietro, *L'Elusione Fiscale nell'Esperienza Europea* (n 174); Pistone, *Abuso del Diritto ed Elusione Fiscale* (n 172); K Perrou, 'The Judicial Application of Anti-Avoidance Doctrines in Greece and its Impact on International Tax Law' (2006) 34 *Intertax* 101.

[193] See however Gestri (n 4) 24–52.

[194] On the existence of such a trend in Belgium, see P Van Ommeslaghe, 'Abus de Droit, Fraude aux Droits des Tiers et Fraude à la Loi' (1976) *Revue Critique de Jurisprudence Belge* 303, 336–50. A similar trend in France is approved by Josserand (n 124) no 198–202; and criticised by Vidal (n 134) 353–62.

As shown in Table 3, most European countries have adopted general doctrines countering abuses of rights, fraudes legis and tax avoidance. The presence of such general doctrines does not exclude per se the existence of particular measures: for instance, most European countries that have adopted a General Anti-Avoidance Rule (GAAR) have also adopted CFC rules, a type of Targeted Anti-Avoidance Rule (TAAR) assessed in *Cadbury Schweppes.*[195] Similarly, certain legal orders may combine a general doctrine of abuse of rights with specific measures, aiming, for instance, at the abuse of legal proceedings.

The notion that such 'abuses' ought to be fought is incredibly pervasive; as a matter of fact, doctrines of abuse have been developed in Latin-American countries,[196] in Japan,[197] under Jewish law[198] and Israeli law,[199] under Islamic law (shari'a)[200] and the civil law of most Arabic countries,[201] under Soviet[202] and contemporary Russian law,[203] under human rights law,[204] public international law[205] and—quite obviously—Union law. Furthermore, similar prohibitions can even be found in private regulatory regimes: for instance, insurance companies most often impose 'qualifying periods' during the first months of an insurance contract, to prevent strategies by which customers would contract a new insurance in anticipation of the forthcoming realisation of a covered risk.[206] This technique of 'qualifying' or 'suspect period' is a legal ground commonly used in Union law to prevent artificial choices of law.[207]

195 See ch 2 section IV.

196 GA Spota, 'El abuso del derecho en la legislacion latinoamericana' in Rotondi (n 181); PB Martins, *O abuso do direito e o ato ilícito*, 3rd edn (Rio de Janeiro, Forense, 1997); MT Ruiz Luján, *El abuso del derecho y la legislación colombiana* (Medellín, Universidad de Antioquia, 1941).

197 Y Noda and T Nomura, 'L'abus du droit en droit privé japonais' in Rotondi (n 181); K Sono and Y Fujioka, 'The Role of the Abuse of Rights in Japan' (1975) 35 *Lousiana Law Review* 1057.

198 A Kirschenbaum, 'Jewish Law and the Abuse of Rights' (1980–82) 5 *Tel Aviv University Studies in Law* 98; S Shilo, 'Kofin Al Midat S'Dom: Jewish Law's Concept of Abuse of Rights' (1980) 15 *Israel Law Review* 49.

199 WZ Zeltner, 'Abuse of right in Israeli law' in Rotondi (n 181).

200 M Shouaib, 'Les origines coraniques de la théorie musulmane de l'abus de droit' (2001) 78 *Revue de Droit International et de Droit Comparé* 340; M Fathy, *La doctrine musulmane de l'abus des droits* (Paris, H Georg & P Geuthner, 1913).

201 A Al-Qasem, 'The Unlawful Exercise of Rights in the Civil Codes of the Arab Countries of the Middle East' (1990) 39 *The International and Comparative Law Quarterly* 396.

202 EL Johnson, 'Abuse of Rights in Soviet Civil Law' (1960) 1 *The Solicitor Quarterly* 320.

203 Reid, 'Abuse of Rights in Scots Law' (n 191) 135.

204 Sajó (n 65); A Spielmann and D Spielmann (n 65).

205 GDS Taylor, 'The Content of the Rule against Abuse of Rights in International Law' (1972–73) 46 *British Yearbook of International Law* 324; G Schwarzenberger, 'Uses and Abuses of the « Abuse of Rights » in International Law' (1956) 42 *Transactions of the Grotius Society* 147; A-C Kiss, *L'abus de droit en droit international* (Paris, LGDJ, 1952); N-S Politis, 'Le problème des limitations de la souveraineté et la théorie de l'abus de droit dans les rapports internationaux' (1925) 6 *Recueil des Cours de l'Académie de Droit International* 1.

206 By way of illustration, the Belgian branch of DKV proposed a medical insurance called 'Plan Z', which subjected the reimbursement of heavy dental treatments to the expiry of a 12-month qualifying period, and the reimbursement of all other medical treatments to the expiry of a 3-month qualifying period.

207 See ch 4 section II.

In sum, each and every legal order (including common law jurisdictions) does prohibit abuses of law; despite certain national idiosyncrasies, the only relevant variable regards the technique deployed (general or particular rules). In other words, *every* national legal order has developed *some* principle of prohibition of abuses of rights and abuses of law. AG Tesauro similarly affirmed the universality of the prohibition of abusive practices:

> Any legal order which aspires to achieve a minimum level of completion must contain self- protection measures, so to speak, to ensure that the rights it confers are not exercised in a manner which [is] abusive, excessive or distorted.[208]

[208] AG Tesauro, Case C-367/96 *Kefalas* [1998] ECR I-2843, para 24.

2

The Formal Doctrine of Abuse of Union Law

THE PREVIOUS CHAPTER proceeded to a preliminary identification of the abuse of Union law, mainly by contrasting it with other phenomena of abuse such as the abuse of rights. The present chapter pursues the investigation of the abuse of Union law by studying the most visible legal ground dealing with abuses of Union law, namely the formal doctrine of abuse developed by the Court of Justice. In more detail, the object of this chapter is to describe the legislative origins (Section I) and the subsequent judicial construction of the doctrine of abuse of Union law (Sections II to V).

I. At the Legislative Origins of the Formal Doctrine of Abuse of Union Law

The wording of the formal doctrine of abuse, famously enounced by the Court of Justice in *Emsland-Stärke*, can be traced back to declarations and propositions made by the Commission and the Council during the years 1994 and 1995, in relation to the adoption of a legislative instrument on the protection of the Community's financial interests.

On 15 June 1994, the Commission made a Proposal for a Council Regulation on the protection of the Community's financial interests, spurred by the need to improve the cooperation between Member States in the prevention of fraudulent practices committed to the detriment of the Community's financial interests,[1] which became Council Regulation 2988/95 on the protection of the European Communities financial interests.[2] In its proposal, the Commission distinguished between frauds, abuses and other irregularities against the Community

[1] Commission (EC), 'Proposal for a Council Regulation (EC, Euratom) on protection of the Community's financial interests' COM (94) 214 final, 7 July 1994.

[2] Council Regulation (EC, Euratom) 2988/95 of 18 December 1995 on the protection of the European Communities financial interests [1995] OJ L312/1.

budget (Article 1), and gave the following definition of 'abuse of Community law' (Article 3(1) of the Proposal):

> 'Abuse of Community law' means an act is done for the purpose of obtaining an unwarranted advantage by means of fictitious or artificial operations designed to create a situation that is formally in accordance with the law but is devoid of any real economic purpose and is contrary to the purpose sought by the material instrument of Community law.

During the Essen European Council of 9 and 10 December 1994, the fight against such frauds and abuses was ranked as a priority policy issue, and the European Council summoned the Council (Economic and Financial Affairs, or ECOFIN) 'to adopt the Regulation on the protection of the Community's financial interests as soon as possible'.[3]

On 20 March 1995, in the course of the subsequent legislative procedure involving the consultation of the European Parliament, the Council made the following declaration in relation to the concept of abuse:

> [The Council] notes that further progress is required in devising a broad legal concept of abuse of Community rules, as proposed by the Commission, in order to reduce the risk of transactions with no valid economic rationale being carried out solely to take advantage of benefits available under Community financial rules.[4]

On 19 June 1995, the ECOFIN Council reached an agreement in principle[5] on a joint guideline on the Regulation on the protection of the financial interests of the Communities, which was formally adopted on 29 June 1995.[6] Although it consulted the Parliament again in relation to the amendments made to the Commission proposal, the Council ignored the amendments suggested by the Parliament on 30 November 1995. On 18 December 1995, it formally adopted the text as it stood following its discussions on 29 June 1995,[7] which became Council Regulation (EC, Euratom) 2988/95 of 18 December 1995 on the protection of the European Communities financial interests.

The final text adopted by the Council is rather ambivalent on the treatment of abusive practices: on the one hand, all explicit references to the concept of 'abuse' have been discarded;[8] on the other hand, the Regulation still includes a general

[3] Essen European Council (EC), 'Presidency Conclusions', 9–10 December 1994, available at www.europarl.europa.eu/summits/.

[4] Council (EC), 'Debate in Council' (Legislative Procedure CNS/1994/0146), 20 March 1995.

[5] Council (EC), '1856th Meeting: ECOFIN' (Press Release) PRES/95/193, 19 June 1995.

[6] Council (EC), '1862nd Meeting: Labour and Social Affairs' (Press Release) PRES/95/199, 29 June 1995.

[7] Council (EC), 'Act adopted by Council after consultation of Parliament' (Legislative Procedure CNS/1994/0146), 18 December 1995.

[8] The scope of the Regulation 2988/95 is based on the notion of irregularity, which is defined by art 1(2) as 'any infringement of a provision of Community law resulting from an act or omission by an economic operator, which has, or would have, the effect of prejudicing the general budget of the Communities or budgets managed by them'.

anti-abuse provision oddly hidden in Article 4, which deals with 'administrative measures and penalties':

> Article 4(3) of Council Regulation 2988/95
>
> Acts which are established to have as their purpose the obtaining of an advantage contrary to the objectives of the Community law applicable in the case by artificially creating the conditions required for obtaining that advantage shall result, as the case shall be, either in failure to obtain the advantage or in its withdrawal.

The adoption of this provision led to a peculiar situation, whereby a Union legislative instrument comprises a half-hidden anti-abuse provision that does not say its name, but whose scope, general in nature,[9] potentially extends to any abuse of law aiming at obtaining an advantage at the expense of the budgets managed by the Union (Article 4(3) read in conjunction with Article 1).

The Court has never addressed abuses of law through a direct application of Article 4(3) of Regulation 2988/95. This can be easily explained in *Emsland-Stärke*, since the Regulation was not applicable *ratione temporis*;[10] and for all the cases of abuse not committed at the expense of Union resources (chiefly cross-border abuses of law committed at the expense of national budgets, such as in *Cadbury Schweppes*, *Thin Cap Group Litigation* or *Oy AA*),[11] which do not fall within the scope *ratione materiae* of the Regulation. But this refusal to rely on Article 4(3) of Regulation 2988/95 becomes harder to justify in cases such as *Vonk Dairy Products*, in which the Court initially applied its judicial doctrine of abuse,[12] and subsequently referred to Regulation 2988/95 with regard to the limitation period.[13] Likewise, in *Pometon*, the Court applied the anti-abuse provision of Regulation 2988/95 only incidentally, when deciding upon the applicable sanction.[14] The absence of reference to Regulation 2988/95 in the *Halifax* judgment has similarly been criticised.[15]

However, irrespective of the motives[16] underlying the Court's reticence to explicitly rely on Article 4(3) of Regulation 2988/95, that reticence does not imply

[9] On the general scope of art 4(3) of Regulation 2988/95, see Case C-158/08 *Pometon* [2009] ECR I-4695, para 27. On the general scope of Regulation 2988/95, see art 1 of the Regulation; see also Case C-94/05 *Emsland-Stärke II* [2006] ECR I-2619, para 50 and Case C-295/02 *Gerken* [2004] ECR I-6369, para 56: 'in the area of checks and penalties for irregularities committed under Community law, the Community legislature has, by adopting Regulation 2988/95, laid down a series of general principles and has required that, as a general rule, all sectoral regulations comply with those principles'.

[10] Case C-110/99 *Emsland-Stärke* [2000] ECR I-11569, paras 37–38.

[11] Case C-196/04 *Cadbury Schweppes* [2006] ECR I-7995; Case C-524/04 *Thin Cap Group Litigation* [2007] ECR I-2107; Case C-231/05 *Oy AA* [2007] ECR I-6373.

[12] Case C-279/05 *Vonk Dairy Products* [2007] ECR I-239, paras 29–38.

[13] Ibid, paras 41–43.

[14] Case C-158/08 *Pometon* [2009] ECR I-4695, paras 27–29.

[15] C Amand, 'Prohibition of Abusive Practices in European VAT: Court Aid to National Legislations Bugs?' (2008) 36 *Intertax* 189, 199.

[16] One could speculate about the Court's willingness to respect the Council's decision to remove every reference to the concept of abuse contained in the initial Commission proposal, or its desire to maintain a unified doctrine of abuse catching all abusive practices: both those committed at the expense of the Union resources, and the others.

a willingness to depart from its substance. Quite on the contrary, there is a striking resemblance between the wording of the doctrine of abuse enounced in *Emsland-Stärke* on the one hand, and the wording of Article 3 in the initial Commission Proposal, of the Council's declaration of 20 March 1995 and of Article 4(3) of Regulation 2988/95, on the other: all four statements refer to *artificial* operations (devoid of valid economic rationale, or carried out solely in order to obtain an advantage under Union law); and they all evoke a contrariety to the *objectives* of the applicable Union rules.

There is accordingly a direct kinship between the doctrine of abuse in Union law, as formulated in *Emsland-Stärke*, and the legislative references to the prohibition of abuses made in the course of the adoption of Regulation 2988/95.[17] In that sense, the doctrine of abuse in Union law can be said to have 'legislative' origins. As a matter of fact, the Commission's position in *Emsland-Stärke* explicitly referred to Article 4(3), although the Regulation was not applicable at the material time: according to the Commission, the latter provision was the mere expression of a general principle of law already in force in the Union legal order.[18]

Including its first appearance in 2000, the Court has applied the formal doctrine of abuse—independently of any 'internal limit' defined by the applicable Union laws[19]—in eight seminal cases during the period 2000-10. These are shown in Table 4.

Table 4 – Judgments Applying the Doctrine of Abuse, Sorted by Chronological Order

Case	Date	Legal Context
Emsland-Stärke	14-12-2000	Export Refunds (CAP)
Halifax	21-02-2006	Sixth Directive VAT
Agip Petroli	06-04-2006	Regulation 3577/92 on Maritime Cabotage
Cadbury Schweppes	12-09-2006	Freedom of Establishment: Direct Taxation
Vonk Dairy Products	11-01-2007	Export Refunds (CAP)
Thin Cap Group Litigation	13-03-2007	Freedom of Establishment: Direct Taxation
ING. AUER	08-11-2007	Directive 69/335 on Capital Duty
Part Service	21-02-2008	Sixth Directive VAT

[17] The connection between art 4(3) of Regulation 2988/95 and the doctrine of abuse was explicitly made by the Commission in Case C-110/99 *Emsland-Stärke* [2000] ECR I-11569, paras 37–39.

[18] Case C-110/99 *Emsland-Stärke* [2000] ECR I-11569, paras 37–38.

[19] See ch 4 and ch 5 section III.B.

This chapter mostly refers to the eight seminal cases of abuse of law in which the Court applied the formal doctrine of abuse, examined in the previous chapter: *Emsland-Stärke*, *Halifax*, *Agip Petroli*, *Cadbury Schweppes*, *Vonk Dairy Products*, *Thin Cap Group Litigation*, *ING. AUER*, *Part Service*. Several of those eight judgments have been reaffirmed by the Court in subsequent decisions, such as *Tanoarch* in the field of VAT (reaffirming *Halifax*), *Etling* in relation to export refunds (reaffirming *Emsland-Stärke*) or *Commission v Spain* and *Commission v Greece* in relation to capital duties (reaffirming *ING. AUER*).[20]

Conceptually, three crucial steps can be identified in the construction of the formal doctrine of abuse by the Court of Justice: its first enunciation in the field of export refunds, in *Emsland-Stärke* (December 2000); the extension of its scope to all 'internal' abuses of law, in *Halifax* (February 2006); and the extension of its scope to 'cross-border' abuses of law, falling within the scope of the Treaty freedoms of movement, in *Cadbury Schweppes* (September 2006). This distinction between internal and cross-border abuses of law is commonly made in the scholarship:

> One may distinguish two main categories of abuse. First, cases where a person seeks to circumvent national law by relying on a fundamental freedom and, second, cases where a person seeks to take improper advantage of a right granted by Union legislation.[21]

> The first type relates to attempts by individuals to rely on Community provisions in order to avoid or evade Member State laws. The second type involves cases in which Community provisions are 'abusively' relied upon in order 'to gain advantages in a manner that conflicts with the purposes and aims of those same provisions'.[22]

In sum, an internal abuse of law consists in the artificial election of a Union legal regime, whereas a cross-border abuse of law consists in the artificial election of a national legal regime. Furthermore, the eight applications of the formal doctrine of abuse mentioned in Table 4 can be sorted in four different areas of law, which form the next four sections: export refunds (*Emsland-Stärke*, *Vonk Dairy Products*), VAT (*Halifax*, *Part Service*), direct taxation (*Cadbury Schweppes*, *Thin Cap Group Litigation*) and other national legal regimes (*Agip Petroli*, *ING. AUER*).

[20] Joined Cases C-230/09 and C-231/09 *Etling* [2011] ECR I-3097, para 78; Case C-504/10 *Tanoarch* [2011] ECR I-10853, paras 49–54; Case C-397/07 *Commission v Spain* [2009] ECR I-6029, paras 29–30; Case C-178/05 *Commission v Greece* [2007] ECR I-4185, para 32.

[21] T Tridimas, 'Abuse of Rights in EU Law: Some Reflections with Particular Reference to Financial Law' in R de la Feria and S Vogenauer (eds), *Prohibition of Abuse of Law: a New General Principle of EU Law?* (Oxford, Hart Publishing, 2011) 190.

[22] P Schammo, 'Arbitrage and Abuse of Rights in the EC Legal System' (2008) 14 *European Law Journal* 351, 358; see also M Gestri, *Abuso del Diritto e Frode alla Legge nell'Ordinamento Comunitario* (Milan, Giuffrè, 2003) 15; D Weber, 'Abuse of Law in the Context of Indirect Taxation: Why We Need the Subjective Intention Test, When is Combating Abuse an Obligation and Other Comments' in de la Feria and Vogenauer, *Prohibition of Abuse of Law* (n 21) 400.

II. Applications of the Formal Doctrine of Abuse in the Field of Export Refunds

After a series of circumvolutions highlighting the illegitimacy of avoidance strategies, starting with *Van Binsbergen* in 1974,[23] the Court of Justice enounced the formal doctrine of abuse in 2000, in the *Emsland-Stärke* case. *Emsland-Stärke* (and *Vonk Dairy Products*) concerned the revocation of decisions granting 'export refunds', namely subsidies promoting the export of Union agricultural products. The amount of export refund granted for a category of products may vary according to the third country of destination ('differentiated export refund', such as in *Vonk Dairy Products*) or not ('non-differentiated export refund', such as in *Emsland-Stärke*).

When the amount of export refund is higher than the aggregate import duties applied by both the third country of destination and the European Union, Union exporters have an incentive to export and immediately re-import products into the Union, irrespective of any commercial benefit (re-importation strategy: see *Emsland-Stärke*). Such strategies are conceivable for both differentiated and non-differentiated export refunds.[24]

When the export refund is differentiated, imaginative Union traders can also export products to a third country for which a high export refund had been defined, and then immediately re-export them to the real third country of destination, to which, by hypothesis, a lower export refund had been assigned (re-exportation strategy: see *Vonk Dairy Products*).[25]

Under the relevant Union legislation, national authorities could defeat both strategies of re-importation and re-exportation by requiring evidence of the products' importation[26] or even marketing[27] in the declared third country of destination. However, in both *Emsland-Stärke* and *Vonk Dairy Products*, national authorities failed to avail themselves of that possibility in due time, which explained the recourse to an autonomous doctrine of abuse.

[23] Case 33/74 *Van Binsbergen* [1974] ECR 1299, paras 12–13. See ch 4 n 83 and accompanying text.

[24] On the risk of re-importation strategies, see Case C-515/03 *Eichsfelder Schlachtbetrieb* [2005] ECR I-7355, paras 29–30; Case C-114/99 *Roquette Frères* [2000] ECR I-8823, paras 17–20; Case C-54/95 *Germany v Commission* [1999] ECR I-35, paras 46–47; Case C-347/93 *Boterlux* [1994] ECR I-3933, paras 23–30.

[25] On the risk of re-export strategies, see Case C-515/03 *Eichsfelder Schlachtbetrieb* [2005] ECR I-7355, paras 26–28 and 30; Case C-54/95 *Germany v Commission* [1999] ECR I-35, paras 44–45 and 47; Case C-347/93 *Boterlux* [1994] ECR I-3933, paras 17–20; Case 125/75 *Eierkontor I* [1976] ECR 771, paras 5–6.

[26] Case C-515/03 *Eichsfelder Schlachtbetrieb* [2005] ECR I-7355, paras 26–30; Case C-110/99 *Emsland-Stärke* [2000] ECR I-11569, paras 31–33; Case C-54/95 *Germany v Commission* [1999] ECR I-35, paras 39–48; Case C-347/93 *Boterlux* [1994] ECR I-3933, paras 18–30.

[27] Case C-279/05 *Vonk Dairy Products* [2007] ECR I-239, para 29; Case C-515/03 *Eichsfelder Schlachtbetrieb* [2005] ECR I-7355, para 29; Case C-110/99 *Emsland-Stärke* [2000] ECR I-11569, paras 34–35; Case C-114/99 *Roquette Frères* [2000] ECR I-8823, para 18; Case 44/76 *Eierkontor II* [1977] ECR 393, para 16.

A. *Emsland-Stärke* (2000)

Case C-110/99 *Emsland-Stärke* [2000] ECR I-11569

i. Facts

Under Regulation 2730/79,[28] which was applicable in the *Emsland-Stärke* case, the payment of export refunds was subject to the proof that the products had left the territory of the Union unaltered (Article 9(1) of Regulation 2730/79). Where there was a risk of artificial re-exportation (Article 10(1)(a)) or re-importation (Article 10(1)(b)), national authorities could also require evidence that the products had been imported in the third country of destination, by proving the completion of the customs entry formalities for home use in that country (Articles 20(2)). They could also require additional proof that the products had actually been placed on the market in the third country of destination (Article 10(1)).

Emsland-Stärke GmbH, a German company, had received non-differentiated export refunds in respect of several consignments of products based on potato starch and wheat starch, which were exported to Switzerland between April and June 1987. The recipients of the goods were Fuga and Lukowa, two companies established at the same address in Lucerne (Switzerland) and managed by the same persons. However, immediately after being released for home use in Switzerland, these consignments were re-introduced into the Union and were released for home use in Germany and Italy, upon payment of the applicable import duties.

When the German customs authorities discovered the final destination of the exported consignments, namely Germany and Italy, they revoked their decisions granting an export refund and demanded repayment of the subsidy for an amount exceeding DEM 300,000. Emsland-Stärke challenged the revocation, arguing that all the goods had been released for home use in Switzerland and that the consignments had been sold in Switzerland by Fuga to Lukowa, before being re-imported. Furthermore, it contended that it was not aware of the purchasers' intentions with respect to the goods exported to Switzerland.

ii. Decision of the Court

The Court first ruled out the possibility for national authorities to require additional proof regarding actual importation or marketing *after* granting the export refund. Indeed, on the basis of the wording of Article 10(1) of Regulation 2730/79 and of the judgment in *Boterlux*,[29] such additional evidences could only be demanded prior to the grant of the refund (paras 48–49). As a consequence,

[28] Commission Regulation (EEC) 2730/79 of 29 November 1979 laying down common detailed rules for the application of the system of export refunds on agricultural products [1979] OJ L317/1.

[29] Case C-347/93 *Boterlux* [1994] ECR I-3933, para 30.

all formal conditions laid down by Regulation 2730/79 for the grant of an export refund were fulfilled, since the goods had left the geographical territory of the Union as required by Article 9(1) (paras 46–47).

However, the 'specific circumstances' of the case, which suggested 'an abuse, that is to say, a purely formal dispatch from Community territory with the sole purpose of benefiting from export refunds', led the Court to examine whether an export refund could be revoked a posteriori (para 50). In that regard, the Court's previous case law had established that the scope of Union law did not cover abuses on the part of traders.[30] This exclusion implied that the benefit of monetary compensatory amounts could be withdrawn in the presence of strategies of re-importation that 'were not realised as bona fide commercial transactions but only in order wrongfully to benefit from the grant of monetary compensatory amounts' (para 51).[31]

In the next step of its reasoning, the Court enounced for the first time the formal doctrine of abuse of Union law, by defining the two constitutive elements of an abusive practice (paras 52–53):

> A finding of an abuse requires, first, a combination of objective circumstances in which, despite formal observance of the conditions laid down by the Community rules, the purpose of those rules has not been achieved.
>
> It requires, second, a subjective element consisting in the intention to obtain an advantage from the Community rules by creating artificially the conditions laid down for obtaining it. The existence of that subjective element can be established, inter alia, by evidence of collusion between the Community exporter receiving the refunds and the importer of the goods in the non-member country.

The presence of those two elements had to be verified by the national court in accordance with the rules of national law, provided that the effectiveness of Union law was not thereby undermined (para 54). Furthermore, the obligation to repay an export refund when the two constitutive elements of an abuse are established did not breach the principle of lawfulness, for it was the mere consequence of a finding that the conditions for its granting were created artificially, turning the refund into an undue payment (para 56).

As for the application of the two tests to Emsland-Stärke's re-importation strategy, the national court considered that the purpose of the Union rules had not been achieved (para 55). Moreover, the fact that the exporter did not re-import the goods itself was irrelevant (para 57), and the fact that the goods were sold by the importer established in the third country of destination to an undertaking with which it has personal and commercial links, before being re-imported into the Union, was one of the factual elements which could be taken into account to establish the artificiality of the operation (para 58).

[30] Case 125/76 *Cremer* [1977] ECR 1593, para 21.
[31] Case C-8/92 *General Milk Products* [1993] ECR I-779, para 21.

B. *Vonk Dairy Products* (2007)

Case C-279/05 *Vonk Dairy Products* [2007] ECR I-239

i. Facts

From 1988 to 1994, Vonk Dairy Products, a company incorporated in the Netherlands, exported about 2000 tons of Italian pecorino cheese per year to the USA, for which it received a differentiated export refund on the basis of Regulation 3665/87.[32] Vonk Dairy Products adduced documents proving that the consignments had been released for free circulation in the US.

An investigation by the US Customs, requested by the Netherlands Customs, revealed that about 1500 tons of pecorino were almost immediately re-exported to Canada by Orlando Food Corporation, an intermediary of Vonk Dairy Products active in the US. Indeed, the rate of export refund for the US was higher than for Canada, which created a financial incentive to set up such re-exportation strategies. The recipient of most consignments was National Cheese & Food Company, a Canadian company established in Ontario. It was established that Vonk Dairy Products was involved in the sale of cheese in Canada and that it had exchanged explicit correspondence with National Cheese & Food Company in that connection.

Following the investigation, the Netherlands customs authorities revoked their decision granting refunds as regards the 75 consignments in dispute, and demanded repayment of a sum of NLG 2,800,000 corresponding to the difference between the differentiated refunds applicable to the US and to Canada, plus a 15 per cent fine.

Vonk Dairy Products argued that it satisfied all the conditions laid down in Articles 4, 17(3) and 18 of Regulation 3665/87 for obtaining differentiated refunds, given that it had furnished evidence of importation and release for consumption in the US. Moreover, it argued that the Netherlands authorities had not established the existence of an abuse under the test set out in *Emsland-Stärke.*

ii. Decision of the Court

As in *Emsland-Stärke*, the national authorities had not availed themselves, before the export refunds became definitive, of the possibility to request evidence that the products had actually been placed on the market of the country of importation, as permitted by Article 5(1)(a) and Article 18(2) of Regulation 3665/87. Therefore, Vonk Dairy Products satisfied, at a formal level, all the conditions provided for by Regulation 3665/87 for the grant of an export refund (para 29; see also paras 35–37).

[32] Commission Regulation (EEC) 3665/87 of 27 November 1987 laying down common detailed rules for the application of the system of export refunds on agricultural products [1987] OJ L351/1.

The Court undertook to provide guidance to the national court regarding the assessment of the re-exportation strategy set up by Vonk Dairy Products, namely the immediate re-exportation of pecorino cheese from the US to Canada (para 30). In that regard, the Court recalled that the scope of Union regulations did not extend to abuses on the part of traders (para 31).[33] Consequently, national authorities could demand repayment of definitively paid refunds if the existence of an abusive practice on the part of the exporter could be established (para 32). The Court finally referred to its well-established doctrine of abuse, paraphrasing its decision in *Emsland-Stärke* (para 33):

> That evidence involves first, a combination of objective circumstances from which it is apparent that, despite formal observance of the conditions laid down by the Community rules, the purpose of those rules has not been achieved, and, second, a subjective element consisting in the intention to obtain an advantage from the Community rules by creating artificially the conditions laid down for obtaining it. The existence of that subjective element can be established, inter alia, by evidence of collusion between the exporter receiving the refunds and the importer of the goods in a non-member country other than the country of importation.

The presence of those two elements had to be verified by the national court in accordance with the rules of national law, provided that the effectiveness of Union law was not thereby undermined (para 34).

III. Applications of the Formal Doctrine of Abuse in the Field of VAT

After its first enunciation in *Emsland-Stärke* (December 2000), the *Halifax* ruling (February 2006) marked a second crucial step in the development of the doctrine of abuse of Union law. Indeed, the *Halifax* ruling[34] made clear that the doctrine of abuse potentially applies to all internal abuses of law, namely artificial elections of a Union legal regime. As we shall see in the next section, *Cadbury Schweppes* completed this evolutionary process a few months later (in September 2006), by extending the scope of the doctrine of abuse to cross-border abuses of law, namely artificial elections of a national legal regime.

Within the scope of the VAT system harmonised at Union level, a common type of tax structuring is designed by taxpayers who cannot recover part of or all the

[33] Case 125/76 *Cremer* [1977] ECR 1593, para 21; Case C-110/99 *Emsland-Stärke* [2000] ECR I-11569, para 51.

[34] See Case C-255/02 *Halifax* [2006] ECR I-1609, para 70: 'That principle of prohibiting abusive practices also applies to the sphere of VAT'.

input VAT.[35] As a rule, taxpayers must request payment of VAT on the goods and services they offer, and subsequently transfer this output VAT to the tax authorities; on the other hand, they are entitled to recover the input VAT they have borne on the goods and services purchased in the context of their economic activity. However, as a credit institution, Halifax was mostly VAT-exempted (no output VAT) and had consequently a very limited right to deduction (about 5 per cent of the input VAT). In order to circumvent that limitation, it sought to delegate the construction of four call centres to a specific entity of the Halifax group, endowed with a full right to deduction (100 per cent of the input VAT on the construction costs).[36]

Another classical example of VAT avoidance exploits the possibility offered by certain national laws to opt for the taxation of the leasing or letting of immovable property,[37] pursuant to Article 137 of VAT Directive 2006/112[38] (ex-Article 13C of the Sixth Directive[39]). When such an option is granted ('taxation—deduction' or 'no taxation—no deduction'), taxpayers have a financial incentive to opt for taxation when they bear heavy refurbishment or construction costs, for the input VAT incurred on the refurbishment or construction works (deduction) is likely to exceed the output VAT due on the lease agreement (taxation). Such VAT avoidance strategies, which lead to a refund of VAT at the expense of the Treasury, were fought by national legislatures through the restriction of the right to opt for taxation or the limitation of the right to deduction, which gave rise to several preliminary references to the Court.[40] The *University of Huddersfield* ruling precisely concerned the exercise of such an option: when planning the refurbishment of two buildings, the University leased them to a special entity created for that purpose, and opted for VAT taxation. Bound by the limited scope of the preliminary reference, the Court (Grand Chamber) merely referred to the doctrine of abuse applied the same day in *Halifax*.[41] *Halifax* was subsequently reaffirmed by the Court's judgment in *Tanoarch*.[42]

[35] M Ridsdale, 'Abuse of Rights, Fiscal Neutrality and VAT' (2005) 2 *EC Tax Review* 82, 82.

[36] See Amand, 'Prohibition of Abusive Practices in European VAT' (n 15) 196; R de la Feria, 'Prohibition of Abuse of (Community) Law: the Creation of a New General Principle of EC Law through Tax' (2008) 45 *Common Market Law Review* 395, 421–22.

[37] R de la Feria, 'The European Court of Justice's Solution to Aggressive VAT Planning—Further towards Legal Uncertainty?' (2006) 15 *EC Tax Review* 27.

[38] Council Directive 2006/112/EC of 28 November 2006 on the Common System of Value Added Tax [2006] OJ L347/1.

[39] Sixth Council Directive 77/388/EEC of 17 May 1977 on the harmonization of the laws of the Member States relating to turnover taxes—Common system of value added tax: uniform basis of assessment [1977] OJ L145/1.

[40] See Case C-376/02 *Goed Wonen II* [2005] ECR I-3445; Joined Cases C-487/01 and C-7/02 *Gemeente Leusden* [2004] ECR I-5337; Case C-326/99 *Goed Wonen* [2001] ECR I-6831; Case C-396/98 *Schloßstraße* [2000] ECR I-4279.

[41] Case C-223/03 *University of Huddersfield* [2006] ECR I-1751, para 52.

[42] Case C-504/10 *Tanoarch* [2011] ECR I-10853.

The *Part Service* case concerned the artificial splitting of taxable leasing services into several transactions, in order to benefit from a partial exemption. In the past, other attempts at artificial splitting were designed to benefit from a favourable tax rate or elect a more favourable place of taxation.[43]

A. *Halifax* (2006)

Case C-255/02 *Halifax* [2006] ECR I-1609

i. Facts

Halifax was founded in 1853 and named after the town of Halifax, where it had its headquarters, and which is located in West Yorkshire near Bradford and Huddersfield.[44] By the early 2000s, Halifax was the fifth largest UK bank in terms of market capitalisation; in 2001, it became a division of the group Halifax Bank of Scotland plc (HBOS), following its merger with the Bank of Scotland.

In 1999, Halifax decided to construct four call centres on four different sites: at Cromac Wood and Dundonald in Northern Ireland (both near Belfast), at Livingston in Scotland (near Edinburgh) and at West Bank, Leeds (near Halifax). For that purpose, Halifax concluded a classical development contract with Cusp Ltd, a property development and contracting company, for the Cromac Wood site. However, Halifax disengaged itself from that contract by a novation agreement of 28 February 2000, following which a complex transactional structure was set up, involving several entities of the group: Halifax itself, Leeds Permanent Development Services Ltd (Leeds), County Wide Property Investments Ltd (County) and Halifax Property Investments Ltd (Property), all three wholly-owned subsidiaries of Halifax. The same type of transactional structure, consisting of seven transactions, was replicated for the three other construction projects, as shown in Table 5.

[43] The Court has underlined that 'temptation' (or incentive) several times: see Case C-425/06 *Part Service* [2008] ECR I-897, para 49; Case C-41/04 *Levob* [2005] ECR I-9433, para 18; Case C-349/96 *CPP* [1999] ECR I-973, para 27.

[44] Halifax is located barely eight miles away from both Huddersfield and Bradford. Surprisingly enough, Halifax and Huddersfield lent their names to two judgments of the Court of Justice endorsing the doctrine of abuse in Union law, whereas the existence in English law of a general doctrine of abuse of rights was famously rejected by the House of Lords in *Bradford Corporation v Pickles* (1895) Appeal Cases 587 (HL): see among others H Foster, 'Abuse of Rights—Civil Law—Legal Reasoning: Bradford v Pickles Revisited' (1973) 8 *University of British Columbia Law Review* 343; M Taggart, *Private Property and the Abuse of Rights in Victorian England: The Story of Edward Pickles and Bradford Water Supply* (Oxford, Oxford University Press, 2002).

Table 5 – *Halifax*: Detail of the Transactional Structure

	Transaction	Parties		Consideration	VAT
1	*Loan*	Halifax	Leeds	62,000,000	–
2	*Construction*	Halifax	Leeds	140,000	25,000
3	*Development*	Leeds	County	41,000,000	7,000,000
4	*Lease*	Halifax	Leeds	Premium	–
5	*Lease Assignment*	Leeds	Property	Premium	–
6	*Under-Lease*	Property	Halifax	Premium	–
7	*Construction Works*	County	Builders	Works Price	Works VAT

First of all, Halifax entered into a loan agreement (VAT-exempted) with Leeds (Agreement 1), under which it agreed to lend a maximum amount of about GBP 62,000,000 for the development of the four sites. Second, Halifax gave Leeds the responsibility of carrying certain construction works on the sites, for a price of GPB 165,000, including VAT of GBP 25,000 (Agreement 2). Subsequently, Leeds entered into a development and funding agreement with County, under which the latter was mandated to carry out construction works on the sites (Agreement 3). In relation to that agreement, County charged Leeds an amount of GPB 48,000,000, including VAT of GPB 7,000,000. Halifax would then grant a lease of each construction site to Leeds (Agreement 4), which would assign the leases to Property upon completion of the works (Agreement 5), which would in turn sublet the call centres 'to be constructed' to Halifax (Agreement 6), all three transactions being made for a premium. Those operations were VAT-exempted, but were carried out during different financial years, so that their exemption had no impact on the right to deduction of the entities involved.[45] Finally, County engaged various independent contractors and professionals (the 'arm's-length builders') to construct call centres on each site (Agreement 7), the latter charging a price including VAT.

The purpose of this transactional structure was undisputed, namely circumventing the limitation imposed upon Halifax, a credit institution, to deduct the input VAT on the construction of the call centres. As a rule, a taxable person[46] has the right to deduct all the input VAT borne on the acquisition of professional goods and services,[47] such as call centres. However, this principle does not apply to goods and services used by a taxable person for both taxable and exempted activities, since exempted activities do not entail a right to deduction. Accordingly, Article 17(5) of the Sixth Directive[48] limits the right to deduction on such goods

[45] AG Maduro, Case C-255/02 *Halifax* [2006] ECR I-1609, para 6.

[46] A taxable person is 'any person who, independently, carries out in any place any economic activity, whatever the purpose or results of that activity': VAT Directive 2006/112 art 9.

[47] VAT Directive 2006/112 art 168.

[48] VAT Directive 2006/112 art 173.

and services, by providing that only a proportion of the input VAT borne on their acquisition is deductible (*proportional* right to deduction). Pursuant to Article 19 of the Sixth Directive,[49] this deductible proportion is made up of a fraction having as *numerator* the yearly turnover of taxable operations effected by the taxable person, and as *denominator* the yearly turnover of both taxable and exempted operations.

Banks and other financial institutions are typically granted such a proportional right to deduction, for they use their professional goods and services to carry out both exempted and taxable activities. Moreover, since most financial activities are VAT-exempted,[50] they usually have a low proportional right to deduction. Halifax was no exception: at the material time, the vast majority of its services were exempted from VAT, so that it was able to recover less than 5 per cent of its input VAT (para 12). Concretely, this meant that Halifax was entitled to deduct less than 5 per cent of the VAT borne on the construction of the four call centres.

Given Halifax's limited right to deduction, the objective of the transactional structure was to allocate most of the input VAT borne on the construction works to an associated company endowed with an integral right to deduction, namely County. The flows of VAT generated by this structure can be schematised as set out in Figure 3. For the sake of the argument, we shall assume that the construction costs paid by County to the independent constructors was of GBP 48,000,000 (the price paid by Leeds to County), including GBP 7,000,000 of VAT.

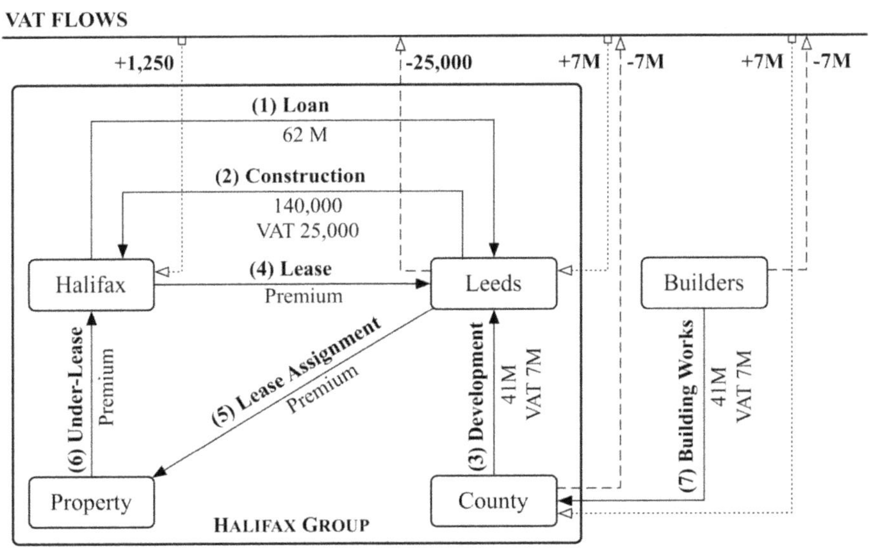

Figure 3 – *Halifax*: Detail of the VAT Flows

[49] VAT Directive 2006/112 art 174.
[50] VAT Directive 2006/112 art 135.

First, on the input VAT of GBP 25,000 paid to Leeds, Halifax was entitled to deduct only GBP 1250 (proportional right to deduction: 5 per cent of GBP 25,000). Thereafter, Leeds paid GBP 25,000 to the tax authorities (output VAT received from Halifax) but deducted GBP 7,000,000 (input VAT paid to County). Finally, County paid GBP 7,000,000 as well (output VAT received from Leeds) and, by hypothesis, deducted GBP 7,000,000 (input VAT paid to the builders, or 'Works VAT' in Figure 3.

The latter deduction, whereby an entity of the Halifax group (County) became entitled to deduct the totality of the input VAT charged by the independent contractors (GBP 7,000,000, by hypothesis), is the very purpose of the whole transactional structure. Indeed, as an ordinary taxable person carrying out a taxable activity of property development and investment, County held a full right to deduction. Overall, this transactional structure allowed the Halifax Group to deduct GBP 6,976,250 (GBP 7,000,000 – GBP 7,000,000 + GBP 7,000,000 – GBP 25,000 + GBP 1250), whereas the entity Halifax would have been allowed to deduct less than 5 per cent of the VAT charged by the same independent contractors, namely less than GBP 350,000 (5 per cent of GBP 7,000,000). In short, thanks to this tax planning, the Halifax Group expected to realise a gain of about GBP 6,600,000 (95 per cent of the VAT charged by the constructors).

However, by decisions of 4 and 7 July 2000, the UK tax authorities rejected Leeds Development's and County's claims for deduction, arguing that Halifax was the real recipient of the construction works, so that only Halifax was entitled to deduct the input VAT on those works, applying its normal recovery percentage.

ii. Decision of the Court

The Court first recalled that the basic concepts of the VAT system, such as 'economic activity', 'supply of goods' or 'supply of services', are objective in nature and apply without regard to the purpose or results of the transactions concerned (paras 55–56).[51] It follows that 'the question whether a given transaction is carried out for the sole purpose of obtaining a tax advantage is entirely irrelevant in determining whether it constitutes a supply of goods or services and an economic activity' (para 59). Even such transactions constitute supplies of goods or services, if they satisfy the objective criteria on which those concepts are based.

However, the fact that a transaction was carried out for the sole purpose of obtaining a tax advantage can have consequences on the right to deduction of the parties involved. In that connection, Union law does not extend to cover abusive practices, namely 'transactions carried out not in the context of normal commercial operations, but solely for the purpose of wrongfully obtaining advantages provided for by Community law' (para 69).[52] Crucially, the Court confirmed that

[51] Joined Cases C-354/03, C-355/03 and C-484/03 *Optigen* [2006] ECR I-483, para 44.

[52] Case 125/76 *Cremer* [1977] ECR 1593, para 21; Case C-8/92 *General Milk Products* [1993] ECR I-779, para 21; Case C-110/99 *Emsland-Stärke* [2000] ECR I-11569, para 51.

the prohibition of abusive practices also applies within the sphere of VAT (para 70), where the prevention of tax evasion, avoidance and abuse is an objective recognised by the Sixth Directive (para 71).[53]

Nevertheless, the principle of legal certainty (para 72) and the right of individuals to minimise their tax liability (para 73) must be protected.[54] Therefore, the notion of abusive practices should be delineated by the test defined in *Emsland-Stärke* (paras 74–75):

> In the sphere of VAT, an abusive practice can be found to exist only if, first, the transactions concerned, notwithstanding formal application of the conditions laid down by the relevant provisions of the Sixth Directive and the national legislation transposing it, result in the accrual of a tax advantage the grant of which would be contrary to the purpose of those provisions.
>
> Second, it must also be apparent from a number of objective factors that the essential aim of the transactions concerned is to obtain a tax advantage. As the AG observed in point 89 of his Opinion, the prohibition of abuse is not relevant where the economic activity carried out may have some explanation other than the mere attainment of tax advantages.

The presence of those two elements should be verified by the national court in accordance with the rules of evidence of national law, provided that the effectiveness of Union law is not undermined (para 76).[55] Yet, by contrast with its decision in *Emsland-Stärke*, the Court gave the national court further guidance concerning the application of those two tests.

As regards the first element – the teleological assessment—, the right to deduction is meant to relieve the taxable trader of the burden of the VAT paid in the course of his economic activities (principle of neutrality: para 78). It is only where the acquisition of goods and services is directly linked to an economic activity giving rise to a deduction entitlement, that the VAT paid on the goods and services acquired can be deducted (para 79). Therefore, concludes the Court (para 80):

> To allow taxable persons to deduct all input VAT even though, in the context of their normal commercial operations, no transactions conforming with the deduction rules of the Sixth Directive or of the national legislation transposing it would have enabled them to deduct such VAT, or would have allowed them to deduct only a part, would be contrary to the principle of fiscal neutrality and, therefore, contrary to the purpose of those rules.

When verifying the presence of the second element, whereby the transactions concerned must essentially seek to obtain a tax advantage, the national court may take into account 'the purely artificial nature of those transactions and the links of a legal, economic and/or personal nature between the operators involved in the

[53] Joined Cases C-487/01 and C-7/02 *Gemeente Leusden* [2004] ECR I-5337, para 76.

[54] Case C-4/94 *BLP* [1995] ECR I-983, para 26; Case C-108/99 *Cantor Fitzgerald International* [2001] ECR I-7257, para 33.

[55] Case C-515/03 *Eichsfelder Schlachtbetrieb* [2005] ECR I-7355, para 40.

scheme for reduction of the tax burden' (para 81). In the case at hand, the national court made clear that the sole purpose of the transactions at issue in the main proceedings was to obtain a tax advantage (para 82).

Finally, the Court specified the consequences of a finding of abusive practice: if it precludes any right to deduction in relation to the vitiated transactions (paras 84–85),[56] which entails an obligation to repay the VAT deducted, it cannot lead to a penalty, for which a clear and unambiguous legal basis would be necessary (para 93).[57] Moreover, the national authorities are under an obligation to restore the situation that would have prevailed in the absence of abusive practice: if they are entitled to claim repayment of the VAT abusively deducted,[58] they must also reimburse any tax charged in relation to the abusive transactions and allow any deduction arising under the 'restored' situation (paras 94–97).

B. *Part Service* (2008)

Case C-425/06 *Part Service* [2008] ECR I-897

i. Facts

When economic operators deal directly with final consumers, they have an incentive to minimise the taxable amount of the goods or services they offer, for final consumers do not have a right to deduct input VAT. As a result, any decrease in the VAT charged to the final consumers entails an equivalent decrease in the price of their goods and services.[59]

The existence of that incentive led two Italian companies, Part Service (formerly Italservice) and IFIM Leasing, to structure their vehicle leasing activity in the following way. Throughout 1987, Italservice and IFIM, two companies belonging to the same financial group, proposed combined services in relation to the leasing of motor vehicles. Instead of concluding a classical leasing transaction, which would have entailed a VAT liability on the whole consideration paid by the customers (the lessees), Italservice and IFIM split their leasing services in several transactions as illustrated by Figure 4 below:

— *first*, IFIM granted the customer the use of the motor vehicle with an option to purchase, in consideration of: lease payments, the setting up of a surety corresponding to the costs of the vehicle not covered by the lease payments and the provision of an unlimited security;

[56] Case C-400/98 *Breitshol* [2000] ECR I-4321, para 41; Case C-396/98 *Schloßstraße* [2000] ECR I-4279, para 42.

[57] Case C-110/99 *Emsland-Stärke* [2000] ECR I-11569, para 56.

[58] Case C-32/03 *Fini H* [2005] ECR I-1599, para 33.

[59] Such an incentive does not exist when a taxable person deals with another taxable person, for the latter is entitled to deduct the VAT charged by the former.

— *secondly*, in consideration of an advance payment by the customer, Italservice insured the vehicle against all risks except civil liability and guaranteed the fulfilment of its obligations in favour of IFIM, by financing the surety and providing the unlimited security. Italservice was then instructed by the customer to transfer the amount financed to IFIM, by way of the surety promised;
— *finally*, Italservice entrusted the performance of the contract agreed with the customer to IFIM, for which it remunerated IFIM. In the event of default of the customer, IFIM was also guaranteed by Italservice an amount equivalent to that promised by Italservice to the customer, by way of refund, if the latter fulfilled his obligations to make the lease payments.

The considerations paid by the customer to Italservice (second transaction) and by Italservice to IFIM (third transaction) were exempted pursuant to Article 13B(a) and (d) of the Sixth Directive. Moreover, as a result of the advance payment made by the customer to Italservice, the total lease payments paid by the customer to IFIM (first transaction) were reduced to an amount barely above the cost of the vehicle (para 11). Since those lease payments were the only taxable amounts, this series of transactions reduced the amount of VAT due on the leasing transaction in the same proportion.

The Italian tax authorities considered that these separate agreements formed a single transaction, and that the consideration paid by the customer for the leasing arrangement had been artificially split to reduce the taxable amount, as the role of lessor was divided between Italservice and IFIM. Therefore, Italservice was served an adjustment notice for VAT in respect of the year 1997. Italservice contested the tax adjustment, claiming that the structure had been chosen not for tax avoidance purposes, but for valid economic reasons regarding marketing, organisation and guarantee (para 19).

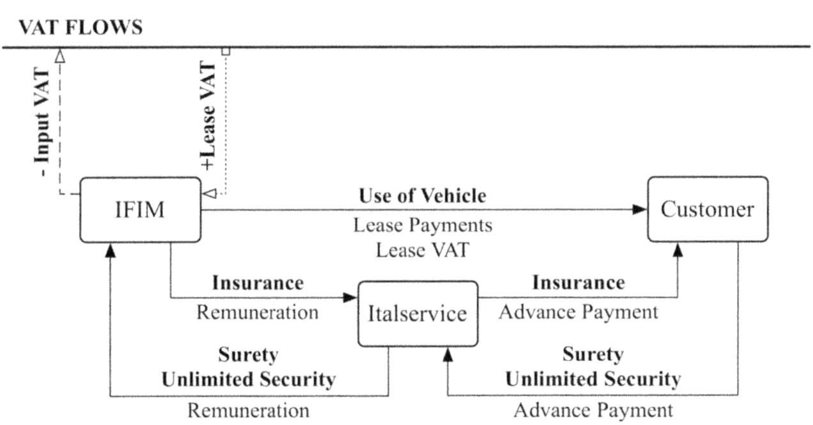

Figure 4 – *Part Service*: Detail of VAT Flows

ii. Decision of the Court

In reply to the first question referred by the national court, the Court refined the second element of the doctrine of abuse formulated in *Halifax*, according to which an abusive practice can only be found when it is apparent from a number of objective factors that the *essential aim* of the transactions concerned was to obtain a tax advantage.[60] The national court wondered whether the expression 'essential aim' meant that the accrual of a tax advantage had to be the principal or the sole aim of the transactions, to the exclusion of other economic objectives. The Court favoured the former option, holding that there could still be a finding of an abusive practice when the accrual of a tax advantage constituted the principal aim of the transaction at issue, alongside other limited economic objectives (paras 40–45).

By its second question, the national court directly asked the Court whether the transactions at issue could be considered as abusive. The Court started by evoking its case law on the splitting of supplies of services. Within the VAT system, the question of whether several services should be considered as a single transaction is of particular importance for applying the tax rate or certain exemptions (paras 48–49).[61] In certain circumstances, several services, although formally distinct and each of which would separately give rise to taxation or exemption, cannot be regarded as independent and must therefore be assessed as a single transaction (para 51). Such is the case when certain services are only ancillary to a principal service, that is when they do not constitute an aim in themselves for the customers, but a means of better enjoying the principal service (para 52).[62] Such is also the case when several services are so closely linked that they form, objectively, a single, indivisible economic supply, which it would be artificial to split (para 53).[63]

The Court then suggested an alternative approach based on the prohibition of abusive practices, and pointed out the following characteristics of the transactions at issue (para 57):

— the two companies taking part in the leasing transaction are part of the same group;
— the service supplied by the leasing company (IFIM) is subject to a division, the financing element is entrusted to another company (Italservice) to be split into a credit service, an insurance service and a brokerage service;
— the service of the leasing company is therefore reduced to a service for renting a vehicle;
— the lease payments made by the customer are of an amount which is only slightly higher than the purchase cost of the vehicle;

60 Case C-255/02 *Halifax* [2006] ECR I-1609, para 75.
61 Case C-349/96 *CPP* [1999] ECR I-973, para 27; Case C-41/04 *Levob* [2005] ECR I-9433, para 18.
62 Case C-349/96 *CPP* [1999] ECR I-973, para 30; Case C-41/04 *Levob* [2005] ECR I-9433, para 21.
63 Case C-41/04 *Levob* [2005] ECR I-9433, para 22.

— that service, considered in isolation, therefore seems to be economically unprofitable, so that the viability of the business cannot be ensured solely by means of contracts concluded with the customers;
— the leasing company receives the consideration of the leasing transaction only through the cumulative lease payments made by the customer and the amounts transferred from the other company of the same group.

Thereafter, the Court recalled the two constitutive elements of an abusive practice, identified in *Emsland-Stärke* and confirmed in *Halifax* (para 58):

> In order to assess whether those transactions can be held to constitute an abusive practice, the national court must verify, first, whether the result sought is a tax advantage, the granting of which would be contrary to one or more of the objectives of the Sixth Directive and, then, whether that constituted the principal aim of the contractual approach adopted (see paragraph 42 of this judgment).

As regards the first element, the expected result of the disputed transactions was the accrual of a tax advantage in the form of an exemption of the services entrusted to Italservice. Since the leasing of vehicles under leasing contracts constituted a taxable supply of services,[64] that exemption would run contrary to the objective of Article 11A(1) of the Sixth Directive, which provides for the taxation of the whole consideration received from the customer (paras 59–61).

As regards the second element, the purely artificial nature of the transactions and the links of a legal, economic and/or personal nature between the operators involved[65] were such as to demonstrate that the accrual of a tax advantage constituted the principal aim pursued, notwithstanding the presence of other economic objectives arising from, for example, marketing, organisation or guarantee considerations (para 62).

IV. Applications of the Formal Doctrine of Abuse in the Field of Direct Taxation

If the *Halifax* ruling (and the subsequent VAT cases of abuse) extended the scope of the doctrine of abuse to all internal abuses of law, *Cadbury Schweppes* completed the 'generalisation' of the doctrine of abuse of Union law by confirming its applicability to cross-border artificial movements, falling within the scope of the Treaty provisions on free movement. By contrast with internal abuses of Union

[64] Case C-451/99 *Cura Anlagen* [2002] ECR I-3193, para 19; Case C-155/01 *Cookies World* [2003] ECR I-8785, paras 44–45.
[65] Case C-255/02 *Halifax* [2006] ECR I-1609, para 81.

law, which consists in artificial attempts to elect a Union legal regime, cross-border abuses aim at electing a hospitable national legal regime.[66]

As explained in the previous chapter,[67] tax avoidance constitutes a specific form of abuse of law in the field of taxation: where abuses of law seek to elect a more favourable regulatory regime, tax avoidance strategies seek to elect a more favourable tax regime and thereby 'avoid' a less favourable one.[68] As a matter of fact, the Court has consistently linked tax avoidance to abusive practices, as in *Halifax*, *ING. AUER*, *Cadbury Schweppes* or *Foggia*.[69]

In a more systematic fashion, tax avoidance amounts to an undesirable choice of tax law, by which taxpayers seek to transfer either a tax liability to a low-tax jurisdiction or a tax deduction to a high-tax jurisdiction. The two cases of tax avoidance in which the Court explicitly relied on the formal doctrine of abuse concerned the first hypothesis: the transfer of a tax liability to a low-tax jurisdiction.[70] Such a transfer occurred through the incorporation of a subsidiary in a low-tax jurisdiction (*Cadbury Schweppes*, para 59) and the payment of interest—instead of a dividend—to a parent company established in a low-tax jurisdiction (*Thin Cap Group Litigation*, para 76).

A. *Cadbury Schweppes* (2006)

Case C-196/04 *Cadbury Schweppes* [2006] ECR I-7995

i. Facts

As with most national tax regimes within the Union, UK tax law provides that resident companies are subject to corporation tax on their worldwide profits, including the profits realised through branches and agencies active outside the United Kingdom. By contrast, resident companies are usually not taxed on the profits realised by their subsidiaries, the latter being endowed with a distinct legal personality. By way of exception, UK tax law provided that a resident company was taxable on the profits of a foreign subsidiary in which it owned a holding of more than 50 per cent (the subsidiary being therefore a 'Controlled Foreign Company' or CFC), and where the tax liability of the subsidiary was less than three-quarters

[66] See nn 21–22 and accompanying text.

[67] See ch 1 section IV, esp n 172 and accompanying text.

[68] See de la Feria, 'Prohibition of Abuse of (Community) Law' (n 36); Gestri, *Abuso del Diritto e Frode alla Legge nell'Ordinamento Comunitario* (n 22) 120; V Edwards and P Farmer, 'The Concept of Abuse in the Freedom of Establishment of Companies: a Case of Double Standards?' in FG Jacobs et al (eds), *Continuity and Change in EU Law: Essays in Honour of Sir Francis Jacobs* (Oxford, Oxford University Press, 2007) 213.

[69] Case C-255/02 *Halifax* [2006] ECR I-1609, paras 68–71; Case C-251/06 *ING. AUER* [2007] ECR I-9689, paras 40–42; Case C-196/04 *Cadbury Schweppes* [2006] ECR I-7995, para 55; Case C-126/10 *Foggia* [2011] ECR I-10923, paras 50–51.

[70] Other cases of tax avoidance are examined in a subsequent chapter: see ch 4 section I.

of the amount of tax which would have been paid in the United Kingdom had the subsidiary been established there. In order to prevent double taxation, the resident parent company was granted tax credits for the tax paid by the CFC abroad, and for the tax paid in the United Kingdom on the eventual dividends received from the CFC. The purpose of such CFC rules—adopted in most OECD countries[71]—is to prevent resident companies from diverting income to subsidiaries in low-tax countries (*Cadbury Schweppes*, paras 48 and 59).[72]

Nevertheless, a resident company could still be exempted from taxation on its CFC's profits if it proved that it satisfied any of the following conditions (paras 8.11):

- the CFC adopted an 'acceptable distribution policy', which meant that a specified percentage (90 per cent in 1996) of its profits were distributed within 18 months of their arising and taxed in the hands of a resident company;
- the CFC was engaged in 'exempt activities' within the meaning of that legislation, such as certain trading activities carried out from a business establishment;
- the CFC satisfied the 'public quotation condition', which meant that 35 per cent of the voting rights were held by the public, the subsidiary was quoted and its securities were dealt in on a recognised stock exchange;
- the CFC's chargeable profits did not exceed an amount set at GBP 50,000 (*de minimis* exception);
- the resident company satisfied the 'motive test' by establishing the following: first, the main purpose of the transactions of the accounting period in question was not a reduction in United Kingdom tax; secondly, the main reason for the CFC's existence was not a reduction in United Kingdom tax by means of a diversion of profits (ie a situation where, in the absence of the CFC, the receipts would have been taxable in the hands of a United Kingdom resident).

Cadbury Schweppes plc (CS), a company incorporated in the United Kingdom, was the parent company of the Cadbury Schweppes Group, which consisted of companies established in the United Kingdom, in other Member States and in third States. The group included two subsidiaries established in the International Financial Services Centre (IFSC) in Dublin, Ireland: Cadbury Schweppes Treasury Services (CSTS) and Cadbury Schweppes Treasury International (CSTI), which CS owned indirectly through a chain of subsidiaries at the head of which was Cadbury Schweppes Overseas Ltd (CSO) (see Figure 5).

CSTS and CSTI, whose business was to raise and provide finance to subsidiaries of the Cadbury Schweppes Group, were subject to a tax rate of 10 per cent at the material time. It is common ground that CSTS and CSTI were established in

[71] Schammo, 'Arbitrage and Abuse of Rights in the EC Legal System' (n 22) 357.

[72] Commission (EC), 'The application of anti-abuse measures in the area of direct taxation' (Communication) COM (2007) 785 final, 10 December 2007, 6; de la Feria (n 36) 429.

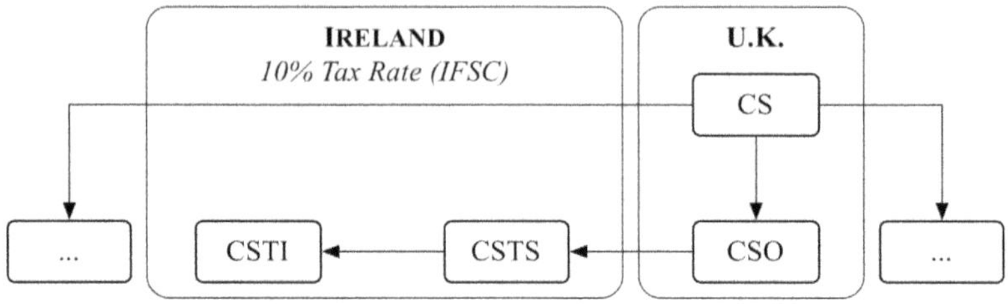

Figure 5 – Structure of the Cadbury Schweppes Group

Dublin solely in order to benefit from the favourable tax regime of the IFSC for the internal financing activities of the Cadbury Schweppes group (para 18).

Given this 10 per cent tax rate, the UK tax authorities applied the CFC legislation and attributed to CSO the profits realised by CSTS and CSTI during the 1996 financial year. By decision of 18 August 2000, they therefore claimed corporation tax in the sum of GBP 8,638,633 from CSO. CS and CSO appealed against that tax notice, arguing that the UK CFC legislation was contrary to Articles 43 EC, 49 EC and 56 EC.

ii. Decision of the Court

If previous case law had established that individuals cannot use the rights created by the Treaty to improperly circumvent national laws (para 35),[73] cross-border abusive practices are not as such excluded from the scope of free movement. Paraphrasing *Centros*,[74] 'the fact that the company was established in a Member State for the purpose of benefiting from more favourable legislation does not in itself suffice to constitute abuse of that freedom' (para 37). Therefore, the establishment of CSTS and CSTI in the IFSC for the avowed purpose of benefiting from a favourable tax regime does not in itself constitute abuse, and those companies are entitled to rely on Articles 43 EC and 48 EC (para 38).[75] It should be noted that this element of the case law is questioned by the subsequent *VALE* ruling, decided by the Grand Chamber of the Court.[76]

Having reaffirmed that abusive practices are not as such excluded from the scope of the freedoms of movement, the Court stated that the UK legislation

[73] Case 115/78 *Knoors* [1979] ECR 399, para 25; Case C-61/89 *Bouchoucha* [1990] ECR I-3551, para 14; Case C-212/97 *Centros* [1999] ECR I-1459, para 24.

[74] Case C-212/97 *Centros* [1999] ECR I-1459, para 27; Case C-167/01 *Inspire Art* [2003] ECR I-10155, para 96; Case C-364/01 *Barbier* [2003] ECR I-15013, para 71.

[75] Case C-212/97 *Centros* [1999] ECR I-1459, para 18; Case C-167/01 *Inspire Art* [2003] ECR I-10155, para 98.

[76] Case C-378/10 *VALE Építési* [2012] ECR I-0000, paras 34–35; see ch 4 n 120 and accompanying text.

on CFCs created a restriction on the freedom of establishment, since resident companies were taxed differently according to the level of taxation of the companies in which they had a controlling holding. Indeed, resident companies were taxed on the profits of CFCs established in a Member State applying 'lower levels of taxation' within the meaning of the legislation on CFCs; by contrast, resident companies were not taxed on the profits of a CFC that was not subject to a 'lower level of taxation' in another Member State. This difference of treatment could hinder the exercise of the freedom of establishment by dissuading a resident company from establishing a subsidiary in a Member State applying a lower level of taxation. In that regard, the fact that UK legislation subjected in effect the resident company to the taxation level of resident companies holding a CFC in the United Kingdom, through the granting of tax credits for the foreign taxes paid by the CFC, was irrelevant (paras 43–46).

The UK Government argued that this restriction on free movement could be justified by the need to counter a specific form of tax avoidance, by which a resident company artificially transfers profits to a subsidiary established in a low-tax Member State (para 48). It is indeed settled case law that 'a national measure restricting freedom of establishment may be justified where it specifically relates to wholly artificial arrangements aimed at circumventing the application of the legislation of the Member State concerned' (para 51).[77]

In that regard, the Court highlighted that the objective pursued by the freedom of establishment is to foster economic and social interpenetration within the Union,[78] by allowing Union nationals to participate on a stable and continuing basis in the economic life of a Member State other than their State of origin (para 53).[79] Given that objective of integration, the freedom of establishment presupposes 'actual establishment of the company concerned in the host Member State and the pursuit of genuine economic activity there' (para 54).[80] As a consequence, the prohibition of such abusive practices represents a legitimate concern for Member States, capable of justifying a restriction on free movement (para 55):

> It follows that, in order for a restriction on the freedom of establishment to be justified on the ground of prevention of abusive practices, the specific objective of such a restriction must be to prevent conduct involving the creation of wholly artificial arrangements which do not reflect economic reality, with a view to escaping the tax normally due on the profits generated by activities carried out on national territory.

[77] Case C-264/96 *ICI* [1996] ECR I-4695, para 26; Case C-324/00 *Lankhorst-Hohorst* [2002] ECR I-11779, para 37; Case C-9/02 *de Lasteyrie du Saillant* [2004] ECR I-2409, para 50; Case C-446/03 *Marks & Spencer* [2005] ECR I-10837, para 57.

[78] Case 2/74 *Reyners* [1974] ECR 631, para 21.

[79] Case C-55/94 *Gebhard* [1995] ECR I-4165, para 25.

[80] Case C-221/89 *Factortame II* [1991] ECR I-3905, para 20; Case C-246/89 *Commission v United Kingdom* [1991] ECR I-4585, para 21.

The Court then proceeded to the assessment of the UK legislation on CFCs in regard of the legitimate objective of preventing abusive practices, by examining whether the legislation was *appropriate* to thwart abusive practices (flaw of under-inclusion) and *proportionate* to that objective (flaw of over-inclusion).[81] As regards the appropriateness of the UK legislation on CFCs, the Court swiftly stated that the inclusion of the profits of CFCs subject to a very favourable tax regime in the tax base of the resident parent company made it possible to thwart incorporations of subsidiaries in low-tax States whose sole purpose was to escape the tax normally due in the United Kingdom (para 59). The UK legislation was accordingly appropriate to the objective of preventing this specific form of wholly artificial arrangements (no under-inclusion).

The proportionality analysis sought to ascertain whether the scope of the UK legislation on CFCs did not go beyond wholly artificial arrangements, by catching non-artificial arrangements (flaw of over-inclusion). First, the Court seemed not entirely convinced that the exceptions formulated in the UK legislation itself, such as the distribution of almost all the CFC's profits, the performance of trading activities by the CFC or the motive test (see above), sufficed to exclude non-artificial arrangements from its scope (paras 61–63). Secondly, it transposed the standard of abuse defined in *Emsland-Stärke* and *Halifax* into the area of free movement (para 64):

> In order to find that there is [a wholly artificial] arrangement there must be, in addition to a subjective element consisting in the intention to obtain a tax advantage, objective circumstances showing that, despite formal observance of the conditions laid down by Community law, the objective pursued by freedom of establishment, as set out in paragraphs 54 and 55 of this judgment, has not been achieved.

Therefore, within the scope of the freedom of establishment, a wholly artificial arrangement involves the existence of tax motives (subjective element) and the absence of genuine economic activity in the Member State of establishment, which is the objective pursued by freedom of establishment (objective element). In light of that standard of abuse, the UK legislation on CFCs could only be proportionate—and thus compatible with Union law—if it did not apply when the incorporation of a CFC reflected economic reality, despite the existence of tax motives (para 65). The presence of genuine economic activities in the host Member State had to be verified on the basis of objective factors, such as the CFC's physical existence in terms of premises, staff and equipment (paras 66–67). The creation of a CFC must be regarded as wholly artificial arrangement where the CFC is a fictitious establishment not carrying out any genuine economic activity in the host Member State, such as 'letterbox' or 'front' subsidiaries (para 68).[82] By contrast, the fact that the CFC's activities could have been carried out in the

[81] On the issues of over- and under-inclusion, see D Kennedy, 'Form and Substance in Private Law Adjudication' (1976) 89 *Harvard Law Review* 1685, 1687–89.

[82] Case C-341/04 *Eurofood IFSC* [2006] ECR I-3813, paras 34–35.

Member State of the parent company does not warrant the conclusion that there is a wholly artificial arrangement (para 69). The resident company, which is best placed for that purpose, must be given an opportunity to adduce evidence that the CFC is actually established and carries out genuine activities in the host Member State (para 70).

Finally, it fell to the national court to determine whether the UK legislation on CFCs, and in particular the motive test, was proportionate to the objective of preventing abusive practices, by excluding non-artificial arrangements from its scope (no over-inclusion: para 72).

B. *Thin Cap Group Litigation* (2007)

Case C-524/04 *Thin Cap Group Litigation* [2007] ECR I-2107

i. Facts

The *Thin Cap Group Litigation* case concerned the thin capitalisation rules applicable in the United Kingdom. Initially, thin capitalisation rules treated the payment of interest as a distribution of dividends in order to prevent domestic strategies by which taxpayers tended to finance a company through debt (loans) rather than equity (capital), leading to a situation of 'thin capitalisation'. Indeed, if both interest (debt) and dividends (equity) were taxable in the recipient's hands (creditor or shareholder), interest was deductible for the paying company whereas dividends were not, thereby creating a tax incentive to favour debt over capital as financing method.

However, the desire to prevent the economic double taxation of dividends led most Member States to exempt recipients (shareholders) from income tax on the dividends received; this exemption even became an obligation within the scope of Council Directive 90/435/EEC (distribution of profit by a subsidiary established in another Member State, holding higher than 10 per cent in the capital of the subsidiary).[83]

The exemption of dividends in the hands of the recipient removed most of the attractiveness exerted by domestic thin capitalisation strategies,[84] but created room for a new form of thin capitalisation strategy, cross-border in nature. Indeed, as a result of that exemption, interest is taxable in the hands of the recipient (and tax exempt for the paying company), whereas dividends are taxable in the hands

[83] Council Directive 90/435/EEC of 23 July 1990 on the common system of taxation applicable in the case of parent companies and subsidiaries of different Member States [1990] OJ L225/6.

[84] The configuration of tax losses within the group of companies could still lead to opportunistic choices between interest and dividend: the existence of tax losses at the level of the parent company would encourage a payment of interest (taxable only in the hands of the parent-lender company), whereas the existence of tax losses at the level of the subsidiary would encourage a distribution of dividend (taxable only in the hands of the borrowing subsidiary).

of the distributing company (and tax exempt for the recipient). This difference of regime generates the possibility, within a group of companies, to decide where a tax liability will arise: in the country of the distributing company (subsidiary), by distributing a dividend; in the country of the recipient company (parent), by paying interest. Therefore, in a cross-border setting, paying *interest* rather than a dividend allows a group of companies to transfer a tax liability from a subsidiary to a parent company located in another Member State, presumably applying lower tax rates (*Thin Cap Group Litigation*, para 76).[85]

In that context, thin capitalisation rules were adopted by Member States to counter such cross-border thin capitalisation strategies. Thin capitalisation rules commonly re-characterise the payment of interest to a foreign parent company as a distribution of dividend, thereby neutralizing such tax schemes, when the loan capital of the distributing company greatly exceeds its equity capital (situation of 'thin capitalisation'). The main proceedings concerned UK thin capitalisation rules and consisted of a number of claims for compensation brought by groups of companies, following the Court's ruling in *Lankhorst-Hohorst*,[86] in which German thin capitalisation rules were found incompatible with Article 43 EC. Essentially, specific provisions of UK tax law provided that interest paid by a resident company was to be treated as a distribution of profits to the extent it exceeded the amount that would have been paid at arm's length. Moreover, the UK tax legislation included a general provision on transfer pricing, which neutralised the tax effects of any transaction—including the payment of interest—between companies under common control, if the terms of the transaction generated a tax advantage for one of the parties, and differed from what they would have been if the companies had not been under common control. However, those provisions were not applicable when both parties to the transaction were subject to income tax in the United Kingdom.

Having regard to those rules, some of the claimant companies had converted part of their debt to equity in order to prevent interest payments from being re-characterised as a distribution of dividends. On the basis of the Court's ruling in *Lankhorst-Hohorst*, they considered that the UK thin capitalisation rules were incompatible with Union law and brought claims for compensation for the tax detriment suffered (mostly the additional corporation tax caused by the limitation on the deduction of interest and by the conversion of debt to equity).

ii. Decision of the Court

First of all, the Court described how UK thin capitalisation rules restricted free movement by treating differently resident borrowing companies according to whether the related lending company was established in the United Kingdom or not (para 40). Those rules, which treated interest paid by a resident company to

[85] Commission Communication on anti-abuse measures (n 72) 7.
[86] Case C-324/00 *Lankhorst-Hohorst* [2002] ECR I-11779.

another company of the same group as a distribution of dividend, to the extent to which that interest exceeded the amount that would have been paid at arm's length, were not applicable when the loan had been granted by a resident company. As a consequence, the tax position of a resident company that had been granted a loan by a related *non-resident* company was less advantageous than that of a resident company that had been granted a loan by a related *resident* company (paras 41–45). The presence of a specific risk related to multinational groups of companies, consisting in the transfer of profits to a low-tax State (Ireland) to avoid taxation in the State of the subsidiary (United Kingdom), was irrelevant in that regard (paras 58–60). Therefore, a difference of treatment between resident companies based on the location of their parent company's seat constituted a restriction on the freedom of establishment, for it might dissuade foreign companies from establishing a subsidiary in that Member State (para 61).

However, a national measure restricting freedom of establishment may be justified 'where it specifically targets wholly artificial arrangements designed to circumvent the legislation of the Member State concerned' (para 72).[87] More precisely, and replicating paragraph 55 of the *Cadbury Schweppes* judgment (para 74):

> In order for a restriction on the freedom of establishment to be justified on the ground of prevention of abusive practices, the specific objective of such a restriction must be to prevent conduct involving the creation of wholly artificial arrangements which do not reflect economic reality, with a view to escaping the tax normally due on the profits generated by activities carried out on national territory.

As the legislation on CFCs at issue in *Cadbury Schweppes*, the UK thin capitalisation rules could only be justified if they were appropriate (no under-inclusion) and proportionate (no over-inclusion) to the objective of preventing abusive practices, ie purely artificial arrangements entered into for tax reasons alone.

As regards their appropriateness, the Court acknowledged that those rules were indeed suitable to counter cross-border practices of thin capitalisation, by which the taxation of a subsidiary's profits is reduced through its financing by way of loan capital (instead of equity capital) and a payment of interest (instead of a distribution of dividend) to a parent company located in a low-tax State. Indeed, treating a payment of interest as a distribution of dividend in such a case sufficed to counter any such practice (no under-inclusion) (paras 76–77).

The proportionality analysis sought to ascertain whether the thin capitalisation rules went beyond what was necessary to prevent abusive practices,[88] by catching non-artificial arrangements (flaw of over-inclusion). In that regard, the Court ascertained that thin capitalisation rules based on an arm's-length test do not go beyond the objective of preventing abusive practices (paras 78–81). More precisely,

[87] Case C-264/96 *ICI* [1996] ECR I-4695, para 26; Case C-324/00 *Lankhorst-Hohorst* [2002] ECR I-11779, para 37; Case C-446/03 *Marks & Spencer* [2005] ECR I-10837, para 57; Case C-196/04 *Cadbury Schweppes* [2006] ECR I-7995, para 51.

[88] Case C-324/00 *Lankhorst-Hohorst* [2002] ECR I-11779, para 37.

the question should be 'whether, had there been an arm's-length relationship between the companies concerned, the loan would not have been granted or would have been granted for a different amount or at a different rate of interest' (para 81). Moreover, the taxpayer should be given an opportunity to provide evidence of any commercial justification supporting the arrangement (para 82) and the re-characterisation of interest paid as a distribution must be limited to the proportion of that interest exceeding what would have been agreed at arm's length (para 83).

V. Other Applications of the Formal Doctrine of Abuse in the Field of Free Movement

As with *Cadbury Schweppes* and *Thin Cap Group Litigation*, the two last seminal cases of abuse concern artificial cross-border movements affecting national legal regimes. In both cases, businesses sought to elect a more favourable national legal regime, in relation to maritime transport services (*Agip Petroli*) and capital duty (*ING. AUER*). However, unlike the three cases analysed in the previous section, the assessment of those cross-border abuses of law was realised within the framework of instruments of secondary legislation (Regulation 3577/92 in *Agip Petroli*, Council Directive 69/335 in *ING. AUER*).

A. *Agip Petroli* (2006)

Case C-456/04 *Agip Petroli* [2006] ECR I-3395

i. Facts

With a view to eliminating restrictions on the provision of maritime transport services within the Union, Regulation 3577/92[89] provides that, as a rule, the law of the Flag State applies to all matters relating to manning (Articles 1 and 3(1) of Regulation 3577/92). As an exception, the law of the host country (namely the State in which the maritime transport services are performed) applies to all matters in respect of island cabotage 'not preceded or followed by an international voyage' (Articles 3(2) and (3)).[90]

[89] Council Regulation (EEC) 3577/92 of 7 December 1992 applying the principle of freedom to provide services to maritime transport within Member States (maritime cabotage) [1992] OJ L364/7.

[90] The conditions relating to the vessels' gross tonnage are omitted in this section, for they were not relevant to the discussion before the Court. For the sake of completeness, one may confidently assume that the tanker *Theodoros IV* chartered by Agip Petroli was over 650 gt, so that both the Flag State principle (art 3(1) of Regulation 3577/92) and the international voyage exception (art 3(3) of Regulation 3577/92) applied in the main proceedings.

Agip Petroli, an Italian company, chartered the Greek-registered tanker Theodoros IV to ship a cargo of crude oil from Magnisi to Gela, both in Sicily ('island cabotage'). Agip Petroli contended that Greek law, the law of the Flag State, was applicable to all matters relating to manning pursuant to Article 3(3) of Regulation 3577/92, since the vessel planned to subsequently make a voyage to a foreign State without cargo on board ('voyage in ballast').

On 6 December 2001, the Italian Harbour authorities refused to grant the Theodoros IV the permission to ship crude oil from Magnisi to Gela, on the following grounds. First, they considered that, for Article 3(3) of Regulation 3577/92 to be applicable, the international voyage following or preceding the island cabotage had to be 'commercially autonomous', which implied that the vessel had cargo on board destined for or coming from a foreign port. That provision could not be invoked in the case of a voyage in ballast or a voyage with a cargo of goods which, in terms of quality and quantity, could not make the voyage autonomous (para 9). As a consequence, the shipment of crude oil from Magnisi to Gela remained subject to Italian law, the Host law, pursuant to Article 3(2) of Regulation 3577/92. Second, and by contrast with Greek law, the Italian Shipping Code required that the crew be exclusively composed of European Union nationals. Noting that the crew of the Theodoros IV included sailors who were nationals of the Philippines, the Harbour authorities refused to grant the permission sought.

ii. Decision of the Court

The Court first observed that nothing in the text of Regulation 3577/92 formally excluded voyages in ballast from the scope of Article 3(3), through a requirement of functional or commercial autonomy (paras 14–15). As a rule, international voyages in ballast should therefore trigger the application of the law of the Flag State, just like any other international voyage.

However, the Court issued an important qualification to that principle: 'in spite of that finding, it is not possible to accept sham voyages in ballast carried out to circumvent Article 3 of the Regulation and the objective of the Regulation itself' (para 18). It is indeed settled case law that the scope of Union law cannot be extended to cover abuses on the part of a trader, ie activities not carried out in the context of normal commercial transactions but only with the aim of circumventing the rules of Union law (para 20).[91]

Consequently, the law of the host country should apply, instead of the law of the Flag State, where the ship-owner has set up an artificial international voyage in ballast in order to fall within the scope of Article 3(3) (para 22). Transposing the standard of abuse defined in *Emsland-Stärke* and *Halifax*, the Court added that such an abuse could only be found to exist if the result of the international voyage in ballast is that the shipowner benefits, for all matters relating to manning, from

[91] Case 125/76 *Cremer* [1977] ECR 1593, para 21; Case C-8/92 *General Milk Products* [1993] ECR I-779, para 21; Case C-255/02 *Halifax* [2006] ECR I-1609, para 69.

the application of the law of the flag State, frustrating the aim of Article 3(2) of the regulation, which is to allow the application of the law of the host State to all matters relating to manning in the case of island cabotage. Moreover, there must be objective evidence that the essential aim of the international voyage in ballast was to circumvent the law of the host country (under Article 3(2)), in favour of the law of the Flag State (under Article 3(3): para 23).[92]

Finally, it is for the national court to verify the presence of those two elements in accordance with the national rules of evidence, provided that the effectiveness of Union law is not undermined (para 24).[93]

B. *ING. AUER* (2007)

Case C-251/06 *ING. AUER* [2007] ECR I-9689

i. Facts

The objective of Council Directive 69/335/EEC was to harmonise the taxes on the raising of capital and to prevent Member States from introducing or maintaining other similar taxes, based on the finding that 'the indirect taxes on the raising of capital … give rise to discrimination, double taxation and disparities which interfere with the free movement of capital and which, consequently, must be eliminated by harmonisation'.[94] In 1973, the normal rate of capital duty was fixed at 1 per cent, whereas the reduced rate had to be between 0 per cent and 0.5 per cent.[95]

Ever since the adoption of Council Directive 85/303/EEC, there has been a constant trend towards the abolition of capital duties,[96] both at the European and national levels. At the European level, the Commission, having regard to their '*detrimental economic effect*', has continuously advocated the abolition of capital duties, most recently in its Proposal for a Council Directive recasting Council Directive 69/335/EEC,[97] which led to the adoption of Directive 2008/7/EC. Owing to the fear of revenue losses expressed by several Member States, Directive 2008/7/EC has not abolished capital duties, although their abolition was again embraced as a legitimate objective.[98] Nevertheless, at the national level, many

[92] Case C-255/02 *Halifax* [2006] ECR I-1609, para 86.

[93] Case C-515/03 *Eichsfelder Schlachtbetrieb* [2005] ECR I-7355, para 40; Case C-255/02 *Halifax* [2006] ECR I-1609, para 76.

[94] Council Directive 69/335/EEC of 17 July 1969 concerning indirect taxes on the raising of capital [1969] OJ L249/25.

[95] Council Directive 73/79/EEC of 9 April 1973 varying the field of application of the reduced rate of capital duty provided for in respect of certain company reconstruction operations by Article 7(1)(b) of the Directive concerning indirect taxes on the raising of capital [1973] OJ L103/13; Council Directive 73/80/EEC of 9 April 1973 fixing common rates of capital duty [1973] OJ L103/15.

[96] See Council Directive 85/303/EEC of 10 June 1985 amending Directive 69/335/EEC concerning indirect taxes on the raising of capital [1985] OJ L156/23 rec 2–3.

[97] Commission (EC), 'Proposal for a Council Directive concerning indirect taxes on the raising of capital (recast version)' COM (2006) 760 final, 4 December 2006.

[98] Council Directive 2008/7/EC of 12 February 2008 concerning indirect taxes on the raising of capital [2008] OJ L46/11 rec 4–6.

Member States have unilaterally decided to abolish capital duties, among which the United Kingdom, Germany, France, Denmark, Italy, Ireland, Belgium and the Netherlands.[99]

The facts of the *ING. AUER* case arose in that context. Whereas Germany had abolished them in 1990, Austria maintained capital duties on certain transactions, including the transfer of the management centre or registered office of a foreign capital company to Austria if, by that transfer, that company became an Austrian company. However, pursuant to Article 4(1) and (3) of Directive 69/335, this transfer was exempt from capital duty if, in the former Member State, the company was regarded as a capital company for the purposes of charging capital duty. *Gesellschaften mit beschränkter Haftung* (GmbH), that is limited liability companies, were indeed regarded as capital companies both in Germany and in Austria.

On 9 September 1999, the company Bausoftware GmbH, the formation of which had been declared on 28 July 1999, was registered in Austria. As shown in Figure 6, its sole member was Nemetschek, a German company, and Bausoftware's effective centre of management was in Germany, where capital duties were not levied anymore.

On 16 September 1999, Nemetschek transferred ATS 102,000,000 to Bausoftware. On 22 September 1999, Bausoftware acquired the one-man undertaking Ing. Auer 'Die Bausoftware', established in Austria, and appointed Mr Auer, an Austrian resident, as additional managing director with a special right to manage the business. Lastly, the name of Bausoftware was changed to ING. AUER—Die Bausoftware (ING. AUER).

In June 2005, following an inspection carried out at the premises of ING. AUER, the Austrian tax authorities claimed payment of capital duty of EUR

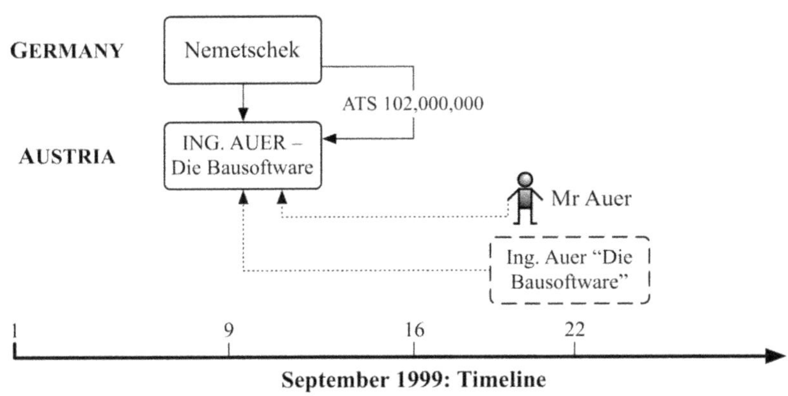

Figure 6 – ING. AUER: Transactional Structure

[99] Proposal for a Council Directive concerning indirect taxes on the raising of capital (n 97) 2.

104,680.20, namely 1 per cent of the value of the rights in the company, by reason of the transfer of its effective centre of management from Germany to Austria. ING. AUER brought an action against that decision, arguing that a GmbH was regarded as a capital company for the purposes of charging capital duty in Germany, so that this transfer had to be exempt of capital duty in Austria pursuant to Article 4(1) and (3) of Directive 69/335. The Austrian tax authorities contended that the exemption was not applicable where the Member State of origin (Germany) had abolished capital duties.

ii. Decision of the Court

The Court started by inserting the dispute within the framework of the Directive. Pursuant to Article 4(1)(g), the transfer of the effective centre of management of a company is subject to capital duty, when the company is considered, for the purposes of charging capital duty, as a capital company in the Member State of destination, but not in the Member State of origin. Article 4(3)(b) only confirms that no capital duty shall be charged when both Member States consider it as a capital company (paras 21–25).

Since the application of Article 4(1)(g) presupposes a discrepancy among Member States in the classification of a given company, it can only apply to companies falling within the scope of Article 3(2), and not of Article 3(1). Indeed, Article 3(1) establishes a list of companies that must be treated as capital companies by all Member States, so that the transfer of their effective centre of management will never be subject to capital duty (paras 28–29). By contrast, Article 3(2) leaves Member States with the option to treat other companies as capital companies, thereby creating a possibility of diverging classification among Member States, and of application of Article 4(1)(g) (paras 30–32).

Within that framework, the fact that the Member State of origin has abolished capital duty is irrelevant: the only relevant criterion for the application of Article 4(1)(g) is the classification as a capital company for the purposes of charging capital duty. Therefore, since ING. AUER had taken the form of a GmbH, it fell within the scope of Article 3(1)(a), which excluded the levying of capital duty upon the transfer of its effective centre of management (paras 26–27 and 33–36).

However, the Court, of its own motion, considered the risk of abusive practices generated by its interpretation of Article 4(1)(g) (paras 37–39). If Directive 69/335 does not contain any specific provision on the prevention of tax avoidance (para 40), it remains that the scope of Union law cannot be extended to cover abusive practices, namely 'transactions carried out not in the context of normal commercial operations, but solely for the purpose of wrongfully obtaining advantages provided for by Community law' (para 41),[100] which includes situations where a person seeks to put itself out of reach of the legislation of a Member State (para 42).

[100] Case C-255/02 *Halifax* [2006] ECR I-1609, para 69.

Within the context of Directive 69/335, the fact that a company has been incorporated in a particular Member State in order to benefit from a more favourable legislation is not sufficient to warrant the conclusion that Union law has been misused (para 43). However, the application of the doctrine of abuse within the scope of Directive 69/335 entails that (para 44):

> [T]he formation of a company in a Member State under wholly artificial arrangements which do not reflect economic reality, with the aim of avoiding the tax normally payable, goes beyond the protection which Directive 69/335 must afford to the companies to which it applies.

It is for the national court to verify whether there is objective evidence of such an abusive practice, consisting in setting up artificial arrangements with the sole aim of obtaining a fiscal advantage (paras 45–47).

3

Definition of the Concept of Abuse of Union Law

THE FRIVOLOUS UTILISATION of the 'abuse' terminology in Union law makes the definition of the concept of 'abuse of Union law' a crucial enterprise: indeed, not only is the expression 'abuse' used to aim at very different phenomena;[1] but also abuses of law are often addressed without any mention of the word 'abuse'.[2] Following the preliminary identification of the abuse of Union law (chapter one), and the study of the formal doctrine of abuse (chapter two), a proper definition of the concept of abuse of Union law can now be proposed.

In the course of this chapter, abuses of Union law will be defined as undesirable choices of law artificially made by private individuals. This definition can be decomposed in three components: a gain-seeking choice of law (Section I), the artificiality requirement (Section II) and the teleological assessment (Section III). The artificiality requirement and the teleological assessment correspond to the so-called 'subjective' and 'objective' elements of the formal doctrine of abuse enounced by the Court in *Emsland-Stärke* (paras 52–53) and *Halifax* (paras 74–75). These three components can be summarised in three simple questions, which arise consciously or not in every case of abuse:

- First, is there a claim by a Union citizen to have his activities governed by a more favourable law (gain-seeking choice of law)?
- Secondly, is this choice of law attempted by means of practices that have no rational explanation other than the regulatory benefit sought (artificial choice of law)?
- Thirdly, should Union citizens have the freedom to elect the law governing their activities (undesirable choice of law)?

As will be shown in the course of this chapter, this definition permits to distinguish the concept of abuses of Union law from seven different situations (Table 6).

[1] See ch 1.

[2] See ch 1 n 9 and accompanying text.

Table 6 – Distinguishing the Abuse of Union Law

Definition of abuse of law	Situations distinguished
Gain-seeking choice of law	Single legal regime Abuse of rights Detrimental change of law Involuntary change of law
Artificiality requirement	Fraud Sound economic transaction
Teleological assessment	Legitimate choice of law

The last section of this chapter dwells upon the practical consequences of a finding of abusive practice, namely the sanction of abuses of law, which concerns the validity of the choice of law attempted, but not the validity of the underlying transactions (Section IV).

Interestingly enough, in his theory of abuse of rights, Josserand identified two requirements that can be easily assimilated to the artificiality requirement and the teleological assessment: on the one hand, abuse of rights are courses of conducts that cannot be justified by a legitimate motive; on the other hand, abuses of rights are actions that run counter to the purpose of the institution, its spirit and finality.[3]

I. The Basics: Abuse of Law as Gain-Seeking Choice of Law

The first component of the definition of abuse of law proposed in this study is the presence of a gain-seeking choice of law: indeed, abusive practices constitute first and foremost attempts to elect a favourable law. Thus, in all seminal cases of abuse of Union law discussed in the previous chapter, the first element systematically underlined by the Court is the intention to obtain a regulatory benefit, namely a benefit offered by the laws of the Union (internal abuses of law) or that of the Member States (cross-border abuses of law):

> [A finding of an abuse] requires … a subjective element consisting in the intention to obtain an advantage from the Community rules by creating artificially the conditions laid down for obtaining it.[4]

[3] L Josserand, *De l'esprit des droits et de leur relativité: théorie dite de l'abus des droits*, 2nd edn (Paris, LGDJ, 1939) no 292 (teleological assessment: see ch 1 n 179 and accompanying text) and 296 (absence of legitimate motive: see n 16 and accompanying text).

[4] Case C-110/99 *Emsland-Stärke* [2000] ECR I-11569, para 53.

Internal abusive practices affect Union laws, such as the Union regulations on export subsidies or the VAT Directive. In the seminal cases of abuse examined in chapter two, businesses attempted to substitute their legal position under Union law for a more favourable one, offering an export subsidy (*Emsland-Stärke*, para 27, 39, 50, 51, 53 and 55), a higher export subsidy (*Vonk Dairy Products*, para 33), a higher VAT deduction (*Halifax*, paras 69 and 74) or a partial VAT exemption (*Part Service*, paras 58–59).

By contrast, cross-border abuses of law affect national laws, and their protagonists seek to 'avoid' or 'circumvent' one national legal order and elect a more favourable one, thereby obtaining a regulatory benefit consisting in the 'difference' between the two legal regimes. The seminal cases of cross-border abuse were mostly attempts to obtain a tax benefit by electing a hospitable tax jurisdiction, either in relation to direct taxation (*Cadbury Schweppes*, paras 51, 55 and 64; *Thin Cap Group Litigation*, paras 74 and 81–82) or capital duty (*ING. AUER*, paras 40–42). *Agip Petroli* concerned an attempt to elect a lighter national law applicable to the manning of vessels carrying out island cabotage (*Agip Petroli*, para 20). This second type of abusive practice comes under the scrutiny of the Union free movement provisions by reason of their intrinsic cross-border element.

In more detail, the very possibility of such 'choice of law' implies the coexistence of several legal regimes that could potentially apply to the same economic transaction. In *Halifax*, the Court observed that the abusive practice originated in national rules entitling taxpayers to decide whether the letting of immovable property should be taxed or exempted (para 67). In practice, the election of a specific legal regime often requires a certain structuring of the intended transaction: in *Halifax*, for instance, the simple development contract led to exemption whereas the complex transactional structure led to taxation. In other words, the same transaction can be wrapped up in various 'legal cloaks',[5] and the gain-seeking choice of law is materialised by the election of the most pleasing legal cloak. The same pattern can be identified in every case of abuse of law (Table 7).

This requirement of a gain-seeking choice of law excludes four types of situations from the notion of abuse of law. The first and most obvious exclusion relates to situations in which only one legal regime may apply. In the presence of a single legal regime, no choice of law is possible, so that no abusive practice can be conceived. This exclusion can be easily illustrated by contrasting the Court's rulings in *Marks & Spencer* and *Papillon*. *Marks & Spencer* concerned the tax treatment of losses incurred by foreign subsidiaries, more precisely the possibility to deduct in the United Kingdom losses incurred by Marks & Spencer's subsidiaries in other Member States. Such a possibility entailed a risk of gain-seeking choice of law,

[5] This terminology has long been used in the field of tax law: see eg SS Surrey, 'Definitional Problems in Capital Gains Taxation' (1956) 69 *Harvard Law Review* 985.

Table 7 – Abuse of Law as Election of a Pleasing Legal Cloak

	Less Pleasing Legal Cloak		More Pleasing Legal Cloak		Economic Transaction
Emsland-Stärke	Direct sale	No export refund	Re-import	Export refund	Sale of starch within Union
Vonk Dairy Products	Direct sale	Low export refund	Re-export	High export refund	Sale of cheese to Canada
Halifax	Simple contract	Partial VAT deduction	Complex contract	Full VAT deduction	Building of call centres
Part Service	Single transaction	Full VAT liability	Split transactions	Partial VAT liability	Leasing of motor vehicles
Cadbury Schweppes	Incorporation in UK	UK direct taxes	Incorporation in Dublin	Irish direct taxes	Intra-group finance
Thin Cap Group Litigation	Dividend	UK direct taxes	Interest	Foreign direct taxes	Corporate activities
Agip Petroli	Island cabotage	Italian manning regime	Voyage in ballast	Greek manning regime	Island cabotage around Sicily
ING. AUER	Incorporation in Austria	Capital duty in Austria	Incorporation in Germany	No capital duty	Corporate activities

if the company was given the right to elect the tax jurisdiction in which the loss could be deducted (Member State of origin or United Kingdom):

> [T]o give companies the option to have their losses taken into account in the Member State in which they are established or in another Member State would significantly jeopardise a balanced allocation of the power to impose taxes between Member States.[6]

By contrast, the tax treatment of corporate losses in *Papillon* only involved companies established in one Member State (France). As a result, the companies could only be subject to French tax law, which excluded the very possibility of a choice of law:

> [T]he question as to whether the profits and losses of companies belonging to the group in question should be taken into account arises only in relation to companies which are resident in a single Member State. Accordingly, the question which is put relates to the taking into account of losses recorded in one and the same Member State, which also excludes, prima facie, a risk of tax avoidance.[7]

The Court's ruling in *Thin Cap Group Litigation* comprises an analogous statement in relation to the tax implications of the financing of a subsidiary:

> [W]ithin a group of companies, the risk that the financing of a subsidiary will be structured in such a way that profits are transferred to a State where they are subject to a lower rate of tax does not normally arise if all of the companies in question are subject, in the same Member State, to the same rate of tax.[8]

The second exclusion aims at abuses of rights, which were already distinguished from abuses of law in a previous chapter. If abuses of law are undesirable acquisitions of a right (choices of law), abuses of rights constitute undesirable exercises of an existing right. Abuses of law question the conditions of application of legal norms and provoke a debate on the very existence of the right at stake. Abuses of rights, by contrast, seek to magnify the effect of legal norms, so that they spur a debate on the precise extent of a right already held. Accordingly, abuses of rights occur within the seams of one single 'legal cloak' (eg the right to initiate proceedings, intellectual property rights or a shareholder's voting rights), which abusers try to stretch in their favour. By contrast, abuses of law seek a substitution of legal cloak: *Emsland-Stärke* attempted to 'move' into the export subsidy scheme; *Halifax* into the (full) VAT deduction scheme; and *Cadbury Schweppes* into the Irish tax jurisdiction.

Thirdly, the concept of abuse of law only covers 'gain-seeking' courses of behaviour, namely actions whereby individuals seek to attract positive legal consequences. Accordingly, the notion of abuse does not extend to transactions implying a detrimental change of law. Thus, assuming that the level of social contributions is substantially higher in Sweden than in Latvia, the temporary

[6] Case C-446/03 *Marks & Spencer* [2005] ECR I-10837, para 46.
[7] Case C-418/07 *Papillon* [2008] ECR I-8947, para 39.
[8] Case C-524/04 *Thin Cap Group Litigation* [2007] ECR I-2107, para 60.

posting of Swedish workers to Latvia could not be suspected of abuse, since it would entail the payment of the higher Swedish social contributions for works carried out on the Latvian territory. Conversely, the temporary posting of Latvian workers to Sweden could amount to abuse as it would entail the payment of the lower Latvian social contributions for works carried out on the Swedish territory, subject to the fulfilment of the other conditions of the definition of abuse of law (artificiality requirement and teleological assessment).[9]

Fourthly and lastly, the concept of abuse of law only covers deliberate 'choices of law', namely courses of behaviour knowingly adopted in order to trigger a change of the applicable law. As a consequence, the concept of abuse of law does not extend to involuntarily changes of law. By way of illustration, in the *Société Pipeline Méditerranée et Rhône* case, the plaintiff in the main proceedings applied for an exemption from excise duties in respect of 795,201 litres of petroleum products lost following leakages and a burst caused by corrosive cracking on its pipeline.[10] The Court was asked to determine whether such event could amount to 'force majeure' within the meaning of the first sentence of Article 14(1) of Directive 92/12.[11] Although Société Pipeline Méditerranée et Rhône sought to obtain a gainful change of law (exemption from excise duties), it was not suspected of abuse of law since this change of law was not the product of a deliberate choice, but rather of 'abnormal and unforeseeable circumstances, extraneous to the operator concerned, the consequences of which, in spite of the exercise of all due care, could not have been avoided' (para 23, definition of force majeure).

To sum up, the first component of the definition of abuse of law is the presence of a gain-seeking choice of law, which excludes situations covered by a single legal regime, abuses of rights, detrimental changes of law and involuntarily changes of law.

II. The Artificiality Requirement: Abuse of Law as Naked Choice of Law

As explained in the previous section, abuses of law amount first and foremost to gain-seeking choices of law. However, a practice designed with the intention of obtaining a regulatory benefit does not suffice to warrant the finding of an abuse of

[9] This example is inspired by the factual setting of the *Laval* case, in which the Swedish trade unions indeed raised the argument of abuse: see Case C-341/05 *Laval* [2007] ECR I-11767, para 40.

[10] Case C-314/06 *Société Pipeline Méditerranée et Rhône* [2007] ECR I-12273.

[11] Council Directive 92/12/EEC of 25 February 1992 on the general arrangements for products subject to excise duty and on the holding, movement and monitoring of such products [1992] OJ L76/1, as amended by Council Directive 94/74/EC of 22 December 1994 [1994] OJ L365/46.

law: in order to be abusive, such practice must be artificial. This idea of artificiality has been expressed in the most diverse ways in the Court's case law:

- discordance with, or absence of economic reality (*Cadbury Schweppes*, para 55; *Thin Cap Group Litigation*, para 74; *ING. AUER*, para 44; *Oy AA*, para 63);
- artificial creation of the conditions laid down for obtaining a regulatory advantage (*Emsland-Stärke*, para 53; *Vonk Dairy Products*, para 33);
- absence of bona fide or normal commercial transactions (*Emsland-Stärke*, para 51; *Halifax*, para 69; *ING. AUER*, para 41);
- transactions carried out with the sole purpose of benefiting from a regulatory gain (export refund: *Emsland-Stärke*, para 50; tax advantage: *Halifax*, para 82 and *Cadbury Schweppes*, para 59; other: *ING. AUER*, para 42);
- absence of genuine economic activity (*Cadbury Schweppes*, paras 65–68);
- justified application of arm's length test (*Thin Cap Group Litigation*, paras 78–81); and
- presence of wholly artificial arrangements aimed at circumventing the application of the legislation of the Member State concerned (*Cadbury Schweppes*, para 51; *Thin Cap Group Litigation*, para 72).

The artificiality requirement is intended to identify practices that are devoid of economic rationality, but for the regulatory benefit claimed (Subsection II.A). Indeed, abuses of Union law amount to 'naked'[12] choices of law, in the sense that they have no other explanation than the regulatory benefit sought. In that connection, it is of crucial importance to defuse a common misconception equating artificiality with absence of economic reality (Subsection II.B). Artificial choices of law are not devoid of economic reality—as they cover real economic transactions—but rather of economic rationality—as their only rationale lies in the regulatory benefit pursued.

A. Artificiality as Economic Irrationality

In the previous section, abuses of law were described as transactions intended to procure a regulatory benefit. To be considered as artificial, a transaction must not only procure a regulatory benefit, but this regulatory benefit must represent its unique purpose.[13] The concept of artificiality implies the *exclusive* intention to

[12] This terminology is inspired by the notion of 'naked restraint on competition' in US law: by contrast with 'ancillary' restraints, which are functionally incidental to some legitimate transaction, naked restraints have no other function than creating and/or allocating market power: see PC Carstensen and B Roth, 'The Per Se Legality of Some Naked Restraints: A [Re]conceptualization of the Antitrust Analysis of Cartelistic Organizations' (2000) 45 *Antitrust Bulletin* 349, 354–58.

[13] See inter alia AG Maduro, Case C-255/02 *Halifax* [2006] ECR I-1609, para 87; D Waelbroeck, 'La notion d'abus de droit dans l'ordre juridique communautaire' in J-V Louis et al (eds), *Mélanges en hommage à Jean-Victor Louis* (Brussels, Éditions de l'université de Bruxelles, 2003) 603.

obtain a regulatory gain, that is: at the *exclusion* of any genuine socioeconomic benefit. Artificial transactions cannot be rationally explained but for the regulatory benefit sought; in other words, they are devoid of economic rationality if one ignores the gain extracted from the legal system:

> A transaction's 'artificiality' in the context of freedom of establishment is revealed by the fact that it has no economic rationale, and so can only be explained in light of the aim to circumvent the law.[14]

> [T]he measuring standard must preferentially lie in analysing whether the operation does make sense or can be understood if we forget about the tax benefits. If we eliminate the tax benefit, the arrangement would not have been reasonable. It then naturally follows that its objective was purely to obtain a tax benefit.[15]

Interestingly enough, in his theory of abuse of rights, Josserand identified a similar requirement: a finding of abuse of rights was dependent on the absence of 'legitimate motive' justifying the course of conduct adopted:

> The act will be normal or abusive depending on whether or not it can be explained by a legitimate motive which constitutes the real cornerstone of the theory of abuse of rights as well as its visible precipitate; we are bound to put our legal powers at the service of a motive appropriate to their spirit and mission, otherwise we do not really exercise them but abuse of them.[16]

By way of illustration, Emsland-Stärke's decision to send consignments of agricultural goods from Germany to Switzerland, whereas their real destinations were Germany and Italy, does not make sense economically for it entails extra costs. Similarly, Halifax's decision to set up a complex transactional structure, involving four subsidiaries and seven agreements, cannot be justified economically as a simple development contract sufficed to build the call centres. Therefore, an artificial choice of law is any course of action that would not be adopted absent the regulatory benefit sought or, put more informally, '[a] deal done by very smart people that, absent tax [regulatory] considerations, would be very stupid'.[17] This

[14] C Costello, 'Citizenship of the Union: Above Abuse?' in R de la Feria and S Vogenauer (eds), *Prohibition of Abuse of Law: a New General Principle of EU Law?* (Oxford, Hart Publishing, 2011) 326.

[15] V Ruiz Almendral, 'Tax Avoidance and the European Court of Justice: What is at Stake for European General Anti-Avoidance Rules?' (2005) 33 *Intertax* 562, 566.

[16] Josserand, *De l'esprit des droits et de leur relativité: théorie dite de l'abus des droits* (n 3) no 296, free translation.

[17] Definition given by Michael Graetz of 'tax shelter' (ie abuse of law in tax matters) in T Herman, 'Tax Report', *Wall Street Journal*, 10 February 1999. The artificiality requirement nurtures an obvious kinship with anti-avoidance measures classically defined by tax legislatures, under the appellation of 'economic substance', 'substance over form' or 'business purpose' tests. See inter alia P Wattel, 'Circumvention of National Law; Abuse of Community Law?' (1995) 32 *Common Market Law Review* 1257, 1265–67; Ruiz Almendral, 'Tax Avoidance and the European Court of Justice' (n 15); F Vanistendael, 'Halifax and Cadbury Schweppes: One Single European Theory of Abuse in Tax Law?' (2006) 15 *EC Tax Review* 192, 195.

assimilation of artificiality with economic irrationality can be identified in the language used by the Court:

> Second, it must also be apparent from a number of objective factors that the essential aim of the transactions concerned is to obtain a tax advantage. As the AG observed in point 89 of his Opinion, the prohibition of abuse is not relevant where the economic activity carried out may have some explanation other than the mere attainment of tax advantages.[18]

In practice, how does one determine whether a given transaction lacks economic rationality? A transaction can be said to be economically irrational or unsound when it entails costs that could be easily avoided. Visually, the presence of such avoidable costs can often be described as a 'detour', namely a costlier path that a rational man would refuse to follow (absent the regulatory benefit sought), such as the Swiss detour in *Emsland-Stärke*. The *Akrich* case regarded a 'detour' to Dublin, as the Akrich spouses moved from the United Kingdom to Ireland in order to manufacture a right to residence in the United Kingdom: absent the regulatory gain sought, their decision to move to Dublin was irrational. Similar irrational detours can be easily identified in other potential cases of abuse: in *Centros*, Danish nationals used a company incorporated in the United Kingdom to sell wine in Denmark; in *Chen*, a Chinese national gave birth alone in Ireland to manufacture a right to residence in the United Kingdom; and in *Agip Petroli*, a vessel made a detour 'in ballast' to a foreign State in order to elect the Greek law on manning.

In other cases, the detour is less obvious as it does not involve a physical detour. In *Halifax* or *Part Service*, the detour was of contractual nature in so far as the protagonists used contractual structures that were more complex than was necessary to carry out their activities (construction of call centres and car rental). The CFC rules assessed in *Cadbury Schweppes* targeted the use of subsidiaries in low-tax jurisdictions for mere tax purposes.

In short, artificial transactions typically entail avoidable real-life costs, or at the very least do not create any real-life value. As a rule, the adoption of a costly course of behaviour is not open to criticism from a legal perspective; it is only the claim to a regulatory benefit that justifies the investigation of artificial transactions. The underlying assumption seems to be that a legal order should not encourage parasitic behaviour that does not create any real-life value, by rewarding it with a regulatory benefit funded by the community. It is in this sense that the Court's reference to 'transactions carried out not in the context of normal commercial operations' must be understood:

> The application of Community legislation cannot be extended to cover abusive practices by economic operators, that is to say transactions carried out not in the context

[18] Case C-255/02 *Halifax* [2006] ECR I-1609, para 75.

> of normal commercial operations, but solely for the purpose of wrongfully obtaining advantages provided for by Community law.[19]

This second component of the definition of abuse of law—artificiality understood as economic irrationality—permits the exclusion of two new types of situations from the notion of abuse of law: frauds and sound economic transactions. On the one hand, both abuse of law and fraud may be viewed as gain-seeking choices of law;[20] however, fraud does not involve artificiality but misrepresentation, namely the concealment of the fact that the conditions of application of a legal rule are not fulfilled in order to wrongfully obtain a benefit. Examples of fraud include the concealment of the end of economic activities under the VAT regime,[21] or the use of fake medical certificates in order to obtain payment of wages during the sickness period.[22]

On the other hand, the notion of artificiality does not extend to sound economic decisions, namely transactions that are grounded in sound economic reasons, even if they entail a gainful change of law. This exclusion relates to the question referred by the national judge in *Agip Petroli*, by which the Court was invited to determine whether transactions lacking 'functional and commercial autonomy' could be ignored as abusive. In effect, the notion of artificiality enquires into the functional and commercial autonomy of transactions entailing a gainful change of law, irrespective of the regulatory gain claimed, and transactions lacking such autonomy must be held artificial:

> [The purpose of the activities in question] is to be objectively determined on the basis of the absence of any other economic justification for the activity than that of creating a tax advantage. Accordingly, this element can be regarded as an element of autonomy. In fact, when applying it, the national authorities must determine whether the activity at issue has some autonomous basis which, if tax considerations are left aside, is capable of endowing it with some economic justification in the circumstances of the case.[23]

A joint discussion of the following cases will aptly illustrate the exclusion of sound economic transactions from the scope of the concept of abuse of law. First of all, *Emsland-Stärke* can be contrasted to *Roquette Frères* and *Eichsfelder*, which both concerned the re-importation into the Union of goods that had undergone substantial processing abroad.[24] In *Roquette Frères*, glucose syrup had been exported from France to Austria (not part of the European Union at the relevant time) and subsequently re-imported into the Union under the form of penicillin. *Eichsfelder* concerned the exportation of boneless beef from Germany to Poland (not part

[19] Case C-255/02 *Halifax* [2006] ECR I-1609, para 69; see also Case C-110/99 *Emsland-Stärke* [2000] ECR I-11569, para 51; Case C-251/06 *ING. AUER* [2007] ECR I-9689, para 41.

[20] See ch 1 section II.B.

[21] Case C-32/03 *Fini H* [2005] ECR I-1599, paras 31–32.

[22] Case C-206/94 *Paletta II* [1996] ECR I-2357, paras 10–13, 23–28.

[23] AG Maduro, Case C-255/02 *Halifax* [2006] ECR I-1609, para 87.

[24] Case C-114/99 *Roquette Frères* [2000] ECR I-8823; Case C-515/03 *Eichsfelder Schlachtbetrieb* [2005] ECR I-7355.

of the European Union at the relevant time), and its subsequent re-importation in Germany under the form of cooked meat roulades. By contrast with *Emsland-Stärke*, the Court explicitly acknowledged that the presence of economic motives (creation of a new product abroad) excluded the risk of abusive re-importation: '[S]uch working or processing, involving as it does the creation of a new product, eliminates the risk … of abusive reimportation of the initial goods into the Community'.[25]

The same contrast opposes the *Cavallera* and *Knoors* cases in the field of professional qualifications.[26] Marco Cavallera, an Italian national, held an Italian diploma of mechanical engineer and wished to pursue the profession of engineer in Italy. Instead of sitting for the State examination in Italy, he obtained the automatic homologation of his Italian diploma in Spain, and then immediately requested the right to work in Italy on the basis of Council Directive 89/48 providing for the mutual recognition of certain higher education diplomas.[27] On the other hand, Knoors was a Dutch national durably employed in a plumbing undertaking in Belgium, where he subsequently ran his own plumbing business from 1970 to 1978. Knoors was not allowed to carry out the same trade in the Netherlands because he did not meet Dutch trade qualifications.

As stated by AG Maduro, the practice set up by Cavallera was indisputably artificial, for his costly detour to Spain could not be explained by any other ground than the desire of circumventing the Italian legislation setting up the requirements for the purpose of taking up the profession of engineer there.[28] By contrast, the number of years worked by Knoors in Belgium provided a genuine economic explanation for his stay there, which excluded the possibility of an artifice:

> [H]aving regard to the nature of the trades in question, the precise conditions set out in Article 3 of Directive 64/427, as regards the length of periods during which the activity in question must have been pursued, have the effect of excluding the risk of abuse … referred to by the Netherlands government.[29]

Lastly, *Thin Capitalisation Group Litigation* and *Lankhorst-Hohorst* concerned thin capitalisation rules. Such rules provide that the payment of interest is to be treated as a distribution of dividend in order to thwart a risk of profit shifting, as paying interest rather than a dividend allows a group of companies to transfer a tax liability from a subsidiary to a parent company located in another Member

[25] Case C-515/03 *Eichsfelder Schlachtbetrieb* [2005] ECR I-7355, para 33; see also Case C-114/99 *Roquette Frères* [2000] ECR I-8823, para 19.

[26] Case C-311/06 *Cavallera* [2009] ECR I-415; Case 115/78 *Knoors* [1979] ECR 399.

[27] Council Directive 89/48/EEC of 21 December 1988 on a general system for the recognition of higher-education diplomas awarded on completion of professional education and training of at least three years' duration [1989] OJ L19/16.

[28] AG Maduro, Case C-311/06 *Cavallera* [2009] ECR I-415, paras 54–58; the Court eventually chose to exclude Cavallera's Spanish title from the scope of Directive 89/48 on the recognition of diplomas: see Case C-311/06 *Cavallera* [2009] ECR I-415, para 58.

[29] Case 115/78 *Knoors* [1979] ECR 399, para 26.

State, presumably applying lower tax rates (*Thin Cap Group Litigation*, para 76).[30] In *Thin Cap Group Litigation*, the Court made clear that such rules could be justified by the need to combat abusive practices in so far as they aim at transactions devoid of economic rationality, and entered into for tax reasons alone (*Thin Capitalisation Group Litigation*, paras 80–82). In the previous *Lankhorst-Hohorst* case, the Court had explicitly ruled out artificiality since the loan recipient was in serious financial difficulties and the loan enabled it to substantially reduce its bank borrowing and interest charges. As a result, the loan transaction had some genuine economic explanation other than the tax benefit claimed (economic rationality).[31]

To sum up, the artificiality test enquires into the economic rationality of the transaction: if the transaction has some genuine economic explanation other than the regulatory benefit claimed, it will not be considered as artificial (*Roquette Frères*, *Knoors* or *Lankhorst-Hohorst*). Conversely, in the absence of genuine economic justification other than the regulatory benefit sought, the transaction must be considered as an artificial choice of law (*Emsland-Stärke*, *Cavallera* or *Thin Cap Group Litigation*).

B. The Fallacy of Economic Reality

Having defined artificiality as absence of economic *rationality*, it is of crucial importance to defuse a common misconception that assimilates artificiality with absence of economic *reality*:

> [T]he purpose test is a proxy for economic reality. If the essential reason for the transaction is not commercial then it can be said to be 'artificial' or 'not genuine'.[32]

> An artificial construction ... is one which creates the form of a business establishment without its substance, a simulacrum which does not represent the economic reality.[33]

The Court's language is not exempt of ambiguity in that regard, as shown by the following classical statement in the *Cadbury Schweppes* judgment:[34]

> In order for a restriction on the freedom of establishment to be justified on the ground of prevention of abusive practices, the specific objective of such a restriction must be

[30] Commission (EC), 'The application of anti-abuse measures in the area of direct taxation' (Communication) COM (2007) 785 final, 10 December 2007, 7.

[31] Case C-324/00 *Lankhorst-Hohorst* [2002] ECR I-11779, paras 15 and 38.

[32] J Freedman, 'The Anatomy of Tax Avoidance Counteraction: Abuse of Law in a Tax Context at Member State and European Union Level' in de la Feria and Vogenauer (n 14) 374.

[33] R Lyal, 'Cadbury Schweppes and Abuse: Comments' in de la Feria and Vogenauer, *Prohibition of Abuse of Law: a New General Principle of EU Law?* (n 14) 432.

[34] Case C-524/04 *Thin Cap Group Litigation* [2007] ECR I-2107, para 74; Case C-251/06 *ING. AUER* [2007] ECR I-9689, para 44; Case C-231/05 *Oy AA* [2007] ECR I-6373, paras 62–63; Case C-105/07 *Lammers and Van Cleef* [2008] ECR I-173, para 28; Case C-330/07 *Jobra* [2008] ECR I-9099, para 35; see also Case C-397/07 *Commission v Spain* [2009] ECR I-6029, para 30; Case C-162/07 *Ampliscientifica* [2008] ECR I-4019, paras 26–28.

> to prevent conduct involving the creation of wholly artificial arrangements which do not reflect economic reality, with a view to escaping the tax normally due on the profits generated by activities carried out on national territory.[35]

However, defining artificiality as absence of economic reality risks reducing the scope of the concept of abuse of law to naught. Indeed, the notion of economic reality tends to focus the debate on the lack of 'economic reality' of the underlying transaction, rather than on the lack of 'economic rationality' of the legal cloak elected. As shown in Table 7 above, every seminal case of abuse examined in this study involves 'real' economic transactions, but which are wrapped up in an artificial legal cloak. For instance, in *Emsland-Stärke*, 'real' agricultural goods were dispatched from Germany to Italy and to another location in Germany, but the national judge wondered whether the Swiss stop had any economic rationality, regardless of the export refund claimed. *Halifax* contracted 'real' independent builders to build 'real' call centres; yet the artificiality test enquired whether the complex transactional structure had any rational explanation beyond its profitable tax consequences. In *Thin Cap Group Litigation*, 'real' sums of money were transferred from a subsidiary to a parent company; the artificiality test only questioned the economic rationality of the legal cloak elected, namely a payment of interest instead of a distribution of a dividend, given its profitable tax consequences. Accordingly, interpreting the artificiality test as an enquiry of the economic reality of the underlying transactions would filter out paramount cases of abuse such as *Emsland-Stärke* or *Halifax*.

Therefore, the question raised by the artificiality test is not whether a real economic transaction is taking place (economic reality), but whether the legal cloak elected to carry out this transaction has some genuine economic explanation other than the regulatory benefit sought (economic rationality). This definition of artificiality as lack of economic rationality implies, on the one hand, the possibility to achieve the same economic outcome with several legal cloaks—or 'routes'—and, on the other, the election of a legal cloak—a 'detour'—that has no other explanation than the regulatory benefit sought. In relation to tax avoidance, Grauberg wrote:

> The test of purpose or the determination of the business goal of the taxpayer's actions refers to the desired results of the transaction, as, in principle, it is possible for the same economic result to be achieved with several legal forms. This may be referred to as a subjective element that attempts to identify the taxpayer's intentions in his tax planning activity. If a transaction carries no business goal, one may conclude that the form assigned to the transaction is incorrect and that characteristics of abuse of the law are present.[36]

[35] Case C-196/04 *Cadbury Schweppes* [2006] ECR I-7995, para 55.

[36] T Grauberg, 'Anti-tax-avoidance Measures and Their Compliance with Community Law' (2009) XVI *Juridica International* 141.

If, on the contrary, artificiality were defined as lack of economic reality, almost no transaction could ever be held artificial—and thus abusive—as the notion of artificiality would be limited to instances of sham, namely situations in which no real good or service is acquired or provided, which would exclude paramount cases of abuse such as *Emsland-Stärke* or *Halifax*. As observed by Weatherill:

> [A sham] is not a cross-border situation at all. This, however, will be rare. And it cannot occur where the undertaking seeking to rely on EU law of free movement needs to set up some distribution or production base, however limited, in another Member State.[37]

This annihilating effect of the interpretation of artificiality as absence of economic reality can be observed in the *RBS Deutschland Holdings* case. Vinci, a company established in the United Kingdom, wished to conclude a car leasing transaction with the Royal Bank of Scotland Group (RBS). If Vinci had directly dealt with the United Kingdom subsidiary of RBS, the rental payments to RBS would have been subject to VAT in the United Kingdom. Instead, Vinci concluded the leasing transaction with the German subsidiary of RBS, and thereby avoided any VAT liability on the rental payments by exploiting a mismatch between the British and German VAT laws:

> Under the relevant United Kingdom legislation, the supplies consisting of the rental of cars were treated as supplies of services made in Germany and accordingly not subject to VAT in the United Kingdom. Under German law, these supplies were treated as supplies of goods in the United Kingdom and accordingly not subject to VAT in Germany. The consequence was that no output tax was charged on those supplies in either Member State.[38]

However, the Court explicitly stated that Vinci's leasing transaction was not artificial (para 50), apparently impressed by the fact that RBS Germany was a 'real' bank active in Germany (para 51) and cars were 'really' leased to Vinci (para 52). In so doing, the Court relied on an interpretation of artificiality as absence of economic reality, which is inconsistent with the interpretation given in seminal cases of abuse such as *Emsland-Stärke*, *Halifax* or *Thin Cap Group Litigation*. In particular, *Part Service* also concerned the VAT regime applicable to the leasing of vehicles.[39] Instead of proposing a classical leasing contract to its customers, Part Service decided to split the agreement into several transactions, which had the effect of reducing the VAT burden on its activities. As in *RBS Deutschland Holdings*, 'real' car leasing services were wrapped up in an artificial legal cloak, elected for no other reason than its profitable tax consequences. The Court's analysis focused on this lack of economic rationality of the 'contractual approach' set up by Part Service:

> In order to assess whether those transactions can be held to constitute an abusive practice, the national court must verify, first, whether the result sought is a tax advantage,

[37] S Weatherill, 'Fitting "Abuse of Rights" into EU Law Governing the Free Movement of Goods and Services' in de la Feria and Vogenauer (n 14) 56.

[38] Case C-277/09 *RBS Deutschland Holdings* [2010] ECR I-13805, para 27.

[39] See ch 2 section III.B.

> the granting of which would be contrary to one or more of the objectives of the Sixth Directive and, then, whether that constituted the principal aim of the contractual approach adopted.[40]

As a consequence, and in stark contrast with *RBS Deutschland Holdings*, the Court decided that the transactional structure set up by Part Service was artificial.[41] If artificiality is interpreted as absence of economic rationality, as in *Part Service*, *Emsland-Stärke* or *Halifax*, it is easy to demonstrate that the transactional structure elected by Vinci and RBS in *RBS Deutschland Holdings* was artificial as well. Indeed, it is hardly debatable that the involvement of the German subsidiary of RBS, instead of the United Kingdom subsidiary, in a car leasing transaction carried out in the United Kingdom, did not respond to any genuine economic need. In other words, the only explanation for the election of that specific legal cloak lay in the accrual of a tax benefit, namely the non-application of VAT on the rental payments.

Arguably, the ambiguity in the *Cadbury Schweppes* ruling stems from ambivalent terminology rather than from erroneous reasoning as in *RBS Deutschland Holdings*. As is usual in the field of direct taxation, the Court refers to the prevention of 'wholly artificial arrangements' (para 57); yet the Court's reasoning becomes more accurate if one reads prevention of 'abusive practices' instead. Indeed, the Court clearly distinguishes between artificiality requirement and teleological assessment. In a first step, which corresponds to the artificiality requirement, the Court observes that the CFC rules are capable of thwarting artificial practices, namely practices which have no purpose other than to escape the tax normally due on the profits generated by activities carried on in national territory (para 59). Resident companies are offered the possibility to adduce evidence of any genuine economic motive supporting the incorporation of the CFC (para 62), which would establish the economic rationality of the legal cloak elected (CFC instead of resident company). In a second step, which corresponds to the teleological assessment, the Court recalls that a finding of artificiality is not sufficient: in addition, there must be objective circumstances showing that the objective of economic and social interpenetration pursued by freedom of establishment has not been achieved (para 64). It is in the context of this teleological assessment that the Court refers to economic reality. Having due regard to the objective of freedom of establishment, the incorporation of a CFC must reflect economic reality, with an actual establishment intended to carry on genuine economic activities in the host Member State (paras 65–67). Conversely, the incorporation of a fictitious CFC not carrying out any genuine economic activity in the territory of the host Member State, such as a 'letterbox' or 'front' subsidiary, would fail the teleological assessment and therefore amount to abuse (para 68).

[40] Case C-425/06 *Part Service* [2008] ECR I-897, para 58.

[41] The Court added that it was sufficient to demonstrate that the accrual of a tax advantage constituted the *principal* aim pursued, notwithstanding the presence of other economic objectives arising from, for example, marketing, organisation or guarantee considerations (para 62).

The Court adds that the fact that the activities of the CFC could just as well have been carried out in the Member State in which the resident company is established does not warrant the conclusion of an abusive practice (para 69). This statement can be easily articulated with the definition of artificiality as absence of economic rationality. Assuming that it has no genuine economic rationality beyond its profitable tax consequences, the transfer of intragroup activities from a resident company to a CFC would be artificial, as it amounts to a substitution of legal cloaks for mere tax reasons. However, a finding of artificiality does not warrant the conclusion of an abusive practice, as such conclusion can only be drawn at the end of the teleological assessment.

To sum up, economic reality does not exclude artificiality, for a real economic transaction may be wrapped up in an artificial legal cloak, whose election has no other genuine explanation than the accrual of a regulatory benefit.

III. The Teleological Assessment: Abuse of Law as Undesirable Choice of Law

The teleological assessment is the last step in the reasoning leading to a finding of abuse of law; its function is to assess the legitimacy of practices previously identified as 'artificial', namely choices of law devoid of economic rationality (beyond the regulatory benefit claimed). By contrast with the two first components of the definition of abuse of law, which enquire into the nature of the practice set up by Union citizens, the teleological assessment enquires into the nature of the law affected by the alleged abuse of law. In essence, the teleological assessment requires the competent judge to determine whether Union citizens should have the freedom to choose the law governing their actions.

The teleological assessment, also called 'objective element' of the formal doctrine of abuse, is by far the most abstruse component of the concept of abuse of law; curiously, it is also the least debated in the scholarship on the abuse of Union law. This lack of interest is all the more puzzling since the function performed by the teleological assessment is of crucial importance: indeed, it permits to distinguish cases such as *Cadbury Schweppes* and *Centros*, in which artificial cross-border movements are respectively proscribed or ratified.[42]

[42] See eg L Cerioni, 'The "Abuse of Rights" in EU Company Law and EU Tax Law: A Re-reading of the ECJ Case Law and the Quest for a Unitary Notion' (2010) 21 *European Business Law Review* 783, 783; also P Schammo, 'Arbitrage and Abuse of Rights in the EC Legal System' (2008) 14 *European Law Journal* 351, 366.

The Court first enounced the teleological assessment, together with a fully fleshed doctrine of abuse, in *Emsland-Stärke*:

> A finding of an abuse requires … a combination of objective circumstances in which, despite formal observance of the conditions laid down by the Community rules, the purpose of those rules has not been achieved.[43]

Unfortunately, this classical statement merely evokes a contrariety to the purpose of the norm at stake, comfortably numbed in the Court's teleological method of interpretation. The Court then deferred to the national court's judgment according to which the objective of the Union rules had not been achieved (para 55). How are we to reconstruct the teleological assessment? In all logic, such reconstruction ought to start from the artificiality requirement, since its function is to assess the legitimacy of artificial practices. In the previous section, artificiality was defined as lack of economic rationality, and artificial choice of law as the election of a legal cloak that has no other explanation than the regulatory benefit sought. In regard of this definition, the question to be solved by the teleological assessment is whether choices of law made by private individuals are desirable or not. In other words, the teleological assessment consists in determining whether Union citizens ought to be granted the freedom to choose the law governing their transactions. AG Maduro propounded a similar reasoning in his Opinion in *Halifax*:

> The basic principle is that of the freedom to opt for the least taxed route to conduct business in order to minimise costs. On the other hand, such freedom of choice exists only within the scope of the legal possibilities provided for by the VAT regime. The normative goal of the principle of prohibition of abuse within the VAT system is precisely that of defining the realm of choices that the common VAT rules have left open to taxable persons.[44]

Consequently, the prohibition of artificial practices as 'abusive' necessarily rests on the assumption that Union citizens should not enjoy the freedom to choose the law governing their transactions. Thus, in the *Halifax* ruling, the Court deemed that granting the freedom to choose between exemption (no right to deduction) and taxation (with right to deduction) would run counter to the fundamental objective of fiscal neutrality of the VAT system:

> To allow taxable persons to deduct all input VAT even though, in the context of their normal commercial operations, no transactions conforming with the deduction rules of the Sixth Directive or of the national legislation transposing it would have enabled them to deduct such VAT, or would have allowed them to deduct only a part, would be contrary to the principle of fiscal neutrality and, therefore, contrary to the purpose of those rules.[45]

[43] Case C-110/99 *Emsland-Stärke* [2000] ECR I-11569, para 52; see also Case C-255/02 *Halifax* [2006] ECR I-1609, para 74.

[44] AG Maduro, Case C-255/02 *Halifax* [2006] ECR I-1609, para 85.

[45] Case C-255/02 *Halifax* [2006] ECR I-1609, para 80.

In *Part Service*, the Court observed that the contractual splitting of a transaction into several individual transactions affords choices of law regarding tax rate or even exemption from VAT (paras 48–49). In order to prevent such choices of law, the Court ruled that several individual transactions must be regarded as one when the contractual splitting is artificial (paras 51–54).

In *Agip Petroli*, the Court ruled that the purpose of Article 3(2) of Regulation 3577/92 is to allow the application of the law of the host State to all matters relating to manning in the case of island cabotage. As the Regulation offered no choice of law in that regard, ship-owners could not be allowed to set up artificially an international voyage in ballast in order that Article 3(3) of the Regulation, and therefore the legislation of the flag State, be applicable, instead of Article 3(2) of the Regulation, and therefore the legislation of the host State (paras 22–23).

In the field of direct taxation, the Court has repeatedly highlighted the need to restrict the possibility for Union citizens to elect the national law governing their transactions, as in *Oy AA*:

> [T]o accept that an intra-group cross-border transfer, such as that at issue in the main proceedings, may be deducted from the taxable income of the transferor would result in allowing groups of companies to choose freely the Member State in which the profits of the subsidiary are to be taxed.
>
> [This] carries the risk that, by means of purely artificial arrangements, income transfers may be organised within a group of companies towards companies established in Member States applying the lowest rates of taxation or in Member States in which such income is not taxed.[46]

The Court issued similar statements in *Marks & Spencer* and *Lidl Belgium* with regard to the tax treatment of corporate losses, underlining the need to avoid offering Union taxpayers the possibility to elect the Member State in which such losses are deducted:

> [T]o accept that the losses of a non-resident permanent establishment might be deducted from the taxable income of the principal company would result in allowing that company to choose freely the Member State in which those losses could be deducted.[47]
>
> As regards ... the risk of tax avoidance, it must be accepted that the possibility of transferring the losses incurred by a non-resident company to a resident company entails the risk that within a group of companies losses will be transferred to companies established in the Member State which apply the highest rates of taxation and in which the tax value of the losses is therefore the highest.[48]

Similarly, CFC and thin capitalisation rules, respectively assessed in *Cadbury Schweppes* and *Thin Cap Group Litigation*, seek to restrict the freedom of corporations to choose the tax jurisdiction in which their profits are located. A hospitable

[46] Case C-231/05 *Oy AA* [2007] ECR I-6373, paras 56 and 58.
[47] Case C-414/06 *Lidl Belgium* [2008] ECR I-3601, para 34.
[48] Case C-446/03 *Marks & Spencer* [2005] ECR I-10837, para 49.

tax jurisdiction can be elected by means of a diversion of profits to a subsidiary established in a low-tax jurisdiction (*Cadbury Schweppes*, para 59); or by paying interest—rather than a dividend—to a parent company established in a low-tax jurisdiction (*Thin Cap Group Litigation*, para 76).[49] The function of CFC and thin capitalisation rules is to thwart artificial arrangements entered into for tax reasons alone. In *Thin Cap Group Litigation*, the Court ruled that thin capitalisation rules are not contrary to free movement in so far as they catch transactions devoid of economic rationality, namely loans that would not have been granted or would have been granted for a different amount or at a different rate of interest, had there been an arm's-length relationship between the companies concerned. As explained above, the Court's teleological assessment is more nuanced in *Cadbury Schweppes*. Under the definition of artificiality as lack of economic rationality, the incorporation of a CFC in a hospitable tax jurisdiction is artificial in so much as it is not justified by genuine economic motives beyond the tax benefit pursued (paras 57–62). However, having due regard to the objective of economic and social interpenetration pursued by the freedom of establishment, such artificial incorporation of a CFC in a hospitable tax jurisdiction is only open to criticism if the CFC is a letterbox company not carrying out any genuine economic activity in the territory of the host Member State (paras 64–67).

The teleological assessment, third and last component of the definition proposed in this chapter, permits to distinguish abuses of law from legitimate choices of law. In every legal order, certain choices of law are indeed consciously offered by the legislature: 'Arrangements lacking economic substance … may be perfectly in line with legislative intent, whether risks are involved or not'.[50]

One obvious example of such legitimate choice of law is the right to incorporate a company, offered in most modern legal orders. Indeed, the possibility to carry out an economic activity through a company can be viewed as a choice between the law applicable to natural persons and the law applicable to legal persons. Decisions to incorporate a company are most often artificial, in the sense intended in the last section, as they are mostly grounded in regulatory considerations, chiefly limited civil liability: shareholders make a choice of law (limited liability or not) by electing a legal cloak (company or not) that has no economic rationality beyond the regulatory benefit sought. Yet despite its artificiality, the decision to incorporate a company is not abusive, for it exploits a choice of law explicitly granted by the legal system. In that connection, Freedman wrote:

> [W]e may need a device set out in legislation or case law to help us draw a line between the legal (sometimes apparently 'artificial') realities we use as the foundation of our legal and therefore our tax system, and the legal realities we are to ignore to get the right economic result. For example, generally the existence of a subsidiary company cannot be ignored in a legal system which endows companies with separate legal personality, even

[49] See ch 2 section IV. See also Commission Communication on anti-abuse measures (n 30) 6–7.

[50] R Karimeri, 'A Critical Review of the Definition of Tax Avoidance in the Case Law of the European Court of Justice' (2011) 39 *Intertax* 296, 300.

> though the corporation is a legal construct and economists would normally ignore the difference between, say, a branch and a subsidiary.[51]

As a rule, decisions to incorporate a company can be viewed as 'artificial', but they cannot be proscribed as 'abusive' since that choice of law is explicitly granted by the legal order. Still, there are instances in which the Court decides to 'lift the corporate veil', thereby ignoring the existence of a legal person used to attempt an undesirable choice of law.[52]

In that context, the teleological assessment permits to filter out legitimate choices of law, which the Union legislature intended to leave open:

> [The objective element] provides a safeguard for those instances where the sole purpose of the activity might be to diminish tax liability but where that purpose is actually a result of a choice between different tax regimes that the Community legislature intended to leave open.[53]

In *Weald Leasing*, the Court faced a choice of law explicitly granted by the Union legal order in the field of VAT. The Churchill Group had acquired a number of assets through a leasing transaction instead of a straight purchase, with the established purpose of deferring its VAT liability (para 31). Therefore, the leasing transaction represented an artificial legal cloak used to attract positive tax consequences. However, by providing for a distinct regime for leasing transactions, the VAT legislation explicitly granted Union taxpayers the freedom to elect the VAT regime governing their transactions: either the VAT regime for purchases or that for leasing. As a consequence, just as the decision to incorporate a company, the artificial choice of law made by the Churchill Group could not be held abusive:

> A taxable person cannot be criticised for choosing a leasing transaction which procures him an advantage consisting … in spreading the payment of his tax liability, rather than a purchase transaction which does not procure him any such advantage.[54]

Similarly, the artificial choice—or circumvention—of national law is not always proscribed as abusive: '[W]hilst an 'abuse' always presupposes a circumvention of the applicable national provisions, vice-versa a circumvention of the applicable national provisions does not necessarily result in an abuse'.[55] As a matter of fact, Union citizens are sometimes granted the freedom to elect the national law governing their activities, as in the seminal *Centros* case. *Centros* concerned a paramount example of artificial cross-border movement. The protagonists were Danish nationals residing in Denmark and starting a wine trading business in Denmark. To that end, they elected an artificial legal cloak, namely a company incorporated in the United Kingdom, which had no other explanation than the avowed purpose of having their activities governed by United Kingdom

[51] Freedman, 'The Anatomy of Tax Avoidance Counteraction' (n 32) 372.
[52] See ch 4 section I, esp nn 40 to 46 and accompanying text.
[53] AG Maduro, Case C-255/02 Halifax [2006] ECR I-1609, para 88.
[54] Case C-103/09 *Weald Leasing* [2010] ECR-13589, para 34.
[55] Cerioni, 'Abuse of Rights' (n 42) 783; Schammo, 'Arbitrage and Abuse of Rights' (n 42) 366.

company law instead of the Danish one. In stark contrast with *Halifax* or *Cadbury Schweppes*, the Court explicitly ratified this artificial choice of law:

> [T]he fact that a national of a Member State who wishes to set up a company chooses to form it in the Member State whose rules of company law seem to him the least restrictive and to set up branches in other Member States cannot, in itself, constitute an abuse of the right of establishment. The right to form a company in accordance with the law of a Member State and to set up branches in other Member States is inherent in the exercise, in a single market, of the freedom of establishment guaranteed by the Treaty.[56]

To paraphrase the Court, artificial choices of law in the context of company law are not abusive, since Union citizens enjoy the freedom to elect the national law governing their companies: 'with [the Centros jurisprudence], the door has been opened for free choice of the applicable company law regime and regulatory competition in the area of company law in Europe'.[57]

To sum up, the function of the teleological assessment is to evaluate the legitimacy of artificial choices of law made by electing a legal cloak that has no other explanation than the regulatory benefit claimed. In practice, the teleological assessment requires the competent judge to determine whether Union citizens should have the freedom to elect the law governing their activities. When Union citizens do not have the freedom to elect the law governing their activities, artificial choices of law will be proscribed as abusive (*Emsland-Stärke*, *Halifax*, *Cadbury Schweppes*); conversely, when the applicable legal regime grants such freedom, artificial choices of law will be ratified as non-abusive (*Weald Leasing*, *Centros*).

IV. The Sanction: Denying the Choice of Law

In the three previous sections, abuses of Union law were successively defined as gain-seeking, artificial and undesirable choices of law; the practical consequences of a finding of abusive practice remain to be determined. In essence, the concept of abuse of law never questions the validity of the economic transactions carried out, but only the validity of the undesirable choice of law attempted.

[56] C-212/97 *Centros* [1999] ECR I-1459, para 27.

[57] H Eidenmüller, 'Abuse of Law in the Context of European Insolvency Law' in de la Feria and Vogenauer (n 14) 137; see also C Barnard and S Deakin, 'Negative and Positive Harmonization of Labor Law in the European Union' (2002) 8 *Columbia Journal of European Law* 389, 395: 'The effect of the incorporation approach [endorsed in Centros] is that the applicable law is a matter of choice for managers of the company or, in the final analysis, for its shareholders'. AG La Pergola similarly deemed that the Treaty guaranteed individuals the 'freedom of choice … of the company instrument best suited to their purposes of all the instruments available under the various national systems of the Member States': AG La Pergola, Case C-212/97 *Centros* [1999] ECR I-1459, para 20.

It is fundamental to understand that the concrete issue raised by the concept of abuse of law is not whether artificial practices ought to be allowed or not, but rather which law should apply to a given economic transaction. Abuses of law amount first and foremost to undesirable choices of law, so that the 'sanction' of abuses of law merely consists in denying the attempted choice of law. Therefore, the transaction in question gets queried only because there is a claim to a benefit offered by the legal order; and the potential consequences of this enquiry are limited to the benefit claimed.

For instance, no one ever considered proscribing the sale of agricultural products made by *Emsland-Stärke*; rather, the concept of abuse of law merely questioned the grant of an export refund when the exported goods are immediately re-imported. As stated by the Court itself:

> Contrary to the assertions of Emsland-Stärke, the obligation to repay refunds received in the event that the two constituent elements of an abuse are established would not breach the principle of lawfulness. The obligation to repay is not a penalty for which a clear and unambiguous legal basis would be necessary, but simply the consequence of a finding that the conditions required to obtain the advantage derived from the Community rules were created artificially, thereby rendering the refunds granted undue payments and thus justifying the obligation to repay them.[58]

The only 'sanction' applied to Emsland-Stärke consists in denying the choice of law attempted through a re-import strategy, by imposing an obligation to repay the export refunds received. In other words, the Court did not prohibit Emsland-Stärke from setting up re-import strategies; rather, it merely ruled that such practices should not benefit from export refunds, owing to their abusive nature.

Similarly, the Court never contemplated the possibility of proscribing the complex contractual structure designed by *Halifax* for the construction of call centres. In particular, it was never claimed that this contractual structure should be declared void; rather, the only practical issue raised by the prohibition of abuses of law was whether Halifax should be entitled to integrally deduct the input VAT borne on the construction of those call centres. Therefore, the only consequence of a finding of abusive practice would consist in the application of the legal regime ordinarily applicable to financial institutions, namely the partial right to deduction:

> [A] finding of abusive practice must not lead to a penalty, for which a clear and unambiguous legal basis would be necessary, but rather to an obligation to repay, simply as a consequence of that finding, which rendered undue all or part of the deductions of input VAT.
>
> It follows that transactions involved in an abusive practice must be redefined so as to re-establish the situation that would have prevailed in the absence of the transactions constituting that abusive practice.[59]

[58] Case C-110/99 *Emsland-Stärke* [2000] ECR I-11569, para 56.

[59] Case C-255/02 *Halifax* [2006] ECR I-1609, para 93 and 94.

Concretely, in order to deny the undesirable choice of law attempted by Halifax and apply the legal regime ordinarily applicable to financial institutions, tax authorities had to demand repayment of the input VAT abusively deducted (para 95), reimburse any output VAT paid in relation to the abusive practice (para 96), and finally allow any deduction that would have been allowed in the absence of abusive practice (para 97). Once again, the Court did not prohibit Halifax from setting up such a complex contractual structure; rather, it merely held that such artificial practice should not procure financial institutions a right to integrally deduct the input VAT.

Lastly, the 'sanction' applied to cross-border abuses of law, as in *Cadbury Schweppes*, responds to the same logic: the consequence of a finding of abusive practice merely consists in denying the attempted choice of national law, made by wilfully electing a specific legal form to carry out economic activities. Thus, it was never argued that the incorporation of subsidiaries in Dublin by the Cadbury Schweppes group should be prohibited or even proscribed, rather, the only practical issue raised by the concept of abuse of law was whether Cadbury Schweppes should pay (low) direct taxes in Ireland or (higher) direct taxes in the United Kingdom. Indeed, the CFC rules examined in *Cadbury Schweppes* provided for the payment of ordinary taxes in the United Kingdom, after reimbursement of the taxes paid in Ireland (para 6). As a result, the Court had to decide whether the Cadbury Schweppes group was entitled to elect Irish tax law for intra-group finance activities carried out by its Irish subsidiaries, or whether it had to remain subject to British tax law:

> By providing for the inclusion of the profits of a CFC subject to very favourable tax regime in the tax base of the resident company, the legislation on CFCs makes it possible to thwart practices which have no purpose other than to escape the tax normally due on the profits generated by activities carried on in national territory.[60]

Eventually, the Court did not prohibit Cadbury Schweppes from setting up subsidiaries in Ireland; rather, it merely permitted the United Kingdom to contest the election of Irish tax law. In other words, a finding of abusive practice in a cross-border context does not lead to the prohibition of the economic transaction carried out, but merely to the non-application of the national law artificially elected, such as Irish tax law in *Cadbury Schweppes*. Similarly, the Court never questioned the validity of economic activities in *Thin Cap Group Litigation* (payment of interest), *ING. AUER* (incorporation of a company in Germany) and *Agip Petroli* (island cabotage); instead, a finding of abusive practice in those cases respectively led to the application of British tax law, Austrian capital duty and the Italian manning regime for island cabotage. Weatherill similarly observed that the concept of abuse of law in a cross-border context dealt exclusively with the jurisdiction of Member States to regulate economic activities:

> Where does 'abuse of rights' fit into the model of the law of free movement? The essence of an allegation of 'abuse' is that host State control should be permitted to apply

[60] Case C-196/04 Cadbury Schweppes [2006] ECR I-7995, para 59.

> without restraint. Put another way, successfully depicting a claim to rely on the free movement rules as an 'abusive' claim entails that the home State's regulatory choices are dismissed as simply not relevant. The host State would enjoy unconditional regulatory competence.[61]

To sum up, the concept of abuse of law does not question the validity of the economic transactions carried out, but only that of the choice of law attempted. Abusive practices amount first and foremost to undesirable choices of law, so that the 'sanction' of abusive practices merely consists in denying the undesirable choice of law attempted.

[61] Weatherill, 'Fitting "Abuse of Rights" into EU Law Governing the Free Movement of Goods and Services' (n 37) 54.

4

Typology of Union Law Reactions to Artificial Practices

IN THE PREVIOUS chapter, artificial practices were defined as transactions devoid of genuine socioeconomic rationale beyond the regulatory benefit sought. On the basis of that definition, the present chapter investigates Union law reactions to such artificial practices other than the recourse to the formal doctrine of abuse. To that end, it seeks to identify and treat a critical mass of Union legal acts addressing artificial choices of law by means of alternative legal grounds, namely without having recourse to the formal doctrine of abuse. As a matter of fact, recourse to the formal doctrine of abuse is arguably the exception, for artificial practices are routinely addressed through informal doctrines of abuse, suspect periods, centre of gravity tests, free choice of law approaches or other legal grounds unrelated to the issue of abuse of law.

The existence of such alternative legal grounds addressing artificial practices under Union law is widely acknowledged in the scholarship:

> Even if we agree that general liberties … or particular rights … require qualification in some way, the question still arises as to the legal mechanism or mechanisms by which such a qualification is to be achieved. In this respect, recourse to a 'general legal principle' … is only one type of legal mechanism, using only one type of language. … Such a qualification can be achieved by restricting the particular conditions under which a particular right (or legal result) arises.[1]

> In the company law cases that were described above the Court's technique is not explicitly based on a specific doctrine of 'abuse of law'. … This approach can be described as construing the 'internal' limit of the law in itself, rather than the 'external' right to make use of the law.[2]

[1] S Whittaker, 'Comments on "Abuse of Law" in European Private Law' in R de la Feria and S Vogenauer (eds), *Prohibition of Abuse of Law: a New General Principle of EU Law?* (Oxford, Hart Publishing, 2011) 259.

[2] W-G Ringe, 'Sparking Regulatory Competition in European Company Law—The Impact of the Centros Line of Case-Law and its Concept of "Abuse of Law"' in de la Feria and Vogenauer, *Prohibition of Abuse of Law* (n 1) 114.

> In many situations, the adjudicative body finds itself in a position to choose, alternatively, between a strict interpretation of the norm used as a 'cover' and the recourse to the technique of fraus legis.[3]

Similarly, the Court has repeatedly acknowledged the existence of alternatives to the formal doctrine of abuse, as Advocates General Maduro and Kokott in their respective Opinions in *Cavallera* and *Centralan*:

> Everything depends, therefore, on the interpretation to be given to the term 'diploma' in the Directive. According to a strict interpretation, the homologation decision cannot be treated as equivalent to a diploma within the meaning of the Directive … . By contrast, on a broad interpretation, such a decision may be regarded as equivalent to a diploma within the meaning of the Directive. … It must be acknowledged from the outset that the choice of a narrow or broad interpretation of the Directive provides the Court with two options of equal value, as the broad interpretation involves application of the principle prohibiting abusive practices.[4]

> It is true that the transactions have an artificial effect and are aimed solely at affording the University the possibility of deducting the VAT paid on the construction of the Harrington Building, even though the University to a great extent provides tax exempt services. The interpretation of the Sixth Directive which I am here advocating, however, precludes these artificial transactions from giving rise to a tax exemption which would run counter to the objectives of the directive and would have to be remedied by recourse to unwritten principles such as the prohibition on the abuse of rights.[5]

In more detail, the alternative reactions of Union law to artificial choices of law include informal doctrines of abuse of law (Section I), suspect periods (Section II), centres of gravity (Section III), legal grounds unrelated to the issue of abuse of law (Section IV) and free choice of law approaches (Section V). As we shall see, both the Court and the Union legislature[6] routinely have recourse to each and every of these alternative legal grounds, so that the following review should demonstrate that abuses of Union law form a much broader phenomenon than one might expect, by no means limited to the cases in which the Court has applied the formal doctrine of abuse.

It must be underlined that all cases presented in this chapter illustrate a specific technique used to address artificial practices, but that their factual settings do

[3] M Gestri, *Abuso del Diritto e Frode alla Legge nell'Ordinamento Comunitario* (Milan, Giuffrè, 2003) 207, free translation; see also KE Sørensen, 'Abuse of Rights in Community Law: a Principle of Substance or Merely Rhetoric?' (2006) 43 *Common Market Law Review* 423, 427–34 (see '3. Alternative approaches to combating abuse of rights').

[4] AG Maduro, Case C-311/06 *Cavallera* [2009] ECR I-415, paras 24–25.

[5] AG Kokott, Case C-63/04 *Centralan* [2005] ECR I-11087, para 61. See also Case C-63/04 *Centralan* [2005] ECR I-11087, para 81; AG Maduro, Case C-419/02 *BUPA Hospitals* [2006] ECR I-1685, paras 100–01; AG Maduro, Case C-452/03 *RAL* [2005] ECR I-3947, para 67. On several occasions, the Court relied on a different legal ground than the one propounded by the advocate general: see eg Case 81/87 *Daily Mail* [1988] ECR 5483; Case C-202/97 *Fitzwilliam* [2000] ECR I-883; Case C-109/01 *Akrich* [2003] ECR I-9607; Case C-298/05 *Columbus* [2007] ECR I-10451.

[6] The formal doctrine of abuse itself is codified in art 4(3) of Regulation 2988/95, whose scope is however limited to internal abuses of law: see ch 2 section I.

not always match the definition of artificial practice. For instance, in *Bidar* and *Förster*, the Court endorsed an anti-abuse technique consisting in imposing a suspect period during which entitlement to social benefits is suspended; yet both Mr Bidar and Ms Förster fulfilled this requirement, thereby proving that they had not set up an artificial practice.

I. Informal Doctrines of Abuse of Law

Formal and informal doctrines of abuse of law share the same objective of precluding undesirable choices of law artificially made by private individuals. In addition, both types of doctrine of abuse constitute autonomous legal grounds, in the sense that Union institutions may base their decisions on formal and informal doctrines of abuse, independently of other legal norms. However, by contrast with the formal doctrine of abuse, informal doctrines of abuse do not rest on a well-structured test, composed of the artificiality requirement and the teleological assessment enounced in *Emsland-Stärke* (paras 52–53) and *Halifax* (paras 74–75).[7] Rather, informal doctrines of abuse merely express the need to combat 'abuse', 'circumvention' or 'avoidance'; in that sense, they form embryonic versions of the formal doctrine of abuse.

Abusive re-importation of goods set up to obtain export refunds were sanctioned as abusive in *Emsland-Stärke*, in which the Court had recourse to the formal doctrine of abuse. In the wake of this judgment, the Union legislature adopted an informal doctrine of abuse now located in Article 27(4)(c) of Regulation 612/2009:

> However, the refund shall be deemed to be unwarranted and shall be reimbursed if the competent authorities find, even after the refund has been paid, that the product exported is reimported into the Community without having undergone any substantial processing or working within the meaning of Article 24 of Regulation (EEC) 2913/92, that the non-preferential duty on import is less than the refund granted, and that export was not carried out as a normal commercial transaction.[8]

Informal doctrines of abuse prohibiting the artificial transport of goods can also be found in the Community Customs Code.[9] In this context, artificial transport of goods is intended to lower the amount of customs duties levied upon importation into the Union, by artificially electing a country of origin benefiting from preferential arrangements with the Union ('preferential origin'). Thus, the rule of

[7] See ch 3.

[8] Commission Regulation (EC) 612/2009 of 7 July 2009 on laying down common detailed rules for the application of the system of export refunds on agricultural products (recast) [2009] OJ L186/1.

[9] Council Regulation (EEC) 2913/92 of 12 October 1992 establishing the Community Customs Code [1992] OJ L302/1.

origin of Article 24 establishes that the origin of imported goods is defined by the place of the last 'economically justified' processing or working:

> Goods whose production involved more than one country shall be deemed to originate in the country where they underwent their last, substantial, economically justified processing or working in an undertaking equipped for that purpose and resulting in the manufacture of a new product or representing an important stage of manufacture.

This rule of origin is complemented by the more robust anti-abuse provision of Article 25:

> Any processing or working in respect of which it is established, or in respect of which the facts as ascertained justify the presumption, that its sole object was to circumvent the provisions applicable in the Community to goods from specific countries shall under no circumstances be deemed to confer on the goods thus produced the origin of the country where it is carried out within the meaning of Article 24.

Moreover, anti-abuse rules can be found in several other provisions of the Community Customs Code.[10]

Abusive re-importations of goods have also been condemned in the context of free movement of goods, through recourse to informal doctrines of abuse. In *Leclerc*, the Court held that the jurisdiction of the host State was pre-empted in favour of the home State (mutual recognition: *Cassis de Dijon* principle[11]), except in the hypothesis of abusive re-importation of goods:[12]

> The above finding [of a restriction to free movement] is not applicable where it is established that the books in question were exported for the sole purpose of re-importation in order to circumvent legislation of the type at issue.[13]

In the field of company law, the Court established an informal doctrine of abuse *pro forma* in *Centros*, when articulating the implications of the freedom of establishment on national company laws:

> [A] Member State is entitled to take measures designed to prevent certain of its nationals from attempting, under cover of the rights created by the Treaty, improperly to circumvent their national legislation or to prevent individuals from improperly or fraudulently taking advantage of provisions of Community law.[14]

This informal doctrine of abuse was, however, emptied of all substance in the remainder of the ruling, which removed every possibility of countering artificial choices of company law.[15] A similar statement can be found in *Singh*, this time

[10] See Community Customs Code, arts 91(1)(b), 133(d), 139, para 2.

[11] Case 120/78 *Rewe-Zentral ('Cassis de Dijon')* [1979] ECR 649.

[12] Case 229/83 *Leclerc* [1985] ECR 1, para 27; see also Case C-322/01 *Deutscher Apothekerverband* [2003] ECR I-14887, para 129; Case C-137/00 *Milk Marque* [2003] ECR I-7975, para 11.

[13] Case 229/83 *Leclerc* [1985] ECR 1, para 27.

[14] Case C-212/97 *Centros* [1999] ECR I-1459, para 24.

[15] Ringe, 'Sparking Regulatory Competition in European Company Law' (n 2) 113: '[I]f situations such as Centros and Cadbury Schweppes are considered to be not "wholly artificial", then the scope for actual abusive behaviour is very small, at least in company law'.

in relation to the free movement of Union citizens married to a third country national.[16] Furthermore, an informal doctrine of abuse was codified in Article 35 of Directive 2004/38/EC on the free movement of Union citizens and their family,[17] to which the Court referred in *Metock*:[18]

> Member States may adopt the necessary measures to refuse, terminate or withdraw any right conferred by this Directive in the case of abuse of rights or fraud, such as marriages of convenience.

In *Knoors*, *Bouchoucha* and *Kraus*, the Court underlined the legitimate interest of Member States in preventing artificial choices of law in relation to the mutual recognition of professional qualifications:

> [I]t is not possible to disregard the legitimate interest which a Member State may have in preventing certain of its nationals, by means of facilities created under the Treaty, from attempting wrongly to evade the application of their national legislation as regards training for a trade.[19]

Similarly, in *Lair*, the Court enabled Member States to fight 'abuses' consisting in taking up residence in a Member State for the sole purpose of enjoying, after a very short period of time, social benefits offered in that State:

> [W]here it may be established on the basis of objective evidence that a worker has entered a Member State for the sole purpose of enjoying, after a very short period of occupational activity, the benefit of the student assistance system in that State, it should be observed that such abuses are not covered by the Community provisions in question.[20]

Numerous applications of informal doctrines of abuse can be identified in the field of direct taxation, where the Court has long established that the fight against tax avoidance can justify restrictions to free movement. In *X and Y*, for instance, the Court held that:

> National courts may, case by case, take account—on the basis of objective evidence—of abuse or fraudulent conduct on the part of the persons concerned in order, where appropriate, to deny them the benefit of the provisions of Community law on which they seek to rely.[21]

[16] Case C-370/90 *Singh* [1992] ECR I-4265, para 24.

[17] Directive 2004/38/EC of the European Parliament and of the Council of 29 April 2004 on the right of citizens of the Union and their family members to move and reside freely within the territory of the Member States [2004] OJ L229/35 art 35.

[18] Case C-127/08 *Metock* [2008] ECR I-6241, para 75.

[19] Case 115/78 *Knoors* [1979] ECR 399, para 25; see also Case C-19/92 *Dieter Kraus* [1993] ECR I-1663, para 34; Case C-61/89 *Bouchoucha* [1990] ECR I-3551, para 14.

[20] Case 39/86 *Lair* [1988] ECR 3161, para 43; see also Case C-413/01 *Ninni-Orasche* [2003] ECR I-13187, paras 36, 41, 45–47.

[21] Case C-436/00 *X and Y* [2002] ECR I-10829, para 42; see also Case C-321/05 *Kofoed* [2007] ECR I-5795, para 36–48; Case C-28/95 *Leur-Bloem* [1997] ECR I-4161, para 40-47; Case C-446/03 *Marks & Spencer* [2005] ECR I-10837, para 49; Case C-9/02 *de Lasteyrie du Saillant* [2004] ECR I-2409, paras 50–54; Case C-324/00 *Lankhorst-Hohorst* [2002] ECR I-11779, paras 37–38; Case C-436/00 *X and Y* [2002] ECR I-10829, paras 40–45; Case C-264/96 *ICI* [1996] ECR I-4695, para 26; Case C-464/02 *Commission v Denmark* [2005] ECR I-7929, paras 55 and 65–69.

In a more systematic fashion, tax avoidance amounts to an undesirable choice of tax law, by which taxpayers seek to transfer either a tax liability to a low-tax jurisdiction or a tax deduction to a high-tax jurisdiction. The *Oy AA* case[22] concerned the first hypothesis, namely a transfer of tax liability to a low-tax jurisdiction, as with the *Cadbury Schweppes* and *Thin Cap Group Litigation* cases in which the Court applied the formal doctrine of abuse.[23] Finnish tax law laid down a system of 'intra-group financial transfers' by which financial transfers could be realised among companies of the same group, such transfers being treated as a taxable income for the transferee and as a deductible expense for the transferor. One of the conditions was the subjection of the transferee to income tax in Finland, in order to prevent artificial transfers of income within groups of companies towards companies established in low-tax jurisdictions. The Court endorsed this restriction to free movement in the following terms:

> [T]o accept that an intra-group cross-border transfer, such as that at issue in the main proceedings, may be deducted from the taxable income of the transferor would result in allowing groups of companies to choose freely the Member State in which the profits of the subsidiary are to be taxed, by removing them from the basis of assessment of the latter and, where that transfer is regarded as taxable income in the Member State of the parent company transferee, incorporating them in the basis of assessment of the parent company. …
>
> Concerning … the prevention of tax avoidance, … the possibility of transferring the taxable income of a subsidiary to a parent company with its establishment in another Member State carries the risk that, by means of purely artificial arrangements, income transfers may be organised within a group of companies towards companies established in Member States applying the lowest rates of taxation or in Member States in which such income is not taxed.
>
> [T]he objectives of safeguarding the balanced allocation of the power to impose taxes between Member States and the prevention of tax avoidance are linked. Conduct involving the creation of wholly artificial arrangements which do not reflect economic reality, with a view to escaping the tax normally due on the profits generated by activities carried out on national territory is such as to undermine the right of the Member State to exercise their tax jurisdiction in relation to those activities and jeopardise a balanced allocation between Member State of the power to impose taxes.[24]

Paraphrasing the Court, the exclusion of recipient companies established in other Member States was justified by the need to avoid granting taxpayers a choice of law: if not for this exclusion, groups of companies would indeed be able to 'choose freely the Member State in which profits are to be taxed' by creating 'wholly artificial arrangements which do not reflect economic reality' (tax avoidance). If the terminology used by the Court in *Oy AA* is very similar to that used in decisions applying the formal doctrine of abuse (chiefly *Cadbury Schweppes* and *Thin Cap*

22 Case C-231/05 *Oy AA* [2007] ECR I-6373.
23 See ch 2 section IV.
24 Case C-231/05 *Oy AA* [2007] ECR I-6373, paras 56, 58 and 62.

Group Litigation), the reasoning is not based on the well-structured doctrine of abuse enounced in *Emsland-Stärke* and *Halifax*, which accounts for its categorisation as 'informal doctrine of abuse'. The Court applied a similar reasoning in *SGI*, which also concerned the risk of transfer of tax liability to a low-tax jurisdiction, by means of unusual or gratuitous advantages granted to a subsidiary established in another Member State.[25]

The *Marks & Spencer* case, in which the Court applied an informal doctrine of abuse, concerned the second hypothesis of tax avoidance, namely the transfer of a tax deduction to a high-tax jurisdiction.[26] Marks & Spencer was a UK company that owned loss-making subsidiaries in Belgium, France and Germany, where they operated sales outlets. Marks & Spencer claimed group tax relief in the United Kingdom, a technique by which a company transfers, for tax purposes, its losses to another company belonging to the same group. However, the tax authorities rejected the claims for relief on the ground that it could only be granted for losses recorded in the United Kingdom. As in *Oy AA*, the rationale behind that requirement was the prevention of tax avoidance, in the form of artificial transfers of losses within groups of companies towards companies established in high-tax jurisdictions ('loss trafficking').[27] The Court ruled that this restriction to free movement was justified in so far as the losses could be deducted by the subsidiaries in their Member State of establishment, on the following grounds:

> In effect, to give companies the option to have their losses taken into account in the Member State in which they are established or in another Member State would significantly jeopardise a balanced allocation of the power to impose taxes between Member States, as the taxable basis would be increased in the first State and reduced in the second to the extent of the losses transferred.
>
> As regards … the risk of tax avoidance, it must be accepted that the possibility of transferring the losses incurred by a non-resident company to a resident company entails the risk that within a group of companies losses will be transferred to companies established in the Member State which apply the highest rates of taxation and in which the tax value of the losses is therefore the highest.
>
> It is also important, in that context, to make clear that Member States are free to adopt or to maintain in force rules having the specific purpose of precluding from a tax benefit wholly artificial arrangements whose purpose is to circumvent or escape national tax law.[28]

As usual, the Court equated tax avoidance with free choice of a tax jurisdiction, by holding that Member States can rightfully prevent a situation where companies would freely elect the jurisdiction in which their losses are taken into account. In essence, the Court's ruling aims at precluding choices of national tax law by

[25] Case C-311/08 *SGI* [2010] ECR I-487, paras 60 ff; see also AG Cruz Villalón, Case C-318/10 *SIAT* [2012] ECR I-0000.

[26] Case C-446/03 *Marks & Spencer* [2005] ECR I-10837.

[27] AG Maduro, Case C-347/04 *Rewe Zentralfinanz* [2007] ECR I-2647, para 32.

[28] Case C-446/03 *Marks & Spencer* [2005] ECR I-10837, paras 46, 49 and 57.

Union taxpayers ('tax avoidance' or 'abuse of law'), as in *Cadbury Schweppes* and *Thin Cap Group Litigation*, by having recourse to an informal doctrine of abuse, as in *Oy AA*. The need to preclude taxpayers from choosing the Member State in which their losses are taken into account was reaffirmed in *Lidl Belgium*, in relation to losses incurred by the Luxembourg permanent establishment of a German company;[29] and in *X Holding*, which concerned the exclusion of foreign subsidiaries from group tax integration in the Netherlands.[30]

Further applications of informal doctrines of abuse can be found in tax directives adopted by the Union legislature. For instance, Article 1(2) of Council Directive 90/435/EEC reads as follows: 'This Directive shall not preclude the application of domestic or agreement-based provisions required for the prevention of fraud or abuse'. Similar provisions on the prevention of tax avoidance can be found in Article 11(1)(a) of Council Directive 90/434/EEC (interpreted in *Foggia, Modehuis A. Zwijnenburg, Kofoed, Leur-Bloem*[31]), Article 5 of Council Directive 2003/49/EC and Article 15(1)(a) of Council Directive 2009/133/EC.[32]

In the area of indirect taxation, the Union legislation on excise duty refers to the need to prevent 'evasion, avoidance or abuse'.[33] If the legislation on capital duty does not refer to the risk of tax avoidance,[34] the Court applied the formal doctrine of abuse in *ING. AUER* and evoked the risk of tax avoidance on other occasions.[35] Similarly, the VAT Directive 2006/112/EC mentions the word 'avoidance' 12 times, the word 'evasion' 17 times and the word 'abuse' twice.[36] Along with the formal

[29] Case C-414/06 *Lidl Belgium* [2008] ECR I-3601, paras 31–51; see also Case C-347/04 *Rewe Zentralfinanz* [2007] ECR I-2647, para 42.

[30] Case C-337/08 *X Holding* [2010] ECR I-1215, paras 28–32.

[31] Case C-126/10 *Foggia* [2011] ECR I-10923, paras 50–51; Case C-352/08 *Modehuis A. Zwijnenburg* [2010] ECR I-4303; Case C-321/05 *Kofoed* [2007] ECR I-5795; Case C-28/95 *Leur-Bloem* [1997] ECR I-4161.

[32] Council Directive 90/435/EEC of 23 July 1990 on the common system of taxation applicable in the case of parent companies and subsidiaries of different Member States [1990] OJ L225/6 art 1(2); Council Directive 90/434/EEC of 23 July 1990 on the common system of taxation applicable to mergers, divisions, transfers of assets and exchanges of shares concerning companies of different Member States [1990] OJ L225/1 art 11(1)(a); Council Directive 2003/49/EC of 3 June 2003 on a common system of taxation applicable to interest and royalty payments made between associated companies of different Member States [2003] OJ L157/49 art 5; Council Directive 2009/133/EC of 19 October 2009 on the common system of taxation applicable to mergers, divisions, partial divisions, transfers of assets and exchanges of shares concerning companies of different Member States and to the transfer of the registered office of an SE or SCE between Member States [2009] OJ L310/34 art 15(1)(a).

[33] Council Directive 2008/118/EC of 16 December 2008 concerning the General Arrangements for Excise Duty and Repealing Directive 92/12/EEC [2008] OJ L9/12 arts 14(3) and 39(3); see also former Council Directive 92/12/EEC of 25 February 1992 on the General Arrangements for Products Subject to Excise Duty and on the Holding, Movement and Monitoring of such Products [1992] OJ L76/1 art 28(3).

[34] Council Directive 2008/7/EC of 12 February 2008 concerning indirect taxes on the raising of capital [2008] OJ L46/11.

[35] Case C-397/07 *Commission v Spain* [2009] ECR I-6029, para 30; Case C-178/05 *Commission v Greece* [2007] ECR I-4185, para 32.

[36] VAT Directive 2006/112; curiously, Amand reaches a different count (respectively 19, 11, 2): C Amand, 'Prohibition of Abusive Practices in European VAT: Court Aid to National Legislations Bugs?' (2008) 36 *Intertax* 189, 194.

doctrine of abuse applied in *Halifax* or *Part Service*, the Court insisted that 'taking account of the economic reality constitutes a fundamental criterion for applying the common system of VAT'.[37] In concrete terms, the principle of economic reality implies, just as the doctrine of abuse, that economic transactions should not be disguised behind abnormal legal forms, intended to provoke a favourable change of law. On that ground, the Court has disregarded two categories of artificial arrangements designed to generate favourable tax consequences: the artificial splitting of economic transactions and the manipulation of fixed establishments. For instance, *Levob* was a Dutch insurance company that sought to reduce its VAT liability on the acquisition of customised software sold by a US company, by artificially splitting the transaction into acquisition of the basic software (VAT-exempt) and customisation (subject to VAT). The Court held that the acquisition of customised software had to be viewed as a single economic transaction, wholly subject to VAT:

> Taking into account ... that a transaction which comprises a single supply from an economic point of view should not be artificially split, so as not to distort the functioning of the VAT system, the essential features of the transaction must in the first place be ascertained in order to determine whether the taxable person is making to the customer, being a typical consumer, several distinct principal supplies or a single supply.[38]

DFDS, on the other hand, concerned a Danish company providing travel agency services in the United Kingdom through a subsidiary incorporated there. Since such services were subject to VAT in the United Kingdom and exempt in Denmark, DFDS sought to elect the Danish VAT regime by presenting the UK subsidiary as the mere executing agent of the Danish parent company. However, the Court disregarded the contractual form given to DFDS' activities in the United Kingdom, in the following unequivocal terms:

> As the AG points out in para 32 to 34 of his Opinion, consideration of the actual economic situation is a fundamental criterion for the application of the common VAT system. The alternative approach for determining the place of taxation of the services of travel agents, based on the fixed establishment from which these services are supplied, is specifically intended to take account of the possible diversification of travel agents' activities in different places within the Community. Systematic reliance on the place where the supplier has established his business could in fact lead to distortions of competition, in that it might encourage undertakings trading in one Member State to establish their businesses, in order to avoid taxation, in another Member State which has availed itself of the possibility of maintaining the VAT exemption for the services in question.[39]

Planzer concerned the right to deduct the VAT paid on fuel supplies, which was denied to businesses established outside the Union. In that context, the German

[37] Case C-73/06 *Planzer* [2007] ECR I-5655, para 43; Case C-260/95 *DFDS* [1997] ECR I-1005, para 23.

[38] Case C-41/04 *Levob* [2005] ECR I-9433, para 20; see also Case C-461/08 *Don Bosco* [2009] ECR I-11079, paras 39–41; Case C-349/96 *CPP* [1999] ECR I-973, paras 29–31.

[39] Case C-260/95 *DFDS* [1997] ECR I-1005, para 23.

authorities contested the economic reality of a Luxembourg subsidiary incorporated by a Swiss transport company (Planzer), apparently with the sole purpose of recovering VAT on its fuel supplies. The Court enabled the German authorities to reject Planzer's claim to VAT deduction, if the Luxembourg establishment did not correspond to any economic reality:

> It is settled case-law that Community law cannot be relied on for abusive or fraudulent ends. That would be the case if a taxable person were to attempt to benefit from the refund system ... in circumstances where the establishment ... does not correspond to any economic reality ... and, moreover, the person concerned is not established in Community territory.[40]

As illustrated by *DFDS* and *Planzer*, unveiling the economic reality may require 'piercing' corporate structures or contractual arrangements conceived by the parties for mere regulatory purposes. In a more systematic fashion, preventing undesirable choices of law requires 'lifting the corporate veil' when companies are used for the sole purpose of electing a favourable law. In *EMU Tabac*, a UK company (ETC) made use of a subsidiary incorporated in Luxembourg (EMU) to purchase tobacco products in Luxembourg, which were then delivered to UK residents through another subsidiary (MBL). This artificial practice was designed for the sole purpose of paying excise duties in Luxembourg, which reduced purchase prices by up to 40 per cent. The Court considered that the products were dispatched or transported by the vendor or on his behalf, so that excise duty was chargeable in the Member State of destination, namely the United Kingdom. To reach that conclusion, the Court lifted the corporate veil and considered that all companies involved in the arrangement formed part of the same entity: 'EMU and MBL are subsidiaries of the same company and as such they can be regarded as forming part of the same economic entity, despite the fact that they are separate legal persons'.[41]

In the seminal *Dyestuffs* judgment, the Court relied on a similar reasoning to uphold a fine imposed by the Commission on businesses established outside the Union territory, following a finding of cartel conduct. According to the Court, when such third country businesses exercise decisive influence over subsidiaries established in the Union, their economic unity outweighs the legal fiction of their separate personalities:

> The applicant was able to exercise decisive influence over the policy of the subsidiaries as regards selling prices in the common market and in fact used this power upon the occasion of the three price increases in question.

[40] Case C-73/06 *Planzer* [2007] ECR I-5655, paras 44–45; see also Case C-231/94 *Faaborg-Gelting Linien* [1996] ECR I-2395.

[41] Case C-296/95 *EMU Tabac* [1998] ECR I-1605, para 47.

> In the circumstances the formal separation between these companies, resulting from their separate legal personality, cannot outweigh the unity of their conduct on the market for the purposes of applying the rules on competition.[42]

The Union legislature may decide to lift the corporate veil as well, as in Regulation 423/2007 on restrictive measures against Iran in relation to its nuclear weapons program.[43] In particular, Article 7(2) provided for fund-freezing measures against entities associated with Iran's proliferation-sensitive nuclear activities, and for 'every legal person owned or controlled by such an entity'. In *Melli Bank*, the Court ruled that the lifting of the corporate veil operated by this provision was necessary to combat the circumvention of asset-freezing measures:

> [W]here the funds of an entity identified as being engaged in nuclear proliferation are frozen there is a not insignificant danger that that entity may exert pressure on the entities it owns or controls in order to circumvent the effect of the measures applying to it and that the freezing of the funds of those entities is necessary and appropriate in order to ensure the effectiveness of the measures adopted and to ensure that those measures are not circumvented.[44]

Nevertheless, in other cases, the Court has proved reluctant to lift the corporate veil and accordingly treat related companies as a single economic entity. In *Laval*, the Swedish trade unions claimed that the Latvian company (Laval) and its Swedish subsidiary (Baltic) formed a single economic entity active in Sweden. They argued that the posting of workers from Latvia amounted to an artificial practice intended to circumvent Swedish law. However, the Court quickly dismissed this argument when examining the admissibility of the reference for a preliminary ruling.[45] The Court rejected a similar plea of inadmissibility in *Hartlauer*, in which an Austrian company had incorporated a subsidiary in Germany apparently with the sole aim of bringing its situation within the scope of Union law.[46]

In the area of public procurement, Article 7 of Directive 2004/18[47] provides for thresholds above which public contracts are subject to the provisions of the Directive. Article 9(3) provides for a specific anti-abuse rule precluding public authorities from splitting up public contracts in order to avoid the obligation to tender:

> No works project or proposed purchase of a certain quantity of supplies and/or services may be subdivided to prevent its coming within the scope of this Directive.

[42] Case 48/69 *ICI v Commission (Dyestuffs)* [1972] ECR 619, para 137 and 140.

[43] Council Regulation (EC) 423/2007 of 19 April 2007 concerning restrictive measures against Iran [2007] OJ L103/1.

[44] Case C-380/09 P *Melli Bank* [2012] ECR I-0000, para 58.

[45] Case C-341/05 *Laval* [2007] ECR I-11767, paras 43–50.

[46] Case C-169/07 *Hartlauer* [2009] ECR I-1721, paras 23–27.

[47] Directive 2004/18/EC of the European Parliament and of the Council of 31 March 2004 on the coordination of procedures for the award of public works contracts, public supply contracts and public service contracts [2004] OJ L134/114.

A similar anti-abuse provision can be found in Article 17(2) of Directive 2004/17 on procurement procedures of entities operating in the water, energy, transport and postal services sectors:[48]

> Contracting entities may not circumvent this Directive by splitting works projects or proposed purchases of a certain quantity of supplies and/or services or by using special methods for calculating the estimated value of contracts.

In Regulation 1370/2007, this anti-abuse principle is recalled in the preamble: 'Competent authorities should not be permitted to split up contracts or networks in order to avoid tendering.'[49]

Lastly, the prevention of abusive practices is sometimes considered necessary to preserve the 'effectiveness' ('*effet utile*') of a legal regime. For instance, in *UsedSoft v Oracle*, the Court adopted a broad interpretation of the concept of sale in the context of Directive 2009/24[50] in order to avoid coexistence of several legal regimes, which would have been exploited to set up circumvention strategies:

> As the Advocate General observes in point 59 of his Opinion, if the term 'sale' within the meaning of Article 4(2) of Directive 2009/24 were not given a broad interpretation as encompassing all forms of product marketing characterised by the grant of a right to use a copy of a computer program, for an unlimited period, in return for payment of a fee designed to enable the copyright holder to obtain a remuneration corresponding to the economic value of the copy of the work of which he is the proprietor, the effectiveness of that provision would be undermined, since suppliers would merely have to call the contract a 'licence' rather than a 'sale' in order to circumvent the rule of exhaustion and divest it of all scope.[51]

To sum up, informal doctrines of abuse form an autonomous legal ground used by Union institutions to prevent undesirable choices of law artificially made by private individuals, just as the formal doctrine of abuse. By contrast with the formal doctrine of abuse, informal doctrines of abuse do not rest on the well-structured test enounced in *Emsland-Stärke* and *Halifax*; rather, they informally express and achieve the objective of preventing abusive practices.

[48] Directive 2004/17/EC of the European Parliament and of the Council of 31 March 2004 coordinating the procurement procedures of entities operating in the water, energy, transport and postal services sectors [2004] OJ L134/1.

[49] Regulation (EC) 1370/2007 of the European Parliament and of the Council of 23 October 2007 on public passenger transport services by rail and by road and repealing Council Regulations (EEC) 1191/69 and 1107/70 [2007] OJ L315/1, rec 23.

[50] Directive 2009/24/EC of the European Parliament and of the Council of 23 April 2009 on the legal protection of computer programs (codified version) [2009] OJ L111/16.

[51] Case C-128/11 *UsedSoft v Oracle* [2012] ECR I-0000, para 49.

II. Suspect Periods

In addition to formal and informal doctrines of abuse, suspect periods are commonly used to preclude undesirable choices of law artificially made by private individuals. Suspect periods subject a change of legal regime to the expiry of a given period of time; by suspending the regulatory benefit sought, suspect periods seek to ensure that decisions of Union citizens are underpinned by socioeconomic motives, and not only by a gain-seeking choice of law. Eidenmüller explicitly identified such suspect periods as anti-abuse instruments in the context of European insolvency law:

> [T]he [European Insolvency Regulation] does not establish a suspect period (i.e. it does not contain a rule to the effect that a former [centre of main interests] remains decisive if the insolvency petition is filed shortly after a [centre of main interests] shift). If such a suspect period existed in the [European Insolvency Regulation], it could be conceived as an 'institutionalised anti-abuse rule'.[52]

Although they did not concern abusive strategies as such, for both protagonists were well integrated in the host society, the *Bidar* and *Förster* decisions offer excellent illustrations of such suspect periods. In both cases, the Court held that the attribution of study grants to migrant Union citizens (not economically active) could be subjected to uninterrupted residence requirements, of respectively three and five years:

> [T]he guarantee of sufficient integration into the society of the host Member State follows from the conditions requiring previous residence in the territory of that State, in this case the three years' residence required by the [national] rules.[53]

> A condition of five years' continuous residence cannot be held to be excessive having regard, inter alia, to the requirements put forward with respect to the degree of integration of non-nationals in the host Member State.[54]

Similar residence requirements had previously been held incompatible with the freedoms of movement, for instance in relation to the Belgian 'minimex', a social benefit intended to cover the minimum means of subsistence.[55] Nevertheless, *Bidar* and *Förster* do not completely break with the previous case law: in *Lair*, several Member States and AG Slynn explicitly supported a requirement of a minimum period of employment, in order to prevent abuses of law by migrant workers applying for study grants shortly after their arrival.[56] Although the Court

[52] H Eidenmüller, 'Abuse of Law in the Context of European Insolvency Law' in de la Feria and Vogenauer (n 1) 147.

[53] Case C-209/03 *Bidar* [2005] ECR I-2119, para 60.

[54] Case C-158/07 *Förster* [2008] ECR I-8507, para 54.

[55] Case 316/85 *Lebon* [1987] ECR 2811; Case 122/84 *Scrivner* [1985] ECR 1027; Case 249/83 *Hoeckx* [1985] ECR 973.

[56] AG Slynn recommended the imposition of a suspect period of one year: AG Slynn, Case 39/86 *Lair* [1988] ECR 3161; see also Case 39/86 *Lair* [1988] ECR 3161, paras 40–44; Case C-413/01 *Ninni-Orasche* [2003] ECR I-13187, paras 36, 41, 45–47.

prohibited Member States from unilaterally imposing such a suspect period (para 42), it subsequently linked the notion of abuse to the period of occupational activity (para 43).

The concrete effect of residence requirements of three and five years endorsed in *Bidar* and *Förster* is to prevent 'benefit tourism',[57] namely undesirable choices of social law by which Union citizens take up residence in a Member State for the sole purpose of enjoying, after a very short period of time, social benefits offered in that State (*Lair*). By requiring a genuine link between Union citizens and a Member State before Union citizens may be entitled to welfare benefits, the Court reduces the scope for 'benefit tourism' or 'abuses of social law'.[58] The Court has reaffirmed the anti-abuse impact of such suspect periods in *Commission v Netherlands* and *Giersch*, which both concerned student funding:

> As regards the risk of abuse relied upon by the Kingdom of the Netherlands, arising in particular from the performance of short periods of employment solely for the purposes of obtaining portable funding, it should be pointed out that the concept of 'worker' for the purposes of Article 45 TFEU has an autonomous meaning specific to EU law and must not be interpreted narrowly. Any person who pursues activities which are real and genuine, to the exclusion of activities on such a small scale as to be purely marginal and ancillary, must be regarded as a 'worker'. The essential feature of an employment relationship is, according to the case-law of the Court, that for a certain period of time a person performs services for and under the direction of another person in return for which he receives remuneration.[59]

> Above all, in order to avoid the risk of 'study grant forum shopping' referred to by all the governments which submitted observations to the Court, and to ensure that the frontier worker who is a taxpayer and who makes social security contributions in Luxembourg has a sufficient link with Luxembourg society, the financial aid could be made conditional on the frontier worker, the parent of the student who does not reside in Luxembourg, having worked in that Member State for a certain minimum period of time. In another context, Article 24(2) of Directive 2004/38 provides that, by derogation from Article 24(1)—according to which all Union citizens residing on the basis of that directive in the territory of the host Member State are to enjoy equal treatment with the nationals of that Member State—the host Member State is not to be obliged to grant maintenance aid for studies before the acquisition of a right of permanent residence which, under Article 16(1) of Directive 2004/38, is subject to a condition of residence of five years in the territory of the Member State concerned.

> It should be noted that, in the cases in the main proceedings, such a risk can be ruled out in so far as it is common ground that Ms Giersch, Mr Stemper, Mr Taminiaux and

[57] C Costello, 'Citizenship of the Union: Above Abuse?' in de la Feria and Vogenauer (n 1) 348; KS Ziegler, '"Abuse of Law" in the Context of the Free Movement of Workers' in de la Feria and Vogenauer (n 1) 311; C Barnard, 'Case C-209/03 Bidar' (2005) 42 *Common Market Law Review* 1465, 1488. Benefit tourism has been defined as 'moving to a Member State with a more congenial social security environment': AG Geelhoed, Case C-456/02 *Trojani* [2004] ECR I-7573, paras 13 and 18.

[58] Sørensen, 'Abuse of Rights in Community Law' (n 3) 428 fn 14 and 445.

[59] Case C-542/09 *Commission v Netherlands* [2012] ECR I-0000, para 68.

> Ms Hodin each has a mother or father who has been working in Luxembourg for 23 years, 32 years, 28 years and 23 years respectively.[60]

Furthermore, according to a broad consensus in the scholarship, this case law is part of a more general trend of Union law, compelling Member States to incrementally extend their solidarity policies to nationals from other Member States, thereby reflecting their degree of integration in the host society (*transnational* solidarity).[61] In particular, the Union legislature structured Directive 2004/38/EC on the free movement of Union citizens around the same incremental approach to transnational solidarity,[62] by defining three categories of migrant citizens whose entitlements increase according to the length of their residence in the host State (short-term, mid-term and long-term residents).[63]

Another instance of continuous residence requirement can be found in the case law on unemployment benefits. In *D'Hoop*, the Court held that Member States could rightfully subject the grant of tideover allowances (granted to young graduates seeking their first employment) to the existence of a 'real link' between recipients and the domestic labour market.[64] The legitimacy of this real link requirement was reinforced in *Collins* and *Vatsouras*, in which the Court held that it could take the form of a continuous residence requirement (suspect period):

> [W]hile a residence requirement is, in principle, appropriate for the purpose of ensuring such a connection, if it is to be proportionate it cannot go beyond what is necessary in order to attain that objective. … In any event, if compliance with the requirement demands a period of residence, the period must not exceed what is necessary in order for the national authorities to be able to satisfy themselves that the person concerned is genuinely seeking work in the employment market of the host Member State.[65]

[60] Case C-20/12 *Giersch and Others* [2013] ECR I-0000, paras 80–81.

[61] S O'Leary, 'Equal Treatment and EU Citizens: A New Chapter On Cross-Border Educational Mobility and Access to Student Financial Assistance' (2009) 34 *European Law Review* 612; C O'Brien, 'Real Links, Abstract Rights and False Alarms: the Relationship between the ECJ's "Real Link" Case Law and National Solidarity' (2008) 33 *European Law Review* 643; L Conant, 'When Courts Decide: Foreigners' Rights and Social Citizenship in Europe and the US' (2008) 7 *European Political Science* 43; FG Jacobs, 'Citizenship of the European Union—A Legal Analysis' (2007) 13 *European Law Journal* 591; O Golynker, 'Analysis and Reflections—Student loans: The European Concept of Social Justice According to Bidar' (2006) 31 *European Law Review* 390; G de Búrca, *EU Law and the Welfare State: in Search of Solidarity* (Oxford, Oxford University Press, 2005); C Barnard, 'EU Citizenship and the Principle of Solidarity' in M Dougan and E Spaventa (eds), *Social Welfare and EU law* (Oxford, Hart Publishing, 2005); K Hailbronner, 'Union Citizenship and Access to Social Benefits' (2005) 42 *Common Market Law Review* 1245; G Davies, 'The High Water Point of Free Movement of Persons: Ending Benefit Tourism and Rescuing Welfare' (2004) 26 *Journal of Social Welfare and Family Law* 211.

[62] Barnard, 'Case C-209/03 Bidar' (n 57) 1478: '[T]he longer migrants reside in the Member State, the more integrated they are in that State and the greater the number of benefits they receive on equal terms with nationals'.

[63] Arts 6, 7 and 16 of Directive 2004/38 on the freedom of movement of Union citizens. See Ziegler, 'Abuse of Law' (n 57) 310; Barnard, 'EU Citizenship and the Principle of Solidarity' (n 61) 166; Golynker, 'Analysis and Reflections' (n 61) 397.

[64] Case C-224/98 *D'Hoop* [2002] ECR I-6191, paras 38–39; see also Case C-258/04 *Ioannidis* [2005] ECR I-8275, paras 30–34.

[65] Case C-138/02 *Collins* [2004] ECR I-2703, para 72, see also paras 65–73. See also Joined Cases C-22/08 and C-23/08 *Vatsouras* [2009] ECR I-4585, paras 38–41.

As stated by the Commission in *Collins*, such a suspect period, consisting in a reasonable period of residence during which the applicant genuinely sought an employment, 'may be justified on objective grounds necessarily intended to avoid "benefit tourism" and thus the possibility of abuse by work-seekers who are not genuine' (para 50).[66]

In relation to the European arrest warrant, Article 4(6) of Council Framework Decision 2002/584/JHA sets out a ground for optional non-execution of a European arrest warrant, where the requested person is a national or a resident of the executing Member State and that State undertakes to execute the sentence.[67] In *Wolzenburg*, the Court ruled that Member States could exclude this possibility for non-nationals not genuinely integrated into their society; as in *Förster*, the Court accepted a five-year residence requirement as a valid measure of genuine integration.[68]

Suspect periods can also be found in Union legislation on the mutual recognition of professional qualifications or abilities, for those instruments classically subordinate mutual recognition to the accomplishment of periods of training or occupational activity in the home State. The prevention of artificial choices of law in relation to professional qualifications derives from the objective of protection enounced in *Kraus*:

> The need to protect a public which will not necessarily be alerted to abuse of academic titles which have not been awarded according to the rules laid down in the country in which the holder of the title intends to make use of it constitutes a legitimate interest such as to justify a restriction, by the Member State in question, of the fundamental freedoms guaranteed by the Treaty.[69]

In that regard, an example of suspect period intended to protect the 'public' can be found in Article 3, first subparagraph, (b), of Directive 89/48 on diploma recognition, which compels host States to authorise Union citizens to take up a profession that they have pursued full-time for at least two years in another Member State in which that profession is not regulated. As explained by the Court in *Toki*, this suspect period of two years seeks to ensure that the professional qualification has not been artificially acquired abroad, but corresponds to an adequate level of skills and abilities:

> Where a profession is not regulated by the State, the guarantee of a certain level of quality of service in the professional field concerned is usually ensured by market forces, in that only those members of the profession concerned who possess skills and abilities at a level deemed adequate by employers or clients will be capable of pursuing that profession full-time in an employed or self-employed capacity, over the prescribed period of

[66] See also Sørensen (n 3) 428 fn 14.

[67] Council Framework Decision 2002/584/JHA of 13 June 2002 on the European Arrest Warrant and the surrender procedures between Member States [2002] OJ L190/1.

[68] Case C-123/08 *Wolzenburg* [2009] ECR I-9621, paras 66–68; see also Case C-66/08 *Kozlowski* [2008] ECR I-6041.

[69] Case C-19/92 *Dieter Kraus* [1993] ECR I-1663, para 35.

> two years. The essence of the requirement of professional experience of that duration is therefore that there is a real possibility that the applicant for recognition can pursue the profession concerned in the Member State of origin.[70]

Similarly, under Article 3 of Council Directive 64/427/EEC, Member States had to accept a period of six consecutive years in an independent capacity as evidence of professional knowledge and ability.[71] In *van de Bijl*, the Court interpreted this provision as requiring genuine and continuous professional activity in the Member State of origin, thereby excluding abusive acquisitions of professional qualifications:

> The directive was designed to make recognition, by a Member State which regulates the activity in question, of the exercise of that activity in another Member State conditional on the fact that such exercise was genuine and real and that it took place over a given number of consecutive years, that is to say, without any interruption other than that resulting from the events of everyday life.[72]

Moreover, the Court explicitly acknowledged the anti-abuse effect of this period of six years in *Knoors*:

> In this case, however, … the precise conditions set out in Article 3 of Directive 64/427, as regards the length of periods during which the activity in question must have been pursued, have the effect of excluding … the risk of abuse referred to by the Netherlands government.[73]

Lastly, the *Cavallera* case offers another illustration of a suspect period preventing artificial choices of law in relation to professional qualifications. Marco Cavallera, an Italian national, held an Italian diploma as a mechanical engineer and wished to pursue the profession of engineer in Italy. Instead of sitting for the State examination in Italy, he obtained the automatic homologation of his Italian diploma in Spain, and then immediately requested the right to work in Italy on the basis of Directive 89/48 on diploma recognition. The Court, however, excluded his Spanish title from the scope of Directive 89/48, since it did not attest any period of training or occupational activity undertaken in Spain:

> The concept of 'diploma' set out [in Article 1(a) of Directive 89/48] does not include a certificate issued by a Member State which does not attest any education or training

[70] Case C-424/09 *Toki* [2011] ECR I-2587, para 31.

[71] Council Directive 64/427/EEC of 7 July 1964 laying down detailed provisions concerning transitional measures in respect of activities of self-employed persons in manufacturing and processing industries falling within ISIC Major Groups 23–40 (Industry and small craft industries) [1964] OJ L117/1863.

[72] Case 130/88 *van de Bijl* [1989] ECR 3039, para 18.

[73] Case 115/78 *Knoors* [1979] ECR 399, para 26; see A Kjellgren, 'On the Border of Abuse—The Jurisprudence of the European Court of Justice on Circumvention, Fraud and Other Misuses of Community Law' (2000) 11 *European Business Law Review* 179, 183.

> covered by the education system of that Member State and is not based on either an examination taken or professional experience acquired in that Member State.[74]

In the field of VAT, the *Ampliscientifica* case concerned an Italian Decree allowing parent companies to consolidate their VAT declaration with their subsidiaries. However, this tax advantage was subject to the following requirement: the parent company was only entitled to act on behalf of the subsidiaries in which it had held more than 50 per cent of the share capital since at least the beginning of the previous calendar year. The Court upheld the validity of this suspect period in the following unambiguous terms:

> Clearly, national legislation ... which requires economic operators to demonstrate, by means of a certain continuity in their activities and operations, that recourse to a mechanism to simplify VAT declarations and payments is not simply motivated by the intention to obtain a tax advantage, ... but is the result of a more long-term economic decision, is not contrary to the principle prohibiting the abuse of rights.[75]

In the area of direct taxation, Article 3(2) the Parent-Subsidiary Directive[76] provides for a similar mechanism, by allowing Member States to subject certain tax exemptions to a suspect period:

> Member States shall have the option of not applying this Directive to companies of that Member State which do not maintain for an uninterrupted period of at least two years holdings qualifying them as parent companies.[77]

The Court, however, relaxed this optional suspect period in *Denkavit International*, by ruling that it would be excessive to deny the tax exemptions during the first two years of holding, but that Member States may rightfully ensure—by other means—that the tax exemptions only benefit companies abiding by this two-year holding requirement.[78] This solution is consistent with a statement of the Court in *Leur-Bloem*, according to which 'a merger by exchange of shares with the aim of creating a specific structure for a limited period of time ... may have valid commercial reasons'.[79]

The imposition of a suspect period may remove the need for recourse to the doctrine of abuse. For instance, Article 8 of Regulation 40/94 entitles the

[74] Case C-311/06 *Cavallera* [2009] ECR I-415, para 58; see also Case C-118/09 *Koller* [2010] ECR I-13627, paras 31–36; Case C-151/07 *Chatzithanasis* [2008] ECR I-9013, para 32; Case C-286/06 *Commission v Spain* [2008] ECR I-8025, paras 71–72.

[75] Case C-162/07 *Ampliscientifica* [2008] ECR I-4019, para 30.

[76] Council Directive 90/435/EEC of 23 July 1990 on the common system of taxation applicable in the case of parent companies and subsidiaries of different Member States [1990] OJ L225/6.

[77] AP Dourado, 'A Single Principle of Abuse in European Union Law: A Methodological Approach to Rejecting a Different Concept of Abuse in Personal Taxation' in de la Feria and Vogenauer (n 1) 475.

[78] Joined Cases C-283/94, C-291/94 and C-292/94 *Denkavit International* [1996] ECR I-5063, paras 30–33.

[79] Case C-28/95 *Leur-Bloem* [1997] ECR I-4161, para 42; see D Weber, 'Abuse of Law in the Context of Indirect Taxation: Why We Need the Subjective Intention Test, When is Combating Abuse an Obligation and Other Comments' in de la Feria and Vogenauer (n 1) 404–06.

proprietor of an earlier trade mark to form opposition to the registration of a new trade mark whenever there is a risk of confusion.[80] In order to prevent abusive registration of trade mark, Article 43(2) provides for the rejection of the opposition if the proprietor cannot prove the genuine use of the earlier trade mark during the period of five years preceding the application for the new trade mark. As this requirement of genuine use effectively prevents abusive practices, the Court rejected the application of the doctrine of abuse within the scope of the Regulation.[81]

To sum up, suspect periods prevent abuses of law by suspending the regulatory benefit sought during a given period of time. By temporarily removing the regulatory incentive, suspect periods ensure that transactions are supported by a socioeconomic incentive, thereby revealing the 'economic reality underlying a legal transaction' (*Ampliscientifica*, para 26). Indeed, by suspending the regulatory benefit sought, suspect periods seek to ensure that decisions by Union citizens are underpinned by socioeconomic motives, and not only by a gain-seeking choice of law.

III. Centres of Gravity

In addition to formal and informal doctrines of abuse as well as suspect periods, centre of gravity approaches are commonly used to prevent undesirable choices of law artificially made by private individuals. By contrast with suspect periods, which are fulfilled over time, centres of gravity 'snapshot' the effectiveness of the link with a specific jurisdiction at a certain point in time. Centre of gravity tests seek to make artificial choices of law costlier, thereby reducing the appeal of setting up artificial practices; in economic terms, they tend to impose costs equal to or higher than the regulatory gain sought, thereby weakening the incentive to set up artificial practices.[82]

More concretely, under a centre of gravity test, a change of legal regime is only allowed where a citizen-taxpayer presents a stronger connection with the new legal regime at a specific point of time. The often-quoted *Van Binsbergen* ruling offers a fine illustration of centre of gravity:

> A Member State cannot be denied the right to take measures to prevent the exercise by a person providing services whose activity is entirely or principally directed towards its

[80] Council Regulation (EC) 40/94 of 20 December 1993 on the Community trade mark [1993] OJ L11/1, repealed by Council Regulation (EC) 207/2009 of 26 February 2009 on the Community trade mark (codified version) [2009] OJ L78/1.

[81] Order in Case C-357/12 P *Wohlfahrt v OHIM* [2013] ECR I-0000.

[82] Noblet similarly identified centre of gravity tests as anti-abuse techniques, and gathered them under the heading 'effectiveness': A Noblet, *La lutte contre le contournement des droits nationaux en droit communautaire* (Lille, ANRT, 2004) 341–71.

> territory of the freedom guaranteed by Article 59 for the purpose of avoiding the professional rules of conduct which would be applicable to him if he were established within that State.[83]

The idea conveyed by the above statement is that a Member State hosting all or most of the activities of a person should have jurisdiction to regulate this person; in other words, the jurisdiction to regulate an economic activity is defined by the location of its centre of main interests. From the perspective of Union citizens, such a centre of gravity test naturally prevents cross-border artificial movements aiming at the election of a given national law by making such strategies costlier. Indeed, a centre of gravity requirement implies that Union citizens wishing to elect the laws of a given Member State need to actually move the majority of their economic activities to its territory; accordingly, centre of gravity test naturally impedes abuses of law, defined as undesirable choices of law artificially made by private individuals.

In a more systematic fashion, Union law regularly applies a centre of gravity approach to legal persons (Subsection III.A) and natural persons (Subsection III.B).

A. Centre of Gravity Approaches for Legal Persons (Real Seat Theory)

The real seat is the most common centre of gravity approach for legal persons. Although originating in company law, the notion of 'real seat' is commonly used in other laws applicable to legal persons, behind concepts such as 'main establishment', 'centre of administration' or 'head office'. According to the classical scholarship on company law, the real seat theory defines the *lex societatis* as the law of the Member State where companies have their 'real seat', that is their centre of administration or head office; conversely, the incorporation theory stipulates that companies should only be subject to the law of their Member State of incorporation.[84] The practical relevance of this distinction is that the incorporation theory grants free choice of law, whereas the real seat theory tends to restrict the freedom to elect the *lex societatis*: 'Since the costs of such a move [of headquarters] will usually outweigh the advantages connected with a more efficient corporate law

[83] Case 33/74 *Van Binsbergen* [1974] ECR 1299, para 13; see also Case 39/75 *Coenen* [1975] ECR 1547, para 9.

[84] Ringe (n 2) 110; E Vaccaro, 'Transfer of Seat and Freedom of Establishment in European Company Law' (2005) 16 *European Business Law Review* 1348, 1349; M Garcia-Riestra, 'The Transfer of Seat of the European Company v Free Establishment Case-Law' (2004) 15 *European Business Law Review* 1295, 1296; E Wymeersch, 'The Transfer of the Company's Seat in European Company Law' (2003) 40 *Common Market Law Review* 661, 661; C Barnard and S Deakin, 'Negative and Positive Harmonization of Labor Law in the European Union' (2002) 8 *Columbia Journal of European Law* 389, 395.

regime, the real seat doctrine effectively prevents free choice'.[85] The contrast between incorporation theory and real seat theory was exposed by the German Bundesgerichtshof in its reference in the *Überseering* case:

> [W]here the connecting factor is taken to be the place of incorporation, the company's founding members are placed at an advantage, since they are able, when choosing the place of incorporation, to choose the legal system which suits them best. …
>
> [B]y contrast, where the connecting factor is taken to be the actual centre of administration, that prevents the provisions of company law in the State in which the actual centre of administration is situated, which are intended to protect certain vital interests, from being circumvented by incorporating the company abroad.[86]

i. Applications of the 'Real Seat Theory' in Union Law

Numerous applications of the real seat theory can be found in the Court's case law and in the secondary legislation. In *Planzer*, which concerned the interpretation of the Thirteenth VAT Directive,[87] the Court established a particularly detailed definition of 'real seat', intended to prevent the use of 'letter box companies' within the VAT regime:[88]

> With regard to a company, as in the case in the main proceedings, the term business for the purposes of Article 1(1) of the Thirteenth Directive refers to the place where the essential decisions concerning the general management of that company are adopted and where the functions of its central administration are carried out.
>
> Determination of a company's place of business requires a series of factors to be taken into consideration, foremost amongst which are its registered office, the place of its central administration, the place where its directors meet and the place, usually identical, where the general policy of that company is determined. Other factors, such as the place of residence of the main directors, the place where general meetings are held, the place where administrative and accounting documents are kept, and the place where the company's financial, and particularly banking, transactions mainly take place, may also need to be taken into account.
>
> Thus, a fictitious presence, such as that of a 'letter box' or 'brass plate' company, cannot be described as a place of business for the purposes of Article 1(1) of the Thirteenth Directive (see, by analogy, Case C-341/04 Eurofood IFSC, para 35, and Cadbury Schweppes, para 68).[89]

The real seat theory is also applied in bank regulation. One of the largest bank frauds in history was set up in the early nineties by the Bank of Credit and

[85] JC Dammann, 'Freedom of Choice in European Corporate Law' (2004) 29 *Yale Journal of International Law* 477, 480.
[86] Case C-208/00 *Überseering* [2002] ECR I-9919, paras 15–16.
[87] Thirteenth Council Directive 86/560/EEC of 17 November 1986 on the harmonization of the laws of the Member States relating to turnover taxes—Arrangements for the refund of value added tax to taxable persons not established in Community territory [1986] OJ OJ L326/40.
[88] See n 40 and accompanying text.
[89] Case C-73/06 *Planzer* [2007] ECR I-5655, paras 60–62.

Commerce International (BCCI), which was a Luxembourg bank mostly active in the United Kingdom.[90] In the wake of the BCCI scandal, the Union legislature revised Banking Directive 2006/48[91] in order to improve the prudential control of banks within the Union, in particular by having recourse to the real seat theory.[92] According to the tenth recital in its preamble:

> Member States' competent authorities should not grant or should withdraw an authorisation where factors such as the content of the activities programmes, the geographical distribution of activities or the activities actually carried on indicate clearly that a credit institution has opted for the legal system of one Member State for the purpose of evading the stricter standards in force in another Member State within whose territory it carries on or intends to carry on the greater part of its activities.

Moreover, Article 11(2) of the Directive provides that:

> Each Member State shall require that:
>
> (a) any credit institution which is a legal person and which, under its national law, has a registered office shall have its head office in the same Member State as its registered office; and
>
> (b) any other credit institution shall have its head office in the Member State which granted its authorisation and in which it actually carries on its business.

By requiring credit institutions to have their head office and actually operate in the Member State whose law is applicable (the 'home State'), the Union legislature pursued two intertwined objectives: first, ensure that the competent authorities of the home State can exercise effective regulation and supervision;[93] and secondly, avoid abusive practices consisting in incorporating a company in a more hospitable jurisdiction while being mostly active in another Member State, on BCCI's model.[94] The other directives on financial services subsequently emulated this centre of gravity approach.[95]

[90] BCCI was a bank chartered in Luxembourg but mostly active in London and in the Cayman Islands. BCCI managed to organise fraudulent activities of an unprecedented scale, generating losses estimated between 10 and 17 billions USD. See 'Timeline: BCCI Case', *The Guardian*, 3 November 2005.

[91] Directive 2006/48/EC of the European Parliament and of the Council of 14 June 2006 relating to the taking up and pursuit of the business of credit institutions [2006] OJ L177/1.

[92] Gestri, *Abuso del Diritto e Frode alla Legge nell'Ordinamento Comunitario* (n 3) 73.

[93] T Tridimas, 'Abuse of Rights in EU Law: Some Reflections with Particular Reference to Financial Law' in de la Feria and Vogenauer (n 1) 188.

[94] P Schammo, 'Comments on Abuse of Rights in EU Law' in de la Feria and Vogenauer (n 1) 194–95.

[95] Directive 2004/39/EC of the European Parliament and of the Council of 21 April 2004 on markets in financial instruments amending Council Directives 85/611/EEC and 93/6/EEC and Directive 2000/12/EC of the European Parliament and of the Council and repealing Council Directive 93/22/EEC [2004] OJ L145/1 art 5(4); arts 1(e), 4 and 6(3) of Directive 2002/83/EC of the European Parliament and of the Council of 5 November 2002 concerning life assurance [2002] OJ L345/1; arts 13(8), 14(2), and 20 of Directive 2009/138/EC of the European Parliament and of the Council of 25 November 2009 on the taking-up and pursuit of the business of Insurance and Reinsurance (Solvency II) [2009] OJ L335/1; art 7(1)(d) of Directive 2009/65/EC of the European Parliament and of the Council of 13 July 2009 on the coordination of laws, regulations and administrative provisions relating to undertakings for collective investment in transferable securities (UCITS) [2009] OJ L302/32.

The Union law on broadcasting services followed a similar evolution.[96] The original text of the First Broadcasting Directive 89/552/EEC[97] vaguely stated that Member States had the power to regulate broadcasters falling under their jurisdiction (Article 2). Confronted with strategies of circumvention seeking to exploit this indeterminacy, the Court applied the *Van Binsbergen* principle in *Veronica* and *TV10*:

> A Member State may regard as a domestic broadcaster a radio and television organization which establishes itself in another Member State in order to provide services there which are intended for the first State's territory, since the aim of that measure is to prevent organizations which establish themselves in another Member State from being able, by exercising the freedoms guaranteed by the Treaty, wrongfully to avoid obligations under national law, in this case those designed to ensure the pluralist and non-commercial content of programmes.[98]

Moreover, the Court explicitly acknowledged the anti-abuse effect of this centre of gravity requirement in the subsequent *Commission v United Kingdom*:

> The Commission has stated … that Member States may find a solution to the problem of double control, without the necessity of further legislation, by interpreting the criterion of establishment as referring to the place in which a broadcaster has the centre of its activities, in particular the place where decisions concerning programme policy are taken and the programmes to be broadcast are finally put together.
>
> The United Kingdom also contends that the criterion of establishment involves a risk of abuse in that a broadcaster could move its seat to another Member State in order to avoid application of the legislation of a Member State.
>
> As to that, the interpretation of the criterion of establishment advocated by the Commission … would considerably reduce the risk of abuse pointed out by the United Kingdom.[99]

In the same sense, AG Lenz observed in his Opinion:

> Finally, it is necessary to consider the defendant's objection that the Commission's favoured criterion creates a danger of abuse. … [T]he criterion advocated by the Commission for determining the competent Member State is also more appropriate inasmuch as it focuses on a relatively stable factor that cannot easily be altered. A transfer

[96] See D Doukas, 'Free Movement of Broadcasting Services and Abuse of Law' in de la Feria and Vogenauer (n 1); R de la Feria, 'Prohibition of Abuse of (Community) Law: the Creation of a New General Principle of EC Law through Tax' (2008) 45 *Common Market Law Review* 395, 400–03; J Harrison and L Woods, *European Broadcasting Law and Policy* (Cambridge, Cambridge University Press, 2007); LH Hansen, 'The Development of the Circumvention Principle in the Area of Broadcasting' (1998) 25 *Legal Issues of European Integration* 111.

[97] Directive 89/552/EEC of the European Parliament and of the Council of 3 October 1989 on the coordination of certain provisions laid down by law, regulation or administrative action in Member States concerning the provision of audiovisual media services (Audiovisual Media Services Directive) [1989] OJ L298/23.

[98] Case C-23/93 *TV10* [1994] ECR I-4795, para 21; see also Case C-148/91 *Veronica* [1993] ECR I-487, 12–13.

[99] Case C-222/94 *Commission v United Kingdom* [1996] ECR I-4025, paras 58–60.

> of establishment in the above sense requires some trouble and effort; in contrast, a change of the Member State from which transmissions are effected is, in the present state of technology, possible in a short space of time without any great expense.[100]

Yet in both *Commission v United Kingdom* and *VT4*, the Court toned down the *Van Binsbergen* principle, centred on the destination of the services provided, in favour of a centre of gravity approach focusing on the main place of establishment:

> Where a television broadcaster has more than one establishment, the competent Member State is the State in which the broadcaster has the centre of its activities. It is therefore for the national court to determine, applying that criteria, which Member State has jurisdiction over VT4's activities, taking into account in particular the place where decisions concerning programme policy are taken and the programmes to be broadcast are finally put together.
>
> [T]he mere fact that all the broadcasts and advertisements are aimed exclusively at the Flemish public does not, as VTM claims, demonstrate that VT4 cannot be regarded as being established in the United Kingdom. The Treaty does not prohibit an undertaking from exercising the freedom to provide services if it does not offer services in the Member State in which it is established.[101]

The *Van Binsbergen* principle, as applied in *Veronica* and *TV10*, formed a centre of gravity focusing on the 'output' of the economic activity, namely the destination of the services provided. This approach was explicitly rejected in *VT4* (para 24), and replaced by a criterion placing emphasis on the 'input' of the economic activity, namely the factors of production (para 19). This evolution is not neutral in terms of gravity, for factors of production ('input') can nowadays be easily moved to another jurisdiction, as shall be explained in the next subsection.

In order to reduce the room for abusive practices stressed by this case law, the Union legislature modified the First Broadcasting Directive 89/552 in 1997[102] and 2007,[103] to eventually recast its content in 2010.[104] Directive 97/36/EC transposed the real seat theory into the current Article 2 of Directive 2010/13/EU, which determines the jurisdiction of Member States by reference to the place of

[100] AG Lenz, Case C-222/94 *Commission v United Kingdom* [1996] ECR I-4025, paras 71 and 73.

[101] Case C-56/96 *VT4* [1997] ECR I-3143, paras 19 and 22; see also Case C-222/94 *Commission v United Kingdom* [1996] ECR I-4025, para 58–60.

[102] Directive 97/36/EC of the European Parliament and of the Council of 30 June 1997 amending Council Directive 89/552/EEC on the coordination of certain provisions laid down by law, regulation or administrative action in Member States concerning the pursuit of television broadcasting activities [1997] OJ L202/60.

[103] Directive 2007/65/EC of the European Parliament and of the Council of 11 December 2007 amending Council Directive 89/552/EEC on the coordination of certain provisions laid down by law, regulation or administrative action in Member States concerning the pursuit of television broadcasting activities [2007] OJ L332/27.

[104] Directive 2010/13/EU of the European Parliament and of the Council of 10 March 2010 on the coordination of certain provisions laid down by law, regulation or administrative action in Member States concerning the provision of audiovisual media services (Audiovisual Media Services Directive) [2010] OJ L95/1.

establishment of broadcasters.[105] In turn, the place of establishment is defined in regard of a combination of factors of production, including the location of the head office, the place where editorial decisions are taken and the location of the workforce. On the other hand, Directive 2007/65/EC introduced a specific anti-abuse measure—the current Article 4 of Directive 2010/13/EU—reflecting the *Van Binsbergen* principle.[106] In sum, Article 2 of Directive 2010/13/EU forms an 'input' centre of gravity (as in *Commission v United Kingdom* and *VT4*), and Article 4 an 'output' centre of gravity (in accordance with *Veronica* and *TV10*).

In *Fitzwilliam* and *Plum*, two rulings issued in 2000, the Court established a centre of gravity with regard to national schemes of social security applicable to posted workers.[107] Article 14(1)(a) of Regulation 1408/71[108] provides that an undertaking posting workers to another Member State for less than 12 months remains subject to the social security of the Member State in which it is established (home regulation).[109] Just as the first directives on financial and broadcasting services, this legal regime remained silent regarding the possibility of artificial establishment in Member States imposing low social contributions, followed by the posting of workers to Member States imposing high social contributions (*Plum*, para 7). The Court effectively prevented such constructions by imposing a centre of gravity approach:

> [I]t is clear ... from the purpose of Article 14(1)(a) ... that only an undertaking which habitually carries on significant activities in the Member State in which it is established may be allowed the benefit of the advantage afforded by the exception provided for by that provision.
>
> [Relevant criteria] include the place where the undertaking has its seat and administration, the number of administrative staff working in the Member State in which it is established and in the other Member State, the place where posted workers are recruited and the place where the majority of contracts with clients are concluded, the law applicable to the employment contracts concluded by the undertaking with its workers, on the one hand, and with its clients, on the other hand, and the turnover during an appropriately typical period in each Member State concerned. That list cannot be exhaustive; the choice of criteria must be adapted to each specific case.[110]

With regard to labour law applicable to posted workers, the *Laval*-line of case law[111] famously precluded host States from applying their domestic laws to posted

[105] See Directive 97/36 rec 10–11.

[106] See Directive 2007/65 rec 32–33; Directive 2010/13 rec 40–43.

[107] Case C-202/97 *Fitzwilliam* [2000] ECR I-883, paras 26–43; Case C-404/98 *Plum* [2000] ECR I-9379, paras 21–23; see Gestri (n 3) 76–81.

[108] Regulation (EEC) 1408/71 of the Council of 14 June 1971 on the application of social security schemes to employed persons and their families moving within the Community [1971] OJ L149/2.

[109] See ch 7 section IV.A.

[110] Case C-202/97 *Fitzwilliam* [2000] ECR I-883, 40 and 43.

[111] Case C-341/05 *Laval* [2007] ECR I-11767; Case C-346/06 *Rüffert* [2008] ECR I-1989; Case C-319/06 *Commission v Luxembourg* [2008] ECR I-4323. See ch 8 section IV.

workers for matters falling outside the scope of Article 3(1) of Directive 96/71.[112] Arguably, this decision reversed the well-established *Rush Portuguesa*-line case of law, in which the Court had judged that host States could 'extend' their labour law to any person who is employed, even temporarily, within their territory.[113] The *Laval* ruling triggered an intense debate among Union institutions, academics and social partners, which led the Commission to propose a directive on the enforcement of Directive 96/71 in 2012.[114] The peculiarity of the Commission's proposal lies in Article 3, entitled 'Preventing abuse and circumvention', which imports the centre of gravity approach already applied for posted workers in the area of social security (Regulation 1408/71, interpreted by *Fitzwilliam*) into the area of labour law (Directive 96/71, interpreted by *Laval*). If adopted, this provision would draw a list of factual elements that competent authorities would take into account to identify the Member State in which the posting undertaking is established (eg registered office, administration, payment of taxes, recruitment of workers, substantial business activity, turnover) and to determine whether the worker is temporarily 'posted' in a Member State other than the one in which he normally works (eg limited duration of posting, expected return to the State of origin, reimbursement of travel and accommodation costs, repetition of posting).

More generally, it should be underlined that the freedom of establishment is frequently interpreted as entailing an 'in-built' centre of gravity. As the Court's classical statement goes:

> [T]he concept of establishment within the meaning of [the Treaty provisions on freedom of establishment] involves the actual pursuit of an economic activity through a fixed establishment in another Member State for an indefinite period.[115]

The criterion of 'actual pursuit of an economic activity', already proposed by AG Darmon in *Daily Mail*,[116] tends to exclude artificial incorporations realised for the sole purpose of benefiting from a more favourable legislation; as Sørensen puts it: 'Thus, the concept of establishment is interpreted so as to limit the risk of abuse'.[117]

[112] Directive 96/71/EC of the European Parliament and of the Council of 16 December 1996 concerning the posting of workers in the framework of the provision of services [1996] OJ L18/1.

[113] Case C-113/89 *Rush Portuguesa* [1990] ECR I-1417, para 18; see also Joined Cases C-49/98, C-50/98, C-52/98 to C-54/98 and C-68/98 to C-71/98 *Finalarte and Others* [2001] ECR I-7831; Joined Cases C-369/96 and C-376/96 *Arblade and Others* [1999] ECR I-8453.

[114] Commission (EC), 'Proposal for a Directive of the European Parliament and of the Council on the enforcement of Directive 96/71/EC concerning the posting of workers in the framework of the provision of services' COM (2012) 131 final, 21 March 2012.

[115] Case C-221/89 *Factortame II* [1991] ECR I-3905, para 20; see also Case C-438/05 *Viking* [2007] ECR I-10779, para 70; Case C-196/04 *Cadbury Schweppes* [2006] ECR I-7995, para 54; Case C-411/03 *SEVIC Systems* [2005] ECR I-10805, para 18; Case C-246/89 *Commission v United Kingdom* [1991] ECR I-4585, para 21.

[116] AG Darmon, Case 81/87 *Daily Mail* [1988] ECR 5483, para 3:

> Establishment 'means integration into a national economy'. Thus, it is not contested that establishment within the meaning of the Treaty involves two factors: physical location and the exercise of an economic activity, both, if not on a permanent basis, least on a durable one.

[117] Sørensen (n 3) 428; see also V Edwards and P Farmer, 'The Concept of Abuse in the Freedom of Establishment of Companies: a Case of Double Standards?' in FG Jacobs et al (eds), *Continuity and*

This approach was also followed by the Council in the General Programme for the abolition of restrictions on the freedom of establishment, which required undertakings to have a 'real and continuous link with the economy of a Member State' in order to enjoy freedom of establishment.[118]

This centre of gravity approach to the notion of establishment is far from being uniformly applied by Union institutions as stressed by the *Centros*-line of case law.[119] However, *Centros* is itself questioned by the subsequent *VALE* judgment issued by the Grand Chamber of the Court. In *VALE*, which concerned the cross-border transformation of Italian company into a Hungarian company, the Court indeed held that the notion of establishment presupposed genuine economic activity in the host State:

> As regards the existence of a restriction on the freedom of establishment, the Court notes that the concept of establishment within the meaning of the Treaty provisions on the freedom of establishment involves the actual pursuit of an economic activity through a fixed establishment in the host Member State for an indefinite period. Consequently, it presupposes actual establishment of the company concerned in that State and the pursuit of genuine economic activity there (Case C-196/04 *Cadbury Schweppes and Cadbury Schweppes Overseas* [2006] ECR I-7995, paragraph 54 and the case-law cited).
>
> In the present case, there has been nothing to suggest in the procedure before the Court that the activities of VALE Építési will be restricted to Italy and that the company will not actually seek to establish itself in Hungary, although that is a matter to be determined by the referring court.[120]

In a sense, the Court's judgment in *Cadbury Schweppes* stands at the intersection between formal doctrine of abuse and 'in-built' centre of gravity approach. The Court first paraphrased its ruling *Factortame II* to infer the requirement of genuine economic activity from the objective of the freedom of establishment (paras 52–55), and subsequently merged this requirement with the prohibition of abusive practices (paras 63–69). As noted by Vella:

> If the objective is that identified in Cadbury Schweppes, namely allowing a 'Community national to participate, on a stable and continuing basis, in the economic life of a Member State other than his State of origin', then the setting up of wholly artificial

Change in EU Law: Essays in Honour of Sir Francis Jacobs (Oxford, Oxford University Press, 2007) 219; P Wattel, 'Circumvention of National Law; Abuse of Community Law?' (1995) 32 *Common Market Law Review* 1257, 1266; L Neville Brown, 'Is there a General Principle of Abuse of Rights in European Community Law?' in D Curtin et al (eds), *Institutional Dynamics of European Integration—Essays in Honour of Henry G. Schermers*, vol II (Dordrecht, M Nijhoff, 1994) 517.

[118] Council (EC), 'General Programme for the abolition of restrictions on freedom of establishment' (Resolution), 18 December 1961, C2/36, Title I; see Ringe (n 2) 112; D Triantafyllou, 'L'interdiction des abus de droit en tant que principe général du droit communautaire' (2002) 38 *Cahiers de Droit Européen* 611, 629.

[119] See inter alia Case C-212/97 *Centros* [1999] ECR I-1459, para 30; de la Feria, 'Prohibition of Abuse of (Community) Law' (n 96) 405.

[120] Case C-378/10 *VALE Építési* [2012] ECR I-0000, paras 34–35.

establishments which do not participate in the economic life of the Member State must surely constitute an abuse of that freedom.[121]

In that regard, Lyal considered it more appropriate to interpret the notion of 'establishment' as incorporating a centre of gravity approach, instead of having recourse to the notion of 'abuse':

> [T]he objective pursued by the freedom of establishment is to allow a business to be set up and carried on in another Member State, as part of economic life in that second Member State. In essence, that means the actual pursuit of an economic activity there. An artificial construction, by contrast, is one which creates the form of a business establishment without its substance, a simulacrum which does not represent the economic reality. This is nothing more than an interpretation of the expression 'establishment'. One might therefore ask what added value is to be found in the use of the expression 'abuse of law' here.[122]

A variant of this anti-abuse interpretation of establishment consists in identifying a 'fixed' or 'permanent establishment', namely a portion of a business presenting a genuine connection with the territory of one Member State. This technique is commonly used in tax law to allocate tax jurisdiction among States: for instance, Article 5 of the OECD Model Tax Convention defines permanent establishment as 'a fixed place of business through which the business of an enterprise is wholly or partly carried on'.[123] Furthermore, under Article 43 of VAT Directive 2006/112, services are taxed by the State in which the supplier has established its business or has a fixed establishment from which the service is supplied. As noticed by Genschel, the volume of tax avoidance under an origin-based VAT regime depends on whether 'origin' is interpreted as real seat or place of incorporation.[124] The Court interpreted this notion of fixed establishment in *Planzer*, *DFDS* and *Berkholz*;[125] in all three cases, taxpayers sought to manipulate their place of establishment in order to obtain a tax benefit.[126] The Court fought those artificial establishments by stressing the need for taking account of the economic reality (*Planzer*, para 43), and by affixing a centre of gravity onto the notion of fixed establishment:

> [T]he term fixed establishment implies a minimum degree of stability derived from the permanent presence of both the human and technical resources necessary for the

[121] J Vella, 'Sparking Regulatory Competition in European Company Law: A Response' in de la Feria and Vogenauer (n 1) 131.

[122] R Lyal, 'Cadbury Schweppes and Abuse: Comments' in de la Feria and Vogenauer (n 1) 432.

[123] OECD, 'OECD Model Tax Convention on Income and on Capital 2010', 22 July 2010, available at http://dx.doi.org/10.1787/9789264175181-en.

[124] P Genschel, 'Why no Mutual Recognition of VAT? Regulation, Taxation and the Integration of the EU's Internal Market for Goods' (2007) 14 *Journal of European Public Policy* 743, 759 fn 6.

[125] Case C-73/06 *Planzer* [2007] ECR I-5655, paras 52–57; Case C-260/95 *DFDS* [1997] ECR I-1005, paras 17–24; Case 168/84 *Berkholz* [1985] ECR 2251, paras 17–18.

[126] Planzer claimed to be established in Luxembourg, rather than Switzerland, in order to obtain VAT refunds. DFDS claimed to be established in Denmark, rather than in the United Kingdom, in order to benefit from a full VAT exemption (para 23). Berkholz claimed to have a fixed establishment on ferry boats plying between Germany and Denmark, rather than an establishment in Germany, in order to benefit from a partial VAT exemption.

> provision of given services. It thus requires a sufficient degree of permanence and a structure adequate, in terms of human and technical resources, to supply the services in question on an independent basis.[127]

Centre of gravity tests are commonly used in private international law *stricto sensu* to prevent undesirable choices of law, and Union private international law is no exception.[128] In the *Koelzsch* case, the Court interpreted Article 6 of the Rome Convention,[129] which lays down special conflict rules relating to individual contracts of employment. Having due regard to its protective function, the Court ruled that workers should be subject to the law of their State of employment, before construing this criterion as a centre of gravity:

> In so far as the objective of Article 6 of the Rome Convention is to guarantee adequate protection for the employee, that provision must be understood as guaranteeing the applicability of the law of the State in which he carries out his working activities rather than that of the State in which the employer is established.
>
> [W]here work is carried out in more than one Member State, the criterion of the country in which the work is habitually carried out must be given a broad interpretation and be understood as referring to the place in which or from which the employee actually carries out his working activities and, in the absence of a centre of activities, to the place where he carries out the majority of his activities.[130]

In the field of insolvency proceedings, Council Regulation 1346/2000 is rather explicit on the need to prevent forum shopping, namely choices of forum made by insolvent debtors setting up artificial cross-border movements:

> It is necessary for the proper functioning of the internal market to avoid incentives for the parties to transfer assets or judicial proceedings from one Member State to another, seeking to obtain a more favourable legal position (forum shopping).[131]

To that end, the international jurisdiction in matters of insolvency proceedings is based on the location of the debtor's centre of main interests or 'COMI' (Article 3), yet another variant of centre of gravity.[132] In *Interedil*, the Court commented on the notion of COMI:

> The presumption in the second sentence of Article 3(1) of the Regulation may be rebutted, however, where, from the viewpoint of third parties, the place in which a company's central administration is located is not the same as that of its registered office. …

[127] Case C-73/06 *Planzer* [2007] ECR I-5655, para 54; Case C-260/95 *DFDS* [1997] ECR I-1005, para 20; Case 168/84 *Berkholz* [1985] ECR 2251, para 18.

[128] For a general overview, see Gestri (n 3) 157–82.

[129] Rome Convention on the law applicable to contractual obligations (adopted 19 June 1980, entered into force 1 April 1991) 1605 UNTS 59.

[130] Case C-29/10 *Koelzsch* [2011] ECR I-1595, paras 42 and 45.

[131] Council Regulation (EC) 1346/2000 of 29 May 2000 on Insolvency Proceedings [2000] OJ L160/1 rec 4.

[132] See M Lauterfeld, '"Centros" and the EC Regulation on Insolvency Proceedings' (2001) 12 *European Business Law Review* 79, 83, equating the COMI approach with the real seat theory.

> The factors to be taken into account include, in particular, all the places in which the debtor company pursues economic activities and all those in which it holds assets, in so far as those places are ascertainable by third parties. …
>
> [T]he presence of company assets and the existence of contracts for the financial exploitation of those assets in a Member State other than that in which the registered office is situated cannot be regarded as sufficient factors to rebut the presumption laid down by the European Union legislature unless a comprehensive assessment of all the relevant factors makes it possible to establish, in a manner that is ascertainable by third parties, that the company's actual centre of management and supervision and of the management of its interests is located in that other Member State.[133]

The function of this centre of gravity is to restrict the choice of insolvency law, which is determined by the location of the COMI (Article 4):

> Recital 4 of the Regulation defines forum shopping as the phenomenon that debtors 'transfer assets or judicial proceedings from one Member State to another, seeking to obtain a more favourable legal position'. As under the Regulation both the forum and the applicable law (the lex forum concursus) depend on the 'Centre of Main Interests' (COMI), a successful forum shopping in the context of insolvency law will depend upon the debtor's ability to move this very COMI from one into another jurisdiction.[134]

This anti-abuse function of the COMI—interpreted by the Court as excluding letterbox companies 'not carrying out any business in the territory of the Member State in which their registered office is situated' (*Eurofood*, para 35)[135]—is broadly acknowledged in the scholarship,[136] although not always approved.[137]

ii. 'Output' versus 'Input' Centre of Gravity

As evoked earlier, a shift has occurred in the orientation of centre of gravity tests applied by the Court to undertakings, from the output to the input of economic activities, with far-reaching consequences on their effectiveness. Doukas noted this evolution in the broadcasting case law, from *TV10* to *VT4*, and underlined that this shift implied a far milder approach to abuses of law.[138]

The first version of the centre of gravity test focused on the 'output' of economic activities, namely the location of the recipients of goods and services provided: the *Van Binsbergen* principle, in that regard, targeted activities originating in the Member State of establishment, but 'entirely or principally directed towards' the territory of another Member State (*Van Binsbergen*, para 13;

[133] Case C-396/09 *Interedil* [2011] ECR I-9915, paras 51–53.

[134] W-G Ringe, 'Forum Shopping under the EU Insolvency Regulation', Oxford Legal Studies Research Paper, no 33/2008 (August 2008), available at http://ssrn.com/abstract=1209822, 3.

[135] Case C-341/04 *Eurofood IFSC* [2006] ECR I-3813, paras 35–36; see also Case C-339/07 *Seagon* [2009] ECR I-767, paras 23–24; Case C-1/04 *Staubitz-Schreiber* [2006] ECR I-701, para 25.

[136] Eidenmüller, 'Abuse of Law in the Context of European Insolvency Law' (n 52); J Armour, 'Abuse of European Insolvency Law? A Discussion' in de la Feria and Vogenauer (n 1).

[137] See Ringe, 'Forum Shopping under the EU Insolvency Regulation' (n 134).

[138] Doukas, 'Free Movement of Broadcasting Services and Abuse of Law' (n 96) 78.

Veronica, paras 12–13; *TV10*, paras 20–21).[139] By contrast, the *VT4* ruling explicitly dismissed this 'output' approach, by setting aside the obligation to provide goods and services in the Member State of establishment (*VT4*, para 22).[140] Instead, undertakings must abide by the laws of the Member State in which their main factors of production are located, ie their 'input' centre of gravity (*VT4*, para 19). The same evolution can be identified within the formal doctrine of abuse: in an effort to translate the doctrine into workable terms in *Cadbury Schweppes*, the Court indeed mentioned factors of production such as premises, staff and equipment (*Cadbury*, para 67).[141]

However, this shift from 'output' (patterns of sales) to 'input' (factors of production) centre of gravity is not neutral in a context of globalisation marked by the exponential increase of mobility, and in particular the mobility of factors of production. Indeed, the new communication technologies have dramatically decreased the costs of moving a company's factors of production to another jurisdiction.[142] As early as in 1988, AG Darmon envisioned how 'telephone, telex and telecopier' would enable administrators to manage a company from anywhere in the world.[143] Since then, the Internet has become a basic facility within industrialised societies, whereas the overall level of protectionism has substantially decreased under the WTO's pressure. This combination of modern communication technologies and global economic integration has exponentially reduced the cost of moving production factors to another jurisdiction, even if it includes the dismantling and reassembling of entire factories.[144] As a consequence, input centres of gravity have lost most of their gravity, since they seek to locate the hub of eminently volatile factors of production. By way of illustration, the Court explicitly acknowledged the inefficiency of input centres of gravity in *DFDS*:

> Systematic reliance on the place where the supplier has established his business could in fact lead to distortions of competition, in that it might encourage undertakings trading in one Member State to establish their businesses, in order to avoid taxation, in another Member State which has availed itself of the possibility of maintaining the VAT exemption for the services in question.[145]

[139] Manifestations of the *Van Binsbergen* principle can still be found in the secondary legislation: see eg art 4 of Directive 2010/13 on audiovisual media services; rec 10 and art 11(2) of Directive 2006/48 on credit institutions.

[140] See also Case C-46/08 *Carmen Media Group* [2010] ECR I-8149, para 43.

[141] P Schammo, 'Arbitrage and Abuse of Rights in the EC Legal System' (2008) 14 *European Law Journal* 351, 375: 'The ECJ focused on the means by which an economic activity is exercised. Thus, it referred to the existence of premises, staff and equipment'.

[142] See ch 10 section II.

[143] AG Darmon, Case 81/87 *Daily Mail* [1988] ECR 5483, para 7; see also AG Léger, Case C-196/04 *Cadbury Schweppes* [2006] ECR I-7995, para 138; AG Lenz, Case C-222/94 *Commission v United Kingdom* [1996] ECR I-4025, para 71–73.

[144] This exponential increase of mobility is manifest in the broadcasting sector, where satellite technology permits broadcasting from literally anywhere in the world: see Doukas (n 96) 63; Hansen, 'The Development of the Circumvention Principle in the Area of Broadcasting' (n 96) 113.

[145] Case C-260/95 *DFDS* [1997] ECR I-1005, para 23.

By contrast, output centres of gravity have retained their gravity, for they focus on patterns of sales: on the one hand, consumers remain relatively immobile; on the other, business are not likely to structure their market shares solely in order to benefit from a more favourable law. Indeed, under an output centre of gravity, undertakings are subject to the law of the country in which they realise most of their turnover, a criterion endorsed by the Court in its *Fitzwilliam* ruling: '[relevant criteria] include the turnover during an appropriately typical period in each Member State concerned' (para 43). In order to be subject to the law of another country, businesses would have to realise most of their turnover there, by acquiring market shares in that country and/or by foregoing market shares in other jurisdictions. As a consequence, artificial cross-border movements would become unlikely, for they would require an upheaval in the undertaking's marketing strategy. This explains why output centres of gravity have retained their 'gravity', namely their capacity to restrict choices of law, by contrast with input centres of gravity.

In sum, the shift from output to input centres of gravity, combined with the exponential increase of mobility, drastically reduces the gravity of centre of gravity tests, which as a result increasingly fail to restrict choices of law. This shift is problematic since the very purpose of centre of gravity tests is to constrain the choice of applicable law; de Sousa, for instance, stressed the existential threat posed by Internet to the real seat theory—when viewed as an input centre of gravity:

> In the context of increasingly transnational corporations with managers living in different States and communicating via Internet and video-conference, a transfer of the centre of management of the company to another State (without being fictitious or a sham) becomes more and more feasible in light of the current telecommunications facilities. The real seat theory progressively loses its sense in a world where the Internet has eroded the traditional geographical borders between States.[146]

In that context, it should not come as a surprise that the Court adamantly denied any relevance to the absence of economic activities in the State of incorporation (output centre of gravity) in the *Centros*-line of case law, in which it granted free choice of company law: 'As regards abuse of the law, it follows from Centros that the mere fact that a company does not carry on any activity in the State of formation cannot constitute such abuse'.[147]

However, in stark contrast with the *Centros* ruling, it must be highlighted that the use of output centre of gravity as 'connecting factor' is nothing extraordinary in Union law. In the seminal *Woodpulp* judgment, the Court famously relied on the 'effects doctrine' to justify the extraterritorial application of Union competition law.

[146] AF de Sousa, 'Company's Cross-border Transfer of Seat in the EU after Cartesio', Jean Monnet Working Paper, no 07/09, available at www.JeanMonnetProgram.org, 8.

[147] Case C-167/01 *Inspire Art* [2003] ECR I-10155, para 120; see also Case C-212/97 *Centros* [1999] ECR I-1459, para 29.

The *Woodpulp* case concerned a cartel formed by woodpulp suppliers established outside the Union, which disputed the applicability of Union law by arguing that their anticompetitive conduct had been adopted outside the Union. The Court rejected the argument by establishing the effects doctrine, with the explicit purpose of precluding strategies of avoidance of Union competition law, in an anticipated echo to the doctrine of abuse:

> It should be observed that an infringement of Article [101 TFEU], such as the conclusion of an agreement which has had the effect of restricting competition within the common market, consists of conduct made up of two elements, the formation of the agreement, decision or concerted practice and the implementation thereof. If the applicability of prohibitions laid down under competition law were made to depend on the place where the agreement, decision or concerted practice was formed, the result would obviously be to give undertakings an easy means of evading those prohibitions. The decisive factor is therefore the place where it is implemented.[148]

In essence, Union law applies when the effects[149] of anticompetitive conducts are felt within the Union, irrespective of the places where participating businesses are established or where the concerted practice is actually decided.[150] The rationale underpinning this doctrine is to prevent businesses from making choices of law that would exclude Union competition law, by establishing themselves outside the Union territory.

A similar output centre of gravity, based on the place where the effects of an activity are felt, is established by Article 15(1)(c) of Regulation 44/2001 on jurisdiction and the recognition and enforcement of judgments in civil and commercial matters (Brussels I),[151] which is located in section 4 on jurisdiction over consumer contracts. In order to protect consumers, Article 16 entitles them to decide whether to bring proceedings in the State in which they reside or in the State in which the other party is domiciled. Under Article 15(1)(c), this choice is offered whenever the consumer contract has been concluded with a person who 'pursues commercial or professional activities in the Member State of the consumer's domicile' or, by any means, 'directs such activities to that Member State', and the contract falls within the scope of such activities. In the cases *Pammer*, *Mühlleitner* and *Emrek*, the Court has been asked to interpret the expression 'directs such activities to that Member State', in particular in the case of websites

[148] Joined Cases C-89/85, C-104/85, C-114/85, C-116/85, C-117/85 and C-125/85 to C-129/85 *Ahlström Osakeyhtiö and Others v Commission (Woodpulp)* [1993] ECR I-1307, para 16.

[149] For a comparison with the US effects doctrine, see R Whish and D Bailey, *Competition Law*, 7th edn (Oxford, Oxford University Press, 2012) ch 12.

[150] Commission (EC), 'Guidelines on the effect on trade concept contained in Articles 81 and 82 of the Treaty' (Notice), 27 April 2004, C101/81, no 100 ff.

[151] Council Regulation (EC) 44/2001 of 22 December 2000 on jurisdiction and the recognition and enforcement of judgments in civil and commercial matters [2001] OJ L12/1 (Brussels I).

promoting goods and services and accessed by consumers domiciled in other Member States than that of the seller.[152]

Intellectual property law is another field in which the Court has developed output centres of gravity to preclude choices of law, having due regard to the mobility offered by modern communication technologies. The *L'Oréal* case concerned the protection of trade marks in relation to offers for sale of L'Oréal products originating outside of the Union territory, but which were accessible within the Union through an online marketplace run by eBay.[153] As with the plaintiffs in the *Woodpulp* case, eBay disputed the applicability of Union trade mark law to goods located in a third country. AG Jääskinen rebutted the argument by referring to the effects doctrine established in the *Woodpulp* judgment:

> [I]n the light of the effects doctrine applied in particular in the field of EU competition law, it can be stated that behaviour outside the territory of the Union but directly producing legally relevant effects on the subject-matter of EU legislation cannot escape the application of EU rules merely because the acts causing such effects take place outside the Union territory.
>
> [I]f not only the objective effect but also the subjective intent of the persons concerned is to produce such effects in the EU, the evaluation has to be different. Otherwise activities targeting EU markets could escape the application of EU rules concerning, for example, consumer protection, protection of intellectual property rights, unfair competition and product safety by merely situating the activity or the site of the company responsible for the activity in a third country. Therefore, trade mark protection cannot be limited to cases where the goods in question are put on the market in the EU.[154]

The Court followed the Advocate General, pointing out again the need to preclude artificial choices of law, consisting in establishing businesses outside the Union to exclude the application of Union law:

> As the Advocate General observed at point 127 of his Opinion and as the Commission pointed out in its written observations, the effectiveness of those rules would be undermined if they were not to apply to the use, in an Internet offer for sale or advertisement targeted at consumers within the EU, of a sign identical with or similar to a trade mark registered in the EU merely because the third party behind that offer or advertisement is established in a third State, because the server of the Internet site used by the third party is located in such a State or because the product that is the subject of the offer or the advertisement is located in a third State.[155]

If *Woodpulp* and *L'Oréal* concerned the application of European Union rules to businesses established in third countries, the Court applied the same reasoning to Union businesses seeking to circumvent national copyright laws. The *Stichting*

[152] Joined Cases C-585/08 and C-144/09 *Pammer and Hotel Alpenhof* [2010] ECR I-12527; Case C-190/11 *Mühlleitner* [2012] ECR I-0000; AG Cruz Villalón, Case C-218/12 *Emrek* [2013] ECR I-0000.

[153] Case C-324/09 *L'Oréal* [2011] ECR I-6011.

[154] AG Jääskinen, Case C-324/09 *L'Oréal* [2011] ECR I-6011, paras 125 and 127.

[155] Case C-324/09 *L'Oréal* [2011] ECR I-6011, para 63.

de Thuiskopie case concerned a Germany company (Opus) selling blank media to Netherlands consumers by means of Dutch-language websites. Opus contested its liability for private copying levy in the Netherlands, arguing that it could not be regarded as the importer of the blank media. As in *L'Oréal*, the Court considered that behaviour aimed at the territory of a Member State falls within the reach of intellectual property law in that Member State, irrespective of the actual location of that behaviour or the place of establishment of its author. As a consequence, the Court ruled that:

> [I]t is for the Member State which has introduced a system of private copying levies chargeable to the manufacturer or importer of media for reproduction of protected works, and on the territory of which the harm caused to authors by the use for private purposes of their work by purchasers who reside there occurs, to ensure that those authors actually receive the fair compensation intended to compensate them for that harm. In that regard, the mere fact that the commercial seller of reproduction equipment, devices and media is established in a Member State other than that in which the purchasers reside has no bearing on that obligation to achieve a certain result.[156]

A similar strategy was submitted to the Court in the *Donner* case: an Italian company (Dimensione) sold well-known pieces of furniture (eg Bauhaus) to German customers by means of advertisements and supplements in German newspapers, direct publicity letters and a German-language website.[157] Those pieces of furniture were protected under German copyright law, but not under Italian copyright law. The transport company owned by Titus Donner had delivered several pieces of furniture to German customers; as a consequence, he was convicted in Germany of aiding and abetting the prohibited commercial exploitation of copyright-protected works. In his Opinion, AG Jääskinen underlined the regulatory challenge posed by modern communication technologies (para 7), evoked above: the Internet increases the mobility of factors of production, and facilitates attempts to circumvent unfavourable national law by moving the place of establishment. As a matter of fact, in both *Donner* and *Stichting de Thuiskopie*, contractual arrangements were designed to circumvent copyright protection in the Member State in which goods were eventually used (para 37). In that context, businesses should be precluded from choosing the law applicable to their activity, lest enabling them to evade the rights of copyright holders (para 51). To that end, the Advocate General proposed an interpretation of the act of 'distribution', whose location determines the applicable national law, in accordance with the effects doctrine established in *L'Oréal* and *Stichting de Thuiskopie*:

> In the situation of cross border distance selling arrangements, the assessment of whether copies are made available to the public in the Member State where enforcement of copyright is sought must be based on the criteria elaborated by the Court in L'Oréal and Others. If a seller targets consumers in a given Member State and creates or makes

[156] Case C-462/09 *Stichting de Thuiskopie* [2011] ECR I-5331, para 41.
[157] Case C-5/11 *Donner* [2012] ECR I-0000.

> available to them a specific delivery arrangement and method of payment that enables consumers to purchase copies of copyright protected works in that Member State, then there is distribution by sale in that Member State.[158]

The Court followed the Advocate General's Opinion, effectively preventing artificial relocations of businesses in order to escape national copyright law:

> [A] trader who directs his advertising at members of the public residing in a given Member State and creates or makes available to them a specific delivery system and payment method, or allows a third party to do so, thereby enabling those members of the public to receive delivery of copies of works protected by copyright in that same Member State, makes, in the Member State where the delivery takes place, a 'distribution to the public' under Article 4(1) of Directive 2001/29.[159]

To sum up, the crucial interest of the case law on the effects doctrine (*Woodpulp*, *L'Oréal*, *Stichting de Thuiskopie*, *Donner*) lies in its explicit rationale, namely the impossibility, in the era of Internet, to prevent undesirable choices of law with a connecting factor based on the place of establishment (input centre of gravity). As explained earlier, input centres of gravity have lost most of their gravity with the emergence of modern communication technologies, for they seek to locate factors of production that have become eminently volatile. In all those cases, the Court discarded the place of establishment as connecting factor, and explicitly justified its decision by the need to preclude businesses from freely electing their preferred law by moving their place of establishment.

As a consequence, the case law on the effects doctrine questions solutions reached by the Court in cases such as *VT4*, in which the Court formally expressed its intent to preclude artificial choices of law, and yet decided that businesses should be regulated by the Member State in which they are established.[160] As shown throughout the present section, centre of gravity approaches must nowadays be grounded on the destination of business activities (output centre of gravity), as with the effects doctrine, and not on the place of establishment (input centre of gravity).

B. Centre of Gravity Approaches for Natural Persons (Habitual Residence and Genuine Integration Requirements)

The second category of centre of gravity approach applies to natural persons. In the context of Union law, centres of gravity for natural persons take the form of requirements of habitual residence and genuine integration.

[158] AG Jääskinen, Case C-5/11 *Donner* [2012] ECR I-0000, para 55.
[159] Case C-5/11 *Donner* [2012] ECR I-0000, para 30.
[160] See n 101 and accompanying text.

i. 'Habitual Residence' Requirements

Requirements of habitual residence can be identified in many areas of Union law. In relation to the mutual recognition of driving licences, Article 9 of Council Directive 91/439/EEC[161] provides for the following definition of the concept of 'habitual residence':

> Normal residence means the place where a person usually lives, that is for at least 185 days in each calendar year, because of personal and occupational ties, or, in the case of a person with no occupational ties because of personal ties which show close links between that person and the place where he is living.
>
> However, the normal residence of a person whose occupational ties are in a different place from his personal ties and who consequently lives in turn in different places situated in two or more Member States shall be regarded as being the place of his personal ties, provided that such person returns there regularly

Directive 91/439 determines the jurisdiction of Member States to issue a driving licence on the basis of the normal residence of Union citizens. The function explicitly assigned to the normal residence requirement is to prevent Union citizens from electing the Member State in which they are issued a driving licence. The Court repeatedly underlined this anti-abuse effect of the normal residence requirement:

> [T]he residence condition helps inter alia the fight against 'driving-licence tourism' in the absence of complete harmonisation of the laws of the Member States relating to the issuing of driving licences.[162]

The same definition of habitual residence was used in Article 7(1) of Council Directive 83/182 on tax exemptions for the temporary importation of means of transport,[163] which was interpreted in the *Ryborg* and *Louloudakis* cases.[164] In this context, the function of the normal residence requirement is to prevent natural persons from electing the Member State in which they are taxed on their means of transport. This concern is particularly strong in Member States imposing high taxes on car owners for environmental reasons, such as Denmark (*Ryborg*).

[161] Council Directive 91/439/EEC of 29 July 1991 on driving licences [1991] OJ L237/1 art 7(1)(b) according to which Member States are to issue driving licences only to applicants having their normal residence on their territory.

[162] Case C-184/10 *Grasser* [2011] ECR I-4057, para 27; Joined Cases C-329/06 and C-343/06 *Wiedemann* [2008] ECR I-4635, para 69; Joined Cases C-334/06 to C-336/06 *Zerche* [2008] ECR I-4691, para 66; Case C-1/07 *Weber* [2008] ECR I-8571, para 39.

[163] Council Directive 83/182/EEC of 28 March 1983 on tax exemptions within the Community for certain means of transport temporarily imported into one Member State from another [1983] OJ L105/59 arts 3(1)(aa) and 4(1)(aa) which provide for a definition *a contrario*: Member States are to exempt the temporary importation of vehicles, except when the importer has his normal residence on its territory.

[164] Case C-392/05 *Alevizos* [2007] ECR I-3505, paras 54–62; Case C-262/99 *Louloudakis* [2001] ECR I-5547, paras 50–60; Case C-297/89 *Ryborg* [1991] ECR I-1943, paras 19–29.

The Court has also adopted a centre of gravity approach outside the scope of Directive 83/182,[165] based on the intended use of the vehicle. This line of case law concerns Union citizens residing in one Member State (eg Denmark, Belgium) and employed in another (eg Germany, Luxembourg), and who possess a vehicle registered in the Member State of employment, where taxes are lower. Again, the concern voiced by Member States such as Denmark was that their residents might abusively circumvent (higher) domestic taxes by setting up companies or branches in another Member State, where they acquire and register vehicles that are subsequently used in the Member State of residence.[166] In response, the Court allowed the Member State of residence to levy a registration tax on such vehicles when it is intended that the vehicle should be used essentially in its territory on a permanent basis, or where it is in fact used in that manner.[167]

In the area of social security contributions, a centre of gravity approach thwarts the risk of abusive practice pointed out by the German and Dutch Governments in *Barry Banks*, consisting in becoming affiliated to social security in a Member State in which contributions are modest, with the sole purpose of going to another Member State in order to work there for a year without paying the higher contributions there (*Barry Banks*, para 24). The Court was invited to interpret Article 14a(1)(a) of Regulation 1408/71, which provides that a person normally self-employed in a Member State and who performs work in another Member State shall continue to be subject to the legislation of the first Member State, provided that the anticipated duration of the work does not exceed 12 months. *Barry Banks* concerned opera singers resident in the United Kingdom who had temporarily 'posted themselves' to the opera house La Monnaie in Brussels, and contested their affiliation to social security in Belgium. Referring to its ruling in *Fitzwilliam*,[168] which concerned Article 14(1)(a) of Regulation 1408/71 and the posting of employed persons, the Court ruled that Barry Banks could only remain affiliated to UK social security if he was normally self-employed in the United Kingdom:

> Article 14a(1)(a) of Regulation 1408/71 imposes the preliminary requirement that the person concerned be normally self-employed in the territory of a Member State. That obligation assumes that the person concerned habitually carries out significant activities in the territory of the Member State where he is established. Thus, such a person must already have been carrying out his activity for some time at the moment when he wishes to take advantage of the provision in question. Similarly, during the period in which he works in the territory of another Member State, that person must continue to maintain,

[165] Directive 83/182 applies only where individuals have their normal residence in a Member State other than the Member State of temporary importation: see Case C-464/02 *Commission v Denmark* [2005] ECR I-7929, para 5.

[166] Case C-464/02 *Commission v Denmark* [2005] ECR I-7929, para 55.

[167] Case C-464/02 *Commission v Denmark* [2005] ECR I-7929, paras 75–78; Joined Cases C-151/04 and C-152/04 *Nadin* [2005] ECR I-11203, para 41; Case C-364/08 *Vandermeir* [2008] ECR I-8087, paras 32–36.

[168] See nn 107–10 and accompanying text.

> in his State of origin, the necessary means to carry on his activity so as to be in a position to pursue it on his return.[169]

In the previous *Angenieux* ruling, the Court was asked to interpret that notion of habitual residence with regard to a business representative having his permanent address in France but carrying out continuous business-canvassing tours in Germany for nine months per year. In its judgment issued in 1973, the Court ruled that his residence—which determined the Member State in which he had to be affiliated to social security—was the place in which that worker had established the permanent centre of his interests and to which he returned in the intervals between his tours.[170]

In the area of social benefits, a centre of gravity approach thwarts the risk of 'benefit tourism'. *Swaddling* was a UK national requesting income support in the United Kingdom after a period of employment in France. This factual setting gave the Court the opportunity to propose a set of concrete criteria translating the notion of habitual residence into workable terms:

> The phrase 'the Member State in which they reside' in Article 10a of Regulation 1408/71 refers to the State in which the persons concerned habitually reside and where the habitual centre of their interests is to be found. In that context, account should be taken in particular of the employed person's family situation; the reasons which have led him to move; the length and continuity of his residence; the fact (where this is the case) that he is in stable employment; and his intention as it appears from all the circumstances.
>
> For the purposes of that assessment, however, the length of residence in the Member State in which payment of the benefit at issue is sought cannot be regarded as an intrinsic element of the concept of residence within the meaning of Article 10a of Regulation 1408/71. In particular, when, as in the present case, an employed person, on returning to his State of origin after exercising his right to freedom of movement, has made it clear at the time of applying for income support that he intends to remain in his State of origin, where his close relatives live …, he cannot be deemed not to satisfy the condition concerning residence within the meaning of Article 10a merely because the period of residence completed in his State of origin is too short.[171]

Paraphrasing the Court, the length of residence may not be used as a suspect period (para 30), but rather as one criterion to identify the applicant's habitual residence (para 29). In other words, the habitual residence must be understood as a centre of gravity requirement rather than a suspect period, conditioning the grant of income support.[172]

[169] Case C-178/97 *Bazzy Banks* [2000] ECR I-2005, para 25.

[170] Case 13/73 *Angenieux* [1973] ECR 935, para 32.

[171] Case C-90/97 *Swaddling* [1999] ECR I-1075, paras 29–30.

[172] This case law can be contrasted to the subsequent *Collins* and *Vatsouras* judgments interpreting the freedom of movement of workers, in which the Court allowed the imposition of a suspect period conditioning the grant of jobseekers' benefits, which consisted in a reasonable period of residence during which the applicant genuinely sought employment on the domestic labour market. See section II of this chapter.

In private international law, Articles 3(1) and 8(1) of Council Regulation 2201/2003 determine international jurisdiction in matters of divorce and parental responsibility, respectively on the basis of the habitual residence of the spouses and the child.[173] As explained in the Borrás Report, those grounds seek to establish a 'genuine connection' between the litigant and the Member State having jurisdiction (point 32), with a view to limiting forum shopping.[174] Furthermore, in the *A* case, the Court provided some assistance regarding the identification of a child's habitual residence:

> In addition to the physical presence of the child in a Member State other factors must be chosen which are capable of showing that that presence is not in any way temporary or intermittent and that the residence of the child reflects some degree of integration in a social and family environment.[175]

Lastly, the Staff Regulations of the European Union grant an expatriation allowance to officials that have not habitually resided in the State of employment during the five years preceding their entry into service. This requirement of habitual residence, interpreted as the permanent or habitual centre of interests in *Magdalena Fernández*, prevents artificial relocations in another State for the sole purpose of obtaining an expatriation allowance.[176] The Court gave a similar reading of the notion of residence as 'centre of interests' in *Schäflein*, in relation to geographical weightings applicable to termination of service allowances.[177]

ii. The 'Genuine Integration' Requirement

The Court's approach to centre of gravity for natural persons has progressively evolved from simplistic residence requirements towards a subtler analysis of the degree of integration of Union citizens into the host society.

This expanding requirement of genuine integration accounts for the condemnation of residence requirements in recent social benefit cases. When fulfilled, residence requirements are good indicators of genuine integration into the host society. Problems arise when Union citizens do not fulfil a residence requirement imposed by a Member State although they are genuinely integrated into its society. Thus, the Court precluded the imposition of residence requirements for the grant of pensions by the Netherlands to World War II victims (*Tas-Hagen*), and by Poland

[173] Council Regulation (EC) 2201/2003 of 27 November 2003 concerning jurisdiction and the recognition and enforcement of judgments in matrimonial matters and the matters of parental responsibility, repealing Regulation (EC) 1347/2000 [2003] OJ L338/1.

[174] Council (EC), 'Explanatory Report on the Convention on Jurisdiction and the Recognition and Enforcement of Judgments in Matrimonial Matters' (Borrás Report), 28 May 1998, C221/27. As explained at no 49, the alternative criteria defining the spouses' habitual residence leave some room for undesirable forum shopping.

[175] Case C-523/07 *A* [2009] ECR I-2805, para 38.

[176] Case C-452/93 P *Magdalena Fernández v Commission*, paras 21–23; see also Case C-424/05 P *Commission v Hosman-Chevalier* [2007] ECR I-5027; Case C-10/06 P *De Bustamente Tello* [2007] ECR I-10381.

[177] Case 284/87 *Schäflein* [1988] ECR 4475.

to victims of deportation during the Soviet regime (*Nerkowska*). The motive stated by the Court is identical in both rulings: while acknowledging the legitimate objective of verifying the genuine integration of the beneficiary into the host society, the genuine integration of the applicants was sufficiently attested by their nationality and their extended period of employment in those countries.[178]

The Court was more explicit in *Lucy Stewart*, which concerned the right to short-term incapacity benefit in the United Kingdom, which was made subject to a condition of 'past presence' for not less than 26 weeks in the 52 weeks preceding the date of the claim.[179] The Court stated that it is legitimate for the national legislature to ensure that there is a genuine link between a claimant to a benefit and the host society (para 89). However, measuring the degree of integration through the sole criterion of residence is too exclusive and accordingly disproportionate:

> While the rules for applying that condition do not, in themselves, appear to be unreasonable, none the less that condition is too exclusive in nature. Indeed, by requiring specific periods of past presence in the competent Member State, the condition of past presence unduly favours an element which is not necessarily representative of the real and effective degree of connection between the claimant to short-term incapacity benefit in youth and that Member State, to the exclusion of all other representative elements. It therefore goes beyond what is necessary to attain the objective pursued.[180]

In the main proceedings, the Court observed that other 'representative elements' established the genuine integration of the claimant, such as her connection to the social security system (paras 97–99), her dependence on her parents who received retirement pensions from the United Kingdom and who had lived or worked there (para 100), and the fact that she had passed a significant part of her life there (para 101).

The Court adopted a similar approach in the subsequent *Prinz* judgment,[181] which concerned student funding claimed in Germany by (non-economically active) German citizens who did not reside in Germany and intended to study abroad. The Court recalled that is legitimate for a Member State to grant funding only to students who have demonstrated a certain degree of integration into their society (para 36). However, the Court ruled once again that the use of a sole residence requirement to measure the degree of integration is disproportionate:

> Although the existence of a certain level of integration may be regarded as established by the finding that a student has resided in the Member State where he may apply for an education or training grant for a certain period, a sole condition of residence, such as that at issue in the main proceedings, risks, as the AG observes in point 95 of her Opinion, excluding from funding students who, despite not having resided for an uninterrupted period of three years in Germany immediately prior to studying abroad,

[178] Case C-499/06 *Nerkowska* [2008] ECR I-3993, para 43; Case C-192/05 *Tas-Hagen* [2006] ECR I-10451, para 38.

[179] Case C-503/09 *Lucy Stewart* [2011] ECR I-6497.

[180] Case C-503/09 *Lucy Stewart* [2011] ECR I-6497, para 95.

[181] Case C-523/11 *Prinz* [2013] ECR I-0000.

> are nevertheless sufficiently connected to German society. That may be the case where the student is a national of the State concerned and was educated there for a significant period or on account of other factors such as, in particular, his family, employment, language skills or the existence of other social and economic factors.[182]

This case law marks a clear evolution in the centre of gravity approach applied to natural persons, from simplistic residence requirements to subtler genuine integration requirements. The Court has progressively made clear that habitual residence requirements are expressions of a more general principle, according to which Member States must incrementally include migrant citizens into their solidarity policies in order to mirror their degree of integration into the host society. The criterion of genuine integration accounts for the apparent contradictions in the Court's treatment of residence requirements, as the latter merely serve as indicator of genuine integration: whenever genuine integration can be shown by other representative elements, residence requirements become redundant and therefore disproportionate, as in *Tas-Hagen*, *Nerkowska*, *Lucy Stewart* and *Prinz*. In the absence of other representative elements, the Court usually upholds residence requirements as indicators of genuine integration, as in *Gottwald*, which concerned the grant of free road toll discs to disabled persons in Austria:

> With regard to a measure such as that at issue in the main proceedings, intended to facilitate regular journeys in Austria by disabled persons with a view to their integration in national society, the place of residence or of ordinary residence then appears to be a criterion suitable to establish the existence of a connection between those persons and the society of the Member State concerned such as, in particular, to distinguish them, as the AG observed in point 71 of his Opinion, from other categories of users likely to use the road network of that Member State only occasionally or temporarily.[183]

In essence, this requirement of genuine integration is used by Union institutions to manage the tension between the entitlement of migrant citizens to transnational solidarity and the right of Member States to shape their social security system and prevent abuses in the form of benefit tourism:

> By linking integration and solidarity, the Court captures the nature of the relationships underlying the welfare state, without an appeal to nationalism. It prompts an examination of whether the migrant EU citizen has developed a real link with the host Member State, such as to warrant inclusion within the scope of the solidaristic community. Instrumentally, the solidarity enquiry is apt to ensure equal access for migrant EU citizens who have an established link with the host country, whilst preventing 'welfare tourism'.[184]

[182] Case C-523/11 *Prinz* [2013] ECR I-0000, para 38.

[183] Case C-103/08 *Gottwald* [2009] ECR I-9117, para 36.

[184] Costello, 'Citizenship of the Union: Above Abuse?' (n 57) 348; see also O Golynker, 'Jobseekers' Rights in the European Union: Challenges of Changing the Paradigm of Social Solidarity' (2005) 30 *European Law Review* 111, 117.

Overall, the centre of gravity approach to welfare benefits developed under Union law rests on an assessment of the degree of integration into the host society, of which the habitual residence is only one indicator among others. The broad definition of 'worker', and the correlative tolerance towards potential abuses committed by workers,[185] can be usefully read in light of this global centre of gravity approach, based on the degree of integration into the host society. The liberal stance towards choices of law made by workers does not amount, properly speaking, to an exception to the centre of gravity approach to welfare benefits. Rather, workers are *presumed* to have their centre of gravity in the Member State of employment, so that they should be entitled to full social security coverage there. Indeed, workers integrate themselves into the host society by contributing to the provision of both private and public goods, thanks to their occupational activity and the payment of taxes and social contributions. As explained by the Court in *Commission v Netherlands*:

> As regards migrant workers and frontier workers, the fact that they have participated in the employment market of a Member State establishes, in principle, a sufficient link of integration with the society of that Member State, allowing them to benefit from the principle of equal treatment, as compared with national workers, as regards social advantages. That principle is applicable not only to all employment and working conditions, but also to all the advantages which, whether or not linked to a contract of employment, are generally granted to national workers primarily because of their objective status as workers or by virtue of the mere fact of their residence on the national territory.
>
> The link of integration arises from, inter alia, the fact that, through the taxes which he pays in the host Member State by virtue of his employment, the migrant worker also contributes to the financing of the social policies of that State and should profit from them under the same conditions as national workers.[186]

As employment establishes genuine integration, no further requirement—of residence or other—can be imposed to migrant or frontier workers: '[A] Member State may not make payment of a social advantage within the meaning of Article 7 of Regulation 1612/68 dependent on the condition that recipients are resident in the national territory of that Member State'.[187] Nevertheless, with regard to frontier workers who do not reside in the State of employment, the Court has allowed certain limitations to their equality of treatment with nationals, depending on the extent of their integration in the society of that Member State or their attachment to that State.[188] In *Geven*, for instance, Germany was allowed to restrict the benefit of child-raising allowances to residents and to non-residents engaged in

[185] See section V of this chapter.

[186] Case C-542/09 *Commission v Netherlands* [2012] ECR I-0000, paras 65–66.

[187] Case C-287/05 *Hendrix* [2007] ECR I-6909, para 50 and case law cited.

[188] Case C-20/12 *Giersch and Others* [2013] ECR I-0000, para 64 and case law cited.

substantial occupational activity in Germany (frontier workers employed more than 15 hours per week).[189]

In sum, both migrant citizens and workers are subject to a genuine integration requirement when they claim social benefits in the host State. Genuine integration can be presumed in the case of workers residing in the host State (*Hendrix*). Union citizens—by definition economically inactive—must establish genuine integration into the host society through residence or any other representative element (*Prinz*). Frontier workers find themselves in an intermediate position, as they may be subject to a threshold of employment in the host State or asked to establish genuine integration by other means (*Geven*). As summarised by Catherine Barnard:

> [T]here is a key difference between economically active and non-economically active citizens: those who are economically active enjoy full equal treatment from the first day of their arrival in the host State. And since it is perceived that they contribute to the economy of the host State, the Court does not have to work hard to justify their equality of treatment. By contrast, those who are not economically active do not enjoy full equality of treatment from the first day of their arrival ... Instead, the Court has offered a more nuanced approach to equality, based on the length of stay in the host State and the depth of integration into the society of the host State.[190]

The genuine integration requirement permits an insightful reconstruction of the case law on student funding. Migrant students may derive a right to student funding directly or indirectly, through their parents' employment. On the one hand, migrant students may claim a direct right to student funding either as former workers or as mere citizens. When a migrant person decides to quit his employment in order to undertake studies, the presumption of genuine integration provided by his former employment fades away. In *Lair*, the Court ruled that this shield of genuine integration protects the involuntary loss of employment or the undertaking of studies related to previous employment:

> [M]igrant workers are guaranteed certain rights linked to the status of worker even when they are no longer in an employment relationship.
>
> In the field of grants for university education, such a link between the status of worker and a grant awarded for maintenance and training with a view to the pursuit of university studies does, however, presuppose some continuity between the previous occupational activity and the course of study; there must be a relationship between the purpose of the studies and the previous occupational activity. Such continuity may not, however, be required where a migrant has involuntarily become unemployed and is obliged by

[189] Case C-213/05 *Geven* [2007] ECR I-6347; see also Case C-212/05 *Hartmann* [2007] ECR I-6303.

[190] Barnard (n 57) 1488; see also Golynker, 'Jobseekers' Rights in the European Union' (n 184) 115: 'Economically active migrants such as workers and self-employed persons are a-priory deemed bona fide contributors to the host society entitled to equal treatment'.

conditions on the job market to undertake occupational retraining in another field of activity.[191]

In the alternative, migrant students may claim a direct right as mere—economically inactive—citizens. As they are not covered by former employment, such migrant students may be asked to establish their genuine integration into the host society.[192] In *Förster*, the Court held that a condition of five years' continuous residence was not excessive to ensure genuine integration in the host Member State.[193] Nevertheless, as explained above, the Court ruled in *Prinz* that the use of a sole residence requirement to measure the degree of integration, at the exclusion of other representative elements such as family, employment, language skills or any social and economic factor, is disproportionate.[194]

On the other hand, migrant students may also derive an indirect right to student funding, by seeking the protection of the presumption of genuine integration provided by their parents' employment. The rationale of this extension lies in the Court's well-established analysis of student funding for dependent children as social benefit for the migrant worker. As this indirect claim to student funding is covered by the parents' employment in the host society, the host State cannot subject it to a further requirement of residence of the student on national territory:

> [S]tudy finance granted by a Member State to the children of workers constitutes for a migrant worker a social advantage within the meaning of Article 7(2) of Regulation 1612/68, where the worker continues to support the child. In such a case the child may rely on Article 7(2) in order to obtain study finance under the same conditions as are applicable to the children of national workers, and no additional residence requirement may be imposed upon him.[195]

Furthermore, the Court has consistently ruled that no further requirement of residence could be imposed on the parent workers either. In other words, frontier workers are as genuinely integrated into the State of employment as resident workers, and are therefore entitled to student funding for their dependent children, as in *Meeusen*:

> It is expressly stated in the fourth recital in the preamble to [Regulation 1612/68] that the right of free movement must be enjoyed 'without discrimination by permanent, seasonal and frontier workers and by those who pursue their activities for the purpose of providing services' and Article 7 of the Regulation refers, without reservation, to a 'worker who is a national of a Member State'. The Court deduced from that and ruled, in Meints, that a Member State may not make the grant of a social advantage within the

[191] Case 39/86 *Lair* [1988] ECR 3161, paras 36–37; Case C-357/89 *Raulin* [1992] ECR I-1027, para 22; Case C-413/01 *Ninni-Orasche* [2003] ECR I-13187, para 35.

[192] On this evolution, see O'Leary, 'Equal Treatment and EU Citizens' (n 61); Golynker (n 61).

[193] Case C-158/07 *Förster* [2008] ECR I-8507, para 54.

[194] Case C-523/11 *Prinz* [2013] ECR I-0000, para 38.

[195] Case C-3/90 *Bernini* [1992] ECR I-1071, para 29; see also Case C-337/97 *Meeusen* [1999] ECR I-3289, para 19.

meaning of Article 7 of the Regulation dependent on the condition that the beneficiaries be resident within its territory.[196]

As the Court excluded the possibility to justify residence requirements imposed upon migrant workers' children by the need to ensure their genuine integration into the host society, Member States have attempted to justify them on other grounds. *Commission v Netherlands* and *Giersch* both concerned the legitimacy of a residence requirement to obtain 'portable' funding, namely funding for studies abroad.[197] In *Commission v Netherlands*, the Netherlands put forward the promotion of student mobility: a residence requirement was necessary to ensure that portable funding went only to those students whose mobility outside the Netherlands had to be encouraged, namely the students 'attached' to the Netherlands. In *Giersch*, Luxembourg put forward the objective of increasing the proportion of residents holding a higher education degree. Having due regard to that legitimate objective, Luxembourg argued that portable funding could only be granted to those students who were likely to return to Luxembourg after the completion of their studies abroad. Such return was only likely for those students showing a real 'attachment' to Luxembourg, which could be tested by their residence there.

In practice, both grounds of justification amount to the reintroduction of requirements of 'attachment' to the host society for migrant workers' children claiming student funding. While acknowledging the legitimacy of both objectives and the appropriateness of residence requirements, the Court judged in both cases that the use of a sole residence requirement was too exclusive in such contexts, and thus disproportionate.[198] In *Giersch*, in particular, the Court held that sufficient attachment to Luxembourg, such as to make probable that aid recipients will return to settle there, could be inferred from residence in a border State and economic activity of the parents in Luxembourg for a significant period of time (para 78). The Court added that Luxembourg could impose a requirement of minimum period of employment in its territory in order to prevent abusive practices (para 80). In *Geven*, the Court had accepted that frontier workers could be subject to a requirement of substantial activity in the State of employment (more than 15 hours per week). Accordingly, this case law reaffirms the illegitimacy of residence requirements in the context of student funding granted to frontier workers' children, as the latter are covered, as a rule, by the presumption of genuine integration triggered by their parents' employment.

As explained throughout this chapter, the central function assigned to requirements of genuine integration and/or residence is the prevention of abusive practices, sometimes labelled as 'benefit tourism' in this context. Union citizens

[196] Case C-337/97 *Meeusen* [1999] ECR I-3289, para 21.

[197] Case C-542/09 *Commission v Netherlands* [2012] ECR I-0000; Case C-20/12 *Giersch and Others* [2013] ECR I-0000.

[198] Case C-542/09 *Commission v Netherlands* [2012] ECR I-0000, para 86; Case C-20/12 *Giersch and Others* [2013] ECR I-0000, para 76.

should only be allowed to claim social benefits from the Member States in which they are genuinely integrated. AG Kokott's Opinion in *Teixeira* illustrates the interplay between prohibition of abuses, transnational solidarity and integration requirement:[199]

- Member States find themselves under an obligation of transnational solidarity towards migrant Union citizens (para 82);
- this obligation of solidarity does not extend to abusive practices, as corroborated by Article 35 of Directive 2004/38 (para 83);
- given her high degree of integration in the United Kingdom (para 85), Ms Teixeira's reliance on transnational solidarity could not be considered as abusive (para 84).

Arguably, this requirement of genuine integration can be extended beyond social benefits. In his Opinion in *Cavallera*, which concerned the mutual recognition of professional qualifications, AG Maduro argued that free movement could only be used to assist economic and social interpenetration:

> The recognition of diplomas is thus closely linked to the effective exercise of the freedoms recognised by the Treaty for the purpose of assisting 'economic and social interpenetration within the Community' in that field.[200]

This objective of fostering economic and social interpenetration within the Union is not achieved where the exercise of free movement is not effective (para 53) but only involves wholly artificial arrangements that do not reflect economic reality (para 60). From a broader perspective, national jurisdictions were once fortresses closed behind nationality ramparts; the creation of an internal market based on free movement forced their opening; nowadays, the prevention of abusive claims permits a new closure, based on the suppler requirement of genuine integration.

To sum up, residence and genuine integration requirements are two types of centre of gravity applied to natural persons, assessing the effectiveness of the link with a specific jurisdiction at a certain point in time. Their function is to impede artificial practices, irrespective of the terminology used (eg abuse, benefit tourism, forum shopping), thereby restricting the choice of applicable law. Such requirements tend to impose a global requirement of genuine integration into the host society, thereby provoking an alignment between applicable legal regime and reality.[201]

[199] AG Kokott, Case C-480/08 *Teixeira* [2010] ECR I-1107, paras 82–85.

[200] AG Maduro, Case C-311/06 *Cavallera* [2009] ECR I-415, para 48; see also AG Léger, Case C-196/04 *Cadbury Schweppes* [2006] ECR I-7995, para 42. The Court eventually condemned Mr Cavallera's abusive strategy by excluding his certificate from the notion of 'diploma', another option suggested by AG Maduro (para 25).

[201] As explained above, an artificial strategy amounts to the election of an artificial legal cloak which cannot be justified by a genuine socioeconomic motive: see ch 3 section II.

IV. Incidental Prevention of Artificial Practices

In addition to formal and informal doctrines of abuse, suspect periods and centres of gravity, artificial choices of law can be *incidentally* prohibited through legal grounds unrelated to the issue of abuse of law. By contrast with the previous legal grounds, which were specifically intended to counter artificial practices, the prohibition of abuses is here merely incidental to another legal issue, which represents the true focus of attention.

As a matter of fact, certain legal norms form natural barriers to abuses of law; curiously, this point can be illustrated by contrasting the *Richards* and *Dafeki* cases.[202] The *Richards* case concerned the retirement age applicable in the United Kingdom to man-to-female transsexuals.[203] Under UK law, men were entitled to retire at age 65 and women at age 60. A few months before turning 60, Richards underwent male-to-female gender reassignment surgery, and immediately applied for a retirement pension. On the other hand, the *Dafeki* case questioned the binding force, in Germany, of a birth certificate issued by a single judge in Greece. Mrs Dafeki was a Greek national who had worked in Germany for 20 years. At age 55, she was issued a new birth certificate in Greece attesting that she was 59, and immediately applied for a retirement pension. Irrespective of their outcome, the relevance of those cases lies in the impact of the applicable rules on the possibility of abuse. In *Dafeki*, the Greek procedure to obtain a new birth certificate left room for abusive or fraudulent practices, and this risk clearly prompted the German refusal to recognise Mrs Dafeki's new birth certificate. By contrast, in *Richards*, no one ever raised the argument of abuse despite the dubious timing of the gender reassignment, which occurred a few months before Richards turned 60. The reason is pretty straightforward: it is unthinkable that Richards could change sex for the sole purpose of obtaining an anticipated retirement; in simple terms, the costs of a gender reassignment far exceed the benefits of an early retirement.

The Court's judgment in *Daily Mail* perfectly illustrates how certain legal rules (and interpretations) naturally impede abusive practices.[204] Daily Mail sought to remain subject to UK company law while becoming liable to taxation in the Netherlands, by transferring its real seat in the latter State. This strategy was spurred by the perspective of avoiding UK tax on capital gains, without being subject to equivalent tax in the Netherlands. Under UK tax law, the transfer of tax residence outside the United Kingdom had to be authorised by the domestic tax authorities, which required acquittal of UK tax on capital gains. Daily Mail decided to proceed without the consent of the UK tax authorities and opened an

[202] Case C-423/04 *Richards* [2006] ECR I-3585; Case C-336/94 *Dafeki* [1997] ECR I-6761.

[203] *Richards* was the third episode of a British trilogy on the legal status of transsexuals under Union law: see Case C-117/01 *K.B.* [2004] ECR I-541; Case C-13/94 *P v S* [1996] ECR I-2143.

[204] Case 81/87 *Daily Mail* [1988] ECR 5483, paras 23–24; see also Case C-210/06 *Cartesio* [2008] ECR I-9641, paras 108–10.

investment management office in the Netherlands. By ruling that the transfer of registered office or real head office to another Member State was a problem 'not resolved by the rules on the right of establishment' (para 23), the Court incidentally enabled the United Kingdom to fight the tax avoidance scheme set up by Daily Mail (para 7). As noted by Sørensen,

> This interpretation allowed the case to be solved without discussing the issue of abuse, even though the underlying problem in the case was that the company was trying to avoid paying taxes in the United Kingdom.[205]

Similarly, Fidium Finanz was deprived of any right under Union law following the Court's decision to situate the debate within the freedom to provide services (only applicable to Union businesses), instead of the free movement of capital (applicable to Union and third country businesses).[206] Fidium Finanz had chosen to establish itself in Switzerland while carrying out most of its activity in Germany, in order to escape regulatory supervision in both countries;[207] however, the Court's decision enabled Germany to regulate Fidium Finanz, thereby countering its artificial choice of Swiss law.

In *Daily Mail* and *Fidium Finanz*, the Court ruled that the artificial practices in question fell outside the scope of Union law; in other cases, the Court may set aside the obligation of mutual recognition, thereby erecting a natural barrier to the artificial election of a home State. For instance, the Court excluded the mutual recognition of national licences to provide gambling services;[208] this decision made it impossible for Carmen Media Group to 'avoid' German law by artificially establishing itself in Gibraltar, since Germany was entitled to (re-) regulate its activity.[209] Similarly, Mr Bouchoucha was a French national holding a diploma of osteopathy delivered in the United Kingdom; he sought to practise osteopathy in France, where osteopaths were required to be doctors of medicine. The French authorities were allowed to thwart this artificial practice consisting in electing UK law in order to circumvent the French requirement of being a doctor of medicine,[210] on the ground that osteopathy qualifications were not mutually recognised.[211]

If *Carmen Media Group* and *Bouchoucha* establish general exceptions to mutual recognition, other rules exclude mutual recognition in more specific situations. For instance, Mr Gullung was a French lawyer who got expelled from the Colmar bar for breaching rules relating to professional ethics. Subsequently, he became

[205] Sørensen (n 3) 438 fn 17; see also de la Feria (n 96) 403–04.

[206] Case C-452/04 *Fidium Finanz* [2006] ECR I-9521, para 49.

[207] AG Stix-Hackl, Case C-452/04 *Fidium Finanz* [2006] ECR I-9521, para 83.

[208] Case C-347/09 *Dickinger* [2011] ECR I-8185, para 96; Joined Cases C-316/07, C-358/07 to C-360/07, C-409/07 and C-410/07 *Markus Stoß* [2010] ECR I-8069, para 112–13; Case C-42/07 *Bwin* [2009] ECR I-7633, para 69. See ch 7 n 29 and accompanying text.

[209] Case C-46/08 *Carmen Media Group* [2010] ECR I-8149, paras 43–44.

[210] See Noblet, *La lutte contre le contournement des droits nationaux en droit communautaire* (n 82) 156.

[211] Case C-61/89 *Bouchoucha* [1990] ECR I-3551, para 14. See ch 7 n 30 and accompanying text.

registered as a *Rechtsanwalt* in Offenburg (Germany) and sought unsuccessfully to rely on Directive 77/249[212] to practise again in France.[213] A similar strategy of circumvention[214] was elaborated by German nationals deprived of their right to drive in Germany, who sought to rely on Directive 91/439 after obtaining another driving licence in the Czech Republic. However, the Court repeatedly ruled that Member States do not have to recognise a foreign driving licence where the holder has lost his right to drive on their territory, until the period of withdrawal or suspension has expired:

> To require a Member State to recognise the validity of a driving licence issued by another Member State ..., despite the fact that he is subject to a valid measure withdrawing his right to drive ..., would have the effect of encouraging offenders likely to be subject to such withdrawal to travel without delay to another Member State in order to evade the administrative or criminal consequences of those offences and would ultimately destroy the confidence on which the system of mutual recognition of driving licences rests.[215]

De Agostini is another free movement case in which the Court incidentally prevented circumvention strategies set up by advertisers, but not those committed by broadcasters.[216] Sweden prohibited television advertisements aimed at children; yet De Agostini (a Swedish company) advertised a children's magazine both on TV3 (run by a UK company) and TV4 (run by a Swedish company). The Court's ruling distinguished between measures taken by the Swedish authorities against broadcasters (TV3 and TV4) and measures aimed at advertisers (De Agostini). On the one hand, the Court endorsed a strict home country principle approach with regard to broadcasters, whose regulation had been coordinated by the First Broadcasting Directive 89/552. As a result, Sweden could take measures against the domestic broadcaster TV4, but not against the UK broadcaster TV3, even in a situation of circumvention (paras 60–62). On the other hand, since the Directive did not apply to advertisers such as De Agostini, Sweden was free to apply measures protecting consumers both to domestic and foreign advertisers, and therefore to thwart artificial practices (para 35).[217] Subsequent amendments to the Broadcasting Directive mitigated the risk of abusive practices through centre of gravity approaches (Articles 2 and 4 of Directive 2010/13).[218]

[212] Council Directive 77/249/EEC of 22 March 1977 to facilitate the effective exercise by lawyers of freedom to provide services [1977] OJ L78/17.

[213] Case 292/86 *Gullung* [1988] ECR 111, para 22; see Wattel, 'Circumvention of National Law' (n 117) 1267.

[214] See Costello (n 57) 351: 'The circumvention of home State rules could not be more vivid'.

[215] Case C-1/07 *Weber* [2008] ECR I-8571, para 39. See also Case C-184/10 *Grasser* [2011] ECR I-4057, para 23; Order of 9 July 2009 in Case C-445/08 *Wierer* [2009] ECR I-119, para 51; Joined Cases C-334/06 to C-336/06 *Zerche* [2008] ECR I-4691, para 70; Joined Cases C-329/06 and C-343/06 *Wiedemann* [2008] ECR I-4635, para 73; Costello (n 57) 351–52.

[216] Joined Cases C-34/95 to C-36/95 *De Agostini* [1997] ECR I-3843.

[217] See Hansen (n 96) 132; Sørensen (n 3) 437.

[218] See section III of this chapter.

The Court reaffirmed *De Agostini* in *Mesopotamia Broadcast*, which concerned a Danish company broadcasting, throughout Europe, television programmes describing the Kurdish question. The German authorities decided to prohibit the retransmission of those programmes, which had been explicitly permitted by the Danish authorities. The Court reaffirmed and generalised the *De Agostini* principle:

> In paragraph 38 of [De Agostini], the Court also stated that the Directive does not preclude a Member State from taking, pursuant to general legislation on protection of consumers against misleading advertising, measures against an advertiser in relation to television advertising broadcast from another Member State, provided that those measures do not prevent the retransmission, as such, in its territory of television broadcasts coming from that other Member State.
>
> That reasoning also applies to the legislation of a Member State which does not specifically concern the broadcast and distribution of programmes and which, in general, pursues a public policy objective without however preventing retransmission per se, on its territory, of television broadcasts from another Member State.[219]

Abuses of law are also incidentally prohibited in the field of VAT. As in *Halifax*, *Centralan* concerned a complex transactional structure designed to recover the—normally non-recoverable—VAT borne on the construction of buildings. Nevertheless, by contrast with *Halifax*, the Court merely interpreted Article 20(3) of the Sixth Directive to thwart this tax avoidance strategy, without having recourse to the doctrine of abuse (para 81).[220] The *RAL* case concerned a group restructuring designed to escape a VAT liability on slot gaming machines exploited in the United Kingdom, by establishing the service provider in Guernsey. However, the Court ruled that those services constituted 'entertainment or similar activities' and were therefore taxable at the place of performance (United Kingdom), and not of establishment (Guernsey).[221] Following a legislative reform suppressing its right to deduction, BUPA Hospitals sought to prolong its right to deduct VAT by entering into a series of prepayment arrangements. The Court countered this abusive practice by stating that such transactions were not chargeable under Article 10(2) of the Sixth Directive.[222] Lastly, in *Temco Europe*, the Court interpreted the notion of 'letting of immovable property'—exempted under Article 13(B) of the Sixth Directive—as including the transaction at stake, thereby excluding Temco's right to deduction.[223] Although in all those cases the national court or

[219] Joined Cases C-244/10 and C-245/10 *Mesopotamia Broadcast* [2011] ECR I-8777, paras 49–50.

[220] Case C-63/04 *Centralan* [2005] ECR I-11087, para 81; AG Kokott, Case C-63/04 *Centralan* [2005] ECR I-11087, paras 60–61; R de la Feria, 'The European Court of Justice's Solution to Aggressive VAT Planning—Further towards Legal Uncertainty?' (2006) 15 *EC Tax Review* 27, 28.

[221] Case C-452/03 *RAL* [2005] ECR I-3947, para 34; AG Maduro, Case C-452/03 *RAL* [2005] ECR I-3947, para 67; de la Feria, 'The European Court of Justice's Solution to Aggressive VAT Planning' (n 220) 29.

[222] Case C-419/02 *BUPA Hospitals* [2006] ECR I-1685, para 51; AG Maduro, Case C-419/02 *BUPA Hospitals* [2006] ECR I-1685, para 100.

[223] Case C-284/03 *Temco Europe* [2004] ECR I-11237, para 28.

the Commission suggested having recourse to the doctrine of abuse,[224] the Court thwarted the disputed arrangements by the relevant interpreting provisions of the VAT legislation.

In the area of direct taxation, the Court's ruling in *Columbus* incidentally thwarted an abuse of law consisting in transferring a tax liability to a low-tax jurisdiction,[225] as in *Cadbury Schweppes* or *Oy AA*.[226] Columbus was a partnership established in Belgium by German residents; owing to its status of 'coordination centre' in Belgium, its incomes were subject to a low level of taxation in Belgium. German law sought to prevent artificial practices consisting in establishing partnerships in low-tax jurisdictions, by applying (higher) German taxes to foreign partnerships after offsetting the (low) taxes paid abroad. Without ever evoking the possibility of abusive strategy, the Court found that subjecting foreign partnerships owned by German residents to ordinary German taxes could not restrict free movement, since their taxation was aligned on that of German partnerships (absence of discrimination). By allowing Germany to replace foreign taxation by its domestic taxation, the Court incidentally thwarted artificial cross-border movements consisting in electing a hospitable tax jurisdiction by establishing a partnership there.

The factual setting of the *Kofoed* case offers an additional illustration of the anti-abuse effect of the credit method of prevention of double taxation:[227] Kofoed was a Danish resident receiving dividends from an Irish company, and who was subject to low Irish taxes as long as Denmark exempted his Irish incomes (exemption method). Following a revision of the Danish-Irish Double Tax Treaty, Denmark decided to tax Irish dividends at the normal Danish rate, while reimbursing low taxes paid in Ireland (credit method),[228] with the global economic result that Irish dividends received by Danish residents became subject to ordinary Danish taxation. The tax scheme assessed by the Court was designed by Kofoed to circumvent the upcoming Danish taxation on Irish dividends, by 'emptying' the Irish company of its capital before the entry into force of the amendment.

Lastly, the *Emsland-Stärke* and *Vonk Dairy Product* rulings applied the formal doctrine of abuse to re-import and re-export strategies set up in order to artificially obtain export refunds. Similar schemes were prevented in *Boterlux* (re-import), *Töpfer* (re-export) and *Eierkontor I* (re-export) by requesting evidence of customs clearance and/or marketing in the country of destination, as

[224] Case C-63/04 *Centralan* [2005] ECR I-11087, para 46; Case C-452/03 *RAL* [2005] ECR I-3947, para 21; Case C-419/02 *BUPA Hospitals* [2006] ECR I-1685, para 39; Case C-284/03 *Temco Europe* [2004] ECR I-11237, para 15.

[225] Case C-298/05 *Columbus* [2007] ECR I-10451, paras 39–40.

[226] See ch 2 section IV.A and section I of this chapter.

[227] The 'credit method' consists in applying domestic taxes and reimbursing foreign taxes; the 'exemption method' consists in renouncing to tax an income already taxed in another country. See arts 23 A and 23 B of OECD Model Tax Convention on Income and on Capital (n 123).

[228] Case C-321/05 *Kofoed* [2007] ECR I-5795. Under the credit method, the dividends received by Kofoed would be subject to—higher—Danish tax, whereas they used to be subject to—lower—Irish tax under the exemption method.

foreseen by the relevant secondary legislation.[229] As a matter of fact, it is only because such complementary evidence had not been demanded in due time that recourse was made to the formal doctrine of abuse in *Emsland-Stärke* (paras 48–49) and *Vonk Dairy Products* (para 29).

In all those cases, abusive choices of law were prevented without recourse to a specific anti-abuse technique (doctrine of abuse, suspect period or centre of gravity); rather, they were incidentally prohibited through the use of ordinary tools provided by the relevant legal regimes. In some cases, the Court's interpretation is formally detached from the issue of abuse, although one cannot rule out that it was influenced by the desire to counter abusive practices (eg *Daily Mail*, *Fidium Finanz*, *Bouchoucha*, *De Agostini*). In other cases, the Court more openly links its interpretation to the issue of abuse, as in *Weber* (driving licences), *Boterlux*, *Töpfer* and *Eierkontoor* (export refunds).

V. Free Choice of Law

All the legal grounds studied in this chapter were meant to prevent artificial practices aiming at electing a favourable legal regime, either by proscribing them as 'abusive' (doctrines of abuse), by increasing their realisation costs (suspect period, centre of gravity) or by preventing them incidentally. In stark contrast with those legal grounds, 'free choice of law' approaches explicitly ratify artificial practices. As described in the previous chapter, artificial practices are first and foremost choices of law; accordingly, allowing artificial practices necessarily amounts to granting free choice of law to Union citizens. Under Union law, the best-known example of free choice of law is the *Centros*-line of case law. In *Centros* and its epigones, the Court applied the incorporation theory in European company law:[230]

> [T]he fact that a national of a Member State who wishes to set up a company chooses to form it in the Member State whose rules of company law seem to him the least restrictive and to set up branches in other Member State cannot, in itself, constitute an abuse of the right of establishment.[231]

As explained earlier, the real seat theory forms a centre of gravity restricting the choice of *lex societatis*, by subjecting companies to the law of the Member State in

[229] Case C-347/93 *Boterlux* [1994] ECR I-3933, para 30; Case 250/80 *Töpfer* [1981] ECR 2465, paras 14–18; Case 125/75 *Eierkontor I* [1976] ECR 771, para 5–6. See D Anderson, 'Abuse of Rights' (2006) 11 *Judicial Review* 348, 352: 'The facts [of *Emsland-Stärke*] were similar to [*Töpfer*], in which the ECJ denied the benefit to the company on a straightforward interpretation of the right in the Regulation'.

[230] de la Feria (n 96) 405; Tridimas, 'Abuse of Rights in EU Law' (n 93) 178: '[*Centros*] may be seen as a triumph for the doctrine of incorporation and a corresponding defeat for the real seat doctrine'.

[231] Case C-212/97 *Centros* [1999] ECR I-1459, para 27. See also Case C-210/06 *Cartesio* [2008] ECR I-9641, paras 110–14; Case C-167/01 *Inspire Art* [2003] ECR I-10155; Case C-208/00 *Überseering* [2002] ECR I-9919.

which they have their real seat.[232] By contrast, the incorporation theory stipulates that companies are subject to the law of the Member State of incorporation;[233] as a result, the incorporation theory de facto grants free choice of company law to shareholders, who may elect their preferred national law by a costless act of incorporation in their preferred jurisdiction:

> With [the Centros jurisprudence], the door has been opened for free choice of the applicable company law regime and regulatory competition in the area of company law in Europe.[234]
>
> [In Centros], the Court of Justice has created a market for corporate forms within the European Union, granting de facto a choice between the legal forms of now twenty-seven Member States.[235]

In more detail, *Centros* ratified the artificial incorporation of new companies in a specific Member State for the sole purpose of benefiting from a more favourable legislation ('entry'). When such an act of incorporation abides by the local law, all other Member States are under the obligation to recognise the company and allow it to act on their territory. In addition, *Cartesio* dissipated a doubt left by *Daily Mail* concerning the re-incorporations of existing companies under another national law ('exit'). The Court indeed ruled that Member States cannot prevent a company incorporated under their national law 'from converting itself into a company governed by the law of [another] Member State, to the extent that it is permitted under that law to do so' (para 112). As a consequence, shareholders of both new (*Centros*) and existing (*Cartesio*) companies can freely elect their preferred company law, through an act of incorporation (*Centros*) or re-incorporation (*Cartesio*) in the relevant jurisdiction.[236] So delimited by *Cartesio*, the scope of *Daily Mail* is restricted to existing companies that intend to remain subject to the law of the Member State of incorporation (no 'exit'), but wish to transfer their connecting factor—real seat or place of incorporation—to another Member State.

This line of case law is, however, questioned by the subsequent *VALE* ruling, which concerned the cross-border transformation of an Italian company into a Hungarian company. In this judgment, the Grand Chamber of the Court indeed ruled that the concept of establishment presupposes actual establishment of

[232] See section III.A of this chapter.

[233] Wymeersch, The Transfer of the Company's Seat in European Company Law' (n 84) 661.

[234] Eidenmüller (n 52) 137.

[235] Ringe (n 2) 115; see also Dammann, 'Freedom of Choice in European Corporate Law' (n 85) 477–78; W Kerber and R Van den Bergh, 'Unmasking Mutual Recognition: Current Inconsistencies and Future Chances', Marburg Papers on Economics, no 2007/11 (19 April 2007), available at www.uni-marburg.de/fb02/makro/forschung/MPOE, 7.

[236] de Sousa, 'Company's Cross-border Transfer of Seat in the EU after Cartesio' (n 146); A Johnston and P Syrpis, 'Regulatory Competition in European Company Law after Cartesio' (2009) 34 *European Law Review* 378; A Autenne and J-E Navez, 'Cartesio—Les contours incertains de la mobilité transfrontalière des sociétés revisités' (2009) 1–2 *Cahiers de droit Européen* 91.

the company concerned in the host State and the pursuit of genuine economic activity there.[237]

The *Centros* solution was transposed to road haulage services in the *Andreas Hoves* case, which concerned the establishment by a German GmbH of a subsidiary in Luxembourg, whose activity was limited to the carriage of goods for the German parent company. This subsidiary did not own a garage or parking spaces for the lorries in Luxembourg, and all major decisions were taken in Germany.[238] Given that the centre of activities of the subsidiary was located in Germany, the German tax administration demanded payment of the German tax on motor vehicles. The Court ruled that both Regulation 3118/93 and Directive 93/89[239] preclude host Member States from regulating or taxing road haulage carriers, subject to the exceptions enumerated by Article 6 of Regulation 3118/93. In other words, road haulage carriers may freely elect their preferred national law by establishing themselves in their Member State of preference; once they are lawfully authorised in the Member State of establishment, the other Member States lose their jurisdiction to regulate them.

The free movement of workers is another field in which abuses of law are only loosely fought. Article 45(2) TFEU provides that workers are subject to the labour, social and tax laws of the Member State in which they are employed.[240] In that connection, the Court has consciously constructed a broad notion of migrant 'worker',[241] covering nearly any professional activity, however limited. As a result of this broad interpretation, migrant workers are granted the freedom to elect their preferred labour, social and tax laws by taking up an employment in their Member State of preference (free choice of law). In more detail, the Court's

[237] Case C-378/10 *VALE Építési* [2012] ECR I-0000, paras 34–35; see n 120 and accompanying text.

[238] Case C-115/00 *Andreas Hoves* [2002] ECR I-6077, paras 66–72.

[239] Council Regulation (EEC) 3118/93 of 25 October 1993 laying down the conditions under which non-resident carriers may operate national road haulage services within a Member State [1993] OJ L279/1; Council Directive 93/89/EEC of 25 October 1993 on the application by Member States of taxes on certain vehicles used for the carriage of goods by road and tolls and charges for the use of certain infrastructures [1993] OJ L279/32.

[240] Art 45(2) TFEU: '[The free movement of workers] shall entail the abolition of any discrimination based on nationality between workers of the Member States as regards employment, remuneration and other conditions of work and employment'. See also Regulation (EEC) 1612/68 of the Council of 15 October 1968 on freedom of movement for workers within the Community [1968] OJ L257/2 art 7(2); Regulation (EEC) 1408/71 of the Council of 14 June 1971 on the application of social security schemes to employed persons and their families moving within the Community [1971] OJ L149/2 art 13; Regulation (EC) 593/2008 of the European Parliament and of the Council of 17 June 2008 on the law applicable to contractual obligations [2008] OJ L177/6 (Rome I) art 8.

[241] Case C-292/89 *Antonissen* [1991] ECR I-745, para 11; Case 139/85 *Kempf* [1986] ECR 1741, para 13:

> The provisions laying down [the freedom of movement for workers] and, more particularly, the terms 'worker' and 'activity as an employed person' defining the sphere of application of those freedoms must be given a broad interpretation … whereas exceptions to and derogations from the principle of freedom of movement for workers must be interpreted strictly.

classical definition of a migrant worker, first enounced in *Levin* (1982), reads as follows:

> Any person who pursues activities which are real and genuine, to the exclusion of activities on such a small scale as to be regarded as purely marginal and ancillary, is entitled to freedom of movement as a worker.[242]

The 'genuineness' of an employment is usually tested against three criteria: duration of employment (from employed to unemployed), intensity of employment (threshold of hours worked per week) and level of remuneration. First of all, the level of remuneration has been consistently denied any relevance, as in *Levin* (remuneration below the minimum guaranteed remuneration), *Kempf* (below the level of the minimum means of subsistence) or *Lawrie-Blum* (below the starting salary of a qualified teacher).[243] As summed up by the Court in *Vatsouras*:

> Neither the origin of the funds from which the remuneration is paid nor the limited amount of that remuneration can have any consequence in regard to whether or not the person is a 'worker' for the purposes of Community law.[244]

Secondly, the short duration of the occupational activity can never question the status of worker. When assessing a three-month contract as a waitress in *Ninni-Orasche*, the Court explicitly stated that the short duration of an employment cannot, in itself, exclude that employment from the scope of the freedom of movement for workers (para 25).[245] However, the Court itself qualified this irrelevance of the duration of employment—reiterated in *Vatsouras*—with the '*Lair* principle', according to which the freedoms of movement do not cover strategies consisting in entering a Member State for the sole purpose of enjoying, after a very short period of occupational activity, welfare benefits in that State (para 36).

Lastly, the limited intensity of an occupation rarely questions the status of migrant worker either. In *Levin* (part-time chambermaid) and *Kempf* (12 music lessons per week), the Court explicitly endorsed part-time employment. In *Lawrie-Blum*, the Court considered that trainee teachers giving lessons a few hours per week were workers.[246] Nevertheless, to enjoy the status of worker, a

[242] Case C-456/02 *Trojani* [2004] ECR I-7573, para 15. See among many others Case C-208/07 *von Chamier* [2009] ECR I-6095, para 69; Joined Cases C-22/08 and C-23/08 *Vatsouras* [2009] ECR I-4585, para 26; Case C-213/05 *Geven* [2007] ECR I-6347, para 16; Case C-464/02 *Commission v Denmark* [2005] ECR I-7929, para 64; Case C-138/02 *Collins* [2004] ECR I-2703, para 26; Case C-413/01 *Ninni-Orasche* [2003] ECR I-13187, para 26; Case C-337/97 *Meeusen* [1999] ECR I-3289, para 13; Case C-357/89 *Raulin* [1992] ECR I-1027, paras 10 and 13–15; Case 197/86 *Brown* [1988] ECR 3205, para 21; Case 66/85 *Lawrie-Blum* [1986] ECR 2121, paras 16–17; Case 139/85 *Kempf* [1986] ECR 1741, para 11; Case 53/81 *Levin* [1982] ECR 1035, para 17.

[243] Case 66/85 *Lawrie-Blum* [1986] ECR 2121, para 21; Case 139/85 *Kempf* [1986] ECR 1741, para 14; Case 53/81 *Levin* [1982] ECR 1035, para 16.

[244] Joined Cases C-22/08 and C-23/08 *Vatsouras* [2009] ECR I-4585, para 27; see also Case C-456/02 *Trojani* [2004] ECR I-7573, para 16.

[245] Case C-413/01 *Ninni-Orasche* [2003] ECR I-13187, paras 25, 36 and 46; Joined Cases C-22/08 and C-23/08 *Vatsouras* [2009] ECR I-4585, para 29.

[246] See also Case C-14/09 *Hava Genc* [2010] ECR I-931, para 25 (an employment of less than 10 hours a week is sufficient to obtain the status of worker).

trainee must complete a number of hours sufficient to familiarise himself with the work (*Bernini*). Moreover, when assessing the effective and genuine nature of an activity carried out under a contract for occasional employment, account may be taken of the irregular nature and limited duration of the services actually performed (*Raulin*).[247]

The combined effect of this case law is the emergence of a particularly inclusive notion of migrant worker: nearly any occupational activity—however limited in duration, intensity and remuneration—is capable of granting the status of worker under the free movement provisions. Correlatively, the Court has proved particularly tolerant towards artificial cross-border movements set up by migrant workers,[248] de facto granting them free choice of labour, social and tax laws within the Union.

This free choice of law is however qualified by centres of gravity or suspect periods with regard to welfare benefits, as explained above.[249] Overall, it seems that Union workers are free to take up an employment in another Member State in order to enjoy more favourable labour, social and tax laws; as long as they are employed, workers are shielded from any suspicion of abuse (free choice of law). It is only where the duration (*Lair*, *Ninni-Orasche*) and/or intensity (*Raulin*) of employment are exceptionally low that workers lose the benefit of this presumption of legitimacy, as bona fide contributors to the host society.[250] Ziegler evokes in that regard a 'time-or-scale element': 'if someone has been a worker, but only for a short time or only in an employment on a small scale, it may appear to be "disproportionate" to grant further rights'.[251] In other words, when deprived of a proper employment shield, workers are assimilated to—economically inactive—Union citizens, and therefore required to establish their genuine integration into the host society by other means (centre of gravity approach).

In some exceptional cases, free choice of law is granted in relation to social benefits. In *van Heijningen*, for instance, the Court ruled that a person employed for four hours per week was an 'employed person' under Article 2(1) of Regulation 1408/71, and was entitled to full family allowances in the Netherlands. This decision must be contrasted to the *Geven* judgment interpreting Article 7(2) of Regulation 1612/68,[252] in which Germany was allowed to restrict the benefit of child-raising allowances to persons either residing or engaged in substantial occupational activity in Germany (at least 15 hours per week).

[247] Case 53/81 *Levin* [1982] ECR 1035, para 17; Case 139/85 *Kempf* [1986] ECR 1741, para 14; Case 66/85 *Lawrie-Blum* [1986] ECR 2121, para 21; Case C-3/90 *Bernini* [1992] ECR I-1071, para 16; Case C-357/89 *Raulin* [1992] ECR I-1027, para 14.

[248] E Spaventa, 'Comments on Abuse of Law and the Free Movement of Workers' in de la Feria and Vogenauer (n 1); Ziegler (n 57); de la Feria (n 96) 411.

[249] See section II and subsection III.B.

[250] Golynker (n 184) 115: 'Economically active migrants such as workers and self-employed persons are a-priory deemed bona fide contributors to the host society entitled to equal treatment'.

[251] Ziegler (n 57) 299.

[252] Regulation (EEC) 1612/68 of the Council of 15 October 1968 on freedom of movement for workers within the Community [1968] OJ L257/2.

The *Salzano* case concerned family allowances as well, granted to an Italian national working in Germany, but whose wife and children resided in Italy. Despite periods of employment in Italy, his wife never requested family allowances there, in order to remain under the more generous German regime. According to the German authorities, Italian allowances were 'payable' under Article 76 of Regulation 1408/71, so that the Salzano family had lost their entitlement to German allowances. The Court however ruled that Article 76 required actual payment of allowances in the country of residence, thereby granting free choice of law to the Salzano spouses: they could either request and obtain family allowances in Italy, or not request them and remain under the German regime.[253]

Article 76 of Regulation 1408/71 was subsequently amended, in the wake of the *Salzano* and *Pinna* judgments.[254] Under the new Article 76(1) introduced by Regulation 3427/89,[255] the Member State of employment (eg Germany in *Salzano*) must only pay the eventual difference between its domestic family allowance and the family allowance paid by the Member State of residence (eg Italy). Under the new Article 76(2), explicitly drafted in reaction to the *Salzano*-line of case law, the Member State of employment can take into account any family allowance for which an application has not been made in the Member State of residence.

However, from the perspective of Union citizens, the new Article 76(1) already deprives the '*Salzano* stratagem' of any interest, since Union citizens are guaranteed the higher family allowance offered in both States, even if they apply for them in the State of residence. By contrast, the former Article 76 provided for exclusive jurisdiction of either the State of employment or the State of residence, which spurred the decision not to apply for family allowances in Italy in the *Salzano* case. The new Article 76(2) merely proscribes irrational behaviour of Union citizens, who would by mistake or out of spite omit to apply for family allowances in their State of residence. This was precisely the situation in *Schwemmer*, in which Mr Schwemmer refrained from applying for family benefits under Swiss legislation solely in order to cause detriment to his ex-wife. The Court was asked to interpret Article 10 of Regulation 574/72,[256] whose wording is similar to the new Article

[253] Case 191/83 *Salzano* [1984] ECR 3741; AG Darmon, Case 191/83 *Salzano* [1984] ECR 3741, para 3; see also Case C-2/89 *van Heijningen* [1990] ECR I-1755, para 7-15; Case C-213/05 *Geven* [2007] ECR I-6347, paras 20–30.

[254] Case 41/84 *Pinna* [1986] ECR 1. The *Pinna* ruling condemned the residence criterion for the purpose of granting family allowances, so that the Union legislature amended Regulation 1408/71 in order to implement the employment criterion (*lex loci labori*): see European Economic and Social Committee (EC), 'The Proposal for a Council Regulation amending Regulation 1408/71 on the application of social security schemes to employed persons, to self-employed persons and to members of their families moving within the Community and Regulation 574/72 laying down the procedure for implementing Regulation 1408/71' (Opinion), 23 March 1988, C134/1.

[255] Council Regulation (EEC) 3427/89 of 30 October 1989 amending Regulation (EEC) 1408/71 on the application of social security schemes to employed persons, to self-employed persons and to members of their families moving within the Community and Regulation (EEC) 574/72 laying down the procedure for implementing Regulation (EEC) 1408/71 [1989] OJ L331/1.

[256] Regulation (EEC) 574/72 of the Council of 21 March 1972 fixing the procedure for implementing Regulation (EEC) 1408/71 on the application of social security schemes to employed persons and their families moving within the Community [1972] OJ L74/1.

76(1) of Regulation 1408/71, but without being qualified by a provision similar to the new Article 76(2) of Regulation 1408/71. As a result, the Court reaffirmed the initial *Salzano* solution, entitling Mrs Schwemmer to full family allowance in Italy.[257]

With regard to unemployment benefits, Article 71(1) of Regulation 1408/71 provides that unemployed persons, who reside in a State different from the one in which they were employed, may elect to receive them either in the State of residence or in the State of last employment:

> [B]y virtue of [Article 71(1)(b)], workers who are wholly unemployed are entitled to make a choice between the benefits offered by the Member State in which they were last employed and those offered by the Member State in which they reside. They exercise that option by making themselves available either to the employment services of the State in which they were last employed (Article 71(1)(b)(i)) or to those of the Member State in which they reside (Article 71(1)(b)(ii)).[258]

Nevertheless, this freedom to elect unemployment benefits in the State of employment or of residence was carefully restrained by the Court, in order to prevent artificial relocation strategies in Member States offering the most generous unemployment benefits. For that purpose, the Court explicitly applied a centre of gravity approach to the notion of 'residence':

> [F]or the application of Article 71(1) of Regulation 1408/71 ... the place of 'residence' is determined by the place where the habitual centre of interests is situated. In that regard it is important to consider the family situation of the worker as well as the reasons that have led him to move, and the nature of the work.[259]

Another area in which the Court has proved reluctant to fight artificial practices is the family reunification rights of third country nationals (TCNs) married with Union citizens, when the latter make use of their freedom of movement ('migrant' citizens). In *Akrich*, the protagonists had confessed that their brief stay in Ireland was designed to exploit the *Singh* ruling and manufacture a right of residence in the United Kingdom to Mr Akrich, a Moroccan national who had been previously deported by the UK authorities (para 36).[260] The Court formally rejected the application of the doctrine of abuse in such a hypothesis (para 56), but subjected the freedom of movement sought by Mr Akrich (right of residence in the United Kingdom) to a requirement of prior lawful residence in the Member State of departure, namely Ireland (para 54).[261]

[257] Case C-16/09 *Schwemmer* [2010] ECR I-9717, paras 53–59.

[258] Case C-102/91 *Knoch* [1992] ECR I-4341, para 16; Case 1/85 *Miethe* [1986] ECR 1837, para 9. See also Case C-372/02 *Adanez-Vega* [2004] ECR I-10761, paras 29–40; Case 236/87 *Bergemann* [1988] ECR 5125, paras 18–22; Case 76/76 *Di Paolo* [1977] ECR 315, paras 11–22.

[259] Case C-372/02 *Adanez-Vega* [2004] ECR I-10761, para 37; Case C-102/91 *Knoch* [1992] ECR I-4341, paras 21–23; Case 76/76 *Di Paolo* [1977] ECR 315, paras 17–22.

[260] Case C-109/01 *Akrich* [2003] ECR I-9607; Case C-370/90 *Singh* [1992] ECR I-4265.

[261] C Schiltz, 'Akrich: A Clear Delimitation Without Limits' (2005) 3 *Maastricht Journal of European and Comparative Law* 241, 247: 'This means ... that if Ireland granted Mr. Akrich a residence right, he would be able to rely on Regulation 1612/68 in order to gain leave to enter the UK'.

The concrete impact of *Akrich* is to grant a certain freedom to elect a national immigration regime for TCN family members of Union citizens, subject to a requirement of cross-border movement. Union citizens whose TCN family members face deportation may take up an employment in another Member State to trigger the application of Union law. The choice of the Member State of exile would then be based on its favourable immigration regime (the 'Dublin route'[262] in *Akrich*), facilitating the obtaining of a lawful residence for TCN family members, who would thereafter enjoy the right to accompany the migrant citizen throughout the Union (United Kingdom in *Akrich*).

The Court went further in its subsequent case law, and chiefly in the *Metock* ruling, whereby the Court granted TCNs the unconditional right to accompany the migrant citizen with whom they form a family, irrespective of whether they have lawfully resided in a Member State previously.[263] Under the *Metock* ruling, Union citizens whose family members face deportation only have to exercise their freedom of movement to secure them a right of residence, without having to comply with national immigration regimes, which considerably reduces the scope of the notion of abuse in relation to immigration regimes.[264] The Court moved from free choice of immigration regime (*Akrich*) to no immigration regime (*Metock*) for family members of migrant citizens,[265] always subject to a requirement of cross-border movement.

Furthermore, a first—but limited—relaxation of the requirement of cross-border movement in relation to TCN family members occurred in the *Zambrano* judgment, which compelled Member States to issue a residence and work permit to TCN parents upon whom minor children, who are Union citizens, are dependent:

> Article 20 TFEU ... precludes a Member State from refusing a third country national upon whom his minor children, who are European Union citizens, are dependent, a right of residence in the Member State of residence and nationality of those children, and from refusing to grant a work permit to that third country national, in so far as such decisions deprive those children of the genuine enjoyment of the substance of the rights attaching to the status of European Union citizen.[266]

In the subsequent *Dereci* case, the Court made clear that this relaxation was limited to the factual setting of the *Zambrano* case, in which the refusal to issue residence and work permits to TCN parents would have forced their minor children, Union citizens, to leave the Union as a whole. Moreover, in the later *O* case, the Court ruled that a derived right of residence, for TCN family members of Union citizens returning to their Member State of nationality, could only exist if the stay in the

[262] C Costello, 'Metock: Free Movement and "Normal Family Life" in the Union' (2009) 46 *Common Market Law Review* 587, 592.

[263] Case C-127/08 *Metock* [2008] ECR I-6241, paras 58–70; Case C-291/05 *Eind* [2007] ECR I-10719, para 41; Case C-1/05 *Jia* [2007] ECR I-1, paras 26–33.

[264] Costello, 'Metock' (n 262) 608–11.

[265] A Tryfonidou, 'Family Reunification Rights of (Migrant) Union Citizens: Towards a More Liberal Approach' (2009) 15 *European Law Journal* 634, 640: '[Following Metock] the family member can automatically accompany or join the migrant in the host State, without any additional conditions being imposed by that State'.

[266] Case C-34/09 *Zambrano* [2011] ECR I-1177, para 45.

host Member State was sufficiently 'actual' to develop or consolidate a family life there (paras 51–57). The Court ended its reasoning by recalling that the scope of Union law cannot be extended to cover abusive practices (para 58). If confirmed, this requirement of 'actual stay' in the host Member State would introduce a centre of gravity approach in the field, and accordingly help prevent artificial relocations in a host Member State intended to manufacture a derived right of residence for TCN family members in the Member State of nationality of a Union citizen.[267]

The Court similarly endorsed free choice of law in relation to the nationality of Union citizens. In *Micheletti*, the Spanish authorities deemed that a dual national (Argentinean and Italian) had to be regarded as Argentinean, and accordingly outside the scope of the freedoms of movement, because he had his habitual residence in Argentina. The Court outlawed this centre of gravity approach to nationality, on the following ground:

> Under international law, it is for each Member State, having due regard to Community law, to lay down the conditions for the acquisition and loss of nationality. However, it is not permissible for the legislation of a Member State to restrict the effects of the grant of the nationality of another Member State by imposing an additional condition for recognition of that nationality with a view to the exercise of the fundamental freedoms provided for in the Treaty.[268]

In *Zhu and Chen*, the same free choice of law approach led the Court to allow an artificial practice set up by a Chinese family to manufacture a long-term right of residence in the United Kingdom.[269] Mrs Chen indeed admitted that she had specifically chosen to give birth in Belfast, where Irish nationality was granted to any person born on Irish soil (*ius soli*). The Irish nationality of her newborn daughter, Catherine Zhu, would then secure them a long-term right to reside in the United Kingdom (para 36).[270] However, the Court maintained the strict obligation of recognition enounced in *Micheletti*, precluding Member States from assessing the possibility of an abusive practice (para 40). Costello approves this case law without qualification, as 'any generalised requirement to demonstrate that nationality reflects a "genuine link" would leave many nationals of the Member States vulnerable'.[271]

It should be noted that this case law seems to contradict the stance of the International Court of Justice, which explicitly adopted a centre of gravity approach in the *Nottebohm* case. Nottebohm had acquired Liechtenstein nationality in order to abusively evade the consequences of the international law of war.

[267] Case C-256/11 Dereci [2011] ECR I-11315, paras 65–68; Case C-456/12 *O* [2014] ECR I-0000, paras 51–58; see also Case C-457/12 *S* [2014] ECR I-0000, paras 42–44.

[268] Case C-369/90 *Micheletti* [1992] ECR I-4239, para 10; see also Case C-148/02 *Garcia Avello* [2003] ECR I-11613, para 28.

[269] Case C-200/02 *Zhu and Chen* [2004] ECR I-9925.

[270] See Jacobs, Citizenship of the European Union' (n 61) 596:

> In Chen, in circumstances which might have been regarded as an abuse of rights, [the Court] held that a manoeuvre designed to create a right of residence for a baby and her Chinese mother in the UK did not preclude the recognition of that right.

[271] Costello (n 57) 336.

The ICJ sought to counter this abusive practice by subjecting the recognition (ie 'opposability') of nationality to the existence of a 'genuine link' between the national and the conferring State.[272]

A similar contrast between Union law and international law can be identified with regard to the nationality of ships. Article 5(1) of the Geneva Convention on the High Seas, whose preamble explicitly specifies that its purpose is 'to codify the rules of international law relating to the high sea', explicitly states that there must exist a 'genuine link' between a State and the ships flying its flag:

> Each State shall fix the conditions for the grant of its nationality to ships, for the registration of ships in its territory, and for the right to fly its flag. Ships have the nationality of the State whose flag they are entitled to fly. There must exist a genuine link between the State and the ship; in particular, the State must effectively exercise its jurisdiction and control in administrative, technical and social matters over ships flying its flag.[273]

However, the Convention has been ratified or accessed by a limited number of States, including only 19 Member States of the European Union.[274] Moreover, both the principle and the precise meaning of the genuine link requirement have been debated, so that it cannot be considered as customary international law.[275] Against that background, the Court's stance on flags of convenience in the *Poulsen* case has been viewed as particularly permissive.[276] In 1989, Mr Poulsen, a Danish national, had sold his fishing vessel, the *Onkel Sam*, to a Panamanian company wholly owned by his brother, another Danish national. The company immediately reappointed Mr Poulsen as master of the vessel; the crew remained Danish and paid in Denmark; and between voyages, the vessel was normally berthed in a Danish port. The double purpose of this artificial practice was hardly disputed. First, Mr Poulsen received a final cessation premium upon the sale of his vessel, pursuant to Council

[272] *Nottebohm (Liechtenstein v Guatemala)* [1955] ICJ Rep 5. See inter alia J Verhoeven, 'Abus, Fraude ou Habileté?' in J Verhoeven (ed), *La loyauté: mélanges offerts à Etienne Cerexhe* (Brussels, Larcier, 1997) 420; JL Kunz, 'The Nottebohm Judgment' (1960) 54 *The American Journal of International Law* 536; JM Jones, 'The Nottebohm Case' (1956) 5 *The International and Comparative Law Quarterly* 230; OJ Lissitzyn, 'Nottebohm Case (Liechtenstein v Guatemala)' (1955) 49 *The American Journal of International Law* 396; Costello (n 57) 335.

[273] Geneva Convention on the High Seas (adopted 29 April 1958, entered into force 30 September 1962) 450 UNTS 11. See also AG Mischo, Case C-221/89 *Factortame II* [1991] ECR I-3905, paras 13 ff.

[274] The Member States that have not ratified or accessed the Treaty are Estonia, France, Greece, Ireland, Lithuania, Luxembourg, Malta and Sweden. See https://treaties.un.org/Pages/ShowMTDSGDetails.aspx?src=UNTSONLINE&tabid=1&mtdsg_no=XXI-2&chapter=21&lang=en#Participants.

[275] RR Churchill, 'European Community Law and the Nationality of Ships and Crews' (1991) 5 *European Transport Law* 591, 593. At first, the International Law Commission had laid down a series of objective criteria relating to ownership, but they were removed from the final draft owing to the lack of consensus among national delegations. The main line of division seemed to oppose Americans (in favour of flags of convenience) and Europeans (in favour a genuine link requirement): see Kunz, 'The Nottebohm Judgment' (n 272) 569.

[276] Case C-286/90 *Poulsen* [1992] ECR I-6019; see D Simon and A Rigaux, 'La technique de consécration d'un nouveau principe général de droit communautaire: l'exemple de l'abus de droit' in M Blanquet (ed), *Mélanges en hommage à Guy Isaac: 50 ans de droit communautaire* (Toulouse, Presses de l'Université des sciences sociales de Toulouse, 2004) 585; F Lagondet, 'L'abus de droit dans la jurisprudence communautaire' (2003) 1 *Journal de droit européen* 8, 9; Verhoeven, *La loyauté* (n 272).

Regulation 4028/86,[277] although he pursued his fishing activities as normal aboard the vessel—by then flying the Panamanian flag. Second, the Panamanian flag permitted the vessel to escape the ban on salmon and sea trout fishing imposed by Council Regulation 3094/86,[278] implementing the Convention for the Conservation of Salmon in the North Atlantic,[279] of which Panama is not a signatory.

At the beginning of 1990, the *Onkel Sam* was forced to moor in Denmark after catching 22 tons of salmon in the North Atlantic, owing to a mechanical problem and bad weather conditions. The Danish fishery officers discovered and seized the cargo, while Mr Poulsen was indicted for contravening Regulation 3094/86. In its judgment, the Court explicitly rejected the 'genuine link' approach suggested by the Danish authorities, stating that the vessel's Panamanian nationality could not be set aside.[280] As a consequence, European vessel owners were granted free choice of law: either fly a European Union flag and be subject to the ban on fishing salmon and sea trout, or fly the Panamanian flag (or another flag of convenience) and not be subject to it. It should be mentioned that in the subsequent *AJD Tuna* case, the Court upheld the validity of Regulation 530/2008,[281] in so far as it prohibited Union operators from accepting landings of bluefin tuna or placing them in cages for fattening or farming, even where they were caught by ships flying the flag of a third country.[282]

The Court adopted a similar free choice of law approach in relation to fishing quotas, by famously endorsing the practice of 'quota-hopping'. In accordance with the Montego Bay Convention,[283] the Common Fisheries Policy seeks to conserve fishery resources by restricting the quantity of fish that can be caught in the sea. Under the regime established by Regulations 101/76 and 170/83,[284] the Council sets annual 'Total Allowable Catches' (TACs) for fish stocks threatened by overfishing (Article 3 of Regulation 170/83). The TACs are then divided into national catch quotas attributed to every Member State, with a view to assuring each Member State 'relative stability of fishing activities' for each of the stocks considered (Article 4 of Regulation 170/83). Member States are responsible for issuing detailed rules regarding the utilisation of the national catch quotas allocated to them (Article 5(2) of Regulation 170/83).

[277] Council Regulation (EEC) 4028/86 of 18 December 1986 on Community measures to improve and adapt structures in the fisheries and aquaculture sector [1986] OJ L376/7.

[278] Council Regulation (EEC) 3094/86 of 7 October 1986 laying down certain technical measures for the conservation of fishery resources [1986] OJ L288/1.

[279] Reykjavik Convention for the conservation of salmon in the North Atlantic Ocean (adopted 2 March 1982, entered into force 1 October 1983) 1338 UNTS 33.

[280] Case C-286/90 *Poulsen* [1992] ECR I-6019, paras 12–16.

[281] Commission Regulation (EC) 530/2008 of 12 June 2008 establishing emergency measures as regards purse seiners fishing for bluefin tuna in the Atlantic Ocean, East of longitude 45°W, and in the Mediterranean Sea [2008] OJ L155/9.

[282] Case C-221/09 *AJD Tuna* [2011] ECR I-1655, paras 77–85.

[283] Montego Bay Convention on the Law of the Sea (adopted 10 December 1982, entered into force 16 November 1994) 1834 UNTS 3.

[284] Council Regulation 101/76 of 19 January 1976 laying down a Common Structural Policy for the Fishing Industry [1976] OJ L20/19 art 4; Council Regulation (EEC) 170/83 of 25 January 1983 establishing a Community System for the Conservation and Management of Fishery Resources [1983] OJ L24/1.

It is in that policy context that the practice of 'quota-hopping' appeared with the purpose of artificially circumventing national limitations on fishing activities;[285] the practice consisted in reflagging fishing vessels in order to fish against the fishing quotas of another Member State.[286] Quota-hopping was mostly practised by Spanish interests at the expense of UK fishing quotas,[287] which gave rise to a long series of references for a preliminary ruling before the Court.[288] In *Factortame II*, the Court referred to quota-hopping as a practice whereby the UK fishing quotas were 'plundered by vessels flying the British flag but lacking any genuine link with the United Kingdom' (para 4). In essence, all the questions referred to the Court concerned various measures adopted by the United Kingdom to impose such a 'genuine link' between the vessels fishing against UK quotas and UK society (centre of gravity approach). Again, such genuine link requirement could be inferred from Article 5(1) of the Geneva Convention on the High Seas, quoted above.

Despite a formal declaration allowing the imposition of such a 'genuine link' in *Jaderow* (para 26), between vessels fishing against national quotas and local populations dependent on fisheries, the Court removed every possibility to set up an effective centre of gravity approach[289]—on the model of the *Centros* ruling.[290] In that regard, the boldest statement is indubitably to be found in the *Agegate* ruling, in which the Court proclaimed that a residence requirement, to the effect that 75 per cent of the crew habitually reside ashore in the United Kingdom, was simply 'irrelevant' in a system of quotas designed to protect local populations dependent on fisheries (para 25). Since the socioeconomic toll of fishing quotas should be proportionally allocated among the local populations dependent on fisheries (*Romkes*, para 23: relative stability of fishing activities), the UK authorities decided to exclude non-residents from national quotas.[291] Nevertheless, after striking down all nationality and residence requirements, the Court only allowed Member States to demand that the vessel be operated from domestic ports (regular landings

[285] Quota-hopping was explicitly designated as an 'abuse' by the Irish Government: Case C-93/89 *Commission v Ireland* [1991] ECR I-4569, para 12.

[286] A Hatcher et al, 'Quota-hopping and the Foreign Ownership of UK Fishing Vessels' (2002) 26 *Marine Policy* 1, 1.

[287] C Lequesne, 'Quota Hopping: The Common Fisheries Policy Between States and Markets' (2000) 38 *Journal of Common Market Studies* 779, 783–84.

[288] Case 46/86 *Romkes* [1987] ECR 2671; Case 223/86 *Pesca Valentia* [1988] ECR 83; Order of the President in Case C-246/89 R *Commission v United Kingdom* [1989] ECR 3125; Case C-3/87 *Agegate* [1989] ECR 4459; Case C-216/87 *Jaderow* [1989] ECR 4509; Case C-213/89 *Factortame I* [1990] ECR I-2433; Case C-221/89 *Factortame II* [1991] ECR I-3905; Case C-93/89 *Commission v Ireland* [1991] ECR I-4569; Case C-246/89 *Commission v United Kingdom* [1991] ECR I-4585; Case C-279/89 *Commission v United Kingdom* [1992] ECR I-5785.

[289] In the same sense, M Morin, 'The Fisheries Resources in the European Union—The Distribution of TACs: Principle of Relative Stability and Quota-Hopping' (2000) 24 *Marine Policy* 265, 271: 'The *Jaderow* case permits States to require the condition of a 'real economic link' but does not provide them with true means to control whether this link really exists'.

[290] In *Centros*, the Court formally allowed Member States to fight abuses (para 24), but then prevented them from doing so in practice (paras 25–27).

[291] RR Churchill, 'Quota Hopping: the Common Fisheries Policy Wrongfooted?' (1990) 27 *Common Market Law Review* 209, 226.

and/or visits: *Jaderow*, paras 27–32) and managed through a fixed establishment within their territory, even if the latter acts on instructions from a decision-taking centre located in another Member State (*Factortame II*, paras 34–35).

Overall, by authorising quota-hopping, this case law grants free choice of law in relation to national fishing quotas: investors may easily reflag their fishing vessels in another Member State, and be ipso facto granted the right to fish against its national quota. As such, quota-hopping does not imperil the primary objective of preserving fishery resources in the Union, since quota-hoppers fish against actual quotas (of another Member State) and not 'off-quota'. However, it does contradict the secondary objective of relative stability of fishing activities (Article 4(1) of Regulation 170/83), which stipulates that fishing possibilities must be proportionally allocated among local communities particularly dependent upon fisheries.[292] Indeed, if fishing quotas are determined by taking into account the needs of local populations, then they should be actually used by those local populations,[293] which implies the adoption of a centre of gravity approach and the prohibition of quota-hopping as abusive.[294] The Court's stance on quota-hopping is all the less understandable since it formally endorsed the system of national quotas and the principle of relative stability in the *Romkes* case (para 23)—only to later undermine it by allowing quota-hopping.

A last instance of artificial reflagging is provided by the *Viking* case, in which a Finnish company (Viking) sought to reflag a vessel flying the Finnish flag (the *Rosella*) by registering it in Norway or Estonia, in order to be applied lower labour standards and consequently reduce its exploitation costs.[295] Viking's strategy is a paramount example of an artificial practice, namely a choice of law (high versus low labour standards) made under the cover of interchangeable legal cloaks (Finnish flag versus Estonian flag). Nevertheless, the Court never evoked the possibility of qualifying this strategy as abusive, de facto granting free choice of labour law to ship-owners.

To sum up, all the cases described in this section concerned artificial practices that were not condemned as 'abusive', but explicitly ratified by Union institutions. Those cases can be said to grant free choice of law to Union citizens, since artificial practices are first and foremost choices of law, namely voluntary changes of legal regime provoked by the election of a specific legal cloak.

[292] Case 46/86 *Romkes* [1987] ECR 2671, para 23; Case C-216/87 *Jaderow* [1989] ECR 4509, para 23; Parliament (EC), 'Heavily fisheries-dependent regions, relative stability and access to fishery resources' (Written Question E-3187/02), 7 November 2002, 2003 C155E/106, no 1; Lequesne, 'Quota Hopping' (n 287) 783.

[293] P Chaumette and G Proutière Maulion, 'Quota-hopping et appropriation des ressources halieutiques' (2005) 23 *Annuaire de Droit Maritime et Océanique* 309; Morin, 'The Fisheries Resources in the European Union' (n 289) 266:

> This objective [of relative stability] supposes, as a corollary, that the vessels entitled to this distribution remain largely economically active within the region concerned, in other words that these vessels are still an integral part of the local socioeconomic fabric.

[294] Neville Brown, 'Is there a General Principle of Abuse of Rights in European Community Law?' (n 117) 522–25.

[295] Case C-438/05 *Viking* [2007] ECR I-10779.

5

Abuse of Union Law and Legal Certainty

THE PRESENT CHAPTER is devoted to the long-standing debate on the room for legal uncertainty entailed by the prohibition of abuses of Union law. Without disputing that the prohibition of abusive practices is a source of legal uncertainty, this chapter argues that such criticism is simplistic as it ignores another fundamental value of any legal order, which is designated as legal congruence. Whereas legal certainty focuses on the *predictability* of legal outcomes, legal congruence is concerned with their *equity*. Every legal order is characterised by a well-established trade-off between legal certainty and legal congruence: the more predictable are legal norms, the less equitable they can be in particular cases (Section I). The concept of abuse of law must be appraised in light of this trade-off between legal certainty and legal congruence. Abuses of Union law are manifestations of a lack of legal congruence caused by the rigidity of Union law. In that sense, legal certainty can be viewed as a source of artificial practices (Section II). In turn, the prohibition of artificial practices amounts to a normative decision to reinstate legal congruence at the expense of legal certainty in particular cases (Section III).

I. The Trade-off between Legal Certainty and Legal Congruence

The phenomenon of abuse of Union law cuts across an immemorial debate between two legitimate objectives of any legal order: legal certainty (the tendency to yield predictable legal outcomes) and legal congruence (the tendency to yield equitable legal outcomes). To a great extent, legal certainty and legal congruence represent ideals that are difficult to achieve *individually*; yet the pivotal submission of this chapter is that they can never be achieved *simultaneously*. Indeed, it has long been established that the law is pervaded by an inescapable trade-off: the more predictable are legal outcomes, the less equitable they can be in particular cases (Subsection I.A). This trade-off is present in Union law as in any other legal order, both at the stage of the adoption of legal norms by the legislature and at the stage of their interpretation by the judiciary (Subsection I.B).

A. The Universality of the Trade-off between Legal Certainty and Legal Congruence

In order to describe the trade-off between legal certainty and legal congruence, it is useful to propose a preliminary definition of these notions, although their precise meaning will incrementally emerge in the course of this chapter. Legal certainty can be defined as the tendency of a legal regime to yield predictable outcomes. The virtue inherent in legal certainty is the predictability of legal outcomes for those potentially subject to the dreadful impact of public force. As observed by Holmes:

> [I]n societies like ours the command of the public force is intrusted to the judges in certain cases, and the whole power of the state will be put forth, if necessary, to carry out their judgments and decrees. People want to know under what circumstances and how far they will run the risk of coming against what is so much stronger than themselves.[1]

The fear of legal *un*certainty broadly overlaps with the fear of judicial discretion, which can be defined as the extent to which a judge applying a legal norm has the freedom to choose among various outcomes.[2] Indeed, a legal norm that reduces the ambit of choice for the competent judge tends to yield the same outcome irrespective of the judge seized, thereby generating legal certainty. In that connection, Ihering used the concept of formal realisability:

> By formal realisability … I mean the ease and certainty of application of abstract law to concrete cases. Depending on whether this operation demands a more or less considerable exertion of intellectual force, depending on whether its outcomes are more or less certain, I will say that there is more or less formal realisability.[3]

However, it has long been established that legal norms securing legal certainty are not exempt of defects, and correlatively that judicial discretion has its benefits.[4] Indeed, legal certainty only represents the first panel of a diptych common to every legal order. The second panel has been given many names, such as equity, justice, fairness; in the present study, it will be designated as legal congruence. By contrast with legal certainty, legal congruence is not a term of art in the literature, although the idea it conveys is frequently asserted in a wide variety of contexts. Congruence, whose general meaning is agreement or harmony, comes from the Latin verb *congruere*, literally to come together or correspond with. In geometry, congruence is the relationship between two figures that have the same shape and size, so that they coincide exactly when superimposed. In anatomy, two joints

[1] OW Holmes, 'The Path of the Law' (1897) 110 *Harvard Law Review* 991, 991.

[2] RM Dworkin, 'Judicial Discretion' (1963) 60 *The Journal of Philosophy* 624, 625.

[3] R von Jhering, O de Meulenaere (trans), *L'Esprit du Droit Romain*, 3rd edn, vol 1 (Paris, Librairie A Marescq, 1886) 52, free translation.

[4] See among many others D Kennedy, 'Form and Substance in Private Law Adjudication' (1976) 89 *Harvard Law Review* 1685.

are said to be congruent when they perfectly fit each other. In a legal context, congruence is the quality of a legal regime that perfectly fits the reality it seeks to regulate and therefore tends to yield equitable legal outcomes.

Whereas legal certainty relates to a formal quality of law (predictability), legal congruence is concerned with its substantive qualities (equity). The conflict between both virtues can be summed up as follows: the more predictable are legal outcomes, the less equitable they can be in particular cases. Indeed, laws are drafted and voted by human beings who cannot be expected to foresee the infinite intricacies of reality: 'Since legislators act under the constraints of limited resources, bounded foresight, and inexact human language, unanticipated problems of fit have long been viewed as unavoidable'.[5] As a consequence, casting legal norms into a rigid mould inevitably condemns them to legal *in*congruence, for rigid norms cannot be adapted to unavoidable problems of fit:

> When rigid general law is laid upon the uneven ground of nature it will touch at certain points and miss at others. Aristotle attributes the fault, not to law, but to the unevenness of nature … Wherever one lays the blame, there is undeniably a fault between strict law and nature—including human nature. Sometimes the law fits with nature, and sometimes it does not.[6]

As evoked in the previous excerpt, Aristotle discussed the difficulty of matching law with reality in the *Nicomachean Ethics*, hence the need for 'decrees':

> The reason is that all law is universal but about some things it is not possible to make a universal statement which shall be correct. … And it is none the less correct; for the error is in the law nor in the legislator but in the nature of the thing … In fact this is the reason why all things are not determined by law, that about some things it is impossible to lay down a law, so that a decree is needed. For when the thing is indefinite the rule also is indefinite, like the leaden rule used in making the Lesbian moulding; the rule adapts itself to the shape of the stone and is not rigid, and so too the decree is adapted to the facts.[7]

Masons from Lesbos used a leaden rule, which could be bent to the irregular curves of a moulding, enabling them to reproduce it. Rigid legal rules tend to yield certain but inequitable outcomes, as they cannot be bent to the irregular curves of reality. In short, legal certainty tends to generate absurd outcomes. Conversely, flexible legal rules tend to yield equitable but uncertain outcomes, as the competent judge can bend them to the irregular curves of reality.

[5] JF Manning, 'What Divides Textualists from Purposivists?' (2006) 106 *Columbia Law Review* 70, 71–72.

[6] G Watt, *Equity Stirring: the Story of Justice beyond Law* (Oxford, Hart Publishing, 2009) 8–9.

[7] Aristotle, WD Ross (trans), *The Nicomachean Ethics* (Oxford, Clarendon Press, 1908) book V ch 10. The lesbian rule was a mason's rule of lead used in Lesbos, which could be bent to measure and reproduce the irregular curves of a moulding.

A first illustration of the trade-off between legal certainty and legal congruence can be provided with the following common rule: 'Citizens who have reached the age of 18 have legal capacity'. This rule undeniably provides a high degree of legal certainty, as it invites the competent judge to validate a transaction[8] after a mere verification of the parties' age. Yet, if applied literally, this rule would validate transactions made by mentally disabled persons who have reached the age of 18. Creating an exception for the mentally disabled decreases the degree of legal certainty, as it invites the competent judge to assess whether a person is 'mentally disabled'. The original rule would also, if applied literally, validate transactions made by persons who find themselves under the influence of authority figures, such as priests or doctors. Again, creating another exception to address such situations further undermines legal certainty, as it invites the competent judge to assess whether a person is 'under the influence of an authority figure'. And the list of exceptions could go on, each exception improving legal congruence—and undermining legal certainty.

As illustrated by the former example, a norm offering a high degree of legal certainty presents a linear simplicity that can hardly be fitted to the uneven contours of reality. Accordingly, if absurd outcomes are to be avoided—which amounts to ensuring legal congruence—exceptions must be introduced in order to break the linear simplicity of the applicable norm—which necessarily decreases legal certainty. In other words, the more certain are legal rules, the less they fit reality, and this trade-off pervading every legal order is aggravated by the increasing intricacy of modern reality. In more detail, this trade-off can be identified at the stage of the adoption of a legal norm by the legislature and at that of its application by the judiciary (Table 8).

First of all, the wording of legal norms suffers from a well-established dilemma that has been labelled as the 'question of legal form':[9] legal norms can be rested

Table 8 – The Trade-off between Legal Certainty and Legal Congruence

	Legal Certainty	Legal Congruence
Adoption by the Legislature	Rigid legal commands	Flexible legal commands
Interpretation by the Judiciary	Literal interpretation	Teleological interpretation

[8] Legal capacity can be defined as 'a construct which enables law to recognise and validate the decisions and transactions that a person makes': O Lewis, 'Advancing Legal Capacity Jurisprudence' (2011) 6 *European Human Rights Law Review* 700, 700.

[9] Disputes regarding the form of legal norms are common in legal scholarship and involve stereotypical arguments regardless of the substantive issue at stake: see P Schlag, 'Rules and Standards' (1985–86) 33 *UCLA Law Review* 379, 380. As a matter of fact, a body of legal thought named the 'jurisprudence of rules' is exclusively devoted to that question of legal form; it postulates that the question of legal form is significant and can be analysed in isolation from the substantive issues that legal norms respond to: see Kennedy, 'Form and Substance in Private Law Adjudication' (n 4) 1687; J Braithwaite, 'Rules and Principles: A Theory of Legal Certainty' (2002) 27 *Australian Journal of Legal Philosophy* 47.

on either rigid or flexible legal commands. A legal command is said to be *rigid* when it is highly determinate and cannot be modulated by the competent judge; numerical criteria are the archetype of rigid legal commands. Conversely, a *flexible* legal norm rests on legal commands that are indeterminate and can be modulated by the competent judge, such as standards of reasonableness, good faith, unconscionability, due care or unjust enrichment. The distinction between rigid and flexible legal norms can be easily highlighted with a few illustrations:

Table 9 – Rigid Wording versus Flexible Wording of Legal Norms

	Rigid Norm	**Flexible Norm**
1	Citizens who have reached the age of 18 have legal capacity.	Citizens who enjoy capacity of discernment have legal capacity.[10]
2	Sounds above 70 decibels shall be punished by a USD 10 fine.	Excessive loudness shall be enjoinable upon showing of irreparable harm.[11]
3	Driving in excess of 130 km/h on highways shall be punished by a EUR 100 fine.	Driving at unreasonable speed shall be punished by an appropriate fine.[12]

The relevance of this distinction, as shown in Table 9, resides in the fact that rigid legal norms generate legal certainty (at the expense of legal congruence), whereas flexible legal norms ensure legal congruence (at the expense of legal certainty). In other words, the wording of legal norms calls for a choice between two legitimate objectives: legal certainty or legal congruence.

On the one hand, the choice of legal certainty is materialised by the adoption of rigid legal norms. For instance, rigid norm no 1 guarantees a high degree of legal certainty, as the competent judge is bound to mechanically acknowledge the legal capacity of every citizen who has reached the age of 18. Conversely, flexible norm no 1 requests the competent judge to assess whether individuals enjoy 'capacity of discernment' before acknowledging their legal capacity: such a flexible standard leaves ample room for judicial discretion and accordingly entails a risk of legal uncertainty.[13]

On the other hand, the choice of legal congruence is made through the adoption of flexible legal norms. Flexible norm no1 allows the competent judge to adapt its decisions to the idiosyncrasies of concrete cases. By contrast, rigid norm

[10] Modified version of example borrowed from Kennedy (n 4) 1689.

[11] Example borrowed from Schlag, 'Rules and Standards' (n 9) 382–83; see also M Franklin and R Rabin, *Cases And Materials on Tort Law and Alternatives*, 3rd edn (New York, Foundation Press, 1983) 51–54.

[12] Modified version of example borrowed from L Kaplow, 'Rules versus Standards: An Economic Analysis' (1992) 42 *Duke Law Journal* 557, 559–60.

[13] von Jhering, *L'Esprit du Droit Romain* (n 3) 54–55.

nol mechanically[14] excludes citizens who possess the capacity of discernment before the age of 18, and mechanically includes citizens who lack this capacity after the age of 18. A rigid norm having the shape of a straight line cannot be bent to match a tortuous reality; by contrast, a flexible norm can be adapted to the intricate contours of reality, in order to make its scope perfectly coincide with the reality it intends to regulate.

Accordingly, rigid norms ensure legal certainty but undermine legal congruence. Conversely, the adaptability of flexible norms permits legal congruence and, by the same token, imperils legal certainty. Duncan Kennedy underlined the existence of this zero-sum game in the following terms:

> The use of [rigid] rules, as opposed to [flexible] standards, to deter immoral or antisocial conduct means that sometimes perfectly innocent behaviour will be punished, and that sometimes plainly guilty behaviour will escape sanction. These costs of mechanical over- and under-inclusion are the price of avoiding the potential arbitrariness and uncertainty of a [flexible] standard.[15]

Secondly, this trade-off between legal certainty and legal congruence is also present at the stage of the interpretation of legal norms by the judiciary, where it takes the form of a dilemma between literal and teleological methods of interpretation. This interpretative dilemma tends to be confined to the application of rigid norms for flexible norms already empower the competent judge to take all relevant circumstances into account in order to avoid inequitable outcomes. Conversely, rigid norms tend to guarantee legal certainty at the expense of legal congruence and, as such, entail a risk of inequitable outcomes:

> [A] formal method would highlight the 'ordinary' meaning of the norm as well as values of rule of law and legal certainty, whereas a teleological interpretation would emphasize values of adaptability, coherence, integrity, equality, and indiscrimination.[16]

The dilemma between literal and teleological interpretation arises when judges are actually confronted with a risk of inequitable outcome: a literal interpretation secures legal certainty whereas a teleological interpretation thwarts the risk of inequitable outcome. Countless illustrations of the risk of legal incongruence entailed by the literal interpretation of rigid legal norms can be found in the literature. For instance, Blackstone related that a surgeon who had opened the vein of a person having a fit in the street was prosecuted—but eventually found innocent—under a Bolognian law that 'punished with the utmost severity whoever drew blood in

[14] Duncan Kennedy and Ronald Dworkin use the idea of 'mechanical' jurisprudence in the same sense, namely a mode of judicial interpretation privileging legal certainty at the expense of legal congruence: see Kennedy (n 4) 1695, 1711, 1745, 1754; RM Dworkin, 'The Model of Rules' (1967) 35 *The University of Chicago Law Review* 14, 16.

[15] Kennedy (n 4) 1695. 'Rules' are rigid norms, 'standards' flexible ones.

[16] R Karimeri, 'A Critical Review of the Definition of Tax Avoidance in the Case Law of the European Court of Justice' (2011) 39 *Intertax* 296, 304.

the streets' in order to protect public order.[17] Dworkin discussed the case *Riggs v Palmer*,[18] in which a New York court had to decide whether an heir could inherit from his grandfather in accordance with the applicable law, although he had murdered him to do so.[19] More recently, Lord Mance described a case in which the United Kingdom Supreme Court[20] had to decide whether a property owner, who had built a house within the profile of a barn and invisibly to the outside, could benefit from a time limit protecting unauthorised building from enforcement action after four years.[21] In each of these cases, sticking to the letter of the law on behalf of legal certainty would have led to an absurd outcome, as pointed out by Lord Mance:

> Are there, however, limits to the certainty to which legislators and judges can or should aspire? The infinite circumstances affecting human existence fit uneasily within strait-jackets. Certainty can be pushed too far, and, if it is coupled with governmental suspicion of judicial discretion, it can lead to potential injustice. … In this regard, a purely literal approach, based on the 'natural' meaning of individual words, may lead to absurdity.[22]

In other words, in order to re-establish legal congruence and avoid absurd outcomes, judges may have to go beyond the letter of the law to call upon its spirit (or *telos*), thereby adopting a teleological method of interpretation:

> It is normally unnecessary to reach beyond the letter of the law, but the need to do so is sometimes clear. … Every system of justice has a responsibility to supervise the operation in relation to particular people in particular cases of its general and necessarily imperfect scheme and to intervene to prevent harm caused by routine insistence on legal form and legal norms.[23]

Aristotle advocated the recourse to teleological interpretation when the literal application of a rigid norm leads to such absurd outcome:

> When the law speaks universally, then, and a case arises on it which is not covered by the universal statement, then it is right, where the legislator fails us and has erred by oversimplicity, to correct the omission—to say what the legislator himself would have said had he been present, and would have put into his law if he had known. … And this is the nature of the equitable, a correction of law where it is defective owing to its universality.[24]

[17] W Blackstone, *Commentaries on the Laws of England* (Oxford, Clarendon Press, 1769) Introduction s 2 'Of the Nature of Laws in General'.

[18] *Riggs v Palmer* (1889) 115 NY 506 (Court of Appeals of New York).

[19] Dworkin, 'The Model of Rules' (n 14) 23.

[20] *Secretary of State for Communities and Local Government v Welwyn Hatfield B.C.* (2010) EWCA Civ 26.

[21] J Mance, 'Should the Law be Certain?', The Oxford Shrieval lecture, 11 October 2011, available at www.supremecourt.gov.uk/docs/speech_111011.pdf, no 44–45.

[22] Mance, 'Should the Law be Certain' (n 21) no 13 and 21.

[23] Watt, *Equity Stirring* (n 6) 2.

[24] Aristotle, *The Nicomachean Ethics* (n 7) book V ch 10.

However, by inviting the judge to discover the 'telos' of the applicable law and to overrule its letter if necessary, the teleological method of interpretation inevitably undermines legal certainty:

> Constructing a provision teleologically is by no means a straightforward exercise. The teloi are those of the legislature. A teleological interpretation involves both an element of construction and an element of evaluation. As a result, a teleological interpretation can quickly become a hazardous exercise. From here, it is only a short step to concluding that purposive interpretation allows for a good degree of discretion and a good degree of discretion allows satisfying preferences other than those of the legislature.[25]

In other words, teleological interpretation tends to sacrifice legal certainty in favour of legal congruence, thereby preventing inequitable outcomes. Therefore, the interpretation of rigid norms by the judiciary is subject to the same dilemma as the adoption of norms by the legislature: the judge seized must choose between pursuing legal certainty or legal congruence. A literal interpretation solidifies the rigidity of the applicable norm, thereby securing legal certainty. Conversely, a teleological interpretation instils a measure of flexibility into the rigid scope of the applicable norm, in order to make it coincide with reality, thereby achieving legal congruence. In that connection, Blackstone wrote in his *Commentaries on the Laws of England*, first published in 1769:

> [T]he most universal and effectual way of discovering the true meaning of a law, when the words are dubious, is by considering the reason and spirit of it; or the cause which moved the legislator to enact it. … For since in laws all cases cannot be foreseen or expressed, it is necessary, that when the general decrees of the law come to be applied to particular cases, there should be somewhere a power vested of defining those circumstances, which (had they been foreseen) the legislator himself would have expressed.[26]

In sum, just as the legislature must choose between rigid and flexible norms, the judiciary must choose between literal and teleological interpretation; and both choices are informed, consciously or not, by the trade-off between legal certainty and legal congruence. The dilemma posed by the judicial interpretation of rigid norms is known to every legal order. In the context of US constitutional law, it has taken the form of a dispute between 'textualists' and 'purposivists'. Purposivists argue that applying the letter of a bicentenary text to modern issues entails a great risk of legal incongruence or inequitable outcomes, so that judges should enforce its spirit rather than its letter.[27] Conversely, textualists contend that a

[25] P Schammo, 'Arbitrage and Abuse of Rights in the EC Legal System' (2008) 14 *European Law Journal* 351, 373.

[26] Blackstone, *Commentaries on the Laws of England* (n 17) Introduction, s 2 'Of the Nature of Laws in General'.

[27] Manning, 'What Divides Textualists from Purposivists?' (n 5).

literal interpretation of the US Constitution is necessary in order to guarantee legal certainty:

> [Textualists] demand fidelity to something they call 'the text'. They expound a rule: The text is the authoritative given that judges are bound to follow. Failure to adhere to this rule will bring about all sort of evils, including judicial creativity and arbitrariness.[28]

In the context of English law, the virtues of teleological interpretation have long been established in relation to equity. Historically, equity is a body of law[29] that emerged in order to mitigate the harsh rigidity of the common law.[30] As a consequence, the function of equity was to improve legal congruence, which accordingly reduced legal certainty:

> The 'need' for the equity courts was, by historical consensus, to mitigate the harsh rigors of the common-law courts. The latter had developed increasingly strict and formal pleadings and causes of action, but real-world variety and the need for justice outstripped the narrowness of the common-law forms of action. … The common-law forms of action, in short, applied less and less certainly to the activities of the real world.[31]

To sum up, every legal order is pervaded by an inescapable trade-off between two legitimate objectives: legal certainty or the desire to produce predictable outcomes, on the one hand, and legal congruence or the desire to yield equitable outcomes, on the other. As shown throughout this section, this trade-off takes the form of two dilemmas respectively faced by the legislature and the judiciary: on the one hand, the legislature must choose between rigid and flexible norms; on the other, the judiciary must choose between literal and teleological methods of interpretation.

B. The Trade-off between Legal Certainty and Legal Congruence in Union Law

Legal certainty has the status of a general principle of Union law[32] and, as such, appears regularly in the Court's case law. For instance, the Court recalled the meaning of legal certainty in the *Nelson* judgment, which concerned the obligation of

[28] Schlag (n 9) 390–91.

[29] Equity as a body of English law is not to be confused with the broader notion of equity derived in the Middle Ages from the Aristotelian philosophy: see HE Yntema, 'Equity in the Civil Law and the Common Law' (1966–67) 15 *The American Journal of Comparative Law* 60, esp 81.

[30] MA Glendon, PG Carozza and CB Picker, *Comparative Legal Traditions: Text, Materials, and Cases on Western Law*, 3rd edn (St Paul MN, Thomson/West, 2007) 311; S Worthington, *Equity* (Oxford, Clarendon Press, 2003) 8 ff; HG Hanbury and RH Maudsley, *Modern Equity* (London, Stevens & Sons, 1989) 3–4.

[31] A D'Amato, 'Legal Uncertainty' (1983) 71 *California Law Review* 1, 36–37.

[32] T Tridimas, *The General Principles of EU Law*, 2nd edn (Oxford, Oxford University Press, 2006) ch 6.

airlines to compensate passengers in the event of delay to their flights, previously established in the *Sturgeon* case:

> [A]s regards the clarity of the obligations imposed on air carriers, it should be borne in mind that the principle of legal certainty requires that individuals should be able to ascertain unequivocally what their rights and obligations are and take steps accordingly.[33]

The Court also stated in *Plantanol*:

> [T]he principle of legal certainty, the corollary of which is the principle of the protection of legitimate expectations, requires, on the one hand, that rules of law must be clear and precise and, on the other, that their application must be foreseeable by those subject to them.[34]

However, the relationship between substantive Union law and legal certainty is far more nuanced than the unqualified endorsement of legal certainty as general principle of Union law. Indeed, as with every legal order, the Union legal order is pervaded by a struggle between legal certainty and legal congruence, which can be easily illustrated by re-examining some well-known features of Union law.

First of all, the freedoms of movement represent the cornerstone of the process of economic integration within the Union. Yet the wording of the Treaty provisions establishing the freedoms of movement is laconic, in particular in light of their broad and multiform scope of application. As will be explained throughout part two of this study, the Court's interpretation of the freedoms of movement is characterised by its flexibility, which tends to undermine legal certainty. One central issue raised by the notion of obstacle to free movement is whether goods or services exported from one Member State ('home') to another ('host') may be subject to the laws of both home and host States. Arguably, such multiple regulation amounts to indirect discrimination.[35] As a matter of fact, the Court held in *Cassis de Dijon* that multiple regulation was incompatible with free movement, except where justified by the proportionate pursuit of a legitimate policy objective.[36] However, it is not exceptional for the Court to endorse multiple regulation. In the field of direct taxation, for instance, the Court explicitly ruled that double taxation by two Member States does not amount to restriction to free movement.[37] Similarly, in relation to online gambling services, the Court held that compelling online betting bookers to apply for authorisation in every State in which they provide services does not constitute obstacle to free movement.[38]

[33] Joined Cases C-581/10 and C-629/10 *Nelson* [2012] ECR I-0000, para 66 and case law cited; Joined Cases C-402/07 and C-432/07 *Sturgeon and others* [2009] ECR I-10923.

[34] Case C-201/08 *Plantanol* [2009] ECR I-8343, para 46 and case law cited.

[35] See ch 7 section II.

[36] Case 120/78 *Rewe-Zentral ('Cassis de Dijon')* [1979] ECR 649, para 14; see ch 7 n 16 and accompanying text.

[37] Case C-128/08 *Damseaux* [2009] ECR I-6823, para 27; see ch 7 n 28 and accompanying text.

[38] Joined Cases C-316/07, C-358/07 to C-360/07, C-409/07 and C-410/07 *Markus Stoß* [2010] ECR I-8069, paras 112–13; see ch 7 n 29 and accompanying text.

Quite obviously, this oscillation between single and multiple regulation does not confer much legal certainty to the scope of the freedoms of movement. At the inception of the European Communities, such instability could be attributed to the novelty of the legal norms interpreted by the Court. Yet nowadays, the inconsistency of the 'free movement test' requires a substantive explanation, which has indeed been the object of ample academic thinking.[39] If this inconsistency is examined at length in part two of this study, it is sufficient for the purpose of the present section to contextualise this instability along the eternal struggle between predictability (legal certainty) and equity (legal congruence) of legal outcomes. The freedoms of movement apply to the most diverse factual situations and areas of law. As a consequence, a 'one-size-fits-all' free movement test is an illusion, for this test needs to be sufficiently adaptable to fit the particular reality of each and every case. Thus, although the same provisions apply, it can hardly be disputed that the importation of alcoholic beverages, the direct taxation of dividends and the regulation of gambling services call for differentiated interpretations. As it needs to be adaptable, the notion of obstacle to free movement is bound to remain uncertain.

Moreover, the objective of free movement must be balanced against other legitimate objectives pursued by Member States. This balancing process occurs in the second step of the reasoning, once an obstacle to free movement has been established. The Court has proved rather willing to accept the legitimacy of a wide range of policy objectives argued by Member States.[40] The decisive step of the justification process usually lies somewhere in the proportionality analysis, which questions the necessity of the national measures at stake to achieve the legitimate objective. Arguably, the proportionality analysis promotes more equitable legal outcomes by fine-tuning national law to the subtlety of reality; by the same token, it has adverse effects upon legal certainty. In her Opinion in *Prinz*, which concerned a three-year residence requirement to obtain study financing in Germany, AG Sharpston explicitly identified this twofold effect of the proportionality analysis:

> [T]he three-year rule is too rigid. It risks excluding from funding students who, despite not having resided for an uninterrupted period of three years in Germany immediately prior to studying abroad, are nevertheless sufficiently connected to German society due to their German nationality, residence, schooling or employment there, language skills, family and other social or economic ties, or other elements capable of showing that connection. …

[39] See inter alia A Saydé, 'One Law, Two Competitions: An Enquiry into the Contradictions of Free Movement Law' (2010–2011) 13 *Cambridge Yearbook of European Legal Studies* 365; MP Maduro, *We the Court: the European Court of Justice and the European Economic Constitution* (Oxford, Hart Publishing, 1998) ch 3; C Barnard and S Deakin, 'Market Access and Regulatory Competition' in C Barnard and J Scott (eds), *The Law of the Single Market: Unpacking the Premises* (Oxford, Hart Publishing, 2002).

[40] Nevertheless, in a recent Opinion, AG Bot highlighted the difficulty of accepting a justification based on 'economic protectionism', which was bluntly put forward by the German Government: AG Bot, Case C-628/11 *International Jet Management*, para 72.

> Here I agree with the German Government that the three-year rule is transparent and administratively efficient and offers legal certainty. The relevant information can easily be collected and the decision is mechanical, yes or no. … However, the most transparent and efficient measure is not necessarily a proportionate measure. … A measure like the three-year rule is likely to be more transparent and efficient than one requiring individual circumstances to be examined in each case. The latter would arguably be less restrictive and more inclusive.[41]

To paraphrase AG Sharpston, a three-year suspect period provides legal certainty but generates inequitable outcomes, as it mechanically excludes genuinely integrated persons. By contrast, a centre of gravity approach is less certain but more equitable or 'proportionate', since it enables the competent judge to rely on all individual circumstances to measure the degree of integration into German society. In sum, the demands of proportionality soften the sharp edge of law, thereby promoting more equitable but less predictable legal outcomes.

Secondly, next to the freedoms of movement, another set of fundamental principles maintains an ambiguous relationship with legal certainty: the general principles of Union law. On the one hand, legal certainty has the status of a general principle of Union law.[42] On the other hand, the recourse to general principles of Union law is liable to undermine legal certainty, which can be illustrated with the controversial *Sturgeon* judgment. The *Sturgeon* case, and the subsequent *Nelson* case, concerned the right to compensation for passengers in the event of delay to their flights under Regulation 261/2004.[43] The text of the Regulation indeed provides for a right to compensation, but exclusively for passengers whose flights are cancelled and not merely delayed:

> [T]he referring court asks, in essence, whether, and if so under what conditions, passengers whose flights are delayed enjoy the right to compensation under Regulation 261/2004.
>
> In that connection, it should be noted that neither Article 7 of Regulation 261/2004 nor any other provision of that regulation expressly provides such a right.[44]

Nonetheless, the Court had recourse to the general principle of equal treatment to extend the scope of the right to compensation to passengers whose flights are delayed and who suffer a loss of time of at least three hours:

> [A]ll Community acts must be interpreted in accordance with primary law as a whole, including the principle of equal treatment, which requires that comparable situations must not be treated differently and that different situations must not be treated in the same way unless such treatment is objectively justified.

[41] AG Sharpston, Case C-523/11 *Prinz* [2013] ECR I-0000, paras 95 and 104 to 106.

[42] Tridimas, *The General Principles of EU Law* (n 32) ch 6.

[43] Regulation (EC) 261/2004 of the European Parliament and of the Council of 11 February 2004 establishing common rules on compensation and assistance to passengers in the event of denied boarding and of cancellation or long delay of flights, and repealing Regulation (EEC) 295/91 [2004] OJ L46/1.

[44] Joined Cases C-581/10 and C-629/10 *Nelson* [2012] ECR I-0000, paras 28–29.

> Given that the damage sustained by air passengers in cases of cancellation or long delay is comparable, passengers whose flights are delayed and passengers whose flights are cancelled cannot be treated differently without the principle of equal treatment being infringed. That is *a fortiori* the case in view of the aim sought by Regulation 261/2004, which is to increase protection for all air passengers.
>
> In those circumstances, the Court finds that passengers whose flights are delayed may rely on the right to compensation laid down in Article 7 of Regulation 261/2004 where they suffer, on account of such flights, a loss of time equal to or in excess of three hours, that is to say when they reach their final destination three hours or more after the arrival time originally scheduled by the air carrier.[45]

Quite obviously, the Court's decision to have recourse to general principles, in order to go beyond the letter of Union legislation, undermines legal certainty:

> The use of general principles by the Courts of the EU can entail the exercise of judicial discretion to a considerable degree, unless a legislature provides specific rules for their application. This is not surprising if it is remembered that, as Dworkin has said, principles deal with the requirements of 'justice, fairness or some other dimension of morality'. Professor Melchior Wathelet, formerly a judge in the Court of Justice, of course, has expressed some concern that the predictability and objectivity of the law may suffer from the use of the general principle of proportionality in cases in which the fundamental freedoms are applied to tax law.[46]

As a matter of fact, the extension of the right to compensation in the event of flight delay in the *Sturgeon* and *Nelson* judgments could not be predicted on the basis of the letter of Regulation 261/2004. Surely enough, such reduction of the degree of legal certainty is open to criticism. Nevertheless, any such criticism ought to integrate the trade-off between legal certainty and legal congruence. In that regard, it is useful to recall the factual setting of the main proceedings in *Sturgeon*, namely flight delays of 22 and 25 hours, which questioned the relevance of the distinction between 'cancellation' and 'delay', two notions unfortunately not defined in Regulation 261/2004. In this peculiar factual context, equity indeed required the recourse to the general principle of equal treatment.

Furthermore, the criteria invoked by the parties to distinguish between cancellation and delay (eg change of aircraft, change of flight number, new check-in, declaration of cancellation) did not provide legal certainty and were subject to manipulation by air carriers. In that context, the Court's ruling can be viewed as a rupture of legal certainty in order to preserve equity (by treating long delays as cancellations for the purpose of the right to compensation), followed by a restoration of legal certainty (by issuing a three-hour threshold).

Arguably, the controversy surrounding the *Sturgeon* judgment was not triggered by the initial rupture of legal certainty, as equity ordered the assimilation

[45] Joined Cases C-402/07 and C-432/07 *Sturgeon* [2009] ECR I-10923, paras 48, 60 and 61.

[46] T Lyons, 'State Aid, Taxation and Abuse of Law' in R de la Feria and S Vogenauer (eds), *Prohibition of Abuse of Law: a New General Principle of EU Law?* (Oxford, Hart Publishing, 2011) 508.

of delays of 22 and 25 hours to cancellations. Rather, the controversy originates in the method chosen by the Court to restore equity afterwards: instead of a negative step consisting in declaring the Regulation invalid, the Court took the positive step of laying down a rigid 3-hour threshold beyond which delays have to be treated as cancellations, contrary to what AG Sharpston suggested:

> The actual selection of the magic figure is a legislative prerogative. To the extent that any figure is to some extent arbitrary, its arbitrariness is covered by that prerogative (the margin of legislative discretion). Thus, the Community legislator can select a particular time-limit (23 and a half hours, 24 hours, 25 hours, or 48 hours—whatever it be) triggering a right to compensation. The Court cannot.[47]

According to the learned Advocate General, even if the Regulation might be invalid on the ground that *not* treating long delays as cancellations is inequitable, the selection of a 'magic figure' as threshold necessarily yields inequity itself, which can only be legitimised through the legislative process. Once the Union legislature has selected such a magic figure, the function of the Court should be limited, once again, to verify whether the inequity inherent to this magic figure is sufficiently serious to set it aside—or, in Court's parlance, whether the threshold adopted breaches the general principle of equality.

It is not the object of this section to take position in the heated debate on *Sturgeon*; rather, it seeks to reframe this debate in light of the trade-off between legal certainty and legal congruence. The crucial point is the following: the recourse to general principles of law in order to set aside or complement written provisions adopted by the Union legislature, as in *Sturgeon* and many other judgments, is bound to have adverse effects on legal certainty. Nevertheless, just as the rules of equity in English law, general principles of law promote more equitable legal outcomes by relaxing the rigidity of legal norms, a function often labelled as 'gap-filling':

> [General principles of EU law] enable the European Court of Justice to fill normative gaps left either by the authors of the Treaties or by the EU legislature. The 'gap-filling' function of general principles thus ensures the autonomy and coherence of the EU legal system.[48]

Thirdly, the Court's recourse to the teleological method of interpretation can be similarly re-examined in light of the struggle between legal certainty and legal congruence. It is well known that the Court does not shy away from the teleological method of interpretation, which consists in construing a provision in the

[47] AG Sharpston, Joined Cases C-402/07 and C-432/07 *Sturgeon and others* [2009] ECR I-10923, paras 93–94.

[48] K Lenaerts and JA Gutiérrez-Fons, 'The Constitutional Allocation of Powers and General Principles of EU Law' (2010) 47 *Common Market Law Review* 1629, 1629; Tridimas (n 32) 17.

light of the purpose for which it was enacted.[49] In *CILFIT*, for instance, the Court unambiguously stated that:

> Every provision of Community law must be placed in its context and interpreted in the light of the provisions of Community law as a whole, regard being had to the objectives thereof and to its state of evolution at the date on which the provision in question is to be applied.[50]

Earlier, the Court had 'discovered' that the supremacy and direct effect of Union law flowed from the objectives of the Treaty:

> The executive force of Community law cannot vary from one State to another in deference to subsequent domestic laws, without jeopardizing the attainment of the objectives of the Treaty.[51]

> The objective of the EEC Treaty, which is to establish a common market, … implies that this Treaty is more than an agreement which merely creates mutual obligations between the contracting States.[52]

As the teleological method of interpretation rests on the unwritten 'telos' of legal norms, it is classically associated with legal uncertainty. Following a visit of the Court after the accession of the United Kingdom to the Union, Lord Denning described the Court's method of interpretation in his unmistakable style:

> [European judges] adopt a method which they call in English by strange words—at any rate they were strange to me—the 'schematic and teleological' method of interpretation. … When they come upon a situation which is *to their minds* within the spirit—but not the letter—of the legislation, they solve the problem by looking at the design and purpose of the legislature—at the effect it was sought to achieve. They then interpret the legislation so as to produce the desired effect. This means they fill in gaps, quite unashamedly, without hesitation. They ask simply: what is the sensible way of dealing with this situation so as to give effect to the presumed purpose of the legislation? … To our eyes—short-sighted by tradition—it is legislation pure and simple. But to their eyes it is fulfilling the true role of the courts.[53]

However, the Court's recourse to the teleological method of interpretation preserves the legal congruence of Union law, which is most often ignored in the literature. Maduro highlighted the importance of the teleological method interpretation for the adaptability of Union law:

> As with Constitutions the EU Treaties are based on principles so as to be open to the future. … EU constitutional law is no different. On the contrary, its constitutional

[49] AA Llorens, 'The European Court of Justice, More Than a Teleological Court' (1999–2000) 2 *Cambridge Yearbook of European Legal Studies* 373, 381–82; O Pollicino, 'Legal Reasoning of the Court of Justice in the Context of the Principle of Equality between Judicial Activism and Self-restraint' (2004) 5 *German Law Journal* 283, 289.

[50] Case 283/81 *CILFIT* [1982] ECR 3415, para 20.

[51] Case 6/64 *Costa v ENEL* [1964] ECR 1141.

[52] Case 26/62 *van Gend and Loos* [1963] ECR 3.

[53] *James Buchanan & Co Ltd v Babco Forwarding & Shipping (UK) Ltd* (1977) 2 WLR 107 (HL), 112.

> pluralism requires an ever greater adaptability which, must, at the same time be respectful of the limits imposed by national constitutionalism. In this respect, teleological and meta-teleological interpretation is the mechanism through which such principles are developed in a controllable and transparent manner.[54]

Illustrations of the trade-off between legal certainty and legal congruence can also be found in specific areas of Union law. For instance, in the field of environmental law, Cheyne discussed two possible approaches to the definition of 'waste' in the Framework Waste Directive.[55] The first approach secures legal certainty and the second legal congruence:

> Regulatory techniques such as listing by name have the advantage of providing clarity. However, their inflexibility entails the cost of frequent updating in fast-moving areas or the alternative risk of increasing lack of relevance and effectiveness as the lists become out-of-date. …
>
> Instead of listing waste items by their specific names, therefore, it seems desirable to use the threat posed by waste to the environment. … The disadvantage of this approach, however, is that it gives less precision and may lead to uncertainty.[56]

In the field of State aids, Kelyn Bacon described a long-standing debate on the degree of discretion that competition agencies and courts should have. On the one hand, those in favour of 'discretion' consider that competition agencies and courts should have a broad margin of appreciation to take all relevant factors into account and balance the costs and benefits to overall welfare. On the other hand, those in favour of 'rules' insist that legal norms should be transparent and certain, despite inevitable errors and inconsistencies.[57] The first stance ('discretion') is concerned with legal congruence, the second ('rules') with legal certainty; the adoption of a legal norm by the Union legislature inevitably calls for a choice between legal certainty—offered by rigid norms—and legal congruence—offered by flexible norms.

To sum up, Union law is pervaded by a struggle between legal certainty and legal congruence, which manifests itself both in the wording and the interpretation of Union legal norms. Most importantly for the present study, the trade-off between legal certainty and legal congruence provides an insightful framework of analysis for the concept of abuse of Union law.

[54] MP Maduro, 'Interpreting European Law: Judicial Adjudication in a Context of Constitutional Pluralism' (2007) 1 *European Journal of Legal Studies* 1, 12.

[55] Council Directive 75/442/EEC of 15 July 1975 on waste [1975] OJ L194/39, replaced by Directive 2006/12/EC of the European Parliament and of the Council of 5 April 2006 on waste [2006] OJ L114/9.

[56] I Cheyne, 'The Definition of Waste in EC Law' (2002) 14 *Journal of Environmental Law* 61, 63.

[57] K Bacon, *European Community Law of State Aid* (Oxford, Oxford University Press, 2009) 1.30–1.32.

II. Legal Certainty as Source of Abusive Practices

The object of the present section is to situate the phenomenon of abuse of Union law along the trade-off between legal certainty and legal congruence, established in the previous section. In that regard, it can be said that legal certainty is a source of abusive practices. Indeed, if rigid Union laws do ensure legal certainty, they can be abused in order to obtain a benefit in contradiction with their purpose (Subsection II.A). More generally, norms guaranteeing legal certainty tend to open a congruence gap between law and reality, in which abuses of Union law may flourish (Subsection II.B).

A. Abuses of Rigid Union Laws

Having due regard to the first section of this chapter, abuses of Union law can now be analysed as expressions of a lack of legal congruence, provoked by the rigidity of Union laws. Given their structural imperfection, casting legal norms into a rigid mould inevitably condemns them to legal incongruence, for rigid norms cannot be adapted to 'unavoidable problems of fit'—such as abusive practices. As a matter of fact, it has long been established that abusive practices thrive on the rigidity of legal norms, which may stem from their wording and/or literal interpretation:

> The more unbending the law, the more it resembles a stiff staff with which the cunning may beat the foolish, the trusting and the innocent. No matter how much one might wish to restrict the role of equity in law, it cannot be denied that it must at least restrain calculated abuse of the rigidity and inadequacy of the general formalities and rules of law.[58]

By definition, the scope of a rigid norm cannot be adapted to address an abusive practice that was not envisaged by the legislature. This lack of adaptability in presence of an abusive practice threatens the legal congruence of the applicable norm, since granting the benefit abusively sought might be in contradiction with the objectives pursued by the legislature. This threat of legal incongruence can be conveniently illustrated by re-examining the seminal *Emsland-Stärke* and *Halifax* cases.

Emsland-Stärke concerned Regulation 2730/79 laying down common detailed rules for the application of the system of export refunds on agricultural products.[59] The Union legislature has set up a system of export refunds in order to encourage the export of agricultural goods produced within the Union, which consists in the grant of subsidies intended to compensate the difference between

[58] Watt (n 6) 33.

[59] Commission Regulation (EEC) 2730/79 of 29 November 1979 laying down common detailed rules for the application of the system of export refunds on agricultural products [1979] OJ L317/1.

the level of—higher—Union prices and the level of worldwide market prices. As described earlier, the abusive practice considered in *Emsland-Stärke* can be decomposed in two steps: the exportation of Union agricultural products to Switzerland, where they were marketed for a brief period of time, and their immediate re-importation into the Union. In essence, the Court was asked to determine whether the export refund usually attached to the exportation of agricultural goods had to be granted in case of immediate re-importation into the Union.

Regulation 2730/79 did not specifically envisage the scenario of a brief placing on the market in a third country, in order to benefit from an export refund, followed by a re-importation into the Union. The rigid article 10(1) merely entitled national authorities to require additional proof of 'importation' and 'placing on the market':

> In the following circumstances payment of the refund shall be conditional not only on the product having left the geographical territory of the community but also—save where it has perished in transit as a result of force majeure—on its having been imported into a non-member country and where appropriate into a specific non-member country:
>
> (a) where there is serious doubt as to the true destination of the product; or
> (b) where by reason of the difference between the rate of the refund on the exported product and the import duties applicable to an identical product on the day when customs export formalities are completed it is possible that the product may be reintroduced into the community.
>
> In such cases the provisions of article 20 (2), (3), (4), (5) and (6) shall apply. The competent authorities of the member states may require satisfactory additional proof that the product has in fact been placed on the market in the non-member country of import.

Arguably, Emsland-Stärke could have adduced proof of both importation and placing on the market in Switzerland. Moreover, the Court judged that such additional proof could only be requested before granting the export refund (paras 48–49); yet in the main proceedings, national authorities found out about the re-importation only after granting the export refund, so that they were not even entitled to request such additional proof. In short, the rigidity of Article 10(1) made it impossible to address the specific scenario set up by Emsland-Stärke, so that the latter formally abided by all requirements laid down by Regulation 2730/79:

> It should first be noted that, for the operations at issue in the main proceedings, all the formal conditions for the grant of non-differentiated export refunds laid down by Regulation 2730/79 were fulfilled.[60]

[60] Case C-110/99 *Emsland-Stärke* [2000] ECR I-11569, para 46.

This rigidity of Article 10(1) threatened the legal congruence of Regulation 2730/79, since the Union legislature had all the intentions to counter such abusive re-import strategies, as explained in the ninth recital:

> Whereas certain export transactions can lead to abuses; whereas, in order to prevent such abuses, payment of the refund should be subject to the condition that the product has not only left the geographical territory of the community but has also been imported into a non-member country and, where applicable, actually marketed there.

As a matter of fact, the fight against abusive re-import strategies naturally fitted into the policy objectives of Regulation 2730/79. Export refunds are indeed granted in order to compensate the difference between the level of—higher—Union prices and the level of worldwide market prices, so that they should not artificially improve the competitive position of agricultural goods eventually placed on the market within the Union. AG Alber reached the same finding:

> The point of departure for the further analysis of the matter must therefore be the objective of the export refund scheme. Essentially, the Court has consistently held that non-differentiated refunds are granted in order to compensate for the difference between commodity prices within the Community, and international market prices. … By making Community products competitive on the world market in this way, their sale outside the Community becomes viable in commercial terms and also desirable under the common agricultural policy. …
>
> [O]bjective circumstances, in the form of immediate re-importation of the goods by the same means of transport without their even being unloaded, and the unified invoicing for export and re-import, give rise to a prima facie presumption that claims have been made under Community export refund rules for a purpose other than that intended.[61]

Therefore, as observed by the Court, *Emsland-Stärke* sought to exploit the rigidity of Regulation 2730/79 in order to obtain a benefit in contradiction with its purpose:

> A finding of an abuse requires, first, a combination of objective circumstances in which, despite formal observance of the conditions laid down by the Community rules, the purpose of those rules has not been achieved.[62]

It is noteworthy that the Union legislature later decided to correct the rigidity of Regulation 2730/79 by adopting Regulation 800/1999,[63] which was later recast by Regulation 612/2009 laying down common detailed rules for the application of the system of export refunds on agricultural products.[64] By comparison with Regulation 2730/79, the preamble to Regulation 612/2009 includes many

[61] AG Alber, Case C-110/99 *Emsland-Stärke* [2000] ECR I-11569, paras 70 and 73.

[62] Case C-110/99 *Emsland-Stärke* [2000] ECR I-11569, para 52.

[63] Commission Regulation (EC) 800/1999 of 15 April 1999 laying down common detailed rules for the application of the system of export refunds on agricultural products [1999] OJ 102/11.

[64] Commission Regulation (EC) 612/2009 of 7 July 2009 on laying down common detailed rules for the application of the system of export refunds on agricultural products (recast) [2009] OJ L186/1.

more recitals condemning unambiguously abusive practices in relation to export refunds.[65] Among these, the 25th, 27th and 28th recitals are of particular relevance to the issue of abusive re-import strategies:

> Certain export transactions can lead to deflection of trade. In order to prevent such deflections, payment of the refund should be subject to the condition that the product has not only left the customs territory of the Community but has also been imported into a third country or has undergone substantial processing or working. Moreover, payment of the refund may, in some cases, be subject to the product's having actually been placed on the market in the importing third country or to its having undergone substantial processing or working. …
>
> Community financing of export operations is unjustified where the operation is not a normal commercial transaction, since it has no real economic purpose and is effected solely to obtain a payment from the Community.
>
> Steps should be taken to prevent Community funds from being allocated for transactions which do not correspond to any objective of the system of export refunds. This risk exists for products attracting export refunds which are subsequently reimported into the Community without having undergone substantial processing or working in a third country and on which reduced or zero duty is paid on reimport rather than the normal rate, pursuant to a preferential agreement or a Council decision.

This stronger stance vis-à-vis abusive re-import strategies was reflected in Article 27 of Regulation 612/2009, which replaced Article 10 of Regulation 2730/79. If the first paragraph provides for evidentiary requirements similar to that of former Article 10 (proofs of exportation, importation and placing on the market in a third country), Article 27 was supplemented with a new paragraph 4, which reads as follows:

> Paragraph 1 shall apply before the refund has been paid.
>
> However, the refund shall be deemed to be unwarranted and shall be reimbursed if the competent authorities find, even after the refund has been paid:
>
> …
>
> (c) that the product exported is reimported into the Community without having undergone any substantial processing or working within the meaning of Article 24 of Regulation (EEC) 2913/92, that the non-preferential duty on import is less than the refund granted, and that export was not carried out as a normal commercial transaction.

Arguably, the Union legislature corrected the rigidity of Article 10 of Regulation 2730/79 by inserting this new paragraph 4. Indeed, the requirement of an export 'carried out as a normal commercial transaction' instils a measure of flexibility into the scope of this anti-abuse provision, and reimbursement can be demanded

[65] See esp recitals 23 to 30, 35 and 43.

even after payment of the export refund. As a consequence, judges are better equipped to fight abusive practices that should not fall within the scope of the export refunds regime (legal congruence). The necessary corollary of this increase of legal congruence is a decrease of legal certainty, as judges will enjoy a broader margin of discretion, in particular in their assessment of what constitutes a 'normal commercial transaction', which they can exercise even after payment of the export refund.

Just as *Emsland-Stärke*'s strategy exploited the rigidity of Regulation 2730/79, Halifax's strategy exploited the rigidity of the VAT legislation to seek a benefit in contradiction with its purpose. As explained earlier, economic activities of credit institutions are mostly VAT-exempted under Article 135 of the VAT Directive 2006/112, so that credit institutions usually enjoy a very limited right to deduction by virtue of Article 168 of the same directive. As a matter of fact, the bank Halifax held a right to deduction of about 5 per cent of the input VAT. As a consequence, when it decided to build up four new call centres, a transaction entailing a heavy burden of input VAT, Halifax outsourced their construction to a specific entity of the Halifax group endowed with a full right to deduction, in order to save GBP 6,600,000 of input VAT.

The abusive practice designed by Halifax threatened the legal congruence of the VAT regime as it contradicted its central objective, namely tax neutrality. In pure economic theory, any tax on economic activity is liable to reduce the volume of economic activity as a whole; in that sense, no such tax can claim to be entirely neutral. Nevertheless, beyond this general chilling effect of taxation, the VAT regime vows to affect equally all economic activities, so that no individual business enjoys a competitive advantage through the application of the VAT system. The seventh recital in the preamble to VAT Directive 2006/112 reads as follows:

> The common system of VAT should, even if rates and exemptions are not fully harmonised, result in neutrality in competition, such that within the territory of each Member State similar goods and services bear the same tax burden, whatever the length of the production and distribution chain.

As suggested by this recital, the principle of neutrality of VAT encompasses two axes ('similar goods and services bear the same tax burden'; 'whatever the length of the production and distribution chain'), which are the object of ample and robust case law. The Court explicitly acknowledged the coexistence of these two axes of neutrality in *Zimmerman*:

> [I]n the field of VAT, the concept of neutrality is used in different senses.
>
> On the one hand, recalling that the deduction mechanism provided for under the Sixth Directive is intended to relieve the trader entirely of the burden of the VAT payable or paid in the course of all his economic activities, the Court has held that the common system of VAT seeks to ensure neutrality of taxation of all economic activities, provided that those activities are themselves subject in principle to VAT.

> On the other hand, according to settled case-law, the principle of fiscal neutrality means that supplies of goods or services which are similar, and which are accordingly in competition with each other, may not be treated differently for VAT purposes.[66]

On a vertical axis ('whatever the length of the production and distribution chain'), the VAT is neutral towards all forms of the same economic activity, which is ensured by the deduction mechanism. Thanks to the deduction mechanism, the VAT is a general tax on consumption exactly proportional to the price of the goods and services, however many transactions take place in the production and distribution process before the stage at which the tax is charged, as stated by article 1(2) of VAT Directive 2006/112. The Court summed up this facet of neutrality as follows:

> [The preamble to the First VAT Directive 67/227] refers to the need to achieve such harmonization of legislation concerning turnover taxes as will eliminate factors which may distort conditions of competition and therefore to secure neutrality in competition, in the sense that within each country similar goods should bear the same tax burden, whatever the length of the production and distribution chain.[67]

On a horizontal axis ('similar goods and services bear the same tax burden'), the VAT is neutral towards competing economic activities, which implies that similar goods or services may not be treated differently for VAT purposes. As explained by the Court, 'the principle of fiscal neutrality includes the principle of elimination of distortion in competition as a result of differing treatment for VAT purposes'.[68]

It is fairly easy to demonstrate that both axes of neutrality were breached by the abusive practice designed by Halifax, as the latter sought to manufacture a right to deduction although (most of) its economic activities were VAT-exempted. On the one hand, granting a right to deduction in relation to VAT-exempted activities would lead to the payment of VAT that is not exactly proportional to the price of the services provided by Halifax. On the other hand, Halifax would have gained a competitive advantage over other credit institutions through the application of the VAT system. The Court reached the same finding in its judgment:

> [T]he deduction system under the Sixth Directive is meant to relieve the trader entirely of the burden of the VAT payable or paid in the course of all his economic activities. The common system of VAT consequently ensures complete neutrality of taxation of all economic activities, whatever their purpose or results, provided that they are themselves subject in principle to VAT.
>
> To allow taxable persons to deduct all input VAT even though, in the context of their normal commercial operations, no transactions conforming with the deduction rules

[66] Case C-174/11 *Zimmermann* [2012] ECR I-0000, paras 46–48.

[67] Case 89/81 *Hong-Kong Trade Development Council* [1982] ECR 1277, para 6; see also Case C-520/10 *Lebara* [2012] ECR I-0000, paras 23–25.

[68] See among many others Case C-33/11 *A Oy* [2012] ECR I-0000, para 33; Case C-363/05 *JP Morgan* [2007] ECR I-5517, para 47.

> of the Sixth Directive or of the national legislation transposing it would have enabled them to deduct such VAT, or would have allowed them to deduct only a part, would be contrary to the principle of fiscal neutrality and, therefore, contrary to the purpose of those rules.[69]

Therefore, Halifax had set up an abusive practice exploiting the rigidity of the VAT legislation, whose provisions were indeed complied with, in order to obtain a benefit in contradiction with the purpose of the VAT regime:

> [I]n the sphere of VAT, an abusive practice can be found to exist only if, first, the transactions concerned, notwithstanding formal application of the conditions laid down by the relevant provisions of the Sixth Directive and the national legislation transposing it, result in the accrual of a tax advantage the grant of which would be contrary to the purpose of those provisions.[70]

To sum up, abuses of Union law seek to exploit the rigidity of Union laws in order to obtain a benefit in contradiction with their purpose, as shown by *Emsland-Stärke* and *Halifax*. Indeed, such rigidity precludes the competent judge from adapting its decision to the idiosyncrasies of concrete cases; as a consequence, rigid norms are prone to abusive practices. As will be exposed in Section V.C below, the recourse to the doctrine of abuse in both *Emsland-Stärke* and *Halifax* was precisely intended to instil a measure of flexibility into the rigid scope of the applicable Union laws, in order to reinstate legal congruence.

B. The Congruence Gap as Room for Abusive Practices

This chapter has established so far the existence of a trade-off between legal certainty and legal congruence, as well as a positive correlation between rigid Union laws and the proliferation of abusive practices. It is now time to formalise the relationship between legal certainty, legal congruence and abusive practices into more theoretical terms, by introducing the notion of 'congruence gap'. The premise of this theoretical reconstruction lies in the inherent imperfection of human laws, which are unavoidably exposed to unanticipated problems of fit. Indeed, if human legislatures could anticipate every situation likely to occur in reality, legal certainty and legal congruence could be achieved simultaneously and abusive practices could be equally prevented by rigid and flexible norms.

However, since human legislatures cannot anticipate every such situation, as explained in the previous sections of this chapter, the pursuit of legal certainty inevitably undermines legal congruence, and vice-versa. Laws securing legal certainty have a simplistic rigidity that cannot adapt to the intricate contours of reality, and in particular of modern reality, owing to their inherent rigidity. Indeed, when unanticipated problems of fit actually occur, rigid

[69] Case C-255/02 *Halifax* [2006] ECR I-1609, paras 78 and 80.
[70] Case C-255/02 *Halifax* [2006] ECR I-1609, para 74.

norms guaranteeing legal certainty are not able to adapt themselves in order to preserve legal congruence. This lack of adaptability open a well-identified 'congruence gap' between the rigid scope of a law and the subtle reality. In that connection, Gary Watt wrote:

> The strictness, generality, formality and routine of legal rules combine to create a gap—an 'equity gap'—between the general law and more pleasing justice. Even if we fantasise that there might come a moment when the law, in all its formal and flexible aspects, will be considered perfectly fitting with every eventuality of a given society, one can be sure that such a society will change faster than its law, so time itself will open up the gap between the law and more pleasing justice.[71]

Schematically, the congruence gap between law and reality can be represented as in Figure 7. As shown by this graphical representation, the pursuit of legal certainty inevitably opens a gap between law and reality; and the higher the degree of legal certainty, the greater the congruence gap. Conversely, the pursuit of legal congruence reduces the gap between law and reality, at the expense of legal certainty. In practice, it is within the confines of the congruence gap that legal norms may lead to absurd outcomes. For instance, granting legal capacity to every citizen who has reached the age of 18 entails a congruence gap encompassing, among other situations, the validation of transactions made by the mentally deficient or by persons under the influence of an authority figure.[72]

More importantly for the present study, it is within the congruence gap that abusive practices flourish; in other words, the congruence gap represents the playground in which abusive practices can be designed. To understand this point, it is useful to recall the definition of artificial choice of law proposed above, namely the election of a legal cloak that has no other rationale than the regulatory benefit sought.[73] This possibility of electing a legal cloak that has no logical explanation in the reality, and that can only be understood in its legal context, presupposes the existence of a gap between law and reality. Indeed, when a congruence gap separates law from reality, some legal effects are not

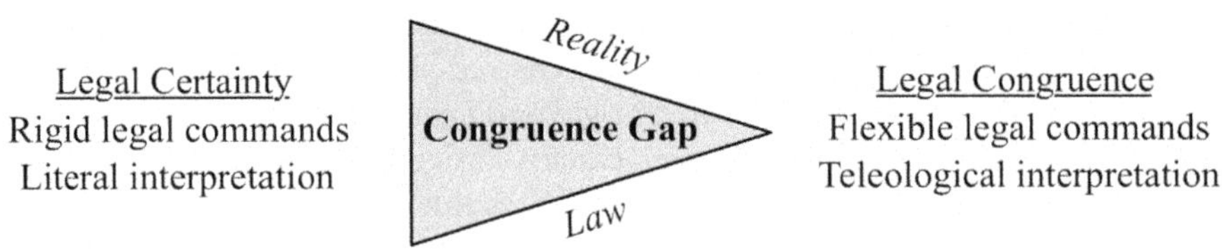

Figure 7 – The Congruence Gap

[71] Watt (n 6) 10. In the same sense, D'Amato wrote that 'there will always be a gap between some actual rules in the legal system and the rules of natural law': see D'Amato (n 31) 50.

[72] See section I.

[73] See ch 3 section II.

aligned with reality, which creates opportunities to artificially elect a fitting legal cloak:

> The fact that so many opportunities for tax avoidance exist is inevitable as long as the legislation (the legislator) is not perfect. The unavoidable deficiencies in tax laws may in themselves largely account for the tensions between substance and form, not least because of the difficulty in forming accurate legal descriptions of the phenomena in a manner that mirrors reality.[74]

In short, if an abuse of Union law consists in the artificial choice among several legal 'cloaks' to dress one and the same transaction, the congruence gap represents the 'cloakroom' in which such a choice can be made. This positive correlation between congruence gap and room for abusive practices has important consequences. On the one hand, legal certainty is a source of abusive practices: indeed, rigid legal commands and literal interpretation tend to open a congruence gap, on which abusive practices may proliferate. In the specific context of tax law, Ruiz Almendral wrote:

> [E]xcessive literalism when interpreting tax legislation, together with an excess of formalism when taking into account legal forms as defined in private law, constitute one of the most important breeding grounds for the proliferation of tax avoidance schemes.[75]

In his Opinion in *Halifax*, AG Maduro similarly associated legal certainty and the proliferation of abusive practices:

> Legal certainty must be balanced against other values of the legal system. Tax law should not become a sort of legal 'wild-west' in which virtually every sort of opportunistic behaviour has to be tolerated so long as it conforms with a strict formalistic interpretation of the relevant tax provisions and the legislature has not expressly taken measures to prevent such behaviour.[76]

On the other hand, the fight against abusive practices irremediably takes its toll on legal certainty: indeed, flexible legal commands and/or teleological interpretation tend to eliminate the congruence gap that can be exploited to set up abusive practices, but they undermine legal certainty. In the context of tax law again, Weisbach wrote:

> [T]axpayers have been able to manipulate the rules endlessly to produce results clearly not intended by the drafters. To respond, lawmakers and regulators have shifted the tax system toward standards, primarily by adopting what are known as 'anti-abuse rules'. A typical anti-abuse rule allows the government (and only the government) to override the literal words of a statute or regulation. … A common reaction to anti-abuse rules is horror. Anti-abuse rules seem to eliminate certainty and reliability in the tax law.[77]

[74] Karimeri, 'A Critical Review of the Definition of Tax Avoidance' (n 16) 299.

[75] V Ruiz Almendral, 'Tax Avoidance and the European Court of Justice: What is at Stake for European General Anti-Avoidance Rules?' (2005) 33 *Intertax* 562.

[76] AG Maduro, Case C-255/02 *Halifax* [2006] ECR I-1609, para 77.

[77] DA Weisbach, 'Formalism in the Tax Law' (1999) 66 *The University of Chicago Law Review* 860, 860–61.

In more general terms, Kjellgren observed that the fight against abusive practices requires the introduction of a measure of discretion for the competent authorities:

> The concept of 'abuse-control' in this sense is therefore—and by necessity—connected with a certain degree of uncertainty. The very raison d'être may very well be to introduce a certain measure of discretion for the authorities in situations where rules technically speaking are applied correctly but where the legal outcome nevertheless is considered 'abusive' by society.[78]

In sum, norms guaranteeing legal certainty tend to open a congruence gap between law and reality, in which abuses of Union law may flourish. Conversely, the fight against abusive practices requires the closing of this congruence gap, which necessarily reduces legal certainty.

III. The Fight against Abusive Practices as Source of Legal Congruence

As explained in the previous section, the fight against abusive practices requires the closing of the congruence gap between law and reality; in other words, fighting abusive practices amounts to reinstating legal congruence at the expense of legal certainty. In that connection, it is often ascertained that the authors of abusive practices, who have engineered unnatural legal constructions to artificially obtain an advantage, have lost their right to legal certainty:

> The position in relation to a right of recovery due to a possible abuse of rights is completely different; the presumption here is that the abuse of rights as such does not merit protection. The abuse of rights causes the protection guaranteed by the legal system to a trader acting in good faith to be forfeited.[79]
>
> Economic activity of that kind, even if not unlawful, deserves no protection from the Community law principles of legal certainty and protection of legitimate expectations because its only likely purpose is that of subverting the aims of the legal system itself.[80]
>
> The principle of legal certainty can only be set aside if there is a matter of abuse. In this circumstance, the abuser, namely, can no longer rely on the foreseeability of the law.[81]

The fight against artificial practices, which amounts to a sacrifice of legal certainty on the altar of legal congruence, can be made in two ways: by having

[78] A Kjellgren, 'On the Border of Abuse—The Jurisprudence of the European Court of Justice on Circumvention, Fraud and Other Misuses of Community Law' (2000) 11 *European Business Law Review* 179, 179.

[79] AG Alber, Case C-110/99 *Emsland-Stärke* [2000] ECR I-11569, para 80.

[80] AG Maduro, Case C-255/02 *Halifax* [2006] ECR I-1609, para 86.

[81] D Weber, 'Abuse of Law in the Context of Indirect Taxation: Why We Need the Subjective Intention Test, When is Combating Abuse an Obligation and Other Comments' in de la Feria and Vogenauer, *Prohibition of Abuse of Law: a New General Principle of EU Law?* (n 46) 396.

recourse to the doctrine of abuse in the presence of rigid legal norms (Subsection III.A) or by modulating the scope of flexible legal norms (Subsection III.B). Arguably, the recourse to the doctrine of abuse amounts to a teleological interpretation of rigid norms: 'The principle [of abuse] reflects the Court's tendency to interpret Community law teleologically, thereby excluding abusive practices from its scope.'[82] The raison d'être of a teleological interpretation triggered by the recourse to the doctrine of abuse lies in the possibility of ignoring the letter of the applicable law in case of conflict with its purposes or '*teloi*', which is precisely the effect of a finding of abuse. Yet there is no need for such teleological interpretation when the wording of the applicable Union law is flexible enough to yield an outcome compatible with its purposes.[83]

Nevertheless, it is important to highlight that both techniques decrease the degree of legal certainty: with the doctrine of abuse, legal uncertainty originates in the teleological interpretation of rigid norms; with flexible legal norms, the source of legal uncertainty lies in their very wording. In sum, the choice is not between doctrine of abuse and legal certainty, but rather between fighting abusive practices (legal congruence) and legal certainty.

A. The Legal Uncertainty Inherent to the Doctrine of Abuse

In the vast literature on the doctrine of abuse, it is commonly asserted that the formal doctrine of abuse threatens legal certainty in so far as it enquires into the 'subjective intentions' of the parties in the context of the artificiality requirement. By contrast with that common assumption, the present section argues that the teleological assessment represents the main source of legal certainty within the doctrine of abuse, but that this threat is justified by the desire to achieve legal congruence.

The artificiality requirement is a subjective test, namely a test sounding out the intentions, thoughts or motivations of a person. By way of illustration, the question 'Does this person show sufficient maturity?' is subjective, whereas the question 'Has this person reached the age of 18?' is objective. The artificiality requirement can be characterised as subjective, as it seeks to ascertain the intention to obtain a regulatory gain, at the exclusion of any socioeconomic gain.[84] This subjectivity inherent to the artificiality requirement has triggered a common fear of judicial discretion in the literature, as it would be impossible to enquire into the state of mind of human beings:

> [The subjective part of the doctrine of abuse] is problematic not so much due to the specific characteristics of legal persons and their distinction from natural persons, but

[82] Karimeri (n 16) 296.
[83] Ruiz Almendral, 'Tax Avoidance and the European Court of Justice' (n 75) 568.
[84] See ch 3 section II.

> rather to the inherently indeterminate nature of any test to assess whether this criterion is met.[85]

> It is never possible to find out what the real intention of a human being is. One always has to look at the factual situation and try to discern why a human being acted in the way he or she did, but in the end, there is always a certain amount of guesswork involved.[86]

Similarly, the Court has highlighted this risk of judicial discretion entailed by subjective tests in a number of occasions,[87] including the following:

> [A]n obligation on the tax authorities to carry out enquiries to determine the intention of the taxable person would be contrary to the objectives of the common system of VAT of ensuring legal certainty.[88]

> The competent national authorities … are not therefore called upon to enquire into the parties' subjective intentions, which would be very difficult to prove and would give rise to legal uncertainty.[89]

> [The Court's reluctance to attach weight to subjective criteria] is inevitable since subjective criteria and thus in particular the aim of those concerned may readily be subject to manipulation.[90]

Despite this widespread fear of judicial discretion, it must be underlined that every legal order commonly has recourse to such subjective tests. As observed by Josserand in his seminal study on the abuse of rights under French law:

> It is not exceptional for our courts to enquire the mentality of the [parties] and to penetrate, through various and most secure means of investigation, their heart of hearts. Those psychological enquiries occur daily, not only in criminal law, but also in private law.[91]

[85] P Koutrakos, 'The Emsland-Stärke Abuse of Law Test in the Law of Agriculture and Free Movement of Goods' in de la Feria and Vogenauer (n 46) 209.

[86] M Lang, 'Cadbury Schweppes' Line of Case Law from the Member States' Perspective' in de la Feria and Vogenauer (n 46) 449; see also A Arnull, 'What is a General Principle of EU Law?' in de la Feria and Vogenauer (n 46) 23; KS Ziegler, '"Abuse of Law" in the Context of the Free Movement of Workers' in de la Feria and Vogenauer (n 46) 307; E Spaventa, 'Comments on Abuse of Law and the Free Movement of Workers' in de la Feria and Vogenauer (n 46) 317; R Lyal, 'Cadbury Schweppes and Abuse: Comments' in de la Feria and Vogenauer (n 46) 430–32; C Amand, 'Prohibition of Abusive Practices in European VAT: Court Aid to National Legislations Bugs?' (2008) 36 *Intertax* 189, 198; J Harrison and L Woods, *European Broadcasting Law and Policy* (Cambridge, Cambridge University Press, 2007) 179.

[87] Case C-4/94 *BLP* [1995] ECR I-983, para 24; Joined Cases C-354/03, C-355/03 and C-484/03 *Optigen* [2006] ECR I-483, para 45; Joined Cases C-439/04 and C-440/04 *Kittel* [2006] ECR I-6161, para 43; Case C-409/04 *Teleos* [2007] ECR I-7797, para 39; Case 53/81 *Levin* [1982] ECR 1035, paras 21–22; Case C-109/01 *Akrich* [2003] ECR I-9607, para 55-56; AG La Pergola, Case C-212/97 *Centros* [1999] ECR I-1459, para 20.

[88] Case C-255/02 *Halifax* [2006] ECR I-1609, para 57.

[89] AG Léger, Case C-196/04 *Cadbury Schweppes* [2006] ECR I-7995, para 119.

[90] AG Geelhoed, Case C-109/01 *Akrich* [2003] ECR I-9607, para 174.

[91] L Josserand, *De l'esprit des droits et de leur relativité: théorie dite de l'abus des droits*, 2nd edn (Paris, LGDJ, 1939) no 256, free translation.

Josserand could have made the same observation in relation to Union law. In *Kittel*, for instance, the Court asserted that tax authorities should not enquire into the parties' intentions (para 42); and yet subsequently stated that a person who 'knew or should have known' that he was participating in a fraud should not be entitled to deduct VAT.[92] In *Uniplex*, the Court held that the period for bringing proceedings seeking to have an infringement of the public procurement rules established starts to run from the date on which the claimant 'knew or ought to have known' of that infringement.[93] Union institutions regularly rely on other subjective criteria such as the 'intention to obtain an advantage,'[94] 'tax motives',[95] the 'intentions' of migrant citizens,[96] the 'fraudulent intent',[97] 'bad faith'[98] or 'good faith'.[99] This frequent recourse to subjective tests under Union law has proved unproblematic, just as the recourse to objective tests.

Arguably, one of the reasons for their smooth application is that subjective tests do not usually entail an unworkable room for judicial discretion. As shown by the examples mentioned above, subjective tests do not involve the psychic reading of a person's mind, but are rather targeted at well-defined subjective intentions that are discovered through the gathering of objective clues. As noted by Ruiz Almendral, 'to a certain extent, the discussion [on motives] is perfectly useless, for

[92] Joined Cases C-439/04 and C-440/04 *Kittel* [2006] ECR I-6161, para 59.

[93] Case C-406/08 *Uniplex* [2010] ECR I-817, para 35.

[94] Case C-162/07 *Ampliscientifica* [2008] ECR I-4019, para 30; Case C-196/04 *Cadbury Schweppes* [2006] ECR I-7995, para 61 and 64; Case C-279/05 *Vonk Dairy Products* [2007] ECR I-239, para 33; Joined Cases C-487/01 and C-7/02 *Gemeente Leusden* [2004] ECR I-5337, para 78; Case C-110/99 *Emsland-Stärke* [2000] ECR I-11569, para 53; Case C-515/03 *Eichsfelder Schlachtbetrieb* [2005] ECR I-7355, para 39.

[95] Case C-196/04 *Cadbury Schweppes* [2006] ECR I-7995, para 65.

[96] Case C-90/97 *Swaddling* [1999] ECR I-1075, para 29; Case C-102/91 *Knoch* [1992] ECR I-4341, para 23; Case C-216/89 *Reibold* [1990] ECR I-4163; Case 76/76 *Di Paolo* [1977] ECR 315, para 22.

[97] Case C-321/05 *Kofoed* [2007] ECR I-5795, para 31.

[98] Council Regulation (EC) 40/94 of 20 December 1993 on the Community trade mark [1993] OJ L11/1 art 51(1)(b); art 3(2)(d) of First Council Directive 89/104/EEC to approximate the laws of the Member States relating to trade marks [1988] OJ L40/1; Case C-569/08 *Internetportal und Marketing* [2010] ECR I-4871, paras 40–77; Joined Cases C-95/07 and C-96/07 *Ecotrade* [2008] ECR I-3457, para 70; Case C-428/05 *Laub* [2007] ECR I-5069, para 25; Case C-159/02 *Turner* [2004] ECR I-3565, para 31.

[99] Case C-271/06 *Netto Supermarkt* [2008] ECR I-771, para 25; Case C-409/04 *Teleos* [2007] ECR I-7797, para 66; Case C-146/05 *Collée* [2007] ECR I-7861, para 35; Case C-209/03 *Bidar* [2005] ECR I-2119, paras 67–69; Case C-336/00 *Huber* [2002] ECR I-7699, paras 53 and 58–59; Case C-400/98 *Breitsohl* [2000] ECR I-4321, para 39; Joined Cases C-110/98 to C-147/98 *Gabalfrisa and Others* [2000] ECR I-1577, para 46; Case C-24/95 *Alcan* [1997] ECR I-1591, paras 39–43; Case C-347/93 *Boterlux* [1994] ECR I-3933, para 32; Case C-8/92 *General Milk Products* [1993] ECR I-779, para 21; Case 25/76 *Galeries Segoura* [1976] ECR 1851, para 11; Case 39/75 *Coenen* [1975] ECR 1547, para 10; Joined Cases 43/59, 45/59 and 48/59 *von Lachmüller* [1960] ECR 463. See also arts 2:101, 2:103, 6:301, 7:101 and 7:102 of the Acquis Principles: Research Group on the Existing EC Private Law (Acquis Group), *Principles of the Existing EC Contract Law (Acquis Principles)—Contract I* (Munich, Sellier European Law Publishers, 2007); Research Group on the Existing EC Private Law (Acquis Group), *Principles of the Existing EC Contract Law (Acquis Principles)—Contract II* (Munich, Sellier European Law Publishers, 2009); Research Group on the Existing EC Private Law (Acquis Group), *Principles of the Existing EC Contract Law (Acquis Principles)—Contract III* (Munich, Sellier European Law Publishers, 2013).

most of those favouring the 'subjective' element admit that it can only be proved with reference to the rest of the (objective) elements of tax avoidance'.[100]

In practice, the room for judicial discretion generated by a subjective test will depend on the type of subjective intention of which enquiry is made, on the one hand, and on the ease with which objective evidence of that specific intention can be adduced, on the other. The former explains why the artificiality requirement, although a subjective test, entails limited room for judicial discretion. Indeed, the artificiality requirement merely seeks to determine the type of benefit (regulatory versus socioeconomic) sought by a person when carrying out a given transaction. In other words, the subjective enquiry implied by the artificiality requirement is confined to the examination of the incentives underpinning a given transaction. Furthermore, when conducting this well-targeted subjective enquiry, the judge may usefully rely on objective evidence of the actual gain brought by the transaction to the parties involved: if the transaction merely brought a regulatory gain to the parties, at the exclusion of any other socioeconomic gain, it must be held as artificial. AG Maduro wrote:

> When the Court takes the view that an abuse exists whenever the activity at issue cannot possibly have any other purpose or justification than to trigger the application of Community law provisions in a manner contrary to their purpose, that is tantamount, in my view, to adopting an objective criterion for the assessment of the abuse. It is true that those objective elements will reveal that the person or persons engaged in that activity had, most likely, the intention of abusing Community law. But it is not that intention that is decisive for the assessment of the abuse. It is instead the activity itself, objectively considered.
>
> In my view it is not therefore a search for the elusive subjective intentions of the parties that ought to determine the existence of the subjective element mentioned in Emsland. Instead, the intentions of the parties to improperly obtain an advantage from Community law are merely inferable from the artificial character of the situation to be assessed in the light of a set of objective circumstances.[101]

Following AG Maduro's invitation, the Court substituted the expression 'intention to obtain an advantage' initially used in *Emsland-Stärke* (para 53) with the expression 'essential aim of the transactions' in the *Halifax* ruling (para 75).[102] The artificiality requirement is accordingly 'objectified', as the subjective intention

[100] Ruiz Almendral (n 75) 567.

[101] AG Maduro, Case C-255/02 *Halifax* [2006] ECR I-1609, paras 70–71; see also AG Léger, Case C-196/04 *Cadbury Schweppes* [2006] ECR I-7995, paras 115–21; Schammo, 'Arbitrage and Abuse of Rights in the EC Legal System' (n 25) 368; J Freedman, 'The Anatomy of Tax Avoidance Counteraction: Abuse of Law in a Tax Context at Member State and European Union Level' in de la Feria and Vogenauer (n 46) 375; V Edwards and P Farmer, 'The Concept of Abuse in the Freedom of Establishment of Companies: a Case of Double Standards?' in FG Jacobs et al (eds), *Continuity and Change in EU Law: Essays in Honour of Sir Francis Jacobs* (Oxford, Oxford University Press, 2007) 227.

[102] S Vogenauer, 'The Prohibition of Abuse of Law: an Emerging General Principle of EU Law' in de la Feria and Vogenauer (n 46) 538.

to artificially obtain a regulatory advantage is translated into the objective aim of the transaction:

> [W]hen we talk about the intention or aim of a person, we talk about subjective considerations. That is, 'subjective' in the sense that we talk about the mental state of a person. However, if we talk about the aim of a transaction, we talk about objective considerations.[103]

In practice, the artificiality requirement leaves little room for judicial discretion, since a finding of artificiality requires the identification of a choice of law made by a private individual through a transaction that has no other explanation than the regulatory benefit sought.[104] The evidentiary dimension of the artificiality requirement has two aspects: on the one hand, authorities must rest a finding of abuse on objective evidence (*Emsland-Stärke*, para 54; *Halifax*, para 76; *ING. AUER*, paras 45–47; *Agip Petroli*, para 24), on the other hand, the parties to the transaction must have the opportunity to provide objective evidence of any commercial justification supporting it (*Cadbury Schweppes*, para 70; *Thin Cap Group Litigation*, para 82). Once the competent judge may conclude on the basis of such objective evidence that a transaction has no other explanation than the regulatory benefit sought, he may safely infer that this transaction amounts to an artificial choice of law. As summarised by Snell,

> Subjective intent is obviously difficult to determine, but the law is generally quite prepared to infer intent from objective evidence. Judges and juries everywhere have proven willing to convict in the absence of a confession on the basis of evidence that points to the requisite mens rea. Indeed, the focus on the artificial nature of the transaction can be understood as such objective evidence of intent. If the only possible reason for a transaction is to obtain an advantage from EU rules, this has to be the real reason for it. In fact, it is almost tautological to require an artificial arrangement and an intention to take advantage of EU rules. If the artificial arrangement is found, the intent is overwhelmingly likely to be there as well.[105]

Thus understood, the artificiality requirement of the doctrine of abuse presents a fairly confined threat to legal certainty.

In contrast, the teleological assessment represents the focal point of tension between legal certainty and legal congruence. The teleological assessment is indisputably objective as it does not enquire into the intentions of the parties, but rather determines the legitimacy of the artificial choice of law in dispute.[106] Yet it is within the framework of the teleological assessment that the competent judge

[103] Schammo (n 25) 368; see also, among many others, Freedman, 'The Anatomy of Tax Avoidance Counteraction' (n 101) 375; D Triantafyllou, 'L'interdiction des abus de droit en tant que principe général du droit communautaire' (2002) 38 *Cahiers de Droit Européen* 611, 628; Weber, 'Abuse of Law in the Context of Indirect Taxation' (n 81) 397.

[104] See ch 3 section II.

[105] J Snell, 'The Notion of and a General Test for Abuse of Rights: Some Normative Reflections' in de la Feria and Vogenauer (n 46) 226.

[106] See ch 3 section III.

must decide whether the outcome artificially sought is sufficiently inequitable for the wording of the applicable Union law to be set aside; or, in other words, whether legal certainty deserves to be sacrificed on the altar of legal congruence.

As explained in Subsection II.A above, abuses of Union law represent attempts to exploit the rigidity of Union laws in order to obtain a benefit in contradiction with their purpose. From this perspective, the formal doctrine of abuse can be reconstructed as an injection of flexibility into the scope of a rigid Union law, in order to mitigate the risk of legal incongruence flowing from its literal interpretation:

> When abuse of law occurs, the purpose of the norm is circumvented, relying on the literal interpretation. This brings the tension between the ratio and the wording of the norm to the fore. It follows quite logically that it is of relatively little use to study tax avoidance as a separate phenomenon, since the questions relate to the flexibility of methods of interpretation of law. ... The doctrine of abuse of rights gives clear precedence to a substantive rather than formal or literal interpretation of Community law provisions.[107]

The legal history surrounding the seminal *Emsland-Stärke* case aptly illustrates this submission, as shown in Figure 8 below. The abusive practice set up by Emsland-Stärke sought to exploit the rigidity of Article 10(1) in order to obtain a benefit in contradiction with the purpose of Regulation 2730/79. Article 10(1) of Regulation 2730/79 merely entitled national authorities to demand, before granting the export refund, proof of 'importation' and 'placing on the market'. Such rigidity has the virtue of ensuring legal certainty but threatened legal congruence, as it precluded the judge seized from modulating the scope of the export refund regime in order to exclude artificial re-importations of goods.

The Court's recourse to the doctrine of abuse in the *Emsland-Stärke* judgment had the effect of relaxing the rigidity of Article 10(1) of Regulation 2730/79. The Court invited the national judge seized to consider whether 'despite formal observance of the conditions laid down by the [Union] rules, the purpose of those rules has not been achieved' (para 52). In that sense, the doctrine of abuse is essentially teleological for it empowers the competent judge to discard the letter of Union law, if a literal interpretation leads to an outcome that runs counter to its purposes:

> Provided that those objective circumstances are found to exist one must conclude that a person who relies upon the literal meaning of a Community law provision to claim a right that runs counter to its purposes does not deserve to have that right upheld. In such circumstances, the legal provision at issue must be interpreted, contrary to its literal meaning, as actually not conferring the right.[108]
>
> A finding of abuse resulting in the non-application of the rule does indeed resemble a purposive or teleological interpretation whereby the wording of the rule (being found to be 'over-inclusive' for the situation in question) is 'read down' in order to 'restrict'

[107] Karimeri (n 16) 297 and 304.
[108] AG Maduro, Case C-255/02 *Halifax* [2006] ECR I-1609, para 71.

or 'reduce' the scope of the rule. Writings on legal methodology in the German legal tradition would describe such an outcome as a 'teleological reduction' (*teleologische Reduktion*).[109]

It is noteworthy that the later adoption of Article 27(4) of Regulation 612/2009 by the legislature preserved the state of affairs ensuing from the Court's recourse to the doctrine of abuse in *Emsland-Stärke*. This provision amounts to a codification of the case law on abusive practices in relation to export refunds, and chiefly of the *Emsland-Stärke* judgment; in particular, the notion of 'normal commercial transaction' is directly inspired by paragraph 51 of this judgment. This criterion of 'normality' provides the competent judge with enough flexibility to exclude abusive transactions, just as the doctrine of abuse did.

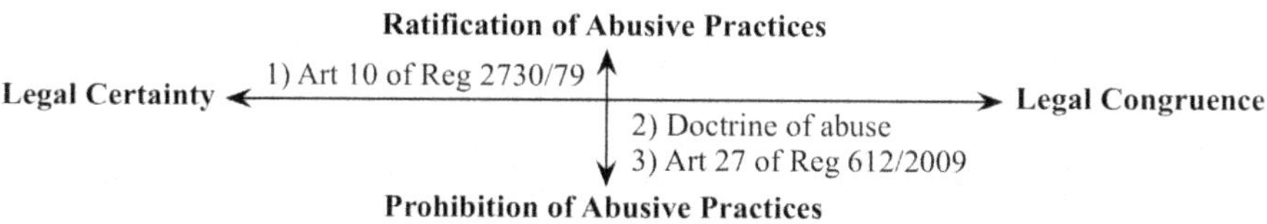

Figure 8 – *Emsland-Stärke* between Legal Certainty and Legal Congruence

As illustrated by *Emsland-Stärke*, the doctrine of abuse thwarts the risk of legal incongruence entailed by rigid Union laws, but generates a risk of legal uncertainty. Both effects of the doctrine of abuse have been abundantly acknowledged in the literature, although almost systematically in isolation from each other. On the one hand, it is well established that the doctrine of abuse restores legal congruence:

> Such a rule, conceived as a principle of interpretation, constitutes an indispensable safety-valve for protecting the aims of all provisions of Community law against a formalistic application of them based solely on their plain meaning.[110]

> [When] the tension between the strict application of a rule and the true spirit of that rule is at stake, ... the principle of the prohibition of abuse of rights functions as a corrective mechanism to the strict application of a rule of law.[111]

In that sense, the function of the doctrine of abuse can be compared to that of general principles of law or rules of equity,[112] which are also invoked to fill the

[109] Vogenauer, 'The Prohibition of Abuse of Law' (n 102) 558. This teleological element had already been identified by Josserand in his theory of abuse of rights: Josserand, *De l'esprit des droits et de leur relativité* (n 91) n°292 (see ch 1 n 179 and accompanying text); commented by J Gordley, 'The Abuse of Rights in the Civil Law Tradition' in de la Feria and Vogenauer (n 46) 36.

[110] AG Maduro, Case C-255/02 *Halifax* [2006] ECR I-1609, para 74.

[111] A Lenaerts, 'The General Principle of the Prohibition of Abuse of Rights: A Critical Position on Its Role in a Codified European Contract Law' (2010) 18 *European Review of Private Law* 1121, 1122.

[112] See nn 29–31, 46–48 and accompanying text.

congruence gap between law and reality.[113] Sooner or later, the application of rigid legal norms calls for such 'gap-filling' mechanisms: 'Where a code is rigid, it is important to allow judges discretion to adjudicate problematic cases going beyond the letter of the code'.[114]

On the other hand, owing to the trade-off between legal certainty and legal congruence, any attempt to reduce the rigidity of a legal norm necessarily comes at a cost, in the form of an increased room for judicial discretion. Thus, if the recourse to the doctrine of abuse restores legal congruence by condemning undesirable choices of law, it must undermine legal certainty by the same token, which as a matter of fact has been the object of recurrent criticism:

> Any abuse-based reasoning can therefore be expected to diminish legal certainty and to increase judicial discretion. National doctrines of abuse are frequently criticised for this reason.[115]

> [T]he doctrine of abuse serves the purpose of transforming something that would be otherwise legal into unlawful behaviour. And … the transformation from legality to illegality happens via means of judicial interpretation in the case at issue and therefore might raise problems of legal certainty as well as democratic accountability.[116]

Indeed, the perspective of a judge going beyond the letter of the relevant Union law and seeking to grasp its elusive 'spirit', in order to outlaw as 'abusive' transactions that he finds in contradiction with the latter, awakens fears of legal uncertainty:

> The first part of the test [of the doctrine of abuse] has been uncontroversial. It fits well with the teleological method of interpretation familiar to EU lawyers, and reserves an important role to the Court …. Nevertheless, there are some instances where it is likely to lead to considerable difficulties.[117]

> The real difficulty lies with ascertaining the purposes of the statute, although this may be easier with EU legislation than with UK provisions, where the very detailed drafting style adopted can sometimes seem devoid of any principle whatsoever. But even EU legislation may not always be founded on a coherent and obvious economic principle and thus it can be difficult for the courts to decide these issues.[118]

It should be underlined that this harmful effect of the fight against abusive practices upon legal certainty is inevitable, owing to the trade-off between legal

[113] Tridimas (n 32) 17 ff; Arnull, 'What is a General Principle of EU Law?' (n 86) 7–8; R de la Feria, 'Prohibition of Abuse of (Community) Law: the Creation of a New General Principle of EC Law through Tax' (2008) 45 *Common Market Law Review* 395, 434; M Dougan, 'Some Comments on the Idea of a General Principle of Union Law Prohibiting Abuses of Law in the Field of Free Movement for Union Citizens' in de la Feria and Vogenauer (n 46); P Farmer, 'Prohibition of Abuse of (European) Law: The Creation of a New General Principle of EU Law through Tax: A Response' in de la Feria and Vogenauer (n 46); A Lenaerts, 'The General Principle of the Prohibition of Abuse of Rights' (n 111) 1124–25.

[114] C Costello, 'Citizenship of the Union: Above Abuse?' in de la Feria and Vogenauer (n 46) 328.

[115] Vogenauer (n 102) 545.

[116] Spaventa, 'Comments on Abuse of Law and the Free Movement of Workers' (n 86) 316.

[117] Snell, 'The Notion of and a General Test for Abuse of Rights' (n 105) 225.

[118] Freedman (n 101) 376.

certainty and legal congruence. Thus, designing an anti-abuse rule with a view to preserve legal certainty will necessarily decrease its anti-abuse capacity. By way of illustration, in his comment on the *Halifax* judgment, Lyal wrote:

> There was also some concern that the introduction of an open-ended rule [prohibiting abusive practices] could have harmful consequences for legal certainty. That worry merited close attention, though problems of legal certainty can be minimised by formulating a narrow rule aimed at clear cases of manipulation.[119]

Quite obviously, compared to a general doctrine of abuse, a 'narrow rule aimed at clear cases of manipulation' provides more legal certainty, but also less legal congruence as it is not capable of catching every type of abusive practice. In sum, the broader the fight against abusive practices, the higher the degree of legal uncertainty:

> In the eternal tension that law faces, in either considering the single case (by using general principles, or by being vague, leading to legal indeterminacy) or the typical case (the average typical case or the frequent typical case) through a typified method that drastically reduces or eliminates discretionary application (using legal fictions or irrebuttable presumptions), the principle of abuse of EU law clearly favours the first-mentioned purpose, in contrast to certainty, as it implies a case-by-case analysis.[120]

The fear of legal uncertainty partly accounts for the fact that the Court does not always have recourse to a teleological interpretation of rigid norms. For instance, in the quota-hopping saga (*Agegate*, *Jaderow*, *Factortame II*), the Court refused to read an implicit requirement of a genuine link with the State of the flag in the scope of Regulations 101/76 and 170/83, although such requirement was undoubtedly commanded by the purpose of the fishing quotas, namely the proportional allocation of available catches among local communities dependent upon fisheries, and could moreover be derived from Article 5(1) of the 1958 Geneva Convention on the High Seas.[121] By reinforcing the rigidity of the legal regime on fishing quotas, the Court secured legal certainty at the expense of legal congruence.

To sum up, the formal doctrine of abuse can be reconstructed as an injection of flexibility into the scope of a rigid Union law, in order to mitigate the risk of legal incongruence flowing from a literal interpretation. This flexibility brought by the doctrine of abuse empowers the competent judge to assess abusive practices in light of the purposes of the applicable Union law and beyond its letter (teleological interpretation), thereby ensuring legal congruence at the expense of legal certainty.

[119] Lyal, 'Cadbury Schweppes and Abuse' (n 86) 428.

[120] AP Dourado, 'A Single Principle of Abuse in European Union Law: A Methodological Approach to Rejecting a Different Concept of Abuse in Personal Taxation' in de la Feria and Vogenauer (n 46) 472.

[121] See ch 4 n 273 and accompanying text.

B. Fighting Abusive Practices by Enacting Flexible Legal Norms

The previous section described the need to have recourse to the doctrine of abuse when abusive practices affect rigid legal norms. However, as abusive practices thrive on rigid and detailed legal rules, they can also be fought by enacting flexible and more general legal rules: '[P]lanning around a vague rule is difficult and the creation of such uncertainty may be a significant deterrent in precluding artificial arrangements'.[122] As their scope is malleable, flexible norms entail a degree of legal uncertainty but permit legal congruence: indeed, the competent judge has the possibility of countering abusive practices by modulating their scope. As observed by Kjellgren,

> Circumvention in many cases thrives on detailed rules, making use of the more textual—albeit seldom purpose-oriented—interpretations of applicable legal norms. What, then, can the legislator do? One of the possibilities is to introduce legal norms of more general applicability in order to combat 'abuse' of legal rights. The concept of 'abuse-control' in this sense is therefore—and by necessity—connected with a certain degree of uncertainty.[123]

In his Opinion in *Kefalas*, AG Tesauro questioned the usefulness of an autonomous doctrine of abuse in Union law, precisely by reason of its flexibility:

> [T]he risk of there being a gap in the system—which is, after all, what the abuse of rights principle, like all other so-called catch-all provisions, seeks to avoid—is minor, or non-existent, in a legal order like that of the Community which, through judicial interpretation and case-law in general, is more promptly amenable to adaptation to the needs of society.
>
> That said, it is none the less true that any legal order which aspires to achieve a minimum level of completion must contain self-protection measures, so to speak, to ensure that the rights it confers are not exercised in a manner which is abusive, excessive or distorted. This requirement is not at all alien to Community law; on the contrary, it has been repeatedly recognised in the Court's case-law.[124]

In that regard, it is important to defuse a common misconception according to which legal certainty is better preserved when abusive practices are fought through statutory construction, rather than by having recourse to the doctrine of abuse. By way of illustration, Costello confessed a preference for the latter option in relation to the *Weber* and *Wiedemann* cases, in which the Court interpreted Directive 91/439 in a way that prevented 'driving-licence tourism':[125] '*The Court's approach is preferable, in that there is no need to rely on the concept of abuse in these cases*'.[126] In more general terms, Snell wrote:

> Ideally of course the doctrine of abuse of rights should be utilised extremely sparingly. Instead, the legislature and the courts should craft carefully circumscribed rights that

[122] Karimeri (n 16) 304.
[123] Kjellgren, 'On the Border of Abuse' (n 78) 179.
[124] AG Tesauro, Case C-367/96 *Kefalas* [1998] ECR I-2843, para 23–24.
[125] See ch 4 n 162 and accompanying text.
[126] Costello, 'Citizenship of the Union' (n 114) 352.

> contain their own limitations. Abusive attempts to invoke a right should generally be met with the finding that the situation is outside the scope of the right altogether, as in the case of a person seeking to rely on the free movement of workers but engaged in a purely marginal and ancillary activity. The less frequently the notion of abuse is employed the more successful has the Union legal system been, and under no circumstances should the doctrine be allowed to become a substitute for detailed legislation and case law.[127]

Such criticism is oblivious to the fact that fighting abusive practices necessarily undermines legal certainty, irrespective of the technique applied. Admittedly, having recourse to the doctrine of abuse does generate legal uncertainty, as it amounts to a teleological interpretation of the applicable norm. But countering abusive practices through statutory construction of flexible legal norms, such as Directive 91/439 or the Treaty provisions on free movement, equally generates legal uncertainty, for such norms offer per se an important room for judicial discretion. Legal uncertainty originates either in the teleological interpretation of rigid norms or in the wording of flexible norms. In sum, the choice is not between doctrine of abuse and legal certainty, but rather between fighting abusive practices and legal certainty—and more generally between legal congruence and legal certainty.

Therefore, if *Emsland-Stärke* and *Halifax*, examined in the previous section, illustrate the need to have recourse to an 'external' doctrine of abuse in the presence of abusive practices affecting rigid Union laws, such practices can also be fought through the 'internal' interpretation of flexible Union laws. In that connection, mention can be made of Article 27(4) of Regulation 612/2009, evoked above, or of the anti-abuse provisions commonly adopted in the tax legislation.[128] Thanks to their flexibility, the scope of such norms can be modulated to address abusive practices, whose emergence is inevitable but whose concrete manifestations are unpredictable. However, as explained in the inception of this section, fighting abusive practices with flexible legal norms does not provide more legal certainty than the recourse to an autonomous doctrine of abuse: their adaptability implies legal uncertainty in itself, precisely because their scope can be modulated by the competent judge.

Within Union law, the Treaty provisions on free movement constitute a paramount example of flexible norms; as a matter of fact, the indeterminacy of the

[127] Snell (n 105) 231.

[128] Council Directive 90/435/EEC of 23 July 1990 on the common system of taxation applicable in the case of parent companies and subsidiaries of different Member States [1990] OJ L225/6 art 1(2); Council Directive 90/434/EEC of 23 July 1990 on the common system of taxation applicable to mergers, divisions, transfers of assets and exchanges of shares concerning companies of different Member States [1990] OJ L225/1 art 11(1)(a); Council Directive 2003/49/EC of 3 June 2003 on a common system of taxation applicable to interest and royalty payments made between associated companies of different Member States [2003] OJ L157/49 art 5; Council Directive 2009/133/EC of 19 October 2009 on the common system of taxation applicable to mergers, divisions, partial divisions, transfers of assets and exchanges of shares concerning companies of different Member States and to the transfer of the registered office of an SE or SCE between Member States [2009] OJ L310/34 art 15(1)(a).

'free movement test' has been highlighted on numerous occasions.[129] This flexibility of the free movement provisions has one important implication: abusive practices can be addressed by modulating their scope, without having recourse to an 'external' doctrine of abuse. Thus, when interpreting the free movement provisions, the Court often merges the treatment of abusive practices with the conditions of application of the relevant free movement right, as shown in Figure 9.[130]

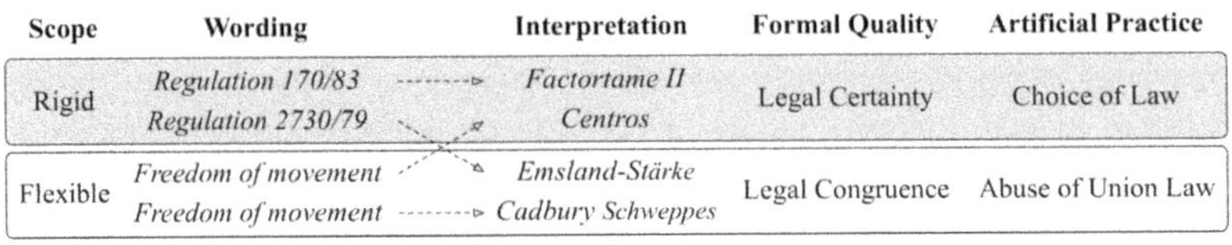

Figure 9 – Artificial Practices, Legal Congruence and Legal Certainty

Cadbury Schweppes illustrates the fight against abusive practices through the interpretation of the free movement provisions. The national proceedings in *Cadbury Schweppes* concerned the compatibility with the freedom of establishment of CFC (for 'Controlled Foreign Company') rules adopted by the United Kingdom. CFC rules are intended to counter a form of tax avoidance by which companies attempt to artificially shift profits from the Member State in which they are made to a low-tax State by means of the establishment of a subsidiary in that State (the 'controlled foreign company'). In order to prevent such artificial choice of law, CFC rules reintegrate the profits of the subsidiary into the taxable profits of the parent company. In its judgment, the Court found that CFC rules restricted the freedom of establishment but could be justified in so far as they were aimed at letterbox companies, as the objective of the freedom of establishment is to foster genuine economic integration:

> Having regard to that objective of integration in the host Member State, the concept of establishment within the meaning of the Treaty provisions on freedom of establishment involves the actual pursuit of an economic activity through a fixed establishment in that State for an indefinite period. Consequently, it presupposes actual establishment of the company concerned in the host Member State and the pursuit of genuine economic activity there.
>
> In order for a restriction on the freedom of establishment to be justified on the ground of prevention of abusive practices, the specific objective of such a restriction must be to prevent conduct involving the creation of wholly artificial arrangements which do not reflect economic reality, with a view to escaping the tax normally due on the profits generated by activities carried out on national territory.[131]

[129] See n 39 and accompanying text.
[130] Ziegler, 'Abuse of Law' (n 86) 306; see also Spaventa (n 86) 315–20.
[131] Case C-196/04 *Cadbury Schweppes* [2006] ECR I-7995, paras 54–55.

Furthermore, from a dynamic perspective, the interpretation given by the Court will itself have an impact on the degree of flexibility of the norm interpreted, and as a consequence on the room for abusive practices. In the presence of flexible norms such as the freedoms of movement, abusive practices can be viewed as attempts to 'rigidify' their scope in order to open a congruence gap between law and reality. Various techniques can be used to reject such attempt and preserve the flexibility necessary to counter abusive practices. In *Cadbury Schweppes* (as in *Thin Cap Group Litigation*), the Court integrated the doctrine of abuse within the scope of the free movement provisions, explicitly referring to *Emsland-Stärke* and *Halifax*:

> In order to find that there is [a wholly artificial arrangement] there must be, in addition to a subjective element consisting in the intention to obtain a tax advantage, objective circumstances showing that, despite formal observance of the conditions laid down by Community law, the objective pursued by freedom of establishment, as set out in paragraphs 54 and 55 of this judgment, has not been achieved (see, to that effect, Case C-110/99 Emsland-Stärke [2000] ECR I-11569, paragraphs 52 and 53, and Case C-255/02 Halifax and Others [2006] ECR I-0000, paragraphs 74 and 75).[132]

However, abusive practices are most of the time addressed without reference to the doctrine of abuse: as explained above, common reactions of Union law to abusive practices include centres of gravity, suspect periods and free choice of law approaches.[133] The effect of a centre of gravity is similar to that of the doctrine of abuse: it permits legal congruence and the fight against abusive practices, but undermines legal certainty. As explained above, the real seat theory constitutes a paramount example of centre of gravity approach.[134] Concrete applications of the real seat theory can be found in *Fitzwilliam* and *Plum*, in which the Court decided that posted workers remained subject to the social security of their home State only if the posting undertaking habitually carries on significant activities in the Member State in which it is established (*Fitzwilliam*, para 40). To that end, the Court drew a non-exhaustive list of 'relevant criteria':

> [Relevant criteria] include the place where the undertaking has its seat and administration, the number of administrative staff working in the Member State in which it is established and in the other Member State, the place where posted workers are recruited and the place where the majority of contracts with clients are concluded, the law applicable to the employment contracts concluded by the undertaking with its workers, on the one hand, and with its clients, on the other hand, and the turnover during an appropriately typical period in each Member State concerned. That list cannot be exhaustive; the choice of criteria must be adapted to each specific case.[135]

[132] Case C-196/04 *Cadbury Schweppes* [2006] ECR I-7995, para 64.
[133] See ch 4.
[134] See ch 4 section III.A and III.B.
[135] Case C-202/97 *Fitzwilliam* [2000] ECR I-883, para 43.

On the one hand, the flexibility of this centre of gravity test increases legal congruence, as it enables the national judge to take into account idiosyncrasies of concrete cases in order to measure the genuineness of the link between an undertaking and its home State, thereby preventing artificial relocations in jurisdictions levying low social contributions. On the other hand, such a test tends to reduce legal certainty, since the possibility for the judge seized to rely on an open list of relevant criteria renders the outcome less certain. The risk of legal uncertainty entailed by centre of gravity tests is well identified in the scholarship. As a matter of fact, the legal uncertainty inherent to such tests was one of the central arguments raised by AG La Pergola to endorse a free choice of law approach in *Centros*:

> [T]he requirement that the parent company effectively carry on business is not only debatable as to substance but difficult to apply owing to its indeterminate nature. What kind of business must the parent company conduct, for how long and on what scale, for it to be at liberty to exercise the right to set up a secondary establishment?[136]

Similarly, in matters of cross-border insolvency proceedings, Article 3 of Regulation 1346/2000 provides that the courts of the Member State within the territory of which the 'centre of a debtor's main interests' is situated shall have jurisdiction to open insolvency proceedings. The use of the centre of main interests or 'COMI' to determine both the competent judge (Article 3) and the applicable law (Article 4) has been criticised on the ground that it imperils legal certainty:

> The second problem I see with the COMI standard is that the definition of the COMI is still widely unclear or 'fuzzy', as Eidenmüller puts it. ... The 'fuzziness' of the COMI standard (including the uncertainty as to the conditions for the rebuttability of the presumption) is most likely to create legal uncertainty both for the respective company and for third parties who are in business relations with the company. Again, the unpredictability and the vagueness of the 'head office' criterion (which was the main element of the 'real seat' theory) was one of the major criticisms that were raised against the real seat theory.[137]

By contrast with doctrines of abuse and centres of gravity, suspect periods offer more legal certainty but less legal congruence: indeed, they tend to draw a straight line that rarely espouses the winding aspects of real-life cases. In other words, the formal rigidity of suspect periods precludes judges from adapting their decisions to idiosyncrasies of concrete cases; conversely, they are commonly praised for leaving little or no room for judicial discretion. Thus, in *Förster*, the Court ruled that a five-year residence requirement imposed on Union citizens requesting a

[136] AG La Pergola, Case C-212/97 *Centros* [1999] ECR I-1459, para 17.

[137] W-G Ringe, 'Forum Shopping under the EU Insolvency Regulation' (2008) Oxford Legal Studies Research Paper no 33/2008, available at http://ssrn.com/abstract=1209822, 26; see also J Armour, 'Abuse of European Insolvency Law? A Discussion' in de la Feria and Vogenauer (n 46) 159.

study grant was compatible with the Treaty, having due regard to the legal certainty it offered:

> By enabling those concerned to know, without any ambiguity, what their rights and obligations are, the residence requirement laid down by the Policy rule of 9 May 2005 is, by its very existence, such as to guarantee a significant level of legal certainty and transparency in the context of the award of maintenance grants to students.[138]

However, the use of suspect periods decreases legal congruence, as their rigidity precludes the competent judge from apprehending the intricacies of reality. For instance, the five-year residence requirement endorsed in *Förster* mechanically excludes migrant citizens who are highly integrated in the host State before the expiry of that period. This was precisely the criticism issued by AG Mazák in his Opinion in *Förster*, later echoed in the scholarship:

> [A] five-year residence requirement [is not proportionate], since it can reasonably be assumed that a number of students may have established a substantial degree of integration into society well before the expiry of that period. That is especially the case with students who, like Ms Förster, have also pursued occupational activities in the host Member State in addition to their studies.[139]

> The five-year residence condition precluded any examination of her actual degree of integration in the host Member State, as the Court's previous case law seemed to require. … As the Court itself highlighted in Förster, the advantage of the five-year residence requirement is the clarity and legal certainty which it affords benefit claimants and, presumably, host Member States.[140]

Moreover, if the use of suspect periods risks excluding legitimate transactions, as the five-year residence in *Förster*, it also entails the reverse risk, namely the inclusion of abusive practices. The latter risk led AG Geelhoed to reject the imposition of a minimum residence period in *Akrich*, which was also echoed in the literature:

> [O]bjective criteria lend themselves to being circumvented. In my view legal certainty requires that the factors taken into account by the national authorities in reviewing the issue of misuse be discernible. That entails the risk that persons concerned may adjust their situation so as to satisfy the conditions laid down. I would point to the statement by Mrs Akrich to the effect that she was assuming that her period of residence in Ireland together with her husband had to be of at least six months' duration.[141]

[138] Case C-158/07 *Förster* [2008] ECR I-8507, para 57.

[139] AG Mazák, Case C-158/07 *Förster* [2008] ECR I-8507, para 130.

[140] S O'Leary, 'Equal Treatment and EU Citizens: A New Chapter On Cross-Border Educational Mobility and Access to Student Financial Assistance' (2009) 34 *European Law Review* 612, 621 and 627; see also C O'Brien, 'Real Links, Abstract Rights and False Alarms: the Relationship between the ECJ's "Real Link" Case Law and National Solidarity' (2008) 33 *European Law Review* 643, 649.

[141] AG Geelhoed, Case C-109/01 *Akrich* [2003] ECR I-9607, paras 175–76.

> [A] test for abuse based on objective criteria, such as minimum residence periods, can be opposed on the basis that such criteria are subject to circumvention.[142]

In matters of insolvency proceedings, Eidenmüller discussed in similar terms the possibility to substitute the criterion of 'centre of main interests' used by Article 3 of Regulation 1346/2000 with a suspect period:

> Would it be advisable to combine the proposal made here with a suspect period such that not the actual registered office is decisive with respect to the opening of main insolvency proceedings, but the registered office at some earlier point in time—eg a few months or a year before the insolvency petition? … Although arguments can be put forward in favour of it, especially its deterrent effect on last-minute forum shoppers and its clear-cut character (legal certainty), the length of such a suspect period is always arbitrary.[143]

This analysis of centres of gravity and suspect periods demonstrates the pervasiveness of the trade-off between legal certainty and legal congruence. Rigid criteria such as suspect periods increase legal certainty but entail a risk of inequitable outcomes (such as abusive practices); yet any attempt to prevent inequitable outcomes necessarily rests on more flexible criteria such as centres of gravity, which reduces the degree of legal certainty. AG Sharpston identified this ineluctable trade-off in her Opinion in *Prinz*, which concerned a three-year residence requirement imposed by Germany to obtain study financing.[144] In essence, she observed that a three-year suspect period provides certain but inequitable outcomes, as it mechanically excludes genuinely integrated persons. By contrast, a centre of gravity approach is less certain but more equitable for it enables the competent judge to rely on all individual circumstances to measure the degree of integration into German society.

Furthermore, anti-abuse rules are themselves subject to the same trade-off between legal certainty and legal congruence, as every legal norm: adopting general anti-abuse rules provides more legal congruence, whereas specific anti-abuse rules provide more legal certainty. This tension was underlined both by the Commission and the scholarship:

> As tax planning structures are ever more elaborate and national legislators are frequently left with insufficient time for reaction, specific anti-abuse measures often turn out to be inadequate for successfully catching up with novel aggressive tax planning structures. Such structures can be harmful to national tax revenues and to the functioning of the internal market. Therefore, it is appropriate to recommend the adoption by Member States of a common general anti-abuse rule, which should also avoid the complexity of many different ones.[145]

[142] Ziegler (n 86) 307; see also Costello (n 114) 340.

[143] H Eidenmüller, 'Abuse of Law in the Context of European Insolvency Law' in de la Feria and Vogenauer (n 46) 155.

[144] AG Sharpston, Case C-523/11 *Prinz* [2013] ECR I-0000; see n 41 and accompanying text.

[145] Commission (EC), 'Aggressive tax planning' (Recommendation) C (2012) 8806 final, 6 December 2012, rec 8.

> The less detailed the definition, the less predictable the application is prone to be. This is perhaps the main criticism against general anti-avoidance doctrines. The alternative is the use of specific norms targeting only certain forms of tax avoidance. ... Yet, a detailed formulation may also lend itself to further abuse as it is sometimes held that through an a contrario interpretation, that which is left out is implicitly allowed.[146]

The last possible reaction to the presence of abusive practices is to ratify them by adopting a free choice of law approach. A free choice of law approach classically rests on a literal interpretation that 'rigidifies' the applicable Union law, thereby creating a congruence gap between law and reality; as such, it represents the choice of legal certainty over legal congruence. In *Centros*, AG La Pergola proposed such a reading of the freedom of establishment, later followed by the Court:

> The Danish authorities insist that the principal establishment must really pursue the activities stated to be the object of the company. However, that line of reasoning leads them to see in Article [54 TFUE] an additional condition to which the right to set up a secondary establishment is subject. However, in my view, the formal requirements set out in Article [54 TFUE], for the purpose of identifying companies that have that right, are definitive.[147]

A literal reading of Article 54 TFEU precludes the competent judge from taking into account any circumstance other than the fact that the company has been formed in accordance with the law of a Member State, thereby guaranteeing a high degree of legal certainty. By the same token, such an approach undermines legal congruence, as it does not permit any judicial correction of the mechanical application of the applicable Union law:

> While forcing a Court to stick to a literal interpretation would undoubtedly limit its judicial discretion—thus affecting the allocation of powers between the legislature and the Courts—a formalistic literal interpretation does not allow capturing the abuse/avoidance problematic. The vice is the rule itself.[148]

In matters of insolvency proceedings, this pursuit of legal certainty led several scholars to advocate the replacement of the current centre of gravity approach (based on the debtor's centre of main interests) by a free choice of law approach (based on the debtor's registered office): 'This radical approach would have the clear advantage of a predictable jurisdiction venue and a predictably applicable insolvency law'.[149]

This effect of a free choice of law approach can be easily identified in the field of nationality as well, another field in which legal certainty is often preferred to legal congruence. As a matter of fact, both attributions of nationality by descent

[146] Karimeri (n 16) 298.
[147] AG La Pergola, Case C-212/97 *Centros* [1999] ECR I-1459, para 18.
[148] Schammo (n 25) 375.
[149] Ringe (n 137) 27; see also Eidenmüller, 'Abuse of Law in the Context of European Insolvency Law' (n 143) 154; Armour (n 137) 167.

and by birth are prone to abusive practices, as they are not apt to guarantee the existence of a genuine link with the country of nationality:

> [A]ll systems of nationality by descent (*jus sanguinis*) may end up attributing nationality to individuals who have never set foot in their country of nationality. … Nationality by birth on the territory (*jus soli*) also fails to map onto a genuine link with state of nationality in some instances, as birth in the territory may be sufficient to attribute nationality, without the child's family having any established links to the country. In the EU, only Ireland maintained a system of absolute *jus soli*, the underlying source of controversy in *Chen.*[150]

Owing to the trade-off between legal congruence and legal certainty, the pursuit of legal congruence necessarily undermines legal certainty: for instance, the use of a genuine link requirement (centre of gravity) would 'replace a clear and objective criterion by vague and subjective criteria' so that 'its overall effect would … be international uncertainty and insecurity'.[151] For this very reason, Costello approved the *Micheletti* and *Zhu and Chen* jurisprudence:

> A 'real link' test would be in danger of undermining the crucial clarity and certainty of regimes of citizenship by birth. … Accordingly, Member States are under a strict duty to recognise each other's designations of nationality, precluding claims that an EU citizen acquired nationality in an abusive manner.[152]

To sum up, the flexibility of legal norms such as the Treaty provisions on free movement provides legal congruence at the expense of legal certainty. Thanks to their flexibility, the competent judge can modulate the scope of such norms to address abusive practices, whose emergence is inevitable but whose concrete manifestations are unpredictable. Yet from a dynamic perspective, the interpretation of such norms will affect their degree of flexibility, and accordingly alter their positioning along the trade-off between legal congruence and legal certainty: the integration of a doctrine of abuse (*Cadbury Schweppes*) or a centre of gravity approach (*Fitzwilliam*) tends to preserve legal congruence at the expense of legal certainty, whereas a suspect period (*Förster*) or a free choice of law approach (*Centros*) tends to favour legal certainty over legal congruence.

[150] Costello (n 114) 334.

[151] JL Kunz, 'The Nottebohm Judgment' (1960) 54 *The American Journal of International Law* 536, 571.

[152] Costello (n 114) 336 and 352.

Conclusion: The Certainty of Abuse and the Illusion of Legal Certainty

IN THIS PART one, abuses of Union law were identified as private reactions to public actions undertaken by Union institutions (abuse private-public, chapter one). In more detail, they were defined as artificial and undesirable choices of law made by private individuals (chapter three). In reaction, Union institutions may have recourse to the formal doctrine of abuse (chapter two), informal doctrines of abuse, centres of gravity, suspect periods and free choice of law approaches (chapter four). Furthermore, the phenomenon of abuse of Union law cuts across an inescapable trade-off between two formal virtues of law, legal certainty and legal congruence, which are respectively concerned with the predictability and equity of legal outcomes (chapter five).

From a dynamic perspective, abusive practices are best described as reactions of Union citizens to Union laws, themselves giving rise to reactions of the Union legal order. These two chronological sequences form an endless cycle of action by public authorities and reception by private citizens, followed by renewed public action and private reaction, and so on. By way of an epilogue to this part one, the essence of these two chronological sequences can be respectively captured with the following formulae: the certainty of abuse (from Union law to abuse) and the illusion of legal certainty (from abuse to Union law).

The first formula, the 'certainty of abuse', is intended to express the inevitability of abusive practices within the Union legal order, as within any other legal order. Abuses of Union law are unpredictable and yet inevitable reactions to the enactment of Union laws. The paradox of abusive practices lies precisely in that their emergence can be predicted with absolute certainty, whereas their concrete forms can never be predicted:

> [There is a] risk, inherent in every legal system, that actions may be taken which, despite formally complying with a legal provision, amount to abusive exploitation of the possibilities left open by that provision, contrary to its purposes and objectives.[1]

As explained in chapter five, this inevitability was already known in Ancient Greece, and has been later thoroughly examined in English law in relation to

[1] AG Maduro, Case C-255/02 *Halifax* [2006] ECR I-1609, para 73.

equity. In 1718, the poet Samuel Daniel wrote: 'Ten Thousand Laws more cannot reach so far, but Malice goes beyond'.[2] These two lines establish a relationship between public action and private reaction that accounts for the inevitability of abuses of law: law can never perfectly adapt to the intricacies of reality, so that malicious citizens will always find a way to go beyond laws and design unforeseeable abusive practices. The exegesis proposed by Watt reads as follows:

> [Samuel Daniel's] intention was to indicate law's inability to anticipate every nuance of human cunning, but even if a perfect code could be created which anticipated every type of wrong (and right) it would still be a mistake to apply the law rigidly. Malice would still have the capacity to 'go beyond' by turning the very rigidity of the law into an instrument of abuse.[3]

Union legislation—just as national legislation—cannot anticipate every scenario of artificial practice left open by their provisions. In practice, the certainty of abuse means that national and Union judges interpreting Union law are necessarily confronted with artificial strategies, such as those in *Emsland-Stärke*, *Halifax* or *Cadbury Schweppes*.

If the first chronological sequence (from Union law to abuse) is characterised by the certainty of abuse, the second sequence (from abuse to Union law) is shaped by the illusion of legal certainty. This formula is intended to convey the tendency of contemporary legal thought to pursue a unilateral quest for legal certainty, thereby ignoring the virtue of legal congruence. Indeed, legal certainty is often depicted as the supreme value of a legal order:

> [I]t is important to recognise that the principle of legal certainty is the starting point in the application of the rule of law. This principle entails that rules of law must be made known and that situations of law governed by EU law must be foreseeable.[4]

> Since the law should strive to balance certainty and reliability against flexibility, it is on the whole wise legal policy to use [rigid] rules as much as possible for regulating human behaviour because they are more certain than [flexible] principles and lend themselves more easily to uniform and predictable application.[5]

The virtue inherent to legal certainty cannot be disputed; as recalled by Holmes, the risk of encountering public force accounts for the need for predictable legal outcomes.[6] What can be disputed, however, is the supremacy all too often granted to legal certainty in the hierarchy of legal values, and chiefly over legal congruence.

[2] S Daniel, 'Epistle to Sir Thomas Egerton' in S Daniel (ed), *Poetical Works*, vol II (London, R Gosling et al, 1718) 345.

[3] G Watt, *Equity Stirring: the Story of Justice beyond Law* (Oxford, Hart Publishing, 2009) 33.

[4] D Weber, 'Abuse of Law in the Context of Indirect Taxation: Why We Need the Subjective Intention Test, When is Combating Abuse an Obligation and Other Comments' Law' in R de la Feria and S Vogenauer (eds), *Prohibition of Abuse of Law: a New General Principle of EU Law?* (Oxford, Hart Publishing, 2011) 395.

[5] J Raz, 'Legal Principles and the Limits of Law Legal Principles and the Limits of Law' (1972) 81 *Yale Law Journal* 823, 841.

[6] OW Holmes, 'The Path of the Law' (1897) 110 *Harvard Law Review* 991, 991 (see ch 5 n 1 and accompanying text).

If the exercise of the 'whole power of the State' should not be unpredictable, it should not be absurd either; in other words, public force should not enforce absurd legal outcomes. But if law must not lead to absurd legal outcomes, then legal certainty can only be a tantalising ideal, given the trade-off between legal certainty and legal congruence. It is in that sense that the quest for legal certainty—or predictability of legal outcomes—can be described as an illusion since the ideal of 'fidelity to law'[7] is equally conditioned by legal congruence—or equity of legal outcomes. Lord Mance similarly questioned the supremacy of legal certainty in the following terms:

> Are there, however, limits to the certainty to which legislators and judges can or should aspire? The infinite circumstances affecting human existence fit uneasily within straitjackets. Certainty can be pushed too far, and, if it is coupled with governmental suspicion of judicial discretion, it can lead to potential injustice. … Only one thing is therefore certain. It is that, while as much of it as possible is desirable, certainty is not the ultimate or wholly achievable aim of the law.[8]

Other scholars have related concrete system failures provoked by the illusory quest for legal certainty. In the field of private international law, Neuhaus described how private international law fiercely pursued legal certainty in the beginning of the twentieth century. To that end, it relied on fixed choice of law rules such as nationality or domicile. However, the mechanical application of these rules frequently yielded inequitable outcomes, which led to the implosion of that system:

> [In the period of transition from certainty to equity, it] is explicitly pointed out that the decisions of conflict-of-law cases by mechanized rules have not even promoted certainty and uniformity. Indeed, it is the very fact that these rules often lead to inequitable results that militates against their gaining general recognition. … In more concrete terms, the fixed connecting factors of nationality or domicile are frequently replaced by 'domicile in fact' (résidence habituelle). Especially nationality as a connecting factor is abandoned wherever it would lead to unjust decisions [9]

Weisbach identified the same system failure in the field of tax law, where the illusory quest for legal certainty is abandoned under the pressure of taxpayers exploiting the rigidity of tax rules in order to claim inequitable outcomes:

> The tax law is the paradigmatic system of rules. … Yet over the last several years, the purely rule-oriented approach to the tax law has begun to be perceived as a failure. The reason is that taxpayers have been able to manipulate the rules endlessly to produce results clearly not intended by the drafters. Manipulation of this sort is inefficient, loses revenue, and demoralizes others. To respond, lawmakers and regulators have shifted the tax system toward standards, primarily by adopting what are known as 'anti-abuse rules.'

[7] Expression borrowed from LL Fuller, 'Positivism and Fidelity to Law: A Reply to Professor Hart' (1958) 71 *Harvard Law Review* 630.

[8] J Mance, 'Should the Law be Certain?', The Oxford Shrieval lecture, 11 October 2011, available at www.supremecourt.gov.uk/docs/speech_111011.pdf, no 13 and 46.

[9] PH Neuhaus, 'Legal Certainty versus Equity in the Conflict of Laws' (1963) 28 *Law and Contemporary Problems* 795, 800.

> A typical anti-abuse rule allows the government (and only the government) to override the literal words of a statute or regulation.[10]

In sum, the unilateral pursuit of legal certainty, without due consideration to the demands of legal congruence, is an illusion. Yet the converse is also true: the unilateral pursuit of legal congruence without due consideration to the demands of legal certainty is also an illusion.[11] In other words, no definitive choice can ever be made in favour of either value, as both are necessary to foster fidelity to law: 'it is not sufficient that laws and adjudication are predictable: they must also be accepted by the legal community in question'.[12] As a consequence, every legal order—including Union law—is condemned to fluctuate between legal certainty and legal congruence. Neuhaus accurately described this eternal struggle:

> The struggle between legal certainty and equity is as old as the law itself. Only the labels have changed: while formerly discussion proceeded in terms of ius strictum and ius aequum, the expressions currently preferred, especially in Germany, are 'legal certainty' and 'justice (in individual cases).' Whatever terms are used, they refer to two different aspects of the law. One is the public interest in clear, equal, and foreseeable rules of law which enable those who are subject to them to order their behavior in such a manner as to avoid legal conflict or to make clear predictions of their chances in litigation. The other is the need for deciding current, concrete disputes adequately, by giving due weight to the special and perhaps unique circumstances of each case. The former aspect calls for legislation, the latter for judicial decision. … But the conflict between legal certainty and justice (equity) will never come to an end. In different countries and at different times, the one or the other of these twin objectives of the law will dominate; there is no permanent solution. Especially neither goal can replace the other.[13]

Furthermore, as evoked in the previous excerpt, the struggle between legal certainty and congruence has institutional implications. Legislation must be the main source of law if legal certainty is to be guaranteed; conversely, adjudication must be the main source of law if legal congruence becomes the priority. Each source of law, legislation and adjudication, is a source of official arbitrariness representing the reverse side of the virtues of legal certainty and congruence. The legislature is a prospective source of law acting with limited foresight, which entails of a risk of legislative arbitrariness when legislation is not adapted to the specific circumstances of a concrete case (absence of legal congruence). The judiciary is a retrospective source of law acting with the benefit of hindsight, which generates a risk of judicial arbitrariness when judges enjoy room for judicial discretion (absence

[10] DA Weisbach, 'Formalism in the Tax Law' (1999) 66 *The University of Chicago Law Review* 860, 860–61.

[11] See eg W Blackstone, *Commentaries on the Laws of England* (Oxford, Clarendon Press, 1769) Introduction s 2 'Of the Nature of Laws in General': '[T]he liberty of considering all cases in an equitable light, must not be indulged too far; lest thereby we destroy all law, and leave the decision of every question entirely in the breast of the judge'.

[12] E Paunio, 'Beyond Predictability—Reflections on Legal Certainty and the Discourse Theory of Law in the EU Legal Order' (2009) 10 *German Law Journal* 1469, 1469.

[13] Neuhaus, 'Legal Certainty versus Equity in the Conflict of Laws' (n 9) 795–96.

of legal certainty). Kennedy underlined that flexible norms merely 'license' judicial arbitrariness, whereas rigid rules 'require' legislative arbitrariness.[14]

Therefore, in institutional terms, the illusion of legal certainty corresponds to Montesquieu's illusion of judges being 'no more than the mouth that pronounces the words of the law, mere passive beings, incapable of moderating either its force or rigor',[15] sometimes called the 'declaratory' theory of adjudication.[16] Just as laws can never provide absolute certainty, it is not possible to confine judges to a declaratory function. The illusion of legal certainty means that the rigidity of legal norms must often be attenuated in concrete cases in order to avoid absurd legal outcomes. In turn, instilling flexibility into the scope of a legal norm, either through its wording or interpretation, entails of a shift of power from the legislature to the judiciary: the more flexible the scope of a legal norm, the more discretion it offers to judges. When the illusion of legal certainty falls, Montesquieu's illusion must fall by the same token.

The phenomenon of abuse of law can be viewed as a particular expression of the universal struggle between legal certainty and congruence. As a consequence, it is intellectually unsatisfactory to merely point at the legal uncertainty entailed by the fight against abusive practices, without contextualising this issue in the light of the broader trade-off between legal certainty and congruence, as shown in Table 10.

Table 10 – Abuse of Union Law and the Illusion of Legal Certainty

		Legal congruence	**Legal certainty**
Form of legal norms	*Formal virtue*	Equity	Predictability
	Scope	Flexible	Rigid
	Wording	Indeterminate	Determinate
	Interpretation	Teleological	Literal
Institutional balance	*Source of law*	Adjudication	Legislation
	Action	Retrospective	Prospective
	Official arbitrariness	Judicial	Legislative
	Abuses of law	Outlawed	Allowed

[14] D Kennedy, 'Form and Substance in Private Law Adjudication' (1976) 89 *Harvard Law Review* 1685, 1689.

[15] Montesquieu, T Nugent (trans), *The Spirit of the Laws* (New York, Hafner Press, 1949) book XI ch 6.

[16] Mance, 'Should the Law be Certain?' (n 8) no 8.

Fostering fidelity to law requires both legal certainty (predictable outcomes) and congruence (equitable outcomes); in that context, the prohibition of abusive practices must be viewed as a decision to sacrifice predictability in order to preserve equity in particular cases. As observed by AG Maduro,

> [Doctrines of abuse were] originally developed by the courts to prevent the formal and mechanical application of legal rules from leading to unacceptable results with respect to the objectives of the legal system.[17]

Moreover, as shown in Table 10, the decision to fight abusive practices has consequences both for the nature of legal norms and the institutional balance within the Union. On the one hand, the fight against abusive practices necessitates the enactment of flexible legal norms, owing either to a decision of the legislature to use indeterminate wording or a decision of the judiciary to have recourse to the teleological method of interpretation. On the other hand, in institutional terms, the fight against abusive practices must be entrusted to the judiciary. As a consequence, the decision to fight against abusive practices entails a shift of power from the legislature to the judiciary:

> [T]he doctrine [of abuse] enhances the institutional competence of the judiciary at the expense of the legislature. It creates a problem for the separation of powers. It allows the judges to decide a case contrary to the wording of the law, which obviously amounts to a rather extreme version of judicial discretion. A routine use of abuse of rights would tilt the balance between the legislature and the judiciary in the favour of the latter, something which would clearly be a matter for concern in the EU where the courts already occupy an unusually strong institutional position.[18]

However, despite this institutional shift of power, the role attributed to the judiciary in the fight against abuses of law can also be viewed as protective of the democratic nature of the legislative process, as it seeks to prevent legal outcomes that were never intended by the legislature:

> [T]he prevention of abuses can also be defended by reference to the democratic character of the legislative process. It can be conceived as limiting opportunistic behaviour that, through interpretative manipulation of the existent rules, would derive from the legislation effects which were neither intended nor deliberated in the democratic process.[19]

[17] AG Maduro, Case C-255/02 *Halifax* [2006] ECR I-1609, fn 68; see also AG Tizzano, Case C-200/02 *Zhu and Chen* [2004] ECR I-9925, para 115; AG Alber, Case C-110/99 *Emsland-Stärke* [2000] ECR I-11569, para 71.

[18] J Snell, 'The Notion of and a General Test for Abuse of Rights: Some Normative Reflections' in de la Feria and Vogenauer, *Prohibition of Abuse of Law: a New General Principle of EU Law?* (n 4) 224; see also P Schammo, 'Arbitrage and Abuse of Rights in the EC Legal System' (2008) 14 *European Law Journal* 351, 372–74.

[19] MP Maduro, 'Foreword' in de la Feria and Vogenauer (n 4) vii; see also MP Maduro, 'Interpreting European Law: Judicial Adjudication in a Context of Constitutional Pluralism' (2007) 1 *European Journal of Legal Studies* 1, 10.

It is with such considerations in mind that judges, and chiefly the Court, decide whether to condemn artificial strategies and conduct the teleological assessment of the doctrine of abuse. When applying the doctrine of abuse, the Court must strike a delicate balance between the desire to preserve legal certainty and the desire to avoid inequitable outcomes. This is precisely what AG Maduro suggested in his Opinion in *Halifax*:

> In this regard, the objective analysis of the prohibition of abuse has to be balanced against the principles of legal certainty and protection of legitimate expectations.[20]

Similarly, this balancing process operated through the doctrine of abuse is well identified in the literature:

> The formulation of the requirements of the prohibition [of abuses] must strike a balance between the legal values of legal certainty and substantive justice.[21]

> [In Halifax, the Court] saw the doctrine of abuse as a balance between, on the one hand, preventing the claiming of unjustified tax benefits and, on the other hand, the need to ensure certainty and foreseeability in the application of Community legislation.[22]

If only for this reason, the concept of abuse of Union law is bound to remain controversial.[23] As it constitutes a particular expression of the struggle pervading every legal order between legal certainty and congruence, the debate over abusive practices can never come to an end. A preference for legal certainty tends to entail the rejection of the concept of abuse, the ratification of artificial practices, reliance on rigid rules and the choice of legislation as source of law:

> [T]he contra legem decision that a finding of an abuse of right entails should never be made as a matter of routine. Such a decision involves the violation of the fundamental principles and values underpinning the legal order and the rule of law, including the separation of powers, legal certainty and so on.[24]

20 AG Maduro, Case C-255/02 *Halifax* [2006] ECR I-1609, para 84.

21 S Vogenauer, 'The Prohibition of Abuse of Law: an Emerging General Principle of EU Law' in de la Feria and Vogenauer (n 4) 546.

22 T Tridimas, 'Abuse of Rights in EU Law: Some Reflections with Particular Reference to Financial Law' in de la Feria and Vogenauer (n 4) 174.

23 In the same sense, Maduro, 'Foreword' (n 19) vii; J Freedman, 'The Anatomy of Tax Avoidance Counteraction: Abuse of Law in a Tax Context at Member State and European Union Level' in de la Feria and Vogenauer (n 4) 380.

24 Snell, 'The Notion of and a General Test for Abuse of Rights' (n 18) 230.

A preference for legal congruence tends to imply the endorsement of the concept of abuse, the prohibition of artificial practices, reliance on flexible norms and the choice of adjudication as source of law:

> The power to apply some such principle as that embodied in the prohibition of abuse of rights must exist in the background in any system of administration of justice in which courts are not purely mechanical agencies. … [T]he determination of the point at which the exercise of a legal right has degenerated into abuse of a right is a question which cannot be decided by an abstract legislative rule, but only by the activity of courts drawing the line in each particular case.[25]

Yet other factors account for the controversies surrounding the concept of abuse of Union law, and those factors are explored in part two of this study.

[25] H Lauterpacht, *The Development of International Law by the International Court* (London, Stevens & Sons, 1958) 165.

Part II

Abuses of Union Law and Economic Integration

Introduction: The Ambivalent Notion of Free 'Movement'

PART ONE OF this study ended with a first explanation for the inconsistent treatment of artificial choices of law made by private individuals. Indeed, choices of law realised through artificial practices are alternatively proscribed as abusive (*Cadbury Schweppes*) or ratified as non-abusive (*Centros*) under Union law. How can the use of letterbox companies be ratified in *Centros*, and then condemned in *Cadbury Schweppes*? A first explanation is that the phenomenon of abuse of Union law is located on a fault-line between legal certainty and legal congruence, which pervades every legal order. An inclination for legal congruence (or equity of legal outcomes) tends to imply the prohibition of artificial practices as abusive, whereas a preference for legal certainty (or predictability of legal outcomes) tends to entail their ratification.

Part two of this study is devoted to two other fault-lines on which is located the phenomenon of abuse of Union law, which offer alternative explanations for the inconsistent treatment of artificial choices of law made by private individuals. The second fault-line is specific to Union law and divides two conceptions of the regulation of the internal market. If economic integration is conceived as the promotion of cross-border competition among private businesses, choices of law must be proscribed as abusive, for they distort business competition. But if economic integration is intended to promote competition among Member States, choices of law by Union citizens represent a desirable process of arbitrage among national laws. The third fault-line corresponds to the tension between the two poles of the economic constitution of the European Union: the fear of private power and the fear of public power. Those who fear private power (more than public power) tend to endorse the concept of abuse of law, whereas those who fear public power prohibition of abuses (more than private power) tend to reject it.

Overall, the enquiry undertaken in this part questions the type of mobility that the European Union ought to promote. Indeed, in a cross-border context, the issue of artificial choices of law inevitably conflates with the broader issue of free movement: cross-border abuses amount to artificial cross-border movements designed to elect a hospitable jurisdiction, as in *Centros* and *Cadbury Schweppes*. Therefore, the decision to proscribe or not cross-border abuses of law is necessarily influenced by the ideal of mobility that ought to be promoted under free movement law, as illustrated by Table 11.

Table 11 – Regulatory Mobility versus Socioeconomic Mobility

Regulatory Mobility	Socioeconomic Mobility
Across national jurisdictions	Across national markets
Choice of law	Real goods and services
Artificial practices ratified	Artificial practices prohibited
Centros	*Cadbury Schweppes*

On the one hand, artificial practices are elaborated with the exclusive intention to obtain a regulatory gain, at the exclusion of any significant socioeconomic gain.[1] Accordingly, endorsing such artificial practices amounts to promoting *regulatory mobility*, namely the possibility to move from one national jurisdiction to another for mere regulatory considerations. Regulatory mobility is the type of mobility promoted by the *Centros* judgment:

> [T]he fact that a national of a Member State who wishes to set up a company chooses to form it in the Member State whose rules of company law seem to him the least restrictive and to set up branches in other Member States cannot, in itself, constitute an abuse of the right of establishment.
>
> [T]he fact that a company does not conduct any business in the Member State in which it has its registered office and pursues its activities only in the Member State where its branch is established is not sufficient to prove the existence of abuse or fraudulent conduct which would entitle the latter Member State to deny that company the benefit of the provisions of Community law relating to the right of establishment.[2]
>
> [In Centros] the person concerned opted for a Member State having a system of company law favourable to him. That is much more frequently the case as a result of differences in the tax legislation of the Member States. Community law can have no complaint with such mobility; rather it is precisely the objective of Community law to promote mobility.[3]

On the other hand, non-artificial practices are underpinned by a socioeconomic rationale, namely the provision or the acquisition of actual goods and services. Accordingly, prohibiting artificial practices amounts to promoting *socioeconomic mobility*, namely the possibility to move from one national market to another for socioeconomic considerations. Under this conception of mobility, Union citizens should be allowed to move to another Member State in order to integrate in the host society, in accordance with the objective of socioeconomic interpenetration

[1] See ch 3 section II.

[2] Case C-212/97 *Centros* [1999] ECR I-1459, paras 27 and 29; see also Case C-167/01 *Inspire Art* [2003] ECR I-10155, para 120.

[3] AG Geelhoed, Case C-109/01 *Akrich* [2003] ECR I-9607, para 179; see also AG Darmon, Case 79/85 *Segers* [1986] ECR 2375, para 6; AG La Pergola, Case C-212/97 *Centros* [1999] ECR I-1459.

underlying the freedoms of movement. Socioeconomic mobility is the type of mobility promoted in *Cadbury Schweppes* and by AG Maduro in *Cavallera*:

> Having regard to that objective of integration in the host Member State, the concept of establishment within the meaning of the Treaty provisions on freedom of establishment involves the actual pursuit of an economic activity through a fixed establishment in that State for an indefinite period. Consequently, it presupposes actual establishment of the company concerned in the host Member State and the pursuit of genuine economic activity there.[4]

> [T]here are reasonable grounds for doubting whether there has been an effective exercise of free movement inasmuch as no activity has taken place in the host Member State. In short, the economic and social interpenetration underlying the freedom of movement of workers is absent.[5]

The central contention of this part two is that the two solutions brought to the issue of abuse of law, namely regulatory and socioeconomic mobility, correspond to two visions of economic integration that pervade the entire law of the internal market, and which can be designated as the regulatory neutrality and regulatory competition paradigms. In general terms, this part two can be conceived as an enquiry into the contradictions of internal market law—in particular the inconsistent treatment of artificial cross-border movements—and the underlying dialectic generating them.

Union law scholarship has long established that the Court has never been able or willing to settle on a unique *free movement test*, relying instead on highly open-textured concepts such as 'obstacle to free movement', 'barrier to trade', 'restriction to market access', 'discrimination on grounds of nationality' or 'non-discriminatory restriction'.[6] In that regard, the wording of the Treaty provisions on free movement is of limited assistance to execute the complex and multiform mission faced by the Court.[7] At first, this inconstancy has led many scholars to advocate a specific version of the free movement test, based for instance on a strict approach to discrimination (Marenco, 1984),[8] or on a distinction between

[4] Case C-196/04 *Cadbury Schweppes* [2006] ECR I-7995, para 54.

[5] AG Maduro, Case C-311/06 *Cavallera* [2009] ECR I-415, para 52; see also AG Léger, Case C-196/04 *Cadbury Schweppes* [2006] ECR I-7995, para 42.

[6] The indeterminacy of the 'free movement test' has been highlighted on numerous occasions: see inter alia A Saydé, 'One Law, Two Competitions: An Enquiry into the Contradictions of Free Movement Law' (2010–11) 13 *Cambridge Yearbook of European Legal Studies* 365; MP Maduro, *We the Court: the European Court of Justice and the European Economic Constitution* (Oxford, Hart Publishing, 1998) ch 3; C Barnard and S Deakin, 'Market Access and Regulatory Competition' in C Barnard and J Scott (eds), *The Law of the Single Market: Unpacking the Premises* (Oxford, Hart Publishing, 2002); J Snell, 'The Notion of Market Access: A Concept or a Slogan?' (2010) 47 *Common Market Law Review* 437; S Deakin, 'Regulatory Competition after Laval' (2007–08) 10 *Cambridge Yearbook of European Legal Studies* 581, 584 ff.

[7] S Weatherill, 'Fitting "Abuse of Rights" into EU Law Governing the Free Movement of Goods and Services' in R de la Feria and S Vogenauer (eds), *Prohibition of Abuse of Law: a New General Principle of EU Law?* (Oxford, Hart Publishing, 2011) 54.

[8] G Marenco, 'Pour une interprétation traditionnelle de la notion de mesure d'effet équivalent à une restriction quantitative' (1984) 20 *Cahiers de droit Européen* 291.

product requirements and market circumstances (White, 1989; prefiguring the *Keck* jurisprudence of 1993).[9] In the 1990s, however, a few scholars engaged in holistic analyses of the Court's case law, with the purpose of embracing all versions of the free movement test elaborated by the Court. Weiler (1999), for instance, adopted an evolutionary approach by identifying five 'generations' in the Court's case law.[10] In a ground-breaking study, Maduro (1998) argued that the various free movement tests applied by the Court in the context of the free movement of goods corresponded to three 'constitutional models' of economic integration: centralised, competitive and decentralised.[11] Nowadays, Union law scholars frequently rely on similar analyses, associating specific versions of the free movement test with different institutional arrangements and visions of the European Union.[12]

Building on this rich stream of scholarship, this part two argues that the contradictions of internal market law are caused by the unconscious and yet permanent reference to two overarching visions of economic integration. The first conception seeks to ensure that the *competition among private businesses* is not distorted by national regulations, which corresponds to the paradigm of regulatory neutrality. The second vision of economic integration seeks to ensure the proper functioning of the *competition among Member States*, and is embodied by the paradigm of regulatory competition. The paradigms of regulatory neutrality and regulatory competition represent two poles of attraction on the compass of economic integration, between which the pointer of internal market law fluctuates constantly, thereby generating contradictions within the free movement jurisprudence (chapter six).

Unfortunately, both makers (Union institutions) and commentators (scholars) of Union law are often unaware of the coexistence of two competing paradigms of economic integration within internal market law. As a consequence, their adoption of one paradigm, upon making or commenting upon internal market law, remains often unconscious or fragmentary at best.[13] This obliviousness is

[9] EL White, 'In Search of the Limits to Article 30 of the EEC Treaty' (1989) 26 *Common Market Law Review* 235.

[10] JHH Weiler, 'Mutual Recognition, Functional Equivalence and Harmonization in the Evolution of the European Common Market and the WTO' in FK Padoa-Schioppa (ed), *The Principle of Mutual Recognition in the European Integration Process* (Basingstoke, Palgrave Macmillan, 2005).

[11] Maduro, *We the Court* (n 6) ch 5.

[12] See eg, KA Armstrong, 'Mutual Recognition' in Barnard and Scott, *The Law of the Single Market* (n 6) 228–30; Barnard and Deakin, 'Market Access and Regulatory Competition' (n 6) 204 ff; Deakin, 'Regulatory Competition after Laval' (n 6) 584 ff.

[13] By way of illustration, the awareness of regulatory competition as a paradigm of economic integration shaping free movement law is roughly limited to its association with the 'home country principle'. Maduro, for instance, conflates home country regulation and regulatory competition into a 'competitive model', before conceding that the 'decentralized model' of host regulation 'is still, to a great extent, a model based on competition': Maduro (n 6) 126 ff and 143. See also Armstrong, 'Mutual Recognition' (n 12) 243; J Pelkmans, 'Mutual Recognition in Goods and Services: an Economic Perspective' in Padoa-Schioppa, *The Principle of Mutual Recognition in the European Integration Process* (n 10) 114; W Kerber and R Van den Bergh, 'Mutual Recognition Revisited: Misunderstandings, Inconsistencies, and a Suggested Reinterpretation' (2008) 61 *Kyklos* 447, 452; JP Trachtman, 'Embedding Mutual Recognition at the WTO' (2007) 14 *Journal of European Public Policy* 780, 785.

problematic because regulatory neutrality and regulatory competition imply different prescriptions for the regulation of the internal market; more accurately, the trade-off between those two paradigms of economic integration materialises in three central 'nodes' of internal market law: positive harmonisation (Union regulation or not), negative harmonisation (home or host regulation) and regulatory mobility (restricted or free choice of law). In other words, while mostly ignored, the conflicting influences of the regulatory neutrality and regulatory competition paradigms account to a considerable extent for the inconsistency of free movement jurisprudence (chapter seven).

This causal link between the coexistence of two paradigms of economic integration, on the one hand, and the contradictions of internal market law, on the other, is best highlighted by re-examining a few practical issues of free movement law, such as the ambivalent status of differentials of regulation, the acceptance of reverse discriminations, the inconsistent prohibition of abuses of law (eg *Centros* versus *Cadbury Schweppes*) or the ambiguity towards social dumping (eg *Laval* versus *Rush Portuguesa*). Indeed, the solutions advocated to those practical issues entirely depend on the adoption, most often unconscious, of either regulatory neutrality or regulatory competition as paradigm of economic integration (chapter eight).

Furthermore, the dialectic between the paradigms of regulatory neutrality and regulatory competition suggests an alternative reading of the State aid regime, another crucial component of internal market law. Indeed, the very principle of a prohibition of State aids can only be accounted for by the regulatory neutrality paradigm; on the other hand, restrictions to the scope of that prohibition (through the criteria of selectivity and transfer of State resources) are best understood in light of regulatory competition. Incidentally, this alternative reading provides a common framework of analysis for the freedoms of movement and the State aid regime (chapter nine).

Lastly, from a broader perspective, the emergence of the concept of abuse of Union law can be interpreted as an evolution of the economic constitution of the European Union, by which public power seeks to reaffirm its capacity to control private power within the internal market. The combination of low moving costs, high regulatory diversity and high territorial unity has led to the emergence of a new form of private power originating in mobility, enabling private individuals to escape the deployment of public power. The practical effect of the prohibition of abusive practices is to restrict this new private power originating in mobility, to the benefit of public power. In that context, the ambivalence towards abusive practices can be usefully reconstructed in light of the tension between fear of private power and fear of public power: those who are more fearful of private power tend to advocate the prohibition of abusive practices, whereas those who are more fearful of public power tend to reject it (chapter ten).

Having regard to the object of this part two, the remainder of this study will focus on cross-border abuses of law. Internal abuses of law do not question the type of mobility that the European Union ought to promote across Member States, but merely consist in the artificial election of a Union legal regime (export refund in *Emsland-Stärke*, VAT deduction in *Halifax*).[14] Inconsistency in the treatment of internal abuses of law can be explained by the struggle between legal certainty and legal congruence, common to every legal order, which was explored in part one of this study. By contrast, the creation of an internal market among several Member States gives rise to a new type of abuse of law, cross-border in nature and characteristic of multilevel polities such as the European Union. In that regard, the decision of a supranational polity to grant or remove the freedom to elect the applicable national law throughout an economically integrated territory entails important legal, political and socioeconomic consequences, which go far beyond the decision of a polity to proscribe internal abuses of law on its territory.

[14] An internal abuse of law consists in the artificial election of a Union legal regime, whereas a cross-border abuse of law consists in the artificial election of a national legal regime: see ch 2 nn 21–22 and accompanying text.

6

The Competing Paradigms of Economic Integration

THE CENTRAL CONTENTION of this part two is that inconsistency of internal market law—including in the treatment of abusive practices—is caused by the mostly unconscious and yet permanent reference to two overarching conceptions of economic integration. The object of the present chapter is to present these two conceptions of economic integration, designated as the paradigms of regulatory neutrality and regulatory competition.

A process of integration among States may of course be fuelled by other considerations than the economic benefits ensuing from the removal of internal borders, such as political stability or cultural enrichment. Nevertheless, in the context of the European Union, economic considerations have arguably represented the driving force behind the creation of the internal market and the introduction of fundamental freedoms of movement.

Against this economic context, this chapter submits that there are only two paradigms of *economic* integration, namely consistent and complete visions of what a process of economic integration should be. This submission does not exclude the existence of alternative paradigms of integration focusing for instance on political, cultural or institutional aspects of integration.[1] What it does exclude though, is the existence of alternative paradigms of economic integration, next to regulatory neutrality and regulatory competition. These two paradigms of economic integration are moreover of particular relevance given the economic nature of the European process of integration.

In more detail, the basic purpose of a process of economic integration among States is to open national borders, in order to facilitate cross-border economic transactions. However, political economy theory is ambivalent regarding the function to be assumed by local laws in such a process. The question in this regard is whether local laws should be 'magnetised' or 'neutralised', ie whether they should or not divert trade flows within the integrated area (Section I).

[1] For instance, Maduro defines three models of integration based on institutional considerations (centralised, competitive and decentralised): MP Maduro, *We the Court: the European Court of Justice and the European Economic Constitution* (Oxford, Hart Publishing, 1998) ch 5.

From this theoretical ambivalence on the function of local laws stem two visions of economic integration, which can indeed be identified in Union legal acts and in the literature on the internal market.[2] On the one hand, the paradigm of regulatory neutrality seeks to avoid the *competition among private businesses* being distorted by local laws (Section II). On the other hand, regulatory competition seeks to ensure the proper functioning of the process of *competition among Member States*, in which local laws become an important factor of competition (Section III). In sum, regulatory neutrality and regulatory competition represent two poles of attraction on the compass of economic integration, between which the pointer of internal market law constantly fluctuates.

However, these two processes of competition can be simultaneously promoted only up to a certain point, so that a project of economic integration is rapidly facing hard choices between promoting the business competition or State competition.[3] One obvious manifestation of this tension is the ambivalent treatment of differentials of regulation under Union law, alternatively condemned as illegitimate 'distortions of competition' (regulatory neutrality) or hailed as legitimate 'competitive advantages' (regulatory competition).[4] This contradiction—as well as all others explored in subsequent chapters—is best accounted for by the contradictory influence of the paradigms of regulatory neutrality and regulatory competition, which shapes daily law-making within the Union.

Despite their considerable influence upon Union law, it cannot be expected to find these two visions of economic integration clearly articulated in legal acts adopted by Union institutions. Rather, the paradigms of regulatory neutrality and regulatory competition are best conceptualised as two overarching systems of reference inspiring law-making within the Union. In Chen and Hanson's terminology, those two paradigms represent 'meta-scripts' of economic integration, namely general schemas informing our approach to all aspects of internal market law.[5] The adoption of regulatory neutrality or regulatory competition as 'meta-script' of economic integration determines an ideal regulatory mode of the internal market (classically identified as host country principle, home country principle, and harmonisation[6]), which in turn shapes the free movement test applied in concrete cases. As will be shown below, it is not uncommon to find

[2] According to Craig and de Búrca, a single market can be achieved either through positive or negative integration: PP Craig and G de Búrca, *EU Law: Text, Cases, and Materials*, 4th edn (Oxford, Oxford University Press, 2008) 605–06; Barnard distinguishes between centralised and decentralised models of economic integration: C Barnard, *The Substantive Law of the EU: the Four Freedoms*, 2nd edn (Oxford, Oxford University Press, 2007) 17–22; see also Maduro, *We the Court* (n 1) ch 5.

[3] See ch 7 section VI.

[4] See ch 8 section I.

[5] Meta-scripts are general schemas informing our approach to all aspects of a body of law: see R Chen and J Hanson, 'The Illusion of Law: The Legitimating Schemas of Modern Policy and Corporate Law' (2004) 103 *Michigan Law Review* 1; R Chen and J Hanson, 'Categorically Biased: The Influence of Knowledge Structures on Law and Legal Theory' (2004) 77 *US California Law Review* 1103.

[6] See inter alia Maduro (n 1) ch 5; KA Armstrong, 'Mutual Recognition' in C Barnard and J Scott (eds), *The Law of the Single Market: Unpacking the Premises* (Oxford, Hart Publishing, 2002) 228–30.

manifestations of both regulatory neutrality and regulatory competition in the same legal regime.[7]

I. The Function of Local Laws in a Process of Economic Integration

The present section provides a brief theoretical overview of the notion of economic integration. If the objective of economic integration is undisputed (facilitating cross-border activity), the methods are not exempt of ambiguity, in particular with regard to the function of local laws.

Historically, the theory of international trade has been constructed along two milestones: the principles of absolute and comparative advantages.[8] In 1776, Adam Smith enounced the principle of absolute advantage,[9] according to which a polity should not produce goods and services when producing them domestically is more costly than importing them from another polity.[10] Formalised by David Ricardo in 1817, the principle of comparative advantage is less intuitive but farther-reaching than the principle of absolute advantage.[11] In essence, it posits that even where a State holds an absolute advantage in respect of a given set of commodities (because it can produce them at a lower cost), it will have an economic interest in trading with another State as long as there are different ratios of productivity among them.[12] By letting in imports from each other, trading States will jointly produce more with the same resources: this efficiency gain generated by free trade is the central economic justification for removing obstacles to

[7] See ch 7 section V.B, esp the 'restricted choice of Home law' and the 'free choice of Host law'.

[8] J Viner, *Studies in the Theory of International Trade* (New York, Harper & Brothers, 1937) ch VIII no 1–18.

[9] A Smith, E Cannan (trans), *An Inquiry into the Nature and Causes of the Wealth of Nations*, 5th edn (London, Methuen & Co, 1904) book IV ch 2 no 11.

[10] Let us assume that Robinson and Friday are stuck on a desert island. In one working day, Robinson and Friday can respectively pluck 10 and 8 coconuts; they are also capable of catching respectively 4 and 12 fish per day. Assuming that they devote their working hours equally to each activity, Robinson and Friday jointly get 9 coconuts (10/2 + 8/2) and 8 fish (4/2 + 12/2) per day. In such a situation, Friday and Robinson have an obvious interest in cooperating and specialising (Robinson in coconuts, Friday in fish), in order to get 10 coconuts and 12 fish, thereby generating a joint surplus of 1 coconut and 4 fish per day.

[11] D Ricardo, *On the Principles of Political Economy and Taxation*, 3rd edn (London, John Murray, 1821) book 7 no 16.

[12] Let us now assume that Friday is better *both* at getting coconuts (productivity of 15 versus 10 for Robinson) and fish (12 versus 4), that is a situation of absolute advantage in respect of both fish and coconuts. If they remained in autarky, Friday could spend-two thirds of his time fishing and thus get 8 fish and 5 coconuts; on the other hand, by dividing his working time equally, Robinson would get 2 fish and 5 coconuts. By contrast, if they decided to cooperate and specialise (Friday in fish, Robinson in coconuts), they would get 12 fish and 10 coconuts, that is a joint surplus of 2 fish per day compared to autarky.

international trade.[13] From a microeconomic perspective, free trade maximises welfare by optimising the size of the consumer and producer surplus.[14]

Ricardo's intuition on the benefits flowing from free trade is strongly disputed, on economic, social and environmental grounds.[15] Moreover, a process of economic integration is traditionally supported by non-economic considerations as well, more or less related to the gains flowing from freer trade.[16] Nevertheless, the principle of comparative advantage remains the central economic justification for the process of economic integration triggered by the Treaty of Rome establishing the European Economic Community (1957): 'the Internal Market … is premised on the idea of free movement to the Member State with the greatest comparative advantage'.[17] As early as in 1954, Tinbergen noted how negative integration (understood as removal of trade impediments) would increase welfare in the integrated area by virtue of the principle of comparative advantage.[18] Similarly, nearly every Commission policy document on the internal market underlines the economic gains[19] generated by the removal of obstacles to trade:

> [T]ax barriers discourage cross-border economic activity and induce firms to prefer domestic over cross-border operations, thereby directly hindering the achievement

[13] P Kenen, *The International Economy*, 4th edn (Cambridge, Cambridge University Press, 2000) 19: 'Trade serves … to minimize the real resource costs of worldwide production, which is the same as saying that trade serves to maximize the real value of production by allocating worldwide resources most efficiently'.

[14] Consumer (producer) surplus is an aggregate measure of welfare, which measures the difference between the price people are willing to pay (receive) and the price they actually pay (receive). See MN Jovanovic, *The Economics of International Integration* (Cheltenham, Edward Elgar, 2006) 40–42; L Neal, *The Economics of Europe and the European Union* (Cambridge, Cambridge University Press, 2007) 44–46; TH Oatley, *International Political Economy: Interests and Institutions in the Global Economy*, 3rd edn (New York, Pearson, 2008) 48–52.

[15] In a nutshell, the very hypothesis of a surplus created through trade is contested (economic criticism); even assuming the existence of such a surplus, free trade aggravates inequalities both among and within countries (social criticism) and ruins the environment (environmental criticism). See eg R Went, 'Game, Set, and Match for Mr. Ricardo? The Surprising Comeback of Protectionism in the Era of Globalizing Free Trade' (2000) 34 *Journal of Economic Issues* 655; D Rodrik, *Has Globalization Gone Too Far?* (Washington DC, Institute for International Economics, 1997).

[16] This mix of economic and non-economic motives can be identified in the Preamble to the TFEU (see esp Recitals 1, 2, 6 and 8). See BA Balassa, *The Theory of Economic Integration* (London, Allen & Unwin, 1973) 6.

[17] D Doukas, 'Free Movement of Broadcasting Services and Abuse of Law' in R de la Feria and S Vogenauer (eds), *Prohibition of Abuse of Law: a New General Principle of EU Law?* (Oxford, Hart Publishing, 2011) 89; see also the excellent Barnard, *The Substantive Law of the EU* (n 2) 1–24.

[18] J Tinbergen, *International Economic Integration*, 2nd edn (Amsterdam, Elsevier, 1965) no 8.2. See also J Pelkmans, 'Economic Concept and Meaning of the Internal Market' in J Pelkmans et al (eds), *The EU Internal Market in Comparative Perspective* (New York, Peter Lang, 2008) 61–63; Neal, *The Economics of Europe and the European Union* (n 14); F McDonald and S Dearden, *European Economic Integration*, 4th edn (Harlow, Prentice Hall, 2005); BA Balassa (ed), *European Economic Integration* (Amsterdam, North-Holland, 1975).

[19] Eg the Monti Report (2010) estimated that the implementation of the Services Directive represented a growth potential of between 0.6 and 1.5% GDP, noting more generally that 'relaunching the single market serves to re-activate Europe's engine of growth and employment': Monti Commission (EC), 'A new strategy for the single market: at the service of Europe's economy and society' (Monti Report), 9 May 2010, 38 and 53.

> of the Internal market (Article 26 TFEU) and the full exploitation of the benefits of market integration. This implies a lack of a 'level playing field', barriers to a more efficient allocation of resources and foregone opportunities for growth and welfare gains across the EU.[20]

From the perspective of market participants, the objective of economic integration is to facilitate cross-border activity within the integrated area: '[Market integration is] a behavioural notion indicating that activities of market participants in different regions or Member States are geared to supply-and-demand conditions in the entire Union'.[21] Economic integration expands the geographical scope of economic rationality: if beforehand market participants tend to be confined to their national territory, they can thereafter freely extend their activities to the entire integrated area:

> With regard to the definition of the 'Internal Market' in the EC Treaty ('an area without internal frontiers') and the objective, set out in the 'Internal Market Strategy for Services', of making the provision of services between Member States as easy as within a Member State.[22]

The ultimate goal of economic integration is to bring about an internal market extending across the territories of the participant States, which shares the same features as local markets. In this internal market, nationals of every Member State become 'other-regarding' in the sense that they elect the most favourable offers throughout the integrated area, irrespective of their origin. Therefore, economic integration alters trade patterns in the Member States, as domestic transactions are replaced by cross-border dealings whenever the latter are more efficient:

> Economic integration in the framework of the [Union] would basically imply reallocation of the means of production. From the economic order on the basis of national schemes the separate economic processes were to merge into one. New potential for specialisation on a larger scale and on a European-wide basis was envisaged to direct production to those locations with comparative advantages in the respective sectors.[23]
>
> The essential feature of a customs union is to change the pattern of trade of the member countries. The EEC has succeeded in doing this to an extent far beyond the wildest expectations of its founding fathers. From having two-thirds of their imports coming from outside the customs union when it was set up in 1958, by 1990 the original six members had over two-thirds of their imports coming from within the customs union, which by then had doubled its membership to twelve countries. And this level of intra-EU trade compared to extra-EU trade has been maintained to the present.[24]

[20] Commission (EC), 'Impact Assessment: Proposal for a Council Directive on a Common Consolidated Corporate Tax Base' (Staff Working Document) SEC (2011) 315 final, 16 March 2011, 14.

[21] Pelkmans, *The EU Internal Market in Comparative Perspective* (n 18) 30.

[22] Commission (EC), 'The state of the internal market for services' (Report) COM (2002) 441 final, 30 July 2002, 14.

[23] R Wesseling, *The Modernisation of EC Antitrust Law* (Oxford, Hart Publishing, 2000) 12.

[24] Neal (n 14) 56.

There is a however a crucial difference between local and integrated markets. Rival businesses in a local market are subject to the same local environment shaped by the public action of local authorities. By contrast, rival businesses in an integrated market are subject to different local environments, shaped by different local authorities, so that these local environments indirectly become a factor of competition:

> Competition is inherent to the very concept of internal market. … Indeed, the removal of obstacles to trade brought about by the establishment of the internal market inevitably leads companies in each Member State to face competition from rivals in other Member States.[25]

As such, the opening of national borders prompted by economic integration tends to throw local laws into competition, as businesses located in a comparatively hospitable jurisdiction enjoy competitive advantage over rival businesses. This effect of local laws on business competition is the object of contradictory normative appraisals, which express two conceptions of the function of local laws in a process of economic integration. Some argue that local laws should be 'neutralised', since diversity among local laws should not alter the course of behaviour of market participants in the integrated area. Others argue that local laws should on the contrary be 'magnetised': they should act as magnets attracting or repulsing market participants. The factual setting of *Agip Petroli*, one of the seminal cases of abuse examined in part one,[26] usefully offers a visual illustration of the potential effect of local laws on economic decisions (see Figure 10)—which shows all the importance of this theoretical discussion for the issue of abuse of law.

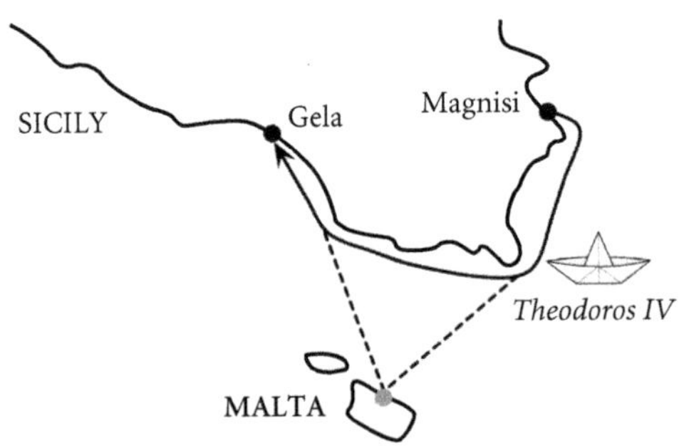

Figure 10 – *Agip Petroli* and the Function of Local Laws in a Process of Economic Integration

[25] M Waelbroeck, 'La place de la concurrence dans le Traité de Lisbonne' in G Vandersanden et al (eds), *Mélanges en hommage à Georges Vandersanden: Promenades au sein du droit européen* (Brussels, Bruylant, 2008) 830, free translation.

[26] See ch 2 section V.A.

Agip Petroli, an Italian company, chartered the Greek-registered tanker *Theodoros IV* to ship a cargo of crude oil from Magnisi to Gela, both located in Sicily. As a rule, island cabotage is subject to the law of the host State, namely Italian law in the main proceedings. However, as explained above, Agip Petroli had organised a voyage in ballast to a foreign State[27] for the host sole purpose of electing the law of the flag State, namely Greek law, for all matters relating to manning.

If local laws are to be 'neutralised', the tanker *Theodoros IV* should not alter its course around Sicily by organising a voyage in ballast to Malta, as its only rationale resides in the election of a hospitable local law. The Malta detour, in this view, amounts to undesirable distortion of trade provoked by local laws. Conversely, if local laws are viewed as legitimate 'magnets', Malta represents a magnetic mermaid to which the *Theodoros IV* should succumb, and the Malta detour a legitimate deflection of trade.

Those two postures towards the function of local laws in a process of economic integration can be easily linked to the inconsistency in the treatment of artificial practices and the ambivalence in the notion of free 'movement'.[28] The desire for neutral local laws calls for the prohibition of artificial practices—namely economic behaviour distorted by local laws—and the promotion of socioeconomic mobility. Conversely, assigning local laws the function of magnets implies the ratification of artificial practices and the promotion of regulatory mobility.

Just as political economy theory is ambivalent regarding the function to be assumed by local laws in a process of economic integration, Union law is ambivalent as to whether national laws should divert trade flows within the internal market, which generates contradictions within the free movement jurisprudence. For instance, partisans of neutralised national laws in the European Union have authored the following quotes:

> [B]arriers created by different national product regulations and standards have a double-edged effect: they not only add extra costs, but they also distort production patterns.[29]

> [D]ivergences in the systems of penalties are likely to lead to distortions in the conditions of competition and to diversions of the natural trade flows of legal goods which would take place if the penalties for intellectual property rights were harmonised throughout the Internal Market.[30]

> Tax induced distortions of competition and diversions of trade are not in accord with the principles of the internal market.[31]

[27] Although the identity of the foreign State is not mentioned in the Court's documents, one may reasonably assume that the *Theodorakis IV* temporarily moored in Malta.

[28] See pt 2 Introduction.

[29] Commission (EC), 'Completing the internal market' (White Paper) COM (85) 310 final, 14 June 1985, no 60.

[30] Commission (EC), 'Proposal for a Directive of the European Parliament and of the Council on measures and procedures to ensure the enforcement of intellectual property rights' COM (2003) 46 final, 30 January 2003.

[31] European Economic and Social Committee (EC), 'The Report from the Commission to the Council, the European Parliament and the European Economic and Social Committee on the rates

> Results of the present lack of harmonisation in the excise field include distortion of competition and diversion of trade and revenue beyond frontiers where taxes are lower.[32]

> [T]he present situation, in the absence of Community legislation, continues to be marked by the application of very different systems which cause distortion of competition and deflection of trade both internally and between Member States.[33]

The opposite posture, in favour of magnetised national laws deflecting trade patterns in the internal market, can be identified in the following quotes:

> Goods should be manufactured wherever the conditions are most favourable. These conditions need not only relate to the economic environment, they should also include the legal environment. If the legal situation in one Member State is particularly favourable for the manufacture of a particular product, then production should be centered there, in the same way as producers should be free to seek out the most favourable economic climate.[34]

> As a general rule, it is clearly legitimate and even desirable that citizens and companies should exploit the differences between regulatory regimes for their own (and, ultimately, for the overall) benefit. As a matter of principle, such choices ought to be protected, rather than being labelled 'abusive' and prohibited'.[35]

> [The issue in Cadbury was] whether the establishment of a subsidiary in another Member State solely because of a more favourable tax regime available there amounts to the abuse of the Treaty freedoms. That is, with all respect, an extraordinary question. It would not occur to anyone to raise the same question in respect of the establishment of a subsidiary in a Member State in order to take advantage of low wages, or for that matter, to benefit from some of the things that paying taxes buys, such as good infrastructure and an educated workforce.[36]

> Laval and the other cases make it clear that it does not amount to abuse of Union law to make use of free movement of services to exploit the comparative advantage of cheaper labour. Many would say hurrah to that.[37]

In sum, two conceptions of the function of national laws are at play within Union law. The first conception considers that national laws ought to be neutralised,

of excise duty applied on alcohol and alcoholic beverages (presented pursuant to Article 8 of Council Directive 92/84/EEC on the approximation of excise duty on alcohol and alcoholic beverages)' (Opinion), 18 January 2006, C69/10, no 4.1.

[32] Parliament (EC), 'Indirect tax harmonization' (Written Question no 1898/98), 16 June 1998, C50/111.

[33] Council Directive 94/5/EC of 14 February 1994 supplementing the common system of value added tax and amending Directive 77/388/EEC—Special arrangements applicable to second-hand goods, works of art, collectors' items and antiques [1994] OJ L60/16 rec 2.

[34] EL White, 'In Search of the Limits to Article 30 of the EEC Treaty' (1989) 26 *Common Market Law Review* 235, 245–46.

[35] S Vogenauer, 'The Prohibition of Abuse of Law: an Emerging General Principle of EU Law' in de la Feria and Vogenauer, *Prohibition of Abuse of Law* (n 17) 549.

[36] R Lyal, 'Cadbury Schweppes and Abuse: Comments' in de la Feria and Vogenauer (n 17) 431.

[37] C Barnard, 'The Notion of Abuse and the Freedom to Provide Services: A Labour Lawyer's Perspective' in de la Feria and Vogenauer (n 17) 100.

which can be expressed in a variety of ways: national laws should not influence economic decisions, which must be based on socioeconomic factors, and should not generate distortions of trade. This conception can be developed into a fully-fledged paradigm of integration designated as regulatory neutrality (Section II). The second conception postulates that national laws ought to be magnetised: they should influence economic decisions and may cause deflections of trade. This conception of national laws as magnets is the basic intuition of the paradigm of regulatory competition (Section III).

II. The Paradigm of Regulatory Neutrality: Economic Integration as Business Competition

If the contradictory influence of the paradigms of regulatory neutrality and regulatory competition can nowadays be identified within internal market law, they emerged at different historical moments of the European project of economic integration. The ideal of regulatory neutrality prevailed within the law of the internal market roughly from the creation of the European Coal and Steel Community (1951) until the landmark *Cassis de Dijon* ruling (1979).[38]

The central feature of the economic integration prompted by the European Union is the creation of an area without internal frontiers: 'The internal market shall comprise an area without internal frontiers in which the free movement of goods, persons, services and capital is ensured in accordance with the provisions of the Treaties' (Article 26(2) TFEU). In concrete terms, what does this classical formula of 'area without internal frontiers'—introduced by the Single European Act (1986)—mean? This formula does not aim at the actual suppression of internal frontiers, but rather at their neutralisation. Indeed, under the regulatory neutrality paradigm, economic integration leads to a territory in which firms and individuals conceive their actions irrespective of national frontiers. Such neutralisation is expected to suppress the economic 'frontiers' or 'barriers' among Member States, which are liable to deflect trade patterns within the internal market:

> A purely economic definition of market integration is based on the concept of 'economic frontiers'. Markets are integrated if economic frontiers between them have been eliminated. An economic frontier is any demarcation over which actual or potential mobilities of goods, services, capital, labour, technology as well as communication flows are low or absent.[39]

> [Economic integration is] a process whereby the outcomes of economic decisions become less dependent on the existence of borders. In integrated markets, firms will be able to consider entry into a product market ignoring the costs of selling across a

[38] Case 120/78 *Rewe-Zentral ('Cassis de Dijon')* [1979] ECR 649.

[39] Pelkmans (n 18) 41; see also Jovanovic, *The Economics of International Integration* (n 14) 17.

> national border. They will compete with other firms across geographic markets that are no longer determined by national borders, except where natural geographic features impose transport costs along borders (eg coastlines).[40]

Economic frontiers or barriers can be said to be 'economic' given their effects on economic activity; but they are also commonly labelled as 'legal' for they originate in the legal environment:

> The term 'legal barriers' covers all obstacles to the development of [economic] activities between Member States deriving directly or indirectly from a legal constraint and which are liable to prohibit, impede or otherwise render less advantageous such activities.[41]

> What does Article 8A mean when it speaks of 'an area without internal frontiers'? ... It is clear that nobody thinks of removing political frontiers. ... In fact, these 'frontiers' seem to concern nothing else than obstacles maintained by divergent national legislation, the so-called 'non-tariff barriers to trade'.[42]

In sum, the concept of 'area without internal frontiers' aims at the neutralisation of national laws, which are liable to create economic frontiers. As explained in the previous section, national laws are neutral when they do not influence economic decisions in the internal market, which is precisely the idea conveyed by the expression 'regulatory neutrality'. A regulation is neutral when market participants ignore it in their decision-making process. In practice, the reasoning applied to determine whether regulation is neutral is a counterfactual analysis, which seeks to determine whether economic decisions would have been identical in the absence of regulation.[43] Regulatory neutrality is preserved when trade flows remain impervious to the hypothetical adoption or repeal of the national laws in question: 'Market integration [is] a state where the outcomes of economic decisions are independent of national frontiers—more succinctly, borders do not matter'.[44]

Having clarified the notion of regulatory neutrality, the next question to be answered is the following: why should regulatory neutrality be preserved in a process of economic integration; in other words, what is the normative framework accounting for the objective of regulatory neutrality? In a project of economic integration, regulatory neutrality is necessary to ensure the proper functioning

[40] London Economics, *Competition Issues*, The Single Market Review, subseries V, vol 3 (London, Kogan Page, 1997) 20.

[41] Commission Report on the state of the internal market for services (n 22) 14.

[42] P Pescatore, 'Some Critical Remarks on the Single European Act' (1987) 24 *Common Market Law Review* 9, 16–17.

[43] Counterfactual analysis is evoked in relation to tax neutrality in U Paschen, *Steuerumgehung im Nationalen und Internationalen Steuerrecht* (Wiesbaden, DUV, 2001) 74. Counterfactual analysis is common in relation to State aids: see Commission (EC), 'State Aid Action Plan—Less and better targeted state aid: a roadmap for state aid reform 2005–2009' (Communication) COM (2005) 107 final, 7 June 2005, no 7; see also Commission (EC), 'Community law on State aid' (Vademecum), 30 September 2008, available at http://ec.europa.eu/competition/state_aid/studies_reports/studies_reports.html, 12.

[44] London Economics, *Competition Issues* (n 40) 23.

of the process of competition among businesses. AG Tesauro explicitly connected the disappearance of internal frontiers with the preservation of undistorted business competition throughout the Union:

> It seems to me to be fully consistent with the logic underlying the Single European Act to conclude that the 'area without internal frontiers' referred to in Article 8a is to be seen as a truly integrated area where the prevailing conditions are as close as possible to those of a single internal market: an area, therefore, in which there is harmonization not only of the rules concerning products but also of those which more generally affect the conditions of competition between undertakings. Indeed, I do not see how it is possible to achieve a genuinely single, integrated market without eliminating divergences between national legislation which, by having a differing impact on production costs, prevents the development of competition on the basis of real equality within the Community.[45]

The prime concern of the regulatory neutrality paradigm is thus the competition among private businesses, which should not be distorted by disparity among national laws. As economic integration leads businesses in each Member State to face competition from rivals in other Member States,[46] the regulatory neutrality paradigm seeks to ensure that competing businesses are subject to equivalent conditions of competition:

> [T]he creation of fair and equal conditions of competition between all economic operators in the field of intellectual property is essential in order to allow these operators to make effective use of the fundamental freedoms set out in the EC Treaty.[47]

> [Food supplements] are regulated in Member States by differing national rules that may impede their free movement, create unequal conditions of competition, and thus have a direct impact on the functioning of the internal market.[48]

> Whereas the laws, regulations and administrative provisions in force in the various Member States relating to the safety characteristics of toys differ in scope and content; whereas such disparities are liable to create barriers to trade and unequal conditions of competition within the internal market.[49]

[45] AG Tesauro, Case C-300/89 *Commission v Council ('Titanium Dioxide')* [1991] ECR I-2867, para 10; see also Commission (EC), *Les distorsions globales de la concurrence et leurs répercussions sur le Marché commun (Rapport Regul)*, Série Concurrence—Rapprochement des Législations no 11 (Brussels, Office des Publications Officielles Des Communautés Européennes, 1971) 5.

[46] Waelbroeck, 'La place de la concurrence dans le Traité de Lisbonne' (n 25) 830.

[47] Commission (EC), 'Proposal for a Directive of the European Parliament and of the Council on measures and procedures to ensure the enforcement of intellectual property rights' COM (2003) 46 final, 30 January 2003.

[48] Commission Directive 2002/36/EC of 29 April 2002 amending certain Annexes to Council Directive 2000/29/EC on protective measures against the introduction into the Community of organisms harmful to plants or plant products and against their spread within the Community [2002] OJ L116/16 rec 2.

[49] Council Directive 88/378/EEC of 3 May 1988 on the approximation of the laws of the Member States concerning the safety of toys [1988] OJ L187/1 rec 1. See also among countless others Directive 2004/48 on the enforcement of intellectual property rights rec 8; Directive 2000/13/EC of the European Parliament and of the Council of 20 March 2000 on the approximation of the laws of the Member States relating to the labelling, presentation and advertising of foodstuffs [2000] OJ L109/29 rec 2; Directive 94/47/EC of the European Parliament and the Council of 26 October 1994 on the

Accordingly, the ultimate strategic goal of the regulatory neutrality paradigm is the creation of the so-called 'level playing field', an idealised situation in which all businesses active in the internal market are subject to identical regulatory conditions throughout the internal market:

> [T]he regulatory ideal of the common market consisted in the creation of a 'level playing-field' on which all economic actors could operate under equal competitive conditions, and across which goods, persons and services could be exchanged unhindered.[50]

Indeed, the regulatory neutrality paradigm aims at neutralising internal frontiers in order to recreate the conditions of an ordinary domestic market, by suppressing the impact of national regulatory idiosyncrasies on trade flows competing within the internal market, as evoked in Schul:

> The concept of a common market … involves the elimination of all obstacles to intra-Community trade in order to merge the national markets into a single market bringing about conditions as close as possible to those of a genuine internal market.[51]

The notion of 'distortion of competition' created by disparity among national laws presupposes the adoption of regulatory neutrality as paradigm of economic integration. Regulatory distortions of competition amount to breaches of regulatory neutrality. The notion of 'distortion' implies a departure from an ideal situation, which is represented by the level playing field where national laws are neutral vis-à-vis business competition. National laws distort competition whenever they create unequal conditions of competition among businesses:

> [F]ollowing the establishment of the single market in goods and services, differences in the cost structure of member states brought about by variations in relative burdens of taxation and regulation will produce 'distortions of competition'.[52]

> [D]iscrepancies between the arrangements currently in force in Member States, which give rise in some cases to deflection of trade and distortion of competition, should be eliminated.[53]

protection of purchasers in respect of certain aspects of contracts relating to the purchase of the right to use immovable properties on a timeshare basis [1994] OJ L280/83 rec 1; Directive 94/25/EC of the European Parliament and of the Council of 16 June 1994 on the approximation of the laws, regulations and administrative provisions of the Member States relating to recreational craft [1994] OJ L164/15 rec 2; Council Directive 93/42/EEC of 14 June 1993 concerning medical devices [1993] OJ L169/1 rec 2; Council Regulation (EEC) 793/93 of 23 March 1993 on the evaluation and control of the risks of existing substances [1993] OJ L84/1 rec 1; Council Directive 92/59/EEC of 29 June 1992 on general product safety [1992] OJ L228/24 rec 2.

50 M Dougan, 'Minimum Harmonization and the Internal Market' (2000) 37 *Common Market Law Review* 853, 860.

51 Case 15/81 *Schul* [1982] ECR 1409, para 33; see also Case 207/83 *Commission v United Kingdom (Original Marking)* [1985] ECR 1201, para 17; Case 159/78 *Commission v Italy* [1979] ECR 3247, para 7; Case 78/70 *Deutsche Grammophon* [1971] ECR 487, para 12.

52 S Deakin and F Wilkinson, 'Rights vs Efficiency? The Economic Case for Transnational Labour Standards' (1994) 23 *Industrial Law Journal* 289, 301–02.

53 Eighth Council Directive 79/1072/EEC of 6 December 1979 on the harmonisation of the laws of the Member States relating to turnover taxes—Arrangements for the refund of value added tax to taxable persons not established in the territory of the country [1979] OJ L331/11 rec 3.

> It is true that the differences between certain regulations on tobacco advertising may give rise to appreciable distortions of competition. ... [T]he fact that sponsorship is prohibited in some Member States and authorised in others gives rise, in particular, to certain sports events being relocated, with considerable repercussions on the conditions of competition for undertakings associated with such events.[54]

> The principle of fiscal neutrality includes the principle of elimination of distortion in competition as a result of differing treatment for VAT purposes.[55]

Two arguments are usually advanced to support the objective of regulatory neutrality: fairness and efficiency. From the perspective of businesses, national laws can be viewed as unfair when they offer competitive advantages to rival businesses, which are less or not regulated. Fairness indeed requires all businesses to compete on an equal footing:

> [I]f the courts begin to recognize the regulatory arbitrage occurring in the communications industry, they may decide to grant disadvantaged companies relief from unfair or other 'legacy' regulations. Our society was founded on the notions of fairness and equality, so it is hard to believe that the courts will ignore the issues of regulatory disparity forever. As it stands, the disparity in our communications regulatory system promotes competitive inequality by allowing companies offering converging technologies to gain competitive advantages through loopholes in the system. This is a problem that must be resolved. If the FCC is not going to level the playing field, the courts have the ability to do so on constitutional grounds.[56]

> This legislative diversity within the EU leads to distortion of competition and thus acts as a barrier to the smooth operation of the European market in contemporary and modern art. These distortions within the EU often work to the advantage of leading auction houses in countries which do not recognise the artist's resale right, as it gives these auction houses a competitive advantage with respect to sales of European works.[57]

From the broader perspective of economic competition, regulatory distortions generate inefficiency. There is indeed a risk that incentives created by State policies lead to the location of economic activities in inappropriate places:

> [I]ncentives distort business-location choices, inducing firms to locate in inefficient locations (the 'banana-plantation-in-Alaska' criticism).[58]

[54] Case C-376/98 *Germany v Parliament and Council ('Tobacco Advertising I')* [2000] ECR I-8419, para 110.

[55] See among many others Case C-33/11 *A Oy* [2012] ECR I-0000, para 33; Case C-363/05 *JP Morgan* [2007] ECR I-5517, para 47.

[56] RK Mullady, 'Regulatory Disparity: The Constitutional Implications of Communications Regulations that Prevent Competitive Neutrality' (2007) 7 *Pittsburgh Journal of Technology Law & Policy* 1, 16.

[57] European Economic and Social Committee (EC), 'The Proposal for a European Parliament and Council Directive on the resale right for the benefit of the author of an original work of art' (Opinion), 18 December 1996, C75/17, no 1.5.

[58] JR Rogers, 'The Law and Policy of State Tax Competition: Much Ado About Nothing?' (2006) 4 *Georgetown Journal of Law & Public Policy* 101, 107, who borrows the 'banana-plantation-in-Alaska' criticism from TJ Holmes, 'Analyzing a Proposal to Ban State Tax Breaks to Businesses' (1995) 19 *Federal Reserve Bank of Minneapolis Quarterly Review* 29, 30.

> On the assumption that factors of production have considerable geographic mobility and that markets are, in general, reasonably competitive, there is some likelihood that locational decisions will entail departures from allocative optimality. That is, businesses, and perhaps individuals, will locate in places which do not involve maximum efficiency in the use of resources, rather than in the places with lowest overall costs, ignoring state-local taxes.[59]

> [C]ompanies have an incentive to make their investments in the country with the lowest tax burden for their situation, which is not necessarily the most economically efficient location.[60]

In sum, the regulatory neutrality paradigm seeks to preserve the spontaneous allocation of resources within the internal market, which must remain undistorted by national laws. In that sense, national laws should be neutral towards competition among businesses, and businesses ought to remain impervious to diversity among national laws. As early as in the ECSC Treaty (1951), the distorting impact of differentials of regulation on competition among private businesses raised sufficiently ample concerns to set up explicit corrective mechanisms in the Treaty itself. Article 67 ECSC provided for the correction of Member State actions liable to 'seriously distort the conditions of competition in the coal and steel industries';[61] whereas Article 68 ECSC prohibited the lowering of wages, decided by undertakings or Member States, when used 'as a weapon of competition among enterprises'.[62] Similarly, the Spaak Report (1956), which led to the adoption of the Treaties of Rome a year later, devoted a great deal of attention to distortions of competition generated by the disparity among national laws, in accordance with the regulatory neutrality paradigm:

> Apart from open discriminations and interventions intended to favour certain undertakings or productions, legislative or regulatory provisions have such an incidence on cost prices that it is appropriate to examine with the greatest care whether, by their own incidence or by their disparity among one or several countries, some of them do not distort the competition among national economies as a whole or in specific sectors.[63]

[59] D Netzer, *State-Local Finance and Intergovernmental Fiscal Relations* (Washington, Brookings Institution, 1969) 39.

[60] TA Kaye, 'The Gentle Art of Corporate Seduction: Tax Incentives in the United States and the European Union' (2008) 57 *Kansas Law Review* 93, 106.

[61] Art 67(1) ECSC provided for the notification to the High Authority of 'any action of a Member State which might have noticeable repercussions on the conditions of competition in the coal and steel industries'. The High Authority had the power to impose corrective measures if such an action was 'liable to provoke a serious disequilibrium by increasing the differentials in costs of production' (art 67(2) ECSC).

[62] In such a case, the High Authority addressed to the enterprise or government concerned a recommendation 'intended to assure the labour force of compensatory benefits to be paid for by the enterprise in question' (art 68(3) ECSC). If the enterprise failed to comply with the recommendation, the High Authority could even impose 'fines and daily penalty payments not to exceed twice the amount of the savings in labour costs unjustifiably effected' (art 68(6) ECSC).

[63] Rapport du Comité intergouvernemental créé par la Conférence de Messine ('Rapport Spaak'), 21 April 1956, aei.pitt.edu/996/01/Spaak_report_french.pdf, 60, free translation. More generally, see Rapport Spaak, Title II ch 2 '*Correction of Distortions and Approximation of Legislations*'.

This vision of economic integration as cross-border competition among businesses was warranted by former Article 3(1)(g) EC, which has been moved to Protocol no 27 on the internal market and competition, annexed to the Treaty of Lisbon.[64] The Court observed in that regard:

> Article 3(3) TEU states that the European Union is to establish an internal market, which, in accordance with Protocol nº 27 on the internal market and competition, annexed to the Treaty of Lisbon, is to include a system ensuring that competition is not distorted.
>
> Article 102 TFEU is one of the competition rules referred to in Article 3(1)(b) TFEU which are necessary for the functioning of that internal market.
>
> The function of those rules is precisely to prevent competition from being distorted to the detriment of the public interest, individual undertakings and consumers, thereby ensuring the well-being of the European Union.[65]

Furthermore, the influence of the regulatory neutrality paradigm on the Court's interpretation of the freedoms of movement is tangible, as will be shown in the subsequent chapters. By way of illustration, the seminal *Dassonville* formula condemns distortions of trade caused by national laws, in conformity with the regulatory neutrality paradigm:

> All trading rules enacted by Member States which are capable of hindering, directly or indirectly, actually or potentially, intra-Community trade are to be considered as measures having an effect equivalent to quantitative restrictions.[66]

As a matter of fact, the *Dassonville* formula closely reflects the wording of the Court's judgment in *Consten and Grundig*, a case of concerted practice restricting competition among private businesses (cartel):

> The concept of 'agreements which may affect trade between Member States' [aims at those agreements] capable of constituting a threat, either direct or indirect, actual or potential, to freedom of trade between Member States in a manner which might harm the attainment of the objectives of a single market between States.[67]

This resemblance, which has been acknowledged in the literature,[68] should not be surprising since the prime concern of the regulatory neutrality paradigm is undistorted business competition. From this perspective, any extra cost imposed upon cross-border trade amounts to restriction to free movement, as it distorts business competition:

> Taxes and regulations may bias economic decisions towards domestic activities because they impose extra-costs on cross-border trade. ... Market integration aims at the removal

[64] J Drexl, 'La Constitution économique européenne—L'actualité du modèle ordoliberal' (2011) XXV *Revue internationale de droit économique* 419, 440.
[65] Case C-52/09 *TeliaSonera* [2011] ECR I-527, paras 20–22.
[66] Case 8/74 *Dassonville* [1974] ECR 837, para 5.
[67] Joined Cases 56 and 58/64 *Consten and Grundig* [1966] ECR 429, point 6 of the summary.
[68] K Mortelmans, 'Towards Convergence in the Application of the Rules on Free Movement and on Competition?' (2001) 38 *Common Market Law Review* 613, 623; S Stadlmeier, 'Milestones on the Road to Keck' (2006) 2 *Croatian Yearbook of European Law and Policy* 51, 55–58.

of trade barriers. The goal is to reduce differences in the tax and regulatory treatment of domestic and cross-border trade. In the fully integrated market, no such difference remains. Borders lose their economic significance. This is, of course, is the promised land of market integration in the EU, a Single Market 'without internal frontiers'.[69]

III. The Paradigm of Regulatory Competition: Economic Integration as State Competition

Next to regulatory neutrality, manifestations of another paradigm of economic integration can be identified in Union law, namely the paradigm of regulatory competition. This observation is nothing revolutionary, for many scholars have devoted a great deal of attention to the articulation of the regulatory competition paradigm within Union law,[70] to the extent that regulatory (or 'inter-jurisdictional') competition has been described as 'an integral part of the constitutional structure of the European Union' and 'a concept for European integration'.[71] According to Weatherill, '[diversity] may also be the road, albeit a controversially mapped one, towards regulatory competition as a competing paradigm of internal market law'.[72]

By contrast with the regulatory neutrality paradigm, which focused on competition *among private businesses* and the potential distortions created by national laws, the regulatory competition paradigm is concerned with a process of competition *among Member States* by means of national laws. In essence, it postulates the existence—and proper functioning—of a '*law market*',[73] on which States compete to attract private interests, a process that would ultimately lead to optimal laws.

If the existence of a competition among jurisdictions was reported as early as in the 1850s,[74] the phenomenon only turned into a fully-fledged theoretical

[69] P Genschel, 'Mutual Recognition in Regulation and Taxation', European Union Studies Association, 2005 Biennial Conference, available at aei.pitt.edu/3087/01/eusa-genschel-290305.pdf, 3.

[70] See among many others P Schammo, 'Arbitrage and Abuse of Rights in the EC Legal System' (2008) 14 *European Law Journal* 351; C Barnard and S Deakin, 'Market Access and Regulatory Competition' in Barnard and Scott, *The Law of the Single Market* (n 6); S Deakin, 'Regulatory Competition after Laval' (2007–08) 10 *Cambridge Yearbook of European Legal Studies* 581; S Deakin, 'Is Regulatory Competition the Future for European Integration?' (2006) 13 *Swedish Economic Policy Review* 71; W Kerber, 'Interjurisdictional Competition within the European Union' (1999–2000) 23 *Fordham International Law Journal* 217; J Pelkmans and J-M Sun, 'Regulatory Competition in the Single Market' (1995) 33 *Journal of Common Market Studies* 67.

[71] Kerber, 'Interjurisdictional Competition within the European Union' (n 70) 234 and 247.

[72] S Weatherill, 'Why Harmonise?' in T Tridimas and P Nebbia (eds), *European Union Law for the Twenty-First Century—Volume 2: Internal Market and Free Movement Community Policies* (Oxford, Hart Publishing, 2004) 18.

[73] LE Ribstein and EA O'Hara, *The Law Market* (Oxford, Oxford University Press, 2009).

[74] See S Deakin, 'Legal Diversity and Regulatory Competition: Which Model for Europe?' (2006) 12 *European Law Journal* 440, 442 fn 5, referring to J Saville, 'Sleeping Partnership and Limited Liability, 1850–1856' (1956) 8 *Economic History Review (NS)* 418.

firms, and factors of production between jurisdictions that allows them to choose between different bundles offered by various jurisdictions.[85]

In addition, consumer arbitrage is 'polluted' by preferences for the private goods themselves: for instance, one may rightfully prefer a glass of Cassis de Dijon to a glass of Jägermeister, despite a clear fondness for German law. By contrast, producer arbitrage permits the immediate confrontation of national laws, independently of private goods: when production factors are granted the right to freely elect their preferred law, as in *Centros*, national laws are the only element taken into consideration.

In US scholarship, the concept of regulatory competition has been widely used to describe the Delaware effect, ie the fact that the State of Delaware has attracted a disproportionately high number of incorporations since the early-twentieth century, by offering a favourable regulatory environment to corporations.[86] The Delaware effect has drawn extensive academic interest for regulatory competition in the field of company law, setting off a fierce debate on whether it leads to a depression of regulatory standards (a 'race to the bottom').[87] What is not disputed is that the State of Delaware has imposed its legislation as the 'national' company law of the United States, by winning the regulatory competition in company law.[88]

In the context of the European Union, ever since the Schuman Declaration (1950),[89] political and trade union leaders have been aware of the risk of intensified State competition ensuing from economic integration. However, in normative terms, such a competition among Member States was viewed *as a threat* to be thwarted,[90] which led to the adoption of corrective devices in the ECSC Treaty itself (regulatory neutrality paradigm);[91] rather than *an opportunity* to be

[85] Kerber, 'Interjurisdictional Competition within the European Union' (n 70) 224.

[86] See WL Cary, 'Federalism and Corporate Law: Reflections upon Delaware' (1974) 83 *Yale Law Journal* 663, 663, in which he famously coined the expression 'race to the bottom'.

[87] See, among countless others, M Kahan and E Kamar, 'The Myth of State Competition in Corporate Law' (2002) 55 *Stanford Law Review* 679; L Bebchuk, A Cohen and A Ferrell, 'Does the Evidence Favor State Competition in Corporate Law?' (2002) 90 *California Law Review* 1775; K Greenfield, 'Democracy and the Dominance of Delaware in Corporate Law' (2004) 67 *Law and Contemporary Problems* 135; G Subramanian, 'The Disappearing Delaware Effect' (2004) 20 *Journal of Law, Economics, & Organization* 32; MJ Roe, 'Delaware's Competition' (2003) 117 *Harvard Law Review* 588; Cary, 'Federalism and Corporate Law' (n 86).

[88] L Bebchuk, 'The Desirable Limits in State Competition in Corporate Law' (1992) 105 *Harvard Law Review* 1435, 1495; referring to 'State Competition: Panel Response', 8 *Cardozo Law Review* (1986–87) 779–94, 783.

[89] R Schuman, 'Declaration of 9 May 1950', available at http://europa.eu/abc/symbols/9-may/decl_en.htm.

[90] Wesseling, *The Modernisation of EC Antitrust Law* (n 23) 14. The threat posed by foreign competition was relayed in the press, as illustrated by the following articles (all available at www.cvce.eu): P Drouin, 'Le projet de pool charbon-acier: les chances et les risques de l'économie française', *Le Monde*, 24 May 1950; 'Les Dangers du Plan Schuman', L'Écho de la Bourse, 10 December 1950; J Duclos, 'Lettre de Jacques Duclos', *L'Humanité*, 5 December 1951; 'Plan Schuman et Souveraineté Fiscale des Etats', *Luxemburger Wort*, 9 July 1954; L Charvet, 'La Sidérurgie Française Devant le « Pool »' (1951) 16–17 *Nouvelle Revue de l'Economie Contemporaine* 36; D Gobbi, 'La CECA ha ridotto ancora la produzione di carbone belga', *L'Unità*, 30 May 1959.

[91] See nn 61–62 and accompanying text.

pursued, namely a competitive process potentially leading to optimal regulation (regulatory competition paradigm). In other words, regulatory competition was not conceptualised as a paradigm of economic integration at the inception of the European Communities; as a matter of fact, the Treaties establishing the European Union have been described as 'agnostic' about regulatory competition; as having no 'explicit preference' for such a process; and as pursuing 'not regulatory competition, but market integration'.[92]

Indeed, if many Treaty provisions have an impact on the room available for regulatory competition (such as the possibility of adopting harmonising measures or the prohibition of State aids[93]), they were initially designed to promote undistorted competition among private businesses, pursuant to the regulatory neutrality paradigm. Regulatory competition emerged as an *unintended side effect*[94] of the contrasting fortunes encountered by Union institutions in their efforts to achieve economic integration through regulatory neutrality. The Union legislature, on the one hand, got rapidly stuck in political deadlocks, making (full) harmonisation at the Union level at best illusory in many fields.[95] The Court of Justice, on the other hand, was much more successful in promoting economic integration, through the 'constitutionalisation'[96] and expansive interpretation of the free movement provisions:

> In the late 1970s, harmonisation was seen as a good deal more politically feasible and economically desirable than it is today. … We know today that a great many obstacles to inter-State trade caused by diversity between national laws that might have been expected to be tackled by legislative harmonisation have instead been left in the hands of the judiciary, at national and EU level.[97]

In particular, the landmark *Cassis de Dijon* ruling (1979) marked the judicial advent of the mutual recognition principle, whose purpose was to reduce the relative cost of cross-border trade by precluding multiple regulation, in conformity with the regulatory neutrality paradigm.[98] Accordingly, Schmitt Von Sydow distinguished three periods in the regulation of the internal market: the 'initial surge of the Sixties' (Union harmonisation), the 'decline of the Seventies' (harmonisation stalemate) and the 'new momentum of the Eighties' (mutual recognition),

[92] Schammo (n 70) 370; Weatherill (n 72) 18; Barnard and Deakin (n 70) 197.

[93] See ch 9.

[94] Barnard and Deakin, 'Market Access and Regulatory Competition' (n 70) 198; Deakin, 'Legal Diversity and Regulatory Competition' (n 74) 440; Deakin (n 70) 76.

[95] Craig and de Búrca, *EU Law* (n 2) 606 ff; S Weatherill, 'Fitting "Abuse of Rights" into EU Law Governing the Free Movement of Goods and Services' in de la Feria and Vogenauer (n 17) 56; SK Schmidt, 'The Impact of Mutual Recognition—Inbuilt Limits and Domestic Responses to the Single Market' (2002) 9 *Journal of European Public Policy* 935, 937.

[96] See the seminal E Stein, 'Lawyers, Judges, and the Making of a Transnational Constitution' (1981) 75 *American Journal of International Law* 1; GF Mancini, 'The Making of a Constitution for Europe' (1989) 26 *Common Market Law Review* 595; and JHH Weiler, 'The Transformation of Europe' (1991) 100 *Yale Law Journal* 2403.

[97] Weatherill, 'Fitting "Abuse of Rights" into EU Law Governing the Free Movement of Goods and Services' (n 95) 56.

[98] See ch 7 section II.

prompted by *Cassis de Dijon* and the Commission's White Paper on completing the internal market (1985):[99]

> In the past, internal market policies relied mainly on harmonisation directives introducing common rules for each individual sector. Despite initial success, a number of shortcomings had been identified over the years, and the authors of the White Paper knew very well that a genuine internal market could not be realised by 1992 under the traditional strategy. The new strategy, which runs through all parts of the White Paper as a red line, is based on a shift from the drawing up of new, harmonised regulations to the principle of mutual recognition of national rules and situations.[100]

The consequence of the contrasting fortunes encountered by the Union legislature and judiciary in the promotion of regulatory neutrality was that the regulation of the internal market became characterised by diversity among national laws (no Union harmonisation) and the increasing mobility of Union citizens (free movement). This combination of regulatory diversity and mobility offered Union citizens an ever-increasing room for regulatory arbitrage, the first and necessary step to trigger a regulatory competition process:

> [B]y facilitating the mobility of persons and resources ..., the free movement provisions also facilitate regulatory and tax arbitrage. This is because legal mobility is a basic pre-condition for arbitrage. Thus, if persons and resources can move at low cost between jurisdictions and provided that mobile actors are informed about differences in regulatory regimes, differences between regulatory regimes can a priori also be exploited.[101]

> When courts review laws of Member States against criteria of how far such laws obstruct, or promote, economic mobility, they are necessarily defining the scope and nature of regulatory competition. ... [W]hile regulatory competition may not be the aim of the Court's interventions, it is certainly one of its most significant effects.[102]

In other words, 'negative integration' without 'positive integration'—even if intended to promote regulatory neutrality—inevitably leads to more intense forms of regulatory competition within the internal market: 'The core of the problem is that simultaneous realization of mobility and decentralization logically implies the existence of competition among jurisdictions'.[103] At first, regulatory competition was unconsciously fostered by the Court's judicial activism;

[99] White Paper on completing the internal market (n 29) no 61–63, in which the Commission announces a change a 'strategy' in its internal market policy, from harmonisation to mutual recognition. For a concrete admission of the need to have recourse to mutual recognition given the 'difficulty of harmonising', see Directive 2001/24/EC of the European Parliament and of the Council of 4 April 2001 on the reorganisation and winding up of credit institutions [2001] OJ L125/15, rec 6.

[100] H Schmitt von Sydow, 'The Basic Strategies of the Commission's White Paper' in R Bieber et al (eds), *1992: One European Market?* (Baden-Baden, Nomos, 1988) 92.

[101] Schammo (n 70) 360.

[102] Barnard and Deakin (n 70) 198 and 223; see also Deakin (n 74) 440.

[103] Kerber (n 70) 221.

it is only afterwards that it was rationalised as a paradigm of economic integration by the scholarship, with the help of Tiebout's model:

> The constitutional rules and principles which have brought about the conditions for regulatory competition in the U.S. and EU were not devised with that aim explicitly in mind … Regulatory competition came about as an unintended side effect of legislative or judicial action, and only afterwards was given the appearance of being the product of rational design.[104]

Arguably, it is only in 1999 that the first conscious institutional move towards regulatory competition was made, with the *Centros* ruling,[105] an attempt of the Court of Justice's to emulate the Delaware effect.[106] Since then, the *Centros*-line of case law has generated an abundant literature on regulatory competition in Union law.[107] Historically, an important evolution has therefore marked the theoretical foundations of the process of economic integration within the European Union. If regulatory neutrality was originally viewed as the only way to achieve economic integration, regulatory competition progressively emerged as an alternative, for both pragmatic (regulatory competition does not require Union harmonisation) and theoretical reasons (the growing influence of Tiebout's model). Kaye perfectly captured this evolution, in relation to direct taxation in the internal market:

> The original view of the Commission was that any disparity between the tax systems of the Member States had to be alleviated in order to optimize productivity within the European Community as differing tax systems could be one of those internal frontiers. Tax harmonization would improve neutrality and guarantee that companies located in nations because of efficiency of resources, not simply because of advantageous tax schemes. …
>
> Although tax harmonization is still considered desirable by the Commission, modern economic evaluation stresses the benefits that can be derived from healthy tax competition. The basic economic principle is that tax competition permits taxpayers to exert some influence over governments' tax policies.[108]

104 Deakin (n 70) 76.

105 Case C-212/97 *Centros* [1999] ECR I-1459. See also Case C-210/06 *Cartesio* [2008] ECR I-9641; Case C-167/01 *Inspire Art* [2003] ECR I-10155; Case C-208/00 *Überseering* [2002] ECR I-9919.

106 See esp AG La Pergola, Case C-212/97 *Centros* [1999] ECR I-1459, 20: '[I]n the absence of harmonisation, competition among rules must be allowed free play in corporate matters'.

107 See, among many others, W-G Ringe, 'Sparking Regulatory Competition in European Company Law—The Impact of the Centros Line of Case-Law and its Concept of "Abuse of Law"' in de la Feria and Vogenauer (n 17); A Johnston and P Syrpis, 'Regulatory Competition in European Company Law after Cartesio' (2009) 34 *European Law Review* 378; MV Benedettelli, 'Conflicts of Jurisdiction and Conflicts of Law in Company Law Matters Within the EU "Market for Corporate Models": Brussels I and Rome I after Centros' (2005) 16 *European Business Law Review* 55; C Kirchner, RW Painter and WA Kaal, 'Regulatory Competition in EU Corporate Law after Inspire Art: Unbundling Delaware's Product for Europe' (2005) 2 *European Company and Financial Law Review* 159; C Holst, 'European Company Law After Centros: is the EU on the Road to Delaware?' (2002) 8 *Columbia Journal of European Law* 323; S Lombardo, *Regulatory Competition in Company Law in the European Community: Prerequisites and Limits* (Frankfurt am Main, Peter Lang, 2002); S Deakin, 'Two Types of Regulatory Competition: Competitive Federalism versus Reflexive Harmonisation' (1999) 2 *Cambridge Yearbook of European Legal Studies* 231.

108 Kaye, 'The Gentle Art of Corporate Seduction' (n 60) 104 and 107.

7

Dilemmas in the Regulation of the Internal Market

THE CENTRAL SUBMISSION of this chapter is that the law of the internal market is constantly shaped by two distinct paradigms of economic integration: regulatory neutrality and regulatory competition. As described in the previous chapter, the regulatory neutrality paradigm seeks to ensure the proper functioning of *competition among businesses* by shielding it from regulatory distortions. By contrast, the regulatory competition paradigm seeks to ensure the proper functioning of *competition among States*, in which regulation becomes the very object of the competitive process. Given their different premises and objectives, the regulatory neutrality and regulatory competition paradigms are bound to entail different prescriptions regarding the regulation of the internal market.

In practice, all issues raised by the regulation of the internal market boil down to one admittedly multiform questioning: how should cross-border flows be regulated? To clarify the implications of this question, three groups of persons ought to be distinguished:

— the *home society*, namely the group of Union citizens whose activities are confined to the State of origin or home State;
— the *host society*, namely the group of Union citizens whose activities are confined to the State of destination or host State; and
— the *cross-border flows*, namely the group of Union citizens moving from the home State to the host State.

Internal market law is not concerned with the two first groups, namely home society and host society, which are respectively subject to the ordinary laws of the home State (home law) and the host State (host law).[1] Internal market law is

[1] Issues regarding the regulation of home society or host society are usually dismissed as purely internal situations: see among many others M Mataija, 'Internal Situations in Community Law: An Uncertain Safeguard of Competences Within the Internal Market' (2009) 5 *Croatian Yearbook of European Law and Policy* 31; C Dautricourt and S Thomas, 'Reverse Discrimination and Free Movement Of Persons under Community Law: All for Ulysses, Nothing for Penelope?' (2009) 34 *European Law Review* 433; A Tryfonidou, 'Reverse Discrimination in Purely Internal Situations: An Incongruity in a Citizens' Europe' (2008) 35 *Legal Issues of Economic Integration* 43; MP Maduro, 'The Scope of European Remedies: the Case of Purely Internal Situations and Reverse Discrimination' in

exclusively concerned with the actions taken by Member States in relation to the third group, namely the cross-border flows. In more detail, the issues raised by the regulation of cross-border flows can be sorted into five categories: protectionism, multiple regulation, positive harmonisation, negative harmonisation and regulatory mobility.

First, the issue of protectionism questions whether home State and host State should be allowed to impose extra burdens upon cross-border flows, namely measures that do not apply to members of home society and host society (Section I). The second issue, multiple regulation, seeks to determine whether cross-border flows should be subject to both home and host laws (Section II). Thirdly, the eventuality of positive harmonisation concerns the possibility to replace both home and host laws by a unique Union law (Section III). Fourthly, the negative harmonisation conundrum explores the choice between applying home law or host law to cross-border flows (Section IV). Fifthly, the regulatory mobility dilemma regards the ease with which trade flows should be able to move from the home jurisdiction to the host jurisdiction (Section V).

These five issues logically derive from the tension between the survival of national polities, each with their own power to regulate (regulatory diversity), and the objective of intermingling their respective economies (territorial unity); or, in other words, the tension between 'market integration' and 'market regulation'.[2] As shall be described below, regulatory neutrality and regulatory competition concur in disapproving of protectionism and multiple regulation, but irreconcilably disagree about positive harmonisation, negative harmonisation and regulatory mobility.

I. Protectionism

Protectionism is the most basic issue of economic integration, and indeed the most basic issue of internal market law. Protectionism can be defined as State action intended to impose extra burdens upon cross-border flows, namely measures that do not apply to 'sedentary' citizens. In theory, such extra burdens may target incoming (protectionism from the host State) or outgoing flows (protectionism from the home State). In practice, however, protectionist measures classically target out-of-staters in order to protect in-staters: indeed, it is much more

C Kilpatrick et al (eds), *The Future of European Remedies* (Oxford, Hart Publishing, 2000); E Cannizzaro, 'Producing "Reverse Discrimination" Through the Exercise of EC Competences' (1997) 17 *Yearbook of European Law* 29; DMW Pickup, 'Reverse Discrimination and Freedom of Movement for Workers' (1986) 23 *Common Market Law Review* 135.

[2] KA Armstrong, 'Mutual Recognition' in C Barnard and J Scott (eds), *The Law of the Single Market: Unpacking the Premises* (Oxford, Hart Publishing, 2002) 225.

common for host States to burden incoming flows in order to shield their host society—chiefly local businesses—from external competition. In the context of US law, Sunstein defined protectionism as follows:

> The first [purpose of the commerce clause] is to control what we might call naked protectionism: measures adopted by one state in order to protect its citizens—most likely its producers—against competition from outsiders. Protectionist measures are designed to safeguard the interests of insiders at the expense of outsiders. It is thus likely to be a product of the exercise of political power by well-organized private groups; and by hypothesis, no other goal is involved.[3]

It is of crucial importance to clearly distinguish protectionism from multiple regulation, which is the object of the next section, as they both tend to impose extra burdens upon cross-border flows. The first criterion of distinction (*unilateral v multilateral*) is that protectionism only concerns measures unilaterally adopted by one State; whereas multiple regulation aims at the concomitant action of two or more States. The second criterion of distinction (*special v ordinary*) is that protectionism concerns special measures targeted at cross-border flows; whereas multiple regulation aims at the impact of ordinary national laws that are applicable to everyone. This distinction between protectionism and multiple regulation is regularly underlined in Commission policy documents:

> An individual or corporate taxpayer who is in a cross-border situation may suffer discrimination or double taxation or face additional compliance costs. This creates a disincentive for individuals who wish to work or invest in other Member States.[4]

Given their different natures, protectionist measures are often designated as 'distinctly applicable measures', 'direct' or 'overt discrimination', since the discriminatory effect is intended by the State. By contrast, multiple regulation is often labelled as 'indistinctly applicable measures', 'indirect' or 'covert discrimination', as the discriminatory effect may only be incidental to the desire of Member States to apply their ordinary laws:

> Distinctly applicable measures expressly treat imported goods less favourably than domestic goods. By contrast, indistinctly applicable measures appear on their face to treat domestic and imported goods alike, but in fact disadvantage imported goods by requiring them to satisfy an additional set of rules[5]

So defined as special and unilateral measures targeted at cross-border flows, protectionist measures can be of two sorts. First, States may regulate the crossing of an internal border, by imposing border taxes (chiefly customs duties: Article 30 TFEU), quantitative restrictions (quotas: Articles 34 and 35 TFEU) or border

[3] CR Sunstein, 'Protectionism, the American Supreme Court, and Integrated Markets' in R Bieber et al (eds), *1992: One European Market?* (Baden-Baden, Nomos, 1988) 129.

[4] Commission (EC), 'Co-ordinating Member States' direct tax systems in the Internal Market' (Communication) COM (2006) 823 final, 19 December 2006, 3.

[5] C Barnard, *The Substantive Law of the EU: the Four Freedoms*, 2nd edn (Oxford, Oxford University Press, 2007) 97.

controls (designated as 'physical barriers' in the 1985 White Paper[6]). By definition, such at-the-border measures only affect cross-border flows and are therefore protectionist. The Court has proved particularly strict with at-the-border measures, as in the early *Statistical Levy* case, which concerned a charge levied by Italy on imported and exported goods, whose purpose was to collect statistical data on Italy's foreign trade. The Court ruled that such a levy constituted an obstacle to trade, despite its small amount and irrespective of its actual effects on the market:

> [A]ny pecuniary charge, however small and whatever its designation and mode of application, which is imposed unilaterally on domestic or foreign goods by reason of the fact that they cross a frontier, and which is not a customs duty in the strict sense, constitutes a charge having equivalent effect within the meaning of Articles 9, 12, 13 and 16 of the Treaty, even if it is not imposed for the benefit of the State, is not discriminatory or protective in effect and if the product on which the charge is imposed is not in competition with any domestic product.[7]

Secondly, the prevention of protectionism also requires the prohibition of internal measures openly discriminating against foreign trade flows.[8] The 1962 General Programmes are particularly revealing of the initial mind-set of the European construction, which precisely focused on discriminations imposed against foreign nationals *within* one Member State.[9] There are moreover numerous examples of openly discriminatory measures struck down by the Court,[10] including the seminal *Costa v Enel* in which the Court stated:

> Article 53 of the EEC treaty is satisfied so long as no new measure subjects the establishment of nationals of other Member States to more severe rules than those prescribed for nationals of the country of establishment.[11]

Another example of a protectionist measure can be found in the more recent *International Jet Management* case. German law obliged non-German airlines to obtain permission to make inward flights in respect of charter flights, and to

[6] Commission (EC), 'Completing the internal market' (White Paper) COM (85) 310 final, 14 June 1985, nos 11–12, 24–56 and 60: 'physical barriers impede trade flows and add unacceptable administrative costs'.

[7] Case 24/68 *Commission v Italy ('Statistical Levy')* [1969] ECR 193, para 9.

[8] White Paper on completing the internal market (n 6), no 57: 'Goods and people moving within the Community should not find obstacles inside the different Member States as opposed to meeting them at the border'.

[9] Council (EC), 'General Programme for the abolition of restrictions on freedom of establishment' (Resolution), 18 December 1961, C2/36; Council (EC), 'General Programme for the abolition of restrictions on freedom to provide services' (Resolution), 18 December 1961, C2/32.

[10] Case 2/74 *Reyners* [1974] ECR 631 (Belgian nationality requirement to exercise the profession of lawyer in Belgium); Case C-47/08 *Commission v Belgium (Notaries)* [2011] ECR I-4105 (Belgian nationality requirement to exercise the profession of notary in Belgium); Case 197/84 *Steinhauser* [1985] ECR 1819 (French nationality requirement to participate in a public tendering procedure in France); Case 21/84 *Commission v France* ('Postal franking machine') [1985] ECR 1355 (French manufacture requirement for letter-franking machines used by French postal services).

[11] Case 6/64 *Costa v ENEL* [1964] ECR 1141, para 9.

obtain this permission non-German airlines had to adduce evidence that German airlines were not in a position to carry out the flights (a non-availability declaration). Having reached the obvious conclusion that the measure was discriminatory, AG Bot could not hide his surprise at the ground of justification based on 'economic protectionism' bluntly put forward by the German Government:

> Regarding economic protectionism, we do not see how, in a Union of 27, such a goal could be considered as legitimate and justify a violation of the principle of non-discrimination. … In any event, we do not see how the protection of the national economy could be regarded as being based on objective considerations independent of the nationality of the persons concerned.[12]

The next question to be examined is whether this prohibition of protectionism under Union law can be normatively explained in light of the objective of economic integration, defined either as regulatory neutrality or regulatory competition.

On the one hand, the regulatory neutrality paradigm seeks to ensure that domestic and cross-border flows are subject to the same regulatory burden (level playing field), in order to preserve competition among private goods.[13] Therefore, regulatory neutrality requires the suppression of protectionist measures, whose very purpose is to impose an extra burden upon cross-border flows, thereby distorting the competition between local businesses and cross-border flows. By way of illustration, this conceptualisation of protectionism in light of regulatory neutrality can be identified in the following excerpt:

> [W]ith the implementation of the Single Market Programme, border controls within the EU area were abolished … because border formalities tended to increase the transactions costs of cross-border trade, thereby inhibiting the creation of a truly integrated European market.[14]

On the other hand, regulatory competition functions as a chain of information conveying individual preferences regarding national laws, from consumers to producers (consumer arbitrage) and from producers to national governments (producer arbitrage).[15] Protectionist measures tamper with both consumer and producer arbitrages. First, consumers indirectly arbitrate among national laws by choosing among products subject to different national laws. As incoming goods are subject to an extra burden imposed by the host State, consumers residing in the host State cannot compare the respective virtues of host law and foreign law. Secondly, producers directly arbitrate among national laws by electing the most hospitable jurisdiction. Quite obviously, whenever their relocation is hampered

[12] AG Bot, Case C-628/11 *International Jet Management* [2014] ECR I-0000, para 72, free translation. See also Case C-628/11 *International Jet Management* [2014] ECR I-0000, para 70.

[13] See ch 6 section II.

[14] For instance, on border controls, see PB Sørensen, 'Tax Coordination in the European Union: What are the Issues?' (2001) 8 *Swedish Economic Policy Review* 143, 157.

[15] See ch 6 sections II and III.

by protectionist measures adopted by the host State, producers cannot usefully compare the respective virtues of (ordinary) host law and other national laws.

To sum up, protectionism is incompatible with both regulatory neutrality and regulatory competition, although for different reasons: under regulatory neutrality, protectionist measures distort competition among private businesses, whereas they hamper consumer and producer arbitrages under regulatory competition.

II. Multiple Regulation

The issue of multiple regulation marks the passage from a single-jurisdiction perspective, characteristic of protectionism, to a multiple-jurisdiction perspective. Conceptually, there is indeed a stark difference between applying a harsher regulation to foreign trade flows (protectionism) and applying ordinary domestic law to trade flows already subject to the law of their country of origin (multiple regulation), as explained in the previous section.

Cassis de Dijon is widely acknowledged as the judgment in which the Court established the principle according to which multiple regulation erects obstacles to trade incompatible with the objective of economic integration, but which can be justified by the proportionate pursuit of a legitimate policy objective. The facts are well known: the French blackcurrant liqueur Cassis de Dijon could not be sold in Germany as German law imposed a threshold of alcohol content (25 per cent) in fruit liqueurs. The Court ruled that:

> There is therefore no valid reason why, provided that they have been lawfully produced and marketed in one of the member states, alcoholic beverages should not be introduced into any other Member State; the sale of such products may not be subject to a legal prohibition on the marketing of beverages with an alcohol content lower than the limit set by the national rules.[16]

In his Opinion in the first *Sunday Trading* case, AG Van Gerven highlighted the evolution of the free movement jurisprudence triggered by *Cassis de Dijon*, which shifted the emphasis from discriminatory measures (protectionism) to national measures applying 'without distinction' (multiple regulation):

> At the outset it was made clear that a national measure which was discriminatory … towards imported goods was caught by the prohibition laid down in Article [34 TFEU]. … The Court subsequently considered the prohibition laid down in Article [34 TFEU] also applicable in the case of measures applying to national and imported products without distinction.[17]

[16] Case 120/78 *Rewe-Zentral ('Cassis de Dijon')* [1979] ECR 649, para 14.

[17] AG Van Gerven, Case 145/88 *B and Q (Sunday Trading)* [1989] ECR 3851, paras 14–15.

Since then, the Court has routinely distinguished between protectionism and multiple regulation as well, as in the *Gouda* case:

> Article [56 TFEU] entails, in the first place, the abolition of any discrimination against a person providing services on account of his nationality or the fact that he is established in a Member State other than the one in which the service is provided.
>
> In the absence of harmonisation of the rules applicable to services, or even of a system of equivalence, restrictions on the freedom guaranteed by the Treaty in this field may arise, in the second place, as a result of the application of national rules which affect any person established in the national territory to persons providing services established in the territory of another Member State who already have to satisfy the requirements of that State's legislation.[18]

In concrete terms, multiple regulation implies that cross-border flows merely benefit from national treatment: protectionist measures (chiefly by the host State) are prohibited, but cross-border flows are subject to both home law and ordinary host law:

> In the decentralised model, States will retain regulatory powers, but are, at the same time, prevented from developing protectionist policies. … [They are] required not to discriminate against foreign products or persons in their exercise of those powers.[19]

> [A]part from this right to equality of treatment with host state nationals, market access is premised upon full compliance with the laws of the host state.[20]

> A large number of services encounter the same problem: the Member State of destination treats the service provider as if he were established on its territory, and hence subjects him fully to its legal system. … [T]his approach amounts to reducing the principle of the free movement of services to a simple obligation not to discriminate.[21]

In normative terms, multiple regulation is incompatible with the objective of economic integration, be it defined as regulatory neutrality or regulatory competition, and for the reasons already exposed in relation to protectionism. On one hand, multiple regulation is incompatible with regulatory neutrality as it imposes an extra burden upon cross-border flows, in comparison with local competitors who are subject to one set of national laws. In that connection, the 1985 White Paper used the notion of 'technical barriers to trade' formed by the coexistence of different national standards for products.[22] The distortionary impact of

[18] Case C-288/89 *Gouda* [1991] ECR I-4007, paras 10 and 12.

[19] MP Maduro, *We the Court: the European Court of Justice and the European Economic Constitution* (Oxford, Hart Publishing, 1998) 109 and 143.

[20] Armstrong, 'Mutual Recognition' (n 2) 229.

[21] Commission (EC), 'The state of the internal market for services' (Report) COM (2002) 441 final, 30 July 2002, 51.

[22] White Paper on completing the internal market (n 6) no 57-159 and 13: 'An example of [technical barrier] are the different standards for individual products adopted in different Member States for health or safety reasons, or for environmental or consumer protection'.

multiple regulation upon business competition is abundantly acknowledged in the literature, in accordance with the regulatory neutrality paradigm:

> The main consideration underlying [Cassis de Dijon] is that such disparities between national laws may result in serious obstacles to intra-Community trade since they may necessitate extra expense or additional efforts in order to make the manufacture or the marketing of the product comply with laws differing from one Member State to another.[23]

> [A] regulation also creates a fixed cost which is entirely supported by the foreign firm. This asymmetric fixed cost comes from the additional burden supported by a firm when it decides to export and comply to the regulation of a foreign country: it runs from the one-time cost of re-designing a product or its packaging to the more subtle cost entailed by conformity assessment.[24]

> The elimination of multiple regulation of traders is central to achieving an integrated market.[25]

> The lack of harmonisation of national rules places a burden on economic agents in the extra costs of having to comply with more than one set of rules.[26]

On the other hand, multiple regulation is incompatible with the regulatory competition paradigm as well, as it disturbs both consumer and producer arbitrages. Consumers cannot validly arbitrate among national laws, by choosing among products subject to different laws: if domestic goods are only subject to host law, incoming goods are indeed subject to both home *and* host laws. To enable consumer arbitrage, incoming goods must be subject to the sole home law (mutual recognition).[27] In addition, producers cannot validly arbitrate among national laws either, since any election of a hospitable home jurisdiction will be neutralised by the simultaneous application of home and host laws to their cross-border activities.

In sum, the objective of economic integration requires the suppression of multiple regulation, both under regulatory neutrality and regulatory competition. However, it must be strongly underlined that the objective of economic integration does not systematically prevail over other legitimates objectives pursued by Member States. Indeed, endorsement of multiple regulation is not exceptional within the free movement jurisprudence. Such endorsement may happen at either of two different stages: the Court may decide that multiple regulation does not

[23] AG Van Gerven, Case 145/88 *B and Q (Sunday Trading)* [1989] ECR 3851, para 15.

[24] A Suwa-Eisenmann and T Verdier, 'Reciprocity and the Political Economy of Harmonization and Mutual Recognition of Regulatory Measures', Centre for Economic Policy Research, Discussion Paper no 3147 (January 2002), available at www.cepr.org/pubs/dps/DP3147.asp, 4.

[25] S Weatherill, 'Pre-emption, Harmonisation and the Distribution of Competence to Regulate the Internal Market' in Barnard and Scott, *The Law of the Single Market* (n 2) 66.

[26] Maduro, *We the Court* (n 19) 69.

[27] See section IV.C.

constitute an obstacle to trade at all; or it may decide that the obstacle to trade is justified by the proportionate pursuit of a legitimate policy objective.

For instance, the Court has repeatedly endorsed multiple regulation in the field of direct taxation, by judging that double taxation by two Member States does not amount to a restriction prohibited by the Treaty. For instance, the Court decided in *Damseaux* that:

> [D]isadvantages which could arise from the parallel exercise of tax competences by different Member States, to the extent that such an exercise is not discriminatory, do not constitute restrictions prohibited by the EC Treaty.[28]

Accordingly, Member States have no obligation to prevent international double taxation under Union law. Similarly, in relation to online gambling services, the Court held that compelling online betting bookers to apply for authorisation in every State in which they provide services does not constitute an obstacle to free movement. This principle was clearly established in *Markus Stoß*:

> Having regard to that margin of discretion and the absence of any Community harmonisation in the matter, a duty mutually to recognise authorisations issued by the various Member States cannot exist having regard to the current state of EU law.
>
> It follows in particular that each Member State retains the right to require any operator wishing to offer games of chance to consumers in its territory to hold an authorisation issued by its competent authorities, without the fact that a particular operator already holds an authorisation issued in another Member State being capable of constituting an obstacle.[29]

Migrant workers may be similarly required to obtain a new professional qualification in the host State in the absence of mutual recognition, as in *Bouchoucha*:

> It must therefore be stated … that in the absence of harmonisation at Community level regarding activities which fall solely within the scope of the practice of medicine, Article 52 EEC does not preclude a Member State from restricting an activity ancillary to medicine such as, in particular, osteopathy exclusively to persons holding the qualification of doctor of medicine.[30]

In all these cases, the Court held that multiple regulation did not restrict the freedoms of movement, irrespective of the possibility of a subsequent justification. In addition, the Court may find that a legitimate policy objective ought to prevail over the objective of economic integration, and accept that a restriction to free

[28] Case C-128/08 *Damseaux* [2009] ECR I-6823, para 27; see also Case C-67/08 *Block* [2009] ECR I-883, paras 28–31; Case C-194/06 *Orange European Smallcap Fund* [2008] ECR I-3747, para 47; Case C-513/04 *Kerckhaert and Morres* [2006] ECR I-10967, paras 20–24; J Englisch, 'Taxation of Cross-Border Dividends and EC Fundamental Freedoms' (2010) 38 *Intertax* 197, 208.

[29] Joined Cases C-316/07, C-358/07 to C-360/07, C-409/07 and C-410/07 *Markus Stoß* [2010] ECR I-8069, paras 112–13; see also Case C-347/09 *Dickinger* [2011] ECR I-8185, para 96; Case C-42/07 *Bwin* [2009] ECR I-7633, para 69.

[30] Case C-61/89 *Bouchoucha* [1990] ECR I-3551, paras 14–16; see also Case 136/78 *Auer* [1979] ECR 437.

movement is justified. In *Cassis de Dijon*, the Court explicitly acknowledged the existence of this balancing exercise between the objective of economic integration and other legitimate objectives:

> It is clear from the foregoing that the requirements relating to the minimum alcohol content of alcoholic beverages do not serve a purpose which is in the general interest and such as to take precedence over the requirements of the free movement of goods, which constitutes one of the fundamental rules of the Community.[31]

In more detail, Treaty derogations can justify both protectionism (discriminatory measures, irrespective of measures imposed by other States) and multiple regulation, whereas the so-called 'mandatory requirements' evoked by the Court in *Cassis de Dijon* can only justify multiple regulation.[32] As is well known,[33] Treaty derogations and mandatory requirements pursue various objectives of public interest whose protection is better guaranteed under protectionism or multiple regulation, such as:

— public morality, public policy or public security; the protection of health and life of humans, animals or plants; the protection of national treasures possessing artistic, historic or archaeological value; or the protection of industrial and commercial property (Treaty derogations: see Articles 36, 45(3), 52(1) and 65(1)(b) TFEU); and
— the effectiveness of fiscal supervision; the financial balance of the social security system; the protection of the environment, of consumers, of working conditions, of press diversity, and of fundamental rights (mandatory requirements).

Overall, the free movement jurisprudence oscillates between single regulation and multiple regulation: in some cases multiple regulation amounts to obstacle to trade (*Cassis de Dijon*), in other cases it does not (*Damseaux*, *Markus Stoß*, *Bouchoucha*); even when it obstructs trade, multiple regulation can be justified by the proportionate pursuit of a legitimate policy objective. As the freedoms of movement apply to the most diverse factual situations and areas of law, a 'one-size-fits-all' free movement test is an illusion, for this test needs to be sufficiently adaptable to fit the particular reality of each and every case. Thus, although the same provisions apply, it can hardly be disputed that the importation of alcoholic beverages, the direct taxation of dividends or the regulation of broadcasting and gambling services call for differentiated interpretations. In that connection, Weatherill extensively wrote on the 'conditional regulatory autonomy' of the host State, which derives from the free movement jurisprudence:

> The space allowed to a host State to justify its rules means that it is at least possible that dual regulation will occur. But these circumstances are limited by the rules of the

[31] Case 120/78 *Rewe-Zentral ('Cassis de Dijon')* [1979] ECR 649, para 14.
[32] See section IV.A.
[33] See eg Barnard, *The Substantive Law of the EU* (n 5) chs 5, 6 and 16.

> Treaty, boldly interpreted by the Court. ... The host State enjoys conditional regulatory autonomy—the precise determination of whether or not it has met the necessary conditions belongs with the Court. ... It is in this regard noticeable that at least rhetorically the Court has accepted the importance of balancing the several interests at stake. Free movement does not have any automatic priority and in this sense the Court is in such cases particularly sensitive to protection of the host State's (admittedly conditional) regulatory autonomy, declaring it to enjoy a margin of discretion in such circumstances.[34]

To sum up, multiple regulation is incompatible with economic integration, be it defined as regulatory neutrality or regulatory competition, for the reasons evoked in relation to protectionism: multiple regulation distorts business competition and hampers both consumer and producer arbitrage. However, multiple regulation may be endorsed under Union law, when other legitimate policy objectives pursued by Member States prevail over the objective of economic integration.

III. The Eventuality of Positive Harmonisation

Although for different reasons, both the regulatory neutrality and the regulatory competition paradigms advocate that every trade flow competing throughout the internal market be regulated *only once* (suppression of protectionism and multiple regulation). Three regulatory modes subject cross-border flows to a single regulation: Union regulation, host regulation and home regulation, which confer exclusive jurisdiction respectively to the Union, the host State and the home State.

Union regulation, often labelled as 'positive harmonisation' by Union legislature,[35] is the most obvious way to achieve the objective of single regulation, as it consists in replacing all national laws by one unique legislation adopted at the Union level. At the inception of the European Communities, harmonisation by the Union legislature was perceived as the only method that would permit the achievement of the internal market from a multiple jurisdiction perspective, once protectionism (single jurisdiction perspective) had been outlawed.[36] For instance, the 1968 and 1969 Council General Programmes explicitly relied on harmonisation

[34] S Weatherill, 'Fitting "Abuse of Rights" into EU Law Governing the Free Movement of Goods and Services' in R de la Feria and S Vogenauer (eds), *Prohibition of Abuse of Law: a New General Principle of EU Law?* (Oxford, Hart Publishing, 2011) 53–54.

[35] The concept of 'positive harmonization' aims at the role of the Union legislature in a particular area of law, and 'negative harmonization' at the role of the Court of Justice: see C Barnard and S Deakin, 'Negative and Positive Harmonization of Labor Law in the European Union' (2002) 8 *Columbia Journal of European Law* 389.

[36] See eg Weatherill, 'Fitting "Abuse of Rights" into EU Law' (n 34) 56: 'In the late 1970s, harmonisation was seen as a good deal more politically feasible and economically desirable than it is today'; SK Schmidt, 'The Impact of Mutual Recognition—Inbuilt Limits and Domestic Responses to the Single Market' (2002) 9 *Journal of European Public Policy* 935, 937: 'Originally, the European Community (EC) attempted to achieve the common market by fully harmonizing divergent national regulations'.

to eliminate technical barriers to trade resulting respectively from 'disparities between national legislations' and 'disparities between the provisions laid down by law, regulation or administrative action in Member States'.[37]

As a matter of fact, through the prism of regulatory neutrality, diversity among national laws generates differentials of regulation between domestic and cross-border flows, which by hypothesis are regulated by different Member States ('host' and 'home'). Therefore, diversity among national laws creates distortions originating in regulation and affecting competition among private goods and services; in other words, regulatory diversity creates obstacles to economic integration when the latter is defined as regulatory neutrality:

> Inter-State regulatory diversity causes a barrier to inter-State trade.[38]

> [Legal barriers] stem from difficulties caused by divergent national regulations.[39]

> National treatment, Commission officials argued, was not sufficient to guarantee the completion of the internal market. … In product regulation the major trade impediment was considered to be regulatory diversity.[40]

Positive harmonisation by the Union legislature constitutes the only possibility of removing those distortions of competition stemming from regulatory diversity among national laws: as stated by von Quitzow, '[differences in national laws] result in distortions of cross-border competitive relations. The only way to clear away such distortions according to the existing Treaty rules is harmonisation'.[41] This explains why harmonisation was once considered as a 'superior alternative' to mutual recognition, 'because it aimed straight at the root cause of the problem of regulatory diversity'.[42] Only harmonisation can create a true level playing field throughout the internal market: in Maduro's terminology, '[the centralised model] not only allows access to national markets but also guarantees equal conditions of competition in regard to the legal regimes to which products are subjected'.[43] Under the influence of the regulatory neutrality paradigm, uniformity has always been an objective of internal market law:

> After all, internal market rhetoric, with its insistence on the removal of 'distortions' of competition and equalisation of the conditions of competition and the fundamental

[37] Council (EC), 'General Programme for the elimination of technical barriers to trade which result from disparities between national legislations' (Resolution), 7 March 1968, C48/24; Council (EC), 'General Programme for the elimination of technical barriers to trade which result from disparities between the provisions laid down by law, regulation or administrative action in Member States' (Resolution), 28 May 1969, C76/1.

[38] Weatherill (n 34) 51.

[39] Commission Report on the state of the internal market for services (n 21) 14.

[40] P Genschel, 'Why no Mutual Recognition of VAT? Regulation, Taxation and the Integration of the EU's Internal Market for Goods' (2007) 14 *Journal of European Public Policy* 743, 745.

[41] CM von Quitzow, *State Measures Distorting Free Competition in the EC* (The Hague, Kluwer Law International, 2002) 29 and chs 7 to 9.

[42] Genschel, 'Why no Mutual Recognition of VAT?' (n 40) 747.

[43] Maduro (n 19) 110.

(economic) rights of all (market) citizens in the Community-wide single market, points towards uniformity rather than diversity and flexibility. While exceptions to the paradigm of uniformity might be tolerated, they would still be perceived as exceptional and anomalous.[44]

In stark contrast with regulatory neutrality, the regulatory competition paradigm adamantly opposes any attempt to suppress diversity among national laws, for this diversity is a prerequisite of any competitive process: 'When regulatory competition is a substitute for harmonization, internal market forces would respond to differences in national regulation'.[45] Indeed, harmonisation by the Union legislature removes every possibility of comparison and ipso facto of arbitrage among national laws by consumers or producers, since every trade flow is made subject to the sole Union legislation: 'Full harmonisation would eliminate … regulatory competition'.[46] Under the regulatory competition paradigm, harmonisation can thus be described as a situation of monopoly—with all related anticompetitive evils: '[Regulatory competition] would damn harmonisation itself as anti-competitive',[47] for 'how can it be ensured that the activities of such a state as a monopolist will fulfill the preferences of its constituents?'.[48]

As a consequence, Treaty provisions enabling the Union legislature to adopt harmonising measures constitute archetypal manifestations of the regulatory neutrality paradigm.[49] Article 114 TFEU (former 95 EC) provides a general legal basis for the adoption of 'measures for the approximation of the provisions laid down by law, regulation or administrative action in Member States which have as their object the establishment and functioning of the internal market'. In the first *Tobacco Advertising* judgment, the Court ruled that Article 114 TFEU did not vest in the Union legislature a general power to regulate the internal market, but a limited power to adopt measures that contribute to eliminating likely obstacles to free movement and to removing appreciable distortions of competition.[50] As a matter of fact, if economic integration is defined as regulatory neutrality, diversity among national laws distorts competition among private goods, and *therefore* amounts to

[44] N Bernard, 'Flexibility in the European Single Market' in Barnard and Scott (n 2) 101–02.
[45] J Pelkmans and J-M Sun, 'Regulatory Competition in the Single Market' (1995) 33 *Journal of Common Market Studies* 67, 70.
[46] W Kerber and R Van den Bergh, 'Mutual Recognition Revisited: Misunderstandings, Inconsistencies, and a Suggested Reinterpretation' (2008) 61 *Kyklos* 447, 453.
[47] S Weatherill, 'Why Harmonise?' in T Tridimas and P Nebbia (eds), *European Union Law for the Twenty-First Century—Volume 2: Internal Market and Free Movement Community Policies* (Oxford, Hart Publishing, 2004) 14. See also C Barnard and S Deakin, 'Market Access and Regulatory Competition' in Barnard and Scott (n 2) 199 and 201; S Deakin, 'Legal Diversity and Regulatory Competition: Which Model for Europe?' (2006) 12 *European Law Journal* 440, 441; S Deakin, 'Is Regulatory Competition the Future for European Integration?' (2006) 13 *Swedish Economic Policy Review* 71, 75.
[48] W Kerber, 'Interjurisdictional Competition within the European Union' (1999–2000) 23 *Fordham International Law Journal* 217, 223.
[49] See arts 67, 81, 82, 83, 113, 114, 115 and 191 TFEU.
[50] Case C-376/98 *Germany v Parliament and Council ('Tobacco Advertising I')* [2000] ECR I-8419, paras 83 and 95.

an obstacle to trade. Taken to its extreme, regulatory neutrality would confer an infinite scope to Article 114 TFEU. De Witte wrote:

> Those two aims correspond to the two justifications for making legal rules and principles more uniform across jurisdictions that are most often cited in the economic analysis literature, namely: transboundary externalities and fair competition.[51]

This reading of Article 114 TFEU in light of the regulatory neutrality paradigm helps an understanding of why, in practice, the Court almost never annuls Union legislation (with the notable exception of the first *Tobacco Advertising* judgment), thereby conferring considerable autonomy from judicial review upon the Union legislature. Once there is a consensus to view diversity among national laws as a source of distortions of business competition, in accordance with the regulatory neutrality paradigm, any harmonising measure is likely to pass the test set out in *Tobacco Advertising*. Thus, Weatherill could rightly observe that the Court's case law in this field has become little more than a 'drafting guide' for the Union legislature:

> The pattern is circular: the Court presents a formula which defines the proper scope of legislative harmonization and which sets out the control exercised by the principles of proportionality and subsidiarity, the EU legislature duly adopts the approved but reliably vague vocabulary and, provided the drafting is well chosen, the Court has no plausible basis on which to set aside the legislative act. Case law dealing with the limits of EU competence has been converted into no more than a 'drafting guide' for the EU legislature.[52]

Countless harmonising laws are explicitly justified by the need to suppress 'distortions of competition' generated by disparity among national laws, which necessarily aims at competition among private businesses (regulatory neutrality).[53] Conversely, whenever regulatory competition is—consciously or not—adopted as paradigm of economic integration, a positive harmonisation by Union legislature is unlikely. In that connection, it must be underlined that the regulatory competition paradigm demonstrates natural affinities with the principle of subsidiarity, formalised by the Maastricht Treaty (1992).[54]

[51] B de Witte, 'A Competence to Protect: The Pursuit of Non-Market Aims through Internal Market Legislation' in P Syrpis (ed), *The Judiciary, the Legislature and the EU Internal Market* (Cambridge, Cambridge University Press, 2011) 26; citing A Ogus, 'Competition between National Legal Systems: A Contribution of Economic Analysis to Comparative Law' (1999) 48 *International and Comparative Law Quarterly* 405, 416.

[52] S Weatherill, 'The Limits of Legislative Harmonization Ten Years after Tobacco Advertising: How the Court's Case Law has become a "Drafting Guide"' (2011) 12 *German Law Journal* 827, 828.

[53] See ch 6 nn 47–49 and accompanying text.

[54] See European Economic and Social Committee (EC), 'Mutual recognition in the single market' (Opinion), 29 November 2000, C116/14, no 3.6.1; Commission (EC), 'Mutual recognition in the context of the follow-up to the action plan for the single market' (Communication) COM (99) 299 final, 16 June 1999; Kerber, 'Interjurisdictional Competition within the European Union' (n 48) 218; Pelkmans and Sun, 'Regulatory Competition in the Single Market' (n 45) 88; G Majone, 'Mutual Recognition in Federal Type Systems', EUI Working Paper, SPS 1993/1, available at http://hdl.handle.net/1814/231, 11:

> [T]he great merit of the principle [of mutual recognition] is that it replaces centralized by decentralized decision making, in the spirit of the subsidiarity principle, and thus makes possible competition among different regulatory approaches.

By way of illustration, this vision of economic integration as regulatory neutrality was clearly exposed by the Union legislature in the preamble to Directive 2001/84 on the resale right for the authors of works of art:

> The resale right is currently provided for by the domestic legislation of a majority of Member States. Such laws, where they exist, display certain differences, notably as regards the works covered, those entitled to receive royalties, the rate applied, the transactions subject to payment of a royalty, and the basis on which these are calculated. The application or non-application of such a right has a significant impact on the competitive environment within the internal market, since the existence or absence of an obligation to pay on the basis of the resale right is an element which must be taken into account by each individual wishing to sell a work of art. This right is therefore a factor which contributes to the creation of distortions of competition as well as displacement of sales within the Community.
>
> Such disparities with regard to the existence of the resale right and its application by the Member States have a direct negative impact on the proper functioning of the internal market in works of art as provided for by Article 14 of the Treaty. In such a situation Article 95 of the Treaty constitutes the appropriate legal basis.[55]

In short, the Union legislature justified the need for Union harmonisation by pointing to the distortions of competition and the displacement of sales provoked by diversity among national laws. The negative appraisal of 'displacement of sales' recalls the controversy on the function of national laws in a process of economic integration:[56] if national laws are to be neutral, they should not provoke displacements of sales, which explains the need for Union harmonisation (regulatory neutrality); conversely, if national laws ought to act as magnets, displacements of sales are desirable indeed and no harmonisation is needed (regulatory competition). This dilemma on the function of national laws, which is reflected in opposite approaches to Union harmonisation, can also be identified in the following statement:

> The concept of internal market rests on a paradox: it encourages cross-border movement but the latter is fostered by the preservation of national disparities ..., which on the other hand constitute hindrances to international exchanges.[57]

To sum up, harmonisation by the Union legislature raises a first dilemma in the regulation of the internal market owing to the ambivalence of the notion of economic integration: Union regulation represents the ideal regulatory mode for regulatory neutrality, but the worst one for regulatory competition.

[55] Directive 2001/84/EC of the European Parliament and of the Council of 27 September 2001 on the resale right for the benefit of the author of an original work of art [2001] OJ L272/32, rec 9–10.

[56] See ch 6 section I.

[57] M Fallon, 'La délocalisation comme instrument de fraude lié à la circulation des biens et des personnes' in J Verhoeven (ed), *La loyauté: mélanges offerts à Etienne Cerexhe* (Brussels, Larcier, 1997), 166, free translation.

IV. The Negative Harmonisation Conundrum

Whenever a harmonisation by the Union legislature is viewed as undesirable (regulatory competition) or unachievable (regulatory neutrality), the objective of single regulation ineluctably leads to another hard choice, captured by the negative harmonisation conundrum. Indeed, in the absence of positive harmonisation, single regulation can be achieved through either home regulation or host regulation.

A. Home Regulation and Host Regulation

There is considerable uncertainty as to the exact meaning of commonly used concepts such as 'mutual recognition', 'home country principle' or 'host country principle'. Host country principle, for instance, suggest that cross-border flows are subject to host law, but is commonly used for situations characterised by multiple regulation.[58] Home country principle or home state control usually describes situations in which the host State is deprived of all regulatory powers, so that cross-border flows are only subject to home law. Mutual recognition is by far the most ambiguous concept of the three. The principle of mutual recognition is traditionally associated with the following excerpts of the *Cassis de Dijon* ruling:

> Obstacles to movement within the Community resulting from disparities between the national laws relating to the marketing of the products in question must be accepted in so far as those provisions may be recognized as being necessary in order to satisfy mandatory requirements relating in particular to the effectiveness of fiscal supervision, the protection of public health, the fairness of commercial transactions and the defence of the consumer. ...
>
> There is therefore no valid reason why, provided that they have been lawfully produced and marketed in one of the Member States, [products] should not be introduced into any other Member State.[59]

The importance of these two foundational paragraphs cannot be overstated, as they establish the principle according to which incoming goods should not be subject to multiple regulation. Unfortunately, this principle has been the object of contrasted interpretations. The Commission initially interpreted *Cassis de Dijon* as imposing automatic mutual recognition, which would lead to home state control:

> Any product imported from another Member State must in principle be admitted to the territory of the importing Member State if it has been lawfully produced, that is, conforms to rules and processes of manufacture that are customarily and traditionally accepted in the exporting country, and is marketed in the territory of the latter. ... Only under very strict conditions does the Court accept exceptions to this principle.[60]

[58] See eg Armstrong (n 2) 229.

[59] Case 120/78 *Rewe-Zentral ('Cassis de Dijon')* [1979] ECR 649, paras 8 and 14.

[60] Commission (EC), 'The consequences of the judgment given by the Court of Justice on 20 February 1979 in case 120/78 (Cassis de Dijon)' (Communication), 3 October 1980, C256/2.

This interpretation by the Commission of *Cassis de Dijon* is implicitly grounded on the assumption that the laws of the Member States are roughly equivalent:

> In principle, therefore, given the Council's recognition of the essential equivalence of the objectives of national legislation, mutual recognition could be an effective strategy for bringing about a common market in a trading sense.[61]

However, this interpretation has been criticised for minimising the impact of the 'mandatory requirements' exception.[62] Having due regard to this exception, a first group of scholars considered that *Cassis de Dijon* endorses conditional mutual recognition based on substantive equivalence. Under this approach, the host State retains the power to apply ordinary host law, but has the obligation to take into account the 'regulatory history' of cross-border flows:

> Mutual recognition requires that the regulatory history of a product, service or worker acquired in the home state cannot be ignored when it comes to considering what legitimate regulatory controls may be applied in the host state.[63]

The concrete impact of this interpretation is that the host State remains free to impose its own standards, when the standards of the home State are substantially lower:

> Where [mandatory] requirements are involved, mutual recognition is not automatically applicable: the host Member State retains the possibility of requiring that the degree of protection afforded by a product from another Member State is equivalent to that provided for in its national regulations.[64]

Another group of scholars, led by Weiler, argue that *Cassis de Dijon* imposes conditional mutual recognition based on functional equivalence, by virtue of which goods complying with the standards of the home State can be marketed in the host State provided the standards of the first State are functionally parallel to those of the second.[65] In more detail, Pelkmans wrote:

> The notion of mutual recognition [implies] that a good entering this member state from another EU country must be allowed unhindered access, even if the detailed specifications in the relevant domestic regulation differ from those in the country of origin, as long as the regulatory objectives are equivalent.[66]

[61] White Paper on completing the internal market (n 6) no 63.

[62] K Alter and S Meunier-Aitsahalia, 'Judicial Politics in the European Community: European Integration and the Pathbreaking Cassis de Dijon Decision' (1994) 26 *Comparative Political Studies* 535.

[63] Armstrong (n 2) 230.

[64] Commission (EC), 'Second biennial report on the application of the principle of mutual recognition in the single market' COM (2002) 419 final, 23 July 2002, 5; see also A Mattera, 'The Principle of Mutual Recognition and Respect for National, Regional and Local Identities and Traditions' in FK Padoa-Schioppa (ed), *The Principle of Mutual Recognition in the European Integration Process* (Basingstoke, Palgrave Macmillan, 2005) 17.

[65] JHH Weiler, 'Mutual Recognition, Functional Equivalence and Harmonization in the Evolution of the European Common Market and the WTO' in Padoa-Schioppa, *The Principle of Mutual Recognition in the European Integration Process* (n 64) 45–47.

[66] J Pelkmans, 'Mutual Recognition in Goods and Services: an Economic Perspective' in Padoa-Schioppa (n 64) 87.

The difference—if any—between substantive equivalence and functional equivalence would be the following: substantive equivalence compares the level of protection afforded under host and home laws, whereas functional equivalence compares their functions (eg protection of environment versus protection of consumers).

This high degree of terminological uncertainty accounts for the use of the notions of multiple regulation, home regulation and host regulation in this study. As explained above, *multiple regulation* means that cross-border flows are subject to both home and host laws. Under *home regulation*, cross-border flows must only abide by the standards of the home State, even when the standards imposed by the host state are higher. Conversely, under *host regulation*, cross-border flows must abide by the higher standards imposed by the host State. Union law regularly has recourse to both home and host regulation.

On the one hand, home regulation has been endorsed in directives creating a 'single passport' in the financial area. In the preamble to Directive 2006/48 on credit institutions, this technique is described as follows:

> It is appropriate to effect only the essential harmonisation necessary and sufficient to secure the mutual recognition of authorisation and of prudential supervision systems, making possible the granting of a single licence recognised throughout the Community and the application of the principle of home Member State prudential supervision.[67]

Accordingly, Article 16 of the directive provides that 'Host Member States may not require authorisation or endowment capital for branches of credit institutions authorised in other Member States'. In other words, the 'single passport' technique is another appellation for home regulation:

> All 'single passport' Financial Services Directives (banks, insurance, investment services) have a principle in common: a financial services provider which has been incorporated in accordance with the laws of a Member State (and has its head office therein) is entitled to a so-called 'single passport' which gives it the right to sell its services in all other Member States.[68]

Reorganisation measures and winding up of credit institutions are similarly subject to home regulation. The sixth recital of Directive 2001/24 on the reorganisation and winding up of credit institutions reads as follows:

> The administrative or judicial authorities of the home Member State must have sole power to decide upon and to implement the reorganisation measures provided for in the law and practices in force in that Member State. Owing to the difficulty of harmonising Member States' laws and practices, it is necessary to establish mutual recognition by the

[67] Directive 2006/48/EC of the European Parliament and of the Council of 14 June 2006 relating to the taking up and pursuit of the business of credit institutions [2006] OJ L177/1, rec 7; see also ch 4 nn 91–95 and accompanying text.

[68] M Dassesse, 'Localization of Financial Services: Regulatory and Tax Implications' in M Andenas and W-H Roth (eds), *Services and Free Movement in EU Law* (Oxford, Oxford University Press, 2003) 385; see also E Lomnicka, 'The Home Country Control Principle in the Financial Services Directives and the Case Law' in Andenas and Roth, *Services and Free Movement in EU Law* (n 68).

> Member States of the measures taken by each of them to restore to viability the credit institutions which it has authorised.[69]

Article 3 provides that the administrative or judicial authorities of the home State shall alone be empowered to decide on the implementation of reorganisation measures in a credit institution, and that these reorganisation measures shall be applied in accordance with the laws of the home State. Directive 2001/17 sets up a similar regime for the reorganisation and winding-up of insurance undertakings.[70] Another illustration of home regulation is provided by Directive 91/439 on the mutual recognition of driving licences, whose Article 2(1) provides that 'driving licences issued by Member States shall be mutually recognized'.[71]

Home regulation may also be imposed by the Court when interpreting the freedoms of movement. In the *Centros* line of case law, for instance, the Court ruled that the host State (Denmark) could not apply its national laws to a company incorporated according to the laws of another State (United Kingdom), even where the company exclusively conducted business in the host State. The Court systematically rejected hypothetical 'mandatory requirements' that could justify the application of host law to companies present in several Member States. In *Überseering*, the Court made clear that companies are subject to home regulation:

> Thus, despite the general terms in which paragraph 23 of Daily Mail and General Trust is cast, the Court did not intend to recognise a Member State as having the power, vis-à-vis companies validly incorporated in other Member States and found by it to have transferred their seat to its territory, to subject those companies' effective exercise in its territory of the freedom of establishment to compliance with its domestic company law.[72]

On the other hand, and by contrast with home regulation, host regulation subjects cross-border flows to the standards of the host State, without however leading to multiple regulation. Accordingly, host regulation demands that the 'regulatory history' of cross-border flows be taken into account, which can be done in two different ways: either the impact of home law is erased before applying ordinary host law; or the application of host law is adjusted in order to take into account the impact of home law.

The first method, consisting in erasing the impact of home law before applying host law, can be usefully illustrated with the VAT system set up at Union level. Indeed, every time a good crosses an internal border, a 'border tax adjustment' occurs by which the home State reimburses the VAT perceived, and the host

[69] Directive 2001/24/EC of the European Parliament and of the Council of 4 April 2001 on the reorganisation and winding up of credit institutions [2001] OJ L125/15.

[70] Directive 2001/17/EC of the European Parliament and of the Council of 19 March 2001 on the reorganisation and winding-up of insurance undertakings [2001] OJ L110/28.

[71] Council Directive 91/439/EEC of 29 July 1991 on driving licences [1991] OJ L237/1.

[72] Case C-208/00 *Überseering* [2002] ECR I-9919, para 72; see also Case C-210/06 *Cartesio* [2008] ECR I-9641; Case C-167/01 *Inspire Art* [2003] ECR I-10155; Case C-212/97 *Centros* [1999] ECR I-1459; Case 79/85 *Segers* [1986] ECR 2375.

State demands payment of the VAT at its domestic rate. As better explained by Genschel,

> Border tax adjustments are necessary in order to ensure that imports and domestic goods compete on an equal VAT footing: exports have to receive a refund for VAT paid to the exporting country (country of origin) and imports have to pay VAT to the importing country (destination country) in order to ensure that they are taxed at the same level as products originating from the import country.[73]

In other situations, the regulatory history of a trade flow can be easily 'severed' (instead of 'erased', as in the VAT regime), because the laws at stake impose recurrent obligations that can be divided over time. This severability is characteristic of tax, labour and social obligations imposed upon workers, who as a rule are subject to the laws of the Member State in which they are employed, as provided for by Article 45(2) TFEU and several instruments of secondary legislation.[74] Article 3 of Regulation 1408/71 on social security schemes applicable to migrant workers provides that migrant workers 'shall be subject to the same obligations and enjoy the same benefits under the legislation of any Member State as the nationals of the State'. Under Article 7 of Regulation 1612/68, migrant workers are entitled to equal treatment with national workers, in particular with regard to remuneration, tax and social advantages.[75] In other words, whenever a worker moves to another Member State, the regulatory powers of the country of origin (home) are automatically pre-empted to the benefit of the country of destination (host), without giving rise to multiple regulation. As a consequence, migrant workers are not entitled to 'export' the laws of their State of origin; rather, they are immediately subject to the laws of their State of destination:

> [T]here is no basis in Community law for a principle of regime portability in favour of workers—in other words, a worker moving from a more to a less regulative Member State cannot insist on taking the protection of the labour law of the state of origin with them.[76]

As nicely summed up by AG Fennelly, 'the migrant worker must take the national employment market as he finds it'.[77] Moreover, the Court has validated the application of host regulation to migrant workers on countless occasions.[78] Similarly, host regulation is commonly applied within the scope of the freedom of establishment,

[73] Genschel (n 40) 746.

[74] See ch 4 n 240.

[75] See KS Ziegler, '"Abuse of Law" in the Context of the Free Movement of Workers' in de la Feria and Vogenauer, *Prohibition of Abuse of Law* (n 34) 299.

[76] S Deakin, 'Regulatory Competition after Laval' (2007–08) 10 *Cambridge Yearbook of European Legal Studies* 581, 607; Ziegler, 'Abuse of Law' (n 75) 299.

[77] AG Fennelly, Case C-190/98 *Graf* [2000] ECR I-493, para 32.

[78] See, among many others, Case C-269/07 *Commission v Germany* [2009] ECR I-7811; Case C-158/07 *Förster* [2008] ECR I-8507; Case C-138/02 *Collins* [2004] ECR I-2703; Case 316/85 *Lebon* [1987] ECR 2811, para 11; Case 175/78 *Saunders* [1979] ECR 1129, para 10; Case C-164/99 *Portugaia Construções* [2002] ECR I-787, para 21; Joined Cases C-369/96 and C-376/96 *Arblade and Others* [1999] ECR I-8453, para 41; Case C-113/89 *Rush Portuguesa* [1990] ECR I-1417, para 18.

which presupposes 'the actual pursuit of an economic activity through a fixed establishment in the host Member State for an indefinite period'.[79] For instance, in relation to corporation tax, the Court judged in *National Grid Indus* that the preservation of the allocation of powers of taxation between the Member States justified that a transfer of tax residence entail a transfer of taxing powers to the host State:

> [L]egislation such as that at issue in the main proceedings is appropriate for ensuring the preservation of the allocation of powers of taxation between the Member States concerned. The final settlement tax levied at the time of the transfer of a company's place of effective management is intended to subject to the Member State of origin's tax on profits the unrealised capital gains which arose within the ambit of that State's power of taxation before the transfer of the place of management. Unrealised capital gains relating to an economic asset are thus taxed in the Member State in which they arose. Capital gains realised after the transfer of the company's place of management are taxed exclusively in the host Member State in which they have arisen, thus avoiding double taxation.[80]

The second method permitting to achieve host regulation consists in adjusting the application of host law in order to take into account the impact of home law. This second method is commonly used in the field of professional qualifications, in which Member States are obliged to take into account the qualifications received in other Member States, as clearly stated by the Court in *Vlassopoulou*:

> It must be stated in this regard that, even if applied without any discrimination on the basis of nationality, national requirements concerning qualifications may have the effect of hindering nationals of the other Member States in the exercise of their right of establishment guaranteed to them by Article 52 of the EEC Treaty. That could be the case if the national rules in question took no account of the knowledge and qualifications already acquired by the person concerned in another Member State.
>
> Consequently, a Member State which receives a request to admit a person to a profession to which access, under national law, depends upon the possession of a diploma or a professional qualification must take into consideration the diplomas, certificates and other evidence of qualifications which the person concerned has acquired in order to exercise the same profession in another Member State by making a comparison between the specialized knowledge and abilities certified by those diplomas and the knowledge and qualifications required by the national rules.[81]

The subsequent Directive 2005/36 on the recognition of professional qualifications is founded on the same principle: Article 14, entitled 'compensation measures', empowers the host State to require the applicant to complete an adaptation period of up to three years or to take an aptitude test, whenever there is a substantial difference between the requirements imposed in the home and

[79] Case C-378/10 *VALE Építési* [2012] ECR I-0000, para 34.
[80] Case C-371/10 *National Grid Indus* [2011] ECR I-12273, para 48.
[81] Case C-340/89 *Vlassopoulou* [1991] ECR I-2357, paras 15–16.

host States.[82] This second method is also commonly used in relation to tests and analyses imposed by Member States. According to settled case law, the host State is compelled to take account of any test carried out in another Member State:

> [W]hilst a Member State is free to require a product of the type in question, which has already received approval in another Member State, to undergo a fresh procedure of examination and approval, the authorities of the Member States are nevertheless required to assist in bringing about a relaxation of the controls existing in intra-Community trade and to take account of technical or chemical analyses or laboratory tests which have already been carried out in another Member State.[83]

In practice, compliance with this obligation requires a proactive attitude from the authorities of the host State:

> It follows that [the authorities of the Member States] are not entitled unnecessarily to require technical or chemical analyses or laboratory tests where those analyses and tests have already been carried out in another Member State and their results are available to those authorities, or may at their request be placed at their disposal.
>
> Strict compliance with that obligation requires an active approach on the part of the national body to which an application is made for approval of a product or recognition, in that context, of the equivalence of a certificate issued by an approval body of another Member State.[84]

In light of this distinction between home regulation and host regulation, how can the *Cassis de Dijon* principle be reinterpreted? Unfortunately, there is no easy or definitive answer to that question, for the type of regulation ensuing from *Cassis de Dijon* entirely depends on the impact of the mandatory requirements exception in concrete cases. When this exception is broadly interpreted, for instance as allowing the host State to enforce a level of regulation equivalent to its own standards (substantive equivalence), *Cassis de Dijon* tends to lead to host regulation.[85] When this exception is interpreted restrictively, for instance as precluding the application of host law whenever the objective pursued has been taken into account under home law (functional equivalence), *Cassis de Dijon* tends to lead to home regulation.[86]

[82] Directive 2005/36/EC of the European Parliament and of the Council of 7 September 2005 on the recognition of professional qualifications [2005] OJ L255/22; Bernard, 'Flexibility in the European Single Market' (n 44) 109.

[83] Case C-293/94 *Brandsma* [1996] ECR I-3159, para 12; see also Case 272/80 *Frans-Nederlandse Maatschappij voor Biologische Producten* [1981] ECR 3277, para 14; Case C-400/96 *Harpegnies* [1998] ECR I-5121, para 35.

[84] Case C-432/03 *Commission v Portugal* [2005] ECR I-9665, paras 46–47; see also Case 188/84 *Commission v France ('Woodworking Machines')* [1986] ECR 419, para 33.

[85] See eg Case C-110/05 *Commission v Italy ('Motorcycle Trailer')* [2009] ECR I-519, paras 59–69; Case C-142/05 *Mickelsson* [2009] ECR I-4273, paras 34–39; Case C-433/05 *Sandström* [2010] ECR I-2885, paras 32–40.

[86] See eg Case C-30/99 *Commission v Ireland ('Precious Metals')* [2001] ECR I-4619, paras 29–33; Case C-12/00 *Commission v Spain ('Chocolate')* [2003] ECR I-459, paras 85–94 (in which the objective pursued under host law had already been addressed under Union law, namely Directive 73/241).

However, as the Court interprets restrictively the justifications put forward by Member States in the presence of restrictions to free movement, it is commonly considered that *Cassis de Dijon* tends to promote home regulation in practice. In this pragmatic vein, Bernard wrote:

> [A]lthough the Court justifies its results on the basis of functional equivalence, by 'demonstrating' that there exist alternative means less restrictive of trade to satisfy the legitimate objective invoked by the host state, there is in reality rarely true functional parallelism. To take Weiler's own example drawn from Cassis de Dijon, labelling will not prevent some consumers from being misled as to the alcohol contents of a liqueur that does not correspond to their traditional expectations: 'some cannot read, others do not read'. To that extent, under the cover of functional parallelism, there may in fact lie de facto mutual recognition.[87]

Irrespective of the interpretation adopted in concrete cases, it cannot be denied that *Cassis de Dijon* imposes an obligation of mutual recognition upon the host State in order to overcome the problem of multiple regulation. Yet the scope of this obligation of mutual recognition is greater when *Cassis* is interpreted as requiring home regulation, rather than host regulation, as the host State is obliged to forego its higher standards.

In comparison, the interpretation of the subsequent *Keck* ruling appears rather simpler. *Keck* concerned the compatibility with the free movement of goods of a general prohibition on resale at a loss imposed under French law. Since it can be readily assumed that the home State does not regulate sales occurring onto the French territory, the French prohibition on resale at a loss does not lead to multiple regulation but only to host regulation. *Cassis de Dijon*, by contrast, concerned product requirements (minimum alcohol content) that were regulated by both home and host States, so that a choice had to be made between home regulation or host regulation in order to avoid multiple regulation.

> It is established by the case-law beginning with 'Cassis de Dijon' that, in the absence of harmonization of legislation, obstacles to free movement of goods which are the consequence of applying, to goods coming from other Member States where they are lawfully manufactured and marketed, rules that lay down requirements to be met by such goods (such as those relating to designation, form, size, weight, composition, presentation, labelling, packaging) constitute measures of equivalent effect prohibited by Article 30. This is so even if those rules apply without distinction to all products unless their application can be justified by a public-interest objective taking precedence over the free movement of goods.
>
> By contrast, contrary to what has previously been decided, the application to products from other Member States of national provisions restricting or prohibiting certain selling arrangements is not such as to hinder directly or indirectly, actually or potentially, trade between Member State within the meaning of the Dassonville judgment, so long as those provisions apply to all relevant traders operating within the national territory and

[87] In the same sense, see Bernard (n 44) 104.

> so long as they affect in the same manner, in law and in fact, the marketing of domestic products and of those from other Member States.[88]

Keck endorses host regulation with respect to aspects of cross-border flows that are not regulated by the home State, so that the application of host law affects 'in the same manner, in law and in fact, the marketing of domestic products and of those from other Member States' (absence of multiple regulation).[89] AG La Pergola elaborated a similar reasoning in the *Foie Gras* case: France could freely apply its domestic standards to imported 'foie gras' products without restricting free movement, since no other Member State had adopted legislative measures concerning the composition or production of such products.[90]

To sum up, home regulation subjects cross-border flows to the standards of the home State, whereas host regulation subjects them to the standards of the host State. Home regulation imposes an obligation of 'full' recognition upon the host State since it must forego its—eventual—higher standards. Host regulation can be achieved either by erasing the impact of home law before applying ordinary host law; or by obliging the host State to take it into account when applying host law, which implies a milder form of mutual recognition.

B. The Negative Harmonisation Conundrum

In a more systematic fashion, the consequences of home regulation and host regulation on the regulation of the internal market can be distinguished from the perspective of Member States, from the perspective of cross-border flows and from the perspective of equality among Union citizens.

First, from the perspective of Member States, home regulation implies that only one State, the 'home State' or country of origin, has jurisdiction to regulate cross-border flows, irrespective of the place in which activities are carried out:

> In this approach, provided there is compliance with the substantive and procedural regulatory requirements of the home state (or state in which market access is first sought), thereafter, market access to other markets ought to be permitted.[91]

In practice, home regulation deeply shakes the traditional conception of regulation, for Member States lose the power to regulate their domestic market as a whole, solely retaining the power to regulate domestic producers.[92] By contrast, under host regulation, every Member State retains jurisdiction to regulate activities carried out in their territory, but their interventions are coordinated in order to avoid multiple regulation of cross-border flows.

[88] Joined Cases C-267/91 and C-268/91 *Keck and Mithouard* [1993] ECR I-6097, paras 15–16.
[89] See also Case C-292/92 *Hünermund* [1993] ECR I-6787, paras 21–23.
[90] AG La Pergola, Case C-184/96 *Commission v France (Foie Gras)* [1998] ECR I-6197, para 37. The Court judged that the general prohibition imposed under French law was disproportionate.
[91] Armstrong (n 2) 299.
[92] See Kerber and Van den Bergh, 'Mutual Recognition Revisited' (n 46) 454.

Secondly, from the perspective of cross-border flows, home regulation entitles them to 'export' the standards of their home State throughout the internal market, which accordingly remain applicable irrespective of the State in which activities are carried out. By contrast, under host regulation, cross-border flows become subject to the standards of the new host State upon border crossing; to paraphrase AG Fennely, cross-border flows must take the host market as they find it.[93]

Thirdly and most importantly, home regulation and host regulation fulfil two different conceptions of equality, which can only be reconciled through Union harmonisation. On the one hand, host regulation subjects cross-border flows to the standards of the host State, thereby ensuring equal treatment between cross-border flows and the host society (country of destination). As such, host regulation generates 'host equality', namely identical regulatory conditions within the confines of every host State (level playing field). For instance, under Article 3 of Regulation 1408/71 and Article 7 of Regulation 1612/68, migrant workers become subject to the tax, labour and social laws of the host State, just as any other domestic worker.

On the other hand, under home regulation, cross-border flows remain subject to the standards of the home State, which preserves equal treatment between cross-border flows and the home society (country of origin). Accordingly, home regulation promotes another conception of equality,[94] usefully labelled as 'home equality', which creates identical regulatory conditions across borders and among activities originating in the same home State. In *Cassis de Dijon*, for instance, the liquor Cassis de Dijon remained subject to French law, just as the other liquors produced in France and sold throughout the internal market; and it was allowed to compete on the German market with liquors subject to German law.[95]

Therefore, home regulation and host regulation correspond to two conceptions of equality for cross-border flows, respectively host equality (equal treatment with host society) and home equality (equal treatment with home society). Maduro identified these two conceptions of equality under a different terminology, when he opposed reverse discriminations (breaches of host equality) to differences of treatment deriving from legislative disparities (breaches of home equality).[96]

This distinction between host and home equality permits to articulate the *negative harmonisation conundrum*. The negative harmonisation conundrum postulates that host and home equality cannot be simultaneously achieved through negative harmonisation. Indeed, absent positive harmonisation, cross-border flows cannot simultaneously benefit from equal treatment with their home society and with their host society. This conundrum, identified by Graetz and Warren

[93] See n 77 and accompanying text.

[94] In *Auer*, the Court observed that mutual recognition (home regulation) promoted a type of equality in conformity with the prohibition of discrimination on grounds of nationality: Case 136/78 *Auer* [1979] ECR 437, para 24.

[95] Armstrong (n 2) 299.

[96] Maduro (n 19) 154–57.

in the context of tax law,[97] can be usefully illustrated with a simple numerical example:

— *Proposition 1*: Danish and British laws impose different regulatory burdens of respectively 6 and 1 (absence of positive harmonisation);
— *Proposition 2*: Under host regulation, a British undertaking active in Denmark must be subject to the Danish burden of 6 (host equality);
— *Proposition 3*: Under home regulation, a British undertaking active in Denmark must be subject to the British burden of 1 (home equality).

The conundrum consists in that only two out of those three propositions can hold simultaneously. The simultaneous realisation of host and home equality (propositions 2 and 3) requires identical laws in both jurisdictions, which can only occur through positive harmonisation (proposition 1). Union regulation is indeed the only regulatory mode that suppresses regulatory diversity altogether within the internal market. Conversely, in the absence of positive harmonisation (proposition 1), a choice must be made between host and home equality (proposition 2 or 3); in other words, cross-border flows can benefit from equal treatment either with their home society or with their host society, but not with both simultaneously.

This conundrum accounts for numerous inconsistencies in the Court's case law on the freedoms of movement, in which host and home equality are successively upheld. For instance, the regulation of migrant workers is traditionally effectuated under host regulation, so that all workers of a national market are subject to the same tax, social and labour laws (host equality).[98] As a corollary, breaches of home equality, which result from disparities among the laws of Member States, do not amount to restrictions to free movement. In other words, workers cannot expect their migration to another Member State to be neutral in terms of regulation, which is indeed confirmed by countless statements of the Court regarding taxation, social security or criminal law:

> By prohibiting every Member State from applying its law differently on the ground of nationality, within the field of application of the Treaty, Articles [18 and 45 TFEU] are not concerned with any disparities in treatment which may result, between Member States, from divergences existing between the laws of the various Member States, so long as the latter affect all persons subject to them in accordance with objective criteria and without regard to their nationality.[99]

> [T]he Treaty offers no guarantee to a citizen of the Union that transferring his activities to a Member State other than that in which he previously resided will be

[97] MJ Graetz and AC Warren, Jr., 'Income Tax Discrimination and the Political and Economic Integration of Europe' (2006) 115 *Yale Law Journal* 1186, 1216–17. Under this version of the conundrum, 'capital export neutrality' (host equality) and 'capital import neutrality' (home equality) cannot be simultaneously achieved, except if taxation is identical in both countries.

[98] See nn 74–78 and accompanying text.

[99] Case 1/78 *Kenny* [1978] ECR 1489, para 18 (free movement of workers, social security).

> neutral as regards taxation. Given the relevant disparities in the tax legislation of the Member States, such a transfer may be to the citizen's advantage or not, according to circumstances.[100]

In a nutshell, if cross-border flows benefit from host equality, they cannot possibly be guaranteed home equality; as a consequence, their cross-border movement will not be neutral in terms of regulation, given the change of applicable host law. Full regulatory neutrality could only be achieved through Union harmonisation, which would indeed ensure both host and home equality.

Conversely, whenever home regulation is applied, breaches of home equality become restrictions to free movement, and conversely breaches of host equality become compatible with free movement, including reverse discriminations.[101] For instance, in the controversial *Laval* case,[102] the Court ruled that Laval should be allowed to export Latvian standards to Sweden (home equality); as a consequence, the Swedish trade unions' claim to host equality between Swedish workers and posted Latvian workers became a restriction to free movement. In so doing, the Court emulated the solution adopted by the Union legislature in the field of social security, under Article 14(1)(a) of Regulation 1408/71,[103] but reversed its own previous case law in the field of labour law (*Rush Portuguesa*).[104]

In sum, the negative harmonisation conundrum postulates that, absent positive harmonisation by Union legislature, the Court must choose between two irreconcilable conceptions of equality, which alternatively mould the concept of 'restriction to free movement': host equality, ensured by host regulation (equality between cross-border flows and host society, as in *Kenny* or *Schulz*); or home equality, guaranteed by home regulation (equality between cross-border flows and home society, as in *Laval*).

[100] Case C-240/10 *Schulz* [2011] ECR I-8531, para 42 (free movement of workers, taxation). See also among countless others Case C-403/03 *Schempp* [2005] ECR I-6421, para 34 (free movement of citizens, taxation); Case C-67/08 *Block* [2009] ECR I-883, para 35 (free movement of capital, taxation); Case C-379/92 *Peralta* [1994] ECR I-3453, para 34 (freedom of establishment, criminal law); Case C-365/02 *Lindfors* [2004] ECR I-7183, para 34 (free movement of citizens, taxation); Case C-208/07 *von Chamier* [2009] ECR I-6095, para 85 (free movement of citizens, social security); Case C-392/05 *Alevizos* [2007] ECR I-3505, para 76 and Case C-387/01 *Weigel* [2004] ECR I-4981, para 55 (free movement of workers, taxation); Case C-3/08 *Leyman* [2009] ECR I-9085, para 45; Joined Cases C-393/99 and C-394/99 *Hervein II* [2002] ECR I-2829, para 51; Case C-177/94 *Perfili* [1996] ECR I-161, para 17 (freedom to provide services, criminal law).

[101] See ch 8 section II.

[102] Case C-341/05 *Laval* [2007] ECR I-11767; see ch 8 section IV.

[103] Under art 14(1)(a) of Regulation 1408/71, home regulation applies to the social security of posted workers: see Case 35/70 *Manpower* [1970] ECR 1251, para 11; Case C-404/98 *Plum* [2000] ECR I-9379, para 20; Case C-202/97 *Fitzwilliam* [2000] ECR I-883, para 29.

[104] Case C-113/89 *Rush Portuguesa* [1990] ECR I-1417, para 18.

C. Addressing the Negative Harmonisation Conundrum

The previous subsection established the existence of the negative harmonisation conundrum, namely the impossibility to simultaneously achieve host and home equality in the absence of positive harmonisation. The central contention of this chapter is that the Court's choice between host and home equality is informed by two contradictory paradigms of economic integration: regulatory neutrality and regulatory competition. In a nutshell, regulatory neutrality requires host regulation, whereas regulatory competition demands home regulation.

On the one hand, the regulatory neutrality paradigm seeks to eliminate regulatory distortions affecting the competition among private businesses. As a consequence, it approves host regulation for it subjects trade flows competing within every national market to the same regulatory burden, as in *Kenny*, *Rush Portuguesa* or *National Grid Indus* (national level playing field). Quite obviously, in order to achieve regulatory neutrality, Union harmonisation remains a superior alternative to host regulation for it creates a Union-wide level playing field. For instance, Article 3(1) of Directive 96/71 on the posting of workers imposes host equality,[105] and its ratio legis was the creation of a national level playing field, as host equality eliminates distortions of competition both among employers and among employees competing in a given national market:

> [T]he equal treatment principle in the Posting of Workers Directive cuts both ways, guaranteeing, on the one hand, the equal treatment of undertakings in the context of the freedom to provide services, and, on the other, under Article 3, the equal treatment of posted employees under the locally applicable minimum terms and conditions of employment.[106]

By contrast, under home regulation, every trade flow competing in a national market remains subject to its respective home law. As a consequence, home regulation leads to differentials of regulation and ipso facto distortions of competition among businesses active in a given national market (absence of host equality). Armstrong observed:

> As will be evident, a pure model of home state control gives rise to a market in which each good or service only complies with one set of regulatory controls (the home state), but within the market as a whole, different goods and services will have complied with different home state controls.[107]

[105] Directive 96/71/EC of the European Parliament and of the Council of 16 December 1996 concerning the posting of workers in the framework of the provision of services [1996] OJ L18/1 art 3(1).

[106] Parliament (EC), 'Application of Directive 96/71/EC on the posting of workers' (Resolution), 20 December 2006, C313E/452, G; Case C-341/05 *Laval* [2007] ECR I-11767, paras 74–75; Case C-445/03 *Commission v Luxembourg* [2004] ECR I-10191, para 28; Case C-43/93 *Vander Elst* [1994] ECR I-3803, para 25.

[107] Armstrong (n 2) 299.

From a static perspective, such distortions of business competition flow from the mere coexistence of different legal regimes. Yet from a dynamic perspective, home regulation is also liable to generate trade deflections towards the most hospitable jurisdiction. Thus, the Court observed in *X* that the taxation of means of transport in the country in which the purchaser has his habitual residence (host State), instead of the country in which he acquires the means of transport (home State) is aimed at avoiding undesirable diversions of trade:

> [T]he rules pertaining to the taxation of acquisitions of new means of transport ... aim to prevent distortions of competition between the Member States liable to result from the application of differing rates of tax. If there were no transitional arrangements, the marketing of new means of transport would tend to be confined to Member States having a low VAT rate, to the detriment of the other Member States and their taxation revenue.[108]

On the other hand, the regulatory competition paradigm demands home regulation, since host regulation impairs both consumer and producer arbitrages. First, host regulation makes consumer arbitrage impracticable. Within every host State, consumers purchase goods and services abiding by the standards of the host State (host equality). In theory, consumers can still move to other Member States in order to acquire products regulated under other national laws. However, transportation costs make such consumer arbitrage likely to be severely restricted in volume and limited to adjacent Member States; in addition, certain host regulation regimes seek to prevent this form of consumer arbitrage, such as the VAT regime on the acquisition of new means of transport, evoked above. Conversely, under home regulation, consumers can choose among products subject to different national laws, since imported products remain subject to the standards of their home State (home equality). As a result, home regulation permits the confrontation of national laws within every national market, through the proxy of products subject to different national laws. By purchasing their preferred products, consumers indirectly arbitrate among national laws; thus, under the *Cassis de Dijon* ruling, consumers choosing between French and German liquors (eg Jägermeister versus Cassis de Dijon) indirectly arbitrage between French and German laws. In other words, the competition between Jägermeister and Cassis de Dijon acts as a proxy for the competition between German and French laws:

> The Cassis de Dijon principle can be seen as speeding-up regulatory competition, since in requiring free movement of goods subject to a mutual recognition principle, it not only sets into competition producers from different countries, but does the same for the different regulatory regimes under which they were producing.[109]

[108] Case C-84/09 *X* [2010] ECR I-11645, para 24.
[109] Deakin (n 47) 443.

Barnard and Deakin accurately described this effect of home regulation on regulatory competition:

> In practice, regulatory competition within the EC does not rest on migration alone. Given the practical barriers to free movement within the EC, in general, it is easier (or, less costly) for goods to move to persons rather than the other way round: therefore, free movement of goods acts as a proxy for free movement of persons. Thus the *Cassis de Dijon* principle, by requiring the receiving or 'host state' to open its markets to goods legitimately produced in any other Member State (the 'home state'), provides a vital additional mechanism for subjecting laws to the forces of regulatory competition. This is the essence of 'mutual recognition'. Consumers in the host state now have a choice of goods produced under different regulatory regimes. Competition between goods produced under different legal systems means, in effect, that the laws of those systems are thrown into competition with each other too.[110]

Secondly, host regulation impairs producer arbitrage as well, by which producers move their activities to another home State by reason of its more hospitable laws. As host regulation requires cross-border flows to abide by the standards of the host State, the eventual relocation of a producer in a new home State cannot alter the applicable (host) standards. For instance, under the common VAT regime, goods marketed in Germany by a French producer are subject to VAT in Germany (host regulation); the eventual relocation of this French producer to Romania is irrelevant in that regard. Kerber and Van den Bergh observed:

> The country of destination rule does not allow direct regulatory competition between product regulations, because even a relocation of firms does not change the requirement of compliance with the domestic regulations of the import countries.[111]

By contrast, home regulation enables producer arbitrage. Indeed, under home regulation, producers are entitled to export their home law throughout the internal market: the standards of the home State remain applicable irrespective of the place in which activities are carried out. Centros, for instance, was entitled to conduct business in Denmark while remaining subject to company law in the United Kingdom. Laval was entitled to post workers to Sweden while remaining subject to Latvian standards. Accordingly, home regulation facilitates both producer arbitrage as well as consumer arbitrage:

> Following this principle a company will only need to comply with one national rule for its products to be able to move freely throughout the entire common market. Firms could choose among the different national regulations, and consumers among the products complying with those different rules.[112]
>
> Regulatory competition between Member States would seem to be a natural consequence of mutual recognition … Mutual recognition will expose national regulation to the forces of arbitrage: consumers may choose between domestic regulation and that of

[110] Barnard and Deakin, Market Access and Regulatory Competition (n 47) 203.
[111] Kerber and Van den Bergh (n 46) 452.
[112] Maduro (n 19) 132.

any other member state by importing the relevant goods or services. To the extent that even production factors find it profitable to respond to regulatory differences, mutual recognition and free movement may induce cross-border factor flows.[113]

To sum up, the regulatory neutrality paradigm requires host regulation, for it establishes a national level playing field among private competitors within every Member State (host equality). By contrast, the regulatory competition paradigm demands home regulation for it enables both consumer and producer arbitrages (home equality). In the same sense, Weatherill sharply observed that home regulation distorts business competition but promotes State competition:

> [Home regulation] is typically characterised as creating distortions of competition within the Community, for costs incurred by economic operators vary State by State according to the chosen legal regime, and yet, on another level, it generates competition—between States as regulators.[114]

V. The Regulatory Mobility Dilemma

The present section is devoted to the fifth and last issue raised by the regulation of the internal market, namely regulatory mobility. Regulatory mobility represents the dynamic dimension of differentials of regulation; in other words, it seeks to capture the reaction of private individuals to differentials of regulation.

The issue of regulatory mobility is of crucial importance for the topic of the present study, namely the abuse of Union law. From the perspective of Union citizens, regulatory mobility measures the freedom to elect one's preferred national law. Accordingly, regulatory mobility overlaps with the issue of abuse of law, which was defined as an undesirable choice of law made by a private individual;[115] as explained above, ratifying cross-border abusive practices amounts to promoting regulatory mobility.[116] From the perspective of Member States, regulatory mobility can be defined as the ease with which private interests can be moved from one jurisdiction to another, with regulatory powers being transferred from the first State to the second.

The first objective of this section is to examine the relationship between regulatory mobility and the various regulatory modes of the internal market identified in the course of this chapter. Regulatory mobility is indeed not conceivable under multiple regulation or Union regulation (Subsection V.A), but well under home regulation or host regulation (Subsection V.B). Its second objective is to describe the

[113] Pelkmans, 'Mutual Recognition in Goods and Services' (n 66) 114.
[114] Weatherill, 'Pre-emption, Harmonisation and the Distribution of Competence' (n 25) 54.
[115] See ch 3.
[116] See pt II Introduction.

opposite normative assessments reached by the paradigms of regulatory neutrality and regulatory competition on the issue of regulatory mobility (Subsection V.C).

A. Regulatory Immobility under Multiple Regulation and Union Regulation

The impact of multiple regulation on regulatory mobility is quite straightforward, for it suppresses regulatory mobility altogether. Regulatory mobility aims at movements from a home jurisdiction to a host jurisdiction; that is, from one legal order to another. Multiple regulation, which consists in the cumulative application of home and host laws,[117] forces to regulatory immobility for it precludes Union citizens from 'putting [themselves] out of reach of the legislation of a Member State'.[118] Union citizens do not enjoy the freedom to move to another jurisdiction when both home and host States have the power to regulate their activities. For instance, the Court's decision to allow multiple regulation in the gambling sector[119] made it impossible for *Carmen Media Group* to circumvent German law by establishing itself in Gibraltar.[120] Similarly, in *Bouchoucha*, the Court endorsed multiple regulation on the ground that osteopathy qualifications were not mutually recognised, thereby allowing the French authorities to thwart a likely circumvention strategy:[121]

> [A]ccording to Knoors ... it is not possible to disregard the legitimate interest which a Member State may have in preventing certain of its nationals, by means of facilities created under the Treaty, from attempting to evade the application of their national legislation as regards vocational training.
>
> That is true in particular where the fact that a national of a Member State has obtained in another Member State a diploma whose scope and value are not recognized by any Community provision might place his Member State of origin under an obligation to allow him to exercise the activities covered by that diploma within its territory even though access to those activities is restricted there to the holders of a higher qualification ...
>
> It must therefore be stated ... that in the absence of harmonisation at Community level regarding activities which fall solely within the scope of the practice of medicine, Article 52 EEC does not preclude a Member State from restricting an activity ancillary to

[117] See section II.

[118] Case C-251/06 *ING. AUER* [2007] ECR I-9689, para 42:
The protection afforded by Community law does not therefore apply to situations in which a natural or legal person intends to rely abusively or fraudulently on Community provisions with the sole aim of putting itself out of reach of the legislation of a Member State.

[119] Case C-42/07 *Bwin* [2009] ECR I-7633, para 69; Joined Cases C-316/07, C-358/07 to C-360/07, C-409/07 and C-410/07 *Markus Stoß* [2010] ECR I-8069, paras 112–13; Case C-347/09 *Dickinger* [2011] ECR I-8185, para 96. See ch 4 n 209, ch 5 n 38 and accompanying text.

[120] Case C-46/08 *Carmen Media Group* [2010] ECR I-8149, paras 43–44. AG Mengozzi suggested that the behaviour at stake might qualify as abuse of law: AG Mengozzi, Case C-46/08 *Carmen Media Group* [2010] ECR I-8149, para 46.

[121] See A Noblet, *La lutte contre le contournement des droits nationaux en droit communautaire* (Lille, ANRT, 2004) 156.

medicine such as, in particular, osteopathy exclusively to persons holding the qualification of doctor of medicine.[122]

Similarly, a harmonisation by the Union legislature removes all possibilities of 'movement' across national legal orders, by unifying all existing national laws into a single Union legislation. Quite obviously, no choice of law can be made in presence of a unique legal regime. Barnard noted that '[centralisation] reduces the costs that stem from evasion, through forum shopping, externalisation, and extraterritoriality'.[123] In the context of US company law, Dammann similarly observed that free choice of law could be suppressed by having recourse either to a real seat theory or harmonisation at the federal level:

> Of course, the real seat rule, which gives the real seat state a regulatory monopoly vis-à-vis the corporation's internal affairs, is only one of two ways in which free choice can be eliminated. The other method is the imposition of a uniform 'federal' corporate law regime.[124]

On several occasions, the Court indirectly acknowledged the anti-abuse effect of a Union harmonisation:

> It is also important, in that context, to make clear that Member States are free to adopt or to maintain in force rules having the specific purpose of precluding from a tax benefit wholly artificial arrangements whose purpose is to circumvent or escape national tax law. Furthermore, in so far as it may be possible to identify other, less restrictive measures, such measures in any event require harmonisation rules adopted by the Community legislature.[125]

> Community law does not preclude a Member State from adopting, in the absence of harmonisation, measures designed to prevent the opportunities created under the Treaty from being abused in a manner contrary to the legitimate interests of the State.[126]

> [T]he residence condition helps inter alia the fight against 'driving-licence tourism' in the absence of complete harmonisation of the laws of the Member States relating to the issuing of driving licences.[127]

It was even more explicit in the *Knoors* ruling, in which it openly acknowledged that harmonisation at Union level 'removes the causes of any abuse of law':

> [I]t should be emphasised that it is always possible for the Council … to remove the causes of any abuses of the law by arranging for the harmonisation of the conditions of training for a trade in the various Member States.[128]

[122] Case C-61/89 *Bouchoucha* [1990] ECR I-3551, paras 14–16.

[123] Barnard (n 5) 22; see also JC Dammann, 'Freedom of Choice in European Corporate Law' (2004) 29 *Yale Journal of International Law* 477, 480.

[124] Dammann, 'Freedom of Choice in European Corporate Law' (n 123) 480.

[125] Case C-446/03 *Marks & Spencer* [2005] ECR I-10837.

[126] Case C-19/92 *Dieter Kraus* [1993] ECR I-1663, para 34.

[127] Case C-184/10 Grasser [2011] ECR I-4057, para 27; Joined Cases C-329/06 and C-343/06 Wiedemann [2008] ECR I-4635, para 69.

[128] Case 115/78 *Knoors* [1979] ECR 399, para 27; see also Case C-446/03 *Marks & Spencer* [2005] ECR I-10837, para 58; Case C-212/97 *Centros* [1999] ECR I-1459, para 28.

Unification measures taken by the Union legislature can be explicitly spurred by their anti-abuse potential. For instance, Directive 98/84 created a common EU legal framework for combating illicit devices which allow unauthorised access to television services offered against payment.[129] This Directive was supplemented by a convention providing for the same legal regime and directed to non-Member States,[130] whose explicit function was the prevention of artificial relocations in non-Member States in order to avoid the legal regime set up by the Directive:

> Extensive, effective protection for services based on, or consisting of, conditional access appeared to be particularly necessary. In fact, may European states which are not members of the European Union may provide havens to the development or distribution of devices for hacking into conditional access services if their legal system does not provide for sanctions against this very specific hacking activity. It was therefore necessary to extend the provisions of Directive 98/84/EC and to create a common and effective framework at European level for the protection of these services.[131]

With regard to the mutual recognition of criminal penalties, the Commission advocated a minimum harmonisation, in order to prevent offenders from taking advantage of divergences between penalties in the Member States, by moving to a Member State in order to evade prosecution or the enforcement of penalties.[132] For the same motive, the Commission noted that the harmonising directives on insurance services had significantly mitigated the risk of abuse in relation to insurance regulations.[133]

Admittedly, 'internal' abuses of law can still be committed within the scope of harmonising legislation adopted at Union level, where such legislation establishes various legal regimes, as demonstrated by the *Emsland-Stärke* and *Halifax* cases. Nevertheless, a 'unification' of those legal regimes similarly removes the possibility of choice of law, and therefore the risk of internal abuse of law.[134] For instance,

[129] Directive 98/84/EC of the European Parliament and of the Council of 20 November 1998 on the legal protection of services based on, or consisting of, conditional access [1998] OJ L320/54.

[130] European Convention on the legal protection of services based on, or consisting of, conditional access (adopted 24 January 2001, entered into force 1 July 2003) 2246 UNTS 29; Council (EC), Council Decision 2011/853/EU of 29 November 2011 on the signing, on behalf of the Union, of the European Convention on the legal protection of services based on, or consisting of, conditional access [2011] OJ L336/1.

[131] Commission (EC), 'Proposal for a Council Decision concerning the conclusion of the European Convention on the legal protection of services based on, or consisting of, conditional access' COM (2010) 755 final, 15 December 2010, no 9; see also Case C-137/12 *Commission v Council* [2013] ECR I-0000, para 61.

[132] Commission (EC), 'Approximation, mutual recognition and enforcement of criminal sanctions in the European Union' (Green Paper) COM (2004) 334 final, 30 April 2004, 9.

[133] Commission (EC), 'Freedom to provide services and the general good in the insurance sector' (Interpretative Communication), 16 February 2000, C43/5, 8:

> [T]his risk of abuse has been eliminated to a significant degree in the insurance sector as a result of the harmonisation achieved ... by the Community directives concerning the conditions for taking up and carrying on insurance activities.

[134] It is commonly observed that the common VAT regime has suppressed regulatory mobility by harmonising tax bases across Member States, and has conversely left room for abusive practices by not harmonising VAT rates and exemptions. Case C-255/02 *Halifax* [2006] ECR I-1609, para 67; Case C-240/05

in *UsedSoft v Oracle*, the Court adopted a broad interpretation of the concept of sale within the meaning of Article 4(2) of Directive 2009/24 in order to avoid the coexistence of several legal regimes, which would have been exploited to design circumvention strategies.[135]

In sum, regulatory mobility requires single regulation, but without Union regulation.

B. Regulatory Mobility under Home Regulation and Host Regulation

By contrast with multiple regulation and Union regulation, host regulation and home regulation structurally permit regulatory mobility, which does not imply that these regulatory modes are bound to promote regulatory mobility. Indeed, regulatory movements can be either impeded or encouraged under both host regulation and home regulation. As a consequence, each of them must be subdivided into two *alternative regulatory modes*, which are defined by their stance towards regulatory mobility (Figure 11).

The regulatory mobility dilemma consists in that, whenever recourse is made to host regulation or home regulation, a choice must be made between impeding or facilitating regulatory movements across national jurisdictions (restricted versus free choice of law).

Home regulation can be turned into two distinct regulatory modes: restricted choice of home law or free choice of home law. This choice is well known in the field of company law, where it takes the form of an opposition between incorporation

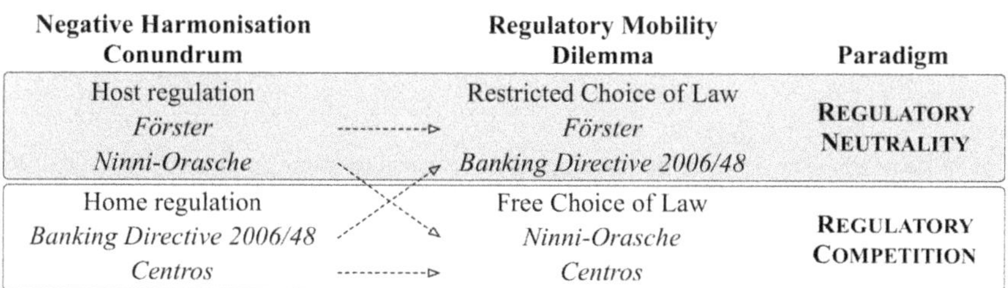

Figure 11– Negative Harmonisation Conundrum and Regulatory Mobility Dilemma

Eurodental [2006] ECR I-11479, para 57; Commission (EC), 'Towards tax co-ordination in the European Union: a package to tackle harmful tax competition' (Communication) COM (97) 495 final, 1 October 1997, no 21; White Paper on completing the internal market (n 114) no 161–69; C Amand, 'Prohibition of Abusive Practices in European VAT: Court Aid to National Legislations Bugs?' (2008) 36 *Intertax* 189, 194–95; R de la Feria, 'The European Court of Justice's Solution to Aggressive VAT Planning—Further towards Legal Uncertainty?' (2006) 15 *EC Tax Review* 27, 33. On the need for harmonisation in order to abolish the distortions of competition stemming from the transitional arrangements of the Sixth Directive, see Case C-240/05 *Eurodental* [2006] ECR I-11479, para 57; Case C-36/99 *Idéal Tourisme* [2000] ECR I-6049, para 39; Case C-305/97 *Royscot* [1999] ECR I-6671, para 31.

[135] Case C-128/11 *UsedSoft v Oracle* [2012] ECR I-0000, para 49; see ch 4 n 51 and accompanying text.

and real seat theories, which was described above.[136] The incorporation theory stipulates that companies are regulated by the Member State in which they are incorporated.[137] As a result, the incorporation theory de facto grants free choice of company law, since the election of the most convenient national law is made by a costless administrative act of incorporation in the relevant jurisdiction. It is common ground that the *Centros*-line of case law[138] marked the 'triumph' of the incorporation theory in European company law,[139] and accordingly constitutes a paramount illustration of free choice of home law. Indeed, Union citizens are entitled to freely elect the national law that will remain applicable to their company throughout the internal market, by an act of incorporation ('entry': *Centros*) or re-incorporation ('exit': *Cartesio*)[140] in their Member State of preference:

> [In Centros], the Court of Justice has created a market for corporate forms within the European Union, granting de facto a choice between the legal forms of now twenty-seven Member States.[141]

> The effect of the incorporation approach is that the applicable law is a matter of choice for managers of the company or, in the final analysis, for its shareholders.[142]

Conversely, home regulation is turned into restricted choice of home law when artificial movements across national jurisdictions are impeded. Under the real seat theory, companies are regulated by the Member State in which they have their 'real seat', that is their centre of administration or head office. As a consequence, the real seat theory tends to restrict the choice of the *lex societatis*: 'Since the costs of such a move [of headquarters] will usually outweigh the advantages connected with a more efficient corporate law regime, the real seat doctrine effectively prevents free choice'.[143] For instance, the Union legislature has required credit institutions to have their 'head office' and actually operate in their home country, namely the Member State whose law is applicable; this model was subsequently emulated

[136] See ch 4 section III.A and V.

[137] E Wymeersch, 'The Transfer of the Company's Seat in European Company Law' (2003) 40 *Common Market Law Review* 661, 661.

[138] Case C-212/97 *Centros* [1999] ECR I-1459, para 27; Case C-210/06 *Cartesio* [2008] ECR I-9641, paras 110–14; Case C-167/01 *Inspire Art* [2003] ECR I-10155; Case C-208/00 *Überseering* [2002] ECR I-9919.

[139] R de la Feria, 'Prohibition of Abuse of (Community) Law: the Creation of a New General Principle of EC Law through Tax' (2008) 45 *Common Market Law Review* 395, 405; T Tridimas, 'Abuse of Rights in EU Law: Some Reflections with Particular Reference to Financial Law' in de la Feria and Vogenauer (n 34) 178: '[Centros] may be seen as a triumph for the doctrine of incorporation and a corresponding defeat for the real seat doctrine'.

[140] See A Johnston and P Syrpis, 'Regulatory Competition in European Company Law after Cartesio' (2009) 34 *European Law Review* 378; AF de Sousa, 'Company's Cross-border Transfer of Seat in the EU after Cartesio' (2009) Jean Monnet Working Paper no 07/09, available at www.JeanMonnetProgram.org.

[141] W-G Ringe, 'Sparking Regulatory Competition in European Company Law—The Impact of the Centros Line of Case-Law and its Concept of "Abuse of Law"' in de la Feria and Vogenauer (n 34) 115.

[142] Barnard and Deakin, 'Negative and Positive Harmonization of Labor Law in the European Union' (n 35) 395.

[143] Dammann (n 123) 480; see also Barnard and Deakin (n 35) 395; Case C-210/06 *Cartesio* [2008] ECR I-9641, para 105; Case C-208/00 *Überseering* [2002] ECR I-9919, paras 15–16.

in other directives on financial services and in broadcasting directives.[144] In its reference for a preliminary ruling in the *Überseering* case, the Bundesgerichtshof highlighted the opposite repercussions of the incorporation and real seat theories upon the possibility to elect one's preferred company law:

> [W]here the connecting factor is taken to be the place of incorporation, the company's founding members are placed at an advantage, since they are able, when choosing the place of incorporation, to choose the legal system which suits them best. Therein lies the fundamental weakness of the incorporation principle, which fails to take account of the fact that a company's incorporation and activities also affect the interests of third parties and of the State in which the company has its actual centre of administration, where that is located in a State other than the one in which the company was incorporated.
>
> [W]here the connecting factor is taken to be the actual centre of administration, that prevents the provisions of company law in the State in which the actual centre of administration is situated, which are intended to protect certain vital interests, from being circumvented by incorporating the company abroad.[145]

In sum, the incorporation theory leads to free choice of home law, and the real seat theory to restricted choice of home law. Just as home regulation, host regulation can be turned into two regulatory modes as well: restricted choice of host law or free choice of host law. This choice is well known in relation to the free movement of natural persons, in which host regulation is ordinarily applied: as a rule, migrant citizens are indeed subject to the laws of the host State.[146]

On the one hand, the entitlement of Union citizens to welfare benefits tends to be subject to a requirement of genuine integration into the host society (restricted choice of host law).[147] In essence, Union institutions use this requirement of genuine integration to manage the tension between the right of migrant citizens to transnational solidarity and the right of Member States to safeguard the integrity of their social security system by preventing 'abuses of host law' in the form of benefit tourism.[148] For instance, in *Bidar* and *Förster*, the Court held that the attribution of study grants to migrant citizens could be subjected to uninterrupted residence requirements of three and five years.[149] Similarly, the Union legislature structured Directive 2004/38 on the free movement of Union citizens around an incremental approach to transnational solidarity,[150] by defining three categories

144 See ch 4 section III.A.

145 Case C-208/00 *Überseering* [2002] ECR I-9919, paras 15–16.

146 See section IV.A.

147 See ch 4 section III.B.ii.

148 O Golynker, 'Jobseekers' Rights in the European Union: Challenges of Changing the Paradigm of Social Colidarity' (2005) 30 *European Law Review* 111, 117.

149 Case C-209/03 *Bidar* [2005] ECR I-2119, paras 57–60; Case C-158/07 *Förster* [2008] ECR I-8507, paras 51–60.

150 C Barnard, 'Case C-209/03 Bidar' (2005) 42 *Common Market Law Review* 1465, 1478: '[T]he longer migrants reside in the Member State, the more integrated they are in that State and the greater the number of benefits they receive on equal terms with nationals'; see also C O'Brien, 'Real Links, Abstract Rights and False Alarms: the Relationship between the ECJ's "Real Link" Case Law and National Solidarity' (2008) 33 *European Law Review* 643; FG Jacobs, 'Citizenship of the European Union—A Legal Analysis' (2007) 13 *European Law Journal* 591; C Barnard, 'Solidarity and New

of migrant citizens whose entitlements expand according to the length of their residence in the host State (short-, mid- and long-term residents).[151]

On the other hand, the Court has constructed a particularly inclusive notion of migrant 'worker': nearly any occupational activity is capable of granting the status of worker under the free movement provisions—however limited in duration (three-month contract as a waitress in *Ninni-Orasche*),[152] intensity (12 music lessons per week in *Kempf*)[153] and remuneration (below statutory minimum remuneration in *Levin*).[154] Accordingly, Union workers are entitled to elect their preferred labour, social and tax laws by taking up any occupational activity in their Member State of preference; as long as they are employed, they are shielded from any suspicion of abuse.

In short, migrant workers enjoy free choice of host law, whereas migrant citizens are only granted restricted choice of host law. This difference of regime between migrant workers (free choice of host law) and migrant citizens (restricted choice of host law) explains why litigants often claim to be workers:

> For these reasons, it is still much easier to invoke the status of a worker, which automatically entails equal treatment, and especially the same social and tax advantages as nationals according to Article 7 of Regulation 1216/68. Hence there is extensive case law around social benefits, much of it concerning student maintenance grants or loans, and around residence rights of TCN family members of a person claiming to be a worker.[155]

In sum, whenever recourse is made to home regulation or host regulation, a choice must be made between impeding or facilitating regulatory movements (restricted versus free choice of law).

C. Addressing the Regulatory Mobility Dilemma

As for the negative harmonisation conundrum, the central submission of this chapter is that Union institutions facing the regulatory mobility dilemma are inspired by two contradictory paradigms of economic integration: regulatory neutrality, which advocates restricted choice of law, and regulatory competition,

Governance in Social Policy' in G De Búrca and J Scott (eds), *Law and New Governance in the EU and the US* (Oxford, Hart Publishing, 2006).

[151] Arts 6, 7 and 16 of Directive 2004/38 on the freedom of movement of Union citizens. See Ziegler (n 75) 310; C Barnard, 'EU Citizenship and the Principle of Solidarity' in M Dougan and E Spaventa (ed), *Social welfare and EU law* (Oxford, Hart Publishing, 2005) 166; O Golynker, 'Analysis and Reflections—Student Loans: The European Concept of Social Justice according to Bidar' (2006) 31 *European Law Review* 390, 397.

[152] Case C-413/01 *Ninni-Orasche* [2003] ECR I-13187, paras 25, 36 and 46; Joined Cases C-22/08 and C-23/08 *Vatsouras* [2009] ECR I-4585, para 29.

[153] Case 53/81 *Levin* [1982] ECR 1035, para 17; Case 139/85 *Kempf* [1986] ECR 1741, para 14; Case 66/85 *Lawrie-Blum* [1986] ECR 2121, para 21; Case C-3/90 *Bernini* [1992] ECR I-1071, para 16; Case C-357/89 *Raulin* [1992] ECR I-1027, para 14.

[154] Case 66/85 *Lawrie-Blum* [1986] ECR 2121, para 21; Case 139/85 *Kempf* [1986] ECR 1741, para 14; Case 53/81 *Levin* [1982] ECR 1035, para 16.

[155] Ziegler (n 75) 299.

which demands free choice of law. This submission is central to the object of the present study, as it provides a second explanation for the controversies surrounding the concept of abuse of Union law.[156]

On the one hand, private individuals should not enjoy the freedom to elect their preferred national law if regulatory neutrality is to be preserved. The notion of regulatory mobility aims at the reaction of private individuals to differentials of regulation. From a static perspective, differentials of regulation distort business competition by subjecting competitors to different regulatory environments.[157] From a dynamic perspective, differentials of regulation distort business competition by encouraging businesses to change their regulatory environment; this dynamic dimension is often captured by the expression 'deflection of trade'.

Regulatory neutrality implies that national regulations should not influence private decision-making within the internal market, in order to ensure undistorted business competition and the spontaneous allocation of resources.[158] In this normative context, choices of law made by private individuals amount to breaches of regulatory neutrality, as their behaviour is dictated by regulatory considerations. For instance, the relocation of a business lured by hospitable laws represents an undesirable deflection of trade, as it is not grounded in genuine socioeconomic considerations. Thus, in *DFDS*, the Court observed that taxation in the country of origin (home regulation) could lead to undesirable deflections of trade:

> Systematic reliance on the place where the supplier has established his business could in fact lead to distortions of competition, in that it might encourage undertakings trading in one Member State to establish their businesses, in order to avoid taxation, in another Member State which has availed itself of the possibility of maintaining the VAT exemption for the services in question.[159]

Similar breaches of regulatory neutrality can be identified in every abusive practice identified in the part one of this study. In *Agip Petroli*, a ship altered its ordinary course in order to elect Greek law for its island cabotage activities around Sicily.[160] In *Cadbury Schweppes*, a British company incorporated subsidiaries in Dublin in order to elect the lower Irish direct taxation.[161] In *Cavallera*, an Italian engineer obtained a qualification of engineer in Spain in order to escape a State exam in Italy.[162] Moreover, the Union legislature explicitly equated abusive practices in relation to anti-dumping duties and export refunds (addressed in *Emsland-Stärke* and *Vonk Dairy Products*) to undesirable deflections of trade:

> Anti-dumping duties imposed pursuant to this Regulation may be extended to imports from third countries of like products, or parts thereof, when circumvention of the

[156] See ch 8 section III. The first explanation lies in the trade-off between legal certainty and legal congruence: see ch 5.

[157] See section III and subsection IV.C.

[158] See ch 6 section I.

[159] Case C-260/95 *DFDS* [1997] ECR I-1005, para 23.

[160] See ch 2 section V.A.

[161] See ch 2 section IV.A.

[162] See ch 4 n 74 and accompanying text.

> measures in force is taking place. Circumvention shall be defined as a change in the pattern of trade between third countries and the Community which stems from a practice, process or work for which there is insufficient due cause or economic justification other than the imposition of the duty, and where there is evidence that the remedial effects of the duty are being undermined in terms of the prices and/or quantities of the like products and there is evidence of dumping in relation to the normal values previously established for the like or similar products.[163]
>
> Certain export transactions can lead to deflection of trade. In order to prevent such deflections, payment of the refund should be subject to the condition that the product has not only left the customs territory of the Community but has also been imported into a third country or has undergone substantial processing or working.[164]

The Union legislature also justified the adoption of Directive 2003/48 on the taxation of interests by the need to prevent 'distortions incompatible with the internal market' originating in tax avoidance strategies:

> In the absence of any coordination of national tax systems for taxation of savings income in the form of interest payments, particularly as far as the treatment of interest received by non-residents is concerned, residents of Member States are currently often able to avoid any form of taxation in their Member State of residence on interest they receive in another Member State.
>
> This situation is creating distortions in the capital movements between Member States, which are incompatible with the internal market.[165]

The distortionary effect of artificial choices of law on the competition among private businesses is well established in the literature as well:

> The theory [of fiscal federalism] asserts that in a world with suboptimal taxes, any cross-border movement motivated by tax-related fiscal concerns rather than pure productivity concerns is a distortionary event.[166]

[163] Council Regulation (EC) 384/96 of 22 December 1995 on protection against dumped imports from countries not members of the European Community [1995] OJ L56/1.

[164] Commission Regulation (EC) 612/2009 of 7 July 2009 on laying down common detailed rules for the application of the system of export refunds on agricultural products (recast) [2009] OJ L186/1 rec 25. In its Proposal for Single Common Market Organisation Regulation, the Commission also inserted a provision according to which it may establish further conditions for the granting of export refunds in order to prevent 'diversion of trade': see Commission (EC), 'Proposal for a Regulation of the Parliament and the Council establishing a common organisation of agricultural markets and on specific provisions for certain agricultural products (Single CMO Regulation)' COM (2010) 799 final, 21 December 2010, art 274(7). Abusive practices were also assimilated to diversions of trade in Case C-7/08 *Har Vaessen* [2009] ECR I-5581, para 42, and Commission Regulation (EEC) 2287/83 of 29 July 1983 laying down provisions for the implementation of Article 127 of Council Regulation (EEC) 918/83 setting up a Community system of reliefs from customs duty [1983] OJ L220/12 rec 3.

[165] Council Directive 2003/48/EC of 3 June 2003 on taxation of savings income in the form of interest payments [2003] OJ L157/38 rec 5–6.

[166] WW Bratton and JA McCahery, 'Tax Coordination and Tax Competition in the European Union: Evaluating the Code of Conduct on Business Taxation' (2001) 38 *Common Market Law Review* 677, 707.

> Alongside the harmonization of tax systems, the establishment of conditions of effective competition also requires specific action to combat tax avoidance. … For each Member State, it results in budgetary losses and infringements of the principle of tax equity; for the Community, it is liable to cause distortions in capital movements and in the conditions of competition.[167]

> Perhaps the main objection to state-tax competition is that it ultimately induces firms to alter their location choices. To the extent that, without tax incentives, firms choose to locate in areas that minimize their costs, the argument is that location incentives can only distort location choices and induce inefficiencies.[168]

In sum, under regulatory neutrality, private individuals should not enjoy the freedom to elect their preferred law as such freedom would distort private competition and deflect trade patterns; as a consequence, artificial choices of law ought to be prohibited as abusive.

On the other hand, regulatory competition has been described as a chain of information conveying preferences regarding national laws from consumers to producers (consumer arbitrage) and from producers to governments (producer arbitrage). As explained earlier, home regulation enables consumer arbitrage.[169] The freedom to directly elect a national law has no relevance in a process of consumer arbitrage, for consumers only indirectly arbitrate among national laws, by purchasing goods and services already moulded by a national law.

However, free choice of law is of crucial importance in a process of regulatory competition, for it enables producer arbitrage. As explained above, producer arbitrage conveys direct signals to national governments, through the relocation of factors of production among national jurisdictions.[170] Free choice of law enables producer arbitrage by offering businesses the right to elect their preferred jurisdiction at no cost. Thus, in the field of company law, producers can freely elect their preferred national law through a costless administrative act of incorporation (*Centros*) or re-incorporation (*Cartesio*) in their Member State of preference: 'With [the Centros jurisprudence], the door has been opened for free choice of the applicable company law regime and regulatory competition in the area of company law in Europe'.[171]

Conversely, a restricted choice of law approach impairs producer arbitrage by making the election of a national law more costly. For instance, the real seat doctrine requires producers to move their real seat to their preferred jurisdiction in order to elect its national law: 'The effect [of the real seat doctrine] is to render impossible the land of market for corporate charters … since a company

[167] Commission (EC), 'The scope for convergence of tax systems in the Community' (Report) COM (80) 139 final, 27 March 1980, no 16.

[168] JR Rogers, 'The Law and Policy of State Tax Competition: Much Ado About Nothing?' (2006) 4 *Georgetown Journal of Law & Public Policy* 101, 101.

[169] See section IV.C.

[170] See ch 6 section III.

[171] H Eidenmüller, 'Abuse of Law in the Context of European Insolvency Law' in de la Feria and Vogenauer (n 34) 137.

cannot switch its state of incorporation at will'.[172] As a consequence, the regulatory competition paradigm endorses free choice of law and opposes the prohibition of artificial choices of law. Indeed, under regulatory competition, artificial choices of law are not 'abusive' but form a desirable process of arbitrage among national laws. As plainly stated by Schammo, 'arbitrage and abuse of rights can be situated at opposing ends'.[173]

Furthermore, the effect of producer arbitrage is maximised when free choice of law is combined with home regulation (free choice of home law), since the free election of hospitable national laws will produce effects throughout the internal market. By contrast, under free choice of host law, the effects of the choice of law will be limited to the activities located in the host State. As a matter of fact, free choice of home law constitutes the apex of regulatory competition, just as Union harmonisation is the apex of regulatory neutrality. This magnifying effect of free choice of home law on a process of regulatory competition has long been identified in the literature:

> The most intensive type of regulatory competition can emerge under a regime of free choice of law. Under this scheme, firms can choose between national regulations without having to move their location. Regulatory competition initiated by mutual recognition is of a different type, since only the consumers (in the import country), but not the producers, can choose between diverging regulations.[174]

> Following this principle a company will only need to comply with one national rule for its products to be able to move freely throughout the entire common market. Firms could choose among the different national regulations, and consumers among the products complying with those different rules. This will create a competitive process among the different national rules: the choice of producers of where to produce and of consumers of what to buy will determine the 'best rules'.[175]

To sum up, whenever recourse is made to host regulation or home regulation, a normative decision must be made as to whether to impede or encourage regulatory mobility. In Union law, this normative decision is alternatively informed by the paradigms of regulatory neutrality and regulatory competition. Through the lens of the regulatory neutrality paradigm, granting free choice of law to private individuals is liable to distort business competition and is accordingly not desirable. Through the lens of regulatory competition, granting free choice of law to private individuals enables them to arbitrate among national laws, which promotes competition among Member States. Accordingly, if artificial choices of law represent undesirable 'abuses of law' under regulatory neutrality, they amount to desirable 'regulatory arbitrage' under regulatory competition.

[172] Deakin (n 47) 81.

[173] P Schammo, 'Arbitrage and Abuse of Rights in the EC Legal System' (2008) 14 *European Law Journal* 351, 352.

[174] Kerber and Van den Bergh (n 46) 452.

[175] Maduro (n 19) 132.

VI. Synthesis: The Trade-off between Regulatory Neutrality and Regulatory Competition

The previous sections were assigned two objectives: first, describing the five issues raised by the regulation of the internal market (protectionism, multiple regulation, the eventuality of positive harmonisation, the negative harmonisation conundrum and the regulatory mobility dilemma); secondly, describing the stance of the paradigms of regulatory neutrality and regulatory competition on each of these five issues. The findings of these five sections can be summarised as follows in Table 12: both paradigms disapprove of protectionism and multiple regulation, but they disagree about positive harmonisation, negative harmonisation and regulatory mobility.

Both agreement on the two former issues and disagreement on the three latter have important consequences for the heuristic potential of the tension between regulatory neutrality and regulatory competition. On the one hand, neither regulatory neutrality nor regulatory competition can account for decisions taken at Union level to allow protectionism or multiple regulation. Indeed, protectionism and multiple regulation are incompatible with economic integration, be it defined as regulatory neutrality or regulatory competition, for they distort business competition and hamper consumer and producer arbitrage. It should be recalled in that connection that the limited ambition of these paradigms is to encapsulate two visions of economic integration.[176] Yet other economic considerations and above all non-economic considerations may rightfully influence decision-making at Union level; in the Court's case law, such considerations are usually examined as potential grounds of justifications for restrictions on free movement. Thus,

Table 12 – Five Issues in the Regulation of the Internal Market

	Regulatory Neutrality	**Regulatory Competition**
Protectionism	Suppression	Suppression
Multiple regulation	Suppression	Suppression
Eventuality of positive harmonisation	Union legislation	No Union legislation
Negative harmonisation conundrum	Host regulation	Home regulation
Regulatory mobility dilemma	Restricted choice of law	Free choice of law

[176] It was submitted above that there are only two paradigms of *economic* integration, namely consistent and complete visions of what a process of economic integration should be. This submission does not exclude the existence of alternative paradigms of integration focusing for instance on political, cultural or institutional aspects of integration, but rather the existence of other paradigms of economic integration beyond regulatory neutrality and regulatory competition: see ch 6.

if protectionism and multiple regulation are undeniably incompatible with economic integration, be it understood as regulatory neutrality or regulatory competition, other considerations might lead the Court or the Union legislature to allow them.

On the other hand, the disagreement between regulatory neutrality and regulatory competition represents a major explaining factor for the inconsistency of Union law on positive harmonisation, negative harmonisation and regulatory mobility. In plain language, as there is no agreement as to what economic integration actually means within the Union, and since the two potential visions of economic integration are contradictory, the Union law of economic integration is bound to be inconsistent on these issues. Again, other factors than the objective of economic integration may partly account for this inconsistency, but their existence does not undermine the central influence of the objective of economic integration in the law and policy of the European Union, which is corroborated by the legislation, case law and literature used throughout this study.

The practical consequence of this disagreement is the existence of *a trade-off* between regulatory neutrality and regulatory competition: once protectionism and multiple regulation are overcome, the pursuit of one paradigm of economic integration comes necessarily at the expense of the other. Achieving regulatory neutrality undermines the competitive process among Member States; as a matter of fact, the elimination of all distortions to cross-border business competition requires positive harmonisation, which would suppress all room for regulatory competition. Weatherill wrote:

> [Regulatory competition] would damn harmonisation itself as anti-competitive. Why should there not be regulatory variation among Member States, with the market, populated by consumers of regulation, inter alia commercial firms, dictating which approach is 'best' by selecting the jurisdiction judged most hospitable, and using that as a base to supply the wider market? This, one might argue, is not State laws causing a distortion of competition—it is competition![177]

Conversely, promoting competition among Member States leads to distortions of business competition; thus, allowing relocation in hospitable jurisdictions 'offering' lenient laws heightens competition among States, but generates inefficiency in private competition (the 'banana-plantation-in-Alaska' example[178]). Bratton and McCahery clearly identified this distortionary effect of tax competition within the Union:

> [T]ax competition … may be seen as beneficial or distortionary depending on the observer's point of view. Tax competition's defenders argue that it encourages operational efficiency in government and keeps States responsive to citizen preferences. … Opponents of tax competition take this scenario and describe the result in terms of economic distortions.[179]

[177] Weatherill, 'Why Harmonise?' (n 47) 14.
[178] See ch 6 n 58 and accompanying text.
[179] Bratton and McCahery (n 166) 680–81.

In more systematic terms, this trade-off between regulatory neutrality and regulatory competition materialises in three dilemmas located at central 'nodes' of free movement law: positive harmonisation (Union regulation or not: Section III), negative harmonisation (host versus home regulation: Section IV) and regulatory mobility (restricted versus free choice of law: Section V). These three nodes can be easily translated into 'regulatory modes' of the internal market, which can then be ranked in two contrary orders of preference reflecting the tenets of regulatory neutrality and regulatory competition (Table 13).

The paradigms of regulatory neutrality and regulatory competition concur in advocating the suppression of protectionism and multiple regulation, which is likely to create a strong pressure to overcome them under Union law. Beyond protectionism and multiple regulation, they have exact opposite preferences regarding the regulation of the internal market. The regulatory neutrality paradigm seeks to ensure regulatory equality and impede regulatory mobility in order to ensure undistorted business competition: as a consequence, it supports Union regulation (its apex), host regulation and restricted choice of host law. By contrast, regulatory competition opposes regulatory equality and thrives on regulatory mobility, in order to enable regulatory arbitrage: accordingly, it adamantly opposes Union regulation (its nadir), and advocates home regulation[180] or even better: free choice of home law (its apex).

Union institutions are inevitably confronted with these hard choices located on the three central nodes of free movement law, and their decisions are commonly informed by the contradictory paradigms of regulatory neutrality and regulatory competition. Moreover, Union institutions are not equals before these hard choices: if the Union legislature may act on all three nodes (positive harmonisation,

Table 13 – Regulatory Modes of the Internal Market

Jurisdiction	Regulatory Mode	Regulatory Equality	Regulatory Mobility	RN	RC
Union	Union regulation	Full equality	Suppressed	1	5
Host State	Restricted choice of host law	Host equality	Impeded	2	4
Host State	Free choice of host law	Host equality	Facilitated	3	3
Home State	Restricted choice of home law	Home equality	Impeded	4	2
Home State	Free choice of home law	Home equality	Facilitated	5	1

'RN' stands for regulatory neutrality, 'RC' for regulatory competition
Descending order of preference: from 1 (apex) to 5 (nadir)

[180] Host regulation ensures regulatory equality within one national jurisdiction (host equality), whereas home regulation preserves diversity throughout the internal market by instilling home equality. See section IV.

negative harmonisation and regulatory mobility),[181] the Court cannot proceed to a positive harmonisation, so that it only faces hard choices between home regulation (*Laval*) and host regulation (*Rush Portuguesa*), and between restricted (*Cadbury Schweppes*) and free choice of law (*Centros*).

The practical importance of the trade-off between regulatory neutrality and regulatory competition cannot be overstated. Indeed, this trade-off between regulatory neutrality and regulatory competition accounts for long-established contradictions of free movement law, and in particular the inconsistency of the free movement test applied by the Court. If we exclude the 'basic' cases of protectionism and the rare occasions in which the Court allows multiple regulation, the actual content of the free movement test—irrespective of the terminology used[182]—entirely depends on the solutions brought by the Court to the negative harmonisation conundrum (host versus home regulation) and the regulatory mobility dilemma (free versus restricted choice of law). In turn, the solutions brought to those two dilemmas are informed by the paradigms of regulatory neutrality and regulatory competition. Moreover, this trade-off offers an insightful framework of analysis to re-examine the literature on free movement law. By way of illustration, the following statement by Pelkmans is necessarily inspired by the paradigm of regulatory neutrality: 'regulatory competition is distortive; by contrast, EU regulation removes distortions'.[183]

In sum, the free movement jurisprudence is torn between two incompatible missions, namely to ensure the proper functioning of competition among private businesses (regulatory neutrality) and among Member States (regulatory competition) throughout the internal market. Kerber lucidly exposed this tension in a passage worth reproducing *in extenso*:

> If the elimination of competitive distortions means that competition between firms must proceed entirely uninfluenced by economic policies of jurisdictions within the EC, and different cost conditions between Member States are only allowed due to differences in 'natural conditions,' then the effects of policies of lower-level jurisdictions on the competition between firms must be neutralized through, for example, centralization or harmonization of those policies within the EC. …
>
> But this consequent interpretation of 'undistorted competition' leads to the abolition of any meaningful form of decentralization, implying the complete elimination of any

[181] *First*, the Union legislature can harmonise a given legal field (eg VAT Directive: see ch 4 n 36; regulations on export refunds: see ch 2 nn 28 and 32); *secondly*, it may impose home regulation (eg directives on financial services: see ch 4 nn 91 and 95) or host regulation (eg directive on posted workers: see n 105); and *thirdly*, it may grant a restricted choice of law (eg directives on financial services, broadcasting or driving licences: see ch 4 section III) or a free choice of law (eg family allowances under art 76 of Regulation 1408/71 or art 10 of Regulation 574/72: see ch 4 section V).

[182] Eg 'obstacle to free movement', 'barrier to trade', 'restriction to market access', 'discrimination on grounds of nationality' or 'non-discriminatory restriction'.

[183] Pelkmans (n 66) 116–17; see also S Deakin, 'Reflexive Governance and European Company Law' (2009) 15 *European Law Journal* 224, 224–25.

> interjurisdictional competition by experimenting with different forms of bundles of public goods, institutions, and taxes for the improvement of locational conditions. …
>
> A tension, thus, appears to exist between undistorted competition among firms on the European markets for private goods and interjurisdictional competition on the European markets for public goods and services.[184]

In this passage lies the quintessential dialectic shaping the law of the internal market: removing distortions of competition among private businesses (regulatory neutrality) ineluctably impairs the competition among Member States; conversely, promoting the competition among Member States (regulatory competition) distorts the competition among private businesses.

[184] Kerber (n 48) 237–38.

8

Reviewing Practical Issues of Free Movement Law

THE PREVIOUS CHAPTER sought to demonstrate the existence of a trade-off between regulatory neutrality and regulatory competition, which materialises in three central nodes of internal market law: positive harmonisation (Union regulation or not), negative harmonisation (home or host regulation) and regulatory mobility (restricted or free choice of law).

The present chapter intends to illustrate how, in practice, the trade-off between regulatory neutrality and regulatory competition generates contradictions within the free movement test, by re-examining a few practical issues of free movement law: the ambivalent status of differentials of regulation, the acceptance of reverse discriminations, the inconsistent prohibition of abuses of law (eg *Centros* versus *Cadbury Schweppes*) and the ambiguity towards social dumping (eg *Laval* versus *Rush Portuguesa*). Indeed, the promotion of a specific solution to each of those practical issues rests on the adoption, most often unconscious, of regulatory neutrality or regulatory competition as a paradigm of economic integration.

I. The Ambivalent Status of Differentials of Regulation

The ambivalent status of differentials of regulation is a practical application of the positive harmonisation dilemma and of the negative harmonisation conundrum, described in chapter seven, Sections III and IV. In the absence of positive harmonisation by the Union legislature, undertakings competing throughout the internal market are necessarily subject to different national laws. Depending on the paradigm of economic integration elected, such differentials of regulation will be viewed as legitimate 'competitive advantages' flowing from national laws (regulatory competition) or illegitimate 'distortions of competition' among private businesses (regulatory neutrality).

As mentioned earlier, the conception of differentials of regulation as 'distortions of competition' underpins Treaty provisions enabling the Union legislature to adopt harmonising measures, such as Articles 113, 114 and 115 TFEU.[1] According to the Court's seminal judgment in the first *Tobacco Advertising* case, harmonising measures must remove disparities among national laws that hinder free movement and distort conditions of competition, which necessarily aims at competition among private businesses (regulatory neutrality).[2]

By contrast, the Court's rulings in *Van Tiggele* and *Leclerc* explicitly endorsed the idea that foreign undertakings should be allowed to keep the 'competitive advantages' they derive from their regulatory environment of origin. *Van Tiggele* concerned Dutch legislation imposing minimum prices for domestic and imported alcoholic beverages, which promoted host equality. The Court held that such legislation restricted free movement:

> Thus imports may be impeded in particular when a national authority fixes prices or profit margins at such a level that imported products are placed at a disadvantage in relation to identical domestic products either because they cannot profitably be marketed in the conditions laid down or because the competitive advantage conferred by lower cost prices is cancelled out.[3]

The free movement test adopted by the Court in *Van Tiggele* imposes home regulation, as host regulation would cancel out the competitive advantage conferred by lower cost prices in the home State. The *Leclerc* case concerned French legislation that imposed an alignment of the price of imported books onto the price of domestic books, in order to level the prices of books sold on the French domestic market. It is particularly insightful to contrast the respective arguments of the Commission and the French Government in this case, as they can be directly associated to the contradictory visions of economic integration embodied by the paradigms of regulatory neutrality and regulatory competition:

> The Commission considers that the legislation in question constitutes a measure equivalent in effect to a quantitative restriction on imports, contrary to Article 30 of the Treaty. … In the Commission's view, those … provisions impede imports by making it impossible for importers to charge lower prices and preventing them from penetrating the French market by means of price competition.
>
> The French government argues that legislation of the type at issue is not contrary to Article 30. … The restriction on retail price competition does not in any way restrict imports. Imported and domestic books are treated identically in that respect.[4]

The Commission's argument was dictated by the regulatory competition paradigm, under which importers should keep the competitive advantages they derive from their regulatory environment of origin (home regulation). By contrast, the French Government's argument was inspired by the regulatory neutrality

[1] See ch 7 section III.

[2] Case C-376/98 *Germany v Parliament and Council ('Tobacco Advertising I')* [2000] ECR I-8419.

[3] Case 82/77 *Van Tiggele* [1978] ECR 25, para 14.

[4] Case 229/83 *Leclerc* [1985] ECR 1, paras 21–22. See also Case C-531/07 *LIBRO* [2009] ECR I-3717.

paradigm, under which all competitors active on a national market should be subject to the same standards (host regulation). As in *Van Tiggele*, the Court decided that the French law levelling the prices of books sold on its domestic market was contrary to free movement of goods, on the ground that it precluded importers from charging a retail price reflecting the cost price obtained in the home State.

The central submission of this section is the following: the legitimacy of competitive advantages flowing from national laws entirely depends on the paradigm of economic integration adopted. In *Van Tiggele* and *Leclerc*, the Court promoted home equality by holding that the loss of such competitive advantage was a restriction to free movement, thereby furthering the process of regulatory competition among Member States. However, those decisions undermine host equality, by creating discriminations between domestic and imported products competing in the host market, which breaches regulatory neutrality. By way of illustration, the following criticism is inspired by the idea of regulatory neutrality:

> In Van Tiggele the Court links squarely the loss of a competitive advantage enjoyed by imported goods to a market where a State has retail price maintenance laws as a form of discrimination bringing into play Article 28 EC. The classification of such cases as discrimination cases is difficult to justify since often the national measures are being attacked by nationals of the Member State for the simple reason that the regulatory control hinders their commercial freedom to trade on their own terms. Equally, in order to show that there is discrimination there should be evidence that imported goods are at a disadvantage as a result of the national regulation.[5]

The same tension regarding differentials of regulation can be identified with regard to labour protection, by contrasting the Court's decisions in *Rüffert* and *Defrenne II*. Under regulatory competition, the fact that an employer derives competitive advantages from the labour law of its home State (home regulation) corresponds to the ordinary functioning of a process of economic integration. This conception of economic integration undoubtedly inspired the Court's ruling in *Rüffert*:

> [The obligation to abide by the German minimum wages] causes those undertakings to lose the competitive advantage which they enjoy by reason of their lower wage costs; [this requirement] may impose on service providers established in another Member State where minimum rates of pay are lower an additional economic burden that may prohibit, impede or render less attractive the provision of their services in the host Member State.[6]

Yet under regulatory neutrality, the very same 'competitive advantages' become 'distortions of competition', for they disturb the competition among private

[5] E Szyszczak, 'State Intervention and the Internal Market' in T Tridimas and P Nebbia (eds), *European Union Law for the Twenty-First Century—Volume 2: Internal Market and Free Movement Community Policies* (Oxford, Hart Publishing, 2004) 224.

[6] Case C-346/06 *Rüffert* [2008] ECR I-1989, paras 14 and 37.

goods by subjecting domestic and cross-border flows to different regulatory conditions:

> [The Laval and Rüffert-line of case law] creates distortions of competition domestically and in the internal market where domestic companies have to follow national rules or collective agreements while competitors from other Member States could apply minimum rules.[7]

At the inception of the European Communities, the French Government argued that labour and social costs had to be levelled among Member States, in order to prevent distortions of competition between undertakings subject to high standards (ie in France) and undertakings subject to lower ones.[8] The French claim was only partly welcomed by the other Founding States, eventually leading to the adoption of provisions on equal pay and paid holiday schemes (Articles 157 and 158 TFEU). The ratio legis of these provisions is diametrically opposed to the ratio decidendi of *Rüffert*, as supported by the following passage of *Defrenne II*:

> [T]he aim of [Article 157 TFEU] is to avoid a situation in which undertakings established in States which have actually implemented the principle of equal pay suffer a competitive disadvantage in intra-Community competition as compared with undertakings established in States which have not yet eliminated discrimination against women workers as regards pay.[9]

Rüffert and *Defrenne II* illustrate two irreconcilable visions of economic integration respectively championed by the paradigms of regulatory neutrality and regulatory competition. *Rüffert* stipulates that Union undertakings should enjoy competitive advantages resulting from their national regulatory environment (regulatory competition), whereas *Defrenne II* states that Union undertakings should not enjoy such competitive advantages (regulatory neutrality).

A similar contradiction can be identified in the tax case law of the Court, in which the decision of levelling the taxation of domestic and cross-border activities is alternatively held compatible or incompatible with free movement. Cadbury Schweppes concerned the CFC ('controlled foreign companies') provisions in the United Kingdom, whose object is to prevent resident companies from diverting income to their subsidiaries in low-tax countries.[10] To that end, CFC provisions usually treat such foreign income as domestic income, by subjecting it to domestic taxation after offsetting the low foreign taxes (host regulation). In *Cadbury Schweppes*, the Court held that CFC provisions hindered the freedom of

[7] Own European Economic and Social Committee (EC), 'The social dimension of the internal market' (Own-Initiative Opinion), 14 July 2010, C44/90, no 3.4.5.3.

[8] C Barnard, 'Fifty Years of Avoiding Social Dumping? The EU's Economic and Not So Economic Constitution' in M Dougan and S Currie (eds), *50 Years of the European Treaties* (Oxford, Hart Publishing, 2009); C Barnard and S Deakin, 'Negative and Positive Harmonization of Labor Law in the European Union' (2002) 8 *Columbia Journal of European Law* 389, 400–01; CM von Quitzow, *State Measures Distorting Free Competition in the EC* (The Hague, Kluwer Law International, 2002) 205–06.

[9] Case 43/75 *Defrenne II* [1976] ECR 455, para 9.

[10] See ch 2 section IV.A.

establishment, by dissuading resident companies from establishing a subsidiary in a Member State applying a lower level of taxation:

> That difference in treatment creates a tax disadvantage for the resident company to which the legislation on CFCs is applicable. Even taking into account [the fact] that such a resident company does not pay, on the profits of a CFC within the scope of application of that legislation, more tax than that which would have been payable on those profits if they had been made by a subsidiary established in the United Kingdom, the fact remains that under such legislation the resident company is taxed on profits of another legal person. That is not the case for a resident company with a subsidiary taxed in the United Kingdom or a subsidiary established outside that Member State which is not subject to a lower level of taxation.

The Court however considered that this restriction on free movement could be justified by the prevention of abusive practices.[11] Conversely, in *Columbus*, the Court considered that subjecting foreign partnerships to German taxation after offsetting Belgian taxes (host regulation) did not amount to a restriction to free movement, on the ground that no discrimination could be found between German and foreign partnerships:

> By applying the set-off method to such foreign partnerships, that legislation merely subjects, in Germany, the profits made by such partnerships to the same tax rate as profits made by partnerships established in Germany.
>
> Since partnerships such as Columbus do not suffer any tax disadvantage in comparison with partnerships established in Germany, there is no discrimination resulting from a difference in treatment between those two categories of partnerships.
>
> In the light of all those considerations and the principle of equality of fiscal treatment between limited partnerships such as Columbus, on the one hand, and partnerships established in Germany, on the other hand, [such legislation] cannot be classified as constituting restrictions on the freedom of establishment within the meaning of Article 43 EC.[12]

Therefore, the *Cadbury Schweppes* ruling applied a free movement test based on home equality (regulatory competition), later qualified by a justification based on the prevention of abusive practices (regulatory neutrality); whereas the *Columbus* ruling applied a free movement test based on host equality (regulatory neutrality).

In sum, the outspoken rationales of these judgments—and countless others—can simply not be reconciled, because they flow from different visions of economic integration. Depending on the paradigm of economic integration elected, differentials of regulation among competing undertakings will be viewed as generating illegitimate 'distortions of competition' among private goods (regulatory neutrality: *Defrenne II*, *Columbus*) or legitimate 'competitive advantages' in

[11] Case C-196/04 *Cadbury Schweppes* [2006] ECR I-7995, para 46.

[12] Case C-298/05 *Columbus* [2007] ECR I-10451, paras 39, 40 and 54.

a competition among public goods (regulatory competition: *Van Tiggele*, *Rüffert*, *Cadbury Schweppes*).

II. The Acceptance of Reverse Discriminations

The controversy surrounding reverse discriminations is a practical application of the negative harmonisation conundrum, described in Section IV. Reverse discrimination is one of the most debated issues of Union law.[13] In essence, a reverse discrimination is said to occur whenever, within the confines of a national market, domestic trade flows are subject to stricter regulatory standards than cross-border flows, thereby suffering a competitive disadvantage on their own domestic market.[14] As is well known, the Court has consistently refused to proscribe reverse discriminations as such, often relying on the concept of purely internal situations to exclude them from the scope of Union law.[15] Many authors have criticised the Court's reticence to outlaw reverse discriminations, arguing that the general principle of equality or non-discrimination implies the prohibition of every type of discrimination within the Union, and even more so following the creation of the Union citizenship:

> The just and common sense principle must be that the nationals of all Member States are entitled to the same treatment by any given Member State. To say otherwise is to promote discrimination which is, in effect, based upon the difference in nationality of the victim.[16]

[13] See, inter alia, C Dautricourt and S Thomas, 'Reverse Discrimination and Free Movement of Persons under Community Law: All for Ulysses, Nothing for Penelope?' (2009) 34 *European Law Review* 433; D Garcia, 'Are There Reasons to Convert Reverse Discrimination into a Prohibited Measure?' (2009) 18 *EC Tax Review* 179; A Tryfonidou, 'Reverse Discrimination in Purely Internal Situations: An Incongruity in a Citizens' Europe' (2008) 35 *Legal Issues of Economic Integration* 43; C Ritter, 'Purely Internal Situations, Reverse Discrimination, Guimont, Dzodzi and article 234' (2006) 31 *European Law Review* 690; MP Maduro, 'The Scope of European Remedies: the Case of Purely Internal Situations and Reverse Discrimination' in C Kilpatrick, et al (eds), *The Future of European Remedies* (Oxford, Hart Publishing, 2000); E Cannizzaro, 'Producing "Reverse Discrimination" Through the Exercise of EC Competences' (1997) 17 *Yearbook of European Law* 29; DMW Pickup, 'Reverse Discrimination and Freedom of Movement for Workers' (1986) 23 *Common Market Law Review* 135.

[14] AG Léger, Case C-152/03 *Ritter-Coulais* [2006] ECR I-1711, para 46; Dautricourt and Thomas, 'Reverse Discrimination and Free Movement of Persons under Community Law' (n 13) 433; Garcia, 'Are There Reasons to Convert Reverse Discrimination into a Prohibited Measure?' (n 13) 180; Tryfonidou, 'Reverse Discrimination in Purely Internal Situations' (n 13) 46; Ritter, 'Purely Internal Situations' (n 13) 691.

[15] See, inter alia, Case 44/84 *Hurd* [1986] ECR 29, para 55; Case 98/86 *Mathot* [1987] ECR 809, para 9; see esp Case C-379/92 *Peralta* [1994] ECR I-3453, para 27; Joined Cases C-29/94 to C-35/94 *Aubertin and others* [1995] ECR I-301, paras 6 and 13; Joined Cases C-64 and C-65/96 *Uecker and Jacquet* [1997] ECR I-3171, paras 22–23; Case C-127/08 *Metock and others* [2008] ECR I-6241, paras 76–78.

[16] Pickup, 'Reverse Discrimination and Freedom of Movement for Workers' (n 13) 156.

> [T]he introduction of the status of Union citizenship and the interpretation afforded by the Court to the citizenship provisions seems to have created a new impetus for the extension of the scope of application of human rights as general principles of EC law and, in particular, the Community principle of equality. … [O]ne of the main aims of the Community, now, is that no discrimination of any kind should arise as a result of the application of Community law and the process of European integration.[17]

However, owing to the negative harmonisation conundrum, such broad statements enjoining the Court to prohibit every type of discrimination throughout the internal market are—quite literally—fallacies. If we discard the hypothetical replacement of all national laws by Union laws, which in effect would enact the suppression of Member States and the creation of a European State, the suppression of all discriminations under Union law is a logical impossibility. Indeed, in the absence of positive harmonisation, it is logically impossible to suppress every type of discrimination within the internal market: the Court must choose between host and home equality, that is between prohibiting reverse discriminations or discriminations resulting from legislative disparities.[18]

On the one hand, host equality ensures equal treatment between cross-border flows and the host society, by subjecting them to host regulation. Whenever host equality is elected, in conformity with the regulatory neutrality paradigm, differences of treatment within every national market should be outlawed as restrictions to free movement, including reverse discriminations occurring when cross-border flows seek to 'import' a more favourable home law. In *Perfili*, for instance, the Court stated the following:

> [T]he principle of non-discrimination on grounds of nationality must be interpreted as not precluding a Member State [Italy]'s legislation from requiring a victim of a criminal offence [Lloyd's of London] who wishes to bring suit as a civil party in criminal proceedings to grant his representative a special power of attorney, even when the law of the Member State [United Kingdom] of which the victim is a national does not lay down such a formality.[19]

As a necessary consequence of host equality, cross-border flows (such as Lloyd's of London in *Perfili*) have to suffer inequalities resulting from legislative disparities, namely breaches of home equality, as explicitly acknowledged by the Court in *Schempp*, *Block* or *Peralta*.[20]

Conversely, home equality ensures equal treatment between cross-border flows and their home society, by subjecting them to home regulation. Whenever home equality is elected, in accordance with the tenets of regulatory competition,

[17] Tryfonidou (n 13) 62; see also Garcia (n 13) 191.

[18] See ch 7 section IV. Maduro similarly identifies two types of equality, by distinguishing between reverse discriminations (breaches of host equality) and discriminations resulting from legislative disparities (breaches of home equality): MP Maduro, *We the Court: the European Court of Justice and the European Economic Constitution* (Oxford, Hart Publishing, 1998) 154–57.

[19] Case C-177/94 *Perfili* [1996] ECR I-161, para 19.

[20] See ch 7 n 100 and accompanying text.

goods competing within a given national market are subject to their respective home laws, which by definition entails 'discriminations' among competing goods, including 'reverse discriminations' potentially affecting domestic goods:

> Under a mutual recognition rule, the Member States lose their power to enact mandatory regulations for domestic markets. They are only able to enact mandatory regulations for domestic producers, who still have to comply with domestic regulations. The puzzling point is that the introduction of mutual recognition turns a former regulation for the domestic market into a regulation applying only to domestic producers.[21]

Reverse discriminations are the logical consequence of the solution adopted in *Cassis de Dijon*, *Leclerc* (goods), *Aubertin* (diplomas), *Centros* (corporations), *Laval* or *Rüffert* (posted workers), which defines restrictions to free movement as breaches of home equality; in Maduro's words, home regulation entails the 'acceptance of reverse discriminations'.[22] By way of illustration, if the professional qualification of hairdresser (or ski instructor[23]) is mutually recognised, French nationals must accept that hairdressers educated in another Member State and active in France are subject to their home professional requirements, which are possibly milder than the French ones:

> Community law, in particular Directive 82/489, must be interpreted as not precluding national rules which require that nationals of that Member State hold a diploma in order to operate a hairdressing salon, while permitting hairdressers who are nationals of other Member States to operate a hairdressing salon without holding such a diploma.[24]

The Court's rulings in *Aubertin* and *Perfili* can be usefully contrasted: in *Aubertin*, cross-border flows were allowed to 'import' their more favourable home law (home equality); whereas in *Perfili*, they were compelled to abide by the more severe host standards (host equality). As a matter of fact, the negative harmonisation conundrum postulates that, absent positive harmonisation, the law of the internal market is split into two irreconcilable axes of equality: one must either promote home equality and accordingly tolerate breaches of host equality, including reverse discriminations (*Aubertin*); or promote host equality and accept breaches of home equality, in the form of discriminations resulting from legislative disparities (*Perfili*).

[21] W Kerber and R Van den Bergh, 'Mutual Recognition Revisited: Misunderstandings, Inconsistencies, and a Suggested Reinterpretation' (2008) 61 *Kyklos* 447, 453–54.

[22] Maduro, *We the Court* (n 18) 131, describing the 'new approach to harmonisation'; see also AG Jacobs, Case C-168/91 *Konstantinidis* [1993] ECR I-1191, para 49.

[23] 'Europe: après le plombier polonais, le moniteur de ski anglais', *Libération*, 8 February 2011; AG Sharpston, Case C-200/08 *Commission v France ('Snowboarders')*, removed.

[24] Joined Cases C-29/94 to C-35/94 *Aubertin and others* [1995] ECR I-301, para 13; see also Case C-286/06 *Commission v Spain* [2008] ECR I-8025, paras 80–81 (on the obligation to recognise foreign diplomas of engineering obtained after a shorter period of education than domestic diplomas); Case 246/80 *Broekmeulen* [1981] ECR 2311, para 27 (obligation to recognise foreign diplomas of medicine despite lesser training requirements than domestic diplomas); L Driguez, 'Reconnaissance mutuelle des diplômes' (2008) 12 *Europe* 412, 412, free translation: 'Member States had first to get used … to admitting the value of diplomas granted abroad'.

To sum up, the suppression of all discriminations under Union law is a logical impossibility in the absence of total Union harmonisation, which obliges the Court to choose between home equality and host equality. As suggested throughout this study, the choice of one conception of equality will ultimately depend on the paradigm of economic integration elected. The adoption of home equality entails the acceptance of reverse discriminations (regulatory competition: *Aubertin*, *Leclerc*), whereas the pursuit of host equality implies their suppression (regulatory neutrality: *Perfili*, *Peralta*).

III. The Inconsistent Prohibition of Abuses of Union Law

The inconsistent prohibition of abuses of Union law, which is naturally of prime importance for the present study, is a practical application of the regulatory mobility dilemma, described in chapter seven Section V. The point of departure of this part two was a finding of inconsistent treatment of artificial choices of law made by private individuals. Indeed, such artificial choices of law are alternatively proscribed as abuses of law (*Cadbury Schweppes*) or ratified as non-abusive (*Centros*). The Court's inconstancy in the treatment of artificial choices of law has often been criticised, in particular in relation to the opposite solutions reached in *Centros* and *Cadbury Schweppes*.[25] This inconstancy of the free movement test with regard to artificial choices of law can be further illustrated by contrasting the following excerpts of the *Centros* and *Oy AA* rulings:

> [T]he fact that a national of a Member State who wishes to set up a company chooses to form it in the Member State whose rules of company law seem to him the least restrictive and to set up branches in other Member States cannot, in itself, constitute an abuse of the right of establishment.[26]
>
> [A]llowing groups of companies to choose freely the Member State in which the profits of the subsidiary are to be taxed … would undermine the system of the allocation of the power to tax between Member States.[27]

[25] See eg V Edwards and P Farmer, 'The Concept of Abuse in the Freedom of Establishment of Companies: a Case of Double Standards?' in FG Jacobs et al (eds), *Continuity and Change in EU Law: Essays in Honour of Sir Francis Jacobs* (Oxford, Oxford University Press, 2007).

[26] Case C-212/97 *Centros* [1999] ECR I-1459, para 27; see also Case C-210/06 *Cartesio* [2008] ECR I-9641; Case C-167/01 *Inspire Art* [2003] ECR I-10155; Case C-208/00 *Überseering* [2002] ECR I-9919; Case 79/85 *Segers* [1986] ECR 2375.

[27] Case C-231/05 *Oy AA* [2007] ECR I-6373, para 56; see also Case C-196/04 *Cadbury Schweppes* [2006] ECR I-7995; Case C-524/04 *Thin Cap Group Litigation* [2007] ECR I-2107; Case C-414/06 *Lidl Belgium* [2008] ECR I-3601, paras 32–34; Case C-446/03 *Marks & Spencer* [2005] ECR I-10837, paras 46–49.

In sum, the Court explicitly stated in *Centros* that freedoms of movement grant Union citizens the right to freely choose their preferred national company law; by contrast, the free movement test in *Oy AA* allowed Member States to preclude choices of national tax law. The decision to proscribe (*Cadbury Schweppes*, *Oy AA*) or not (*Centros*) such artificial choices of law is a particular expression of the regulatory mobility dilemma, which is solved by alternatively resorting to restricted or free choice of law approaches.[28] Indeed, the inconsistency of the free movement test with regard to artificial choices of law can be reconstructed as a manifestation of the broader dialectic pervading the law of the internal market: artificial choices of law ought to be proscribed as abusive under regulatory neutrality (*Cadbury Schweppes*), but ratified as legitimate regulatory arbitrage under regulatory competition (*Centros*).

Under the regulatory neutrality paradigm, artificial choices of law distort the competition among private businesses, whose decisions should 'spontaneously' allocate economic resources within the internal market without having regard to the disparity among national laws. Hansen observed:

> The wish to circumvent national legislation is caused by the differences in national legislation. It is obvious that circumvention of national law leads directly to inequality of position between the person established in Member State B and the person that has moved to Member State A. If this unequal position was ignored it could lead to a distortion of competition.[29]

Furthermore, the correlation between the objective of regulatory neutrality and the prevention of abusive practices was firmly established by AG Maduro in his Opinions in *Marks & Spencer* and *Rewe Zentralfinanz*:

> In accordance with this principle of neutrality [of Community law towards national tax systems], the right of establishment may not be used by economic operators to gain advantages that are not connected with the exercise of the freedoms of movement. That would, however, be the case if a transfer of activity in the Community were determined solely by tax considerations, irrespective of any intention to seek real establishment and to integrate with the economy of the host society, with the sole aim of circumventing national laws or artificially exploiting differences between those laws.[30]
>
> On the one hand, the national tax rules must be neutral in regard to the exercise of the freedoms of movement. In that connection, it should be recalled that Article 43 EC lays down a requirement of fiscal neutrality in regard to the establishment of undertakings in the Community. On the other hand, the exercise of the freedoms of movement must be as neutral as possible in regard to the tax arrangements adopted by the Member States. The right of establishment cannot be used by traders with the sole purpose of endangering

[28] See ch 7 section V. This logical sequence appears very clearly in *Fitzwilliam*, in which the Court recalled that under art 14(1)(a) of Regulation 1408/71, home regulation applies to the social security of posted workers (para 29), before impeding regulatory mobility (para 30).

[29] LH Hansen, 'The Development of the Circumvention Principle in the Area of Broadcasting' (1998) 25 *Legal Issues of European Integration* 111, 111.

[30] AG Maduro, Case C-347/04 *Rewe Zentralfinanz* [2007] ECR I-2647, para 33.

> the equilibrium and the cohesion of national tax systems. That would be the case if use were made thereof either abusively to evade national laws or artificially to exploit differences between those laws.[31]

By contrast, under the regulatory competition paradigm, choices of law by Union citizens form a desirable process of regulatory arbitrage by which Union citizens freely compare and elect their preferred national law. Such regulatory arbitrage represents the first step of a process of competition among States, the latter being expected to adjust their national laws in order to match mobile citizens' preferences. As a consequence, if competition among Member States it to be encouraged, artificial choices of law should not be prohibited as abusive. Weatherill observed:

> An allegation of 'abuse' in this sense, if successfully advanced, has the consequence that regulatory competition is blocked: the host State's regulatory choices are not undermined by entry on to its market of goods or services which comply only with the regulatory regime set by their home State.[32]

Explicitly inspired by the regulatory competition paradigm, Vogenauer advocated a restrictive interpretation of the concept of abuse of Union law:

> Keeping the prohibition of abuse of law within narrowly confined boundaries is particularly important in cases of rule avoidance where persons 'escape' from the application of the more stringent regulatory regime of their home State by exercising one of the fundamental freedoms. They thereby choose a more favourable regime, a process frequently referred to as 'regulatory arbitrage'. From the perspective of EU law, this is arguably a good thing. The freedoms are meant to promote the Union's key goal of market integration and thus to encourage the movement of persons, goods, services and capital between jurisdictions. As a general rule, it is clearly legitimate and even desirable that citizens and companies should exploit the differences between regulatory regimes for their own (and, ultimately, for the overall) benefit. As a matter of principle, such choices ought to be protected, rather than being labelled 'abusive' and prohibited.[33]

Accordingly, the very existence of the concept of abuse of law presupposes the adoption of regulatory neutrality as paradigm of economic integration; under regulatory competition, the concept of 'abuse of law' simply does not exist, for artificial choices of law amount to desirable regulatory arbitrage. As summed up by Schammo, 'arbitrage and abuse of rights can be situated at opposing ends'.[34] This contrasted appraisal of artificial choices of law has important practical consequences, for it leads to two versions of the free movement test: the first proscribes

[31] AG Maduro Case C-446/03 *Marks & Spencer* [2005] ECR I-10837, para 67.

[32] S Weatherill, 'Fitting "Abuse of Rights" into EU Law Governing the Free Movement of Goods and Services' in R de la Feria and S Vogenauer (eds), *Prohibition of Abuse of Law: a New General Principle of EU Law?* (Oxford, Hart Publishing, 2011) 60.

[33] S Vogenauer, 'The Prohibition of Abuse of Law: an Emerging General Principle of EU Law' in de la Feria and Vogenauer, *Prohibition of Abuse of Law* (n 32) 549.

[34] P Schammo, 'Arbitrage and Abuse of Rights in the EC Legal System' (2008) 14 *European Law Journal* 351, 352.

abuses of law (*Oy AA*, *Cadbury*), the second ratifies them (*Centros*, *Cartesio*); and these two versions of the free movement test derive from the decision, conscious or not, to strive either for regulatory neutrality or regulatory competition (paradigms of economic integration). As a result, the regulatory neutrality paradigm promotes 'socioeconomic' mobility, whereas the regulatory competition paradigm promotes 'regulatory' mobility (choice of law).

In practice, when confronted with an artificial choice of law, the competent judge must decide whether the applicable legal norm is neutral or not; or, in other terms, whether it is intended to influence private decision-making. As better explained by Ruiz Almendral:

> In [a tax avoidance] analysis it is necessary to take into account the purpose of the tax norm and, specifically, whether or not that norm provides an incentive for that arrangement. ... This of course means that it will be essential to determine whether the tax provision intends to be neutral or not, with regard to that specific arrangement .... As a general departing point, where there is a neutral tax provision, a tax-influenced behaviour stands a good chance of being an avoidance (tax driven) transaction.
>
> [I]n some cases the tax norms mean to bring about other effects, such as influencing the behaviour of the taxpayer. ... [T]he (tax) norm may be implicitly asking the taxpayer to do something for tax reasons. If that is the case, it is obvious that one cannot deny the benefit to the taxpayer on the grounds that it was a tax driven transaction, for that is precisely one of the elements that has been taken into account by the norm.[35]

Thus, in a case like *Centros*, the Court judged that the Treaty provisions on freedom of establishment were not neutral, but were intended to encourage companies to move to the most hospitable jurisdiction. This is evident from the Opinion of AG La Pergola in the same case:

> [A] company is incorporated in the United Kingdom because the founders wish to avail themselves of the opportunity to operate with paid-up capital commensurate with the resources at their disposal and less than is required under Danish law. That situation, whether one likes it or not, is the logical consequence of the rights guaranteed under the Treaty. Moreover, it is consistent with the objective behind the inclusion of the freedom of establishment in the Treaty, namely the need to promote the free movement of persons (and capital) and, by the same token, the achievement of a common market. 'In that respect, the fact that a national of a Member State may take advantage of the flexibility of United Kingdom company law ... must be viewed in that context [that is, in the context of the Community system]'. In short, in the absence of harmonisation, competition among rules must be allowed free play in corporate matters.[36]

However, the *Centros* ruling did not logically flow from the Treaty; rather, a normative decision had to be made as to whether the freedom of establishment ought to be neutral or not towards national company laws. In his Opinions in

[35] V Ruiz Almendral, 'Tax Avoidance and the European Court of Justice: What is at Stake for European General Anti-Avoidance Rules?' (2005) 33 *Intertax* 562, 566 and 578.

[36] AG La Pergola, Case C-212/97 *Centros* [1999] ECR I-1459, para 20.

Marks & Spencer and *Rewe Zentralfinanz*, quoted at the inception of this section, AG Maduro insisted on the neutrality of the freedoms of movement towards national tax systems, with the consequence that artificial choices of law must be fought. By contrast, in *Centros*, AG La Pergola and the Court considered that the freedoms of movement were not intended to be neutral towards national company laws, so that artificial choices of law were legitimate. As observed by Ringe, this decision came as a surprise to many:

> The *Centros* ruling turned out to be a landmark decision on the interpretation of the freedom of establishment and produced substantial reverberations in legal doctrine. This is hardly surprising, since a course of conduct that comes close to abuse—and was widely believed to be a circumvention of national law—was not only declared legal, but even acknowledged as the very essence of the freedom of establishment. From this moment on, it seemed very tempting for businesses to set up a company in the Member State with the most flexible company law system—a development which we will deal with later.[37]

In terms of legal reasoning, the normative decision that a legal provision is neutral is made through the teleological assessment of the formal doctrine of abuse, which leads to the election of the correlated paradigm of economic integration (regulatory neutrality or regulatory competition). The function assigned to the teleological assessment is indeed the appraisal of the desirability of artificial choices of law realised by Union citizens, having due regard to the nature of the legal regime in question.[38] The presence of the teleological assessment is explicit in the formal doctrine of abuse, so that its application logically follows the decision to have recourse to the formal doctrine of abuse. With the other legal grounds dealing with artificial choices of law, the teleological assessment is only implicit so that the logical sequence is reversed: it must be first decided whether an artificial choice of law ought to be condemned or allowed, before having recourse to the given legal ground (eg informal doctrine of abuse, suspect period, centre of gravity or free choice of law).[39]

To sum up, the inconsistent prohibition of abuses of law is yet another expression of the dialectic shaping internal market law, opposing the paradigms of regulatory neutrality and regulatory competition. If economic integration is conceived as the promotion of cross-border competition among private businesses (regulatory neutrality), choices of law must be proscribed as abusive, for they distort business competition. But if economic integration is intended to promote competition among Member States (regulatory competition), choices of law by Union citizens represent a desirable process of arbitrage among national laws. In short, regulatory arbitrage and abuse of law are two normative masks covering one phenomenon: the election of a hospitable national law by a private individual.

[37] W-G Ringe, 'Sparking Regulatory Competition in European Company Law—The Impact of the Centros Line of Case-Law and its Concept of "Abuse of Law"' in de la Feria and Vogenauer (n 32) 110.

[38] See ch 3 section III.

[39] See ch 4.

IV. The Ambiguity Towards Social Dumping

The ambiguity towards social dumping is a practical application of both the negative harmonisation conundrum and the regulatory mobility dilemma, described in chapter seven, Sections IV and V. The present section argues that the trade-off between regulatory neutrality and regulatory competition accounts for the fundamental ambiguity of internal market law towards social dumping.

It is particularly hard to find a real definition of 'social dumping', even in the best literature on the phenomenon.[40] As is well known, the original concept of 'dumping' aims at distortions of competition created by undertaking selling products at below-cost price. In this context, Article 1(2) of Regulation 1225/2009 provides the following definition of dumping:

> A product is to be considered as being dumped if its export price to the Community is less than a comparable price for the like product, in the ordinary course of trade, as established for the exporting country.[41]

In a social context, the notion of dumping has taken on a more specific meaning, namely 'the idea that you replace an employee with a cheaper one coming from somewhere else'.[42] In this sense, the notion of social dumping concentrates all three practical issues of free movement law evoked in the previous sections: differentials of regulation, reverse discriminations and abuses of law. The first idea conveyed by the expression social (or regulatory) dumping is that of a distortion of competition created by a differential of regulation between undertakings subject to high standards and undertakings subject to low (or non-existent) standards. Accordingly, the issue of social dumping questions the legitimacy of differentials of social regulation, affecting competing undertakings established in different Member States (Section I). In his Opinion in *Vergani*, AG Colomer stated:

> The scant provisions which granted rights specifically with regard to employment, such as equal pay for men and women (former Article 119 of the EC Treaty), were designed to avoid 'social dumping', which would distort competition between the Member States.[43]

Secondly, social dumping may constitute a form of reverse discrimination, when foreign businesses are allowed to 'export' the lower social standards imposed by their home State into the host market (Section II). Davies wrote:

> In relation to services the issue raised is none other than the fundamental but often frustrating question of what is 'social dumping'. With regard to services involving the

[40] See esp C Barnard, 'Social Dumping And the Race to the Bottom: Some Lessons for the European Union from Delaware?' (2000) 25 *European Law Review* 57.

[41] Council Regulation (EC) 1225/2009 of 30 November 2009 on protection against dumped imports from countries not members of the European Community [2009] OJ L343/51.

[42] C Barnard, 'Fifty Years of Avoiding Social Dumping? The EU's Economic and Not So Economic Constitution' in M Dougan and S Currie (eds), *50 Years of the European Treaties* (Oxford, Hart Publishing, 2009) 311 fn 2 (quoting Mr Zitting, chairman of the FSU).

[43] See AG Colomer, Case C-207/04 *Vergani* [2005] ECR I-7453, para 21.

> supply of labour, mutual recognition of regulatory regimes could mean that the labour law standards of the Member State of establishment will govern the employment terms of workers hired in the state of establishment by the provider of the services, even if the services are to be provided through those employees in another Member State (the 'host' Member State), which has higher regulatory standards.[44]

Thirdly and lastly, from a dynamic perspective, social dumping represents a risk of abuse of law consisting in the artificial election of a hospitable social jurisdiction (Section III). Barnard observed:

> [C]apital may well be attracted to particular locations, not because of the abundance of the location's workforce or capital, but for other, less worthy reasons such as a more favourable social security regime for employers ... and cheaper wage costs. ... This migration is often referred to ... as social dumping.[45]

In the *Limosa* case, the Court conflated prevention of abuse, unfair competition and social dumping into one ground of justification:

> [T]he objective of combating fraud, particularly social security fraud, and preventing abuse, in particular detecting 'bogus self-employed persons' and combating undeclared work, can form part not only of the objective of the financial balance of social security systems, but also of the objectives of preventing unfair competition and social dumping and protecting workers, including self-employed service providers.[46]

Although the object of the present section is limited to social dumping, the issue of regulatory dumping is by no means limited to labour or social protection, but potentially extends to every type of regulation. For instance, the notion of regulatory dumping is commonly used in relation to environmental protection, as in the following Commission Communication:

> The absence of mandatory waste treatment standards at EU level undermines the creation of a high level of protection across the Community and has also raised concerns about 'standards dumping'. The argument that different environmental standards lead to significant differences in costs incurred by waste management facilities is in principle plausible, although little factual information is available about these economic issues and the actual waste flows involved. Nevertheless, there have been allegations that waste destined for recycling tends to be driven out of countries with higher standards and that, as a consequence, installations in these countries do not receive sufficient quantities of waste to be economically viable. It is therefore argued that Member States are impeded from developing and enforcing environmentally superior waste treatment technologies and requirements in the field of recycling, as waste tends to flow towards countries with lower standards.[47]

[44] P Davies, 'Market Integration and Social Policy in the Court of Justice' (1995) 24 *Industrial Law Journal* 49, 71.

[45] Barnard, 'Fifty Years of Avoiding Social Dumping?' (n 42) 314.

[46] Case C-577/10 *Commission v Belgium ('Limosa')* [2012] ECR I-0000, para 45.

[47] Commission (EC), 'Towards a thematic strategy on the prevention and recycling of waste' (Communication) COM (2003) 301 final, 27 May 2003, no 3.2.4.

As for the three practical issues evoked in the previous sections, the central submission of the present section is that the solutions advocated in the social dumping debate entirely depend on the election, conscious or not, of one overarching conception of economic integration: regulatory neutrality or regulatory competition. In that regard, it is particularly insightful to describe the evolution of the Court's case law on posted workers, and in particular the lines of case law respectively initiated by the *Rush Portuguesa* and *Laval* judgments.

In *Rush Portuguesa*, the Court unambiguously promoted host equality, namely equal treatment between migrant workers and the host society, by ruling that the host State was entitled to apply its labour law to every worker employed in its territory, irrespective of the place of establishment of their employer:

> Community law does not preclude Member States from extending their legislation, or collective labour agreements entered into by both sides of industry, to any person who is employed, even temporarily, within their territory, no matter in which country the employer is established; nor does Community law prohibit Member States from enforcing those rules by appropriate means.[48]

The *Rush Portuguesa* ruling, which is consistent with the usual Union policy of applying host regulation to migrant workers,[49] drastically reduced the room for social dumping strategies. On the one hand, employers bringing workers from their home State were not allowed to 'import' their home labour law, but had to abide by the host labour law (host equality). On the other hand, employers had no incentive to relocate in hospitable labour jurisdictions, since their workers remained subject to host law when employed in the host State. This deterring effect of host equality upon social dumping has been repeatedly underlined in both the case law and the scholarship:

> Thus, in one (unreasoned) paragraph, the Court put a stop to a threat of social dumping—without using this language—by allowing the host state to extend its labour laws and conditions to the staff employed by service providers working in its country.[50]

> Finally, as regards the defence based on the prevention of social dumping, the Court has held that the Member States may extend their legislation or collective agreements relating to minimum wages to any person who is employed, even temporarily, within their territory. That prerogative is also recognised by Article 3 of Directive 96/71.[51]

> In my view, the Law in question is also an appropriate means of preventing social dumping, in that one of its main aims is to harmonise the terms on which service providers, whether they are established in Germany or not, must pay their workers in the framework of the performance of a public contract. It thus ensures that local workers and posted workers on the same site will be paid equally.[52]

[48] Case C-113/89 *Rush Portuguesa* [1990] ECR I-1417, para 18; see also Joined Cases C-49/98, C-50/98, C-52/98 to C-54/98 and C-68/98 to C-71/98 *Finalarte and Others* [2001] ECR I-7831; Joined Cases C-369/96 and C-376/96 *Arblade and Others* [1999] ECR I-8453.

[49] See ch 7 section IV.A.

[50] Barnard (n 42) 314.

[51] Case C-244/04 *Commission v Germany* [2006] ECR I-885, para 61.

[52] AG Bot, Case C-346/06 *Rüffert* [2008] ECR I-1989, para 119.

To the surprise of many, the Court initiated a reversal of the *Rush Portuguesa* logic of host equality in the *Laval* case, which was confirmed in *Rüffert*, by precluding host States from applying their domestic laws to posted workers for matters falling outside the scope of Article 3(1) of Directive 96/71. As in *Van Tiggele* and *Leclerc*,[53] the Court had recourse to home equality, namely equal treatment between migrant workers and their home society, to assess the existence of a restriction on free movement:

> [T]he right of trade unions of a Member State to take collective action by which undertakings established in other Member States may be forced to sign the collective agreement for the building sector ... is liable to make it less attractive, or more difficult, for such undertakings to carry out construction work in Sweden, and therefore constitutes a restriction on the freedom to provide services within the meaning of Article 49 EC.[54]

> [The obligation to abide by the German minimum wages] causes those undertakings to lose the competitive advantage which they enjoy by reason of their lower wage costs; [this requirement] may impose on service providers established in another Member State where minimum rates of pay are lower an additional economic burden that may prohibit, impede or render less attractive the provision of their services in the host Member State.[55]

By reversing the axis of equality, from host equality to home equality, the Court necessarily found that the application of host law to migrant workers amounted to a restriction to free movement, owing to the negative harmonisation conundrum.[56] In this sense, *Laval* represents a radical departure from the host equality traditionally applied to migrant workers under free movement. Deakin commented:

> [T]here is no basis in Community law for a principle of regime portability in favour of workers—in other words, a worker moving from a more to a less regulative Member State cannot insist on taking the protection of the labour law of the state of origin with them. This is precisely the converse of *Laval*, where an employer moving from a less regulative state to a more regulative one was entitled to the protection (from its point of view) of the (weak) labour law of the country of origin. ... What is surprising, in the context of such decisions, is that Laval was decided the way it was.[57]

In so ruling, the *Laval*-line of case law dismantled the natural bulwark formed by *Rush Portuguesa* to social dumping, by enabling employers to 'import' their home labour law when bringing workers from their home State:

> Laval and the other cases make it clear that it does not amount to abuse of Union law to make use of free movement of services to exploit the comparative advantage of cheaper labour. Many would say hurrah to that.[58]

[53] See section I.
[54] Case C-341/05 *Laval* [2007] ECR I-11767, para 99.
[55] Case C-346/06 *Rüffert* [2008] ECR I-1989, para 14 and 37.
[56] See ch 7 section IV.B.
[57] S Deakin, 'Regulatory Competition after Laval' (2007–08) 10 *Cambridge Yearbook of European Legal Studies* 581, 607.
[58] C Barnard, 'The Notion of Abuse and the Freedom to Provide Services: A Labour Lawyer's Perspective' in de la Feria and Vogenauer (n 32) 100.

> The legal aspects of the social dimension have been brought into question because ECJ rulings in four cases (Viking, Laval, Rüffert and Luxemburg) have led to lively debates particularly in political and academic circles about potential fears of increasing risks of social dumping. The European Parliament, the academic world and employee representative organisations have expressed their concern about the decisions. Others are convinced that the ECJ judgements in these cases will contribute to improved functioning of the internal market.[59]

If the respective effects of *Rush Portuguesa* (host equality) and *Laval* (home equality) on social dumping are not questioned, the desirability of social dumping has proved highly controversial, as shown by the last quote. These controversies have led the Commission to propose a directive on the enforcement of Directive 96/71 in 2012, whose Article 3, entitled 'Preventing abuse and circumvention', seeks to prevent abusive relocations of undertakings seeking to elect a hospitable jurisdiction.[60]

The central submission of the present section is that the social dumping debate is yet another manifestation of the dialectic between regulatory neutrality and regulatory competition pervading the law of the internal market. On the one hand, the regulatory neutrality paradigm seeks to avoid competition among private businesses being distorted by national laws. Host equality creates a level playing field within the host State, thereby ensuring neutrality of labour law vis-à-vis businesses competing in the host State. In this context, social dumping distorts competition among employers and among workers, by enabling migrant workers to 'export' their home labour law. Accordingly, partisans of regulatory neutrality view 'social dumping' as an obstacle to a proper economic integration, and advocate a solution *à la Rush Portuguesa* (host equality):

> Freedom of establishment and open transport markets are often used … to establish companies in EU countries with lower labour costs, lower social security contributions and/or tax advantages without offering services in these countries. They exploit social and wage differences between countries for competitive advantage. This results in difficulties in tracing work contracts, ensuring social security schemes, and controlling and enforcing health and safety rules. In order to avoid social dumping it is necessary to ensure that the host country principle is applied, which means the application of the social conditions of the country in which the service is carried out.[61]

On the other hand, the regulatory competition paradigm seeks to ensure the proper functioning of the competition among Member States. In that context, differentials of regulation are legitimate and businesses are encouraged to elect their

[59] Opinion of the Economic and Social Committee on the social dimension of the internal market (n 7) no 1.6.

[60] Commission (EC), 'Proposal for a Directive of the European Parliament and of the Council on the enforcement of Directive 96/71/EC concerning the posting of workers in the framework of the provision of services' COM (2012) 131 final, 21 March 2012. See ch 4 n 114 and accompanying text.

[61] European Economic and Social Committee (EC), 'How EU policies have impacted on the job opportunities, the training needs and the working conditions of transport workers' (Explanatory Opinion), 15 June 2011, C248/22, no 5.2.

preferred labour law, a process called regulatory arbitrage. As a result, supporters of regulatory competition view 'social dumping' as the natural functioning of economic integration, and therefore endorse a solution *à la Laval* (home equality):

> The use of the term of 'social dumping' directed against the new Member States is offensive and should be avoided. To indicate the differences in wages and labour conditions as a problem of the Single Market is contradictory to the simple fact that wages are always part of the competition among the companies which is the basis of the free market economy and is beneficial to the consumers.[62]

In other words, just as the concept of abuse of law, the concept of social dumping simply does not exist under regulatory competition, for a process of competition among Member States is founded on the legitimacy of 'social dumping' strategies, otherwise called 'regulatory arbitrage'. As a consequence, the social dumping debate can never be solved, for it reproduces a broader dialectic opposing the paradigms of regulatory neutrality and regulatory competition. This tension between two irreconcilable visions of 'social dumping' has been explicitly acknowledged on various occasions:

> This rhetoric highlights a problem central to the whole debate on social dumping. What is 'social dumping' to the French—and something to be condemned—is 'inward investment' to the British—and something to be condoned. The single market is premised on the idea of movement by natural or legal persons to the state with the greatest comparative advantage. This was recognised by the Court in Centros.[63]

> [F]rom the beginning of discussions on the AEntG project, it was pointed out several times that such a law was intended, above all, to combat unfair competitive conditions resulting from low-pay competition in Europe and wage and social dumping. The referring court asks to what extent foreign employers who exploit the fact that lower wages are paid in their home country, as a result of different standards of living, are engaged in unfair competition. It considers that, in the European Union, the opening of markets, as an essential aspect of the internal market project, must allow more intense competition and greater international sharing of labour.[64]

To sum up, the ambiguity of the free movement jurisprudence towards social dumping is yet another manifestation of the fundamental dialectic pervading the law of the internal market. Partisans of regulatory neutrality consider social dumping as an obstacle to a proper economic integration as it distorts competition among private businesses, and therefore advocate a solution *à la Rush Portuguesa*. Supporters of regulatory competition view social dumping as the natural functioning of economic integration understood as competition among Member States, and therefore endorse a solution *à la Laval*.

[62] European Economic and Social Committee (EC), 'The Lisbon Agenda and the Internal Market' (Own-Initiative Opinion), 17 February 2010, C347/8, appendix.

[63] Barnard, 'Social Dumping And the Race to the Bottom' (n 40) 68.

[64] AG Mischo, Joined Cases C-49/98, C-50/98, C-52/98 to C-54/98 and C-68/98 to C-71/98 *Finalarte and Others* [2001] ECR I-7831, paras 32–33.

9

State Aids and Economic Integration

THE PREVIOUS CHAPTERS showed that the freedoms of movement host a tension between two paradigms of economic integration, designated as regulatory neutrality and regulatory competition. In turn, the present chapter intends to show that the Union rules on the prohibition of State aids are pervaded by the same tension (Section I). The definition of 'State aid' in Union law, and in particular the exclusion of both general and regulatory measures, can be usefully reinterpreted in light of this paradigmatic tension (Section II). Furthermore, the concept of abuse of Union law represents a useful starting point for the construction of a common framework of analysis of free movement and State aid laws. Abuses of law were defined as undesirable choices of law artificially made by private individuals. There is an obvious affinity between private strategies consisting in *electing* a hospitable jurisdiction—which may be sanctioned as abuses of law—and public strategies consisting in *offering* a hospitable jurisdiction—which may be prohibited as State aids. In essence, the prohibitions of abuses of law and State aids aim at the same phenomenon, but from opposite perspectives (Section III).

I. The State Aids Regime between Regulatory Neutrality and Regulatory Competition

Next to the freedoms of movement, internal market law encompasses another set of rules intended to ensure that State actions comply with the objective of economic integration, namely the *prohibition of State aids*. Article 107(1) TFEU (former 87(1) EC) provides that:

> Save as otherwise provided in the Treaties, any aid granted by a Member State or through State resources in any form whatsoever which distorts or threatens to distort competition by favouring certain undertakings or the production of certain goods shall, in so far as it affects trade between Member States, be incompatible with the internal market.

In comparison with the freedoms of movement, the State aids regime has been described as a 'latecomer in terms of legal development'.[1] Despite their common target (public measures)[2] and shared objective (economic integration), the freedoms of movement and the prohibition of State aids have seldom been articulated within a common framework of analysis.[3] The Court of Justice has referred to their shared objective on a few occasions, such as *Commission v France*:

> The provisions relating to the free movement of goods, the repeal of discriminatory tax provisions and aid have a common objective, namely to ensure the free movement of goods between Member States under normal conditions of competition. … The mere fact that a national measure may possibly be defined as an aid within the meaning of Article [107 TFEU] is not an adequate reason for exempting it from the prohibition contained in Article [34 TFEU].[4]

In addition to their formal separation within the European Treaties (distinct sets of rules), their opposite dynamics may account for this lack of joint analysis: while the freedoms of movement are concerned with *barriers* erected by Member States to cross-border movements, the prohibition of State aids aims at *baits* created by Member States to lure cross-border flows into their territory. Despite their seemingly opposite dynamics, the freedoms of movement and the prohibition of State aids deal with the same fundamental issue raised by economic integration, described above:[5] should national laws be neutral towards trade flows, or should they act as magnets throughout the internal market? Put differently, should Member States' actions be neutral towards competition among private businesses, or should competition among Member States be promoted? As early as 1961, AG Lagrange considered that both 'barriers' and 'baits' were incompatible with economic integration, in accordance with the paradigm of regulatory neutrality:

> [T]here is no common market if there are national customs duties. In the same way there is no real common market in an industry straddling several countries if one of those countries subsidizes its own industry.[6]

[1] M Ross, 'State Aids: Maturing into a Constitutional Problem' (1995) *Yearbook of European Law* 79, 79.

[2] Free movement and State aid laws seek to discipline State interventions within the internal market. By contrast, competition law scrutinises anticompetitive behaviour adopted by private undertakings and affecting the internal market (abuses of a dominant position and cartels). In that sense, free movement and State aid laws are concerned with interactions between public authorities and private individuals, whereas competition law is concerned with interactions among private individuals. The only qualification to the 'private' scope of competition law concerns situations in which a Member State compels private undertakings to adopt anticompetitive behaviour: see the seminal Case 13/77 *G.B.-INNO-B.M. v Association des Détaillants en Tabac (ATAB)* [1977] ECR 2115, paras 28–34.

[3] See, however, A Biondi, P Eeckhout and J Flynn, *The Law of State Aid in the European Union* (Oxford, Oxford University Press, 2004).

[4] Case 18/84 *Commission v France* [1985] ECR 1339, para 13; see also Case 103/84 *Commission v Italy* [1986] ECR 1759, para 19; Case C-21/88 *Du Pont de Nemours* [1990] ECR I-889, para 20.

[5] See ch 6 section I.

[6] AG Lagrange, Case 30/59 *Mines du Limbourg* [1961] ECR 3.

In terms of trade, State aids indeed breach regulatory neutrality as they tend to provoke deflections of trade to the benefit of the subsidising State:

> The crucial point in [the Court's] analysis is the diversion of trade flows which would normally occur. According to the Court, [State aid] is capable of distorting competition, where competition between companies in various Member States exists as the aid artificially strengthens the position of the recipient company.[7]
>
> Indeed, subsidies that are not of a general nature have, by definition, an impact on relative prices and therefore on the allocation of resources among sectors. In an open economy, this implies that the terms of trade are affected. If the effect is significant enough it may shift the comparative advantage of the country.[8]

More generally, prohibiting State aids contributes to regulatory neutrality (competition among businesses), whereas allowing them fosters regulatory competition (competition among Member States). In that connection, it is particularly insightful to contrast the United States and European Union approaches to State aids. US law adopts a permissive approach towards State aids. Schenk observed that 'State aid in the form of both direct subsidies and tax incentives is very common in the United States and operates with little judicial and legislative restriction'.[9] Furthermore, regulatory competition is widely acknowledged as the rationale for such permissiveness in the US law literature: 'There is widespread support in the U.S. for States competing to offer the greatest amount of public services in exchange for tax dollars'.[10] According to the US Supreme Court itself, 'competition among the States for a share of interstate commerce is a central element of our free-trade policy'.[11] As underlined by Barnard, for regulatory competition to function optimally, citizens must be free to arbitrate among local laws and local governments must be free to adjust their laws:

> For competitive federalism to function, two conditions need to be satisfied. First, the federal (central) authorities must lay down and enforce the rules giving goods, persons, and capital freedom to exit one Member State and enter another. Secondly, the states (the decentralized authorities) must remain free to regulate … according to their own standards so as to enable regulators to respond to the competition.[12]

[7] C Nordberg, 'Judicial Remedies for Private Parties Under the State Aid Procedure' (1997) 24 *Legal Issues of Economic Integration* 35, 40.

[8] L Hancher, T Ottervanger and PJ Slot, *EC State Aids* (London, Sweet & Maxwell, 2006), no 2-005.

[9] DH Schenk, 'The Cuno Case: A Comparison of U.S. Subsidies and European State Aid' (2006) 3 *European State Aid Law Quaterly* 3, 3; see also US Federal Trade Commission, 'Competition, State Aids And Subsidies', OECD Global Forum on Competition, 12 February 2010, DAF/COMP/GF/WD(2010)67, no 4: 'States and local authorities regularly provide tax breaks and other incentives to attract new investors'.

[10] Schenk, 'The Cuno Case' (n 9) 6; see also TA Kaye, 'The Gentle Art of Corporate Seduction: Tax Incentives in the United States and the European Union' (2008) 57 *Kansas Law Review* 93.

[11] *Boston Stock Exchange v State Tax Commission* (1977) 429 US 318 (USSC), 328.

[12] C Barnard, *The Substantive Law of the EU: the Four Freedoms*, 2nd edn (Oxford, Oxford University Press, 2007) 20. Regulatory competition has been defined as an iterative process of regulatory arbitrage (by citizens) and adjustment (by local governments), allegedly leading to optimal regulation: see ch 6 section III.

In this context, the prohibition of State aids would have the effect of restraining the power of local States to adjust their laws, in order to match the preferences expressed by mobile citizens, thereby impairing the process of regulatory competition.

Under Union law, by contrast, State aids granted by Member States are subject to strict scrutiny by the Commission. As a rule, State aids falling within the scope of Article 107(1) TFEU are prohibited; they can, however, be deemed compatible with the internal market if they fall within the scope of mandatory or optional derogations respectively listed in Articles 107(2) and (3), or if they contribute to the operation of services of general economic interest within the conditions set out by Article 106(2). The central justification for this broad prohibition of State aids within the European Union is unquestionably regulatory neutrality, which seeks to avoid the competition among private businesses being distorted by national regulations.[13] In that connection, the Commission stated in the *State Aid Action Plan* and the *Vademecum*:

> State aid control comes from the need to maintain a level playing field for all undertakings active in the Single European Market, no matter in which Member State they are established. There is a particular need to be concerned with those State aid measures, which provide unwarranted selective advantages to some firms, preventing or delaying the market forces from rewarding the most competitive firms, thereby decreasing overall European competitiveness.[14]
>
> The negative effects [of State aids] are primarily distortive effects on competition and trade. They may include prevention of exit and keeping inefficient firms afloat, crowding out of private investment, disrupting dynamic incentives, costs of State aid linked to fiscal spending, etc.[15]

This concern was already present in the Spaak Report, which evidently prefigured the actual phrasing of the current Article 107(1) TFEU:

> One of the essential safeguards that must be offered to undertakings is that the game will not be distorted by artificial advantages that would benefit their competitors. Therefore, aids granted by States must be examined very closely, regardless of the external form they take ... The general rule is that aids that distort competition and the allocation of activities by favouring certain undertakings or certain productions are incompatible with the common market, no matter in what form they are granted.[16]

[13] See ch 6 section I.

[14] Commission (EC), 'State Aid Action Plan—Less and better targeted state aid: a roadmap for state aid reform 2005–2009' (Communication) COM (2005) 107 final, 7 June 2005, no 7.

[15] Commission (EC), 'Community law on State aid' (Vademecum), 30 September 2008, available at http://ec.europa.eu/competition/state_aid/studies_reports/studies_reports.html, 12.

[16] Rapport du Comité intergouvernemental créé par la Conférence de Messine ('Rapport Spaak'), 21 April 1956, aei.pitt.edu/996/01/Spaak_report_french.pdf, 57, free translation; see also Commission (EC), 'Completing the internal market' (White Paper) COM (85) 310 final, 14 June 1985, no 157–58.

Prohibition of State aids and regulatory neutrality are regularly associated in the literature as well. Kelyn Bacon, for instance, describes the justification for State aid control as follows:

> State aid has the capacity to distort competition by interfering with the level playing field on which companies compete, with the potential consequence that less efficient companies can account for a larger share of output. State aid control gives the Commission a role in preventing such distortions, unless there is a good enough reason why the aid should be granted.[17]

It should be underlined that the justifications offered in support of the opposite approaches adopted in US and Union law are remarkably consistent with the trade-off between regulatory neutrality and regulatory competition.[18] Indeed, if prohibiting State aids promotes regulatory neutrality (Union law), then allowing State aids should logically promote regulatory competition (US law), given the inherent trade-off between regulatory neutrality and regulatory competition (Figure 12).

In addition, there is a clear awareness on both sides of the Atlantic that the approach adopted towards State aids entails some drawbacks, in accordance with the trade-off between regulatory neutrality and regulatory competition. Thus, within the European Union, many scholars have underlined that the prohibition of State aids impairs the process of regulatory competition within the internal market. For instance, Maduro noted in relation to his 'competitive model' that 'Article [107 TFEU] on State aids limits competition with regard to state support to undertakings'.[19] This argument was explored more extensively by Kerber, who submitted that the ideal of a 'level playing field' underlying the prohibition of State aids implied 'the complete elimination of any interjurisdictional competition'.[20] For the same reason, Besley and other economists argued in favour of a more liberal approach towards State aids within the European Union.[21]

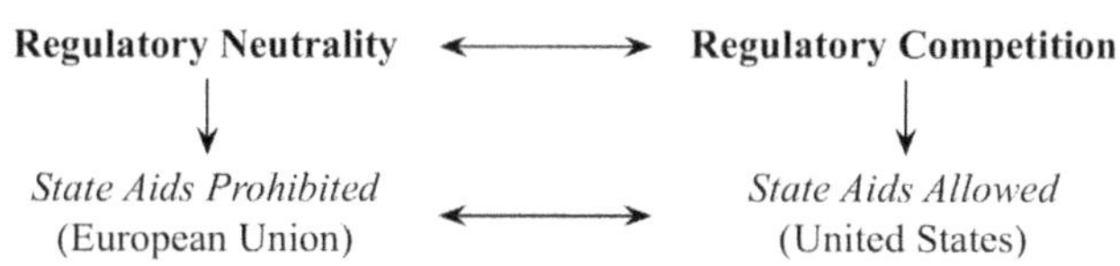

Figure 12 – State Aids and Paradigms of Economic Integration

[17] K Bacon, *European Community Law of State Aid* (Oxford, Oxford University Press, 2009) no 1.13; see also, among many others, Hancher, Ottervanger and Slot, *EC State Aids* (n 8) no 2-018; B Kurcz and D Vallindas, 'Can General Measures be … Selective? Some Thoughts on the Interpretation of a State Aid Definition' (2008) 45 *Common Market Law Review* 159, 159; D Waelbroeck, 'La notion d'aide d'État dans la jurisprudence récente de la Cour de Justice' in G Vandersanden et al (eds), *Mélanges en hommage à Georges Vandersanden: Promenades au sein du droit européen* (Brussels, Bruylant, 2008) 827.

[18] See ch 7 section VI.

[19] MP Maduro, *We the Court: the European Court of Justice and the European Economic Constitution* (Oxford, Hart Publishing, 1998) 134.

[20] W Kerber, 'Interjurisdictional Competition within the European Union' (1999–2000) 23 *Fordham International Law Journal* 217, 238.

[21] T Besley et al, 'The Effects and Policy Implications of State Aids to Industry: An Economic Analysis' (1999) 14 *Economic Policy* 13.

Conversely, US law literature regularly points out that allowing State subsidies generates distortions of competition among private businesses, in accordance with the regulatory neutrality paradigm.[22] The most powerful charge against the US permissive approach towards State aids was led by Enrich, in a seminal article published in 1996.[23] In essence, Enrich advocated an interpretation of the Dormant Commerce Clause ensuring regulatory neutrality, which would preclude States from distorting competition among businesses:

> An antidiscrimination principle that focuses on the distortion of decisions about locating economic activity will subsume as a corollary the more familiar prohibition on protectionist measures that favor in-state businesses by 'burdening out-of-state competitors' or by 'providing a direct commercial advantage to local business.' … Thus, the Court has the opportunity to strengthen and clarify its Commerce Clause jurisprudence … The reframed antidiscrimination principle would prohibit state tax measures that discriminate against interstate commerce by distorting the decisions of economic actors in favor of expenditures on in-state activities.
>
> Under this reframed antidiscrimination principle, business location incentives would be virtually per se unconstitutional … because their central function is to influence economic location decisions and to divert investment into the state.[24]

Under this interpretation, both restrictions on free movement and State aids would as a rule be prohibited. Enrich had the opportunity to plead his thesis during the *Cuno v DaimlerChrysler* litigation, in which he represented the plaintiffs, a group of individual taxpayers residing in Ohio. The *Cuno* case concerned a tax incentive package of $280 million granted by the City of Toledo (Ohio) in order to persuade DaimlerChrysler to build a new vehicle-assembly plant in an economically depressed area of Toledo, which represented an investment of $1.2 billion and the creation of thousands of jobs. To the surprise of most commentators, the Court of Appeals for the Sixth Circuit partly welcomed the plaintiffs' claim by ruling that the franchise tax credit offered to DaimlerChrysler violated the Dormant Commerce Clause;[25] however, the Supreme Court vacated the judgment on procedural grounds.[26]

[22] See among many others Schenk (n 9) 8: 'Despite the widespread use of subsidies in the U.S., there is increasing concern, just as there is in the EU, that the use of subsidies distorts market competition'; Kaye, 'The Gentle Art of Corporate Seduction (n 10) 120: 'Although interstate competition to attract economic development has raised concerns regarding the smooth functioning of the national economy, the proliferation of tax credits and incentives has continued relatively unabated'; DP Wood, 'Cuno v Daimler Chrysler, Inc.: State "Aids" from an American Perspective' (2007) 6 *European State Aid Law Quarterly* 3, 9: '[M]arket distortions caused by State subsidies and State participation in the market have not, in the final analysis, disrupted competition in the U.S. market enough to become a salient political *issue*'.

[23] P Enrich, 'Saving the States from Themselves: Commerce Clause Constraints on State Tax Incentives for Business' (1996) 110 *Harvard Law Review* 377.

[24] Enrich (n 23) 457–58.

[25] *Cuno v DaimlerChrysler* 386 F.3d 738 (6th Cir 2004).

[26] *DaimlerChrysler v Cuno* (2006) 547 US 332 (USSC). The Court ruled that the taxpayers lacked standing to pursue their complaint before a federal jurisdiction; as a result, the Court did not discuss the merits of the case and questions regarding the constitutionality of such tax credits remain unanswered.

If the outcome and apparently limited meaning of the *Cuno* litigation[27] are of secondary importance for the present purpose, Enrich's work corroborates the correlation between State aids and regulatory competition, on the one hand, and between the prohibition of State aids and regulatory neutrality, on the other. Moreover, it is remarkable that restrictions to free movement and State aids should be assessed against the same constitutional rule under US law, namely the Dormant Commerce Clause. This formal unity supports the central submission of the present chapter, namely that the Union freedoms of movement and the prohibition of State aids perform the same function: managing the tension between the objectives of regulatory neutrality and regulatory competition in a context of economic integration.

To sum up, a broad prohibition of State aids preserves undistorted competition among businesses (regulatory neutrality) but reduces the room for competition among Member States (regulatory competition);[28] conversely, allowing State aids distorts business competition but increases the room for State competition.

II. Reviewing the Classical Definition of 'State Aid' under Union Law

As explained in the previous chapters, the paradigms of regulatory neutrality and regulatory competition entail very different prescriptions for the interpretation of the free movement test.[29] Their differences are even more radical in relation to State aids.

If the regulatory competition paradigm were fully endorsed, the scope of the prohibition of State aids would be *null* since, for regulatory competition to function optimally, Member States should be entirely free to adjust their laws in order to match citizens' preferences. This is roughly the solution adopted under US law.

Conversely, under a system of full regulatory neutrality, the scope of the prohibition of State aids would be *infinite* for any divergence among national laws is liable to distort competition among businesses active in the internal market. The

[27] The *Cuno* judgment condemned a State aid for the first time in US law; however, its ambit was limited for it did not concern direct subsidies and only covered certain types of tax credit. Moreover, the Supreme Court would have probably reversed the judgment on the merits as well; and in the alternative, Congress was expected to overrule the decision. For more detail, see among others Kaye (n 10); Schenk (n 9); V Iyer, 'Cuno v DaimlerChrysler, Inc.: Dormant Commerce Clause Limits State Location Tax Incentives' (2005) 40 *Harvard Civil Rights-Civil Liberties Law Review* 523; MJ Graetz, AC Warren, Jr and R Yablon, 'From the Court's Docket: DaimlerChrysler Corp. v Cuno and the European Experience' (2005) 115 *Yale Law Journal Pocket Part* 99.

[28] In the same sense, see 'Les aides d'État sous forme fiscale' (2008) 48 *Revue de Droit Fiscal* 9, no 11–13.

[29] See esp ch 7 section VI.

same argument was made in relation to the eventuality of positive harmonisation at Union level: full regulatory neutrality would confer an infinite scope to the Treaty provisions on harmonisation since legislative disparity distorts competition among private businesses.[30] Thus, under the regulatory neutrality paradigm, legislative disparity justifies a systematic recourse to both harmonisation by the Union legislature and to the prohibition of State aids by the Commission. However, the opposite force exerted by the regulatory competition paradigm reduces the scope of both sets of rules to a middle ground.

As a matter of fact, the ambit of the prohibition of State aids in Union law has navigated between these two extremes, under the influence of the evolving case law of the Court. A fresh reading of the classical definition of State aid can be proposed in light of the tension between regulatory neutrality and regulatory competition.

A State aid is classically defined as any measure satisfying four criteria listed in Article 107(1) TFEU: the measure confers an economic advantage on the recipient; favours certain undertakings or the production of certain goods (condition of 'selectivity'); involves a transfer of State resources; and is liable to distort competition and affect trade between Member States.[31] Of these four conditions, selectivity and transfer of State resources are by far the most controversial. As we shall see, these controversies are chiefly triggered by a blind adherence to regulatory neutrality, whereas these two conditions arguably draw the dividing line between regulatory neutrality and regulatory competition within State aid law. The central contention of this chapter is indeed that State aid law is used to manage the tension between regulatory neutrality and regulatory competition.

According to this classical definition, a State aid must, first of all, confer an economic advantage to the recipient undertaking, whose presence is assessed through the so-called 'private operator test'. This requirement assesses the *private availability* of the advantage received by the recipient undertaking: the question is whether competitors would have been able to obtain on the market the same advantage as the beneficiary.[32] The first case in which the Court explicitly acknowledged the existence of the private operator test, in the wake a strong opinion by AG Lenz, concerned a public subscription of capital in an undertaking in difficulty:

> An appropriate way of establishing whether such a measure is a State aid is to apply the criterion … of determining to what extent the undertaking would be able to obtain the sums in question on the private capital markets. In the case of an undertaking whose capital is held by the public authorities, the test is, in particular, whether in similar circumstances a private shareholder, having regard to the foreseeability of obtaining a

[30] See ch 7 section III.

[31] Case C-140/09 *Fallimento Traghetti del Mediterraneo* [2010] ECR I-5243, para 31; Joined Cases C-182/03 and C-217/03 *Belgium and Forum 187 v Commission* [2006] ECR I-5479, para 84; Case C-280/00 *Altmark* [2003] ECR I-7747, paras 74–75; Kurcz and Vallindas, 'Can General Measures be … Selective?' (n 17) 160; Bacon, *European Community Law of State Aid* (n 17) no 2.02; Vademecum on State aid (n 15) 6–7.

[32] Hancher, Ottervanger and Slot (n 8) no 3-021.

> return and leaving aside all social, regional-policy and sectoral considerations, would have subscribed the capital in question.[33]

The classical formula used by the Court now refers to 'an economic advantage which the recipient undertaking would not have obtained under normal market conditions'.[34] In essence, the private operator test seeks to determine whether the State behaved according to economic rationality: 'a State aid … is that part of a financial flow between a state and a private enterprise in excess of that which would be provided by a private investor'.[35] If no rational private operator would behave as the State did, the measure in question must originate in public power, which justifies Union law's scrutiny.

Although unambiguous in appearance, the private operator test may lead to very different outcomes depending on whether regulatory neutrality or regulatory competition is pursued. Member States have indeed tried to argue that the private operator test should take into account the public benefits accruing from State aids, such as a reduction in the unemployment rate, an increase in tax incomes, or the redevelopment of a depressed region. The inclusion of such public benefits would substantially reduce the scope of the notion of 'State aid', since most decisions to grant an aid rest on their likely public benefits. Correlatively, this inclusion would increase the room enjoyed by States to distort competition among businesses (regulatory neutrality) and compete against each other (regulatory competition). The Court has however consistently excluded public benefits from the private investor test, which increases regulatory neutrality and decreases regulatory competition:

> [I]n order to assess whether the same measure would have been adopted in normal market conditions by a private investor in a situation as close as possible to that of the State, only the benefits and obligations linked to the situation of the State as shareholder—to the exclusion of those linked to its situation as a public authority—are to be taken into account.[36]

> [A] distinction must be drawn between the obligations which the State must assume as owner of the share capital of a company and its obligations as a public authority. Since the three companies in question were constituted as limited companies, the Patrimonio del Estado, as owner of the share capital, would only have been liable for their debts up to the liquidation value of their assets. That means in the present case that the obligations arising from the cost of redundancies, payment of unemployment benefits and aid for

[33] Case 234/84 *Belgium v Commission* [1986] ECR 2263, para 14; AG Lenz, Case 234/84 *Belgium v Commission* [1986] ECR 2263.

[34] Case C-280/00 *Altmark* [2003] ECR I-7747, para 84; Case C-342/96 *Spain v Commission* [1999] ECR I-2459, para 41; Case C-39/94 *SFEI* [1996] ECR I-3547, para 60. See also AG Léger, Case C-280/00 *Altmark* [2003] ECR I-7747.

[35] London Economics, *Competition Issues*, The Single Market Review, subseries V, vol 3 (London, Kogan Page, 1997) 228. See also M Heidenhain (ed), *European State Aid Law* (Munich, Verlag CH Beck, 2010) 23–24; Hancher, Ottervanger and Slot (n 8) no 3-021; Besley, 'The Effects and Policy Implications of State Aids to Industry' (n 21) 17–18.

[36] Case C-124/10 P *Commission v EDF* [2012] ECR I-0000, para 79 and case law cited.

the restructuring of the industrial infrastructure must not be taken into consideration for the purpose of applying the private investor test.[37]

The second constitutive element of a 'State aid' consists in the selectivity of the measure in question; according to the wording of Article 107(1) TFUE, a State aid favours 'certain undertakings or the production of certain goods'. If the first constitutive element (economic advantage) assessed private availability and questioned whether competitors could obtain a similar advantage on the market, this second element (selectivity) assesses public availability and questions whether every domestic undertaking could obtain a similar advantage from the State—or from an autonomous local authority within the State.[38] As a consequence, 'general' measures, namely advantages available to all domestic undertakings, escape State aids scrutiny. Classical examples of such general measures are the reduction of social security contributions or the lowering of tax rates and other general rules of taxation. In *3M Italia*, for instance, the Court judged that national legislation providing for the conclusion of tax proceedings, where such proceedings had lasted for more than 10 years, and in return for payment of a sum equivalent to 5 per cent of the value of the claim, was a general measure:

> [A]dvantages resulting from a general measure applicable without distinction to all economic operators do not constitute State aid within the meaning of that article.
>
> [I]t must be noted, with respect to the selectiveness of the measure, that it applies generally to all taxpayers who are parties to tax proceedings pending before the Corte suprema di cassazione, whatever the nature of the tax at issue, where those proceedings originate in an application at first instance made more than 10 years before the date of the entry into force of that provision and the tax authorities have been unsuccessful at first and second instance.
>
> The fact that only taxpayers satisfying those conditions can benefit from the measure cannot in itself make it into a selective measure.[39]

The exclusion of general measures from State aid scrutiny offers another illustration of the trade-off between the objectives of regulatory neutrality and regulatory competition. General measures distort cross-border competition among businesses, as they are only made available to domestic undertakings, which breaches regulatory neutrality in the internal market.[40] Yet their exclusion from State aid scrutiny

[37] Joined Cases C-278/92, C-279/92 and C-280/92 *Spain v Commission* [1994] ECR I-4103, para 22.

[38] Regional general measures, namely measures adopted by local authorities within a Member State, escape State aid scrutiny as well when they are adopted in institutional, procedural and economic autonomy from central authorities. See Joined Cases C-428/06 to C-434/06 *UGT-Rioja* [2008] ECR I-6747; Case C-88/03 *Portugal v Commission (Azores)* [2006] ECR I-7115; J Bousin and J Piernas, 'Developments in the Notion of Selectivity' (2008) *European State Aid Law Quarterly* 634; C Zatschler, 'Review of the Judgment in Case C-88/03, Portugal v Commission (Azores Tax Regime)' (2006) *European State Aid Law Quarterly* 779.

[39] Case C-417/10 *3M Italia* [2012] ECR I-0000, paras 39, 41 and 42.

[40] Selective advantages distort *both* internal competition and cross-border competition among businesses, as they are only granted to 'certain' domestic undertakings, and accordingly undermine regulatory neutrality even more.

allows Member States to compete by means of general measures, in accordance with the objective of regulatory competition. Conversely, their prohibition would promote regulatory neutrality but suppress a substantial room for regulatory competition. In practice, the exclusion of general measures implies that the selectivity requirement rests on a domestic comparator, as acknowledged by the Court in *Adria-Wien*:[41] an economic advantage can be said general when it is available for all *domestic* undertakings, and the fact that it is not enjoyed by undertakings in other Member States—thereby distorting cross-border competition—is irrelevant.[42]

Whereas it is not disputed that the purpose of the selectivity requirement is to screen out general measures from State aid scrutiny, namely those measures available across the board to all domestic undertakings in all economic sectors in a Member State,[43] the normative justification of this exclusion has proved notoriously controversial. Most of the controversy stems from a blind adherence to regulatory neutrality. This exclusion is indeed untenable in light of the regulatory neutrality paradigm, for general measures distort competition among undertakings in the internal market just as selective measures do. AG Caportorti famously put forward this argument in the *Buy Irish* case, which concerned an advertising campaign financed by the Irish Government in order to promote domestic products:

> [I]t is perfectly justifiable to speak of a general principle of the prohibition of public aids to domestic products, if one wishes to avoid the incongruous view that sectorial aids are prohibited and those of wider scope are permitted. …
>
> In this case, the advertising campaign inspired and financed by the Irish Government, in my opinion, clearly constitutes a form of aid … That campaign … obviously reduces the costs of Irish products—thus distorting competition in the common market—in so far as the burden of paying for the advertising is borne by an institution closely linked to the State.[44]

However, ever since the Spaak Report, the rationale for the exclusion of general measures—or selectivity requirement—is not to be found in regulatory neutrality, but rather in the regulatory competition paradigm. Indeed, the Spaak Report distinguished between public measures granting artificial advantages, which had to be scrutinised by the Commission, and the mere disparity among national regulations, which must be harmonised by the Council.[45] As explained by Di Bucci,

[41] Case C-143/99 *Adria-Wien Pipeline* ECR [2001] I-8365, para 35: 'A State measure which benefits all undertakings in national territory, without distinction, cannot therefore constitute State aid'.

[42] Bacon (n 17) no 2.111; K Bacon, 'State Aids and General Measures' (1997) *Yearbook of European Law* 269, 293–95.

[43] Vademecum on State aid (n 15) 6.

[44] AG Capotorti, Case 249/81 *Commission v Ireland (Buy Irish)* [1982] ECR I-4005, para 7.

[45] Rapport Spaak (n 16) 59, free translation:

> [C]ertain regimes of intervention that formally constitute aids or subsidies are not specifically aimed at certain undertakings or sectors, but affect the general economy. In such case, the Commission has no jurisdiction to decide by itself on the incompatibility, but needs the approval of the Council acting unanimously during the first stage, by a qualified majority thereafter.

> The idea behind this distinction was that Member States may compete with each other by choices of general economic policy, capable of shaping their respective economic environments in different ways, but should not create niches of privilege for certain undertakings or certain sectors.[46]

According to Di Bucci, the rationale for the exclusion of general measures under Article 107(1) TFUE is regulatory competition: Member States are allowed to compete against each other by means of general measures.[47] Two main reasons can be advanced to explain why Member States should be allowed to compete with general measures and not with selective ones. First, it is much more 'expensive' for a State to compete with general measures, since they have to be made available to all domestic undertakings. As a result, the risk of significant distortions of competition on the private market is more limited. By contrast, allowing selective measures would permit Member States to multiply punctual interventions in the economy, which would greatly amplify the risk of distortion.

Secondly, State aid law has no vocation to redress every distortion of business competition left by diversity among national laws. Although general measures do indeed distort competition within the internal market (between domestic and foreign undertakings[48]), such distortions must be resolved through harmonisation by the Union legislature acting under Articles 114 to 118 TFEU. This institutional divide was already envisioned in the Spaak Report (see above), and is often recalled in the literature.[49] In addition, this institutional framework was further refined by the Court in the *Buy Irish* case, in which it held that general measures could be contrary to the freedoms of movement when they intend to substitute domestic products for imported products and are liable to affect the volume of trade between Member States.[50]

The third constitutive element of a State aid consists in that the selective economic advantage identified must distort competition in the internal market and affect inter-State trade. The requirement that inter-State trade be affected aims at distinguishing between aids granted in cross-border and in purely internal situations: only the former falls within the Union's jurisdiction, while the latter falls

[46] V Di Bucci, 'Quelques Aspects Institutionnels du Droit des Aides d'Etat' in F Santaolalla Gadea (ed), *EC State Aid Law: Liber Amicorum Francisco Santaolalla Gadea* (The Hague, Kluwer Law International, 2008) 44, free translation.

[47] In the same sense, see Waelbroeck, 'La notion d'aide d'État' (n 17) 810, free translation:

> The mere fact that a tax regime is more favourable in one Member State than in another does certainly not mean that there is aid. In that regard, a certain degree of tax competition among Member States is in itself not necessarily condemnable.

[48] By contrast, selective measures create distortions of competition between domestic and foreign undertakings as well as among domestic undertakings: see Commission (EC), 'Second Survey on State Aids in the European Community in the manufacturing and certain other sectors' (Communication) SEC (90) 1165/3, 10 July 1990, no 10.

[49] Heidenhain, *European State Aid Law* (n 34) 43; Hancher, Ottervanger and Slot (n 8) no 3-084; Bacon, 'State Aids and General Measures' (n 43) 269.

[50] Case 249/81 *Commission v Ireland (Buy Irish)* [1982] ECR I-4005, esp para 25.

within the Member States' jurisdiction.[51] On the other hand, and as noted by AG Capotorti, the requirement of a distortion of competition seems to be less a defining element of a State aid than the logical implication of the other requirements, namely the grant of a selective advantage to an undertaking.[52] Indeed, the attribution of an advantage that could not be received in the 'normal course of business'[53] is per se liable to disturb allocative efficiency, namely the spontaneous allocation of resources by market forces.[54] In that connection, the Commission observed that such public bounty is likely to prevent or delay market forces from rewarding the most competitive firms active in the internal market, eventually leaving customers with higher prices, lower quality and less innovation.[55]

As a matter of fact, the Court has proved lenient in its interpretation of this third requirement ever since the *Philip Morris* case,[56] in which it ruled that the Commission must only examine whether the aid is liable to affect trade between Member States and distort competition, rather than establish an actual effect on trade and competition.[57] The recipient undertaking is not even required to partake in intra-Union trade, but only to carry out an economic activity that is subject to Union trade[58]—which encompasses most economic activities within the Union. The Commission similarly underlined this low evidentiary threshold in its *Vademecum on State aids*:

> Effect on competition and trade: Aid must have a potential effect on competition and trade between Member States. It is sufficient if it can be shown that the beneficiary is involved in an economic activity and that it operates in a market in which there is trade between Member States.[59]

The fourth and last component of the definition of State aid consists in a transfer of State resources. Although this requirement remains debated, it was firmly established by the Court in three cases involving German legislation: *Sloman*

[51] Bacon (n 17) no 2.142.

[52] AG Capotorti, Case 730/79 *Philip Morris Holland* [1980] ECR I-2671, para 4, free translation: The wording of [Article 107(1) TFEU] lends itself to an interpretation according to which the distortion of competition is a constant and necessary consequence of the benefit granted through the aid of the State to certain undertakings or certain products. This interpretation is confirmed by the logic of economy: an external intervention of a selective nature is bound to distort the game of competition. It can therefore be readily assumed that any public aid granted to an undertaking distorts competition—or threatens to distort it, if the aid is only planned and not yet granted—unless there are exceptional circumstances.

[53] Vademecum on State aid (n 15) 6.

[54] London Economics, *Competition Issues* (n 34) 222, 238 and 260.

[55] State Aid Action Plan (n 14) no 7.

[56] Case 730/79 *Philip Morris Holland* [1980] ECR I-2671, paras 11–12.

[57] Case C-66/02 *Italy v Commission* [2005] ECR I-10901, paras 103–25; Case C-372/97 *Italy v Commission* [2004] ECR I-3679, para 44.

[58] Cases C-393/04 and C-41/05 *Air Liquide Industries Belgium* [2006] ECR I-5293, para 35; Case C-66/02 *Italy v Commission* [2005] ECR I-10901, para 117; Case C-310/99 *Italy v Commission* [2002] ECR I-2289, para 84.

[59] Vademecum on State aid (n 15) 7.

Neptun, *Kirsammer-Hack* and *PreussenElektra*.[60] *Sloman Neptun* concerned a measure exempting ship-owners from ordinary labour law if they registered their vessel in the German international shipping register, instead of the ordinary German shipping register. Sloman Neptun, a German shipping company, sought to hire Filipino seafarers at a rate of pay that was less than one fifth of the ordinary wage of German seafarers.[61] The German Seafarers' Committee refused to give its consent, and argued that this derogatory regime constituted prohibited State aid under Union law. Another derogation to ordinary labour law was at stake in *Kirsammer-Hack*, namely the exclusion of small businesses from the system of protection of workers against unfair dismissal, which effectively precluded Mrs Kirsammer-Hack from suing her employer for unfair dismissal. Lastly, *PreussenElektra* concerned a German law designed to promote the production of electricity from renewable energy sources. On the one hand, electricity distributors were required to purchase electricity from renewable energy sources at fixed minimum prices. On the other hand, upstream electricity suppliers were requested to share the financial burden of this measure, by partially compensating distribution undertakings for the additional costs caused by their purchase obligation.

In all three cases, the Court ruled out the existence of a State aid, on the ground that none of those measures entailed directly or indirectly a transfer of State resources.[62] Indeed, although imposed by the German State, all three laws only entailed transfers of resources among private operators, without involving State resources. In effect, by imposing this requirement of a transfer of State resources,[63] the Court distinguished between 'financial' measures—involving a transfer of State resources—and 'regulatory' measures—which do not.[64] Only financial measures can constitute prohibited State aids, regulatory measures being excluded from State aid scrutiny.

This exclusion of regulatory measures, implied by the requirement of a transfer of State resources, has been heavily criticised by reference to the paradigm of regulatory neutrality, which aims at undistorted competition among private

[60] A precursor was the Court's judgment in Case 82/77 *Van Tiggele* [1978] ECR 25, paras 23–25, on the fixing of minimum retail prices for spirits.

[61] The French version of the conclusions of AG Darmon unequivocally states that 'le salaire proposé à ces marins est inférieur à 20 % de celui des marins allemands' ('less than 20% of'), which was erroneously translated into English as 'the rate of pay offered to those seafarers is 20% lower than that paid to German seafarers'. See AG Darmon, Joined Cases C-72/91 and C-73/91 *Sloman Neptun* [1993] ECR I-887, para 5.

[62] Case C-379/98 *PreussenElektra* [2001] ECR I-2099, paras 58–61; Case C-189/91 *Kirsammer-Hack* [1993] ECR I-6185, paras 16–19; Joined Cases C-72/91 and C-73/91 *Sloman Neptun* [1993] ECR I-887, paras 19–22.

[63] See also Joined Cases C-52/97 to C-54/97 *Epifanio Viscido* [1998] ECR I-2629, paras 13–15, on a derogation allowing Italian postal service to recruit on the basis of fixed-term contracts.

[64] In the same sense, see AG Maduro, Case C-237/04 *Enirisorse* [2006] ECR I-7907, para 44: '[T]he Court seems to wish to draw a distinction between distortions resulting from the adoption of measures to regulate economic activities and those caused by a transfer of public resources to certain undertakings'.

businesses. The scholarship unanimously opines that regulatory measures can distort private competition just as much as financial measures do—or even more so. From the point of view of undertakings, it is indeed irrelevant whether selective advantages are granted through State resources (financial measures) or private resources (regulatory measures): both types of advantages improve the competitive position of the beneficiary undertakings, at the expense of the non-beneficiary undertakings. Regulatory measures may even be a greater source of distortions of competition, where non-beneficiary undertakings are required to grant an advantage to beneficiary undertakings with which they compete. As summarised by AG Jacobs in *PreussenElektra*:

> [A] State measure conferring specific advantages on certain undertakings does not become less anticompetitive where it is financed through private and not through public resources. On the contrary, the distortion of competition might be greater where the cost of the measure is borne by competitors of the aided undertakings and not by the general public.[65]

A kindred criticism was developed by AG Darmon in *Sloman Neptun*, who rightly insisted that Member States could achieve the very same socioeconomic effect by either subsidising undertakings with tax money (financial measure: potential State aid) or by organising direct payments among their citizens (regulatory measure: no State aid). As a consequence, excluding regulatory measures from State aid scrutiny entailed a serious risk that Member States would circumvent the State aid regime by privileging recourse to regulatory rather than financial measures.[66]

If the exclusion of measures not entailing a transfer of State resources could not be justified on substantive grounds, it was apparently grounded in institutional motives. Indeed, in a world of limited institutional resources,[67] the State aid regime cannot deal with every distortion of private competition generated by national laws, and all the more so since State aid scrutiny is exercised by the Commission.[68] As explained earlier, if that premise of regulatory neutrality was adopted, the scope of the State aid regime would be infinite. Therefore, the

[65] AG Jacobs, Case C-379/98 *PreussenElektra* [2001] ECR I-2099, para 139; see also Bacon (n 17) no 2.92; C Ahlborn and C Berg, 'Can State Aid Control Learn from Antitrust? The Need for a Greater Role for Competition Analysis under the State Aid Rules' in Biondi, Eeckhout and Flynn, *The Law of State Aid in the European Union* (n 3) 58.

[66] AG Darmon, Joined Cases C-72/91 and C-73/91 *Sloman Neptun* [1993] ECR I-887, paras 40–43; see also AG Jacobs, Case C-379/98 *PreussenElektra* [2001] ECR I-2099, paras 143–45; Bacon (n 43) 288–89; Ahlborn and Berg, 'Can State Aid Control Learn from Antitrust?' (n 66) 59.

[67] On the idea of limited institutional resources, see MP Maduro, 'Harmony and Dissonance in Free Movement' (2001) 4 *Cambridge Yearbook of European Legal Studies* 315, esp at 338–41.

[68] H van Vliet, 'State Resources and PreussenElektra: When is a State Aid not a State Aid?' in Santaolalla Gadea, *EC State Aid Law* (n 47) 87: '[S]hould the concept of State aid be greatly expanded far beyond covering situations like PreussenElektra …, the number of supplementary notifications to the Commission of measures could be very considerable'; Heidenhain (n 35) 43: 'The regulation of State aid … cannot … provide a comprehensive solution to all problems associated with the distortion of competition'.

primary function of the State resources requirement is to pragmatically restrain the scope of the State aid regime, as confessed by AG Jacobs in *Epifanio Viscido*:

> It might be asked why, given their potential effect on competition, Article [107 TFEU] does not cover all labour and other social measures which by virtue of being selective in their impact might distort competition and thereby have an equivalent effect to State aid. The answer is perhaps essentially a pragmatic one: to investigate all such regimes would entail an enquiry on the basis of the Treaty alone into the entire social and economic life of a Member State.[69]

If the need to restrain the scope of the State aid regime is unanimously accepted, voices such as AG Maduro or Kelyn Bacon consider that such restraint should be made through the selectivity requirement (excluding general measures), rather than through the formalistic requirement of a transfer of State resources (excluding regulatory measures).[70] Therefore, the posture towards the requirement of State resources seems to be eventually dictated by the degree of faith into the effectiveness of the selectivity requirement acting as a restraint on the scope of the State aid regime. In *PreussenElektra*, AG Jacobs, in pragmatic supporter of the State resources requirement, underlined:

> Since [the assessment of selectivity] is a difficult exercise with an uncertain outcome, it seems preferable that legislation regulating the relationship between private actors is as a matter of principle excluded from the scope of the State aid rules.[71]

Although the rationale for the exclusion of regulatory measures was not explicitly grounded in the regulatory competition paradigm, its obvious effect is to considerably broaden the room for regulatory competition by permitting Member States to compete by means of regulatory measures. Under the State aid regime, Member States are indeed entirely free to favour certain undertakings—or even one single undertaking as in *Epifanio Viscido*[72]—by means of regulatory measures:

> State measures which favor specific undertakings, for example by exempting them from economically significant obligations relative to environmental, building, or employment law, but which involve no transfer of State resources in some form, are not covered by Article [107(1) TFEU].[73]

The distortions of private competition entailed by such regulatory measures can only be addressed through Union harmonisation of the Treaty provisions on free movement.[74]

[69] AG Jacobs, Joined Cases C-52 to C-54/97 *Epifanio Viscido* [1998] ECR 1-2629, para 16.

[70] AG Maduro, Case C-237/04 *Enirisorse* [2006] ECR I-7907, paras 45–51; Bacon (n 43) 289.

[71] AG Jacobs, Case C-379/98 *PreussenElektra* [2001] ECR I-2099, para 157; see also AG Jacobs, Case C-241/94 *France v Commission* [1996] ECR I-4551, para 30; Kurcz and Vallindas (n 17) 160; Waelbroeck (n 17) 774.

[72] Joined Cases C-52 to C-54/97 *Epifanio Viscido* [1998] ECR 1-2629, which concerned a derogation allowing Italian postal service to recruit on the basis of fixed-term contracts.

[73] Heidenhain (n 34) 40.

[74] Ross, 'State Aids' (n 1) 82: 'The effect of the stricter Sloman Neptun approach is thus to divert the consideration of such measures into other Treaty mechanisms, if subject to review at all'.

To sum up, a State aid can be defined as a benefit granted to an undertaking and involving a transfer of State resources, which is not made available to every domestic undertaking (selectivity) and that could not be obtained under normal market conditions (economic advantage). The central submission of this chapter is that the actual definition of State aid crystallises a trade-off between regulatory neutrality and regulatory competition, just as the actual version of the free movement test does. An expansive prohibition of State aids furthers regulatory neutrality within the internal market, at the expense of regulatory competition; in other words, the broader the notion of State aid, the broader the level playing field among businesses competing in the internal market:

> [T]he biggest advantage of an interpretation of 'State aid' which would also cover also situations like PreussenElektra ..., would be that it would improve the 'level playing field' between Member States, and limit their possibilities to distort competition between operators in various Member States.[75]

Conversely, any restraint on the scope of the State aid regime increases the room for regulatory competition, at the expense of regulatory neutrality. Excluding general (selectivity requirement) and regulatory measures (transfer of State resources) from State aid scrutiny means, in effect, endorsing the correlated distortions of competition among private businesses active in the internal market (regulatory neutrality). Yet, on another level, these exclusions promote regulatory competition, by entitling Member States to compete against each other by means of general and/or regulatory measures:

> The prohibition of State aid in Article [107(1) TFEU] thus covers only such interventions by the Member States in competition as far as the Member States allocate financial resources ... which are under their control. All other interventions by the Member States in competition are not covered by the provisions regulating State aid.[76]

In sum, Member States may not compete against each other by means of selective financial measures (eg individual subsidies), but they are free to do so by means of general measures (eg progressive taxation) or selective regulatory measures (eg selective exemption from labour or environmental obligations).

III. The Functional Parallelism between Prohibition of Abuses of Law and Prohibition of State Aids

The present section seeks to demonstrate the functional parallelism between the prohibition of abuses of law and the prohibition of State aids. The previous

[75] van Vliet, 'State Resources and PreussenElektra' (n 69) 83.
[76] Heidenhain (n 35) 43.

sections sketched a common framework of analysis of the freedoms of movement and the State aid regime. As mentioned earlier, regulatory neutrality and regulatory competition represent two poles of attraction on the compass of economic integration, between which the pointer of internal market law constantly fluctuates. In that global context, the actual contents respectively attributed to the free movement test, on the one hand, and the concept of State aids, on the other, crystallise a specific trade-off between the objectives of regulatory neutrality (competition among private businesses) and regulatory competition (competition among Member States).

This common framework of analysis of free movement and State aid laws can be further enriched with the concept of abuse of law, which has progressively pervaded free movement law, and represents a useful point of intersection between both sets of rules.[77] Abuses of law were indeed defined as undesirable choices of law artificially made by private individuals. A parallel can easily be drawn between private strategies consisting in *electing* a hospitable jurisdiction—which may be proscribed as abuses of law—and public strategies consisting in *offering* a hospitable jurisdiction—which may be prohibited as State aids.

In essence, the concepts of abuse of law and of State aid seek to apprehend the same phenomenon, namely the attraction exerted by national laws upon businesses active in the internal market, but from opposite perspectives. On the one hand, the prohibition of abuses of law censors businesses' reactions to attractive laws; on the other hand, the prohibition of State aids scrutinises Member States' attempts to lure businesses with attractive laws:

> Of particular concern in an integrated market is the use of State aids to influence the location of productive capacity. In an integrated market there is presumably enhanced flexibility in the location of production facilities. Under such circumstances there may be greater incentives for State aids to be used as a means of influencing location decisions.[78]

As explained earlier, the attraction exerted by national laws upon businesses is diversely assessed by the two paradigms of economic integration.[79] Under regulatory neutrality, such attraction is condemned since national laws should not distort the competition among businesses in the internal market; accordingly, the regulatory neutrality paradigm advocates a broad prohibition of both abuses of law and State aids. Conversely, the attraction exerted by national laws upon businesses is condoned by the regulatory competition paradigm for it represents the very essence of a process of competition among Member States; as a result, the regulatory competition paradigm opposes the prohibition of abuses of law and State aids.

[77] This connection was attempted in T Lyons, 'State Aid, Taxation and Abuse of Law' in R de la Feria and S Vogenauer (eds), *Prohibition of Abuse of Law: a New General Principle of EU Law?* (Oxford, Hart Publishing, 2011); C Quigley, 'Comments on State Aid, Taxation and Abuse of Law' in de la Feria and Vogenauer *Prohibition of Abuse of Law* (n 77) 509–18.

[78] London Economics (n 34) 226.

[79] See ch 6 section I.

The parallelism between the prohibitions of abuses of law and of State aids can be formalised with the conceptual tools offered by the regulatory competition paradigm. Regulatory competition has been defined as an iterative process of regulatory arbitrage by Union citizens (electing their preferred national law) and regulatory adjustment by Member States (adapting their national laws to match Union citizens' preferences), allegedly leading to optimal regulation.[80] If the prohibition of abuses of law restrains the room for regulatory *arbitrage* by Union citizens, the prohibition of State aids restrains the room for regulatory *adjustment* by Member States.

Furthermore, it ought to be underlined that the room for regulatory adjustment by Member States has an impact on the room for regulatory arbitrage by Union citizens. Precluding Member States from making their laws attractive through the State aid regime decreases regulatory diversity within the internal market. As a result, Union citizens have a lesser incentive to elaborate an abusive practice: the strength of the incentive to arbitrate indeed depends on the degree of diversity among national laws, as citizens are less likely to move to another jurisdiction for regulatory motives when national laws are broadly similar.[81] Therefore, prohibiting State aids helps prevent abuses of law by reducing diversity among national legal systems.

The functional parallelism between prohibition of abuses of law, on the one hand, and prohibition of State aids, on the other, can be illustrated with parallel lines of case law in which the Court assessed national laws in light of both concepts. A first 'parallel case study' is provided by a series of judgments on the regulation of ships. The Court's permissive stance towards artificial practices set up in relation to the law applicable to maritime activities was underlined in part one of this study.[82] The Court ratified strategies consisting in reflagging fishing vessels in order to fish against the fishing quotas of another Member State ('quota-hopping': *Jaderow*, *Agegate*, *Factortame II*) or to escape altogether the ban on salmon and sea trout fishing (*Poulsen*). *Viking* concerned the reflagging of a Finnish vessel (the *Rosella*) under the Norwegian or Estonian flag, in order to have lower labour standards apply and consequently reduce exploitation costs.[83] The Court did not even evoke the possibility of qualifying this strategy as abusive, de facto granting free choice of labour law to ship-owners.

Under State aid law, on the other hand, the Court's ruling in *Sloman Neptun* concerned the labour law applicable to crewmembers, just as *Viking*. As explained earlier, the Court ruled that a selective advantage granted through labour law does not constitute state aid, for it does not entail directly or indirectly a transfer of State resources. *Sloman Neptun* accordingly established that economic advantages

[80] See ch 6 section III.

[81] A business taxed at a rate of 50% in Member State A has a strong incentive to move to Member State B if the tax rate is of 10%, but not if it is of 49.9%.

[82] See ch 4 nn 273–295 and accompanying text.

[83] Case C-438/05 *Viking* [2007] ECR I-10779.

granted through the regulation of ships are not, as a rule, prohibited as State aid, for they do not involve a transfer of State resources.

The combined outcome of those two lines of case law is to maximise the room for regulatory competition in the field of ship regulation: on the one hand, ship-owners are free to elect the most hospitable flag law without being suspected of abuse; on the other, Member States are free to make their flag law hospitable by granting selective advantages to ship-owners without being suspected of State aid. As a matter of fact, many scholars have criticised the current state of affairs in ship regulation, pointing at the deleterious regulatory competition among States, and in particular at the widespread offer (by States) and use (by ship-owners) of flags of convenience.[84] The *Poulsen* case, for instance, concerned the reflagging of a Danish fishing vessel under the Panamanian flag, while the vessel maintained its fishing activities in European Union waters. In reaction, traditional high-regulation States have created 'secondary registries', which are in effect flags of convenience, to retain maritime activities within their jurisdiction.[85] The *Sloman Neptun* case was precisely about the German secondary registry, and the exemption granted to ship-owners from ordinary obligations imposed under German labour law. *Sloman Neptun* was confirmed in *3F*, which concerned the establishment of a Danish International Register of Shipping ('the DIS register'), in addition to the ordinary Danish register of ships ('the DAS register'), in order to combat the flight from Community flags to flags of convenience. Ship-owners whose vessels were registered in the DIS register were allowed to pay seafarers from non-member countries according to their national laws. The Court ruled that the establishment of the DIS register did not constitute State aid.[86]

Direct taxation is another field in which the concepts of abuse of law and State aid are applied in parallel; indeed, there is an obvious affinity between tax avoidance (or 'arbitrage') by Union citizens and tax aids (or 'adjustment') granted by Member States. On the one hand, the Court has firmly established the prohibition of abuses of law in relation to direct taxation. Thus, in the seminal *Cadbury*

[84] See among many others JLS de Vivero and JCR Mateos, 'Ocean Governance in a Competitive World. The BRIC Countries as Emerging Maritime Powers—Building New Geopolitical Scenarios' (2010) 34 *Marine Policy* 967; J Wakefield, 'Fisheries: a Failure of Values' (2009) 46 *Common Market Law Review* 431; ER DeSombre, *Flagging Standards: Globalization and Environmental, Safety, and Labor Regulations at Sea* (Cambridge MA, MIT Press, 2006); O Fotinopoulou Basurko, 'Reflexiones acerca de la ley del pabellon como criterio de conexion conflictual a efectos de la determinacion de la ley aplicable al contracto de embarque' (2006) 24 *Annuaire de Droit Maritime et Océanique* 261; P Chaumette and G Proutière Maulion, 'Quota-hopping et appropriation des ressources halieutiques' (2005) 23 *Annuaire de Droit Maritime et Océanique* 309; D Vaughan, 'Factortame and after: A Fishy Story' (2005) 16 *European Business Law Review* 511; J Verhoeven, 'Abus, Fraude ou Habileté?' in J Verhoeven (ed), *La loyauté: mélanges offerts à Etienne Cerexhe* (Brussels, Larcier, 1997); G Assonitis, 'Les Pavillons de Libre Immatriculation' (1991) 4 *Droit Européen des Transports* 435.

[85] AG Darmon, Joined Cases C-72/91 and C-73/91 *Sloman Neptun* [1993] ECR I-887, paras 2–3.

[86] Case C319/07 P *3F* [2010] ECR I-5963, para 67; see also the subsequent Case C-646/11 P *3F* [2013] ECR I-0000.

Schweppes judgment, the Court held that restrictions to free movement are justified in so far as they are intended to prevent artificial arrangements designed to benefit from a more favourable tax regime.[87] *Cadbury Schweppes*, a British company, had incorporated subsidiaries in the International Financial Service Centre (IFSC) of Dublin for mere tax reasons (tax arbitrage); indeed, businesses established in the IFSC benefited from a privileged taxation rate of 10 per cent. Interestingly enough, this IFSC tax regime had been subject to State aid scrutiny a few years earlier, with the Commission ruling that it constituted prohibited State aid.[88] Following the Commission decision, Ireland decided in 2002 to impose a new 12.5 per cent tax rate for all domestic companies, thereby escaping State aid scrutiny (general measure).[89]

The same parallel treatment can be identified in relation to a favourable tax regime designed by Belgium to attract 'coordination centres', namely headquarters of multinational groups. On the one hand, the Court ruled that this special tax regime constituted prohibited State aid in favour of coordination centres.[90] On the other hand, the *Columbus* case concerned a Belgian partnership owned by German residents, which was subject to the 'coordination centres' tax regime.[91] The German legislature had adopted a legislation explicitly intended to counter abusive strategies of German residents consisting in establishing partnerships in low-tax jurisdictions solely for tax purposes.[92] This legislation provided that such partnerships would be liable to ordinary taxation in Germany, after deduction of—by hypothesis, lower—foreign taxes. The Court ruled that such legislation did not restrict the freedoms of movement, since German and foreign partnerships owned by German residents were treated equally, thereby effectively preventing the abusive practice at stake.[93]

Lastly, the tax regime in Gibraltar has similarly given rise to cases involving potential abuses of law and State aids. In its judgment in *Carmen Media Group*, the Court mentioned that the plaintiff was suspected of having established itself in Gibraltar, encouraged in that respect by a tax incentive, only in order to escape the stricter rules that would have been applicable if it had established itself in the

[87] See ch 2 section IV.A.

[88] Commission (EC), 'Proposal for appropriate measures under Article 93(1) of the EC Treaty concerning the International Financial Service Centre and Shannon customs-free airport zone' (State Aid E/1/98), 18 December 1998, C395/14 (ordinary tax rates in Ireland were of 25% on the first IEP 50.000 of taxable profits and 32% on the balance). See C Quigley, 'General Taxation and State Aid' in Biondi, Eeckhout and Flynn (n 3) 214–15.

[89] WW Bratton and JA McCahery, 'Tax Coordination and Tax Competition in the European Union: Evaluating the Code of Conduct on Business Taxation' (2001) 38 *Common Market Law Review* 677, 711.

[90] Joined Cases C-182/03 and C-217/03 *Belgium and Forum 187 v Commission ('Coordination Centres')* [2006] ECR I-5479.

[91] Case C-298/05 *Columbus* [2007] ECR I-10451.

[92] Law on combating abuse and harmonising taxation (Missbrauchsbekämpfungs- und Steuerbereinigungsgesetz) of 21 December 1993 (BGBl 1993 I, p 2310).

[93] See ch 4 n 225 and accompanying text.

territory of the Member State towards which its business was directed. Carmen Media Group had indeed the status of 'exempt company' under Gibraltar tax law, and accordingly paid little or no corporate tax.[94] On the other hand, this favourable tax regime granted by Gibraltar to so-called 'exempt companies' had been subject to State aid scrutiny by the Commission, but the General Court annulled the formal investigation procedure initiated by the Commission on procedural grounds.[95] Nevertheless, in the wake of that procedure, Gibraltar decided to introduce a new corporate tax regime in 2002. Following a new decision taken by the Commission, the Court ruled that the new corporate tax regime constituted prohibited State aid in favour of 'offshore' companies, namely companies without any physical presence in Gibraltar, since they were de facto exempted from corporate taxation.[96]

In short, the prohibitions of both abuses of law and of State aids is firmly established in the field of direct taxation, thereby reducing the room for both regulatory arbitrage and regulatory adjustment—by contrast with ship regulation, an area in which the Court rejected both concepts. The case law on abuses of law and State aids in the field of taxation ought to be reframed in its global policy context, in which tax competition among Member States has raised growing concern over the years.[97] At the inception of the Communities, harmonisation of national taxes was regarded as the ideal technique to achieve economic integration, as for every legal area.[98] However, given the political resistance to Union harmonisation, particularly marked in the tax field, tax integration was more effectively pursued through the freedoms of movement and State aid law.[99] It is in that context that the Commission issued its 'notice on the application of the State aid rules to measures relating to direct business taxation',[100] while the Economy and Finance Council (ECOFIN) adopted a non-binding 'code of conduct for

[94] Case C-46/08 *Carmen Media Group* [2010] ECR I-8149, para 47.

[95] Joined Cases T-195/01 and T-207/01 *Gibraltar v Commission* [2002] ECR II-2309, para 115.

[96] Joined Cases C-106/09 P and C-107/09 P *Commission and Spain v Gibraltar and United Kingdom* [2011] ECR I-11113, para 85–108.

[97] OECD, 'Harmful Tax Competition: an Emerging Global Issue' (Report), 8 April 1998; CM Radaelli, 'Harmful Tax Competition in the EU: Policy Narratives and Advocacy Coalitions' (1999) 37 *Journal of Common Market Studies* 661; Bratton and McCahery, Tax Coordination and Tax Competition in the European Union (n 90) 677–718; PB Sørensen, 'Tax Coordination in the European Union: What are the Issues?' (2001) 8 *Swedish Economic Policy Review* 143; Quigley, 'General Taxation and State Aid' (n 89) 214: 'The problem of tackling distortions of competition caused by low-tax jurisdictions has become more urgent in recent years'.

[98] See ch 6 section III.

[99] A detailed account of this policy switch can be found in Kaye (n 10) 104–21; see also R Plender, 'Definition of Aid' in Biondi, Eeckhout and Flynn (n 3) 26; AG Jääskinen, Joined Cases C-106/09 P and C-107/09 P *Commission and Spain v Gibraltar and United Kingdom* [2011] ECR I-11113, paras 125–28.

[100] Commission (EC), 'Application of the State aid rules to measures relating to direct business taxation' (Notice), 10 December 1998, C384/3.

business taxation'[101] whose signatories accept to repeal tax measures that constitute harmful tax competition.[102]

State aid law has accordingly been attributed a central role in the process of tax integration within the Union; and yet its integrative potential is restrained by one serious limitation: the selectivity requirement.[103] Indeed, if tax measures necessarily involve a transfer of State resources, they are not necessarily selective—the exact opposite of ship regulation.[104] In particular, a general measure imposing a low level of taxation for every domestic undertaking (eg 12.5 per cent tax rate in Ireland; tax-free system in Jersey, Guernsey and the Isle of Man[105]) escapes State aid scrutiny and is only subject to harmonisation by the Union legislature. In addition, it seems that general tax measures do not fall within the scope of the (non-binding) code of conduct on harmful tax competition.[106]

Lastly, an interesting contrast can be drawn between the respective treatments of social security and labour laws, in light of the concepts of abuse of law and State aid. As explained in the previous section, the Court excluded labour law from State aid scrutiny in *Kirshammer-Hack* (and *Sloman Neptun*), on the ground that derogations from ordinary labour law do not involve a transfer of State resources. Conversely, social security measures do, as a rule, involve a transfer of State resources and are therefore subject to State aid scrutiny.[107] This implies that Member States are free to grant selective advantages to one or several undertakings through labour law,[108] whereas they are obliged to extend any economic advantage related to social security to every domestic undertaking.

On the other hand, the Court has enforced a strict prohibition of abusive practices in relation to social security schemes. In *Fitzwilliam*, *Plum* and *Barry Banks*,

[101] Council (EC), 'A code of conduct for business taxation' (Resolution), 1 December 1997, C2/2.

[102] Schenk (n 9) 7:

> There is of course a link between the application of the State aid rules to tax measures and the debate over tax harmonisation. The distortion of competition caused by low tax jurisdictions has been a major concern in the Community for a number of years and the Code of Conduct for Business Taxation reflects this.

[103] Bacon (n 43) 271:

> In the absence of fiscal harmonization, the Commission is increasingly using article [107 TFEU] as a tool for tackling market-distorting tax measures. It is true that fiscal provisions are normally of general application, and therefore outside the scope of article [107(1) TFEU].

[104] Ship regulation is necessarily selective (since it aims at the shipping industry) but does not, as a rule, involve a transfer of State resources.

[105] Kaye (n 10) 112.

[106] According to point B of the Code of conduct, are to be regarded as 'potentially harmful' the tax measures that provide for a significantly lower effective level of taxation than those levels which generally apply in the Member State in question. See AC dos Santos, 'Aides d'État, Code de Conduite et Concurrence Fiscale dans l'Union Européenne' (2004) XVIII *Revue internationale de droit économique* 9, 34–36.

[107] See eg Case C-203/82 *Commission v Italy* [1983] ECR 2525; Case C-75/97 *Belgium v Commission (Maribel)* [1999] ECR I-3671.

[108] Joined Cases C-52/97 to C-54/97 *Epifanio Viscido* [1998] ECR I-2629, paras 13–15, on a derogation allowing Italian postal service to recruit on the basis of fixed-term contracts.

the Court precluded abusive strategies consisting in the artificial establishment of undertakings in Member States levying low social security contributions, followed by the posting of workers to more generous jurisdictions, in the hope that they would remain subject to the social security of the home State.[109] In the field of labour law, the case law on the posting of workers (chiefly the *Laval* ruling) does not, in its present state, conclusively ratify or prohibit artificial choices of law.[110] Nevertheless, in its proposal for a directive on the enforcement of Directive 96/71, the Commission inserted an Article 3, entitled 'Preventing abuse and circumvention', which is explicitly intended to prohibit artificial relocations of undertakings in hospitable jurisdictions.[111]

The policy context of these cases relates to the theme of social dumping, evoked above.[112] The idea conveyed by the expression 'social dumping' is that of a distortion of competition created by a differential of regulation between undertakings respectively subject to high and low social standards. Social dumping can be examined from two different ends: the decision of businesses to relocate in hospitable social jurisdictions (regulatory arbitrage) and the decision of Member States to make their social laws hospitable (regulatory adjustment). On the one hand, the prohibition of abuses of law in cases such as *Fitzwilliam*, *Barry Banks* or *Plum* seeks to prevent social dumping strategies designed by businesses:

> A race to the bottom is said to arise when, in a deregulated internal market, a state unilaterally lowers its social standards in an attempt to attract business from other states. Businesses moving their place of operations in response are said to be engaged in social dumping.[113]

On the other hand, the prohibition of State aids in the field of social security intends to limit social dumping strategies pursued by Member States. For instance, when commenting upon the German derogatory regime at stake in the *Kirshammer-Hack* case, Davies wrote:

> In effect, what Germany was being accused of was 'social dumping' by exempting small employers from its unfair dismissal laws to a greater extent than was the case in other Member States.[114]

[109] Case C-202/97 *Fitzwilliam* [2000] ECR I-883, paras 26–43; Case C-404/98 *Plum* [2000] ECR I-9379, paras 21–23; Case C-178/97 *Barry Banks* [2000] ECR I-2005, paras 24–27. See ch 4 nn 107 and 169 and accompanying text.

[110] Case C-346/06 *Rüffert* [2008] ECR I-1989; Case C-341/05 *Laval* [2007] ECR I-11767; Joined Cases C-49/98, C-50/98, C-52/98 to C-54/98 and C-68/98 to C-71/98 *Finalarte and Others* [2001] ECR I-7831; Joined Cases C-369/96 and C-376/96 *Arblade and Others* [1999] ECR I-8453; Case C-113/89 *Rush Portuguesa* [1990] ECR I-1417.

[111] Commission (EC), 'Proposal for a Directive of the European Parliament and of the Council on the enforcement of Directive 96/71/EC concerning the posting of workers in the framework of the provision of services' COM (2012) 131 final, 21 March 2012. See ch 4 n 114 and accompanying text.

[112] See ch 8 section IV.

[113] C Barnard, 'Social Dumping And the Race to the Bottom: Some Lessons for the European Union from Delaware?' (2000) 25 *European Law Review* 57, 57.

[114] P Davies, 'Market Integration and Social Policy in the Court of Justice' (1995) 24 *Industrial Law Journal* 49, 60.

Overall, the enforcement of the prohibitions of abuses of law and State aids in these four areas (ship regulation, direct taxation, social security and labour law) can be summarised as follows (Table 14).

Table 14 – Parallel Case Studies of Abuse of Law and State Aid

	Abuses of Law Regulatory arbitrage by citizens	**State Aids** Regulatory adjustment by States
Ship Regulation	Permitted (*Poulsen*)	Permitted (*Sloman Neptun*)
Direct Taxation	Proscribed (*Cadbury Schweppes*)	Proscribed (*Gibraltar*)
Social Security	Proscribed (*Fitzwilliam*)	Proscribed (*Maribel*)
Labour Law	Unknown (*Laval*)	Permitted (*Kirshammer-Hack*)

Beyond the particulars of each field, the crucial point is the following: the prohibition of abuses of law and the prohibition of State aids aim at the same phenomenon, namely the attraction exercised by national laws upon the location of businesses in the internal market. Those two prohibitions operate from opposite ends. The prohibition of *abuses of law* reduces the room for regulatory arbitrage by private businesses; in other words, it seeks to limit the margin of reaction of businesses to attractive national laws. The prohibition of *State aids* reduces the room for regulatory adjustment by Member States, namely the margin within which Member States can make their national laws more attractive.

To sum up, the decision to prohibit or not abuses of law and/or State aids is informed by two conceptions of economic integration, designated as regulatory neutrality and regulatory competition. The regulatory competition paradigm opposes the prohibition of abuses of law, for citizens should be free to arbitrate among national laws, as well as the prohibition of State aids, as Member States should be free to adjust their laws to match citizens' preferences. On the other hand, the regulatory neutrality paradigm, which seeks to avoid the competition among businesses in the internal market being distorted by national laws, supports the prohibition of abuses of law and of State aids.

10

Abuse of Union Law and the Economic Constitution of the European Union

THIS CHAPTER IS devoted to the last of three fault-lines of Union law accounting for the contradictions and controversies surrounding the concept of abuse of Union law. In essence, it will be submitted that the emergence of the concept of abuse of Union law can be interpreted as an evolution of the economic constitution of the European Union, by which public power seeks to reaffirm its capacity to control private power within the internal market.

The first section is devoted to the notion of economic constitution of the European Union, which can be defined as a set of fundamental choices regarding the economic system that cannot be overridden by the dominant legislature. Substantively, the function of the economic constitution is to direct the deployment of public power onto private power in the economic sphere (Section I).

The second section describes the historical conditions of the emergence of the phenomenon of abuse of Union law, which consist in a conjunction of socioeconomic and legal factors. On the one hand, new communication technologies and modern transportation means have provoked an explosion of private mobility. On the other hand, the European process of integration has reached a specific moment in which territorial unity is secured but regulatory diversity preserved, which enables private individuals to set up cross-border movements in order to elect a more hospitable jurisdiction. This legal environment opens a space for artificial cross-border movements, which can be exploited thanks to the new communication technologies and modern transportation means (Section II).

Overall, the combination of low moving costs, high regulatory diversity and high territorial unity has led to the emergence of a new form of private power originating in mobility, enabling private individuals to escape the deployment of public power. Admittedly, private mobility has always been a sporadic thorn in the side of public power, but this phenomenon has taken on a systemic dimension in the last three decades, thereby acquiring the status of 'mobility-power'. Abuses of law are manifestations of mobility-power, in which the public cat is confined to a national territory, whereas private mice may run across the Union territory; by outlawing artificial choices of law, the prohibition of abusive practices allows the public cat to catch runaway mice. In a context of low moving costs and high regulatory diversity, the prohibition of abusive practices represents the only course of action available to counter private mobility-power (Section III).

However, the study of the issue of abuse of Union law is complicated by the inconsistent treatment of abusive practices under Union law: escaping national law was held abusive in *Cadbury Schweppes*, but not in *Centros*. Therefore, Union law is fundamentally ambivalent towards private mobility-power and its restraining effect upon national public power. This ambivalence towards private mobility-power can be usefully reconstructed in light of the fundamental political division between fear of private power and fear of public power. Those who are more fearful of private power tend to advocate the prohibition of abusive practices, whereas those who are more fearful of public power tend to reject it. In that sense, the emergence of the concept of abuse of Union law can be interpreted, with its inconsistencies, as the progressive adaptation of the economic constitution of the European Union to a new form of private power originating in mobility (Section IV).

I. The Notion of Economic Constitution of the European Union

The concept of 'economic constitution' was popularised in the aftermath of the Second World War by German scholars who formed the so-called 'Freiburg school of ordoliberalism'.[1] The protagonists of the Freiburg school agreed that the failings of the Weimar Republic and the correlative conquest of political power by the Nazis were due to the inability of the legal system to prevent the creation and abuse of economic power.[2] Indeed, the Weimar economy of the 1920s was plagued by the existence of cartels among powerful corporations colluding to eliminate competition and maximise their profits, and the Weimar Republic was ineffective in fighting these concentrations of private power.[3] This analysis of the failings of

[1] On the Freiburg school of ordoliberalism, see esp DJ Gerber, *Law and Competition in Twentieth-Century Europe: Protecting Prometheus* (Oxford, Oxford University Press, 2001); J Drexl, 'Competition Law as Part of the European Constitution' in A von Bogdandy and J Bast (eds), *Principles of European Constitutional Law* (Oxford, Hart Publishing, 2006); J Drexl, 'La Constitution économique européenne—L'actualité du modèle ordoliberal' (2011) XXV *Revue internationale de droit économique* 419; DJ Gerber, 'Constitutionalizing the Economy: German Neo-Liberalism, Competition Law and the "New" Europe' (1994) 42 *American Journal of Comparative Law* 25; DJ Gerber, 'The Origins of European Competition Law in Fin-de-Siècle Austria' (1992) 36 *American Journal of Legal History* 405; DJ Gerber, 'Law and the Abuse of Economic Power in Europe' (1987–88) 62 *Tulane Law Review* 57; C Mongouachon, 'L'ordolibéralisme: Contexte historique et contenu dogmatique' (2011) 4 *Concurrences* 70.

[2] The three main protagonists of ordoliberalism were Walter Eucken (an economist), Franz Böhm and Hans Grossmann-Doerth (two lawyers); all three taught at Freiburg University in the early 1930s. According to Böhm, 'the issue on which [they] focused together was ... the issue of private power in a free society': quoted by Gerber, '*Protecting Prometheus*' (n 1) 235.

[3] Mongouachon 'L'ordolibéralisme' (n 1) 71–73; Drexl, 'La Constitution économique européenne' (n 1) 430–31; J Monnet, *Mémoires* (Paris, Fayard, 1976) 409, 419 and 511.

the Weimar Republic was reflected in the normative premises of ordoliberalism, which is equally concerned with public power and private power:

> For [ordoliberals], it was not sufficient to protect the individual from the power of government, because governments were not the only threats to individual freedom. Having witnessed the use of private economic power to destroy political and social institutions during the Weimar period, the ordoliberals emphasized the need to protect society from the misuse of such power. … [It] led them to demand the dispersion of not only political power, but economic power as well.[4]

Quite obviously, this combined fear of public and private power can be identified in other historical contexts. In the US context, Adams and Brock draw a parallel between the function performed by the US Constitution with regard to public power and the function performed by competition law with regard to private power: 'Like the political framework prescribed by the Constitution, competition rests upon distrust of concentrated power and on a belief in the maximum possible diffusion of rights and opportunities'.[5] In the same way, the US Supreme Court regularly associates antitrust laws and Bill of Rights:

> Antitrust laws … are the Magna Carta of free enterprise. They are as important to the preservation of economic freedom and our free-enterprise system as the Bill of Rights is to the protection of our fundamental personal freedoms.[6]

In the context of common law, Daniel Francis narrated, in a fascinating study, the concomitant emergence of constitutional law and competition law in eighteenth-century England:

> The same forces that drove the resettlement of the patent monopoly—the rise of Parliament and the common law, dissatisfaction with royal discretionary power, and the emerging vocabulary of individual rights and public welfare—would, before long, drive the triumph of Parliament over the Crown in the English Civil War (1642–1651), the Glorious Revolution (1688) and the Bill of Rights (1689): ultimately, nothing less than the reconstitutionalisation of the United Kingdom. The regulation of economic power, on the one hand, and that of political power, on the other, developed together.[7]

In the aftermath of the Second World War, this double fear of public and private power was translated by ordoliberals into a theory of social organisation relying on both a political constitution and an economic constitution, which were intended to protect individual freedom against abuses of political and economic powers. This dual constitutional system was meant to prevent a new rise of totalitarian regimes that had befallen Europe. A political constitution classically enshrines

[4] Gerber, '*Protecting Prometheus*' (n 1) 240.

[5] W Adams and J Brock, *The Bigness Complex: Industry, Labor, and Government in the American Economy*, 2nd edn (Stanford, Stanford University Press, 2004) 97.

[6] *United States v Topco Associates, Inc.* (1972) 405 US 596, 610 (USSC); *N Pac Ry v United States* (1958) 356 US 1, 4 (USSC).

[7] D Francis, 'Exclusion, Invasion and Abuse: Competition Law and its Constitutional Context' (2009–10) 12 *Cambridge Yearbook of European Legal Studies* 183, 192.

fundamental choices regarding the political system[8] by establishing political rights that cannot be overridden by the dominant legislature, thereby imposing limits to public power: 'In democratic polities under the rule of law, all exercise of public power is subject to observance of fundamental rights. This is a main characteristic of constitutionalism'.[9] In the same way, the economic constitution imposes fundamental choices regarding the economic system, which cannot be overridden by the dominant legislature.[10]

However, if the prime objective of a political constitution is the restraint of public power, that of an economic constitution as envisaged by ordoliberals is the restraint of private power, which they thought equally capable of undermining individual freedom. Yet any control of private power requires a *deployment* of public power. In the context of US constitutional law, James Madison sharply underlined this need for public power in order to oversee private power:

> If men were angels, no government would be necessary. If angels were to govern men, neither external nor internal controls on government would be necessary. In framing a government which is to be administered by men over men, the great difficulty lies in this: you must first enable the government to control the governed; and in the next place oblige it to control itself.[11]

The peculiarity of this tension between deploying and restraining public power lies in that it should remain unresolved, for its resolution either leads to public tyranny (absence of restraint) or private tyranny (absence of deployment). Thus, the ordoliberal economic constitution was intended not to restrain public power, but rather to direct and control its deployment onto private power within strict boundaries. The fear of private power led ordoliberals to advocate State intervention to tackle the issues raised by cartels, monopolies or even mere concentrations of economic power. Nevertheless, ordoliberals shared the liberal creed according to which the State should not disturb the spontaneous allocation of resources by private decision-making. Public power was therefore assigned a specific role in the economic sphere: the State must oversee private power by enforcing the rules

[8] This conception of 'political constitution' can be traced back to Plato and Aristotle, who discussed the merits of various '*politeia*': Aristotle, S Everson (trans), *The Politics and the Constitution of Athens*, 2nd edn (Cambridge, Cambridge University Press, 1996); Plato, T Griffith (trans), *The Republic* (Cambridge, Cambridge University Press, 2000).

[9] LFM Besselink, 'The Protection of Fundamental Rights post-Lisbon', General Report of the XXVth FIDE Congress, 30 May–2 June 2012, available at www.fide2012.eu, 1. See also RM Dworkin, 'Constitutionalism and Democracy' (1995) 3 *European Journal of Philosophy* 2, 2: 'Constitutionalism is a system that establishes individual legal rights that the dominant legislature does not have the power to override or compromise'.

[10] Gerber, '*Protecting Prometheus*' (n 1) 245–54; Drexl, 'Competition Law as Part of the European Constitution' (n 1); Drexl, 'La Constitution économique européenne' 2011 (n 1).

[11] J Madison (or A Hamilton), 'Federalist Paper no 51: The Structure of the Government Must Furnish the Proper Checks and Balances Between the Different Departments', in A Hamilton, J Madison, J Jay and RP Fairfield (ed), *The Federalist Papers: a Collection of Essays written in Support of the Constitution of the United States* (Baltimore, Johns Hopkins University Press, 1981).

of economic competition (process), but it should not participate in economic competition itself (substance).[12]

It is in light of this objective of controlled deployment of public power onto private power that the concept of 'undistorted economic competition', which lies at the core of the economic constitution envisaged by ordoliberals, appears in all its strategic splendour. On the one hand, the State must prevent distortions of competition brought about by concentrations of economic power. On the other hand, the State is itself under a duty to avoid interventions that would distort economic competition. The concept of undistorted economic competition single-handedly translates in concrete terms the objective of overseeing both public power and private power in the economic sphere.

As is well known, ordoliberalism had a considerable influence on the European integration process,[13] chiefly because it was perfectly suited to its strategic needs, namely the control of private and public powers in the economic sphere. Indeed, in 1950, occupied Germany represented a dilemma recurring under the guises of economic and political powers.[14] An ailing European economy—heavily dependent upon a US aid embodied by the Marshall Plan (1947–51)—needed to reinstate the full potential of German industries. However, having witnessed how German industrial cartels had fuelled the Reich's military power, the Allies needed guarantees that German industries would not seek to concentrate and abuse their economic power. The same dilemma existed at the political level: with the vivid memory of the humiliating Treaty of Versailles (1919), Germany quickly became hostile to foreign occupation and administration. On the other side, the idea of a sovereign Germany was hardly palatable to the Allies, who needed guarantees against German nationalism.

In 1950, the Schuman Plan proposed a pragmatic and yet revolutionary solution to the twofold dilemma raised by (German) national power. As the Allies wanted German sovereignty to be limited and Germany demanded to be treated equally, the logical solution consisted in a joint delegation of sovereignty to a supranational institution, by Germany *and* other European countries. Weiler commented:

> If we go back in time to the 1950 Schuman Declaration and the consequent 1951 Treaty of Paris establishing the European Coal and Steel Community, these events, despite their

[12] As noted by Georgopoulos, no economic system can subsist without minimal State intervention, if only to enforce economic freedoms: T Georgopoulos, 'Sur le concept de "constitution économique de l'Union Européenne"' in O Debarge et al (eds), *La constitution économique de l'Union Européenne: 2è rencontre du GIEPI, 12-13 mai 2006* (Brussels, Bruylant, 2008) 16.

[13] See inter alia Gerber, '*Protecting Prometheus*' (n 1) 263–65; Drexl 'Competition Law as Part of the European Constitution' (n 1); Drexl 'La Constitution économique (n 1); Mongouachon (n 1); W Sauter, 'The Economic Constitution of the European Union' (1998) 4 *Columbia Journal of European Law* 27; C Joerges, 'Que reste-t-il de la Constitution économique européenne après la constitutionnalisation de l'Europe?—Une rétrospective mélancolique' (2005) Cahiers Européens de Sciences Po no 01/2005, available at www.cee.sciences-po.fr/erpa/docs/wp_2005_1.pdf.

[14] See Monnet, *Mémoires* (n 3) chs XI to XV; Fondation Jean Monnet pour l'Europe, *Jean Monnet, Robert Schuman, Correspondance 1947–1953* (Lausanne, IRL, 1986) 58–59 and 88–89.

> economic content, are best seen as a long-term and transformative strategy for peace among the states of Western Europe, principally France and Germany. This strategy tried to address the 'mischief' embodied in the excesses of the modern nation-state and the traditional model of statal intercourse among them that was premised on full 'sovereignty', 'autonomy', 'independence', and a relentless defense and maximization of the national interest. ... The European Community was to be an antidote to the negative features of the state and statal intercourse; its establishment in 1951 was seen as the beginning of a process that would bring about their elimination.[15]

Many considered this delegation of sovereignty in favour of a supranational institution as an unprecedented event in history.[16] Thus, in 1951, the Treaty of Paris establishing the European Coal and Steel Community (ECSC) created a common market in the limited but eminently strategic[17] areas of coal and steel (Article 1). Germany, France, Italy, Belgium, the Netherlands and Luxembourg had consented to delegate their sovereignty in those areas to a High Authority whose decisions, adopted by simple majority vote (Article 13), were binding in the Member States' territories (Article 14). In that common market, Member States refrained from imposing customs duties, quantitative restrictions or discriminatory measures, and from granting subsidies (Article 4). Moreover, the High Authority held the general power to oversee State interventions distorting the conditions of competition (Article 67). Finally, detailed antitrust provisions were intended to fight monopolies, cartels and concentrations of economic power (Articles 65 and 66).

Intentionally or not,[18] the ESCS Treaty was designed in accordance with the economic commandments of ordoliberalism: control of public power and private

[15] JHH Weiler, 'The Transformation of Europe' (1991) 100 *Yale Law Journal* 2403, 2478.

[16] The underlying political objective was to 'create a breach into the battlement of national sovereignties, limited enough to rally consents but deep enough to lead States towards the unity needed for peace': Monnet (n 3) 429, free translation. This supranationalism inherent to the Schuman Plan explains why Monnet adamantly refused the creation of the European Community under the aegis of the Council of Europe, whose mode of functioning was merely intergovernmental: see Fondation Jean Monnet pour l'Europe, *Jean Monnet, Robert Schuman, Correspondance 1947–1953* (n 14) 49–53, 76–77 and 158–59.

[17] The production of coal and steel was of crucial importance for both economic and military purposes: Monnet (n 3) ch XII.

[18] At the end of the war, members of the Freiburg school were quickly propelled to the forefront of German politics, as they had no ties to Nazism and propounded market-oriented ideas backed by US authorities. Franz Böhm, for example, was a member of the Bundestag from 1953 to 1961. Ludwig Erhard served as German minister of economy from 1949 until 1963, when he replaced Adenauer as Chancellor, and successfully implemented ordoliberal ideas in post-war Germany. Similarly, German representatives in the founding of the European Communities, as Walter Hallstein and Hans von der Groeben, were closely associated with ordoliberalism. Hallstein was appointed by Adenauer as German negotiator at the Conference of the Schuman Plan, and later became the first President of the European Commission. Von der Groeben was one of the two main drafters of the Spaak Report, and later became the first Commissioner for Competition Policy of the European Commission. See Gerber, *Protecting Prometheus* (n 1) 257–64; Drexl, 'Competition Law as Part of the European Constitution' (n 1) 648. Monnet also recounts that during the Conference on the Schuman Plan, Erhard and Hallstein adamantly rejected the idea of interventions by the High Authority into the common market: Monnet (n 3) 476.

power in the economic sphere, enforced through the strategic goal of undistorted economic competition. In 1957, the Treaty of Rome establishing a European Economic Community expanded the ordoliberal pattern endorsed in 1951 by the ESCS Treaty to the entire economy of Member States. It is against that background that the Treaty on the Functioning of the European Union (TFEU), heir of the Treaty of Rome, can be understood as the economic constitution of the European Union, namely a set of fundamental choices regarding the economic system that cannot be overridden by Member States.[19] The Court confirmed this 'constitutional' status of the European Treaties in the seminal *van Gend and Loos* judgment.[20]

The essence of the economic constitution of the European Union, in the sense envisaged by ordoliberals, consists in the control of public power and private power in the economic sphere, through the strategic goal of undistorted economic competition. In the current law of the European Union, this economic project is chiefly pursued by four sets of Treaty provisions, most of which have been thoroughly examined in the course of this study: the provisions on Union harmonisation, the freedoms of movement, the rules on competition and the rules on State aids. The provisions on Union harmonisation and free movement supervise the intervention of public power in the economy of the Union; the rules on competition oversee private power; the rules on State aids arguably deal with both public power and private power.

First of all, Articles 113 to 118 TFEU provide legal bases for the harmonisation or approximation of national laws, thereby overseeing the action of public power within the internal market. The explicit purpose assigned to Union harmonisation is to ensure that diversity among national laws does not impede the 'functioning of the internal market' (Articles 113, 114, 115 and 118 TFEU) and/or 'distort the conditions of competition' (Articles 113, 116 and 117 TFEU). In other words, the Treaty provisions on Union harmonisation seek to prevent distortions of competition ensuing from State actions.[21]

The same function of appraising public action within the internal market is fulfilled by the freedoms of movement guaranteed to citizens (Article 21 TFEU), goods (Article 28 TFEU), workers (Article 45 TFEU), self-employed persons and

[19] Sauter, 'The Economic Constitution of the European Union' (n 13) 50 ff; A Hatje, 'The Economic Constitution' in von Bogdandy and Bast, *Principles of European Constitutional Law* (n 1) 590–92.

[20] Case 26/62 *van Gend and Loos* [1963] ECR 3:

> The objective of the EEC Treaty, which is to establish a common market, … implies that this Treaty is more than an agreement which merely creates mutual obligations between the contracting States. … [T]he Community constitutes a new legal order of international law for the benefit of which the States have limited their sovereign rights, albeit within limited fields, and the subjects of which comprise not only Member States but also their nationals. Independently of the legislation of Member States, Community law therefore not only imposes obligations on individuals but is also intended to confer upon them rights which become part of their legal heritage.

[21] See ch 7 section III.

companies (Article 49 TFEU), services (Article 56 TFEU) and capital (Article 63 TFEU).[22] As stated by the Court in *Schul*:

> The concept of a common market ... involves the elimination of all obstacles to intra-Community trade in order to merge the national markets into a single market bringing about conditions as close as possible to those of a genuine internal market.[23]

In other words, an effective Union-wide competition requires the freedom of Union citizens to deploy their activities everywhere in the internal market; as a consequence, public interventions hindering private mobility are, as a rule, incompatible with the Treaty.

By contrast with the Treaty provisions on harmonisation and free movement, which are concerned with public power, the rules on competition oversee private power in the internal market.[24] On the one hand, Article 101 TFEU outlaws the artificial creation of economic power by prohibiting agreements and concerted practices among undertakings (cartels) that restrict or distort competition within the internal market. On the other hand, Article 102 TFEU deals with situations of economic dominance held by a single undertaking in the internal market (monopolies): if it does not demand the dispersion of such economic power, it prohibits 'abuses of a dominant position'. These two Treaty provisions are completed by Merger Regulation 139/2004, which aims at preventing excessive concentrations of private power.[25] Article 2(3) of this regulation provides:

> A concentration which would significantly impede effective competition, in the common market or in a substantial part of it, in particular as a result of the creation or strengthening of a dominant position, shall be declared incompatible with the common market.

Lastly, the State aids regime is located at the intersection of public and private powers in the internal market.[26] On its face, Article 107 TFEU oversees public power as it precludes Member States from granting aids that distort competition by favouring certain undertakings or the production of certain goods. However,

[22] Although the Treaty provisions on free movement were originally designed to apply to Member States (vertical application), the Court incrementally expanded their scope to private actors holding a quasi-public power (horizontal application), such as professional associations endowed with regulatory power: see AG Maduro, Case C-438/05 *Viking* [2007] ECR I-10779, paras 29–56.

[23] Case 15/81 *Schul* [1982] ECR 1409, para 33; see also Case 207/83 *Commission v United Kingdom (Original Marking)* [1985] ECR 1201, para 17; Case 159/78 *Commission v Italy* [1979] ECR 3247, para 7; Case 78/70 *Deutsche Grammophon* [1971] ECR 487, para 12.

[24] See L Boy, 'Le droit de la concurrence, élément d'une constitution européenne?' in Debarge, *La constitution économique de l'Union Européenne* (n 12); Drexl, 'Competition Law as Part of the European Constitution' (n 1).

[25] Council Regulation (EC) 139/2004 of 20 January 2004 on the control of concentrations between undertakings [2004] OJ L24/1. See esp rec 4 and 5.

[26] See O Rabaey, 'L'interventionisme libéral, paradoxe de la constitution économique européenne: une approche constitutionnelle dialectique du régime communautaire des aides d'État' in Debarge (n 12).

it can also be argued that the State aids regime protects public power from private power: indeed, if State aids were permitted, businesses would be in a position to use blackmail tactics against national governments, by demanding public subsidies to locate their economic activities on their territory.[27]

To sum up, the economic constitution as envisaged by ordoliberals aims at controlling both public power and private power in the economic sphere. To that end, the economic constitution enshrines fundamental choices that cannot be overridden by the dominant legislature. In the context of the European Union, this function is chiefly performed by the Treaty provisions on harmonisation, free movement, competition and State aids.

II. Historical Conditions of the Emergence of the Phenomenon of Abuse of Union Law

The present section describes the historical conditions accounting for the emergence and exponential growth of the phenomenon of abuse of Union law, which can be decomposed into socioeconomic and legal factors.

From a socioeconomic perspective, the phenomenon of abuse of Union can be linked to the apparition of the new communication technologies, and chiefly of the Internet. Combined with modern and affordable means of transportation, these new communication technologies have considerably increased private mobility. In his Opinion in *Daily Mail* issued in 1988, namely years before the commercial exploitation of the Internet, AG Darmon prophetically quoted the following statement:

> Owing to the progress made by means of communication, it is no longer necessary to arrange formal board meetings. The telephone, telex and telecopier enable each director to state his point of view and to take part in the decision-making without being physically present in a given place. The board meetings each director will attend via television will soon form part of a company's everyday life. The board of directors can meet in a place chosen arbitrarily, which bears no real relation with the decision centre of the company.[28]

[27] For a reading of State aids as 'extortion' of public monies by mobile businesses, and the correlative risk of 'State aid races' among States, see eg London Economics, *Competition Issues*, The Single Market Review, subseries V, vol 3 (London, Kogan Page, 1997) 222; L Hancher, T Ottervanger and PJ Slot, *EC State Aids* (London, Sweet & Maxwell, 2006) no 2-005; D Spector, 'State Aids: Economic Analysis and Practice in the European Union' in X Vives (ed), *Competition Policy in the EU: Fifty Years on from the Treaty of Rome* (Oxford, Oxford University Press, 2009) 178 ff.

[28] AG Darmon, Case 81/87 *Daily Mail* [1988] ECR 5483, para 7.

AG Léger's opinion in *Cadbury Schweppes*, delivered in 2006, acknowledged the fulfilment of this prophecy by highlighting the volatility of businesses:

> Thus, when the services in question consist, as in this case, of raising funds and providing them to subsidiaries in the worldwide Cadbury group, because of modern communication methods they can be carried out in the name of the CFC by staff and information technology which is not physically and materially located in Ireland. In the case of such services, the company formally established in Dublin may have no real substance and be exclusively what is termed a 'letter-box' company.[29]

The strategies set up by *Cadbury Schweppes* or *Centros* are only conceivable in a world characterised by a high degree of private mobility, in which businesses can relocate entire segments of their activities at low or zero cost. In that sense, the explosion of private mobility has contributed to the emergence and growth of the phenomenon of abuse of Union law.

In addition to socioeconomic factors, the emergence of the phenomenon of abuse of Union law can be related to legal factors. Indeed, the phenomenon of abuse of Union law reflects a specific moment reached by the European process of integration, more particularly of the dialectic between unity and diversity within the internal market. On 9 May 1950, Robert Schuman opened his famous declaration with a terse finding: 'A united Europe was not achieved and we had war'.[30] On 4 May 2000, 50 years after the Schuman Declaration and four years before the enlargement to 10 new Member States, the European Parliament adopted the official motto of the European Union, '*Unity in Diversity*'.[31] Arguably, much of the appeal of the expression 'unity in diversity' lies in the inherent tension it hosts, namely the paradox of how many things can become one and still remain different things or, in other words, of how diversity can be preserved in unity. The dialectic between unity and diversity is constitutive of every 'society of States'[32] such as the European Union or the United States.[33] In that connection, it can be

[29] AG Léger, Case C-196/04 *Cadbury Schweppes* [2006] ECR I-7995, para 138.

[30] R Schuman, 'Declaration of 9 May 1950', available at http://europa.eu/abc/symbols/9-may/decl_en.htm.

[31] Following an original idea by journalist Patrick La Prairie, working for the newspaper *Ouest France*, the official motto of the European Union was adopted at the end of a non-official contest inviting students of secondary schools to propose a motto through a dedicated website: see P La Prairie, 'Une Devise pour l'Europe', *Ouest France*, 27 February 2009. The motto was later slightly modified to '*United in Diversity*', which was the version proposed in art I-8 of the Draft Treaty establishing a Constitution for Europe.

[32] H Bull, *The Anarchical Society: a Study of Order in World Politics*, 3rd edn (Basingstoke, Palgrave Macmillan, 2002) 13: a 'society of states' comes into existence 'when a group of states, conscious of certain common interests and common values, form a society in the sense that they conceive themselves to be bound by a common set of rules in their relations with one another, and share in the working of common institutions'.

[33] The official seal of the United States, adopted six years after the Declaration of Independence (1776), carries the phrase '*E Pluribus Unum*' ('*Out of Many, One*'). In a fascinating study, WC Harris identified the tension between unity and diversity, embodied by the phrase '*E Pluribus Unum*', as the constitutional paradox of the United States. Relying on seminal texts of nineteenth-century American

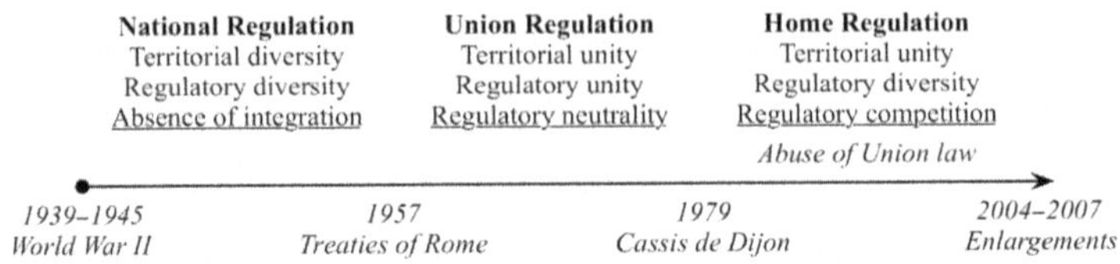

Figure 13 – A Conceptual Timeline of the Regulation of the Internal Market

argued that the phenomenon of abuse of Union law crystallises a specific moment of the dialectic between unity and diversity inherent to the European Union.

The main objective of the European project of integration has been the curtailment of national sovereignty to the benefit of the Union's supranational unity. Since its inception as the European Coal and Steel Community (1951), the structure and functioning of the European Union have permanently fluctuated between unity and diversity. In more detail, the evolution of this tension between unity and diversity defines three moments in the regulation of the internal market, as shown by the following conceptual timeline (Figure 13).[34]

The above timeline is not strictly 'historical', as all three regulatory modes (national, Union and home regulation) have been concurrently used throughout the existence of the internal market; yet it defines three 'conceptual' moments during which each mode successively became the prevalent conception in the regulation of the internal market. The first moment, from World War II (1945) to the Treaties of Rome (1957) predates the creation of the internal market: it covers the pre-integration era, during which national sovereignty was unfettered and the European Union did not exist. The European territory was split up along national borders (territorial diversity), and every State remained free to impose its national laws in their respective national territory (regulatory diversity).

The second moment on this conceptual timeline, from the Treaties of Rome (1957) until the *Cassis de Dijon* ruling (1979), represents the early years of the European Union and the initial momentum towards unity. Historically, the Second World War provided the original impetus towards unity, as encapsulated by the Schuman Declaration, which led to the adoption of the Treaties of Rome. During that period, Union regulation replaced national regulation as the ideal regulatory mode within the European Union; as a consequence, the internal market became characterised by both territorial and regulatory unity. Accordingly,

literature, Harris argues that the one-to-the-many problem can never be solved, but rather constitutes a creative tension modelling the Constitution and the functioning of the United States. See WC Harris, *E Pluribus Unum: Nineteenth-Century American Literature and the Constitutional Paradox* (Iowa City, University of Iowa Press, 2005).

[34] In a slightly more detailed fashion, von Sydow distinguishes three post-integration periods: the 'initial surge of the Sixties', the 'decline of the Seventies' and the 'new momentum of the Eighties': see H Schmitt von Sydow, 'The Basic Strategies of the Commission's White Paper' in R Bieber et al (eds), *1992: One European Market?* (Baden-Baden, Nomos, 1988) 92 (see ch 6 n 100 and accompanying text).

this second period favoured an ideal of economic integration based on regulatory neutrality, in which every undertaking would be subject to the same (Union) regulation,[35] and economic competition would not be distorted by diversity among national laws.

The third moment, from *Cassis de Dijon* (1979) to the present day, is characterised by the combination of territorial unity and regulatory diversity, which accounts for the rise of the phenomenon of abuse of law. As the original momentum towards unity progressively waned, political difficulties made harmonisation at Union level at best illusory.[36] The absence of Union harmonisation preserves regulatory diversity within the Union: as a rule, Member States remain free to define the content of their national laws. On the other hand, the freedoms of movement, broadly interpreted by the Court of Justice, ensure territorial unity within the Union: as a rule, Union citizens are free to move from one Member State to another. In that regard, the *Cassis de Dijon* judgment established mutual recognition as a core principle in the regulation of the internal market. The Commission formalised this conceptual shift in the White Paper on the completion of the internal market (1985), which substituted Union harmonisation with mutual recognition as the institutional priority. By no means has this conceptual shift meant that the Union legislature stopped adopting harmonising measures altogether, but rather that Union institutions—and chiefly the Commission—gave preference to mutual recognition over harmonisation:

> In the past, internal market policies relied mainly on harmonisation directives introducing common rules for each individual sector. Despite initial success, a number of shortcomings had been identified over the years, and the authors of the White Paper knew very well that a genuine internal market could not be realised by 1992 under the traditional strategy. The new strategy, which runs through all parts of the White Paper as a red line, is based on a shift from the drawing up of new, harmonised regulations to the principle of mutual recognition of national rules and situations.[37]

The discrepancy between territorial unity and regulatory diversity, which characterises the third moment of the regulation of the internal market, structurally favours the emergence of abusive practices. Indeed, abusive practices amount to cross-border movements solely designed to elect a more favourable national law; in other words, abuses of Union law rely on the territorial unity guaranteed by the freedoms of movement, in order to exploit the regulatory diversity resulting

[35] Admittedly, many believed that regulatory unity would not have to be entirely imposed through Union legislation, but would in part spontaneously ensue from the enmeshment of national economies. For instance, see Rapport du Comité intergouvernemental créé par la Conférence de Messine ('Rapport Spaak'), 21 April 1956, aei.pitt.edu/996/01/Spaak_report_french.pdf, 65, free translation:

> The spontaneous trend towards harmonisation of social systems and wage levels, as well as trade union action aiming at the alignment of working conditions, will be facilitated by the gradual establishment of the common market.

[36] See ch 6 n 95 and accompanying text.

[37] von Sydow, 'The Basic Strategies of the Commission's White Paper' (n 34) 92; see Commission (EC), 'Completing the internal market' (White Paper) COM (85) 310 final, 14 June 1985, no 13.

from the absence of Union harmonisation. Thus, the protagonists of *Centros* or *Cadbury Schweppes* sought to move to another Member State (territorial unity) in order to elect hospitable national laws (regulatory diversity). Conversely, there can be no abuse when there is no attempt to exploit regulatory diversity within the internal market; in *Papillon*, the Court stated:

> In the main proceedings, the question as to whether the profits and losses of companies belonging to the group in question should be taken into account arises only in relation to companies which are resident in a single Member State. Accordingly, the question which is put relates to the taking into account of losses recorded in one and the same Member State, which also excludes, prima facie, a risk of tax avoidance.[38]

In sum, the phenomenon of abuse of Union law exploits regulatory diversity by relying on territorial unity, so that its emergence and growth can be linked to institutional choices specific to the third moment in the regulation of the internal market, whereby Union harmonisation is neglected and the scope of the freedoms of movement expanded.

Furthermore, when territorial unity is secured through the freedoms of movement, the incentive to set up artificial cross-border strategies is positively correlated to the degree of diversity among national laws. Citizens are less likely to relocate to another jurisdiction for regulatory motives alone when national laws are similar;[39] taken to the extreme, full harmonisation suppresses regulatory diversity and ipso facto all room for regulatory arbitrage within the internal market. Conversely, the higher the degree of regulatory diversity within the internal market, the stronger the incentive to design an abusive practice. The Court observed in *Oy AA*:

> [T]he Finnish system of intra-group financial transfers is able to prevent [abusive] practices, likely to be encouraged by the finding of significant disparities between the bases of assessment or rates of tax applied in the various Member States and designed only to avoid the tax normally due in the Member State of the subsidiary on its profits.[40]

Similarly, the Court stated in *Marks & Spencer*:

> As regards … the risk of tax avoidance, it must be accepted that the possibility of transferring the losses incurred by a non-resident company to a resident company entails the risk that within a group of companies losses will be transferred to companies established in the Member State which apply the highest rates of taxation and in which the tax value of the losses is therefore the highest.

[38] Case C-418/07 *Papillon* [2008] ECR I-8947, para 39.

[39] A business taxed at a rate of 50% in Member State A has a strong incentive to move to Member State B if the tax rate is of 10%, but not if it is of 49.9%.

[40] Case C-231/05 *Oy AA* [2007] ECR I-6373, para 59; see also Case C-311/08 *SGI* [2010] ECR I-487, para 68.

> To exclude group relief for losses incurred by non-resident subsidiaries prevents such practices, which may be inspired by the realisation that the rates of taxation applied in the various Member States vary significantly.[41]

It is against that context that the impact of the enlargements of the Union in 2004, 2007 and 2013 upon the phenomenon of abuse of Union law must be assessed. This enlargement to 13 Member States, with different legislative, political and economic traditions, considerably augmented the degree of regulatory diversity. By the same token, this enlargement substantially increased the strength of the incentives to set up relocation strategies, which inevitably led to situations in which undertakings sought to escape the heavier regulations of old Member States in favour of hospitable legal regimes proposed by new Member States, as in *Laval* and *Viking*.[42] Sørensen wrote:

> [T]he latest enlargement of the EU in 2004, with 10 new Member States, seems to have fuelled Member States' fears of abuse of rights. This is probably due to the fact that the social and legal systems in the new Member States differ substantially from those of the 'old' Member States and these differences can be exploited in various ways.[43]

De la Feria similarly noted the magnifying effect of the recent enlargements upon the phenomenon of abuse of Union law:

> This state of affairs has changed radically within the last few years, with abuse of law gaining significant prominence. This marked change has been attributed to various factors, including the increase in the volume of free movement within the internal market and also the 2004 enlargement.[44]

Overall, this third moment of the regulation of the internal market, characterised by the combination of territorial unity and regulatory diversity, mechanically expands the room for regulatory arbitrage by Union citizens. As a result, it favours a conception of economic integration based on regulatory competition, whereby Member States compete to attract mobile citizens who 'arbitrate' among national laws. In that sense, the emergence of the concept of abuse of Union law, which outlaws such regulatory arbitrage, can be viewed as a surge of regulatory neutrality in a historical moment favouring regulatory competition.

To sum up, the emergence and growth of the phenomenon of abuse of Union law can be explained by a conjunction of socioeconomic and legal factors. On the one hand, new communication technologies and modern transportation means have provoked an explosion of private mobility. On the other hand, the European process of integration has reached a specific moment in which territorial unity is

[41] Case C-446/03 *Marks & Spencer* [2005] ECR I-10837, paras 49–50.

[42] Case C-341/05 *Laval* [2007] ECR I-11767; Case C-438/05 *Viking* [2007] ECR I-10779. See ch 8 section IV.

[43] KE Sørensen, 'Abuse of Rights in Community Law: a Principle of Substance or Merely Rhetoric?' (2006) 43 *Common Market Law Review* 423, 424.

[44] R de la Feria, 'Prohibition of Abuse of (Community) Law: the Creation of a New General Principle of EC Law through Tax' (2008) 45 *Common Market Law Review* 395, 397.

secured but regulatory diversity preserved. This legal environment opens a space for cross-border movements designed to elect a more hospitable jurisdiction, which private individuals exploit thanks to the new communication technologies and modern transportation means.

III. The Rise of a New Form of Private Power Originating in Mobility

The explosion of private mobility described in the previous section entails systemic consequences for the economic constitution of the European Union; indeed, the emergence of the phenomenon of abuse of Union law can be correlated to the rise of a new form of private power originating in mobility. As exposed above, the ordo-liberal ideal of economic constitution requires the controlled deployment of public power onto private power, for instance in the form of State intervention against cartels, monopolies or mere concentrations of economic power. Hatje wrote:

> The heart of the matter is, independent of concrete economic systems, the use of law to establish controls and limitations of power, a power which can be exerted by the state as well as private protagonists. The solution to the question of power, which belongs to the fundamental tasks of every constitution, is therefore the key to understanding the legal function of the economic constitution.[45]

The explosion of private mobility challenges this constitutional arrangement that has prevailed since the ECSC Treaty, by undermining the capacity of public power to deploy itself onto private power within the Union. More precisely, the explosion of private mobility forms a new source of power enabling private individuals to escape the deployment of public power. Within an integrated area characterised by regulatory diversity and territorial unity,[46] the scope of public actions undertaken by Member States is limited to their national territory (no harmonisation), whereas the scope of private actions extends to the entire Union territory (free movement). This discrepancy between the national scope of public action and the Union-wide scope of private action enables private individuals to escape public action, by moving to the territory of a more hospitable State. Abuses of law can thus be described as an unequal cat-and-mouse game, in which the public cat is confined to a national territory, whereas the private mice may run across the Union territory.

In practice, this new mobility-power undermines public power by subjecting it to permanent threats of relocation from mobile individuals. Ulrich Beck commented:

> While the power of states (according to the national rationale) grows by conquering foreign territories, the power of the global economy's players grows precisely by doing

45 Hatje, 'The Economic Constitution' (n 19) 590.

46 See section II.

> or threatening to do the opposite, by being in a position to leave the relevant national territory, to not conquer foreign countries and territories. This in turn succeeds to the extent that transnational companies become extraterritorial factors. The power of the state is thus not undermined or broken by state power, i.e., military threat and conquest, but rather deterritorially, exterritorially, by way of a new weightlessness of transnational trade and activity in the digital space.[47]

Artificial practices, which were defined as strategies pursuing a regulatory benefit at the exclusion of any socioeconomic benefit,[48] are concrete manifestations of this threat. In cases such as *Centros* or *Cadbury Schweppes*, corporations sought to escape public action in the State of origin (Danish company law in *Centros*, UK direct taxation in *Cadbury Schweppes*) and place themselves under the public action of a hospitable jurisdiction (UK company law in *Centros*, Irish direct taxation in *Cadbury Schweppes*). In the seminal *Cadbury Schweppes* judgment, the Court explicitly underlined the 'undermining' effect of such artificial practices upon public power:

> [I]n order for a restriction on the freedom of establishment to be justified on the ground of prevention of abusive practices, the specific objective of such a restriction must be to prevent conduct involving the creation of wholly artificial arrangements which do not reflect economic reality, with a view to escaping the tax normally due on the profits generated by activities carried out on national territory.
>
> Like the practices referred to in paragraph 49 of Marks & Spencer, which involve arranging transfers of losses, within a group of companies, to companies established in the Member State which apply the highest rates of taxation and in which the tax value of those losses is therefore the highest, the type of conduct described in the preceding paragraph is such as to undermine the right of the Member States to exercise their tax jurisdiction in relation to the activities carried out in their territory and thus to jeopardise a balanced allocation between Member States of the power to impose taxes.[49]

In more detail, the precise extent of this mobility-power and of its undermining effect on public power depends on three variables evoked in the previous section: the level of socioeconomic costs entailed by cross-border movements, the degree of regulatory diversity and the degree of territorial unity.

First of all, the extent to which private individuals can escape public power depends on the socioeconomic costs entailed by cross-border movements. When the costs of moving to another State are low, private individuals enjoy the freedom to escape State public action. Accordingly, by considerably reducing the cost of moving, the combination of new communication technologies and affordable means of transportation has greatly expanded mobility-power. Conversely, high

[47] U Beck, 'The Cosmopolitan State: Redefining Power in the Global Age' (2005) 18 *International Journal of Politics, Culture and Society* 143, 150.

[48] See ch 3 section II.

[49] Case C-196/04 *Cadbury Schweppes* [2006] ECR I-7995, paras 55–56; see also Case C-524/04 *Thin Cap Group Litigation* [2007] ECR I-2107, paras 74–75; Case C-231/05 *Oy AA* [2007] ECR I-6373, para 54–56; Case C-414/06 *Lidl Belgium* [2008] ECR I-3601, paras 32–34; Case C-446/03 *Marks & Spencer* [2005] ECR I-10837, paras 45–46.

movements costs tend to annihilate this private power originating in mobility. For instance, strategies consisting in relocating economic activities in a hospitable jurisdiction, as in the *Cadbury Schweppes* case, would be naturally[50] thwarted if the use of aeroplanes, Internet or phone lines entailed prohibitive costs. Moreover, as the costs of communication and transportation are highly dependent on the cost of energy (eg oil or electricity), any increase in energy cost, due for instance to the rarefaction of natural resources, is liable to reduce the capacity of mobility-power to undermine public power.

The two other variables determining the extent of private-mobility, namely the degree of regulatory diversity and the degree of territorial unity, flow directly from Union law. Dougan observed:

> One might well disapprove of individuals who appear to engage in [abusive practices], but their behaviour is merely a consequence of the policy decisions which flow from granting universal rights to free movement across the Union's highly diverse regulatory environment, and the legal response to such behaviour lies entirely in the hands of the Union institutions when implementing and interpreting the relevant provisions of primary and secondary EU law.[51]

The degree of regulatory diversity, which forms the second variable, has experienced a sharp increase in the last two decades, following the advent of the mutual recognition principle and the successive waves of enlargement.[52] The high degree of diversity among public actions augments the probability that private individuals find a 'safe haven' where they can escape public action detrimental to their interests. Conversely, the homogeneity of public actions throughout the Union territory would tend to incapacitate private individuals in their quest for a safe haven. In theory, three courses of action could reduce the degree of regulatory diversity within the Union and accordingly diminish mobility-power, but all three are constrained by severe limitations.

A first theoretical course of action consists in restricting Union membership to Member States with similar regulatory environments. However, this course of action seems to go against the sense of history, as shown by the recent enlargements to new Member States with different regulatory environments.[53]

[50] In theory, coordinated public action could artificially increase the costs of communication, transportation and/or energy, for instance by setting up Union- or world-wide taxation on the relevant economic sectors. However, this theoretical possibility is thwarted by the practical difficulty of overcoming regulatory diversity within the Union and beyond.

[51] M Dougan, 'Some Comments on the Idea of a General Principle of Union Law Prohibiting Abuses of Law in the Field of Free Movement for Union Citizens' in R de la Feria and S Vogenauer (eds), *Prohibition of Abuse of Law: a New General Principle of EU Law?* (Oxford, Hart Publishing, 2011) 360.

[52] See section II.

[53] See nn 42–44 and accompanying text.

A second course of action would consist in replacing national public actions by a Union public action. Again, this second course of action is bound to remain largely theoretical given the political difficulties of achieving harmonisation at Union level, which have prompted the adoption of mutual recognition as the institutional priority in the 1985 White Paper.[54] A kindred but less ambitious course of action consists in having recourse to minimum harmonisation, which allows Member States to adopt more stringent regulatory standards than those defined by the harmonising instrument ('floor'), provided that these standards are compatible with the Treaty ('walls').[55] A minimum harmonisation reduces regulatory diversity within the internal market, by precluding Member States from crossing a given regulatory floor; the higher the floor, the lesser the diversity among national laws, and the lower the incentive to move. Simon Deakin extensively studied the effects of minimum harmonisation and propounded in that connection the concept of 'reflexive harmonisation'. In essence, a process of reflexive harmonisation involves the setting of a floor of rights at Union level, above which Member States are encouraged to experiment with innovative regulations. Reflexive harmonisation should promote mutual learning among Member States and avoid the drawback of a convergence towards lower regulatory standards (race-to-the-bottom).[56]

Overall, the increased number and disparity among Member States make Union harmonisation more difficult, despite the extension of qualified majority voting in the Lisbon Treaty. In that connection, the recourse to 'enhanced cooperation', which started in 1992 with the opt-out of the United Kingdom and Denmark from the third phase of the monetary union, and which is now enshrined in Articles 326 to 334 TFEU, can be viewed as the institutionalisation of regulatory diversity within an increasingly heterogeneous Union.[57]

A third course of action resides in the prohibition of State aids, which acts as a constraint upon regulatory diversity by precluding Member States from granting

[54] See section II.

[55] F de Cecco, 'Room to Move? Minimum Harmonization and Fundamental Rights' (2006) 43 *Common Market Law Review* 9, 9; M Dougan, 'Minimum Harmonization and the Internal Market' (2000) 37 *Common Market Law Review* 853, 855; P Rott, 'Minimum Harmonization for the Completion of the Internal Market? The Example of Consumer Sales Law' (2003) 40 *Common Market Law Review* 1107.

[56] S Deakin, 'Two Types of Regulatory Competition: Competitive Federalism versus Reflexive Harmonisation' (1999) 2 *Cambridge Yearbook of European Legal Studies* 231; S Deakin, 'Regulatory Competition versus Harmonization in European Company Law' in DC Esty and D Geradin (eds), *Regulatory Competition and Economic Integration: Comparative Perspectives* (Oxford, Oxford University Press, 2001); S Deakin, 'Legal Diversity and Regulatory Competition: Which Model for Europe?' (2006) 12 *European Law Journal* 440; S Deakin, 'Is Regulatory Competition the Future for European Integration?' (2006) 13 *Swedish Economic Policy Review* 71; S Deakin, 'Regulatory Competition after Laval' (2007–08) 10 *Cambridge Yearbook of European Legal Studies* 581.

[57] D Thym, 'United in Diversity: the Integration of Enhanced Cooperation into the European Constitutional Order' (2005) 6 *German Law Journal* 1731; JM Beneyto (ed), *Unity and Flexibility in the Future of the European Union: the Challenge of Enhanced Cooperation* (Madrid, CEU Ediciones, 2009).

selective advantages to businesses. As a rule, advantages funded through public resources have to be granted to all businesses falling within the jurisdiction of the competent State. However, the impact of the State aid regime upon regulatory diversity is severely limited by the exclusion of general measures (eg general reduction of taxes or social contributions) and regulatory measures (eg labour law, environmental law).[58]

In such a context of low moving costs and high regulatory diversity, the only possibility to reduce mobility-power resides in the third variable, namely the degree of territorial unity; and the effect of the prohibition of abusive practices is precisely to reduce the degree of territorial unity. When territorial unity is at its highest, private individuals are entirely free to move across the Union territory, which enables them to escape public action detrimental to their interests. As a matter of fact, the Court's expansive interpretation of the freedoms of movement ensures a high degree of territorial unity within the Union.

One theoretical possibility of breaking territorial unity resides in leaving the European Union altogether: moving costs would remain low and regulatory diversity high, but States would recover their power to hinder cross-border movements, for instance through hefty exit taxes. Yet a less radical course of action consists in prohibiting artificial cross-border movements as abusive. The prohibition of abusive practices does not reduce regulatory diversity, for it does not suppress the existence of safe havens within the Union; rather, it reduces territorial unity, as it prevents private individuals from moving to such safe havens. By way of illustration, the concrete effect of the *Cadbury Schweppes* judgment was to permit the application of UK tax law to subsidiaries incorporated in Ireland for mere tax reasons. By outlawing artificial choices of law, the prohibition of abusive practices allows the public cat to catch runaway mice.

Overall, the combination of low moving costs, high regulatory diversity and high territorial unity—only qualified by the prohibition of abusive practices—have led to the emergence of a new form of private power originating in mobility. Admittedly, private mobility has always been a sporadic thorn in the side of public power, in a 'Voltairian' fashion;[59] but it has become a structural constraint on public power in the last three decades. Indeed, if strategies designed to elect hospitable laws have always existed, this phenomenon has taken on a systemic dimension with the new communication technologies and the global trend to economic integration, thereby acquiring the status of 'mobility-power'.

The rise of a new form or private power undermining public power and more generally the cohesion of society is not an unprecedented event in modern history. As a matter of fact, the political problems currently associated with the rise of mobility-power remind of those associated with concentrations of economic

[58] See ch 9 sections II and III.

[59] See General Introduction.

power more than a century ago. For instance, when presenting the bill that would become the Sherman Act (1890), Senator John Sherman declared:

> The popular mind is agitated with problems that may disturb social order, and among them all none is more threatening than the inequality of condition, of wealth, and opportunity that has grown within a single generation out of the concentration of capital into vast combinations to control production and trade and to break down competition. These combinations already defy or control powerful transportation corporations and reach State authorities. They reach out their Briarean arms to every part of our country.[60]

Similarly, in 1938, President Roosevelt famously addressed the US Congress with the following words:

> The liberty of a democracy is not safe if the people tolerate the growth of a private power to a point where it becomes stronger than the democratic state itself. … Among us today a concentration of private power without equal in history is growing.[61]

Subject to a few minor edits, these historical statements on the need to control concentrations of economic power oddly mirror recent statements on the necessity to control private mobility-power. For instance, the OECD published in 2013 an 'action plan on base erosion and profit shifting', which starts with the following lines:

> Globalisation is not new, but the pace of integration of national economies and markets has increased substantially in recent years. The free movement of capital and labour, the shift of manufacturing bases from high-cost to low-cost locations, the gradual removal of trade barriers, technological and telecommunication developments, and the ever-increasing importance of managing risks and of developing, protecting and exploiting intellectual property, have had an important impact on the way cross-border activities take place. … These developments have opened up opportunities for [multi-national enterprises] to greatly minimise their tax burden. … Governments are harmed. Many governments have to cope with less revenue and a higher cost to ensure compliance. Moreover, base erosion and profit shifting undermines the integrity of the tax system, as the public, the media and some taxpayers deem reported low corporate taxes to be unfair.[62]

The Commission voiced the same concern in a recommendation on 'aggressive tax planning' issued in December 2012, going as far as encouraging Member States to adopt a general anti-abuse rule in their national legislation:

> Countries around the world have traditionally treated tax planning as a legitimate practice. Over time, however, the tax planning structures have become ever-more sophisticated. They develop across various jurisdictions and effectively, shift taxable profits towards states with beneficial tax regimes. A key characteristic of the practices in question is that they reduce tax liability through strictly legal arrangements which however contradict the intent of the law. …

[60] 21 Cong Rec 3:2456-62; quoted by Francis (n 7) 209–10.

[61] 83 Cong Rec 5992 (1938). More generally, see R Whish and D Bailey, *Competition Law*, 7th edn (Oxford, Oxford University Press, 2012) ch 1; Mongouachon (n 1) 75–76.

[62] OECD, *Action Plan on Base Erosion and Profit Shifting* (Paris, OECD Publishing, 2013) 7–8.

> Member States are encouraged to introduce the following [general anti-abuse] clause in their national legislation: 'An artificial arrangement or an artificial series of arrangements which has been put into place for the essential purpose of avoiding taxation and leads to a tax benefit shall be ignored. National authorities shall treat these arrangements for tax purposes by reference to their economic substance'.[63]

In sum, the emergence of the phenomenon of abuse of Union law must be viewed as a manifestation of a new form of private power originating in mobility and undermining public power. This private mobility-power is heightened by the combination of low moving costs, high regulatory diversity and high territorial unity, which characterises the current state of the European Union.

IV. Dealing with Private Mobility-Power

Having established that the phenomenon of abuse of Union law is a manifestation of a new form of private power, the inconsistent reactions of Union law to abusive practices can now be assessed in light of a tension between fear of private power and fear of public power. In essence, it will be submitted that the ambivalent assessment of abusive practices mirrors the ambivalent appraisal of public power.

As exposed in the previous section, in a context of low moving costs and high regulatory diversity, the prohibition of abusive practices represents the only course of action available to counter private mobility-power. Abusive practices are assessed in regard of the Treaty provisions on free movement,[64] where they induce an epistemological reversal of perspective within free movement law. Indeed, free movement law classically appraises the impact of national public power upon private activities within the Union. Spaventa noted:

> [I]t would be difficult to reconcile the notion of abuse with the hermeneutic principles established by the Court. Thus, the free movement provisions have always been given a teleological interpretation, which is aimed not only at *facilitating* movement, but also at *not deterring* the use of both primary Treaty rights and rights contained in secondary legislation (which, in any event, usually derive directly from the former rights).[65]

[63] Commission (EC), 'Aggressive tax planning' (Recommendation) C (2012) 8806 final, 6 December 2012, no 1 and 4.2.

[64] See eg Case C-524/04 *Thin Cap Group Litigation* [2007] ECR I-2107; Case C-196/04 *Cadbury Schweppes* [2006] ECR I-7995; Case C-109/01 *Akrich* [2003] ECR I-9607; Case C-212/97 *Centros* [1999] ECR I-1459.

[65] E Spaventa, 'Comments on Abuse of Law and the Free Movement of Workers' in de la Feria and Vogenauer (n 51), 318; see also T Tridimas, 'Abuse of Rights in EU Law: Some Reflections with Particular Reference to Financial Law' in de la Feria and Vogenauer, *Prohibition of Abuse of Law* (n 51) 170; D Triantafyllou, 'L'interdiction des abus de droit en tant que principe général du droit communautaire' (2002) 38 *Cahiers de Droit Européen* 611, 614.

Restrictions on free movement consist in public actions impairing legitimate activities of Union citizens, so that the ordinary effect of a finding of restriction on free movement is a shift from public power to private power. In relation to *Cassis de Dijon*, Weatherill wrote:

> Home State control applies in the absence of a sufficiently compelling basis for host State control. And Germany, the host State, had no good reason to insist that such products shall contain more alcohol than required by France, the home State. So host State regulation of the product could not be justified. In the case itself, free movement law exerted a deregulatory impact, transferring power over the future commercial success of the French-made liqueur in Germany away from the German regulator into the hands of the German consumer.[66]

However, it is settled case law that restrictions on free movement can be justified on the ground of prevention of abusive practices; in *Cadbury Schweppes*, the Court stated:

> [A] national measure restricting freedom of establishment may be justified where it specifically relates to wholly artificial arrangements aimed at circumventing the application of the legislation of the Member State concerned.[67]

The phenomenon of abuse of law spurs a reversal of perspective within free movement law, by enquiring into the impact of private activities upon public power within the Union. Abuses of Union law amount to private actions impairing legitimate public activities of Member States. In *Kraus*, the Court judged that:

> [Union] law does not preclude a Member State from adopting, in the absence of harmonisation, measures designed to prevent the opportunities created under the Treaty from being abused in a manner contrary to the legitimate interests of the State.[68]

Therefore, *Cadbury Schweppes* (2006) can be viewed as a reaction to *Cassis de Dijon* (1979), whereby public power seeks to reaffirm its capacity to control private mobility-power within the internal market. It is only natural that public power should adapt itself to the emergence of a new form of private power: the development of competition law similarly responded to the need to address concentrations of economic power.

However, the study of the issue of abuse of Union law is complicated by the fundamental ambivalence of European Union law towards choices of law made by private individuals. Indeed, the phenomenon of abuse of Union law is diversely appreciated under Union law, as illustrated by the opposite solutions reached by the Court in *Centros* and *Cadbury Schweppes*. In *Centros*, the Court held that setting up an artificial cross-border movement to escape national company law

[66] S Weatherill, 'Fitting "Abuse of Rights" into EU Law Governing the Free Movement of Goods and Services' in de la Feria and Vogenauer (n 51) 51–52.

[67] Case C-196/04 *Cadbury Schweppes* [2006] ECR I-7995, para 51.

[68] Case C-19/92 *Dieter Kraus* [1993] ECR I-1663, para 34.

amounted to a legitimate exercise of the freedoms of movement; in *Cadbury Schweppes*, by contrast, the Court held that artificial cross-border movements designed to escape national tax law could be prohibited as abusive. In short, Union law is fundamentally ambivalent towards private mobility-power and its restraining effect upon national public power.

This ambivalence towards private mobility-power can be usefully reconstructed in light of the fundamental political division between the fear of private power and the fear of public power. Amato observed:

> [W]ithin liberal society itself one of the key divisions of political identity (and hence identification) is between these two sides: the side that fears private power more, and in order to fight it is ready to give more room to the power of government; and the side that fears the expansion of government more, and is therefore more prepared to tolerate private power.[69]

On the one hand, those who are more fearful of private power tend to advocate the prohibition of abusive practices, since it represents the only course of action available to counter private mobility-power. Costello wrote:

> An assessment of the relative power of the right- and duty-holder is also relevant to the issue of abuse. When corporations attempt to circumvent EU rules and undermine home State laws (in particular when there is no prospect of re-regulation at the EU level), we should be concerned.[70]

On the other hand, those who are more fearful of public power tend to reject the prohibition of abusive practices, for they praise the restraining effect of private mobility-power upon public power; instead of blaming the private avoider, they blame the public regulator. For instance, the Friedman spouses considered that the 'drive for equality in Britain' had naturally led to avoidance strategies:

> When the law interferes with people's pursuit of their own values, they will try to find a way around. They will evade the law, they will break the law, or they will leave the country. Few of us believe in a moral code that justifies forcing people to give up much of what they produce to finance payments to persons they do not know for purposes they may not approve of. When the law contradicts what most people regard as moral and proper, they will break the law—whether the law is enacted in the name of a noble ideal such as equality or in the naked interest of one group at the expense of another.[71]

[69] G Amato, *Antitrust and the Bounds of Power: The Dilemma of Liberal Democracy in the History of the Market* (Oxford, Hart Publishing, 1997) 4; see also R Chen and J Hanson, 'The Illusion of Law: The Legitimating Schemas of Modern Policy and Corporate Law' (2004) 103 *Michigan Law Review* 1, in which the authors discuss the neoliberal meta-script of US law: 'markets good, regulation bad'.

[70] C Costello, 'Citizenship of the Union: Above Abuse?' in de la Feria and Vogenauer (n 51) 327; see also E Simpson, 'Is There a Role for a European Principle Prohibiting Abuse of Law in the Field of Personal Taxation? A Comment' in de la Feria and Vogenauer (n 51) 492.

[71] M Friedman and R Friedman, *Free to Choose* (New York, Harcourt Brace Jovanovich, 1979) 145.

Interestingly enough, Gordley showed that the theory of abuse of rights developed by Josserand in the early-twentieth century was intended to counter a growing trend towards individualism, which can be related to the excesses of private power:

> The doctrine may have appealed to its proponents, less because it was a sound critique of formalism than because they hoped it would be 'an instrument of progress' toward a less individualistic and more socially concerned society.[72]

On the other side, Gutteridge rejected this theory of abuse on the ground that it dangerously increased the power of the State:

> [The theory of abuse] resembles a drug which at first appears to be innocuous, but may be followed by very disagreeable after effects. Like all indefinite expressions of an ethical principle it is capable of being put to an infinite variety of uses, and it may be employed to invade almost any sphere of human activity for the purpose of subordinating the individual to the demands of the State.[73]

Without having a preconceived bias towards public power, the Court's case law on abusive practices may include, on a case-by-case basis, considerations regarding the legitimacy of public intervention in specific fields. For instance, in his opinion in *Centros*, AG La Pergola conflated his (positive) assessment of the artificial strategy in question with his (negative) assessment of the relevant Danish law:

> [T]he question of abusing the law can arise only if the rule that is apparently being avoided undoubtedly applies to the legal situation at issue. If the apparent avoidance concerns a provision of national law, it is therefore essential to ascertain first that the national provision it is hoped to apply in the case at issue can be relied on by the court as being consistent with Community law.[74]

Conversely, the prohibition of abusive practices rests on the presumption, implicit or not, that public intervention is legitimate: thus, in *Cadbury Schweppes*, the Court judged that abusive practices are '*such as to undermine the right of the Member States to exercise their tax jurisdiction*'.[75] Similarly, in the *TV10* judgment, the Court first stated that the Dutch Media Act pursued legitimate cultural objectives (paras 18–19), before outlawing artificial strategies designed to escape this legislation (paras 20–21). Doukas commented:

> [A]ny restriction on the freedom of a broadcaster from another Member State to provide services can only be justified if it specifically aims to prevent a wrongful avoidance by that broadcaster of the legitimate, public interest objective(s) of the relevant national legislation through the exercise of the fundamental freedoms. In this regard, the legitimacy per

[72] J Gordley, 'The Abuse of Rights in the Civil Law Tradition' in de la Feria and Vogenauer (n 51) 41.
[73] HC Gutteridge, 'Abuse of Rights' (1933–35) 5 *Cambridge Law Journal* 22, 44.
[74] AG La Pergola, Case C-212/97 *Centros* [1999] ECR I-1459, para 20.
[75] Case C-196/04 *Cadbury Schweppes* [2006] ECR I-7995, para 56; see n 49 and accompanying text.

se of a Member State's decision to maintain a non-commercial broadcasting system might justify its power to frustrate an attempt by an undertaking to evade its jurisdiction.[76]

To sum up, the treatment of abusive practices is intimately linked to political beliefs regarding the dangers respectively entailed by private power and public power, which provides a third ground of explanation for the well-established controversies about the concept of abuse of Union law.[77] Abusive practices are expressions of mobility-power, which enables private individuals to escape public power by spinning around the Union territory. Accordingly, those who believe in the legitimacy of public action tend to condemn such avoidance strategies; conversely, they tend to be praised by those who think that public power should be limited. In other words, those who are more fearful of private power tend to advocate the prohibition of abusive practices, whereas those who are more fearful of public power tend to reject it. In that sense, the emergence of the concept of abuse of Union law can be interpreted, with its inconsistencies, as the progressive adaptation of the economic constitution of the European Union to a new form of private power originating in mobility.

[76] See D Doukas, 'Free Movement of Broadcasting Services and Abuse of Law' in de la Feria and Vogenauer (n 51) 70; see also LH Hansen, 'The Development of the Circumvention Principle in the Area of Broadcasting' (1998) 25 *Legal Issues of European Integration* 111.

[77] As explained throughout this study, the concept of abuse of Union law straddles two other fault-lines of Union law, which also accounts for these controversies: the trade-off between legal certainty and legal congruence, and the trade-off between the paradigms of regulatory neutrality and regulatory competition.

Conclusion: One (Internal Market) Law, Two Competitions

THE OBJECTIVE ASSIGNED to this part two was the reconstruction of the phenomenon of abuse of Union law in light of the project of economic integration prompted by the European Union, in order to identify the factors influencing the decision to prohibit or not artificial choices of law as abusive. Throughout this part two, it has been submitted that the inconsistent treatment of artificial choices of law—and more generally the long-established contradictions of internal market law—are caused by the mostly unconscious and yet permanent reference to two overarching conceptions of economic integration: the paradigms of regulatory neutrality and regulatory competition.

Interestingly enough, many controversies surrounding the law of the internal market seem to be inflamed by a change of paradigm, as exemplified by three of the most debated acts of internal market law: the *Centros* judgment, the Services Directive and the *Laval* judgment. The *Centros* judgment triggered a considerable flow of comments, and is still debated both in the scholarship and within the Court.[1] In essence, *Centros* imposed home regulation and free choice of law in the regulation of companies, two decisive steps towards regulatory competition. Similarly, it was the perceived[2] switch from host regulation to home regulation, in conformity with regulatory competition, that triggered the heated debate on the Services Directive. As is well known, the French population feared the possibility of social dumping entailed by home regulation, and embodied by the

[1] See V Edwards and P Farmer, 'The Concept of Abuse in the Freedom of Establishment of Companies: a Case of Double Standards?' in FG Jacobs et al (eds), *Continuity and Change in EU Law: Essays in Honour of Sir Francis Jacobs* (Oxford, Oxford University Press, 2007); AG Maduro, Case C-210/06 *Cartesio* [2008] ECR I-9641, para 29.

[2] Already before the adoption of the Services Directive, the freedom to provide services largely resorted to home regulation, under the influence of the Court's case law and several sectoral directives. The main innovation of the initial Directive Proposal was the generalisation of the principle to all services, subject to certain exceptions. See B de Witte, 'Setting the Scene: How did Services get to Bolkestein and Why?', EUI Working Papers, LAW 2007/20, available at http://hdl.handle.net/1814/6929; V Hatzopoulos, 'Que reste-t-il de la Directive sur les Services?' (2007) 43 *Cahiers de Droit Européen* 299.

figure of the 'Polish plumber'.[3] Lastly, *Laval* imposed a change of script in the regulation of posted workers, from host regulation to home regulation, once again in accordance with the paradigm of regulatory competition. The Court's stance triggered a storm of criticism,[4] for its own previous case law grounded the regulation of migrant workers—including posted workers—in host regulation (*Rush Portuguesa*); and the ratio legis of Directive 96/71 was apparently to formalise that principle.[5]

Overall, *one (internal market) law* is assigned the contradictory mission of ensuring the proper functioning of *two competitive processes*: the competition among private businesses and among Member States (Table 15).

The regulatory neutrality paradigm seeks to avoid the competition among private businesses being distorted by national regulations, therefore aiming at the creation of a level playing field, an idealised situation in which all businesses competing throughout the internal market are subject to identical regulatory conditions. The regulatory competition paradigm seeks to ensure the proper functioning of the process of competition among Member States, and accordingly aims at maximising the opportunities for regulatory arbitrage, a process by which citizens compare national laws and elect the one best suited to their preferences (chapter six).

As a result, under the regulatory neutrality paradigm, Union law promotes socioeconomic mobility (real goods and services); whereas under the regulatory competition paradigm, Union law promotes regulatory mobility (choice of law). Socioeconomic mobility presupposes the alignment of economic and legal realities: when cross-border flows move to the host market, they become subject to the laws of the host State. Conversely, regulatory mobility implies the disjunction of economic and legal realities: activities taking place on the host market are not necessarily subject to the laws of the host State. Moreover, these two paradigms

[3] In May 2005, the 'Polish plumber' became the symbol of cheap labour coming from Eastern Europe into France, during the public debate preceding the referendum in which the proposed EU Constitution was rejected. See A Asthana, 'The Polish Plumber who Fixed the Vote', *The Observer*, 29 May 2005; E Sciolino, 'Unlikely Hero in Europe's Spat: The "Polish Plumber"', *New York Times*, 26 June 2005. See also Hatzopoulos, 'Que reste-t-il de la Directive sur les Services?' (n 2) 313; European Economic and Social Committee (EC), 'The Proposal for a Directive of the European Parliament and of the Council on services in the internal market' (Opinion), 10 February 2005, C221/113, no 3.5.2, 3.5.3 and 4.2.1.

[4] On those questions, see inter alia C Barnard, 'Fifty Years of Avoiding Social Dumping? The EU's Economic and Not So Economic Constitution' in M Dougan and S Currie (eds), *50 Years of the European Treaties* (Oxford, Hart Publishing, 2009); C Barnard, 'Viking and Laval: An Introduction' (2007–08) 10 *Cambridge Yearbook of European Legal Studies* 463; A Dashwood, 'Viking and Laval: Issues of Horizontal Direct Effect' (2007–08) 10 *Cambridge Yearbook of European Legal Studies* 525; S Deakin, 'Regulatory Competition after Laval' (2007–08) 10 *Cambridge Yearbook of European Legal Studies* 581.

[5] See Recitals 5, 12, 13 and 17 in the Preamble to Directive 96/71 on the posting of workers; AG Mengozzi, Case C-341/05 *Laval* [2007] ECR I-11767, para 249; Case C-244/04 *Commission v Germany* [2006] ECR I-885, para 61; AG Geelhoed, Case C-244/04 *Commission v Germany* [2006] ECR I-885, para 36; Parliament (EC), 'Application of Directive 96/71/EC on the posting of workers' (Resolution), 20 December 2006, C313E/452; C Barnard, 'Social Dumping And the Race to the Bottom: Some Lessons for the European Union from Delaware?' (2000) 25 *European Law Review* 57, 74–75.

Table 15 – One (Internal Market) Law, Two Competitions

	Paradigm of Economic Integration	**Regulatory Neutrality**	**Regulatory Competition**
THEORY	*Function of national laws*	Neutral	Magnets
	Competitive process	Among private businesses	Among Member States
	Policy priority	Level playing field	Regulatory arbitrage
	Type of mobility	Socioeconomic	Regulatory
DILEMMAS	*Eventuality of positive harmonisation*	Harmonisation	No harmonisation
	Negative harmonisation conundrum	Host regulation	Home regulation
	Regulatory mobility dilemma	No choice of law	Choice of law
	State aids	Illegitimate	Legitimate
PRACTICE	*Reverse discriminations*	Illegitimate	Legitimate
	Differentials of regulation	Illegitimate	Legitimate
	Abuses of law	Illegitimate	Legitimate
	Social dumping	Illegitimate	Legitimate
	Economic Constitution	**Control of Private Power**	**Control of Public Power**

can be related to different conceptions of the function of national laws in a process of economic integration: under regulatory neutrality, national laws should be neutral towards trade flows; under regulatory competition, national laws should act as magnets creating trade deflections. These two postures towards the function of local laws in a process of economic integration can be easily linked to the inconsistency in the treatment of artificial practices and the ambivalence of the notion of free 'movement'. The desire for neutral laws calls for the sanction of artificial practices—namely economic behaviour distorted by laws—and the promotion of socioeconomic mobility. Conversely, assigning local laws the function of magnets implies the ratification of artificial practices and the promotion of regulatory mobility.

More generally, given their different premises and objectives, the regulatory neutrality and regulatory competition paradigms are bound to entail different prescriptions regarding the regulation of the internal market. In particular, regulatory neutrality and regulatory competition diverge on three central nodes of internal market law: the eventuality of a harmonisation by the Union legislature; the promotion of host or home equality (negative harmonisation conundrum); and the need to proscribe or permit or ratify artificial cross-border movements (regulatory mobility dilemma). The practical consequence of this disagreement along three nodes of free movement law is the existence of a trade-off between regulatory neutrality and regulatory competition: once protectionism and multiple regulation are overcome, the pursuit of one paradigm of economic integration comes necessarily at the expense of the other. In this trade-off lies the quintessential dialectic shaping the law of the internal market: removing distortions of competition among private businesses ineluctably impairs the competition among Member States; conversely, promoting the competition among Member States distorts the competition among private businesses (chapter seven).

Furthermore, the dialectic between regulatory neutrality and regulatory competition clarifies the terms of certain practical issues of internal market law, whose solution depends on the adoption, most often unconscious, of regulatory neutrality or regulatory competition as paradigmatic of economic integration (chapter eight). First, differentials of regulation among competing undertakings amount to illegitimate distortions of competition among private goods (regulatory neutrality: *Defrenne II*, *Columbus*), but legitimate competitive advantages in competition among public goods (regulatory competition: *Van Tiggele*, *Rüffert*, *Cadbury Schweppes*). Secondly, reverse discriminations are the necessary consequence of home regulation, recommended by regulatory competition (home equality: *Aubertin*); conversely, they necessarily disappear under host regulation, advocated by regulatory neutrality (host equality: *Perfili*). Thirdly, and most importantly for the purpose of this study, artificial choices of law constitute illegitimate abuses of law under regulatory neutrality (*Cadbury Schweppes*), but legitimate regulatory arbitrage under regulatory competition (*Centros*). In sum, 'regulatory arbitrage' and 'abuse of law' are two masks covering one phenomenon: the artificial election of a more favourable national law by Union citizens. Fourthly, social dumping creates illegitimate distortions of competition among private businesses under regulatory neutrality (*Rush Portuguesa*), but represents legitimate regulatory arbitrage under regulatory competition (*Laval*).

In chapter nine, it was submitted that the State aid regime, just as the freedoms of movement, constitutes a legal locus where is managed the tension between two paradigms of economic integration, namely regulatory neutrality and regulatory competition. More concretely, the actual definition of State aid crystallises a specific trade-off between the objectives of regulatory neutrality (competition among private businesses) and regulatory competition (competition among Member States), just as the free movement test does. An expansive prohibition of State aids furthers regulatory neutrality within the internal market, at the expense of regulatory competition: the broader the notion of State aid, the broader the level playing field among private businesses competing in the internal market, and the less intense the competition among Member States. Conversely, any restraint on the scope of the State aid regime increases the room for regulatory competition at the expense of regulatory neutrality. Excluding general (selectivity requirement) and regulatory measures (transfer of State resources) from State aid scrutiny means, in effect, endorsing the correlated distortions of competition among private businesses; yet, on another level, those exclusions broaden the room for regulatory competition, by entitling Member States to compete against each other by means of general and/or regulatory measures.

Lastly, chapter ten submitted that the treatment of abusive practices is intimately linked to political beliefs regarding the dangers respectively entailed by private power and public power, which provides a third ground of explanation for the well-established controversies about the concept of abuse of Union law. A conjunction of socioeconomic and legal factors has led to the emergence of a new form of private power originating in mobility, enabling private individuals to escape the deployment of public power. In practice, this new mobility-power subjects public power to permanent threats of relocation from mobile individuals. In a context of low moving costs and high regulatory diversity, the prohibition of abusive practices represents the only course of action available to counter private mobility-power. Therefore, the ambivalence towards the prohibition of abusive practices can be reconstructed in light of the ambivalent fear of power: those who are more fearful of private power tend to advocate the prohibition of abusive practices, whereas those who are more fearful of public power tend to reject it.

General Conclusion: The Concept of Abuse of Union Law as a Privileged Forum for Thinking about Union Law

ABUSES OF UNION law can be defined as undesirable choices of law artificially made by private individuals (chapters 1 and 3). Abusive practices take on the most various forms, such as tax avoidance strategies (addressed by the Court in the *Halifax* and *Cadbury Schweppes* cases), benefit tourism (eg social benefits in *Lair* or export refunds in *Emsland-Stärke*), social dumping (eg *Fitzwilliam, Rush Portuguesa* or *Laval*) and more generally all forms of relocation designed to elect a more hospitable legal regime. This formal diversity of abusive practices is nurtured by the ingenuity of those subject to Union laws: indeed, abuses of Union law are unpredictable, and yet inevitable, reactions to the enactment of Union laws. The fact that their emergence can be predicted with absolute certainty, whereas their concrete forms can never be predicted, is not the least of the paradoxes implicit in the concept of abuse of Union law. As Samuel Daniel put it memorably in 1718: 'Ten Thousand Laws more cannot reach so far, but Malice goes beyond'.[1]

In the *Emsland-Stärke* and *Halifax* cases, the Court famously issued a formal doctrine of abuse resting on the artificiality and teleological tests: a finding of abuse requires, first, an intention to obtain an advantage from Union law by creating artificially the conditions laid down for obtaining it and, second, that the grant of the said advantage would be contrary to the purpose of the relevant provisions (chapter 2). Nevertheless, it is important to underline that the formal doctrine of abuse is only one among other techniques commonly used in Union law to address artificial choices of law. Indeed, other techniques are frequently used, consciously or not, to deter artificial choices of law by making a change of applicable law costlier, and thus less profitable (chapter 4). Suspect periods, for instance, subject a change of applicable law to the expiry of a given period of time (eg *Bidar, Foster* or *Collins* cases); by suspending the regulatory benefit sought, suspect periods seek to ensure that private decisions are underpinned by genuine socioeconomic

[1] S Daniel, 'Epistle to Sir Thomas Egerton' in S Daniel (ed), *Poetical Works*, vol II (London, R Gosling et al, 1718) 345.

motives and not only by the prospect of a gain-seeking choice of law. Similarly, centre of gravity tests make artificial choices of law costlier, as they constrain Union citizens wishing to elect the legal regime of another Member State to move their residence or real seat to its territory (eg *Van Binsbergen*, *Fitzwilliam*).

Yet the pivotal finding of this study resides in the inconsistent treatment of artificial choices of law under Union law, and correlatively in the great number of scholarly controversies prompted by the concept of abuse of Union law: indeed, artificial choices of law are alternatively outlawed (eg *Emsland-Stärke*, *Halifax*, *Cadbury Schweppes*) or ratified (eg *Centros*, *Zhu and Chen*, *Poulsen*) under Union law. This study accordingly undertook to answer the following question: how can the apparently simple concept of abuse of Union law generate so much disagreement among equally intelligent individuals? In light of the definition of abuse of Union law as an *undesirable* choice of law artificially made by a private individual, this question can be rephrased as follows: what makes artificial choices of law desirable or undesirable? In that regard, I have argued that the concept of abuse of Union law is situated at the intersection of three major fault-lines of Union law, which accounts for the amount of contradiction and controversy it creates.

The first fault line opposes two formal virtues of law: legal congruence and legal certainty (chapter five). Every legal order is characterised by a familiar trade-off between legal certainty and legal congruence: the more predictable are legal norms, the less equitable they can be in particular cases. The phenomenon of abuse of Union law cuts across this fault-line; indeed, abusive practices are manifestations of a lack of legal congruence caused by the rigidity of Union law. In that sense, legal certainty must be viewed as a source of abusive practices: the greater the rigidity and predictability of a legal norm, the wider the margin for an individual to abuse that norm in order to obtain benefits inconsistent with the norm's purposes. More generally, norms guaranteeing legal certainty tend to open a congruence gap between law and reality, in which abuses of Union law may flourish. As a consequence, it is intellectually unsatisfactory to criticise the fight against abusive practices on the ground that it undermines legal certainty, without confronting the broader trade-off between legal certainty and congruence. The legitimacy of a system of law is founded upon both legal certainty (predictable outcomes) and legal congruence (equitable outcomes); in that context, the prohibition of abusive practices must be viewed as a normative decision to reinstate legal congruence at the expense of legal certainty in particular cases.

The second fault line divides two visions of economic integration: regulatory neutrality and regulatory competition (chapters six to nine). The regulatory neutrality paradigm seeks to avoid *competition among private businesses* being distorted by national laws. It aims at the creation of a 'level playing field', an idealised situation in which all businesses competing throughout the internal market are subject to identical regulatory conditions. If economic integration is thus conceived as the promotion of cross-border competition among private businesses, artificial choices of law must be proscribed as abusive, for they distort the competition among private businesses, whose decisions should 'spontaneously' allocate economic resources without having regard to the disparity among national laws. By contrast, under the regulatory competition paradigm, economic integration is conceived as the promotion of *competition among Member States*. In this normative context, choices of law by Union citizens form a desirable process of regulatory arbitrage by which Union citizens freely compare and elect their preferred national law. Such regulatory arbitrage represents the first step of a process of competition among States, the latter being expected to adjust their national laws in order to match mobile citizens' preferences. If granting free choice of law to private individuals distorts business competition (regulatory neutrality), it promotes competition among Member States (regulatory competition); as a consequence, abuse of law and regulatory arbitrage are two normative masks covering one phenomenon: the election of hospitable laws by private individuals.

The third fault line separates two orientations of the economic constitution of the European Union: the fear of private power and the fear of public power (chapter ten). The emergence of the concept of abuse of Union law can be interpreted as an evolution of the economic constitution of the European Union, by which public power seeks to reaffirm its capacity to control private power within the internal market. In the last two decades, a conjunction of socioeconomic and legal factors has led to the emergence of a new form of private power originating in cross-border mobility, enabling private individuals to escape the jurisdictional reach of public power. On the one hand, new communication technologies and modern transportation means have triggered an explosion of private mobility. On the other hand, the European process of integration has reached a specific moment in which territorial unity is secured but regulatory diversity preserved, which enables private individuals to engage in cross-border movement in order to elect a more hospitable jurisdiction. In practice, this new mobility-power undermines public power by subjecting it to permanent threats of relocation from mobile individuals. In such a context of low moving costs and high regulatory diversity, the prohibition of abusive practices represents the only course of action available to counter private mobility-power. Therefore, the ambivalence towards the prohibition of abusive practices—and the correlative shift from private power to public power—can be reconstructed in light of the fundamental political division between fear of private power and fear of public power: those who are more fearful of private power tend to advocate the prohibition of abusive practices, whereas those who are more fearful of public power tend to reject it.

As it straddles these three central fault lines of Union law, each of which generates irreconcilable tensions (legal congruence versus legal certainty, regulatory neutrality versus regulatory competition, fear of private power versus fear of public power), the concept of abuse of Union law is bound to remain controversial. For the same reason, the concept of abuse of Union law offers a forum in which fundamental questions about the nature and function of Union law can be confronted and examined in a new light. As a matter of fact, these three fault-lines can be put together to form an analytical 'matrix' for thinking about Union law.

Legal congruence	-------- ✕ --------	Legal certainty
|	*Abuse*	|
Regulatory neutrality	*of*	Regulatory competition
|	*Union law*	|
Control of private power	-------- ✕ --------	Control of public power

Figure 14 – An Analytical Matrix for Thinking about Union Law

If the concept of abuse of Union law marks the intersection of three crucial fault-lines in the fabric of Union law, these fault-lines can be examined in relation to one another, independently of the concept of abuse. This analytical matrix formed by these three fault-lines is characterised by the interdependence of all its components. Thus, in Figure 14, every action on one component has horizontal, vertical and diagonal repercussions within the matrix: for example, in the absence of Union harmonisation, any institutional decision promoting legal certainty, such as the *Centros* judgment, is likely to increase regulatory competition and the control of public power (vertical repercussions); by the same token, it will undermine legal congruence (horizontal repercussions), regulatory neutrality and the control of private power (diagonal repercussions).

In more detail, the horizontal relationships amount to negative correlations and correspond to the three fault-lines examined throughout this study (legal congruence versus legal certainty, regulatory neutrality versus regulatory competition, fear of private power versus fear of public power). Conversely, the vertical relationships within the matrix amount to positive correlations among its components. First of all, it has long been established that legal certainty is indispensable to the smooth functioning of a process of competition, as competitors must be able to rely on predictable rules of the game. In *Economy and Society*, Max Weber observed that the predictability of Occidental law constituted one of the most important conditions for the development of a capitalist economic system.[2] Trubek proposed an insightful exegesis of Weber's intuition, according to which only Europe, among all 'great civilisations', developed the type of legal system fitted to the needs of capitalism.[3] In the same sense, Neuhaus observed how legal certainty prevailed over equity at the inception of the twentieth century, with a view to the promotion of business activities.[4]

This positive correlation between legal certainty and the development of economic competition needs to be refined in the context of economic integration, depending on whether harmonisation has occurred at Union level. Union harmonisation suppresses all room for regulatory competition, with the Union

[2] M Weber, G Roth and C Wittich (eds), *Economy and Society* (Berkeley, University of California Press, 1968) 883.

[3] DM Trubek, 'Max Weber on Law and the Rise of Capitalism' (1972) *Wisconsin Law Review* 720, 734–35.

[4] PH Neuhaus, 'Legal Certainty versus Equity in the Conflict of Laws' (1963) 28 *Law and Contemporary Problems* 795, 797.

acting as a regulatory 'monopolist'. Yet on another level, the existence of one set of (Union) rules only increases the degree of legal certainty, which is beneficial to business competition (regulatory neutrality).[5] In the absence of Union harmonisation, Member States retain their regulatory powers, with the Union acting as a 'coordinator' issuing choice-of-law rules.[6] In this context, increasing legal certainty at Union level promotes State competition at the expense of undistorted business competition. Indeed, legal certainty facilitates regulatory arbitrage as businesses know with certainty how and when they can switch to another national law (regulatory competition). Conversely, a 'choice of law' rule offering more legal congruence, for instance by outlawing artificial choices of law as abusive, hampers regulatory arbitrage (regulatory neutrality).[7]

Secondly, it is well established that legal certainty helps to bridle public power. Legal certainty empowers private individuals in their dealings with public power; indeed, rigid legal norms minimise the discretion enjoyed by public authorities.[8] In this sense, the pursuit of legal certainty entails a shift from public power to private power, thereby contributing to the control of public power. Conversely, the promotion of legal congruence, which comes at the expense of legal certainty, enables public authorities to better control private power. For instance, empowering judges to outlaw abuses of Union law enables them to oversee avoidance strategies designed by corporations acting in a cross-border setting.[9]

Thirdly and lastly, it has long been observed that the mechanism of competition is intimately linked to the question of power.[10] In essence, competition can be viewed as a mechanism permitting the control of power: private power when businesses are set against each other to compete (regulatory neutrality); or public power when States are set against each other to compete (regulatory competition). In a process of competition among businesses, businesses are disciplined by consumer arbitrage for unsatisfied consumers enjoy the freedom to 'move' to rival businesses. Accordingly, business competition contributes to the control of

[5] See J Pelkmans and J-M Sun, 'Regulatory Competition in the Single Market' (1995) 33 *Journal of Common Market Studies* 67, 86.

[6] See H Spamann, 'Choice of Law in a Federal System and an Internal Market', Jean Monnet Working Paper, 8/01 (2001) 33.

[7] K Heine and W Kerber, 'European Corporate Laws, Regulatory Competition and Path Dependence'(2004) 13 *European Journal of Law and Economics* 47, 61: '[u]ncertainty can prevent the switch between different corporate laws'. See also DC Esty and D Geradin, 'Regulatory Co-Opetition' (2000) 3 *Journal of International Economic Law* 235, 242.

[8] See A D'Amato, 'Legal Uncertainty' (1983) 71 *California Law Review* 1, 6.

[9] See eg P Schammo, 'Arbitrage and Abuse of Rights in the EC Legal System' (2008) 14 *European Law Journal* 351, 374: 'While forcing a Court to stick to a literal interpretation would undoubtedly limit its judicial discretion, … a formalistic literal interpretation does not allow capturing the abuse/avoidance problematic.'

[10] FA Hayek, *The Road to Serfdom* (New York, Routledge, 1944) 96 and 149:

> Our freedom of choice in a competitive society rests on the fact that, if one person refuses to satisfy our wishes we can turn to another. But if we face a monopolist we are at his mercy. … To split or decentralise power is necessarily to reduce the absolute amount of power and the competitive system is the only system designed to minimise by decentralisation the power exercised by man over man.

the private power wielded by competing businesses.[11] In a process of competition among States, States are disciplined by producer arbitrage, for unsatisfied producers enjoy the freedom to move to rival States.[12] As a corollary, regulatory competition increases private power to the detriment of public power, as businesses are able to play States against each other. Beck sharply observed how the intensification of the competition among States undermined their capacity to control private power:

> The methodological nationalism of daily life, politics and scholarship strengthens and consolidates the transnational power of big companies. The world of states is split up by the encouragement of national rivalries, egotism and competitiveness, preventing it from discovering and extending the mighty potential strength of co-operation between states and of finding institutional forms for it. On the principle of *dividere et impera*, this yet again enables the economic actors to play the individual states off against each other. In other words, the national fixation of politics constitutes a decisive self-defeating mechanism.[13]

Overall, this analytical matrix highlights the coexistence of two conflicting 'triads' within Union law: legal congruence, regulatory neutrality and control of private power, on the one hand; legal certainty, regulatory competition and control of public power, on the other. Most importantly, this matrix has crucial analytical implications for the study of Union law, for it advocates the adoption of a holistic approach involving all its components. In the context of US law, Duncan Kennedy has long shown that the form of legal norms is not neutral in terms of substance: rules (securing legal certainty) can be associated to individualism, and standards (offering legal congruence) to altruism.[14] In the same fashion, form and substance are intimately intertwined in Union law. By way of illustration, such a holistic approach can be applied to the field of company law, in which the literature is particularly abundant.

[11] W Adams and J Brock, *The Bigness Complex: Industry, Labor, and Government in the American Economy*, 2nd edn (Stanford, Stanford University Press, 2004) 100: '[Competition] is the device that limits and controls economic power, the safeguard against the abuse of private economic decision making.'

[12] Pelkmans and Sun (n 5) 82: 'Regulatory competition has a 'disciplining effect' on national regulatory systems. With a choice of regulatory regimes, consumer and firm behaviour can serve to tame the Leviathan tendencies of government'. See also JP Trachtman, 'Embedding Mutual Recognition at the WTO' (2007) 14 *Journal of European Public Policy* 780, 785: 'Competition facilitates the control and regulation of the exercise of political power.'

[13] U Beck, 'The Cosmopolitan State: Redefining Power in the Global Age' (2005) 18 *International Journal of Politics, Culture and Society* 143, 154.

[14] D Kennedy, 'Form and Substance in Private Law Adjudication' (1976) 89 *Harvard Law Review* 1685, 1776:

> There is a connection, in the rhetoric of private law, between individualism and a preference for rules, and between altruism and a preference for standards. … In practice, the choice between rules and standards is often instrumental to the pursuit of substantive objectives.

Table 16 – Case Study: A Holistic Approach to Union Company Law

Real seat theory	Incorporation theory
Legal congruence	Legal certainty
Regulatory neutrality	Regulatory competition
Control of private power	Control of public power
Prohibition of abusive practices	*Ratification of regulatory arbitrage*

As explained in the course of this study,[15] the main controversy of Union company law opposes the real seat theory to the incorporation theory: on the one hand, the real seat theory postulates that companies should be regulated by the State in which they have their real seat, namely their centre of administration or head office; conversely, the incorporation theory stipulates that companies should be subject to the law of their State of incorporation. The stereotypical arguments classically exchanged in this longstanding debate can be usefully reframed within the matrix constructed above. First, it is often argued that the incorporation theory enables shareholders to elect with great certainty the law applicable to their company.[16] By contrast, allowing national authorities to apply their laws whenever they consider that a corporation has its 'real seat' on their territory offers more legal congruence but less legal certainty.[17] Secondly, the incorporation theory facilitates regulatory arbitrage by private individuals, thereby spurring a process of regulatory competition.[18] Conversely, the real seat theory prevents the company from electing its preferred company law without genuinely moving into the relevant jurisdiction, thereby impeding regulatory competition and preserving regulatory neutrality.[19] Thirdly, the incorporation theory restrains public power in the field of company law. Ringe, for instance, rejoiced at the deregulatory effect of regulatory competition.[20] Ringe's positive appraisal of regulatory competition drastically contrasts with Professor Deakin's strong reservations about the

[15] See inter alia ch 4 sections III. A and V and ch 7 section V.C.

[16] See eg C HJI Panayi, 'Corporate Mobility in Private International Law and European Community Law: Debunking Some Myths' (2009) 28 *Yearbook of European Law* 123, 126–27.

[17] See eg G Hertig, 'Regulatory Competition for EU Financial Services' (2000) 3 *Journal of International Economic Law* 349, 370–71.

[18] See eg AM Sachdeva, 'Regulatory Competition in European Company Law' (2010) 30 *European Journal of Law and Economics* 137, 141.

[19] See eg S Deakin, 'Is Regulatory Competition the Future for European Integration?' (2006) 13 *Swedish Economic Policy Review* 71, 81: 'The effect [of the real seat doctrine] is to render impossible the land of market for corporate charters ... since a company cannot switch its state of incorporation at will'.

[20] W-G Ringe, 'Sparking Regulatory Competition in European Company Law—The Impact of the Centros Line of Case-Law and its Concept of "Abuse of Law"' in R de la Feria and S Vogenauer (eds), *Prohibition of Abuse of Law: a New General Principle of EU Law?* (Oxford, Hart Publishing, 2011) 123:

> [I]n analysing the effects of the current regulatory competition in Europe, it is clear that the response by Member States thus far has produced certainly 'better' company laws. ... When Member States adopt reform statutes reducing these start-up burdens, this surely gives businessmen and

deregulatory effect of regulatory competition, which can be related to the need to regulate private power.[21] Fourthly, and lastly, the incorporation theory leads to the ratification of artificial choices of company law, whereas the real seat theory permits their prohibition as abusive.[22] In short, the real seat theory endorses legal congruence, regulatory neutrality, the control of private power and the prohibition of artificial choices of law; whereas the incorporation theory promotes legal certainty, regulatory competition, the control of public power and the ratification of artificial choices of law.

Viewed in this light, the concrete handling of abuses of Union law reflects intertwined institutional choices along the three fault-lines of Union law identified above, which also explains why disputes regarding abuses of Union law involve stereotypical arguments regardless of the legal field at stake. Different visions of the concept of 'abuse' flow from different views about the nature of Union law, and in particular whether legal congruence is preferred to legal certainty, whether business competition or State competition ought to be promoted, and whether private power is more or less troubling than public power. Arguably, these tensions form a dialectic that can never be solved; the limited ambition of this study was to query this dialectic and describe how it generates contradictions within the concept of abuse of Union law. Hopefully, the benefits yielded by this study go well beyond the concept of abuse of Union law, as the reasons explaining why equally intelligent individuals disagree on the concept of abuse of Union law help explain why the same individuals disagree on many other issues of Union law.

investors the necessary legal framework for swift and uncomplicated practical implementation of their entrepreneurial ideas and is thus beneficial for all.

[21] S Deakin, 'Reflexive Governance and European Company Law' (2009) 15 *European Law Journal* 224, 240; for similar views in the field of labour law, see S Deakin, 'Regulatory Competition after Laval' (2007–08) 10 *Cambridge Yearbook of European Legal Studies* 581:

> Centros and the decisions which followed it led to the incorporation of tens of thousands of small, closely held German and Danish companies in the UK, and to a reduction in the level of creditor protection legislation in several other EU Member States. As a result, creditors, employees and other third parties have been exposed to a higher risk of corporate failure in those countries. Arguably, Centros has undermined the effectiveness of regulatory mechanisms both in the UK (which now has the responsibility of enforcing company registration rules for a large number of businesses which are owned and run outside the jurisdiction) and in the several other Member States in which a large number of UK-incorporated firms are physically located.

[22] See eg E Wymeersch, 'The Transfer of the Company's Seat in European Company Law' (2003) 40 *Common Market Law Review* 661, 662.

Annex

THIS ANNEX DESCRIBES the methodology applied to retrieve the data exploited in chapter one, in particular *Table 1 – Union Official Documents Mentioning the Term 'Abuse' (1954–2009): Data*, and *Table 2 – Evolution of the 'Abuse Distribution' (1954–2009): Data*.

The data were retrieved from the official website of the European Union (EUR-Lex[1]) on 1 February 2010: first, the relevant time period was defined as 1 January 1954 to 31 December 2009; second, the query was refined by searching the term 'abus*', which extends the search to any word starting with the letters 'abus' (abuse, abuses, abusing, abusive, etc). Among the documents retrieved from EUR-lex, three judgments addressed two different situations of abuse, so that they were counted twice: Case C-163/99 *Portugal v Commission* [2001] ECR I-2613 (two abuses of type III); Case C-54/95 *Germany v Commission* [1999] ECR I-35 (two abuses of types II and IV); Case 46/72 *De Greef v Commission* [1973] ECR 543 (two abuses of types II and III).

In the following pages, the 827 judgments, regulations and directives retrieved from EUR-lex are listed in accordance with the typology established in Table 2, namely: abuses public-public (type I), abuses public-private (type II), abuses private-private (type III), abuses private-public (type IV) and irrelevant mentions of abuse.

Court's Judgments Mentioning the Term 'Abuse' (651)

Abuses Public-Public (Type I)

1. Joined Cases 2/62 and 3/62 *Commission v Luxembourg and Belgium* [1962] ECR 813
2. Case 66/63 *Netherlands v ECSC High Authority* [1964] ECR 1047
3. Joined Cases 52 and 55/65 *Germany v Commission* [1966] ECR 227
4. Case 173/73 *Italy v Commission* [1974] ECR 709
5. Case 30/88 *Greece v Commission* [1989] ECR 3711
6. Case C-198/94 *Italy v Commission* [1996] ECR I-2797
7. Case C-93/00 *Parliament v Council* [2001] ECR I-10119
8. Case C-310/99 *Italy v Commission* [2002] ECR I-2289
9. Case C-3/00 *Denmark v Commission* [2003] ECR I-2643
10. Case C-15/00 *Commission v European Investment Bank* [2003] ECR I-7281

[1] http://eur-lex.europa.eu/RECH_menu.do?ihmlang=en.

11. Joined Cases C-57/00 P and C-61/00 P *Volkswagen* [2003] ECR I-9975
12. Case C-176/03 *Commission v Council* [2005] ECR I-7879
13. Case C-399/03 *Commission v Council* [2006] ECR I-5629
14. Case C-133/06 *Parliament v Council* [2008] ECR I-3189
15. Case C-427/07 *Commission v Ireland* [2009] ECR I-6277

Abuses Public-Private (Type II)

16. Joined Cases 7/56 and 3/57 to 7/57 *Algera* [1957] ECR 39
17. Case 1/58 *Stork* [1958] ECR 43
18. Case 20/59 *Italy v ECSC High Authority* [1960] ECR 663
19. Case 25/59 *Netherlands v ECSC High Authority* [1960] ECR 723
20. Case 17/68 *Reinarz v Commission* [1969] ECR 61
21. Case 45/69 *Boehringer Mannheim GmbH v Commission* [1970] ECR 769
22. Case 46/72 *De Greef v Commission* [1973] ECR 543
23. Case 113/75 *Frecassetti* [1976] ECR 983
24. Case 28/76 *Milac GmbH Groß- und Außenhandel* [1976] ECR 1639
25. Case 35/78 *Schouten* [1978] ECR 2543
26. Case 268/80 *Guglielmi v European Parliament* [1981] ECR 2295
27. Joined Cases 140, 146, 221 and 226/82 *Walzstahl-Vereinigung v Commission* [1984] ECR 951
28. Case 8/83 *Officine Fratelli Bertoli v Commission* [1984] ECR 1649
29. Case 346/82 *Pierre Favre v Commission* [1984] ECR 2269
30. Case 126/83 *STS v Commission* [1984] ECR 2769
31. Case 116/82 *Commission v Germany* [1986] ECR 2519
32. Case 314/85 *Foto-Frost* [1987] ECR 4199
33. Joined Cases 277/85 and 300/85 *Canon v Council* [1988] ECR 5731
34. Case C-317/91 *Deutsche Renault* [1993] ECR I-6227
35. Case C-326/91 P *Henri de Compte v European Parliament* [1994] ECR I-2091
36. Case C-76/93 P *Scaramuzza v Commission* [1994] ECR I-5173
37. Joined Cases C-46/93 and C-48/93 *Brasserie du Pêcheur and Factortame* [1996] ECR I-1029
38. Case C-166/95 P *Commission v Daffix* [1997] ECR I-983
39. Case C-27/95 *Bakers of Nailsea* [1997] ECR I-1847
40. Case C-188/96 P *Commission v V* [1997] ECR I-6561
41. Case C-54/95 *Germany v Commission* [1999] ECR I-35
42. Case C-378/97 *Wijsenbeek* [1999] ECR I-6207
43. Case C-433/97 P *IPK-München* [1999] ECR I-6795
44. Case C-273/97 *Sirdar* [1999] ECR I-7403
45. Case C-153/99 P *Commission v Giannini* [2000] ECR I-2891
46. Case C-248/98 P *NV Koninklijke KNP BT* [2000] ECR I-9641
47. Case C-298/98 P *Metsä-Serla Sales* [2000] ECR I-10157
48. Case C-248/99 P *Monsanto* [2002] ECR I-1
49. Case C-41/00 P *Interporc* [2003] ECR I-2125
50. Case C-224/01 *Köbler* [2003] ECR I-10239
51. Case C-313/04 *Franz Egenberger* [2006] ECR I-6331

52. Case C-328/05 P *SGL Carbon* [2007] ECR I-3921
53. Case C-425/08 *Enviro Tech v Etat belge* [2009] ECR I-10035

Abuses Private-Private (Type III)

54. Case 9/61 *Netherlands v ECSC High Authority* [1962] ECR 413
55. Joined Cases 56 and 58/64 *Établissements Consten* [1966] ECR 429
56. Case 32/65 *Italy v Council* [1966] ECR 563
57. Case 24/67 *Centrafarm* [1968] ECR 81
58. Case 40/70 *Sirena* [1971] ECR 69
59. Case 78/70 *Deutsche Grammophon* [1971] ECR 487
60. Case 57/70 *van Eick* [1971] ECR 613
61. Case 6/72 *Europemballage* [1973] ECR 215
62. Case 46/72 *De Greef v Commission* [1973] ECR 543
63. Case 49/72 *Drescig* [1973] ECR 565
64. Case 2/73 *Geddo* [1973] ECR 865
65. Joined Cases 6 and 7/73 *Istituto Chemioterapico Italiano* [1974] ECR 223
66. Case 127/73 *BRT II* [1974] ECR 313
67. Case 155/73 *Sacchi* [1974] ECR 409
68. Case 16/74 *Centrafarm II* [1974] ECR 1183
69. Case 26/75 *General Motors Continental* [1975] ECR 1367
70. Joined Cases 40 to 48, 50, 54 to 56, 111, 113 and 114/73 *Suiker Unie* [1975] ECR 1663
71. Case 51/75 *EMI Records* [1976] ECR 811
72. Case 86/75 *EMI Records* [1976] ECR 871
73. Case 52/76 *Benedetti* [1977] ECR 163
74. Case 31/76 *Hebrant* [1977] ECR 883
75. Case 26/76 *Metro SB-Großmärkte* [1977] ECR 1875
76. Case 13/77 *GB-INNO v ATAB* [1977] ECR 2115
77. Case 27/76 United Brands Company (Chiquita) [1978] ECR 207
78. Case 102/77 Hoffmann-La Roche [1978] ECR 1139
79. Case 77/77 Benzine en Petroleum Handelsmaatschappij [1978] ECR 1513
80. Case 128/78 Commission v United Kingdom [1979] ECR 419
81. Case 85/76 Hoffmann-La Roche [1979] ECR 461
82. Case 22/78 Hugin [1979] ECR 1869
83. Case 177/78 Mc Carren [1979] ECR 2161
84. Case 125/78 GEMA [1979] ECR 3173
85. Case 22/79 Greenwich Film Production [1979] ECR 3275
86. Case 243/78 Simmenthal [1980] ECR 593
87. Case 136/79 National Panasonic (UK) [1980] ECR 2033
88. Joined Cases 209 to 215 and 218/78 Heintz van Landewyck [1980] ECR 3125
89. Case 31/80 L'Oréal [1980] ECR 3775
90. Case 126/80 Maria Salonia [1981] ECR 1563
91. Case 172/80 Züchner [1981] ECR 2021
92. Case 60/81 International Business Machines Corporation [1981] ECR 2639
93. Case 279/80 Webb [1981] ECR 3305

94. Case 246/81 *Nicholas William* [1982] ECR 2277
95. Case 179/80 *Roquette Frères* [1982] ECR 3623
96. Case 12/82 *Joseph Trinon* [1982] ECR 4089
97. Case 32/82 *Petrus Suys* [1982] ECR 4111
98. Case 7/82 *GVL* [1983] ECR 483
99. Case 90/82 *Commission v France* [1983] ECR 2011
100. Case 210/81 *Schmidt* [1983] ECR 3045
101. Case 322/81 *Michelin* [1983] ECR 3461
102. Joined Cases 43/82 and 63/82 *VBVB and VBBB* [1984] ECR 19
103. Joined Cases 228 and 229/82 *Ford of Europe* [1984] ECR 1129
104. Joined Cases 177 and 178/82 *Jan van de Haar* [1984] ECR 1797
105. Case 338/82 *Albertini* [1984] ECR 2123
106. Case 170/83 *Hydrotherm Gerätebau* [1984] ECR 2999
107. Case 232/81 *Agricola Commerciale Olio* [1984] ECR 3881
108. Case 264/81 *SpA Savma* [1984] ECR 3915
109. Case 35/83 *BAT Cigaretten-Fabriken* [1985] ECR 363
110. Case 41/83 *Italy v Commission* [1985] ECR 873
111. Case 298/83 *CICCE* [1985] ECR 1105
112. Case 89/84 *Pierre Ramel* [1985] ECR 1385
113. Case 243/83 *Binon* [1985] ECR 2015
114. Case 134/84 *Williams* [1985] ECR 2225
115. Case 311/84 *CBEM* [1985] ECR 3261
116. Case 145/83 *Adams* [1985] ECR 3539
117. Case 53/84 *Adams* [1985] ECR 3595
118. Joined Cases 209 to 213/84 *Lucas Asjesi* [1986] ECR 1425
119. Case 5/85 *AKZO* [1986] ECR 2585
120. Case 75/84 *Metro SB-Großmärkte* [1986] ECR 3021
121. Case 226/84 *British Leyland* [1986] ECR 3263
122. Case 45/85 *Verband der Sachversicherer* [1987] ECR 405
123. Case 324/85 *Bouteiller* [1987] ECR 529
124. Case 402/85 *Basset* [1987] ECR 1747
125. Case 43/85 *Ancides* [1987] ECR 3131
126. Joined Cases 142 and 156/84 *British-American Tobacco* [1987] ECR 4487
127. Case 30/87 *Bodson* [1988] ECR 2479
128. Case 254/87 *Syndicat des libraires de Normandie* [1988] ECR 4457
129. Case 247/86 *Alsatel* [1988] ECR 5987
130. Case 53/87 *Maxicar* [1988] ECR 6039
131. Case 238/87 *AB Volvo* [1988] ECR 6211
132. Case 341/87 *EMI Electrola* [1989] ECR 79
133. Case 66/86 *Ahmed Saeed Flugreisen* [1989] ECR 803
134. Case 382/87 *Buet* [1989] ECR 1235
135. Case 395/87 *Tournier* [1989] ECR 2521
136. Joined Cases 110/88, 241/88 and 242/88 *Lucazeau* [1989] ECR 2811
137. Case C-204/88 *Jean-Jacques Paris* [1989] ECR 4361
138. Case C-343/87 *Annibale Culin* [1990] ECR I-225
139. Case C-156/87 *Gestetner* [1990] ECR I-781
140. Case C-354/87 *Weddel* [1990] ECR I-3847
141. Case C-202/88 *France v Commission* [1991] ECR I-1223

142. Case C-41/90 *Höfner and Elser* [1991] ECR I-1979
143. Case C-358/89 *Extramet Industrie* [1991] ECR I-2501
144. Case C-260/89 *Elliniki Radiophonia Tiléorassi* [1991] ECR I-2925
145. Case C-62/86 *AKZO* [1991] ECR I-3359
146. Joined Cases C-6/90 and C-9/90 *Francovich* [1991] ECR I-5357
147. Case C-179/90 *Gabrielli* [1991] ECR I-5889
148. Case C-18/88 *RTT* [1991] ECR I-5941
149. Joined Cases C-48/90 and C-66/90 *Netherlands v Commission* [1992] ECR I-565
150. Case C-235/89 *Commission v Italy* [1992] ECR I-777
151. Case C-30/90 *Commission v United Kingdom* [1992] ECR I-829
152. Case C-381/89 *Ekklisias* [1992] ECR I-2111
153. Case C-62/90 *Commission v Germany* [1992] ECR I-2575
154. Case C-358/89 *Extramet Industrie* [1992] ECR I-3813
155. Case C-3/91 *Exportur* [1992] ECR I-5529
156. Joined Cases C-271/90, C-281/90 and C-289/90 *Spain and Belgium v Commission* [1992] ECR I-5833
157. Case C-225/91 *Matra* [1993] ECR I-3203
158. Joined Cases C-259/91, C-331/91 and C-332/91 *Pilar Allué* [1993] ECR I-4309
159. Case C-364/92 *Eurocontrol* [1994] ECR I-43
160. Case C-53/92 P *Hilti* [1994] ECR I-667
161. Case C-387/92 *Banco de Crédito Industrial* [1994] ECR I-877
162. Case C-128/92 *Banks* [1994] ECR I-1209
163. Case C-393/92 *Municipality of Almelo* [1994] ECR I-1477
164. Case C-18/93 *Corsica Ferries Italia* [1994] ECR I-1783
165. Case C-9/93 *IHT Internationale Heiztechnik* [1994] ECR I-2789
166. Case C-55/93 *van Schaik* [1994] ECR I-4837
167. Case C-323/93 *Centre d'Insémination de la Crespelle* [1994] ECR I-5077
168. Case C-250/92 *Gøttrup-Klim* [1994] ECR I-5641
169. Case C-334/93 *Bonapharma Arzneimittel* [1995] ECR I-319
170. Joined Cases C-241/91 P and C-242/91 P *Radio Telefis Eireann* [1995] ECR I-743
171. Case C-310/93 P *BPB Industries* [1995] ECR I-865
172. Case C-384/93 *Alpine Investments* [1995] ECR I-1141
173. Case C-96/94 *Centro Servizi Spediporto* [1995] ECR I-2883
174. Joined Cases C-140/94, C-141/94 and C-142/94 *DIP* [1995] ECR I-3257
175. Case C-244/94 *Fédération Française des Sociétés d'Assurance* [1995] ECR I-4013
176. Case C-387/93 *Banchero* [1995] ECR I-4663
177. Case C-415/93 *Bosman* [1995] ECR I-4921
178. Case C-441/93 *Pafitis* [1996] ECR I-1347
179. Case C-18/94 *Barbara Hopkins* [1996] ECR I-2281
180. Case C-39/94 *SFEI* [1996] ECR I-3547
181. Case C-91/95 P *Tremblay* [1996] ECR I-5547
182. Case C-333/94 P *Tetra Pak* [1996] ECR I-5951
183. Case C-42/95 *Siemens* [1996] ECR I-6017
184. Case C-268/94 *Portugal v Council* [1996] ECR I-6177
185. Case C-302/94 *British Telecommunications* [1996] ECR I-6417
186. Case C-264/95 P *UIC* [1997] ECR I-1287
187. Case C-343/95 *Diego Calì & Figli* [1997] ECR I-1547
188. Case C-70/95 *Sodemare* [1997] ECR I-3395

189. Case C-373/95 *Maso* [1997] ECR I-4051
190. Joined Cases C-114/95 and C-115/95 *Texaco* [1997] ECR I-4263
191. Case C-242/95 *GT-Link* [1997] ECR I-4449
192. Joined Cases C-359/95 P and C-379/95 P *Ladbroke* [1997] ECR I-6265
193. Case C-55/96 *Job Centre* [1997] ECR I-7119
194. Case C-163/96 *Raso* [1998] ECR I-533
195. Joined Cases C-68/94 and C-30/95 *SCPA* [1998] ECR I-1375
196. Case C-403/96 P *Glencore Grain* [1998] ECR I-2405
197. Case C-367/96 *Kefalas* [1998] ECR I-2843
198. Case C-53/96 *Hermès International* [1998] ECR I-3603
199. Case C-266/96 *Corsica Ferries France* [1998] ECR I-3949
200. Case C-203/96 *Chemische Afvalstoffen Dusseldorp* [1998] ECR I-4075
201. Case C-284/95 *Safety Hi-Tech* [1998] ECR I-4301
202. Case C-341/95 *Bettati* [1998] ECR I-4355
203. Case C-209/96 *United Kingdom v Commission* [1998] ECR I-5655
204. Case C-232/96 *France v Commission* [1998] ECR I-5699
205. Case C-233/96 *Denmark v Commission* [1998] ECR I-5759
206. Case C-238/96 *Ireland v Commission* [1998] ECR I-5801
207. Case C-114/97 *Commission v Spain* [1998] ECR I-6717
208. Case C-7/97 *Oscar Bronner* [1998] ECR I-7791
209. Joined Cases C-215/96 and C-216/96 *Bagnasco* [1999] ECR I-135
210. Case C-87/97 *Gorgonzola* [1999] ECR I-1301
211. Case C-119/97 P *Ufex* [1999] ECR I-1341
212. Case C-423/97 *Travel Vac* [1999] ECR I-2195
213. Case C-235/92 P *Montecatini* [1999] ECR I-4539
214. Case C-67/96 *Albany* [1999] ECR I-5751
215. Joined Cases C-115/97 to C-117/97 *Brentjens' Handelsonderneming* [1999] ECR I-6025
216. Case C-219/97 *Maatschappij Drijvende Bokken* [1999] ECR I-6121
217. Case C-251/97 *France v Commission* [1999] ECR I-6639
218. Case C-6/98 *ARD* [1999] ECR I-7599
219. Case C-151/98 P *Pharos* [1999] ECR I-8157
220. Case C-150/98 P *Economic and Social Committee v E.* [1999] ECR I-8877
221. Joined Cases C-147/97 and C-148/97 *Deutsche Post* [2000] ECR I-825
222. Joined Cases C-395/96 P and C-396/96 P *Compagnie Maritime Belge* [2000] ECR I-1365
223. Case C-373/97 *Diamantis* [2000] ECR I-1705
224. Case C-286/95 P *Commission v ICI* [2000] ECR I-2341
225. Joined Cases C-287/95 P and C-288/95 P *Solvay* [2000] ECR I-2391
226. Case C-38/98 *Régie Nationale des Usines Renault* [2000] ECR I-2973
227. Case C-209/98 *FFAD* [2000] ECR I-3743
228. Case C-258/98 *Giovanni Carra* [2000] ECR I-4217
229. Case C-210/98 P *Salzgitter* [2000] ECR I-5843
230. Case C-359/97 *Commission v United Kingdom* [2000] ECR I-6355
231. Joined Cases C-180/98 to C-184/98 *Pavlov* [2000] ECR I-6451
232. Case C-222/98 *Hendrik van der Woude* [2000] ECR I-7111
233. Joined Cases C-432/98 P and C-433/98 P *Chvatal* [2000] ECR I-8535
234. Joined Cases C-300/98 and C-392/98 *Parfums Christian Dior* [2000] ECR I-11307

235. Case C-273/99 P *Connolly* [2001] ECR I-1575
236. Case C-405/98 *Gourmet International Products* [2001] ECR I-1795
237. Case C-163/99 *Portugal v Commission* [2001] ECR I-2613
238. Case C-163/99 *Portugal v Commission* [2001] ECR I-2613
239. Case C-450/98 P *IECC* [2001] ECR I-3947
240. Case C-340/99 *TNT Traco* [2001] ECR I-4109
241. Case C-173/99 *BETCU* [2001] ECR I-4881
242. Case C-212/99 *Commission v Italy* [2001] ECR I-4923
243. Case C-89/99 *Schieving-Nijstad v of* [2001] ECR I-5851
244. Case C-112/99 *Toshiba Europe* [2001] ECR I-7945
245. Case C-475/99 *Firma Ambulanz Glöckner* [2001] ECR I-8089
246. Case C-270/99 P *Z v European Parliament* [2001] ECR I-9197
247. Case C-1/00 *Commission v France* [2001] ECR I-9989
248. Case C-218/00 *Cisal di Battistello Venanzio* [2002] ECR I-691
249. Case C-309/99 *Wouters* [2002] ECR I-1577
250. Case C-132/99 *Netherlands v Commission* [2002] ECR I-2709
251. Case C-143/00 *Swingward* [2002] ECR I-3759
252. Case C-82/01 P *Aéroports de Paris* [2002] ECR I-9297
253. Case C-471/98 *Commission v Belgium* [2002] ECR I-9681
254. Case C-442/00 *Rodríguez Caballero* [2002] ECR I-11915
255. Case C-462/01 *Hammarsten* [2003] ECR I-781
256. Case C-320/01 *Busch* [2003] ECR I-2041
257. Case C-305/00 *Schulin* [2003] ECR I-3525
258. Case C-462/99 *Connect Austria Gesellschaft für Telekommunikation* [2003] ECR I-5197
259. Joined Cases C-83/01 P, C-93/01 P and C-94/01 P *Chronopost* [2003] ECR I-6993
260. Case C-137/00 *Milk Marque* [2003] ECR I-7975
261. Case C-201/01 *Maria Walcher* [2003] ECR I-8827
262. Case C-125/01 *Peter Pflücke* [2003] ECR I-9375
263. Joined Cases C-172/01 P, C-175/01 P, C-176/01 P and C-180/01 P *International Power* [2003] ECR I-11421
264. Case C-245/01 *RTL Television* [2003] ECR I-12489
265. Case C-296/01 *Commission v France (GMO)* [2003] ECR I-13909
266. Joined Cases C-34/01 to C-38/01 *Enirisorse* [2003] ECR I-14243
267. Case C-60/02 *Criminal proceedings against X* [2004] ECR I-651
268. Joined Cases C-19/01, C-50/01 and C-84/01 *Barsotti* [2004] ECR I-2005
269. Case C-359/01 P *British Sugar* [2004] ECR I-4933
270. Case C-418/01 *IMS Health* [2004] ECR I-5039
271. Case C-49/02 *Heidelberger Bauchemie* [2004] ECR I-6129
272. Case C-262/02 *Commission v France* [2004] ECR I-6569
273. Case C-429/02 *Bacardi* [2004] ECR I-6613
274. Case C-332/01 *Greece v Commission* [2004] ECR I-7699
275. Case C-189/03 *Commission v Netherlands* [2004] ECR I-9289
276. Case C-520/03 *Olaso Valero* [2004] ECR I-12065
277. Case C-12/03 P *Tetra Laval* [2005] ECR I-987
278. Case C-134/03 *Viacom Outdoor* [2005] ECR I-1167
279. Case C-141/02 P *T-Mobile Austria* [2005] ECR I-1283
280. Case C-283/03 *Kuipers* [2005] ECR I-4255

281. Case C-53/03 *GlaxoSmithKline* [2005] ECR I-4609
282. Case C-394/02 *Commission v Greece* [2005] ECR I-4713
283. Case C-198/03 P *CEVA Santé Animale* [2005] ECR I-6357
284. Joined Cases C-544/03 and C-545/03 *Mobistar* [2005] ECR I-7723
285. Case C-379/04 *Richard Dahms* [2005] ECR I-8723
286. Case C-443/03 *Leffler* [2005] ECR I-9611
287. Case C-144/04 *Mangold* [2005] ECR I-9981
288. Case C-78/03 P *Commission v Aktionsgemeinschaft Recht* [2005] ECR I-10737
289. Case C-451/03 *Calafiori* [2006] ECR I-2941
290. Case C-173/03 *Traghetti del Mediterraneo* [2006] ECR I-5177
291. Case C-212/04 *Adeneler* [2006] ECR I-6057
292. Case C-205/03 P *FENIN* [2006] ECR I-6295
293. Joined Cases C-295/04 to C-298/04 *Manfredi* [2006] ECR I-6619
294. Case C-519/04 P *Meca-Medina* [2006] ECR I-6991
295. Case C-53/04 *Marrosu* [2006] ECR I-7213
296. Case C-180/04 *Vassallo* [2006] ECR I-7251
297. Case C-81/05 *Cordero Alonso* [2006] ECR I-7569
298. Joined Cases C-392/04 and C-422/04 *i-21 Germany* [2006] ECR I-8559
299. Case C-167/04 P *JCB Service* [2006] ECR I-8935
300. Case C-434/04 *Ahokainen* [2006] ECR I-9171
301. Joined Cases C-94/04 and C-202/04 *Cipolla* [2006] ECR I-11421
302. Case C-321/03 *Dyson* [2007] ECR I-687
303. Case C-95/04 P *British Airways* [2007] ECR I-2331
304. Case C-282/05 P *Holcim* [2007] ECR I-2941
305. Case C-295/05 *Asemfo* [2007] ECR I-2999
306. Case C-381/05 *De Landtsheer Emmanuel* [2007] ECR I-3115
307. Case C-348/04 *Boehringer Ingelheim KG* [2007] ECR I-3391
308. Case C-391/04 *Georgakis* [2007] ECR I-3741
309. Case C-156/04 *Commission v Greece* [2007] ECR I-4129
310. Case C-362/05 P *Wunenburger* [2007] ECR I-4333
311. Case C-181/06 *Lufthansa* [2007] ECR I-5903
312. Case C-307/05 *Del Cerro Alonso* [2007] ECR I-7109
313. Case C-280/06 *Philip Morris* [2007] ECR I-10893
314. Case C-250/06 *United Pan-Europe Communications Belgium* [2007] ECR I-11135
315. Case C-275/06 *Telefónica de España* [2008] ECR I-271
316. Case C-380/05 *Centro Europa 7* [2008] ECR I-349
317. Case C-498/06 *Robledillo Núñez* [2008] ECR I-921
318. Case C-132/05 *Commission v Germany* [2008] ECR I-957
319. Case C-102/07 *Adidas* [2008] ECR I-2439
320. Case C-268/06 *Impact* [2008] ECR I-2483
321. Joined Cases C-329/06 and C-343/06 *Wiedemann* [2008] ECR I-4635
322. Joined Cases C-334/06 to C-336/06 *Zerche* [2008] ECR I-4691
323. Case C-49/07 *MOTOE* [2008] ECR I-4863
324. Case C-413/06 P *Bertelsmann* [2008] ECR I-4951
325. Case C-195/08 PPU *Rinau* [2008] ECR I-5271
326. Case C-303/06 *Coleman* [2008] ECR I-5603
327. Case C-448/06 *cp-Pharma Handels* [2008] ECR I-5685
328. Joined Cases C-468/06 to C-478/06 *Sot. Lélos kai Sia EE* [2008] ECR I-7139

329. Case C-304/07 *Directmedia Publishing* [2008] ECR I-7565
330. Case C-321/07 *Schwarz* [2009] ECR I-1113
331. Case C-350/07 *Kattner Stahlbau* [2009] ECR I-1513
332. Case C-113/07 P *SELEX* [2009] ECR I-2207
333. Case C-202/07 P *France Télécom* [2009] ECR I-2369
334. Joined Cases C-261/07 and C-299/07 *VTB-VAB* [2009] ECR I-2949
335. Joined Cases C-378/07 to C-380/07 *Angelidaki* [2009] ECR I-3071
336. Case C-425/07 P *AEPI* [2009] ECR I-3205
337. Case C-429/07 *X BV* [2009] ECR I-4833
338. Case C-385/07 P *Der Grüne Punkt* [2009] ECR I-6155
339. Case C-535/06 P *Moser Baer India* [2009] ECR I-7051
340. Case C-534/07 P *Prym* [2009] ECR I-7415
341. Case C-52/07 *Kanal 5* [2009] ECR I-9275
342. Joined Cases C-501/06 P, C-513/06 P, C-515/06 P and C-519/06 P *GlaxoSmithKline* [2009] ECR I-9291
343. Case C-45/08 *Spector Photo Group* [2009] ECR I-12073

Abuses Private-Public (Type IV)

344. Case 23/59 *FERAM* [1959] ECR 501
345. Joined Cases 46/59 and 47/59 *Meroni* [1962] ECR 411
346. Case 33/59 *Compagnie des Hauts Fourneaux de Chasse* [1962] ECR 719
347. Case 11/63 *Lepape* [1964] ECR 61
348. Case 2/67 *de Moor* [1967] ECR 197
349. Case 6/71 *Rheinmühlen Düsseldorf* [1971] ECR 823
350. Case 52-72 *Kienle* [1972] ECR 1267
351. Case 3/73 *Schöttler* [1973] ECR 745
352. Case 30/75 *Unil-It* [1975] ECR 1419
353. Case 125/75 *Eierkontor I* [1976] ECR 771
354. Case 49/76 *Gesellschaft für Überseehandel* [1977] ECR 41
355. Case 44/76 *Eierkontor II* [1977] ECR 393
356. Case 125/76 *Cremer* [1977] ECR 1593
357. Case 83/78 *Raymond Redmond* [1978] ECR 2347
358. Case 11/76 *Netherlands v Commission* [1979] ECR 245
359. Case 18/76 *Germany v Commission* [1979] ECR 343
360. Case 115/78 *Knoors* [1979] ECR 399
361. Case 238/78 *Ireks-Arkady* [1979] ECR 2955
362. Case 808/79 *Fratelli Pardini* [1980] ECR 2103
363. Case 823/79 *Carciati* [1980] ECR 2773
364. Case 112/80 *Dürbeck* [1981] ECR 1095
365. Case 158/80 *Rewe-Handelsgesellschaft Nord mbH and Rewe-Markt Steffen* [1981] ECR 1805
366. Case 8/81 *Becker* [1982] ECR 53
367. Case 250/78 *DEKA* [1983] ECR 421
368. Case 156/82 *Nicolas Corman & Fils* [1983] ECR 1627
369. Case 281/82 *Unifrex* [1984] ECR 1969
370. Joined Cases 187 and 190/83 *Nordbutter* [1984] ECR 2553

371. Case 184/83 *Hofmann* [1984] ECR 3047
372. Case 218/83 *Les Rapides Savoyards* [1984] ECR 3105
373. Case 54/84 *Michael Paul* [1985] ECR 915
374. Case 168/84 *Berkholz* [1985] ECR 2251
375. Case 220/84 *Malhé* [1985] ECR 2267
376. Case 119/84 *Pelkmans* [1985] ECR 3147
377. Case 283/84 *Trans Tirreno Express* [1986] ECR 231
378. Case 65/85 *Ericus v Van Houten International* [1986] ECR 447
379. Case 1/85 *Miethe* [1986] ECR 1837
380. Case 79/85 *Segers* [1986] ECR 2375
381. Case 9/85 *Nordbutter* [1986] ECR 2831
382. Case 221/85 *Commission v Belgium* [1987] ECR 719
383. Case 278/85 *Commission v Denmark* [1987] ECR 4069
384. Case 338/85 *Fratelli Pardini* [1988] ECR 2041
385. Case 316/86 *Krücken* [1988] ECR 2213
386. Case 39/86 *Lair* [1988] ECR 3161
387. Case 127/86 *Ledoux* [1988] ECR 3741
388. Case 215/87 *Schumacher* [1989] ECR 617
389. Case 40/88 *Weber* [1989] ECR 1395
390. Case 22/88 *Vreugdenhil* [1989] ECR 2049
391. Case 173/88 *Henriksen* [1989] ECR 2763
392. Case C-333/87 *France v Commission* [1989] ECR 3773
393. Case C-158/88 *Commission v Ireland* [1990] ECR I-2367
394. Case C-208/88 *Commission v Denmark* [1990] ECR I-4445
395. Case C-367/88 *Commission v Ireland* [1990] ECR I-4465
396. Case C-93/89 *Commission v Ireland* [1991] ECR I-4569
397. Case C-370/90 *Singh* [1992] ECR I-4265
398. Case C-19/92 *Dieter Kraus* [1993] ECR I-1663
399. Case C-421/92 *Habermann-Beltermann* [1994] ECR I-1657
400. Case C-371/92 *Elliniko Dimosio* [1994] ECR I-2391
401. Case C-347/93 *Boterlux* [1994] ECR I-3933
402. Case C-437/93 *Temic* [1995] ECR I-1687
403. Case C-478/93 *Netherlands v Commission* [1995] ECR I-3081
404. Case C-482/93 *Klaus* [1995] ECR I-3551
405. Case C-110/94 *INZO* [1996] ECR I-857
406. Case C-468/93 *Gemeente Emmen* [1996] ECR I-1721
407. Case C-206/94 *Paletta II* [1996] ECR I-2357
408. Joined Cases C-153/94 and C-204/94 *Faroe Seafood* [1996] ECR I-2465
409. Case C-222/94 *Commission v United Kingdom* [1996] ECR I-4025
410. Joined Cases C-246/94, C-247/94, C-248/94 and C-249/94 *Zootecnica S Antonio* [1996] ECR I-4373
411. Case C-327/94 *Dudda* [1996] ECR I-4595
412. Joined Cases C-283/94, C-291/94 and C-292/94 *Denkavit International* [1996] ECR I-5063
413. Case C-124/95 *Centro-Com* [1997] ECR I-81
414. Case C-153/95 *ANDRE* [1997] ECR I-311
415. Case C-171/95 *Tetik* [1997] ECR I-329
416. Case C-106/95 *MSG* [1997] ECR I-911

417. Case C-109/95 *Astir* [1997] ECR I-1385
418. Case C-103/96 *Eridania* [1997] ECR I-1453
419. Case C-351/95 *Kadiman* [1997] ECR I-2133
420. Case C-63/96 *Skripalle* [1997] ECR I-2847
421. Case C-2/95 *SDC* [1997] ECR I-3017
422. Case C-97/95 *Pascoal & Filhos* [1997] ECR I-4209
423. Case C-36/96 *Günaydin* [1997] ECR I-5143
424. Case C-37/95 *Ghent Coal Terminal* [1998] ECR I-1
425. Case C-124/96 *Commission v Spain* [1998] ECR I-2501
426. Case C-401/96 P *Somaco* [1998] ECR I-2587
427. Case C-413/96 *Sportgoods* [1998] ECR I-5285
428. Case C-381/97 *Belgocodex* [1998] ECR I-8153
429. Case C-374/96 *Vorderbrüggen* [1998] ECR I-8385
430. Case C-54/95 *Germany v Commission* [1999] ECR I-35
431. Case C-349/96 *CPP* [1999] ECR I-973
432. Case C-212/97 *Centros* [1999] ECR I-1459
433. Case C-159/97 *Trasporti Castelletti* [1999] ECR I-1597
434. Case C-346/97 *Braathens Sverige* [1999] ECR I-3419
435. Case C-392/96 *Commission v Ireland* [1999] ECR I-5901
436. Joined Cases C-175/98 and C-177/98 *Lirussi* [1999] ECR I-6881
437. Case C-44/97 *Germany v Commission* [1999] ECR I-7177
438. Case C-365/97 *Commission v Italy* [1999] ECR I-7773
439. Case C-12/98 *Far* [2000] ECR I-527
440. Case C-202/97 *FTS* [2000] ECR I-883
441. Joined Cases C-110/98 to C-147/98 *Gabalfrisa and Others* [2000] ECR I-1577
442. Case C-443/97 *Spain v Commission* [2000] ECR I-2415
443. Case C-396/98 *Schloßstraße* [2000] ECR I-4279
444. Case C-400/98 *Breitsohl* [2000] ECR I-4321
445. Case C-454/98 *Schmeink & Cofreth* [2000] ECR I-6973
446. Joined Cases C-177/99 and C-181/99 *Ampafrance* [2000] ECR I-7013
447. Case C-114/99 *Roquette Frères* [2000] ECR I-8823
448. Case C-148/99 *United Kingdom v Commission* [2000] ECR I-9453
449. Case C-482/98 *Italy v Commission* [2000] ECR I-10861
450. Case C-99/99 *Italy v Commission* [2000] ECR I-11535
451. Case C-110/99 *Emsland-Stärke* [2000] ECR I-11569
452. Case C-76/99 *Commission v France* [2001] ECR I-249
453. Case C-187/99 *Eru Portuguesa* [2001] ECR I-1429
454. Case C-63/99 *Gloszczuk* [2001] ECR I-6369
455. Case C-235/99 *Kondova* [2001] ECR I-6427
456. Case C-326/99 *Goed Wonen* [2001] ECR I-6831
457. Case C-493/99 *Commission v Germany* [2001] ECR I-8163
458. Case C-268/99 *Jany* [2001] ECR I-8615
459. Case C-101/99 *British Sugar* [2002] ECR I-205
460. Case C-145/99 *Commission v Italy* [2002] ECR I-2235
461. Case C-174/00 *Kennemer Golf & Country Club* [2002] ECR I-3293
462. Case C-232/99 *Commission v Spain* [2002] ECR I-4235
463. Case C-287/00 *Commission v Germany* [2002] ECR I-5811
464. Case C-115/00 *Andreas Hoves* [2002] ECR I-6077

465. Case C-141/00 *Kügler* [2002] ECR I-6833
466. Case C-377/99 *Germany v Commission* [2002] ECR I-7421
467. Case C-136/00 *Danner* [2002] ECR I-8147
468. Case C-436/00 *X and Y* [2002] ECR I-10829
469. Case C-324/00 *Lankhorst-Hohorst* [2002] ECR I-11779
470. Joined Cases C-465/00, C-138/01 and C-139/01 *Rechnungshof* [2003] ECR I-4989
471. Case C-109/01 *Akrich* [2003] ECR I-9607
472. Case C-167/01 *Inspire Art* [2003] ECR I-10155
473. Case C-45/01 *Christoph-Dornier-Stiftung für Klinische Psychologie* [2003] ECR I-12911
474. Case C-413/01 *Ninni-Orasche* [2003] ECR I-13187
475. Case C-185/00 *Commission v Finland* [2003] ECR I-14189
476. Case C-129/00 *Commission v Italy* [2003] ECR I-14637
477. Case C-322/01 *Deutscher Apothekerverband* [2003] ECR I-14887
478. Case C-271/01 *COPPI* [2004] ECR I-1029
479. Case C-9/02 *de Lasteyrie du Saillant* [2004] ECR I-2409
480. Case C-138/02 *Collins* [2004] ECR I-2703
481. Case C-118/02 *Industrias de Deshidratación Agrícola* [2004] ECR I-3073
482. Case C-159/02 *Turner* [2004] ECR I-3565
483. Case C-17/01 *Sudholz* [2004] ECR I-4243
484. Joined Cases C-487/01 and C-7/02 *Gemeente Leusden and Holin Groep* [2004] ECR I-5337
485. Case C-171/02 *Commission v Portugal* [2004] ECR I-5645
486. Joined Cases C-37/02 and C-38/02 *Di Lenardo Adriano* [2004] ECR I-6911
487. Case C-292/02 *Meiland Azewijn* [2004] ECR I-7905
488. Case C-269/03 *Vermietungsgesellschaft Objekt Kirchberg* [2004] ECR I-8067
489. Case C-200/02 *Zhu and Chen* [2004] ECR I-9925
490. Case C-472/02 *Siomab* [2004] ECR I-9971
491. Case C-445/03 *Commission v Luxembourg* [2004] ECR I-10191
492. Case C-32/03 *Fini H* [2005] ECR I-1599
493. Case C-145/03 *Keller* [2005] ECR I-2529
494. Case C-25/03 *HE* [2005] ECR I-3123
495. Case C-376/02 *Goed Wonen II* [2005] ECR I-3445
496. Case C-452/03 *RAL* [2005] ECR I-3947
497. Case C-542/03 *Milupa* [2005] ECR I-3989
498. Case C-212/03 *Commission v France* [2005] ECR I-4213
499. Case C-498/03 *Kingscrest Associates* [2005] ECR I-4427
500. Case C-77/04 *Réunion européenne II* [2005] ECR I-4509
501. Case C-174/04 *Commission v Italy* [2005] ECR I-4933
502. Case C-147/03 *Commission v Austria* [2005] ECR I-5969
503. Case C-515/03 *Eichsfelder Schlachtbetrieb* [2005] ECR I-7355
504. Case C-464/02 *Commission v Denmark* [2005] ECR I-7929
505. Case C-243/03 *Commission v France* [2005] ECR I-8411
506. Case C-63/04 *Centralan* [2005] ECR I-11087
507. Joined Cases C-151/04 and C-152/04 *Nadin* [2005] ECR I-11203
508. Case C-284/03 *Temco Europe* [2005] ECR I-11237
509. Case C-230/03 *Sedef* [2006] ECR I-157
510. Case C-246/04 *Turn- und Sportunion Waldburg* [2006] ECR I-589

511. Case C-244/04 *Commission v Germany* [2006] ECR I-885
512. Case C-137/04 *Rockler* [2006] ECR I-1441
513. Case C-185/04 *Öberg* [2006] ECR I-1453
514. Case C-255/02 *Halifax* [2006] ECR I-1609
515. Case C-419/02 *BUPA Hospitals* [2006] ECR I-1685
516. Case C-223/03 *University of Huddersfield* [2006] ECR I-1751
517. Case C-456/04 *Agip Petroli* [2006] ECR I-3395
518. Case C-417/04 P *Regione Siciliana v Commission* [2006] ECR I-3881
519. Case C-384/04 *Federation of Technological Industries* [2006] ECR I-4191
520. Case C-466/04 *Acereda Herrera* [2006] ECR I-5341
521. Case C-494/04 *Heintz van Landewijck* [2006] ECR I-5381
522. Joined Cases C-182/03 and C-217/03 *Belgium v Commission* [2006] ECR I-5479
523. Joined Cases C-439/04 and C-440/04 *Kittel* [2006] ECR I-6161
524. Case C-196/04 *Cadbury Schweppes* [2006] ECR I-7995
525. Case C-193/05 *Commission v Luxembourg* [2006] ECR I-8673
526. Case C-5/05 *Joustra* [2006] ECR I-11075
527. Case C-401/05 *VDP Dental Laboratory* [2006] ECR I-12121
528. Case C-279/05 *Vonk Dairy Products* [2007] ECR I-239
529. Case C-524/04 *Test Claimants in the Thin Cap Group Litigation* [2007] ECR I-2107
530. Case C-347/04 *Rewe Zentralfinanz* [2007] ECR I-2647
531. Case C-63/06 *UAB Profisa* [2007] ECR I-3239
532. Case C-178/05 *Commission v Greece* [2007] ECR I-4185
533. Case C-73/06 *Planzer* [2007] ECR I-5655
534. Case C-522/04 *Commission v Belgium* [2007] ECR I-5701
535. Case C-321/05 *Kofoed* [2007] ECR I-5795
536. Case C-16/05 *Tum and Dari* [2007] ECR I-7415
537. Case C-409/04 *Teleos and others* [2007] ECR I-7797
538. Case C-146/05 *Collée* [2007] ECR I-7861
539. Case C-375/05 *Geuting* [2007] ECR I-7983
540. Case C-429/05 *Rampion* [2007] ECR I-8017
541. Case C-98/06 *Freeport* [2007] ECR I-8319
542. Case C-97/06 *Navicon* [2007] ECR I-8755
543. Case C-464/06 *Avena Nordic Grain Oy* [2007] ECR I-8907
544. Case C-251/06 *ING. AUER* [2007] ECR I-9689
545. Case C-374/06 *BATIG* [2007] ECR I-11271
546. Case C-105/07 *Lammers & Van Cleef* [2008] ECR I-173
547. Case C-271/06 *Netto Supermarkt* [2008] ECR I-771
548. Case C-425/06 *Part Service* [2008] ECR I-897
549. Joined Cases C-383/06 to C-385/06 *VNOSW* [2008] ECR I-1561
550. Order in Case C-201/05 *Test Claimants in the CFC and Dividend Group Litigation* [2008] ECR I-2875
551. Case C-162/07 *Ampliscientifica* [2008] ECR I-4019
552. Case C-25/07 *Sosnowska* [2008] ECR I-5129
553. Case C-226/07 *Flughafen Köln/Bonn* [2008] ECR I-5999
554. Case C-127/08 *Metock and others* [2008] ECR I-6241
555. Case C-286/06 *Commission v Spain* [2008] ECR I-8025
556. Case C-151/07 *Khatzithanasis* [2008] ECR I-9013
557. Case C-330/07 *Jobra* [2008] ECR I-9099

558. Case C-285/07 *AT* [2008] ECR I-9329
559. Case C-517/07 *Afton* [2008] ECR I-10427
560. Case C-161/07 *Commission v Austria* [2008] ECR I-10671
561. Case C-19/08 *Petrosian* [2009] ECR I-495
562. Case C-169/07 *Hartlauer Handelsgesellschaf* [2009] ECR I-1721
563. Case C-260/07 *Pedro IV Servicios SL* [2009] ECR I-2437
564. Case C-521/07 *Commission v Netherlands* [2009] ECR I-4873
565. Case C-303/07 *Aberdeen Property Fininvest Alpha Oy* [2009] ECR I-5145
566. Case C-7/08 *Har Vaessen* [2009] ECR I-5581
567. Case C-397/07 *Commission v Spain* [2009] ECR I-6029
568. Case C-168/08 *Hadadi* [2009] ECR I-6871
569. Case C-2/08 *Fallimento Olimpiclub* [2009] ECR I-7501
570. Case C-182/08 *Glaxo Wellcome* [2009] ECR I-8591
571. Case C-219/08 *Commission v Belgium* [2009] ECR I-9213

Irrelevant Mentions of the Term 'Abuse'

572. Case 353/85 *Commission v United Kingdom* [1988] ECR 817
573. Case C-185/89 *Velker* [1990] ECR I-2561
574. Case C-111/92 *Lange* [1993] ECR I-4677
575. Case C-281/91 *Muys' en De Winter's Bouw- en Aannemingsbedrijf* [1993] ECR I-5405
576. Case C-63/92 *Lubbock Fine* [1993] ECR I-6665
577. Case C-453/93 *Bulthuis-Griffioen* [1995] ECR I-2341
578. Case C-306/94 *Régie dauphinoise* [1996] ECR I-3695
579. Case C-45/95 *Commission v Italy* [1997] ECR I-3605
580. Joined Cases C-370/95, C-371/95 and C-372/95 *Careda* [1997] ECR I-3721
581. Case C-60/96 *Commission v France* [1997] ECR I-3827
582. Case C-346/95 *Blasi* [1998] ECR I-481
583. Case C-283/95 *Fischer* [1998] ECR I-3369
584. Case C-172/96 *First National Bank of Chicago* [1998] ECR I-4387
585. Case C-149/97 *The Institute of the Motor Industry* [1998] ECR I-7053
586. Case C-216/97 *Gregg* [1999] ECR I-4947
587. Case C-455/98 *Tullihallitus* [2000] ECR I-4993
588. Case C-36/99 *Idéal tourisme* [2000] ECR I-6049
589. Case C-358/97 *Commission v Ireland* [2000] ECR I-6301
590. Case C-384/98 *D v W* [2000] ECR I-6795
591. Case C-150/99 *Stockholm Lindöpark* [2001] ECR I-493
592. Case C-240/99 *Försäkringsaktiebolaget Skandia* [2001] ECR I-1951
593. Case C-34/99 *Primback* [2001] ECR I-3833
594. Case C-409/98 *Mirror Group* [2001] ECR I-7175
595. Case C-108/99 *Cantor Fitzgerald International* [2001] ECR I-7257
596. Case C-235/00 *CSC Financial Services* [2001] ECR I-10237
597. Case C-169/00 *Commission v Finland* [2002] ECR I-2433
598. Case C-267/00 *Zoological Society of London* [2002] ECR I-3353
599. Case C-315/00 *Maierhofer* [2003] ECR I-563
600. Case C-144/00 *Hoffmann* [2003] ECR I-2921

601. Case C-275/01 *Sinclair Collis* [2003] ECR I-5965
602. Case C-305/01 *MKG-Kraftfahrzeuge-Factoring* [2003] ECR I-6729
603. Case C-168/01 *Bosal* [2003] ECR I-9409
604. Case C-437/01 *Commission v Italy* [2003] ECR I-9861
605. Case C-8/01 *Assurandør-Societetet* [2003] ECR I-13711
606. Case C-212/01 *Unterpertinger* [2003] ECR I-13859
607. Case C-307/01 *d'Ambrumenil* [2003] ECR I-13989
608. Case C-389/02 *Deutsche See-Bestattungs-Genossenschaft* [2004] ECR I-3537
609. Case C-222/01 *British American Tobacco* [2004] ECR I-4683
610. Case C-240/01 *Commission v Germany* [2004] ECR I-4733
611. Case C-308/01 *GIL Insurance* [2004] ECR I-4777
612. Case C-382/02 *Cimber* [2004] ECR I-8379
613. Case C-428/02 *Fonden Marselisborg Lystbådehavn* [2005] ECR I-1527
614. Case C-472/03 *Arthur Andersen* [2005] ECR I-1719
615. Case C-186/04 *Housieaux* [2005] ECR I-3299
616. Case C-200/04 *ISt internationale Sprach- und Studienreisen* [2005] ECR I-8691
617. Joined Cases C-394/04 and C-395/04 *Diagnostiko* [2005] ECR I-10373
618. Case C-280/04 *Jyske Finans A/S* [2005] ECR I-10683
619. Case C-415/04 *Stichting Kinderopvang Enschede* [2006] ECR I-1385
620. Case C-245/04 *EMAG* [2006] ECR I-3227
621. Joined Cases C-443/04 and C-444/04 *Solleveld* [2006] ECR I-3617
622. Case C-169/04 *Abbey National* [2006] ECR I-4027
623. Case C-106/05 *L.u.P.* [2006] ECR I-5123
624. Joined Cases C-181/04 to C-183/04 *Elmeka* [2006] ECR I-8167
625. Case C-240/05 *Eurodental* [2006] ECR I-11479
626. Case C-13/06 *Commission v Greece* [2006] ECR I-11563
627. Case C-391/05 *Jan De Nul* [2007] ECR I-1793
628. Case C-455/05 *Velvet & Steel* [2007] ECR I-3225
629. Case C-170/04 *Rosengren* [2007] ECR I-4071
630. Case C-434/05 *Horizon College* [2007] ECR I-4793
631. Case C-445/05 *Haderer* [2007] ECR I-4841
632. Case C-453/05 *Ludwig* [2007] ECR I-5083
633. Case C-363/05 *JP Morgan* [2007] ECR I-5517
634. Joined Cases C-145/06 and C-146/06 *Fendt Italiana* [2007] ECR I-5869
635. Case C-490/04 *Commission v Germany* [2007] ECR I-6095
636. Case C-184/05 *Twoh International* [2007] ECR I-7897
637. Case C-174/06 *CO.GE.P.* [2007] ECR I-9359
638. Case C-298/05 *Columbus Container Services* [2007] ECR I-10451
639. Case C-451/06 *Walderdorff* [2007] ECR I-10637
640. Case C-341/05 *Laval* [2007] ECR I-11767
641. Case C-437/06 *Securenta* [2008] ECR I-1597
642. Case C-124/07 *Beheer* [2008] ECR I-2101
643. Case C-458/06 *Gourmet Classic* [2008] ECR I-4207
644. Case C-500/06 Corporación Dermoestética [2008] ECR I-5785
645. Case C-253/07 *Canterbury Hockey Club* [2008] ECR I-7821
646. Case C-357/07 *TNT Post United Kingdom* [2009] ECR I-3025
647. Case C-572/07 *Tellmer* [2009] ECR I-4983

648. Case C-69/08 *Visciano* [2009] ECR I-6741
649. Case C-407/07 *Stichting Centraal Begeleidingsorgaan voor de Intercollegiale Toetsing* [2009] ECR I-9615
650. Case C-242/08 *Swiss Re Germany* [2009] ECR I-10099
651. Case C-461/08 *Don Bosco* [2009] ECR I-11079

Regulations Mentioning the Term 'Abuse' (104)

Abuses Public-Public (Type I)

1. Regulation (EC) 1745/2003 of the European Central Bank of 12 September 2003 on the application of minimum reserves (ECB/2003/9)

Abuses Public-Private (Type II)

2. Council Regulation (EC) 3287/94 of 22 December 1994 on pre-shipment inspections for exports from the Community
3. Council Regulation (EC) 789/2001 of 24 April 2001 reserving to the Council implementing powers with regard to certain detailed provisions and practical procedures for examining visa applications
4. Council Regulation (EC) 1236/2005 of 27 June 2005 concerning trade in certain goods which could be used for capital punishment, torture or other cruel, inhuman or degrading treatment or punishment
5. Regulation (EC) 1889/2006 of the European Parliament and of the Council of 20 December 2006 on establishing a financing instrument for the promotion of democracy and human rights worldwide
6. Regulation (EC) 1906/2006 of the European Parliament and of the Council of 18 December 2006 laying down the rules for the participation of undertakings, research centres and universities in actions under the Seventh Framework Programme and for the dissemination of research results (2007–2013) (Text with EEA relevance)
7. Commission Regulation (EC) 1580/2007 of 21 December 2007 laying down implementing rules of Council Regulations (EC) 2200/96, (EC) 2201/96 and (EC) 1182/2007 in the fruit and vegetable sector

Abuses Private-Private (Type III)

8. EEC Council: Regulation 17: First Regulation implementing Articles 85 and 86 of the Treaty
9. Regulation (EEC) 2842/72 of the Council of 19 December 1972 concluding an Agreement between the European Economic Community and the Republic of Iceland and adopting provisions for its implementation

10. Regulation (EEC) 2988/74 of the Council of 26 November 1974 concerning limitation periods in proceedings and the enforcement of sanctions under the rules of the European Economic Community relating to transport and competition
11. Commission Regulation (EEC) 1859/81 of 6 July 1981 amending Regulation (EEC) 1727/70 on intervention procedure for raw tobacco
12. Council Regulation (EEC) 3821/85 of 20 December 1985 on recording equipment in road transport
13. Council Regulation (EC) 2135/98 of 24 September 1998 amending Regulation (EEC) 3821/85 on recording equipment in road transport and Directive 88/599/EEC concerning the application of Regulations (EEC) 3820/84 and (EEC) 3821/85
14. Commission Regulation (EC) 1749/1999 of 23 July 1999 amending Regulation (EC) 2214/96, concerning the sub-indices of the harmonized indices of consumer prices (Text with EEA relevance)
15. Council Regulation (EC) 6/2002 of 12 December 2001 on Community designs
16. Regulation (EC) 733/2002 of the European Parliament and of the Council of 22 April 2002 on the implementation of the .eu Top Level Domain (Text with EEA relevance)
17. Commission Regulation (EC) 1400/2002 of 31 July 2002 on the application of Article 81(3) of the Treaty to categories of vertical agreements and concerted practices in the motor vehicle sector
18. Council Regulation (EC) 1/2003 of 16 December 2002 on the implementation of the rules on competition laid down in Articles 81 and 82 of the Treaty (Text with EEA relevance)
19. Commission Regulation (EC) 2273/2003 of 22 December 2003 implementing Directive 2003/6/EC of the European Parliament and of the Council as regards exemptions for buy-back programmes and stabilisation of financial instruments (Text with EEA relevance)
20. Regulation (EC) 725/2004 of the European Parliament and of the Council of 31 March 2004 on enhancing ship and port facility security (Text with EEA relevance)
21. Commission Regulation (EC) 874/2004 of 28 April 2004 laying down public policy rules concerning the implementation and functions of the .eu Top Level Domain and the principles governing registration (Text with EEA relevance)
22. Commission Regulation (EC) 1480/2004 of 10 August 2004 laying down specific rules concerning goods arriving from the areas not under the effective control of the Government of Cyprus in the areas in which the Government exercises effective control
23. Council Regulation (EC) 1175/2005 of 18 July 2005 imposing a definitive anti-dumping duty and collecting definitively the provisional duty imposed on imports of barium carbonate originating in the People's Republic of China
24. Council Regulation (EC) 1212/2005 of 25 July 2005 imposing a definitive anti-dumping duty on imports of certain castings originating in the People's Republic of China
25. Commission Regulation (EC) 2096/2005 of 20 December 2005 laying down common requirements for the provision of air navigation services (Text with EEA relevance)
26. Regulation (EC) 561/2006 of the European Parliament and of the Council of 15 March 2006 on the harmonisation of certain social legislation relating to road transport and amending Council Regulations (EEC) 3821/85 and (EC) 2135/98 and repealing Council Regulation (EEC) 3820/85 (Text with EEA relevance)—Declaration

27. Council Regulation (EC) 1184/2006 of 24 July 2006 applying certain rules of competition to the production of, and trade in, agricultural products (Codified version)
28. Regulation (EC) 1893/2006 of the European Parliament and of the Council of 20 December 2006 establishing the statistical classification of economic activities NACE Revision 2 and amending Council Regulation (EEC) 3037/90 as well as certain EC Regulations on specific statistical domains Text with EEA relevance
29. Commission Regulation (EC) 341/2007 of 29 March 2007 opening and providing for the administration of tariff quotas and introducing a system of import licences and certificates of origin for garlic and certain other agricultural products imported from third countries
30. Council Regulation (EC) 682/2007 of 18 June 2007 imposing a definitive anti-dumping duty and collecting definitively the provisional duty imposed on imports of certain prepared or preserved sweetcorn in kernels originating in Thailand
31. Regulation (EC) 864/2007 of the European Parliament and of the Council of 11 July 2007 on the law applicable to non-contractual obligations (Rome II)
32. Council Regulation (EC) 1184/2007 of 9 October 2007 imposing a definitive anti-dumping duty and collecting definitively the provisional duty imposed on imports of peroxosulphates (persulphates) originating in the United States of America, the People's Republic of China and Taiwan
33. Council Regulation (EC) 1458/2007 of 10 December 2007 imposing a definitive anti-dumping duty on imports of gas-fuelled, non-refillable pocket flint lighters originating in the People's Republic of China and consigned from or originating in Taiwan and on imports of certain refillable pocket flint lighters originating in the People's Republic of China and consigned from or originating in Taiwan
34. Council Regulation (EC) 194/2008 of 25 February 2008 renewing and strengthening the restrictive measures in respect of Burma/Myanmar and repealing Regulation (EC) 817/2006
35. Council Regulation (EC) 361/2008 of 14 April 2008 amending Regulation (EC) 1234/2007 establishing a common organisation of agricultural markets and on specific provisions for certain agricultural products (Single CMO Regulation)
36. Regulation (EC) 451/2008 of the European Parliament and of the Council of 23 April 2008 establishing a new statistical classification of products by activity (CPA) and repealing Council Regulation (EEC) 3696/93 (Text with EEA relevance)
37. Regulation (EC) 683/2008 of the European Parliament and of the Council of 9 July 2008 on the further implementation of the European satellite navigation programmes (EGNOS and Galileo)
38. Regulation (EC) 1137/2008 of the European Parliament and of the Council of 22 October 2008 adapting a number of instruments subject to the procedure laid down in Article 251 of the Treaty to Council Decision 1999/468/EC, with regard to the regulatory procedure with scrutiny—Adaptation to the regulatory procedure with scrutiny—Part One
39. Commission Regulation (EC) 1240/2008 of 10 December 2008 amending Council Regulation (EC) 560/2005 imposing certain specific restrictive measures directed against certain persons and entities in view of the situation in Côte d'Ivoire
40. Commission Regulation (EC) 1313/2008 of 19 December 2008 amending Regulation (EC) 501/2008 laying down detailed rules for the application of Council Regulation (EC) 3/2008 on information provision and promotion measures for agricultural products on the internal market and in third countries

41. Regulation (EC) 80/2009 of the European Parliament and of the Council of 14 January 2009 on a Code of Conduct for computerised reservation systems and repealing Council Regulation (EEC) 2299/89 (Text with EEA relevance)
42. Council Regulation (EC) 169/2009 of 26 February 2009 applying rules of competition to transport by rail, road and inland waterway (Codified version) (Text with EEA relevance)
43. Commission Regulation (EC) 606/2009 of 10 July 2009 laying down certain detailed rules for implementing Council Regulation (EC) 479/2008 as regards the categories of grapevine products, oenological practices and the applicable restrictions
44. Regulation (EC) 714/2009 of the European Parliament and of the Council of 13 July 2009 on conditions for access to the network for cross-border exchanges in electricity and repealing Regulation (EC) 1228/2003 (Text with EEA relevance)
45. Regulation (EC) 715/2009 of the European Parliament and of the Council of 13 July 2009 on conditions for access to the natural gas transmission networks and repealing Regulation (EC) 1775/2005 (Text with EEA relevance)
46. Commission Regulation (EC) 1023/2009 of 29 October 2009 implementing Regulation (EC) 808/2004 of the European Parliament and of the Council concerning Community statistics on the information society (Text with EEA relevance)
47. Commission Regulation (EC) 1143/2009 of 26 November 2009 approving non-minor amendments to the specification for a name entered in the register of protected designations of origin and protected geographical indications (Picodon de l'Ardèche ou Picodon de la Drôme (PDO))

Abuses Private-Public (Type IV)

48. Commission Regulation (EEC) 1391/78 of 23 June 1978 laying down amended rules for the application of the system of premiums for the non-marketing of milk and milk products and for the conversion of dairy herds
49. Commission Regulation (EEC) 1998/78 of 18 August 1978 laying down detailed rules for the offsetting of storage costs for sugar
50. Council Regulation (EEC) 2573/78 of 30 October 1978 on the application of Decision 2/78 of the EEC-Turkey Council of Association relating to proof of origin for certain textile products exported by Turkey
51. Council Regulation (EEC) 2137/85 of 25 July 1985 on the European Economic Interest Grouping (EEIG)
52. Commission Regulation (EEC) 921/89 of 10 April 1989 amending Regulation (EEC) 890/78 laying down detailed rules for the certification of hops
53. Commission Regulation (EEC) 2264/91 of 26 July 1991 amending Regulation (EEC) 3076/78 on the importation of hops from non-member countries
54. Commission Regulation (EEC) 811/92 of 31 March 1992 fixing the export refunds on beef and veal and amending Regulation (EEC) 3846/87 establishing an agricultural product nomenclature for export refunds
55. Council Regulation (EEC) 2913/92 of 12 October 1992 establishing the Community Customs Code
56. Commission Regulation (EEC) 650/93 of 19 March 1993 on special conditions for the granting of private storage aid for pigmeat

57. Commission Regulation (EEC) 1457/93 of 11 June 1993 fixing the export refunds on beef and amending Regulation (EEC) 3846/87 establishing the nomenclature of agricultural products for export refunds
58. Commission Regulation (EEC) 2454/93 of 2 July 1993 laying down provisions for the implementation of Council Regulation (EEC) 2913/92 establishing the Community Customs Code
59. Council Regulation (EEC) 3030/93 of 12 October 1993 on common rules for imports of certain textile products from third countries
60. Commission Regulation (EC) 2193/94 of 8 September 1994 amending Regulation (EEC) 2454/93 laying down provisions for the implementation of Council Regulation (EEC) 2913/92 establishing the Community Customs Code
61. Council Regulation (EC) 3290/94 of 22 December 1994 on the adjustments and transitional arrangements required in the agriculture sector in order to implement the agreements concluded during the Uruguay Round of multilateral trade negotiations
62. Commission Regulation (EC) 2231/96 of 22 November 1996 amending Annexes I, II, III, IV, V, VI, VII, VIII, IX and XI of Council Regulation (EEC) 3030/93 on common rules for imports of certain textile products from third countries
63. Commission Regulation (EC) 88/97 of 20 January 1997 on the authorization of the exemption of imports of certain bicycle parts originating in the People's Republic of China from the extension by Council Regulation (EC) 71/97 of the anti-dumping duty imposed by Council Regulation (EEC) 2474/93
64. Council Regulation (EC) 154/97 of 20 January 1997 amending Regulation (EEC) 619/71 laying down general rules for granting aid for flax and hemp
65. Council Regulation (EC) 1541/98 of 13 July 1998 on proof of origin for certain textile products falling within Section XI of the Combined Nomenclature and released for free circulation in the Community, and on the conditions for the acceptance of such proof
66. Commission Regulation (EC) 1677/98 of 29 July 1998 amending Regulation (EEC) 2454/93 laying down provisions for the implementation of Council Regulation (EEC) 2913/92 establishing the Community Customs Code (Text with EEA relevance)
67. Commission Regulation (EC) 1621/1999 of 22 July 1999 laying down detailed rules for the application of Council Regulation (EC) 2201/96 as regards aid for the cultivation of grapes to produce certain varieties of dried grapes
68. Commission Regulation (EC) 1602/2000 of 24 July 2000 amending Regulation (EEC) 2454/93 laying down provisions for the implementation of Council Regulation (EEC) 2913/92 establishing the Community Customs Code (Text with EEA relevance)
69. Commission Regulation (EC) 1651/2001 of 14 August 2001 amending Regulation (EEC) 1274/91 introducing detailed rules for implementing Council Regulation (EEC) 1907/90 on certain marketing standards for eggs
70. Commission Regulation (EC) 118/2003 of 23 January 2003 fixing the export refunds on beef and veal and amending Regulations (EEC) 3846/87 establishing an agricultural product nomenclature for export refunds and (EC) 1445/95 on rules of application for import and export licences in the beef and veal sector
71. Commission Regulation (EC) 430/2003 of 7 March 2003 fixing the export refunds on white sugar and raw sugar without further processing
72. Commission Regulation (EC) 431/2003 of 7 March 2003 fixing the export refunds on syrups and certain other sugar products exported without further processing

73. Commission Regulation (EC) 2286/2003 of 18 December 2003 amending Regulation (EEC) 2454/93 laying down provisions for the implementation of Council Regulation (EEC) 2913/92 establishing the Community Customs Code (Text with EEA relevance)
74. Council Regulation (EC) 2222/2004 of 19 November 2004 on administering imports of certain steel products from Ukraine
75. Commission Regulation (EC) 883/2005 of 10 June 2005 amending Regulation (EEC) 2454/93 laying down provisions for the implementation of Council Regulation (EEC) 2913/92 establishing the Community Customs Code (Text with EEA relevance)
76. Council Regulation (EC) 1440/2005 of 12 July 2005 on administering certain restrictions on imports of certain steel products from Ukraine and repealing Regulation (EC) 2266/2004
77. Council Regulation (EC) 1441/2005 of 18 July 2005 on administering certain restrictions on imports of certain steel products from the Republic of Kazakhstan and repealing Regulation (EC) 2265/2004
78. Council Regulation (EC) 1899/2005 of 27 June 2005 on administering certain restrictions on imports of certain steel products from the Russian Federation
79. Regulation (EC) 1781/2006 of the European Parliament and of the Council of 15 November 2006 on information on the payer accompanying transfers of funds (Text with EEA relevance)
80. Commission Regulation (EC) 38/2007 of 17 January 2007 opening a standing invitation to tender for the resale for export of sugar held by the intervention agencies of Belgium, the Czech Republic, Spain, Ireland, Italy, Hungary, Poland, Slovakia and Sweden
81. Commission Regulation (EC) 900/2007 of 27 July 2007 on a standing invitation to tender to determine refunds on exports of white sugar until the end of the 2007/2008 marketing year
82. Commission Regulation (EC) 975/2007 of 21 August 2007 fixing the quantitative limit for the exports of out-of-quota isoglucose for the period from 1 August to 30 September 2007
83. Commission Regulation (EC) 1001/2007 of 29 August 2007 amending Regulations (EC) 800/1999 and (EC) 2090/2002 as regards controls in the framework of export refunds on agricultural products
84. Commission Regulation (EC) 1060/2007 of 14 September 2007 opening a standing invitation to tender for the resale for export of sugar held by the intervention agencies of Belgium, the Czech Republic, Ireland, Spain, Italy, Hungary, Slovakia and Sweden
85. Council Regulation (EC) 1234/2007 of 22 October 2007 establishing a common organisation of agricultural markets and on specific provisions for certain agricultural products (Single CMO Regulation)
86. Commission Regulation (EC) 1330/2007 of 24 September 2007 laying down implementing rules for the dissemination to interested parties of information on civil aviation occurrences referred to in Article 7(2) of Directive 2003/42/EC of the European Parliament and of the Council (Text with EEA relevance)
87. Council Regulation (EC) 1342/2007 of 22 October 2007 on administering certain restrictions on imports of certain steel products from the Russian Federation

88. Commission Regulation (EC) 1451/2007 of 4 December 2007 on the second phase of the 10-year work programme referred to in Article 16(2) of Directive 98/8/EC of the European Parliament and of the Council concerning the placing of biocidal products on the market (Text with EEA relevance)
89. Commission Regulation (EC) 1567/2007 of 21 December 2007 fixing the quantitative limit for the exports of out-of-quota isoglucose until the end of the 2007/2008 marketing year
90. Regulation (EC) 106/2008 of the European Parliament and of the Council of 15 January 2008 on a Community energy-efficiency labelling programme for office equipment (recast version)
91. Commission Regulation (EC) 159/2008 of 21 February 2008 amending Regulations (EC) 800/1999 and (EC) 2090/2002 as regards physical checks carried out when agricultural products qualifying for refunds are exported
92. Commission Regulation (EC) 376/2008 of 23 April 2008 laying down common detailed rules for the application of the system of import and export licences and advance fixing certificates for agricultural products (Codified version)
93. Regulation (EC) 450/2008 of the European Parliament and of the Council of 23 April 2008 laying down the Community Customs Code (Modernised Customs Code)
94. Commission Regulation (EC) 499/2008 of 4 June 2008 amending Regulation (EC) 1501/95 and Regulation (EC) 800/1999 as regards the conditions of granting export refunds on agricultural products
95. Commission Regulation (EC) 555/2008 of 27 June 2008 laying down detailed rules for implementing Council Regulation (EC) 479/2008 on the common organisation of the market in wine as regards support programmes, trade with third countries, production potential and on controls in the wine sector
96. Commission Regulation (EC) 692/2008 of 18 July 2008 implementing and amending Regulation (EC) 715/2007 of the European Parliament and of the Council on type-approval of motor vehicles with respect to emissions from light passenger and commercial vehicles (Euro 5 and Euro 6) and on access to vehicle repair and maintenance information (Text with EEA relevance)
97. Commission Regulation (EC) 1276/2008 of 17 December 2008 on the monitoring by physical checks of exports of agricultural products receiving refunds or other amounts
98. Commission Regulation (EC) 164/2009 of 26 February 2009 amending Regulation (EC) 951/2006 in respect of proofs of arrival at destination for out-of-quota exports in the sugar sector
99. Commission Regulation (EC) 274/2009 of 2 April 2009 fixing the quantitative limit for the exports of out-of-quota sugar and isoglucose until the end of the 2009/2010 marketing year
100. Regulation (EC) 443/2009 of the European Parliament and of the Council of 23 April 2009 setting emission performance standards for new passenger cars as part of the Community's integrated approach to reduce CO 2 emissions from light-duty vehicles (Text with EEA relevance)
101. Commission Regulation (EC) 612/2009 of 7 July 2009 on laying down common detailed rules for the application of the system of export refunds on agricultural products (Recast)

102. Regulation (EC) 987/2009 of the European Parliament and of the Council of 16 September 2009 laying down the procedure for implementing Regulation (EC) 883/2004 on the coordination of social security systems (Text with relevance for the EEA and for Switzerland)
103. Commission Regulation (EC) 1120/2009 of 29 October 2009 laying down detailed rules for the implementation of the single payment scheme provided for in Title III of Council Regulation (EC) 73/2009 establishing common rules for direct support schemes for farmers under the common agricultural policy and establishing certain support schemes for farmers
104. Council Regulation (EC) 1186/2009 of 16 November 2009 setting up a Community system of reliefs from customs duty

Irrelevant Mentions of the Term 'Abuse'

Nil

Directives Mentioning the Term 'Abuse' (72)

Abuses Public-Public (Type I)

Nil

Abuses Public-Private (Type II)

1. Council Directive 82/471/EEC of 30 June 1982 concerning certain products used in animal nutrition
2. Council Directive 2004/83/EC of 29 April 2004 on minimum standards for the qualification and status of third country nationals or stateless persons as refugees or as persons who otherwise need international protection and the content of the protection granted

Abuses Private-Private (Type III)

3. Council Directive 91/439/EEC of 29 July 1991 on driving licences
4. Council Directive 93/13/EEC of 5 April 1993 on unfair terms in consumer contracts
5. Council Directive 93/83/EEC of 27 September 1993 on the coordination of certain rules concerning copyright and rights related to copyright applicable to satellite broadcasting and cable retransmission
6. Directive 96/9/EC of the European Parliament and of the Council of 11 March 1996 on the legal protection of databases
7. Council Directive 96/23/EC of 29 April 1996 on measures to monitor certain substances and residues thereof in live animals and animal products and repealing Directives 85/358/EEC and 86/469/EEC and Decisions 89/187/EEC and 91/664/EEC

8. Directive 97/36/EC of the European Parliament and of the Council of 30 June 1997 amending Council Directive 89/552/EEC on the coordination of certain provisions laid down by law, regulation or administrative action in Member States concerning the pursuit of television broadcasting activities
9. Directive 98/44/EC of the European Parliament and of the Council of 6 July 1998 on the legal protection of biotechnological inventions
10. Directive 98/69/EC of the European Parliament and of the Council of 13 October 1998 relating to measures to be taken against air pollution by emissions from motor vehicles and amending Council Directive 70/220/EEC
11. Directive 98/71/EC of the European Parliament and of the Council of 13 October 1998 on the legal protection of designs
12. Council Directive 1999/70/EC of 28 June 1999 concerning the framework agreement on fixed-term work concluded by ETUC, UNICE and CEEP
13. Directive 2000/35/EC of the European Parliament and of the Council of 29 June 2000 on combating late payment in commercial transactions
14. Directive 2001/20/EC of the European Parliament and of the Council of 4 April 2001 on the approximation of the laws, regulations and administrative provisions of the Member States relating to the implementation of good clinical practice in the conduct of clinical trials on medicinal products for human use
15. Directive 2001/29/EC of the European Parliament and of the Council of 22 May 2001 on the harmonisation of certain aspects of copyright and related rights in the information society
16. Directive 2001/83/EC of the European Parliament and of the Council of 6 November 2001 on the Community code relating to medicinal products for human use
17. Directive 2001/82/EC of the European Parliament and of the Council of 6 November 2001 on the Community code relating to veterinary medicinal products
18. Directive 2003/6/EC of the European Parliament and of the Council of 28 January 2003 on insider dealing and market manipulation (market abuse)
19. Directive 2003/54/EC of the European Parliament and of the Council of 26 June 2003 concerning common rules for the internal market in electricity and repealing Directive 96/92/EC—Statements made with regard to decommissioning and waste management activities
20. Directive 2003/55/EC of the European Parliament and of the Council of 26 June 2003 concerning common rules for the internal market in natural gas and repealing Directive 98/30/EC
21. Commission Directive 2003/124/EC of 22 December 2003 implementing Directive 2003/6/EC of the European Parliament and of the Council as regards the definition and public disclosure of inside information and the definition of market manipulation (Text with EEA relevance)
22. Commission Directive 2003/125/EC of 22 December 2003 implementing Directive 2003/6/EC of the European Parliament and of the Council as regards the fair presentation of investment recommendations and the disclosure of conflicts of interest (Text with EEA relevance)
23. Directive 2004/25/EC of the European Parliament and of the Council of 21 april 2004 on takeover bids (Text with EEA relevance)
24. Directive 2004/27/EC of the European Parliament and of the Council of 31 March 2004 amending Directive 2001/83/EC on the Community code relating to medicinal products for human use (Text with EEA relevance)

25. Directive 2004/39/EC of the European Parliament and of the Council of 21 April 2004 on markets in financial instruments amending Council Directives 85/611/EEC and 93/6/EEC and Directive 2000/12/EC of the European Parliament and of the Council and repealing Council Directive 93/22/EEC
26. Directive 2004/48/EC of the European Parliament and of the Council of 29 April 2004 on the Enforcement of Intellectual Property Rights
27. Commission Directive 2004/72/EC of 29 April 2004 implementing Directive 2003/6/EC of the European Parliament and of the Council as regards accepted market practices, the definition of inside information in relation to derivatives on commodities, the drawing up of lists of insiders, the notification of managers' transactions and the notification of suspicious transactions (Text with EEA relevance)
28. Directive 2004/109/EC of the European Parliament and of the Council of 15 December 2004 on the harmonisation of transparency requirements in relation to information about issuers whose securities are admitted to trading on a regulated market and amending Directive 2001/34/EC
29. Directive 2005/1/EC of the European Parliament and of the Council of 9 March 2005 amending Council Directives 73/239/EEC, 85/611/EEC, 91/675/EEC, 92/49/EEC and 93/6/EEC and Directives 94/19/EC, 98/78/EC, 2000/12/EC, 2001/34/EC, 2002/83/EC and 2002/87/EC in order to establish a new organisational structure for financial services committees (Text with EEA relevance)
30. Commission Directive 2005/28/EC of 8 April 2005 laying down principles and detailed guidelines for good clinical practice as regards investigational medicinal products for human use, as well as the requirements for authorisation of the manufacturing or importation of such products (Text with EEA relevance)
31. Directive 2005/29/EC of the European Parliament and of the Council of 11 May 2005 concerning unfair business-to-consumer commercial practices in the internal market and amending Council Directive 84/450/EEC, Directives 97/7/EC, 98/27/EC and 2002/65/EC of the European Parliament and of the Council and Regulation (EC) 2006/2004 of the European Parliament and of the Council ('Unfair Commercial Practices Directive') (Text with EEA relevance)
32. Directive 2006/68/EC of the European Parliament and of the Council of 6 September 2006 amending Council Directive 77/91/EEC as regards the formation of public limited liability companies and the maintenance and alteration of their capital (Text with EEA relevance)
33. Commission Directive 2006/73/EC of 10 August 2006 implementing Directive 2004/39/EC of the European Parliament and of the Council as regards organisational requirements and operating conditions for investment firms and defined terms for the purposes of that Directive (Text with EEA relevance)
34. Directive 2006/126/EC of the European Parliament and of the Council of 20 December 2006 on driving licences (Recast) (Text with EEA relevance)
35. Directive 2007/36/EC of the European Parliament and of the Council of 11 July 2007 on the exercise of certain rights of shareholders in listed companies
36. Directive 2007/59/EC of the European Parliament and of the Council of 23 October 2007 on the certification of train drivers operating locomotives and trains on the railway system in the Community
37. Directive 2007/64/EC of the European Parliament and of the Council of 13 November 2007 on payment services in the internal market amending Directives 97/7/EC,

2002/65/EC, 2005/60/EC and 2006/48/EC and repealing Directive 97/5/EC (Text with EEA relevance)

38. Directive 2008/26/EC of the European Parliament and of the Council of 11 March 2008 amending Directive 2003/6/EC on insider dealing and market manipulation (market abuse), as regards the implementing powers conferred on the Commission
39. Directive 2008/94/EC of the European Parliament and of the Council of 22 October 2008 on the protection of employees in the event of the insolvency of their employer (Codified version) (Text with EEA relevance)
40. Directive 2008/104/EC of the European Parliament and of the Council of 19 November 2008 on temporary agency work
41. Commission Directive 2009/5/EC of 30 January 2009 amending Annex III to Directive 2006/22/EC of the European Parliament and of the Council on minimum conditions for the implementation of Council Regulations (EEC) nos 3820/85 and 3821/85 concerning social legislation relating to road transport activities (Text with EEA relevance)
42. Directive 2009/29/EC of the European Parliament and of the Council of 23 April 2009 amending Directive 2003/87/EC so as to improve and extend the greenhouse gas emission allowance trading scheme of the Community (Text with EEA relevance)
43. Directive 2009/72/EC of the European Parliament and of the Council of 13 July 2009 concerning common rules for the internal market in electricity and repealing Directive 2003/54/EC (Text with EEA relevance)
44. Directive 2009/73/EC of the European Parliament and of the Council of 13 July 2009 concerning common rules for the internal market in natural gas and repealing Directive 2003/55/EC (Text with EEA relevance)
45. Directive 2009/136/EC of the European Parliament and of the Council of 25 November 2009 amending Directive 2002/22/EC on universal service and users' rights relating to electronic communications networks and services, Directive 2002/58/EC concerning the processing of personal data and the protection of privacy in the electronic communications sector and Regulation (EC) 2006/2004 on cooperation between national authorities responsible for the enforcement of consumer protection laws (Text with EEA relevance)

Abuses Private-Public (Type IV)

46. Council Directive 68/297/EEC of 19 July 1968 on the standardisation of provisions regarding the duty-free admission of fuel contained in the fuel tanks of commercial motor vehicles
47. Council Directive 90/435/EEC of 23 July 1990 on the common system of taxation applicable in the case of parent companies and subsidiaries of different Member States
48. Council Directive 91/498/EEC of 29 July 1991 on the conditions for granting temporary and limited derogations from specific Community health rules on the production and marketing of fresh meat
49. Council Directive 91/680/EEC of 16 December 1991 supplementing the common system of value added tax and amending Directive 77/388/EEC with a view to the abolition of fiscal frontiers

50. Council Directive 92/83/EEC of 19 October 1992 on the harmonization of the structures of excise duties on alcohol and alcoholic beverages
51. Council Directive 93/109/EC of 6 December 1993 laying down detailed arrangements for the exercise of the right to vote and stand as a candidate in elections to the European Parliament for citizens of the Union residing in a Member State of which they are not nationals
52. Council Directive 94/74/EC of 22 December 1994 amending Directive 92/12/EEC on the general arrangements for products subject to excise duty and on the holding, movement and monitoring of such products, Directive 92/81/EEC on the harmonization of the structures of excise duties on mineral oils and Directive 92/82/EEC on the approximation of the rates of excise duties on mineral oils
53. Directive 96/71/EC of the European Parliament and of the Council of 16 December 1996 concerning the posting of workers in the framework of the provision of services
54. Directive 2002/30/EC of the European Parliament and of the Council of 26 March 2002 on the establishment of rules and procedures with regard to the introduction of noise-related operating restrictions at Community airports (Text with EEA relevance)
55. Council Directive 2003/48/EC of 3 June 2003 on taxation of savings income in the form of interest payments
56. Council Directive 2003/9/EC of 27 January 2003 laying down minimum standards for the reception of asylum seekers
57. Directive 2003/20/EC of the European Parliament and of the Council of 8 April 2003 amending Council Directive 91/671/EEC on the approximation of the laws of the Member States relating to compulsory use of safety belts in vehicles of less than 3,5 tonnes
58. Council Directive 2003/49/EC of 3 June 2003 on a common system of taxation applicable to interest and royalty payments made between associated companies of different Member States
59. Council Directive 2003/96/EC of 27 October 2003 restructuring the Community framework for the taxation of energy products and electricity (Text with EEA relevance)
60. Council Directive 2003/109/EC of 25 November 2003 concerning the status of third-country nationals who are long-term residents
61. Council Directive 2004/81/EC of 29 April 2004 on the residence permit issued to third-country nationals who are victims of trafficking in human beings or who have been the subject of an action to facilitate illegal immigration, who cooperate with the competent authorities
62. Council Directive 2004/114/EC of 13 December 2004 on the conditions of admission of third-country nationals for the purposes of studies, pupil exchange, unremunerated training or voluntary service
63. Directive 2006/23/EC of the European Parliament and of the Council of 5 April 2006 on a Community air traffic controller licence (Text with EEA relevance)
64. Commission Directive 2006/70/EC of 1 August 2006 laying down implementing measures for Directive 2005/60/EC of the European Parliament and of the Council as regards the definition of politically exposed person and the technical criteria for simplified customer due diligence procedures and for exemption on grounds of a financial activity conducted on an occasional or very limited basis

65. Council Directive 2006/112/EC of 28 November 2006 on the common system of value added tax
66. Directive 2006/123/EC of the European Parliament and of the Council of 12 December 2006 on services in the internal market
67. Directive 2007/46/EC of the European Parliament and of the Council of 5 September 2007 establishing a framework for the approval of motor vehicles and their trailers, and of systems, components and separate technical units intended for such vehicles (Framework Directive) (Text with EEA relevance)
68. Directive 2008/97/EC of the European Parliament and of the Council of 19 November 2008 amending Council Directive 96/22/EC concerning the prohibition on the use in stockfarming of certain substances having a hormonal or thyrostatic action and of beta-agonists (Text with EEA relevance)
69. Council Directive 2008/118/EC of 16 December 2008 concerning the general arrangements for excise duty and repealing Directive 92/12/EEC
70. Council Directive 2009/50/EC of 25 May 2009 on the conditions of entry and residence of third-country nationals for the purposes of highly qualified employment
71. Council Directive 2009/132/EC of 19 October 2009 determining the scope of Article 143(b) and (c) of Directive 2006/112/EC as regards exemption from value added tax on the final importation of certain goods

Irrelevant Mentions of the Term 'Abuse'

72. Council Directive 86/466/EEC of 14 July 1986 concerning the Community list of less-favoured farming areas within the meaning of Directive 75/268/EEC (Spain)

Bibliography

Books

Ackrill, R, *The Common Agricultural Policy*, Contemporary European Studies 9 (Sheffield, Sheffield Academic Press, 2000).

Adams, W and Brock, J, *The Bigness Complex: Industry, Labor, and Government in the American Economy*, 2nd edn (Stanford, Stanford University Press, 2004).

Afschrift, T, *L'Evitement Licite de l'Impôt et la Réalité Juridique*, 2nd edn (Brussels, Larcier, 2003).

Alsina Atienza, DA, *Efectos juridicos de la buena fe en sus relaciones con las modernas tendencias jurídicas: la apariencia, la imprevision, el abuso del derecho* (Buenos Aires, Talleres graficos argentinos, 1935).

Amato, G, *Antitrust and the Bounds of Power: The Dilemma of Liberal Democracy in the History of the Market* (Oxford, Hart Publishing, 1997).

Amos, MS et al, *Amos and Walton's Introduction to French law*, 3rd edn (Oxford, Clarendon Press, 1967).

Aristotle, WD Ross (trans), *The Nicomachean Ethics* (Oxford, Clarendon Press, 1908).

——, S Everson (trans), *The Politics and the Constitution of Athens*, 2nd edn (Cambridge, Cambridge University Press, 1996).

Arnold, BJ, *Comparative Tax Law and Policy – Module 5: Controlling Tax Avoidance, The Role of the Legislature*, Harvard Law School course (Boston, Harvard University, 2007).

Arnull, A, *The European Union and its Court of Justice*, 2nd edn, Oxford EC Law Library (Oxford, Oxford University Press, 2006).

Atkins, WS, *Technical Barriers to Trade*, The Single Market Review, vol III.1 (London, Kogan Page, 1998).

Audit, B, *La fraude à la loi* (Paris, Dalloz, 1974).

Audit, M, Watt, HM and Pataut, É, *Conflits de lois et régulation économique* (Paris, LGDJ, 2008).

Bacon, K, *European Community Law of State Aid* (Oxford, Oxford University Press, 2009).

Baker, JH, *An Introduction to English Legal History*, 3rd edn (London, Butterworths, 1990).

Bakouche, D, *L'excès en droit civil* (Paris, LGDJ, 2004).

Balassa, BA, *The Theory of Economic Integration* (London, Allen & Unwin, 1973).

Barnard, C, *EC Employment Law*, 3rd edn, Oxford EC law library (Oxford, Oxford University Press, 2006).

——, *The Substantive Law of the EU: the Four Freedoms*, 2nd edn (Oxford, Oxford University Press, 2007).

Beck, U, *Pouvoir et Contre-Pouvoir à l'ère de la Mondialisation* (Paris, Aubier, 2003).
Beck, U, *Power in the Global Age: a New Global Political Economy* (Cambridge, Polity Press, 2005).
Bell, AS, *Forum Shopping and Venue in Transnational Litigation*, Oxford Private International Law Series (Oxford, Oxford University Press, 2003).
Berger, S and MIT Industrial Performance Center, *How We Compete: What Companies Around the World are Doing to Make it in Today's Global Economy* (New York, Currency Doubleday, 2006).
Bernhardt, R, Macalister-Smith, P and Max-Planck-Institut für Ausländisches Öffentliches Recht und Völkerrecht., *Encyclopedia of Public International Law* (Amsterdam, North-Holland, 1992).
Bieber, R et al, *An Ever-Closer Union: a Critical Analysis of the Draft Treaty establishing the European Union*, The European Perspective Series (Luxembourg, Office for Official Publications of the European Communities; European Community Information Service distributor, 1985).
Birnie, PW and Boyle, AE, *International law and the environment*, 2nd edn (Oxford, Oxford University Press, 2002).
Blackstone, W, *Commentaries on the Laws of England* (Oxford, Clarendon Press, 1769).
Bowler, T, *Countering Tax Avoidance in the UK: Which Way Forward?*, TLRC Discussion Paper no 7 (London, The Institute For Fiscal Studies, 2009).
Buckland, WW, McNair, ADM and Lawson, FH, *Roman Law and Common Law: a Comparison in Outline*, 2nd edn (London, Cambridge University Press, 1952).
Bull, H, *The Anarchical Society: a Study of Order in World Politics*, 3rd edn (Basingstoke, Palgrave Macmillan, 2002).
Capitant, H, Colin, AVC and Julliot de La Morandière, L, *Cours élémentaire de droit civil français*, 10th edn (Paris, Dalloz, 1953).
——, Colin, AVC and Julliot de La Morandière, L, *Traité de droit civil d'Ambroise Colin et Henri Capitant* (Paris, Dalloz, 1957).
Cecchini, P, Catinat, M and Jacquemin, A, *The European Challenge 1992: the Benefits of a Single Market* (Aldershot, Gower, 1988).
Centre for Economic Policy Research, *Trade Creation and Trade Diversion*, The Single Market Review, vol IV.3 (London, Kogan Page, 1997).
Cerioni, L, *EU Corporate Law and EU Company Tax Law*, Corporations, Globalisation and the Law (Cheltenham, Edward Elgar, 2007).
Chalmers, D et al, *European Union Law* (Cambridge, Cambridge University Press, 2006).
—— and Tomkins, A, *European Union public law: text and materials* (Cambridge, Cambridge University Press, 2007).
Cheng, B, *General Principles of Law as Applied by International Courts and Tribunals* (Cambridge, Grotius Publications, 1987).
Choudin, L et al, *Voltaire à Ferney 1759–2009* (Ferney, Fondation Voltaire à Ferney, 2009).
Cini, M, *European Union Politics* (Oxford, Oxford University Press, 2003).
Clegg, S and Haugaard, M, *The SAGE handbook of power* (Los Angeles, SAGE, 2009).
Cohen, M et al, *Equality and Preferential treatment* (Princeton, Princeton University Press, 1977).
Collins, L, *Essays in International Litigation and the Conflict of Laws* (Oxford, Oxford University Press, 1994).
Commission (EC), *Les distorsions globales de la concurrence et leurs répercussions sur le Marché commun (Rapport Regul)* (Brussels, Office des Publications Officielles Des Communautés Européennes, 1971).

——, *The Common Agricultural Policy*, EDC collection (Luxembourg, Office for Official Publications of the European Communities, 1972).

Cornut, E, *Théorie Critique de la Fraude à la Loi* (Paris, Defrénois, 2006).

Council of Europe, *Abuse of Rights and Equivalent Concepts: the principle and its present day application*, Proceedings of the Nineteenth Colloquy on European Law (Strasbourg, Council of Europe, Publishing and Documentation Service, 1990).

Craig, PP and de Búrca, G, *The Evolution of EU Law* (Oxford, Oxford University Press, 1999).

—— and de Búrca, G, *EU Law: Text, Cases and Materials*, 4th edn (Oxford, Oxford University Press, 2008).

Currie, S, *Migration Work and Citizenship in the Enlarged European Union* (Farnham, Ashgate, 2008).

Davies, G, *Nationality Discrimination in the European Internal Market* 44 (The Hague, Kluwer Law International, 2003).

de Broe, L, *International Tax Planning and Prevention of Abuse* (Amsterdam, IBFD, 2008).

de Búrca, G, *EU Law and the Welfare State: in Search of Solidarity* (Oxford, Oxford University Press, 2005).

——, Weiler, JHH and Academy of European Law, *The European Court of Justice*, The Collected Courses of the Academy of European Law, vol V (Oxford, Oxford University Press, 2001).

De Page, H, *Traité élémentaire de droit civil belge* (Brussels-Paris, Bruylant, 1933).

De Wolf, M, *Souveraineté Fiscale et Principe de Non Discrimination dans la Jurisprudence de la Cour de Justice des Communautés Européennes et de la Cour Suprême des États-Unis* (Brussels, Bruylant, 2005).

Debarge, O, Georgopoulos, T and Rabaey, O, *La constitution économique de l'Union Européenne: 2è rencontre du GIEPI, 12-13 mai 2006* (Brussels, Bruylant, 2008).

Demogue, R, *Notions Fondamentales du Droit Privé - Essai critique* (Paris, Arthur Rousseau, 1911).

——, *Traité des obligations en général*, vol IV (Paris, Rousseau, 1923-1933).

Denning, A, *The Family History* (London, Butterworths, 1981).

Derine, R, *Le Droit de Propriété en France et en Belgique au XIXè Siècle: Droit Absolu et Quasi Illimité?* (Léopoldville, Editions de l'Université de Léopoldville, 1959).

DeSombre, ER, *Flagging Standards: Globalization and Environmental, Safety, and Labor Regulations at Sea* (Cambridge MA, MIT Press, 2006).

Di Pietro, A, *L'elusione fiscale nell'esperienza europea* (Milano, Giuffrè, 1999).

Dicey, AV, Morris, JHC and Collins, L, *Dicey, Morris and Collins on the Conflict of Laws*, 14th edn (London, Sweet & Maxwell, 2006).

dos Santos, AC, *L'Union Européenne et la Régulation de la Concurrence Fiscale* (Brussels, Bruylant, 2009).

Dougan, M, *National Remedies Before the Court of Justice* (Oxford, Hart Publishing, 2004).

Elsener, U, *Les racines romanistes de l'interdiction de l'abus de droit* (Brussels, Bruylant, 2004).

Ernoult, J, Schoppmann, H and European Association of Public Banks, *European Banking and Financial Services Law*, 3rd edn (Brussels, Larcier, 2008).

Esty, DC and Geradin, D, *Regulatory Competition and Economic Integration: Comparative Perspectives* (Oxford, Oxford University Press, 2001).

European Commission, *The Common Organisation of the Markets in Fishery and Aquaculture Products* (Luxembourg, Office for Official Publications of the European Communities, 2002).

——, *European Code of Sustainable and Responsible Fisheries Practices* (Luxembourg, Office for Official Publications of the European Communities, 2004).

——, *The Common Fisheries Policy: a User's Guide* (Luxembourg, Office for Official Publications of the European Communities, 2009).

Fathy, M, *La doctrine musulmane de l'abus des droits* (Paris, H Georg & P Geuthner, 1913).

Fennell, R, *The Common Agricultural Policy: Continuity and Change* (Oxford, Oxford University Press, 1997).

Fleitas, AM, *El abuso del derecho en la reforma del Código civil argentino* (Buenos Aires, Sección Publicaciones del Seminario de ciencias jurídicas y sociales, 1944).

Fondation Jean Monnet pour l'Europe, *Jean Monnet, Robert Schuman, Correspondance 1947-1953* (Lausanne, IRL, 1986).

Franklin, M and Rabin, R, *Cases And Materials on Tort Law and Alternatives*, 3rd edn (New York, Foundation Press, 1983).

Friedman, M and Friedman, R, *Free to Choose* (New York, Harcourt Brace Jovanovich, 1979).

Fuchs, A, Watt, HM and Pataut, E, *Les Conflits de Lois et le Système Juridique Communautaire*, Thèmes & commentaires, actes (Paris, Dalloz, 2004).

Geny, F, *Méthodes d'Interprétation et Sources en Droit Privé Positif: Essai Critique*, 2nd edn (Paris, LGDJ, 1995).

Gerber, DJ, *Law and Competition in Twentieth-Century Europe: Protecting Prometheus* (Oxford, Oxford University Press, 2001).

Gerster, C and European Association of Public Banks, *European Banking and Financial Services Law* (The Hague, Kluwer Law International, 2004).

Gestri, M, *Abuso del Diritto e Frode alla Legge nell'Ordinamento Comunitario* (Milan, Giuffrè, 2003).

Glendon, MA, Carozza, PG and Picker, CB, *Comparative Legal Traditions: Text, Materials, and Cases on Western Law*, 3rd edn (St Paul MN, Thomson/West, 2007).

Grant, W, *The Common Agricultural Policy* (Basingstoke, Macmillan, 1997).

Grossi, P, L Hooper (trans), *A History of European Law* (Chichester, Wiley-Blackwell, 2010).

Habermas, J and Pensky, M, *The Postnational Constellation: Political Essays*, Studies in Contemporary German Social Thought (Cambridge MA, MIT Press, 2001).

Hamilton, A, Madison, J, Jay, J and RP Fairfield (eds), *The Federalist Papers: a Collection of Essays Written in Support of the Constitution of the United States* (Baltimore, Johns Hopkins University Press, 1981).

Hanbury, HG and Maudsley, RH, *Modern Equity* (London, Stevens & Sons, 1989).

Hancher, L, Ottervanger, T and Slot, PJ, *EC State Aids* (London, Sweet & Maxwell, 2006).

Hardin, R, *Liberalism, Constitutionalism, and Democracy* (Oxford, Clarendon Press, 1999).

Harris, WC, *E Pluribus Unum: Nineteenth-Century American Literature and the Constitutional Paradox* (Iowa City, University of Iowa Press, 2005).

Harrison, J and Woods, L, *European Broadcasting Law and Policy* (Cambridge, Cambridge University Press, 2007).

Hart, H and Sacks, A, *The Legal Process: Basic problems in the making and application of law* (New York, Foundation Press, 1994).

Hart, HLA, *The Concept of Law*, 2nd edn (Oxford, Clarendon Press, 1994).

Hayek, FA, *The Road to Serfdom* (New York, Routledge, 1944).

Heideloff, C et al, *Shipping Statistics Yearbook 2009* (Bremen, Institute of Shipping Economics and Logistics, 2009).

Hemetsberger, W and European Association of Public Banks, *European Banking and Financial Services Law* (Alphrn aan den Rijn, Kluwer Law International, 2006).
Heraclitus of Ephesus, CH Kahn (trans), *The Art and Thought of Heraclitus* (Cambridge, Cambridge University Press, 1981).
Hirschman, AO, *Exit, Voice, and Loyalty: Responses to Decline in Firms, Organizations, and States* (Cambridge MA, Harvard University Press, 1978).
Holmes, OW, Jr and Novick, SM, *The Common Law* (New York, Dover, 1991).
—— and Posner, RA, *The Essential Holmes: Selections from the Letters, Speeches, Judicial Opinions, and other Writings of Oliver Wendell Holmes, Jr* (Chicago, University of Chicago Press, 1992).
Holton, RJ, *Globalization and the Nation-State* (Basingstoke, Macmillan, 1998).
International Labour Organisation, *Social Aspects of European Economic Co-operation (Ohlin Report)* (Geneva, International Labour Office, 1956).
International Labour Organisation, *The Global Seafarer: Living and Working Conditions in a Globalized Industry* (Geneva, International Labour Office, 2004).
Ionescu, RN, *L'abus de droit en droit de l'Union européenne* (Brussels, Bruylant, 2012).
Johnston, D, *Roman Law in Context* (Cambridge, Cambridge University Press, 2004).
Jones, G, *Multinationals and Global Capitalism: From the Nineteenth to the Twenty-First Century* (Oxford, Oxford University Press, 2005).
Josserand, L, *De l'esprit des droits et de leur relativité: théorie dite de l'abus des droits*, 2nd edn (Paris, LGDJ, 1939).
Jovanovic, MN, *The Economics of International Integration* (Cheltenham, Edward Elgar, 2006).
Kenen, P, *The International Economy*, 4th edn (Cambridge, Cambridge University Press, 2000).
Kennedy, D, *A critique of adjudication: fin de siècle* (Cambridge MA, Harvard University Press, 1997).
—— and Fisher, WW, *The Canon of American Legal Thought* (Princeton, Princeton University Press, 2006).
Kiss, A-C, *L'abus de droit en droit international* (Paris, LGDJ, 1952).
—— and Beurier, J-P, *Droit international de l'environnement*, 3rd edn (Paris, Pedone, 2004).
Komesar, NK, *Imperfect Alternatives* (Chicago, University of Chicago Press, 1994).
Lagarde, P, *Le Droit International Privé: Esprit et Méthodes – Mélanges en l'Honneur de Paul Lagarde* (Paris, Dalloz, 2005).
Lagarde, P and Hoffmann, B, *L'Européanisation du Droit International Privé*, Serie de publications de l'Academie de Droit Europeen de Treves 8 (Cologne, Bundesanzeiger, 1996).
Larombière, LVLJ, *Théorie et pratique des obligations* (Paris, G Pedone-Lauriel, 1885).
Lasok, D and Stone, PA, *Conflict of laws in the European Community* (Abingdon, Professional Books, 1987).
Laurent, F, *Principes de droit civil*, 3rd edn (Brussels, Bruylant, 1869-87).
Lauterpacht, H, *The Development of International Law by the International Court* (London, Stevens & Sons, 1958).
Lawson, R, Schermers, HG and European Court of Human Rights, *Leading Cases of the European Court of Human Rights*, 2nd edn (Nijmegen, Ars Aequi Libri, 1999).
le Tourneau, P, *La responsabilité civile*, 2nd edn (Paris, Dalloz, 1976).
Lécuyer, Y, *Les droits politiques dans la jurisprudence de la Cour européenne des droits de l'homme* (Paris, Dalloz, 2009).

Lewis, CT et al, *A Latin Dictionary: Founded on Andrews' Edition of Freund's Latin Dictionary* (Oxford, Clarendon Press, 1879).

Ligeropoulo, A, *Le problème de la fraude à la loi* (Paris, Librairie du Recueil Sirey, 1928).

Lombardo, S, *Regulatory Competition in Company Law in the European Community: Prerequisites and Limits* (Frankfurt am Main, Peter Lang, 2002).

London Economics, *Competition Issues*, The Single Market Review, subseries V, vol 3 (London, Kogan Page, 1997).

Lunney, M and Oliphant, K, *Tort Law: Text and Materials*, 3rd edn (Oxford, Oxford University Press, 2008).

Mackintosh, J, *Roman Law in Modern Practice* (Edinburgh, Tagore Law Lectures, 1934).

Maduro, MP, *We the Court: the European Court of Justice and the European Economic Constitution* (Oxford, Hart Publishing, 1998).

—— and Azoulai, L, *The Past and Future of EU Law: The Classics of EU Law Revisited on the 50th Anniversary of the Rome Treaty* (Oxford, Hart Publishing, 2010).

Malaurie, P, Aynès, L and Stoffel-Munck, P, *Les obligations*, 2nd edn, Droit civil (Defrénois) (Paris, Defrénois, 2005).

Markesinis, BS, Johnston, AC and Deakin, SF, *Markesinis and Deakin's Tort Law*, 6th edn (Oxford, Oxford University Press, 2007).

Martins, PB, *O abuso do direito e o ato ilícito*, 3rd edn (Rio de Janeiro, Forense, 1997).

Marty, G and Raynaud, P, *Droit civil – Les obligations. Tome 1: Les Sources*, 2nd edn (Paris, Sirey, 1988).

Matscher, F, Petzold, H and Wiarda, GJ, *Protection des droits de l'homme: la dimension européenne. Mélanges en l'honneur de Gérard J. Wiarda* (Cologne, Heymanns, 1988).

Mattei, U and Nader, L, *Plunder: When the Rule of Law is Illegal* (Malden MA, Blackwell, 2008).

Mattera, A, *Le Marché Unique Européen*, 2nd edn (Paris, Jupiter, 1990).

Mazeaud, H et al, *Obligations: Théorie Générale*, 8th edn, Leçons de droit civil tome 2/1 (Paris, Montchrestien, 1991).

——, Mazeaud, L and Tunc, A, *Traité théorique et pratique de la responsabilité civile délictuelle et contractuelle*, 6th edn, vol I (Paris, Montchrestien, 1965).

McDonald, F and Dearden, S, *European Economic Integration*, 4th edn (Harlow, Prentice Hall, 2005).

McMahon, JA, *Law of the Common Agricultural Policy*, European law series (Harlow, Longman, 2000).

Mommsen, T et al, *Corpus iuris civilis* (Berolini, Apud Weidmannos, 1912).

Monnet, J, *Mémoires* (Paris, Fayard, 1976).

Montesquieu, T Nugent (trans), *The Spirit of the Laws* (New York, Hafner Press, 1949).

Moyle, JB, *The Institutes of Justinian: a Facsimile of the Moyle Latin Edition of 1912, together with the English Edition of 1913*, The Legal Classics Library (Birmingham, Legal Classics Library, 1985).

Muzny, P, *La Technique de Proportionnalité et le Juge de la Convention Européenne des Droits de l'Homme* (Aix-en-Provence, Presses Universitaires d'Aix-Marseille, 2005).

Neal, L, *The Economics of Europe and the European Union* (Cambridge, Cambridge University Press, 2007).

Netzer, D, *State-Local Finance and Intergovernmental Fiscal Relations* (Washington, Brookings Institution, 1969).

Noblet, A, *La lutte contre le contournement des droits nationaux en droit communautaire* (Lille, ANRT, 2004).

Nozick, R, *Anarchy, State, and Utopia* (Oxford, Blackwell, 1974).

Nuyts, A, *L'exception de forum non conveniens: étude de droit international privé comparé* (Brussels, Bruylant, 2003).

Oatley, TH, *International Political Economy: Interests and Institutions in the Global Economy*, 3rd edn (New York, Pearson, 2008).

OECD, *Action Plan on Base Erosion and Profit Shifting* (Paris, OECD Publishing, 2013).

Oppenheim, L, Jennings, RY and Watts, A, *Oppenheim's International Law – Peace*, 9th edn, vol I (Harlow, Longman, 1992).

Padoa-Schioppa, FK, *The Principle of Mutual Recognition in the European Integration Process* (Basingstoke, Palgrave Macmillan, 2005).

Padoa-Schioppa, T et al, *Efficiency, Stability and Equity: A Strategy for the Evolution of the Economic System of the European Community ('Padoa-Schioppa Report')* (Oxford, Oxford University Press, 1987).

Palan, R, Murphy, R and Chavagneux, C, *Tax Havens: How Globalization Really Works* (Ithaca NY, Cornell University Press, 2010).

Paschalidis, P, *Freedom of Establishment and Private International Law for Corporations* (Oxford, Oxford University Press, 2012).

Paschen, U, *Steuerumgehung im Nationalen und Internationalen Steuerrecht* (Wiesbaden, DUV, 2001).

Pataut, E, *Principe de la Souveraineté et Conflits de Juridiction: Etude de Droit International Privé*, Bibliothèque de droit privé no 298 (Paris, LGDJ, 1999).

Perisin, T, *Free movement of goods and limits of regulatory autonomy in the EU and WTO* (The Hague, TMC Asser, 2008).

Peterson, PE, *The Price of Federalism* (Washington DC, Brookings Institution, 1995).

Pezaros, P and Unfried, M, *The Common Agricultural Policy and the Environmental Challenge: Instruments, Problems and Opportunities from Different Perspectives* (Maastricht, European Institute of Public Administration, 2002).

Pinto, C, *Tax Competition and EU Law* (New York, Kluwer Law International, 2003).

Pistone, P, *Abuso del Diritto ed Elusione Fiscale* (Padua, CEDAM, 1995).

Planiol, M, *Traité élémentaire de droit civil*, 4th edn, vol 2 (Paris, LGDJ, 1951).

Plato, T Griffith (trans), *The Republic* (Cambridge, Cambridge University Press, 2000).

Posner, RA, *Economic Analysis of Law*, 3rd edn (Boston, Little, Brown and Company, 1986).

Poste, E et al, *Gai Institutiones or Institutes of Roman Law*, 4th edn (Oxford, Clarendon Press, 1904).

Research Group on the Existing EC Private Law (Acquis Group), *Principles of the Existing EC Contract Law (Acquis Principles) – Contract I* (Munich, Sellier European Law Publishers, 2007).

——, *Principles of the Existing EC Contract Law (Acquis Principles) – Contract II* (Munich, Sellier European Law Publishers, 2009).

——, *Principles of the Existing EC Contract Law (Acquis Principles) – Contract III* (Munich, Sellier European Law Publishers, 2013).

Ribstein, LE and O'Hara, EA, *The Law Market* (Oxford, Oxford University Press, 2009).

Ricardo, D, *On the Principles of Political Economy and Taxation*, 3rd edn (London, John Murray, 1821).

Rijpma, JJ, *Building Borders: the Regulatory Framework for the Management of the External Borders of the European Union* (Florence, EUI Thesis, 2009).

Ripert, G, *La règle morale dans les obligations civiles* (Paris, LGDJ, 1949).

——, Boulanger, J and Planiol, M, *Traité de droit civil, d'après le traité de Planiol* (Paris, LGDJ, 1956).
Rivera-Batiz, L and Oliva, M-A, *International Trade: Theory, Strategies, and Evidence* (Oxford, Oxford University Press, 2003).
Rodotà, S, *Il controllo sociale delle attività private* (Bologna, Il Mulino, 1977).
——, *Alla ricerca delle liberta* (Bologna, Il Mulino, 1978).
——, *Il terribile diritto: Studi sulla proprieta privata*, Collezione di testi e di studi. Diritto. (Bologna, Il Mulino, 1981).
Rodrik, D, *Has Globalization Gone Too Far?* (Washington DC, Institute for International Economics, 1997).
Rogers, WVH, Winfield, PH and Jolowicz, JA, *Winfield and Jolowicz on Tort*, 17th edn (London, Sweet & Maxwell, 2006).
Ross, WD and Stratton-Lake, P, *The Right and the Good*, 2nd edn, British Moral Philosophers (Oxford, Clarendon Press, 2002).
Rotondi, M, *Gli atti in frode alla legge nella dottrina romana e nella sua evoluzione posteriore* (Turin, L'Erma di Bretschneider, 1911).
Ruiz Luján, MT, *El abuso del derecho y la legislación colombiana* (Medellín, Universidad de Antioquia, 1941).
Sajó, A, *Abuse: the Dark Side of Fundamental Rights*, Issues in Constitutional Law 3 (Utrecht, Eleven International Publishing, 2006).
Saleilles, R, *Étude sur la théorie génerale de l'obligation*, 3rd edn (Paris, LGDJ, 1925).
Scharpf, FW, *Governing in Europe: Effective and Democratic?* (Oxford, Oxford University Press, 1999).
Schenk, A and Oldman, O, *Value Added Tax: a Comparative Approach* (Cambridge, Cambridge University Press, 2007).
Schwarze, J, *European Administrative Law* (London, Sweet & Maxwell, 1992).
Scott, SP, *The Civil Law, including the Twelve Tables, the Institutes of Gaius, the Rules of Ulpian, the Opinions of Paulus, the Enactments of Justinian, and the Constitutions of Leo* (Cincinnati, Central Trust Co, 1932).
Shavell, SM, *Foundations of Economic Analysis of Law* (Cambridge, Belknap Press of Harvard University Press, 2004).
—— and Kaplow, L, *Fairness versus Welfare* (Cambridge MA, Harvard University Press, 2002).
Smith, A, E Cannan (trans), *An Inquiry into the Nature and Causes of the Wealth of Nations*, 5th edn (London, Methuen & Co, 1904).
Starck, B, *Les Obligations* (Paris, Litec, 1972).
Stein, E et al, *European Community Law and Institutions in Perspective: Text, Cases and Readings* (Charlottesville, Michie, 1985).
—— and Sandalow, T, *Courts and Free Markets: Perspectives from The United States and Europe* (Oxford, Clarendon Press, 1982).
Stein, P, *Roman Law in European History* (New York, Cambridge University Press, 1999).
Stevens, R, *Torts and Rights* (Oxford, Oxford University Press, 2007).
Stone, P, *EU Private International Law: Harmonization of Laws*, Elgar European law (Cheltenham, Edward Elgar, 2006).
Sudre, F, *Les grands arrêts de la Cour européenne des droits de l'homme*, 5th edn (Paris, PUF, 2009).
Swann, D, *The economics of the Common Market*, 7th edn (London, Penguin, 1992).
Taggart, M, *Private Property and the Abuse of Rights in Victorian England: The Story of Edward Pickles and Bradford Water Supply* (Oxford, Oxford University Press, 2002).

Tarrow, SG, *Power in Movement: Social Movements and Contentious Politics*, 3rd edn (New York, Cambridge University Press, 2011).
Teather, R, *The Benefits of Tax Competition* (London, The Institute of Economic Affairs, 2005).
Terré, F, Simler, P and Lequette, Y, *Droit civil – Les Obligations*, 9th edn, Précis Dalloz. Droit privé. (Paris, Dalloz, 2005).
Tinbergen, J, *International Economic Integration*, 2nd edn (Amsterdam, Elsevier, 1965).
Titus-Livius, D Spillan (trans), *The History of Rome*, vol I (New York, Harper & Brothers, 1871).
Tridimas, T, *The General Principles of EU Law*, 2nd edn (Oxford, Oxford University Press, 2006).
Université de Liège, *La Constitution Economique Européenne: Actes du Colloque* (Liège, Faculte de droit, 1971).
Van Gerven, W, *Torts: Scope of Protection* (Oxford, Hart Publishing, 1998).
——, W, Lever, J and Larouche, P, *Tort law* (Oxford, Hart Publishing, 2000).
Vidal, J, *Essai d'une théorie générale de la fraude en droit français* (Paris, Dalloz, 1957).
Viner, J, *Studies in the Theory of International Trade* (New York, Harper & Brothers, 1937).
——, *The Customs Union Issue* (New York, The Carnegie Endowment for International Peace, 1950).
von Jhering, R, O de Meulenaere (trans), *L'Esprit du Droit Romain*, 3rd edn, vol 3 (Paris, Librairie A Marescq, 1880).
——, *L'Esprit du Droit Romain*, 3rd edn, vol 4 (Paris, Librairie A Marescq, 1880).
——, *L'Esprit du Droit Romain*, 3rd edn, vol 1 (Paris, Librairie A Marescq, 1886).
——, *L'Esprit du Droit Romain*, 3rd edn, vol 2 (Paris, Librairie A Marescq, 1886).
von Jhering, R, JJ Lalor (trans), *The Struggle for Law*, 2nd edn (Chicago, Callaghan & Co, 1915).
Von Mehren, AT and Gordley, J, *The Civil Law System: an Introduction to the Comparative Study of Law*, 2nd edn (Boston, Little, Brown and Company, 1977).
—— and Gordley, J, *An Introduction to the Comparative Study of Private Law: Readings, Cases, Materials* (Cambridge, Cambridge University Press, 2006).
—— and Gottschalk, E, *Conflict of laws in a globalized world* (Cambridge, Cambridge University Press, 2007).
von Quitzow, CM, *State Measures Distorting Free Competition in the EC* (The Hague, Kluwer Law International, 2002).
Watt, G, *Equity Stirring: the Story of Justice beyond Law* (Oxford, Hart Publishing, 2009).
Weatherill, S, *Cases and Materials on EU Law*, 8th edn (Oxford, Oxford University Press, 2007).
——, *Better Regulation*, Studies of the Oxford Institute of European and Comparative Law v 6 (Oxford, Hart Publishing, 2007).
Weber, M, G Roth and C Wittich (eds), *Economy and Society* (Berkeley, University of California Press, 1968).
——, EA Shils and HA Finch (trans), *The Methodology of the Social Sciences* (New York, Free Press, 1997).
Weiler, JHH and Academy of European Law, *The EU, the WTO, and the NAFTA: Towards a Common Law of International Trade* (Oxford, Oxford University Press, 2000).
Wesseling, R, *The Modernisation of EC Antitrust Law* (Oxford, Hart Publishing, 2000).
Whish, R and Bailey, D, *Competition Law*, 7th edn (Oxford, Oxford University Press, 2012).
Woods, L, *Free Movement of Goods and Services within the European Community* (Aldershot, Ashgate, 2004).
Worthington, S, *Equity* (Oxford, Clarendon Press, 2003).

Edited Books

Balassa, BA (ed), *European Economic Integration* (Amsterdam, North-Holland, 1975).
Barnard, C and Scott, J (eds), *The Law of the Single European Market: Unpacking the Premises* (Oxford, Hart Publishing, 2002).
Beneyto, JM (ed), *Unity and Flexibility in the Future of the European Union: the Challenge of Enhanced Cooperation* (Madrid, CEU Ediciones, 2009).
Biondi, A, Eeckhout, P and Flynn, J (eds), *The Law of State Aid in the European Union* (Oxford, Oxford University Press, 2004).
Birks, P, Burrows, AS and Rodger of Earlsferry, A (eds), *Mapping the Law: Essays in Memory of Peter Birks* (Oxford, Oxford University Press, 2006).
Booth, P (ed), *The Euro – the Beginning, the Middle ... and the End?* (London, The Institute of Economic Affairs, 2013).
Bot, Y and Léger, P (eds), *Le Droit à la Mesure de l'Homme: Mélanges en l'Honneur de Philippe Léger* (Paris, Pédone, 2006).
Cafaggi, F and Academy of European Law (eds), *The Institutional Framework of European Private Law* 15/2 (Oxford, Oxford University Press, 2006).
Cappelletti, M, Seccombe, M and Weiler, JHH (eds), *Integration through Law* (Berlin, W de Gruyter, 1985).
de la Feria, R and Vogenauer, S (eds), *Prohibition of Abuse of Law: a New General Principle of EU Law?* (Oxford, Hart Publishing, 2011).
de Vareilles Sommières, P (ed), *Forum Shopping in the European Judicial Area* (Oxford, Hart Publishing, 2007).
Dougan, M and Currie, S (eds), *50 Years of the European Treaties* (Oxford, Hart Publishing, 2009).
Edward, DAO, Hoskins, M and Robinson, W (eds), *A True European: Essays for Judge David Edward* (Oxford, Hart Publishing, 2003).
Engel, S and Kelsen, H (eds), *Law, State, and International Legal Order: Essays in Honor of Hans Kelsen* (Knoxville, University of Tennessee Press, 1964).
Freedman, J (ed), *Beyond Boundaries: Developing Approaches to Tax Avoidance and Tax Risk Management* (Oxford, Oxford University Centre for Business Taxation, 2008).
Heidenhain, M (ed), *European State Aid Law* (Munich, Verlag CH Beck, 2010).
Pelkmans, J, Chang, M and Hanf, D (eds), *The EU Internal Market in Comparative Perspective* (New York, PIE Peter Lang, 2008).
Polinsky, MA and Shavell, SM (eds), *Handbook of Law and Economics* (Amsterdam, North-Holland, 2007).
Rotondi, M (ed), *L'abus de droit* (Padua, CEDAM, 1979).
Snyder, F (ed), *The Europeanisation of Law: The Legal Effects of European Integration* (Oxford, Hart Publishing, 2000).
Tridimas, T and Nebbia, P (eds), *European Union Law for the Twenty-First Century - Volume 2: Internal Market and Free Movement Community Policies* (Oxford, Hart Publishing, 2004).
Vandersanden, G, Levi, L and De Walsche, A (eds), *Mélanges en hommage à Georges Vandersanden: Promenades au sein du droit européen* (Brussels, Bruylant, 2008).
von Bogdandy, A and Bast, J (eds), *Principles of European Constitutional Law* (Oxford, Hart Publishing, 2006).

Book Chapters

'Equity' in J Lehman (ed), *West's Encyclopedia of American Law*, 2nd edn (Farmington Hills MI, Thomson Gale, 1998)

Ahlborn, C and Berg, C, 'Can State Aid Control Learn from Antitrust? The Need for a Greater Role for Competition Analysis under the State Aid Rules' in A Biondi et al (eds), *The Law of State Aid in the European Union* (Oxford, Oxford University Press, 2004) 41–65.

Armour, J, 'Abuse of European Insolvency Law? A Discussion' in R de la Feria and S Vogenauer (eds), *Prohibition of Abuse of Law: a New General Principle of EU Law?* (Oxford, Hart Publishing, 2011) 157–68.

Armstrong, KA, 'Mutual Recognition' in C Barnard and J Scott (eds), *The Law of the Single Market: Unpacking the Premises* (Oxford, Hart Publishing, 2002) 225–68.

Arnull, A, 'What is a General Principle of EU Law?' in R de la Feria and S Vogenauer (ed), *Prohibition of Abuse of Law: a New General Principle of EU Law?* (Oxford, Hart Publishing, 2011) 7–23.

Balassa, BA, 'Trade Creation and Diversion in the European Common Market: an Appraisal of the Evidence' in BA Balassa (ed), *European Economic Integration* 89 (Amsterdam, North-Holland, 1975) 79–118.

Barenberg, M, 'Labour Federalism in the United States: Lessons for Coordinated Decentralization in Supranational Regimes' in DC Esty and D Geradin (eds), *Regulatory Competition and Economic Integration: Comparative Perspectives* (Oxford, Oxford University Press, 2001) 111–34.

Barnard, C, 'EU Citizenship and the Principle of Solidarity' in M Dougan and E Spaventa (eds), *Social Welfare and EU Law* (Oxford, Hart Publishing, 2005) 157–80.

——, 'Solidarity and New Governance in Social Policy' in G de Búrca and J Scott (eds), *Law and New Governance in the EU and the US* (Oxford, Hart Publishing, 2006) 153–77.

——, 'Fifty Years of Avoiding Social Dumping? The EU's Economic and Not So Economic Constitution' in M Dougan and S Currie (eds), *50 Years of the European Treaties* (Oxford, Hart Publishing, 2009) 311–42.

——, 'The Notion of Abuse and the Freedom to Provide Services: A Labour Lawyer's Perspective' in R de la Feria and S Vogenauer (eds), *Prohibition of Abuse of Law: a New General Principle of EU Law?* (Oxford, Hart Publishing, 2011) 93–104.

—— and Deakin, S, 'Market Access and Regulatory Competition' in C Barnard and J Scott (eds), *The Law of the Single Market: Unpacking the Premises* (Oxford, Hart Publishing, 2002) 197–224.

Baudoin, J-L, 'L'abus de droit dans la doctrine et la jurisprudence du Québec' in M Rotondi (ed), *L'abus de droit* (Padua, CEDAM, 1979) 1–14.

Baum, H, 'Globalizing Capital Markets and Possible Regulatory Responses' in J Basedow and T Kono (eds), *Legal Aspects of Globalization: Conflict of Laws, Internet, Capital Markets and Insolvency in a Global Economy* (The Hague, Klumer Law International, 2000) 77–132.

Bebchuk, L and Ferrell, A, 'Federalism and Takeover Law: The Race to Protect Managers from Takeovers' in DC Esty and D Geradin (eds), *Regulatory Competition and Economic Integration: Comparative Perspectives* (Oxford, Oxford University Press, 2001) 68–94.

Bercusson, B, 'Regulatory Competition in the EU System: Labour' in DC Esty and D Geradin (eds), *Regulatory Competition and Economic Integration: Comparative Perspectives* (Oxford, Oxford University Press, 2001) 241–62.
Biondi, A, 'Justifying State Aid: The Financing of Services of General Economic Interest' in T Tridimas and P Nebbia (eds), *European Union Law for the Twenty-First Century - Volume 2: Internal Market and Free Movement Community Policies* (Oxford, Hart Publishing, 2004) 259–72.
—— and Eeckhout, P, 'State Aid and Obstacle to Trade' in A Biondi et al (eds), *The Law of State Aid in the European Union* (Oxford, Oxford University Press, 2004) 103–16.
Boy, L, 'Le droit de la concurrence, élément d'une constitution européenne?' in O Debarge et al (eds), *La constitution économique de l'Union Européenne: 2è rencontre du GIEPI, 12-13 mai 2006* (Brussels, Bruylant, 2008) 123–45.
Bratton, W and McCahery, J, 'Fiscal Federalism, Jurisdictional Competition, and Tax Coordination: Translating Theory to Policy in the European Union' in DC Esty and D Geradin (eds), *Regulatory Competition and Economic Integration: Comparative Perspectives* (Oxford, Oxford University Press, 2001) 157–89.
Briggs, A, 'The Rejection of Abuse in International Civil Procedure' in R de la Feria and S Vogenauer (eds), *Prohibition of Abuse of Law: a New General Principle of EU Law?* (Oxford, Hart Publishing, 2011) 261–77.
Cerny, PG, 'Competition State' in RJB Jones (ed), *Routledge Encyclopedia of International Political Economy* (London, Routledge, 2001) 220–26.
Charny, D, 'Regulatory Competition and the Global Coordination of Labour Standards' in DC Esty and D Geradin (eds), *Regulatory Competition and Economic Integration: Comparative Perspectives* (Oxford, Oxford University Press, 2001) 311–29.
Chevalier, J-P, 'L'esperienza francese' in A Di Pietro (ed), *L'Elusione Fiscale nell'Esperienza Europea* (Milan, Giuffrè, 1999) 5–32.
Cigoj, S, 'L'abus de droit dans la doctrine et la jurisprudence yougoslaves' in M Rotondi (ed), *L'abus de droit* (Padua, CEDAM, 1979) 15–28.
Costello, C, 'Citizenship of the Union: Above Abuse?' in R de la Feria and S Vogenauer (eds), *Prohibition of Abuse of Law: a New General Principle of EU Law?* (Oxford, Hart Publishing, 2011) 321–53.
Cunha De Sa', FA, 'O abuso do direito na doutrina e na jurisprudência de Portugal' in M Rotondi (ed), *L'abus de droit* (Padua, CEDAM, 1979) 29–54.
Cuniberti, G, 'The Discreet Influence of Abuse of Law in International Civil Procedure' in R de la Feria and S Vogenauer (eds), *Prohibition of Abuse of Law: a New General Principle of EU Law?* (Oxford, Hart Publishing, 2011) 279–88.
Dassesse, M, 'Localization of Financial Services: Regulatory and Tax Implications' in M Andenas and W-H Roth (eds), *Services and Free Movement in EU Law* (Oxford, Oxford University Press, 2003) 383–93.
de la Feria, R, 'Introducing the Principle of Prohibition of Abuse of Law' in R de la Feria and S Vogenauer (eds), *Prohibition of Abuse of Law: a New General Principle of EU Law?* (Oxford, Hart Publishing, 2011) xv–xxv.
de Vareilles-Sommières, P, 'Fraude à la loi' in *Répertoire International Dalloz* (Paris, Dalloz, 1998)
De Villavicencio Francisco, F, 'El abuso del derecho en la doctrina y en la jurisprudencia espanolas' in M Rotondi (ed), *L'abus de droit* (Padua, CEDAM, 1979) 75–86.
de Witte, B, 'A Competence to Protect: The Pursuit of Non-Market Aims through Internal Market Legislation' in P Syrpis (ed), *The Judiciary, the Legislature and the EU Internal Market* (Cambridge, Cambridge University Press, 2011) 25–46.

Deakin, S, 'Regulatory Competition versus Harmonization in European Company Law' in DC Esty and D Geradin (eds), *Regulatory Competition and Economic Integration: Comparative Perspectives* (Oxford, Oxford University Press, 2001) 190–217.

Deloukas, NA, 'Der Rechtmissbrauch im griechischen Privatrecht' in M Rotondi (ed), *L'abus de droit* (Padua, CEDAM, 1979) 55–74.

Di Bucci, V, 'Quelques Aspects Institutionnels du Droit des Aides d'Etat' in F Santaolalla Gadea (ed), *EC State Aid Law: Liber Amicorum Francisco Santaolalla Gadea* (The Hague, Kluwer Law International, 2008) 43–64.

Di Francia, A, 'L'abuso di diritto nella legislazione, nella dottrina e nella giurisprudenza italiana' in M Rotondi (ed), *L'abus de droit* (Padua, CEDAM, 1979) 115–42.

Dougan, M, 'Some Comments on the Idea of a General Principle of Union Law Prohibiting Abuses of Law in the Field of Free Movement for Union Citizens' in R de la Feria and S Vogenauer (eds), *Prohibition of Abuse of Law: a New General Principle of EU Law?* (Oxford, Hart Publishing, 2011) 355–62.

Doukas, D, 'Free Movement of Broadcasting Services and Abuse of Law' in R de la Feria and S Vogenauer (eds), *Prohibition of Abuse of Law: a New General Principle of EU Law?* (Oxford, Hart Publishing, 2011) 63–91.

Dourado, AP, 'A Single Principle of Abuse in European Union Law: A Methodological Approach to Rejecting a Different Concept of Abuse in Personal Taxation' in R de la Feria and S Vogenauer (eds), *Prohibition of Abuse of Law: a New General Principle of EU Law?* (Oxford, Hart Publishing, 2011) 469–83.

Doutrelepont, C, 'Le secteur audiovisuel et la libre prestation des services dans l'Union européenne' in C Doutrelepont and M Waelbroeck (eds), *Questions de droit de l'audiovisuel européen* (Brussels, Bruylant, 1997) 145–66.

Drexl, J, 'Competition Law as Part of the European Constitution' in A von Bogdandy and J Bast (eds), *Principles of European Constitutional Law* (Oxford, Hart Publishing, 2006) 633–76.

Edwards, V and Farmer, P, 'The Concept of Abuse in the Freedom of Establishment of Companies: a Case of Double Standards?' in FG Jacobs et al (eds), *Continuity and Change in EU Law: Essays in Honour of Sir Francis Jacobs* (Oxford, Oxford University Press, 2007) 205–27.

Egan, M, 'The Emergence of the US Internal Market' in J Pelkmans et al (ed), *The EU Internal Market in Comparative Perspective* (New York, Peter Lang, 2008) 249–79.

Eidenmüller, H, 'Abuse of Law in the Context of European Insolvency Law' in R de la Feria and S Vogenauer (eds), *Prohibition of Abuse of Law: a New General Principle of EU Law?* (Oxford, Hart Publishing, 2011) 137–56.

Engel, K and Rose-Ackerman, S, 'Environmental Federalism and the United States: The Risks of Devolution' in DC Esty and D Geradin (eds), *Regulatory Competition and Economic Integration: Comparative Perspectives* (Oxford, Oxford University Press, 2001) 135–53.

Eorsi, G, 'The Abuse of Right in Doctrine and Court Practice in Hungary' in M Rotondi (ed), *L'abus de droit* (Padua, CEDAM, 1979) 87–114.

Essers, P and Kemmeren, E, 'L'esperienza olandese' in A Di Pietro (ed), *L'Elusione Fiscale nell'Esperienza Europea* (Milan, Giuffrè, 1999) 77–105.

Esty, DC and Geradin, D, 'Regulatory Co-Opetition' in DC Esty and D Geradin (eds), *Regulatory Competition and Economic Integration: Comparative Perspectives* (Oxford, Oxford University Press, 2001) 30–46.

Fallon, M, 'La délocalisation comme instrument de fraude lié à la circulation des biens et des personnes' in J Verhoeven (ed), *La loyauté: mélanges offerts à Etienne Cerexhe* (Brussels, Larcier, 1997) 165–89.

——, 'Libertés Communautaires et Règles de Conflit de Lois' in A Fuchs et al (eds), *Les Conflits de Lois et le Système Juridique Communautaire* (Paris, Dalloz, 2004) 31–80.
——, 'L'acquis social constitutionnel de l'Union Européenne' in O Debarge et al (eds), *La constitution économique de l'Union Européenne: 2è rencontre du GIEPI, 12-13 mai 2006* (Brussels, Bruylant, 2008) 239–78.
Fantozzi, A, 'L'esperienza italiana' in A Di Pietro (ed), *L'Elusione Fiscale nell'Esperienza Europea* (Milan, Giuffrè, 1999) 251–60.
Farmer, P, 'Prohibition of Abuse of (European) Law: The Creation of a New General Principle of EU Law through Tax: A Response' in R de la Feria and S Vogenauer (eds), *Prohibition of Abuse of Law: a New General Principle of EU Law?* (Oxford, Hart Publishing, 2011) 3–6.
Faull, J, '"Prohibition of Abuse of Law": A New General Principle of EU Law' in R de la Feria and S Vogenauer (eds), *Prohibition of Abuse of Law: a New General Principle of EU Law?* (Oxford, Hart Publishing, 2011) 291–93.
Faure, M, 'Regulatory Competition vs Harmonization in EU Environmental Law' in DC Esty and D Geradin (eds), *Regulatory Competition and Economic Integration: Comparative Perspectives* (Oxford, Oxford University Press, 2001) 263–86.
Fischer, P, 'L'esperienza tedesca' in A Di Pietro (ed), *L'Elusione Fiscale nell'Esperienza Europea* (Milan, Giuffrè, 1999) 203–49.
Forkosch Morris, S, 'Abus du droit under Doctrine and Jurisprudence in the United States' in M Rotondi (ed), *L'abus de droit* (Padua, CEDAM, 1979) 143–80.
Fox, EM, 'Antitrust Law on a Global Scale: Races Up, Down, and Sideways' in DC Esty and D Geradin (eds), *Regulatory Competition and Economic Integration: Comparative Perspectives* (Oxford, Oxford University Press, 2001) 348–63.
Freedman, J, 'The Anatomy of Tax Avoidance Counteraction: Abuse of Law in a Tax Context at Member State and European Union Level' in R de la Feria and S Vogenauer (eds), *Prohibition of Abuse of Law: a New General Principle of EU Law?* (Oxford, Hart Publishing, 2011) 365–80.
Georgopoulos, T, 'Sur le concept de "constitution économique de l'Union Européenne"' in O Debarge et al (eds), *La constitution économique de l'Union Européenne: 2è rencontre du GIEPI, 12-13 mai 2006* (Brussels, Bruylant, 2008) 3–32.
Ghosh, J, 'Cadbury Schweppes: Breach, Abuse Justification and Why They Are Different' in R de la Feria and S Vogenauer (eds), *Prohibition of Abuse of Law: a New General Principle of EU Law?* (Oxford, Hart Publishing, 2011) 459–68.
Gordley, J, 'The Abuse of Rights in the Civil Law Tradition' in R de la Feria and S Vogenauer (eds), *Prohibition of Abuse of Law: a New General Principle of EU Law?* (Oxford, Hart Publishing, 2011) 33–46.
Govaere, I and Demaret, P, 'The TRIPS Agreement: A Response to Global Regulatory Competition or an Exercise in Global Regulatory Coercion?' in DC Esty and D Geradin (eds), *Regulatory Competition and Economic Integration: Comparative Perspectives* (Oxford, Oxford University Press, 2001) 364–81.
Grundmann, S, 'Internal Market Conflict of Laws from Traditional Conflicts of Law to an Integrated Two Level Order' in A Fuchs et al (eds), *Les Conflits de Lois et le Système Juridique Communautaire* (Paris, Dalloz, 2004) 5–29.
Gyselen, L, 'The Emerging Interface between Competition Policy and Environmental Policy in the EC' in J Cameron et al (eds), *Trade and Environment* (London, Cameron May, 1994) 242–60.

Habermas, J, 'Beyond the Nation-State? On Some Consequences of Economic Globalization' in EO Eriksen and JE Fossum (eds), *Democracy in the European Union: Integration through Deliberation?* (London, Routledge, 2000) 29–42.

——, 'The Postnational Constellation and the Future of Democracy' in J Habermas and M Pensky (ed), *The Postnational Constellation: Political Essays* (Cambridge MA, MIT Press, 2001) 58–112.

Hanf, D, 'Legal Concept and Meaning of the Internal Market' in J Pelkmans et al (eds), *The EU Internal Market in Comparative Perspective* (New York, Peter Lang, 2008) 77–91.

Hatje, A, 'The Economic Constitution' in A von Bogdandy and J Bast (eds), *Principles of European Constitutional Law* (Oxford, Hart Publishing, 2006) 587–632.

Hellner, M, 'The Country of Origin Principle in the e-Commerce Directive: a Conflict with Conflicts of Law?' in A Fuchs et al (eds), *Les Conflits de Lois et le Système Juridique Communautaire* (Paris, Dalloz, 2004) 205–24.

Hertig, G, 'Regulatory Competition for EU Financial Services' in DC Esty and D Geradin (eds), *Regulatory Competition and Economic Integration: Comparative Perspectives* (Oxford, Oxford University Press, 2001) 218–40.

Ionasco, A, 'L'abus de droit en Roumanie' in M Rotondi (ed), *L'abus de droit* (Padua, CEDAM, 1979) 181–194.

Jorgensen, S, 'Abuse of Rights according to Nordic Law' in M Rotondi (ed), *L'abus de droit* (Padua, CEDAM, 1979) 195–210.

Kaplow, L, 'Chapter 10: Taxation' in MA Polinsky and SM Shavell (eds), *Handbook of Law and Economics* (Amsterdam, North-Holland, 2007) 651–755.

Kessedjian, C, 'Le Droit entre Concurrence et Coopération' in H Gaudemet-Tallon and J-P Ancel (eds), *Vers de Nouveaux Equilibres entre Ordres Juridiques: Liber Amicorum Hélène Gaudemet-Tallon* (Paris, Dalloz, 2008) 119–32.

Koutrakos, P, 'The Emsland-Stärke Abuse of Law Test in the Law of Agriculture and Free Movement of Goods' in R de la Feria and S Vogenauer (eds), *Prohibition of Abuse of Law: a New General Principle of EU Law?* (Oxford, Hart Publishing, 2011) 203–17.

Kunz, O, 'L'abus de droit dans la doctrine et la jurisprudence tchécoslovaques' in M Rotondi (ed), *L'abus de droit* (Padua, CEDAM, 1979) 211–20.

Lagarde, P, 'Rapport de Synthèse' in A Fuchs et al (eds), *Les Conflits de Lois et le Système Juridique Communautaire* (Paris, Dalloz, 2004) 283–95.

Lage, SM and Sobredo, PM-L, 'Pursuing Market Integration through the Enforcement of EC Competition Rules: a Critical Perspective' in G Vandersanden et al (eds), *Mélanges en hommage à Georges Vandersanden: Promenades au sein du droit européen* (Brussels, Bruylant, 2008) 593–611.

Lang, M, 'Cadbury Schweppes' Line of Case Law from the Member States' Perspective' in R de la Feria and S Vogenauer (eds), *Prohibition of Abuse of Law: a New General Principle of EU Law?* (Oxford, Hart Publishing, 2011) 435–58.

Lomnicka, E, 'The Home Country Control Principle in the Financial Services Directives and the Case Law' in M Andenas and W-H Roth (eds), *Services and Free Movement in EU Law* (Oxford, Oxford University Press, 2003) 295–319.

Lupi, R, 'Elusione: Esperienze Europee tra l'Uso e l'Abuso del Diritto Tributario' in A Di Pietro (ed), *L'Elusione Fiscale nell'Esperienza Europea* (Milan, Giuffrè, 1999) 261–92.

Lyal, R, 'Cadbury Schweppes and Abuse: Comments' in R de la Feria and S Vogenauer (eds), *Prohibition of Abuse of Law: a New General Principle of EU Law?* (Oxford, Hart Publishing, 2011) 427–34.

Lyons, T, 'State Aid, Taxation and Abuse of Law' in R de la Feria and S Vogenauer (eds), *Prohibition of Abuse of Law: a New General Principle of EU Law?* (Oxford, Hart Publishing, 2011) 493–508.

Macey, JR, 'Regulatory Competition in the US Federal System: Banking and Financial Services' in DC Esty and D Geradin (ed), *Regulatory Competition and Economic Integration: Comparative Perspectives* (Oxford, Oxford University Press, 2001) 95–110.

Maddalon, P, 'Pourquoi est-il difficile d'identifier la constitution économique européenne?' in O Debarge et al (eds), *La constitution économique de l'Union Européenne: 2è rencontre du GIEPI, 12-13 mai 2006* (Brussels, Bruylant, 2008) 103–21.

Maduro, MP, 'The Scope of European Remedies: the Case of Purely Internal Situations and Reverse Discrimination' in C Kilpatrick et al (eds), *The Future of European Remedies* (Oxford, Hart Publishing, 2000) 117–40.

——, 'Europe and the Constitution: what if this is as good as it gets?' in JHH Weiler and M Wind (eds), *European Constitutionalism Beyond the State* (Cambridge, Cambridge University Press, 2003) 74–102.

Malherbe, J, 'L'esperienza belga' in A Di Pietro (ed), *L'Elusione Fiscale nell'Esperienza Europea* (Milan, Giuffrè, 1999) 33–75.

Mattera, A, 'The Principle of Mutual Recognition and Respect for National, Regional and Local Identities and Traditions' in FK Padoa-Schioppa (ed), *The Principle of Mutual Recognition in the European Integration Process* (Basingstoke, Palgrave Macmillan, 2005) 1–24.

Mayer-Maly, T and Bohn, H, 'Die Behandlung des Rechtsmissbrauchs im Osterreichischen Privatrecht' in M Rotondi (ed), *L'abus de droit* (Padua, CEDAM, 1979) 221–38.

Meinertzhagen-Limpens, A, 'L'abus de droit dans la doctrine et la jurisprudence belge' in M Rotondi (ed), *L'abus de droit* (Padua, CEDAM, 1979) 239–64.

Metzger, A, 'Abuse of Law in EU Private Law: A (Re-)Construction from Fragments' in R de la Feria and S Vogenauer (eds), *Prohibition of Abuse of Law: a New General Principle of EU Law?* (Oxford, Hart Publishing, 2011) 235–51.

Mischo, J, 'Libre Circulation des Services et Dumping Social' in Y Bot and P Léger (eds), *Le Droit à la Mesure de l'Homme: Mélanges en l'Honneur de Philippe Léger* (Paris, Pédone, 2006) 435–44.

Muir Watt, H, 'L'Expérience Américaine' in A Fuchs et al (eds), *Les Conflits de Lois et le Système Juridique Communautaire* (Paris, Dalloz, 2004) 145–69.

——, 'Integration and Diversity: the Conflict of Laws as a Regulatory Tool' in F Cafaggi and Academy of European Law (eds), *The Institutional Framework of European Private Law* 15/2 (Oxford, Oxford University Press, 2006) 107–48.

Napier, BW, 'Abuse of Rights in British Law' in M Rotondi (ed), *L'abus de droit* (Padua, CEDAM, 1979) 265–82.

Neville Brown, L, 'Is there a General Principle of Abuse of Rights in European Community Law?' in D Curtin et al (eds), *Institutional Dynamics of European Integration – Essays in Honour of Henry G. Schermers*, vol II (Dordrecht, M Nijhoff, 1994) 511–25.

Nicolaïdis, K, 'Globalization with Human Faces: Managed Mutual Recognition and the Free Movement of Professionals' in FK Padoa-Schioppa (ed), *The Principle of Mutual Recognition in the European Integration Process* (Basingstoke, Palgrave Macmillan, 2005) 129–89.

Noda, Y and Nomura, T, 'L'abus du droit en droit privé japonais' in M Rotondi (ed), *L'abus de droit* (Padua, CEDAM, 1979) 283–302.

Nuyts, A, 'Forum shopping et l'abus du forum shopping dans l'espace judiciaire européen' in *Mélanges Kirpatrick* (Brussels, Bruylant, 2004) 745–90.

——, 'The Enforcement of Jurisdiction Agreements further to Gasser and the Community Principle of Abuse of Rights' in P de Vareilles Sommières (ed), *Forum Shopping in the European Judicial Area* (Oxford, Hart Publishing, 2007) 55–72.

Ohanowicz, A, 'L'abuso del diritto soggettivo nella dottrina e nella giurisprudenza della Polonia' in M Rotondi (ed), *L'abus de droit* (Padua, CEDAM, 1979) 303–12.

Oliver, P, 'Competition and Free Movement: Their Place in the Treaty' in T Tridimas and P Nebbia (eds), *European Union Law for the Twenty-First Century - Volume 2: Internal Market and Free Movement Community Policies* (Oxford, Hart Publishing, 2004) 159–76.

Olivier, DT, 'Roman Law in Modern Cases in English Courts' in *Cambridge Legal Essays Written in Honour of Dr. H. Bond, Prof. W. W. Buckland and Prof. C. S. Kenny* (Cambridge, W Heffer & Sons, Ltd, 1926) 243–58.

Padoa-Schioppa, FK, 'Mutual Recognition, Unemployment and the Welfare State' in FK Padoa-Schioppa (ed), *The Principle of Mutual Recognition in the European Integration Process* (Basingstoke, Palgrave Macmillan, 2005) 191–223.

Pataut, E, 'Lois de Police et Ordre Juridique Communautaire' in A Fuchs et al (eds), *Les Conflits de Lois et le Système Juridique Communautaire* (Paris, Dalloz, 2004) 117–43.

Pelkmans, J, 'Mutual Recognition in Goods and Services: an Economic Perspective' in FK Padoa-Schioppa (ed), *The Principle of Mutual Recognition in the European Integration Process* (Basingstoke, Palgrave Macmillan, 2005) 85–128.

——, 'Economic Concept and Meaning of the Internal Market' in J Pelkmans et al (ed), *The EU Internal Market in Comparative Perspective* (New York, Peter Lang, 2008) 29–76.

Perez Royo, F, 'L'esperienza spagnola' in A Di Pietro (ed), *L'Elusione Fiscale nell'Esperienza Europea* (Milano, Giuffrè, 1999) 173–202.

Pirovano, A, 'L'abus de droit dans la doctrine et la jurisprudence françaises' in M Rotondi (ed), *L'abus de droit* (Padua, CEDAM, 1979) 313–60.

Pistone, P, 'Abuse of Law in the Context of Indirect Taxation: From (Before) Emsland-Stärke 1 to Halifax (and Beyond)' in R de la Feria and S Vogenauer (eds), *Prohibition of Abuse of Law: a New General Principle of EU Law?* (Oxford, Hart Publishing, 2011) 381–93.

Plender, R, 'Definition of Aid' in A Biondi et al (eds), *The Law of State Aid in the European Union* (Oxford, Oxford University Press, 2004) 3–39.

Quigley, C, 'General Taxation and State Aid' in A Biondi et al (eds), *The Law of State Aid in the European Union* (Oxford, Oxford University Press, 2004) 207–17.

——, 'Comments on State Aid, Taxation and Abuse of Law' in R de la Feria and S Vogenauer (eds), *Prohibition of Abuse of Law: a New General Principle of EU Law?* (Oxford, Hart Publishing, 2011) 509–18.

Rabaey, O, 'L'interventionisme libéral, paradoxe de la constitution économique européenne: une approche constitutionnelle dialectique du régime communautaire des aides d'État' in O Debarge et al (eds), *La constitution économique de l'Union Européenne: 2è rencontre du GIEPI, 12-13 mai 2006* (Brussels, Bruylant, 2008) 147–78.

Radicati di Brozolo, LG, 'Libre Circulation dans la CE et Règles de Conflit' in P Lagarde and B Hoffmann (eds), *L'Européanisation du Droit International Privé* (Cologne, Bundesanzeiger, 1996) 87–103.

Ranieri, F, 'Norma scritta e prassi giudiziale nell'evoluzione della dottrina tedesca del Rechtsmissbrauch' in M Rotondi (ed), *L'abus de droit* (Padua, CEDAM, 1979) 361–84.

Revesz, RL, 'Federalism and Regulation: Some Generalizations' in DC Esty and D Geradin (eds), *Regulatory Competition and Economic Integration: Comparative Perspectives* (Oxford, Oxford University Press, 2001) 3–29.

Ringe, W-G, 'Sparking Regulatory Competition in European Company Law – The Impact of the Centros Line of Case-Law and its Concept of "Abuse of Law"' in R de la Feria and S Vogenauer (eds), *Prohibition of Abuse of Law: a New General Principle of EU Law?* (Oxford, Hart Publishing, 2011) 107–25.

Schammo, P, 'Comments on Abuse of Rights in EU Law' in R de la Feria and S Vogenauer (eds), *Prohibition of Abuse of Law: a New General Principle of EU Law?* (Oxford, Hart Publishing, 2011) 193–99.

Scharpf, FW, 'Legitimacy in the Multi-Level European Polity' in M Loughlin and P Dobner (eds), *The Twilight of Constitutionalism?* (Oxford, Oxford University Press, 2010) 89–119.

——, 'Democratic Legitimacy under Conditions of Regulatory Competition: Why Europe Differs from the United States' in FW Scharpf (ed), *Community and Autonomy: Institutions, Policies and Legitimacy in Multilevel Europe* (Frankfurt am Main, Campus, 2010) 173–92.

Schmitt von Sydow, H, 'The Basic Strategies of the Commission's White Paper' in R Bieber et al (eds), *1992: One European Market?* (Baden-Baden, Nomos, 1988) 92.

Shaviro, D, 'Some Observations Concerning Multijurisdictional Tax Competition' in DC Esty and D Geradin (eds), *Regulatory Competition and Economic Integration: Comparative Perspectives* (Oxford, Oxford University Press, 2001) 49–67.

Shipwright, A, 'L'esperienza britannica' in A Di Pietro (ed), *L'Elusione Fiscale nell'Esperienza Europea* (Milan, Giuffrè, 1999) 107–72.

Simon, D and Rigaux, A, 'La technique de consécration d'un nouveau principe général de droit communautaire: l'exemple de l'abus de droit' in M Blanquet (ed), *Mélanges en hommage à Guy Isaac: 50 ans de droit communautaire* (Toulouse, Presses de l'Université des Sciences Sociales de Toulouse, 2004) 559–88.

Simpson, E, 'Is There a Role for a European Principle Prohibiting Abuse of Law in the Field of Personal Taxation? A Comment' in R de la Feria and S Vogenauer (eds), *Prohibition of Abuse of Law: a New General Principle of EU Law?* (Oxford, Hart Publishing, 2011) 485–92.

Snell, J, 'The Notion of and a General Test for Abuse of Rights: Some Normative Reflections' in R de la Feria and S Vogenauer (eds), *Prohibition of Abuse of Law: a New General Principle of EU Law?* (Oxford, Hart Publishing, 2011) 219–31.

Sørensen, KE, 'What is a General Principle of EU Law? A Response' in R de la Feria and S Vogenauer (eds), *Prohibition of Abuse of Law: a New General Principle of EU Law?* (Oxford, Hart Publishing, 2011) 25–32.

Spaventa, E, 'Comments on Abuse of Law and the Free Movement of Workers' in R de la Feria and S Vogenauer (eds), *Prohibition of Abuse of Law: a New General Principle of EU Law?* (Oxford, Hart Publishing, 2011) 315–20.

Spector, D, 'State Aids: Economic Analysis and Practice in the European Union' in X Vives (ed), *Competition Policy in the EU: Fifty Years on from the Treaty of Rome* (Oxford, Oxford University Press, 2009) 176–202.

Spielmann, A, 'La protection des droits de l'homme. Quid des droits des détenus?' in F Matscher et al (eds), *Protection des droits de l'homme: la dimension européenne. Mélanges en l'honneur de Gérard J. Wiarda* (Köln, Heymanns, 1988) 589–94.

—— and Spielmann, D, 'The Concept of Abuse of Rights and the European Convention for the Protection of Human Rights and Fundamental Freedoms' in Council of Europe (ed), *Abuse of Rights and Equivalent Concepts: the Principle and its Present Day Application* (Strasbourg, Council of Europe, Publishing and Documentation Service, 1990) 61–80.

Spota, GA, 'El abuso del derecho en la legislacion latinoamericana' in M Rotondi (ed), *L'abus de droit* (Padua, CEDAM, 1979) 385–440.

Sunstein, CR, 'Protectionism, the American Supreme Court, and Integrated Markets' in R Bieber et al (eds), *1992: One European Market?* (Baden-Baden, Nomos, 1988) 129.

Swank, D, 'The Effect of Globalization on Taxation, Institutions, and Control of the Macroeconomy' in D Held and AG McGrew (ed), *The Global Transformations Reader: an Introduction to the Globalization Debate*, 2nd edn (Cambridge, Polity Press, 2003) 204–12.

Szyszczak, E, 'State Intervention and the Internal Market' in T Tridimas and P Nebbia (eds), *European Union Law for the Twenty-First Century – Volume 2: Internal Market and Free Movement Community Policies* (Oxford, Hart Publishing, 2004) 217–38.

Tebbens, HD, 'Les Règles de Conflit Contenues dans les Instruments de Droit Dérivé' in A Fuchs et al (eds), *Les Conflits de Lois et le Système Juridique Communautaire* (Paris, Dalloz, 2004) 101–15.

Tercier, P, 'L'abus de droit en droit privé suisse' in M Rotondi (ed), *L'abus de droit* (Padua, CEDAM, 1979) 441–44.

Trachtman, JP, 'Regulatory Competition and Regulatory Jurisdiction in International Securities Regulation' in DC Esty and D Geradin (eds), *Regulatory Competition and Economic Integration: Comparative Perspectives* (Oxford, Oxford University Press, 2001) 289–310.

Triantafyllou, D, 'State Aids and Bankruptcy' in T Tridimas and P Nebbia (eds), *European Union Law for the Twenty-First Century – Volume 2: Internal Market and Free Movement Community Policies* (Oxford, Hart Publishing, 2004) 273–89.

Tridimas, T, 'Abuse of Rights in EU Law: Some Reflections with Particular Reference to Financial Law' in R de la Feria and S Vogenauer (eds), *Prohibition of Abuse of Law: a New General Principle of EU Law?* (Oxford, Hart Publishing, 2011) 169–91.

Tunc, A, 'The French Concept of abus de droit' in NE Eastman and B Krivy (eds), *The Cambridge lectures 1981* (London, Butterworths, 1981) 151–60.

van Vliet, H, 'State Resources and PreussenElektra: When is a State Aid not a State Aid?' in F Santaolalla Gadea (ed), *EC State Aid Law: Liber Amicorum Francisco Santaolalla Gadea* (The Hague, Kluwer Law International, 2008) 65–88.

Vanistendael, F, 'Cadbury Schweppes and Abuse from an EU Tax Law Perspective' in R de la Feria and S Vogenauer (eds), *Prohibition of Abuse of Law: a New General Principle of EU Law?* (Oxford, Hart Publishing, 2011) 407–25.

Vella, J, 'Sparking Regulatory Competition in European Company Law: A Response' in R de la Feria and S Vogenauer (eds), *Prohibition of Abuse of Law: a New General Principle of EU Law?* (Oxford, Hart Publishing, 2011) 127–36.

Verhoeven, J, 'Abus, Fraude ou Habileté?' in J Verhoeven (ed), *La Loyauté: Mélanges offerts à Etienne Cerexhe* (Brussels, Larcier, 1997) 407–25.

Vogel, D, 'Environmental Regulation and Economic Integration' in DC Esty and D Geradin (eds), *Regulatory Competition and Economic Integration: Comparative Perspectives* (Oxford, Oxford University Press, 2001) 330–47.

Vogenauer, S, 'The Prohibition of Abuse of Law: an Emerging General Principle of EU Law' in R de la Feria and S Vogenauer (eds), *Prohibition of Abuse of Law: a New General Principle of EU Law?* (Oxford, Hart Publishing, 2011) 521–71.

Voyame, J, Cottier, B and Rocha, B, 'Abuse of Rights in Comparative Law' in Council of Europe (ed), *Abuse of Rights and Equivalent Concepts: the Principle and its Present Day Application* (Strasbourg, Council of Europe, Publishing and Documentation Service, 1990) 23–56.

Vrellis, S, '"Abus" et "Fraude" dans la Jurisprudence de la Cour de Justice des Communautés Européennes' in H Gaudemet-Tallon and J-P Ancel (eds), *Vers de Nouveaux Equilibres entre Ordres Juridiques: Liber Amicorum Hélène Gaudemet-Tallon* (Paris, Dalloz, 2008) 633–46.

Waelbroeck, D, 'La notion d'abus de droit dans l'ordre juridique communautaire' in J-V Louis et al (eds), *Mélanges en hommage à Jean-Victor Louis* (Brussels, Éditions de l'Université de Bruxelles, 2003) 595–616.

——, 'La notion d'aide d'État dans la jurisprudence récente de la Cour de Justice' in G Vandersanden et al (eds), *Mélanges en hommage à Georges Vandersanden: Promenades au sein du droit européen* (Brussels, Bruylant, 2008) 771–827.

Waelbroeck, M, 'La place de la concurrence dans le Traité de Lisbonne' in G Vandersanden et al (eds), *Mélanges en hommage à Georges Vandersanden: Promenades au sein du droit européen* (Brussels, Bruylant, 2008) 829–41.

Weatherill, S, 'Pre-emption, Harmonisation and the Distribution of Competence to Regulate the Internal Market' in C Barnard and J Scott (eds), *The Law of the Single European Market: Unpacking the Premises* (Oxford, Hart Publishing, 2002) 41–74.

——, 'Why Harmonise?' in T Tridimas and P Nebbia (eds), *European Union Law for the Twenty-First Century – Volume 2: Internal Market and Free Movement Community Policies* (Oxford, Hart Publishing, 2004) 11–32.

——, 'Fitting "Abuse of Rights" into EU Law Governing the Free Movement of Goods and Services' in R de la Feria and S Vogenauer (eds), *Prohibition of Abuse of Law: a New General Principle of EU Law?* (Oxford, Hart Publishing, 2011) 49–61.

Weber, D, 'Abuse of Law in the Context of Indirect Taxation: Why We Need the Subjective Intention Test, When is Combating Abuse an Obligation and Other Comments' in R de la Feria and S Vogenauer (eds), *Prohibition of Abuse of Law: a New General Principle of EU Law?* (Oxford, Hart Publishing, 2011) 395–406.

Weiler, JHH, 'The Constitution of the Common Market Place: Text and Context in the Evolution of the Free Movement of Goods' in PP Craig and G de Búrca (eds), *The Evolution of EU Law* (Oxford, Oxford University Press, 1999) 349–76.

——, 'Mutual Recognition, Functional Equivalence and Harmonization in the Evolution of the European Common Market and the WTO' in FK Padoa-Schioppa (ed), *The Principle of Mutual Recognition in the European Integration Process* (Basingstoke, Palgrave Macmillan, 2005) 25–84.

Whittaker, S, 'Comments on "Abuse of Law" in European Private Law' in R de la Feria and S Vogenauer (eds), *Prohibition of Abuse of Law: a New General Principle of EU Law?* (Oxford, Hart Publishing, 2011) 253–60.

Zeltner, WZ, 'Abuse of Right in Israeli Law' in M Rotondi (ed), *L'abus de droit* (Padua, CEDAM, 1979) 465–80.

Ziegler, KS, '"Abuse of Law" in the Context of the Free Movement of Workers' in R de la Feria and S Vogenauer (eds), *Prohibition of Abuse of Law: a New General Principle of EU Law?* (Oxford, Hart Publishing, 2011) 295–314.

Zonderland, P, 'L'abus de droit et Ie titre introductif du projet de Code civil néerlandais' in M Rotondi (ed), *L'abus de droit* (Padua, CEDAM, 1979) 481–500.

Journal Articles

'Allen v Flood' (1898) 11 *Harvard Law Review* 405.

'State Competition: Panel Response' (1986-87) 8 *Cardozo Law Review* 779.

'Case C-110/99 Emsland' (2001) 3 *Journal de droit européen* 65.

'Les aides d'État sous forme fiscale' (2008) 48 *Revue de Droit Fiscal* 9.

Ackermann, T, 'Case C-148/02 *Garcia Avello* [2003] ECR I-11613' (2007) 44 *Common Market Law Review* 141.

Airs, GJ et al, 'Abuse of Tax Law across Europe – Part One' (2010) 19 *EC Tax Review* 85.

——, 'Abuse of Tax Law across Europe – Part Two' (2010) 19 *EC Tax Review* 123.

Al-Qasem, A, 'The Unlawful Exercise of Rights in the Civil Codes of the Arab Countries of the Middle East' (1990) 39 *The International and Comparative Law Quarterly* 396.

Alderton, T and Winchester, N, 'Globalisation and De-regulation in the Maritime Industry' (2002) 26 *Marine Policy* 35.

Alter, K and Meunier-Aitsahalia, S, 'Judicial Politics in the European Community: European Integration and the Pathbreaking Cassis de Dijon Decision' (1994) 26 *Comparative Political Studies* 535.

Amand, C, 'Prohibition of Abusive Practices in European VAT: Court Aid to National Legislations Bugs?' (2008) 36 *Intertax* 189.

Ames, JB, 'How Far an Act May be a Tort because of the Wrongful Motive of the Actor' (1905) 18 *Harvard Law Review* 411.

Amos, MS, 'Abusive Exercise of Rights According to French Law' (1900) 2 *Journal of the Society of Comparative Legislation* 453.

Anagnostopoulou, D, 'Case C-373/97 *Diamantis*: Do Francovich and the Principle of Proportionality Weaken Simmenthal (II) and Confirm Abuse of Rights?' (2001) 38 *Common Market Law Review* 767.

Anderson, D, 'Abuse of Rights' (2006) 11 *Judicial Review* 348.

Angelette, B, 'The Revolution That Never Came and the Revolution Coming: De Lasteyrie Du Salliant, Marks & Spencer, Sevic Systems and the Changing Corporate Law in Europe' (2006) 92 *Virginia Law Review* 1189.

Armour, J, 'Who Should Make Corporate Law? EC Legislation Versus Regulatory Competition' (2005) 58 *Current Legal Problems* 369.

Armstrong, GMJ and LaMaster, JC, 'Retaliatory Eviction as Abuse of Rights: A Civilian Approach to Landlord-Tenant Disputes' (1986) 47 *Lousiana Law Review* 1.

Arnull, AM, 'Reflections on Judicial Attitudes at the European Court' (1985) 34 *The International and Comparative Law Quarterly* 168.

——, 'The Use and Abuse of Article 177 EEC' (1989) 52 *The Modern Law Review* 622.

——, 'Refurbishing the Judicial Architecture of the European Community' (1994) 43 *The International and Comparative Law Quarterly* 296.

Assonitis, G, 'Les Pavillons de Libre Immatriculation' (1991) 4 *Droit Européen des Transports* 435.

Autenne, A and De Wolf, M, 'La mobilité transfrontalière des sociétés en droit européen: le cas particulier du transfert de siège social' (2007) 5-6 *Cahiers de droit Européen* 647.

—— and Navez, J-E, 'Cartesio – Les contours incertains de la mobilité transfrontalière des sociétés revisités' (2009) 1–2 *Cahiers de droit Européen* 91.

Azoulai, L, 'The Court of Justice and the Social Market Economy: The Emergence of an Ideal and the Conditions for its Realization' (2008) 45 *Common Market Law Review* 1335.
Bacon, K, 'State Aids and General Measures' (1997) *Yearbook of European Law* 269.
Baird, DG and Weisberg, R, 'Rules, Standards, and the Battle of the Forms: A Reassessment of § 2-207' (1982) 68 *Virginia Law Review* 1217.
Balassa, BA, 'Trade Creation and Trade Diversion in the European Common Market' (1967) 77 *The Economic Journal* 1.
Barbou Des Places, S, 'Taking Legal Rules into Consideration: EU Asylum Policy and Regulatory Competition' (2004) 24 *Journal of Public Policy* 75.
Barendt, E, 'Separation of Powers and Constitutional Government' (1995) 95 *Public Law* 599.
Barents, R, 'Community Agricultural Law and the Court's Case Law in 1986-1988' (1989) 26 *Common Market Law Review* 391.
Barnard, C, 'Social Dumping And the Race to the Bottom: Some Lessons for the European Union from Delaware?' (2000) 25 *European Law Review* 57.
——, 'Case C-209/03 Bidar' (2005) 42 *Common Market Law Review* 1465.
——, 'Viking and Laval: An Introduction' (2007-08) 10 *Cambridge Yearbook of European Legal Studies* 463.
——, 'Social Dumping or Dumping Socialism?' (2008) 67 *Cambridge Law Journal* 262.
—— and Deakin, S, 'Negative and Positive Harmonization of Labor Law in the European Union' (2002) 8 *Columbia Journal of European Law* 389.
Basedow, J, 'The Communitarization of the Conflict of Laws under the Treaty of Amsterdam' (2000) 37 *Common Market Law Review* 687.
Bebchuk, L, 'The Desirable Limits in State Competition in Corporate Law' (1992) 105 *Harvard Law Review* 1435.
——, Cohen, A and Ferrell, A, 'Does the Evidence Favor State Competition in Corporate Law?' (2002) 90 *California Law Review* 1775.
Becht, M, Mayer, C and Wagner, HF, 'Where Do Firms Incorporate? Deregulation and the Cost of Entry' (2008) 14 *Journal of Corporate Finance* 241.
Beck, U, 'The Cosmopolitan State: Redefining Power in the Global Age' (2005) 18 *International Journal of Politics, Culture and Society* 143.
Becker, F, 'Case C-386/04, Centro di Musicologia Walter Stauffer' (2007) 44 *Common Market Law Review* 803.
Becker, J and Fuest, C, 'Internationalization and Business Tax Revenue – Evidence from Germany' (2010) 17 *International Tax and Public Finance* 174.
Behar-Touchais, M, 'Abus de puissance économique et droit international privé' (2010) XXIV *Revue internationale de droit économique* 37.
Bell, LL, 'Economic Substance – A New Regulatory Tool or the Kitchen Sink' (2005) 8 *Journal of Retirement Planning* 5.
Bellayer-Roille, A, 'Le Contrôle par l'Etat de Pavillon: vers des Conditions Communautaires d'Immatriculation?' (2007) 25 *Annuaire de Droit Maritime et Océanique* 225.
Benedettelli, MV, 'Conflicts of Jurisdiction and Conflicts of Law in Company Law Matters Within the EU "Market for Corporate Models": Brussels I and Rome I after Centros' (2005) 16 *European Business Law Review* 55.
Berger, A, 'Encyclopedic Dictionary of Roman Law' (1953) 43 *Transactions of the American Philosophical Society* 333.
Besley, T et al, 'The Effects and Policy Implications of State Aids to Industry: An Economic Analysis' (1999) 14 *Economic Policy* 13.

Birkmose, HS, 'Regulatory Competition and the European Harmonisation Process' (2006) 17 *European Business Law Review* 1075.

Block, W, 'Hayek's Road To Serfdom' (1996) 12 *Journal of Libertarian Studies* 339.

Bloomfield, AI, 'On the Centenary of Jacob Viner's Birth: A Retrospective View of the Man and His Work' (1992) 30 *Journal of Economic Literature* 2052.

Bolgar, V, 'Abuse of Rights in France, Germany and Switzerland' (1975) 35 *Lousiana Law Review* 1015.

Bouckaert, B and Geest, GD, 'Private Takings, Private Taxes, Private Compulsory Services: The Economic Doctrine of Quasi Contracts' (1995) 15 *International Review of Law and Economics* 463.

Bousin, J and Piernas, J, 'Developments in the Notion of Selectivity' (2008) *European State Aid Law Quarterly* 634.

Braakman, G, 'Monetary Evolutions and the Common Agricultural Policy' (1978) 15 *Common Market Law Review* 157.

Braithwaite, J, 'Rules and Principles: A Theory of Legal Certainty' (2002) 27 *Australian Journal of Legal Philosophy* 47.

Bratton, WW and McCahery, JA, 'Tax Coordination and Tax Competition in the European Union: Evaluating the Code of Conduct on Business Taxation' (2001) 38 *Common Market Law Review* 677.

Brevik, F and Gärtner, M, 'Can Tax Evasion Tame Leviathan Governments?' (2008) 136 *Public Choice* 103.

Brunner, CJH, 'Abuse of Rights in Dutch Law' (1977) 37 *Louisiana Law Review* 729–46.

Buchanan, JM, 'Federalism and Fiscal Equity' (1950) 40 *American Economic Review* 583.

Buigues, P-A and Sekkat, K, 'Public Subsidies to Business: An International Comparison' (2010) *Journal of Industry, Competition and Trade* 1.

Burgio, 'The Abuse of Law in the Framework of the European Tax Law' (1991) 19 *Intertax* 82.

Byers, M, 'Abuse of Rights: An Old Principle, A New Age' (2002) 47 *McGill Law Journal* 389.

Cameron, LA and Berg, GC, 'The U.S. Countervailing Duty Law and the Principle of General Availability' (1985) 19 *Journal of World Trade Law* 497.

Cannizzaro, E, 'Producing "Reverse Discrimination" Through the Exercise of EC Competences' (1997) 17 *Yearbook of European Law* 29.

Carlier, J-Y, 'Case C-200/02 *Zhu and Chen* [2004] ECR I-9925' (2005) 42 *Common Market Law Review* 1121.

——, 'La libre circulation des personnes dans l'Union européenne (1er janvier – 31 décembre 2004)' (2005) 3 *Journal de droit européen* 71.

——, 'Le devenir de la libre circulation des personnes dans l'Union européenne: regard sur la directive 2004/38' (2006) 1-2 *Cahiers de droit Européen* 13.

Carney, WJ, 'The Political Economy of Competition for Corporate Charters' (1997) 26 *Journal of Legal Studies* 303.

Carruthers, J and Villiers, C, 'Company Law in Europe – Condoning the Continental Drift' (2000) 11 *European Business Law Review* 91.

Carstensen, PC and Roth, B, 'The Per Se Legality of Some Naked Restraints: A [Re]conceptualization of the Antitrust Analysis of Cartelistic Organizations' (2000) 45 *Antitrust Bulletin* 349.

Cary, WL, 'Federalism and Corporate Law: Reflections upon Delaware' (1974) 83 *Yale Law Journal* 663.

Catala, P and Weir, JA, 'Delict and Torts: A Study in Parallel – Part II' (1964) 38 *Tulane Law Review* 221.
Cerioni, L, 'The "Überseering" Ruling: the Eve of a "Revolution" for the Possibilities of Companies' Migration throughout the European Community?' (2003) 10 *Columbia Journal of European Law* 117.
——, 'The "Abuse of Rights" in EU Company Law and EU Tax Law: A Re-reading of the ECJ Case Law and the Quest for a Unitary Notion' (2010) 21 *European Business Law Review* 783.
Cerny, PG, 'Paradoxes of the Competition State: The Dynamics of Political Globalization' (1997) 32 *Government and Opposition* 251.
Chalmers, D, 'Free Movement of Goods within the European Community: An Unhealthy Addiction to Scotch Whisky?' (1993) 42 *The International and Comparative Law Quarterly* 269.
——, 'Judicial Preferences and the Community Legal Order' (1997) 60 *The Modern Law Review* 164.
Charny, D, 'Competition among Jurisdictions in Formulating Corporate Law Rules: An American Perspective on the Race to the Bottom in the European Union' (1991) 32 *Harvard International Law Journal* 423.
——, 'Regulatory Competition and the Global Coordination of Labor Standards' (2000) 3 *Journal of International Economic Law* 281.
Charvet, L, 'La Sidérurgie Française Devant le "Pool"' (1951) 16-17 *Nouvelle Revue de l'Economie Contemporaine* 36.
Chaumette, P, 'Le contrôle des navires par les Etats riverains' (1999) 35 *Cahiers Scientifiques du Transport* 55.
——, 'Les marins sont-ils encore à bord?' (2005) 23 *Annuaire de Droit Maritime et Océanique* 179.
—— and Proutière Maulion, G, 'Quota-hopping et appropriation des ressources halieutiques' (2005) 23 *Annuaire de Droit Maritime et Océanique* 309.
Chautard, S, 'Colloque de l'IFM: Le Pavillon National' (2001) 5 *Défense Nationale* 81.
Chen, R and Hanson, J, 'The Illusion of Law: The Legitimating Schemas of Modern Policy and Corporate Law' (2004) 103 *Michigan Law Review* 1.
—— and Hanson, J, 'Categorically Biased: The Influence of Knowledge Structures on Law and Legal Theory' (2004) 77 *US California Law Review* 1103.
Cheyne, I, 'The Definition of Waste in EC Law' (2002) 14 *Journal of Environmental Law* 61.
Chirelstein, MA and Zelenak, LA, 'Tax Shelters and the Search for a Silver Bullet' (2005) 105 *Columbia Law Review* 1939.
Churchill, RR, 'Quota Hopping: the Common Fisheries Policy Wrongfooted?' (1990) 27 *Common Market Law Review* 209.
——, 'European Community Law and the Nationality of Ships and Crews' (1991) 5 *European Transport Law* 591.
Cohn, EJ and Simitis, C, "'Lifting the Veil' in the Company Laws of the European Continent" (1963) 12 *The International and Comparative Law Quarterly* 189.
Conant, L, 'When Courts Decide: Foreigners' Rights and Social Citizenship in Europe and the US' (2008) 7 *European Political Science* 43.
Cordewener, A, Kofler, G and Van Thiel, S, 'The Clash Between European Freedoms and National Direct Tax Law: Public Interest Defences Available to the Member States' (2009) 46 *Common Market Law Review* 1951.

Cornut, E, 'Forum shopping et abus du choix de for en droit international privé' (2007) 134 *Journal de Droit International* 27.

Costello, C, 'Market Access All Areas – The Treatment of Non-discriminatory Barriers to the Free Movement of Workers' (2000) 27 *Legal Issues of Economic Integration* 267.

——, 'Metock: Free Movement and "Normal Family Life" in the Union' (2009) 46 *Common Market Law Review* 587.

Cozian, M, 'What is Abuse of Law?' (1991) 19 *Intertax* 103.

Crabb, JH, 'The French Concept of Abuse of Rights' (1964) 6 *Inter-American Law Review* 1.

Craig, PP, 'Once upon a Time in the West: Direct Effect and the Federalization of EEC Law' (1992) 12 *Oxford Journal of Legal Studies* 453.

——, 'Pringle: Legal Reasoning, Text, Purpose and Teleology' (2013) 20 *Maastricht Journal of European and Comparative Law* 3.

Cruz, N, 'Abuse of Rights in Title VII Cases: The Emerging Doctrine' (1981) 67 *American Bar Association Journal* 1472.

Cueto-Rua, J, 'Abuse of Rights' (1975) 35 *Lousiana Law Review* 965.

D'Amato, A, 'Legal Uncertainty' (1983) 71 *California Law Review* 1.

Dalimov, RT, 'The Dynamics of Trade Creation and Trade Diversion Effects Under International Economic Integration' (2009) 1 *Current Research Journal of Economic Theory* 1.

Dammann, JC, 'Freedom of Choice in European Corporate Law' (2004) 29 *Yale Journal of International Law* 477.

Danby, GA, 'The Use and Abuse of Rights' (1985) 12 *Journal of Law and Society* 375.

Dashwood, A, 'Viking and Laval: Issues of Horizontal Direct Effect' (2007-08) 10 *Cambridge Yearbook of European Legal Studies* 525.

Dautricourt, C and Thomas, S, 'Reverse Discrimination and Free Movement Of Persons under Community Law: All for Ulysses, Nothing for Penelope?' (2009) 34 *European Law Review* 433.

Davies, G, 'The High Water Point of Free Movement of Persons: Ending Benefit Tourism and Rescuing Welfare' (2004) 26 *Journal of Social Welfare and Family Law* 211.

Davies, P, 'Market Integration and Social Policy in the Court of Justice' (1995) 24 *Industrial Law Journal* 49.

de Baere, G, '"Is this a Conflict Rule which I see Before Me?" Looking for a Hidden Conflict Rule in the Principle of Origin as Implemented in Primary European Community Law and in the "Directive on Electronic Commerce"' (2004) 11 *Maastricht Journal of European and Comparative Law* 287.

de Cecco, F, 'Room to Move? Minimum Harmonization and Fundamental Rights' (2006) 43 *Common Market Law Review* 9.

De Cet Bertin, C, 'Bribes Jurisprudentielles Communautaires de Droit International Privé Maritime' (2005) 23 *Annuaire de Droit Maritime et Océanique* 109.

De Geest, G et al, 'Cass. fr. 15.12.1998, Enrichissement Sans Cause' (2000) 8 *European Review of Private Law* 613.

de Kluiver, H-J, 'Inspiring a New European Company Law?' (2004) 1 *European Company and Financial Law Review* 121.

de la Feria, R, 'The European Court of Justice's Solution to Aggressive VAT Planning – Further towards Legal Uncertainty?' (2006) 15 *EC Tax Review* 27.

——, 'Prohibition of Abuse of (Community) Law: the Creation of a New General Principle of EC Law through Tax' (2008) 45 *Common Market Law Review* 395.

de Vivero, JLS, 'The European Vision for Oceans and Seas – Social and Political Dimensions of the Green Paper on Maritime Policy for the EU' (2007) 31 *Marine Policy* 409.
—— and Mateos, JCR, 'Ocean Governance in a Competitive World. The BRIC Countries as Emerging Maritime Powers – Building New Geopolitical Scenarios' (2010) 34 *Marine Policy* 967.
De Vos, M, 'European Flexicurity and Globalization: A Critical Perspective' (2009) 25 *International Journal of Comparative Labour Law and Industrial Relations* 209.
Deakin, S, 'Two Types of Regulatory Competition: Competitive Federalism versus Reflexive Harmonisation' (1999) 2 *Cambridge Yearbook of European Legal Studies* 231.
——, 'Reinventing the Market? Competition and Regulatory Change in Broadcasting' (1999) 26 *Journal of Law and Society* 323.
——, 'Legal Diversity and Regulatory Competition: Which Model for Europe?' (2006) 12 *European Law Journal* 440.
——, 'Is Regulatory Competition the Future for European Integration?' (2006) 13 *Swedish Economic Policy Review* 71.
——, 'Regulatory Competition after Laval' (2007-08) 10 *Cambridge Yearbook of European Legal Studies* 581.
——, 'Reflexive Governance and European Company Law' (2009) 15 *European Law Journal* 224.
—— and Wilkinson, F, 'Rights vs Efficiency? The Economic Case for Transnational Labour Standards' (1994) 23 *Industrial Law Journal* 289.
Denning, A, 'The Need for a New Equity' (1952) 5 *Current Legal Problems* 1.
Devereux, MP and Griffith, R, 'The Impact of Corporate Taxation on the Location of Capital: A Review' (2002) 9 *Swedish Economic Policy Review* 79.
Devine, DJ, 'Some Comparative Aspects of the Doctrine of Abuse of Rights' (1964) *Acta Juridica* 148.
di Robilant, A, 'Abuse of Rights: the Continental Drug and the Common Law' (2010) 61 *Hastings Law Journal* 687.
Díaz Mora, C, 'The Role of Comparative Advantage in Trade within Industries: A Panel Data Approach for the European Union' (2002) 138 *Weltwirtschaftliches Archiv* 291.
Dobson, JM, '"Lifting the Veil" in Four Countries: The Law of Argentina, England, France and the United States' (1986) 35 *The International and Comparative Law Quarterly* 839.
Donsimoni, P, 'Suisse: développements en matière de fiscalité internationale – La problématique des paradis fiscaux' (2010) 8 *Droit fiscal* 207.
dos Santos, AC, 'Aides d'État, Code de Conduite et Concurrence Fiscale dans l'Union Européenne' (2004) XVIII *Revue internationale de droit économique* 9.
Dougan, M, 'Minimum Harmonization and the Internal Market' (2000) 37 *Common Market Law Review* 853.
——, 'Free Movement: The Workseeker as Citizen' (2001) 4 *Cambridge Yearbook of European Legal Studies* 93.
——, 'Cross-border Educational Mobility and the Exportation of Student Financial Assistance' (2008) 33 *European Law Review* 723.
——, 'The Treaty Of Lisbon 2007: Winning Minds, Not Hearts' (2008) 45 *Common Market Law Review* 617.
Drexl, J, 'La Constitution économique européenne – L'actualité du modèle ordoliberal' (2011) XXV *Revue internationale de droit économique* 419.
Driguez, L, 'Reconnaissance mutuelle des diplômes' (2008) 12 *Europe* 412.

Drukker, RT, 'Spite Fences and Spite Wells: Relevancy of Motive in the Relations of Adjoining Landowners' (1938) 26 *California Law Review* 691.
Dworkin, RM, 'Judicial Discretion' (1963) 60 *The Journal of Philosophy* 624.
——, 'The Model of Rules' (1967) 35 *The University of Chicago Law Review* 14.
——, 'Hard Cases' (1975) 88 *Harvard Law Review* 1057.
——, 'Constitutionalism and Democracy' (1995) 3 *European Journal of Philosophy* 2.
Ebke, WF, 'Centros – Some Realities and Some Mysteries' (2000) 48 *The American Journal of Comparative Law* 623.
——, 'The European Conflict-of-Corporate-Laws Revolution: Überseering, Inspire Art and Beyond' (2005) 16 *European Business Law Review* 9.
Editorial, 'Two-speed European Citizenship? Can the Lisbon Treaty Help Close the Gap?' (2008) 45 *Common Market Law Review* 1.
Ehlermann, CD, 'Compétition entre Systèmes Réglementaires' (1995) 387 *Revue du Marché Commun et de L'Union Européenne* 220.
Elkind, JB, 'Footnote to the Nuclear Test Cases: Abuse of Right – A Blind Alley for Environmentalists' (1976) 9 *Vand. J. Transnat'l L.* 57.
Enchelmaier, S and Oliver, P, 'Free Movement of Goods: Recent Developments in the Case Law' (2007) 44 *Common Market Law Review* 649.
Englisch, J, 'Taxation of Cross-Border Dividends and EC Fundamental Freedoms' (2010) 38 *Intertax* 197.
Enrich, P, 'Saving the States from Themselves: Commerce Clause Constraints on State Tax Incentives for Business' (1996) 110 *Harvard Law Review* 377.
Esty, DC and Geradin, D, 'Regulatory Co-Opetition' (2000) 3 *Journal of International Economic Law* 235.
Evans, AE, 'Case Concerning the Barcelona Traction, Light and Power Company, Limited (Belgium v Spain), Second Phase' (1970) 64 *The American Journal of International Law* 653.
Evers, M and de Graaf, A, 'Limiting Benefit Shopping: Use and Abuse of EC Law' (2009) 18 *EC Tax Review* 279.
Fahey, E, 'Going Back to Basics: Re-embracing the Fundamentals of the Free Movement of Persons in Metock' (2009) 36 *Legal Issues of Economic Integration* 83.
Fallon, M, 'Les conflits de lois et de jurisictions dans un espace economique integré: l'expérience de la Communauté Européenne' (1995) 253 *Recueil des Cours de l'Académie de Droit International* 9.
Fawcett, JJ, 'Evasion of Law and Mandatory Rules in Private International Law' (1990) 49 *Cambridge Law Journal* 44.
Fernoux, P, 'Abus de droit: revisitons le passé à l'aune de la nouvelle définition' (2010) 49 *Droit fiscal* 584.
Filios, CP, 'Unjustified Enrichment Based on Interference With Another's Property in French and Greek Legal Order – The Specific Problem of the Requirement 'At the Expense of Another' (2006) 14 *European Review of Private Law* 327.
Fletcher, GP, 'The Right and the Reasonable' (1985) 98 *Harvard Law Review* 949.
——, 'Law and Morality: A Kantian Perspective' (1987) 87 *Columbia Law Review* 533.
Foster, H, 'Abuse of Rights – Civil Law – Legal Reasoning: Bradford v Pickles Revisited' (1973) 8 *University of British Columbia Law Review* 343.
Fotinopoulou Basurko, O, 'Reflexiones acerca de la ley del pabellon como criterio de conexion conflictual a efectos de la determinacion de la ley aplicable al contracto de embarque' (2006) 24 *Annuaire de Droit Maritime et Océanique* 261.

Fougner, T, 'The State International Competitiveness and Neoliberal Globalisation: is There a Future Beyond "the Competition State"?' (2006) 32 *Review of International Studies* 165.

Fouquet, O, 'Fraude à la loi et abus de droit' (2006) 47 *Droit fiscal* 65.

Francis, D, 'Exclusion, Invasion and Abuse: Competition Law and its Constitutional Context' (2009–10) 12 *Cambridge Yearbook of European Legal Studies* 183.

Freedman, J, 'Converging Tracks? Recent Developments in Canadian and UK Approaches to Tax Avoidance' (2005) 53 *Canadian Tax Journal* 1038.

——, 'Improving (Not Perfecting) Tax Legislation: Rules and Principles Revisited' (2010) *British Tax Review* 717.

Fridman, GHL, 'Motive in the English Law of Nuisance' (1954) 40 *Virginia Law Review* 583.

Friedmann, D, 'Unjust Enrichment, Pursuance of Self-Interest, and the Limits of Free Riding' (2002–03) 36 *Loyola of Los Angeles Law Review* 831.

Friedmann, W, 'The Uses of "General Principles" in the Development of International Law' (1963) 57 *The American Journal of International Law* 279.

Frommel, SN, 'United Kingdom Tax Law and Abuse of Rights' (1991) 19 *Intertax* 54.

Fuller, LL, 'Positivism and Fidelity to Law: A Reply to Professor Hart' (1958) 71 *Harvard Law Review* 630.

Fumenier, P, 'Délocalisations: difficultés posées par l'arrêt de la fabrication en France des produits d'un groupe étranger' (2010) 49 *La Semaine Juridique Entreprise et Affaires* 2095.

Gabor, B, 'Restructurations et Interaction entre Politiques Sociales et Fiscales Nationales: une Réponse Européenne au Dumping Social?' (2008) XXII *Revue internationale de droit économique* 247.

Gambaro, A, 'Abuse of Rights in Civil Law Tradition' (1995) 4 *European Review of Private Law* 561.

Ganesh, AR, 'Appointing Foxes to Guard Henhouses: the European Posted Workers' Directive' (2008) 15 *Columbia Journal of European Law* 123.

Garbarino, C, 'The Development of a Judicial Anti-Abuse Principle in Italy' (2009) 2 *British Tax Review* 186.

Garcia, D, 'Are There Reasons to Convert Reverse Discrimination into a Prohibited Measure?' (2009) 18 *EC Tax Review* 179.

Garcia-Riestra, M, 'The Transfer of Seat of the European Company v Free Establishment Case-Law' (2004) 15 *European Business Law Review* 1295.

Gardner, J, 'Legal Positivism: 5 1/2 Myths' (2001) 46 *American Journal of Jurisprudence* 199.

Gardner, LI, 'An Elephant in the Room: Double Deductions and the Economic Substance Doctrine in Coltec Industries, Inc. v U.S.' (2006–07) 60 *Tax Lawyer* 519.

Gaudemet-Tallon, H, 'Le pluralisme en droit international privé: richesses et faiblesses (Le funambule et l'arc-en-ciel)' (2005) 312 *Recueil des Cours de l'Académie de Droit International* 9.

Gautier, M, 'Cour de justice, 19 octobre 2004, Kunqian Catherine Zhu et Man Lavette Chen c/ Secretary of State for the Home Department' (2003-04) 4 *Revue des affaires européennes* 673.

Genschel, P, 'Why No Mutual Recognition of VAT? Regulation, Taxation and the Integration of the EU's Internal Market for Goods' (2007) 14 *Journal of European Public Policy* 743.

—— Kemmerling, A and Seils, E, 'Accelerating Downhill: How the EU Shapes Corporate Tax Competition in the Single Market' (2011) 49 *Journal of Common Market Studies* 585.

Gerber, DJ, 'Law and the Abuse of Economic Power in Europe' (1987–88) 62 *Tulane Law Review* 57.
——, 'The Origins of European Competition Law in Fin-de-Siècle Austria' (1992) 36 *American Journal of Legal History* 405.
——, 'Constitutionalizing the Economy: German Neo-Liberalism, Competition Law and the "New" Europe' (1994) 42 *American Journal of Comparative Law* 25.
Ghinamo, M, Panteghini, PM and Revelli, F, 'FDI Determination and Corporate Tax Competition in a Volatile World' (2010) 17 *International Tax Public Finance* 532.
Gibbons, T, 'The Impact of Regulatory Competition on Measures to Promote Pluralism and Cultural Diversity in the Audiovisual Sector' (2006-2007) 9 *Cambridge Yearbook of European Legal Studies* 239.
Golynker, O, 'Jobseekers' Rights in the European Union: Challenges of Changing the Paradigm of Social Solidarity' (2005) 30 *European Law Review* 111.
——, 'Analysis and Reflections – Student Loans: The European Concept of Social Justice According to Bidar' (2006) 31 *European Law Review* 390.
González Laxe, F, 'Dysfunctions in Common Fishing Regulations' (2010) 34 *Marine Policy* 182.
Graetz, MJ and Warren, AC, Jr, 'Income Tax Discrimination and the Political and Economic Integration of Europe' (2006) 115 *Yale Law Journal* 1186.
—— and Warren, AC, Jr, 'Dividend Taxation in Europe: When the ECJ Makes Tax Policy' (2007) 44 *Common Market Law Review* 1577.
——, Warren, AC, Jr and Yablon, R, 'From the Court's Docket: DaimlerChrysler Corp. v Cuno and the European Experience' (2005) 115 *Yale Law Journal Pocket Part* 99.
Grauberg, T, 'Anti-tax-avoidance Measures and Their Compliance with Community Law' (2009) XVI *Juridica International* 141.
Graveson, R, 'The Doctrine of Evasion of the Law in England and America' (1937) 19 *Journal of Comparative Legislation and International Law* 21.
Green, SP, 'What is Wrong with Tax Evasion?' (2009) 9 *Houston Business and Tax Law Journal* 220.
Greenfield, K, 'Democracy and the Dominance of Delaware in Corporate Law' (2004) 67 *Law and Contemporary Problems* 135.
Griffith, WH, 'Allen v Flood: In Roman Law' (1899) 1 *Journal of the Society of Comparative Legislation* 309.
Gruber, J and Saez, E, 'The Elasticity of Taxable Income: Evidence and Implications' (2002) 84 *Journal of Public Economics* 1.
Gunn, A, 'Tax Avoidance' (1978) 76 *Michigan Law Review* 733.
Gutteridge, HC, 'Abuse of Rights' (1933–35) 5 *Cambridge Law Journal* 22.
Hailbronner, K, 'Union Citizenship and Access to Social Benefits' (2005) 42 *Common Market Law Review* 1245.
Handl, G, 'Territorial Sovereignty and the Problem of Transnational Pollution' (1975) 69 *The American Journal of International Law* 50.
Hansen, JL, 'A New Look at Centros – From a Danish Point of View' (2002) 13 *European Business Law Review* 85.
Hansen, LH, 'The Development of the Circumvention Principle in the Area of Broadcasting' (1998) 25 *Legal Issues of European Integration* 111.
Hanson, J and Yosifon, D, 'The Situation: an Introduction to the Situational Character, Critical Realism, Power Economics, and Deep Capture' (2003) 152 *University of Pennsylvania Law Review* 129.

Harbo, T-I, 'The Function of the Proportionality Principle in EU Law' (2010) 16 *European Law Journal* 158.

Hariton, DP, 'When and How Should the Economic Substance Doctrine be Applied?' (2006–07) 60 *Tax Law Review* 29.

Hart, HLA, 'Positivism and the Separation of Law and Morals' (1958) 71 *Harvard Law Review* 593.

Hatcher, A et al, 'Quota-hopping and the Foreign Ownership of UK Fishing Vessels' (2002) 26 *Marine Policy* 1.

Hatzopoulos, V, 'Que reste-t-il de la Directive sur les Services?' (2007) 43 *Cahiers de droit Européen* 299.

——, 'Assessing the Services Directive' (2007–08) 10 *Cambridge Yearbook of European Legal Studies* 215.

——, 'Le principe de reconnaissance mutuelle dans la libre prestation des services' (2010) 46 *Cahiers de droit Européen* 47.

Heine, K and Kerber, W, 'European Corporate Laws, Regulatory Competition and Path Dependence' (2004) 13 *European Journal of Law and Economics* 47.

Héritier, A, 'Mutual Recognition: Comparing Policy Areas' (2007) 14 *Journal of European Public Policy* 800.

Herman, S, 'Classical Social Theories and the Doctrine of Abuse of Right' (1977) 37 *Louisiana Law Review* 747.

Hertig, G, 'Regulatory Competition for EU Financial Services' (2000) 3 *Journal of International Economic Law* 349.

Hins, W, 'Case C-148/91 Veronica Omroep Organisatie [1993] ECR I-487' (1994) 31 *Common Market Law Review* 901.

Hirschman, AO, 'Exit, Voice, and the State' (1978) 31 *World Politics* 90.

Hirt, HC, 'Freedom of Establishment, International Company Law and the Comparison of European Company Law Systems after the ECJ's Decision in Inspire Art Ltd' (2004) 15 *European Business Law Review* 1189.

HJI Panayi, C, 'Corporate Mobility in Private International Law and European Community Law: Debunking Some Myths' (2009) 28 *Yearbook of European Law* 123.

Holmes, OW, Jr, 'Privilege, Malice, and Intent' (1894) 8 *Harvard Law Review* 1.

——, 'The Path of the Law' (1897) 110 *Harvard Law Review* 991.

Holmes, TJ, 'Analyzing a Proposal to Ban State Tax Breaks to Businesses' (1995) 19 *Federal Reserve Bank of Minneapolis Quarterly Review* 29.

Holst, C, 'European Company Law After Centros: is the EU on the Road to Delaware?' (2002) 8 *Columbia Journal of European Law* 323.

Holzinger, K and Sommerer, T, '"Race to the Bottom" or "Race to Brussels"? Environmental Competition in Europe' (2011) 49 *Journal of Common Market Studies* 315.

Hood, J and Freeze, A, 'Stop the State Bidding Wars for Big Business' (1994) 68 *Policy Review* 62.

Horst, T, 'A Note on the Optimal Taxation of International Investment Income' (1980) 94 *The Quarterly Journal of Economics* 793.

Idot, L, 'Cabotage et contournement de la loi de l'État d'accueil' (2006) 6 *Europe* 196.

Iyer, V, 'Cuno v DaimlerChrysler, Inc.: Dormant Commerce Clause Limits State Location Tax Incentives' (2005) 40 *Harvard Civil Rights-Civil Liberties Law Review* 523.

Jackel, MA, 'Dawn of a New Era: Congress Codifies Economic Substance' (2010) 127 *Tax Notes* 289.

Jacobs, FG, 'Citizenship of the European Union – A Legal Analysis' (2007) 13 *European Law Journal* 591.

Joerges, C, 'Que reste-t-il de la Constitution économique européenne après la constitutionnalisation de l'Europe? – Une rétrospective mélancolique' (2005) 1 *Cahiers Européens de Sciences Po* 1.
—— and Rödl, F, 'Informal Politics, Formalised Law and the "Social Deficit" of European Integration: Reflections after the Judgments of the ECJ in Viking and Laval' (2009) 15 *European Law Journal* 1.
Johnson, EL, 'Abuse of Rights in Soviet Civil Law' (1960) 1 *The Solicitor Quarterly* 320.
Johnston, A and Syrpis, P, 'Regulatory Competition in European Company Law after Cartesio' (2009) 34 *European Law Review* 378.
Jones, JM, 'The Nottebohm Case' (1956) 5 *The International and Comparative Law Quarterly* 230.
Józon, Mn, 'The Enlarged EU and Mandatory Requirements' (2005) 11 *European Law Journal* 549.
Kaczorowska, A, 'Gourmet Can Have His Keck and Eat It!' (2004) 10 *European Law Journal* 479.
Kahan, M and Kamar, E, 'The Myth of State Competition in Corporate Law' (2002) 55 *Stanford Law Review* 679.
Kamar, E, 'A Regulatory Competition Theory of Indeterminacy in Corporate Law' (1998) 98 *Columbia Law Review* 1908.
Kammas, P, 'Strategic Fiscal Interaction among OECD Countries' (2010) 148 *Public Choice* 459.
Kan, A, 'Commission v Netherlands, Case C-299/02' (2005) 99 *The American Journal of International Law* 867.
Kaplow, L, 'Rules versus Standards: An Economic Analysis' (1992) 42 *Duke Law Journal* 557.
Karayannis, VS, 'L'abus des droits découlant de l'ordre juridique communautaire à propos de l'arrêt C-367/96 Kefalas' (1999) 35 *Cahiers de droit Européen* 521.
Karimeri, R, 'A Critical Review of the Definition of Tax Avoidance in the Case Law of the European Court of Justice' (2011) 39 *Intertax* 296.
Kaye, TA, 'The Gentle Art of Corporate Seduction: Tax Incentives in the United States and the European Union' (2008) 57 *Kansas Law Review* 93.
Kazzi, H, 'Aides d'Etat et Compétitivité des Entreprises Communautaires' (2007) XXI *Revue internationale de droit économique* 441.
Keinan, Y, 'It is time for the Supreme Court to Voice its Opinion on Economic Substance' (2006-07) 7 *Houston Business & Tax Lax Journal* 93.
Kennedy, D, 'Form and Substance in Private Law Adjudication' (1976) 89 *Harvard Law Review* 1685.
Kenney, SJ, 'Référendaires at the European Court of Justice and Law Clerks at the U.S. Beyond Principals and Agents: Seeing Courts As Organizations by Comparing Référendaires at the European Court of Justice and Law Clerks at the U.S. Supreme Court' (2000) 33 *Comparative Political Studies* 593.
Kerber, W, 'Interjurisdictional Competition within the European Union' (1999–2000) 23 *Fordham International Law Journal* 217.
—— and Van den Bergh, R, 'Mutual Recognition Revisited: Misunderstandings, Inconsistencies, and a Suggested Reinterpretation' (2008) 61 *Kyklos* 447.
Kiekebeld, B, 'Anti-abuse in the Field of Taxation: Is There One Overall Concept?' (2009) *EC Tax Review* 144.
Kilpatrick, C, 'Laval's Regulatory Conundrum: Collective Standard-Setting and the Court's New Approach to Posted Workers' (2009) 34 *European Law Review* 844.

Kirchner, C and Painter, RW, 'Takeover Defenses under Delaware Law, the Proposed Thirteenth EU Directive and the New German Takeover Law: Comparison and Recommendations for Reform' (2002) 50 *The American Journal of Comparative Law* 451.

——, Painter, RW and Kaal, WA, 'Regulatory Competition in EU Corporate Law after Inspire Art: Unbundling Delaware's Product for Europe' (2005) 2 *European Company and Financial Law Review* 159.

Kirschenbaum, A, 'Jewish Law and the Abuse of Rights' (1980–82) 5 *Tel Aviv University Studies in Law* 98.

Kjellgren, A, 'On the Border of Abuse – The Jurisprudence of the European Court of Justice on Circumvention, Fraud and Other Misuses of Community Law' (2000) 11 *European Business Law Review* 179.

Klinke, U, 'European Company Law and the ECJ: The Court's Judgements in the Years 2001 to 2004' (2005) 2 *ECFR* 270.

Korving, J et al, 'ECJ AG Kokott Opines on Anti-Abuse Provisions of EC Merger Directive' (2007) 35 *Intertax* 294.

Kramer, J-D, 'Abuse of Law by Tax Saving Devices' (1991) 19 *Intertax* 96.

Kübler, F, 'A Shifting Paradigm of European Company Law?' (2005) 11 *Columbia Journal of European Law* 219.

Kuehrer, N, 'Cross-border Company Establishment' (2001) 12 *European Business Law Review* 110.

Kunz, JL, 'The Nottebohm Judgment' (1960) 54 *The American Journal of International Law* 536.

Kurcz, B and Vallindas, D, 'Can General Measures be... Selective? Some Thoughts on the Interpretation of a State Aid Definition' (2008) 45 *Common Market Law Review* 159.

Kuyper, PJ, 'European Community Law and Extraterritoriality: Some Trends and New Developments' (1984) 33 *The International and Comparative Law Quarterly* 1013.

Lagondet, F, 'L'abus de droit dans la jurisprudence communautaire' (2003) 1 *Journal de droit européen* 8.

Latty, ER, 'Pseudo-Foreign Corporations' (1955) 65 *Yale Law Journal* 137.

Lauterfeld, M, '"Centros" and the EC Regulation on Insolvency Proceedings' (2001) 12 *European Business Law Review* 79.

Lavenex, S, 'Mutual Recognition and the Monopoly of Force: Limits of the Single Market Analogy' (2007) 14 *Journal of European Public Policy* 762.

Lawson, FH, 'Notes on the History of Tort in the Civil Law' (1940) 22 *Journal of Comparative Legislation and International Law* 136.

Leibrecht, M, Klien, M and Onaran, O, 'Globalization, Welfare Regimes and Social Protection Expenditures in Western and Eastern European Countries' (2010) 148 *Public Choice* 569.

Lenaerts, A, 'The General Principle of the Prohibition of Abuse of Rights: A Critical Position on Its Role in a Codified European Contract Law' (2010) 18 *European Review of Private Law* 1121.

Lenaerts, K, 'Some Reflections on the Separation of Powers in the European Community' (1991) 28 *Common Market Law Review* 11.

——, 'Federalism: Essential Concepts in Evolution – The Case of European Union' (1997–98) 21 *Fordham International Law Journal* 746.

——, 'The Rule of Law and Coherence of the Judicial System of the European Union' (2007) 44 *Common Market Law Review* 1625.

—— and Bernardeau, L, 'L'Encadrement Communautaire de la Fiscalité Directe' (2007) 43 *Cahiers de droit Européen* 19.

—— and Gutiérrez-Fons, JA, 'The Constitutional Allocation of Powers and General Principles of EU Law' (2010) 47 *Common Market Law Review* 1629.

Lequesne, C, 'Quota Hopping: The Common Fisheries Policy Between States and Markets' (2000) 38 *Journal of Common Market Studies* 779.

Lever, J, 'EU State Aid Law – Not a Pretty Sight' (2013) *European State Aid Law Quarterly* 5.

Lewis, O, 'Advancing Legal Capacity Jurisprudence' (2011) 6 *European Human Rights Law Review* 700.

Lipsey, RG, 'The Theory of Customs Unions: Trade Diversion and Welfare' (1957) 24 *Economica* 40.

——, 'The Theory of Customs Unions: A General Survey' (1960) 70 *The Economic Journal* 496.

Lissitzyn, OJ, 'Nottebohm Case (Liechtenstein v Guatemala)' (1955) 49 *The American Journal of International Law* 396.

Littlewood, M, 'Tax Competition: Harmful to Whom?' (2005) 26 *Michigan Journal of International Law* 411.

Llorens, AA, 'The European Court of Justice, More Than a Teleological Court' (1999–2000) 2 *Cambridge Yearbook of European Legal Studies* 373.

Looijestijn-Clearie, A, 'Centros Ltd: A Complete U-Turn in the Right of Establishment for Companies?' (2000) 49 *The International and Comparative Law Quarterly* 621.

Lopez, C, 'L'Harmonisation Fiscale: un Elan ou une Limite à la Construction Européenne?' (2000) 61 *Petites Affiches* 5.

MacDonald, G, 'Substance, Form and Equity in Taxation and Accounting' (1991) 54 *The Modern Law Review* 830.

Maduro, MP, 'Reforming the Market or the State? Article 30 and the European Constitution: Economic Freedom and Political Rights' (1997) 3 *European Law Journal* 55.

Maduro, MP, 'Harmony and Dissonance in Free Movement' (2001) 4 *Cambridge Yearbook of European Legal Studies* 315.

——, 'So Close and Yet So Far: the Paradoxes of Mutual Recognition' (2007) 14 *Journal of European Public Policy* 814.

——, 'Interpreting European Law: Judicial Adjudication in a Context of Constitutional Pluralism' (2007) 1 *European Journal of Legal Studies* 1.

—— and Weiler, JHH, 'Editorial' (1999) 5 *European Law Journal* 85.

Maisto, G, 'The Abuse of Rights under Italian Tax Law: an Outline' (1991) 19 *Intertax* 93.

Malherbe, J et al, 'Simulation in Belgian Fiscal Law: a Modest Proposal for a Clear Legislative Solution' (1991) 19 *Intertax* 88.

Mancini, GF, 'The Making of a Constitution for Europe' (1989) 26 *Common Market Law Review* 595.

Manning, JF, 'What Divides Textualists from Purposivists?' (2006) 106 *Columbia Law Review* 70.

Marceau, G and Reiman, C, 'When and How Is a Regional Trade Agreement Compatible with the WTO?' (2001) 28 *Legal Issues of Economic Integration* 297.

Marenco, G, 'Pour une interprétation traditionnelle de la notion de mesure d'effet équivalent à une restriction quantitative' (1984) 20 *Cahiers de droit Européen* 291.

Marsh, NS, 'Deduction and Induction in the Law of Torts: A Comparative Approach' (1951) 33 *Journal of Comparative Legislation and International Law* 59.

Martin Osante, JM, 'European Union Maritime Legislation at the Crossroad' (2009) 26 *Annuaire de Droit Maritime et Océanique* 235.
Masciandaro, D, 'Offshore Financial Centres: the Political Economy of Regulation' (2008) 26 *European Journal of Law and Economics* 307.
Mataija, M, 'Internal Situations in Community Law: An Uncertain Safeguard of Competences Within the Internal Market' (2009) 5 *Croatian Yearbook of European Law and Policy* 31.
Matteotti, R, 'Interpretation of Tax Treaties and Domestic General Anti-Avoidance Rules – A Sceptical Look at the 2003 Update to the OECD Commentary' (2005) 33 *Intertax* 336.
Maubernard, C, 'Cour de justice, 30 septembre 2003, Kamer van Koophandel en Fabrieken voor Amsterdam et Inspire Art Ltd.' (2003-04) 2 *Revue des affaires européennes* 304.
Maublanc, J-P, 'Réévaluation de l'abus de droit à la lumière de la jurisprudence communautaire sur les pratiques abusives' (2007) 507 *Revue du Marché Commun et de L'Union Européenne* 267.
Mayes, DG, 'The Effects of Economic Integration on Trade' (1978) 17 *Journal of Common Market Studies* 1.
Mayrand, A, 'Abuse of Rights in France and Quebec' (1974) 34 *Lousiana Law Review* 993.
Mazzoni, 'Atti emulativi, utilità sociale e abuso del diritto' (1969) 15 *Rivista di diritto civile* 601.
McCarthy, HL, 'Abuse of Rights: the Effect of the Doctrine on VAT Planning' (2007) 2 *British Tax Review* 160.
Merks, P, 'Dutch Dividend Withholding Tax in Corporate Cross-border Scenarios, Dividend Stripping and Abuse-of-Law (Part I)' (2003) 31 *Intertax* 450.
——, 'Dutch Dividend Withholding Tax in Corporate Cross-border Scenarios, Dividend Stripping and Abuse-of-Law (Part II)' (2004) 32 *Intertax* 51.
Meyer, MJ, 'When not to Claim your Rights: the Abuse and the Virtuous Use of Rights' (1997) 5 *Journal of Political Philosophy* 149.
Michaels, R, 'The Re-State-ment of Non-State Law: The State, Choice of Law, and the Challenge from Global Legal Pluralism' (2005) 51 *Wayne Law Review* 1209.
——, 'Two Paradigms of Jurisdiction' (2006) 27 *Michigan Journal of International Law* 1003.
——, 'The New European Choice-of-Law Revolution' (2008) 82 *Tulane Law Review* 1607.
—— and Jansen, N, 'Private Law beyond the State – Europeanization, Globalization, Privatization' (2006) 54 *American Journal of Comparative Law* 843.
Mitchell, AD, 'Good Faith in WTO Dispute Settlement' (2006) 7 *Melbourne Journal of International Law* 339.
Mongouachon, C, 'L'ordolibéralisme: Contexte historique et contenu dogmatique' (2011) 4 *Concurrences* 70.
Morgan, B, 'Oh, Reason Not the Need: Rights and Other Imperfect Alternatives for those without Voice' (1999) 24 *Law & Social Inquiry* 295.
Morin, M, 'La Condition de Nationalité du Capitaine de Navire Français' (1999) 17 *Annuaire de Droit Maritime et Océanique* 153.
——, 'The Fisheries Resources in the European Union – The Distribution of TACs: Principle of Relative Stability and Quota-Hopping' (2000) 24 *Marine Policy* 265.
Morse, G, 'HMRC v Principal and Fellows of Newnham College in the University of Cambridge: VAT Anti-avoidance – the End of an Era?' (2008) 5 *British Tax Review* 542.
Mortelmans, K, 'Towards Convergence in the Application of the Rules on Free Movement and on Competition?' (2001) 38 *Common Market Law Review* 613.

Muir Watt, H, 'Choice of Law in Integrated and Interconnected Markets: A Matter of Political Economy' (2002–03) 9 *Columbia Journal of European Law* 383.
——, 'Aspects économiques du droit international privé – Réflexions sur l'impact de la globalisation économique sur les fondements des conflits de lois et de juridictions' (2005) *Recueil des Cours de l'Académie de Droit International* 25.
Mullady, RK, 'Regulatory Disparity: The Constitutional Implications of Communications Regulations that Prevent Competitive Neutrality' (2007) 7 *Pittsburgh Journal of Technology Law & Policy* 1.
Neuhaus, PH, 'Legal Certainty versus Equity in the Conflict of Laws' (1963) 28 *Law and Contemporary Problems* 795.
Neville Brown, L and Boyron, S, 'L'Affaire Factortame: Droit Communautaire contre Droit Public Anglais' (1994) 10 *Revue Française de Droit Administratif* 70.
Nicolaides, P, 'Fiscal Aid in the EC: A Critical Review of Current Practice' (2001) 24 *World Competition* 319.
Nicolaïdis, K, 'Trusting the Poles? Constructing Europe through Mutual Recognition' (2007) 14 *Journal of European Public Policy* 682.
—— and Schmidt, SK, 'Mutual Recognition "on Trial": the Long Road to Services Liberalization' (2007) 14 *Journal of European Public Policy* 717.
Nielsen, SB, Schou, P and Søbygaard, JK, 'Elements of Income Tax Evasion and Avoidance in Denmark' (2002) 9 *Swedish Economic Policy Review* 139.
Nizzo, C, 'L'abuso dei "diritti comunitari": un quesito non risolto' (1997) 11 *Diritto del Commercio Internazionale* 761.
Nordberg, C, 'Judicial Remedies for Private Parties Under the State Aid Procedure' (1997) 24 *Legal Issues of Economic Integration* 35.
Norman Veasey, E and Di Guglielmo, CT, 'What Happened in Delaware Corporate Law and Governance from 1992-2004? A Retrospective on Some Key Developments' (2005) 153 *University of Pennsylvania Law Review* 1399.
Nuyts, A, 'Les principes directeurs de l'Institut de droit international sur le recours à la doctrine du forum non conveniens et aux antisuit injunctions' (2003) 2 *Revue Belge de Droit International* 536.
O'Brien, C, 'Real Links, Abstract Rights and False Alarms: the Relationship between the ECJ's "Real Link" Case Law and National Solidarity' (2008) 33 *European Law Review* 643.
O'Leary, S, 'Equal Treatment and EU Citizens: A New Chapter On Cross-Border Educational Mobility and Access to Student Financial Assistance' (2009) 34 *European Law Review* 612.
O'Shea, T, 'The UK's CFC Rules and the Freedom of Establishment: Cadbury Schweppes plc and its IFSC Subsidiaries – Tax Avoidance or Tax Mitigation?' (2007) 16 *EC Tax Review* 13.
Ogus, A, 'Competition between National Legal Systems: A Contribution of Economic Analysis to Comparative Law' (1999) 48 *International and Comparative Law Quarterly* 405.
Ohlin, B et al, 'Social Aspects of European Economic Co-operation (Summary of the Ohlin Report)' (1956) 74 *International Labour Review* 99.
Olson, M, Jr, 'The Principle of "Fiscal Equivalence": The Division of Responsibilities among Different Levels of Government' (1969) 59 *American Economic Review* 479.
Orrego, C, 'H.L.A. Hart's Understanding of Classical Natural Law Theory' (2004) 24 *Oxford Journal of Legal Studies* 287.

Ortino, M, 'The Role and Functioning of Mutual Recognition in the European Market of Financial Services' (2007) 56 *International & Comparative Law Quarterly* 309.

Ottolenghi, S, 'From Peeping behind the Corporate Veil, to Ignoring It Completely' (1990) 53 *The Modern Law Review* 338.

Palmer, VV, 'From Embrace to Banishment: A Study of Judicial Equity in France' (1999) 47 *The American Journal of Comparative Law* 277.

Panopoulos, G, 'Pour une nouvelle compréhension du droit international des sociétés à la lumière de la jurisprudence de la Cour de justice: du conflit de lois au conflit d'autorités' (2006) 5–6 *Cahiers de droit Européen* 697.

Parai, AK and Yu, ESH, 'Factor Mobility and Customs Unions Theory' (1989) 55 *Southern Economic Journal* 842.

Park, WW, 'Fiscal Jurisdiction and Accrual Basis Taxation: Lifting the Corporate Veil to Tax Foreign Company Profits' (1978) 78 *Columbia Law Review* 1609.

Parleani, G, 'Relocation and Taxation: the European Court of Justice Disallows the French Rule of Direct Taxation of Unrealised Gains' (2004) 1 *European Company and Financial Law Review* 379.

Paunio, E, 'Beyond Predictability – Reflections on Legal Certainty and the Discourse Theory of Law in the EU Legal Order' (2009) 10 *German Law Journal* 1469.

Peglow, K, 'Le libre prestation de services dans la Directive 2006/123/CE' (2008) 44 *Revue Trimestrielle de Droit Européen* 67.

Pelkmans, J, 'Economic Theories of Integration Revisited' (1980) 18 *Journal of Common Market Studies* 333.

——, 'Mutual Recognition in Goods: On Promises and Disillusions' (2007) 14 *Journal of European Public Policy* 699.

—— and Sun, J-M, 'Regulatory Competition in the Single Market' (1995) 33 *Journal of Common Market Studies* 67.

Perillo, JM, 'Abuse of Rights: a Pervasive Legal Concept' (1995) 27 *Pacific Law Journal* 37.

Perrou, K, 'The Judicial Application of Anti-Avoidance Doctrines in Greece and its Impact on International Tax Law' (2006) 34 *Intertax* 101.

Pescatore, P, 'Some Critical Remarks on the Single European Act' (1987) 24 *Common Market Law Review* 9.

Petkova, S, 'Treaty Shopping? The Perspective of National Regulators' (2004) 32 *Intertax* 543.

Piantavigna, P, 'Tax Abuse in European Union Law: A Theory' (2011) 20 *EC Tax Review* 134.

Pickup, DMW, 'Reverse Discrimination and Freedom of Movement for Workers' (1986) 23 *Common Market Law Review* 135.

Pildes, RH and Sunstein, CR, 'Reinventing the Regulatory State' (1995) 62 *The University of Chicago Law Review* 1.

Pirovano, A, 'La fonction sociale des droits: Réflexions sur le destin des théories de Josserand' (1972) 2nd Chronique *Recueil Dalloz Sirey* 67.

Pirsl, K, 'Trends, Developments, and Mutual Influences between United States Corporate Law(s) and European Community Company Law(s)' (2007–08) 14 *Columbia Journal of European Law* 277.

Plender, R, 'Quo vadis? Nouvelle orientation des règles sur la libre circulation des personnes suivant l'affaire Akrich' (2004) 1–2 *Cahiers de droit Européen* 261.

Pochet, C, 'Fédéralisme, Droit des Sociétés et Gouvernance d'Entreprise: quelles Leçons l'Europe peut-elle tirer de l'Expérience Américaine?' (2006) XX *Revue internationale de droit économique* 285.

Pogorelova, L, 'Transfer Pricing and Anti-abuse Rules' (2009) 37 *Intertax* 683.
Politis, N-S, 'Le problème des limitations de la souveraineté et la théorie de l'abus de droit dans les rapports internationaux' (1925) 6 *Recueil des Cours de l'Académie de Droit International* 1.
Pollicino, O, 'Legal Reasoning of the Court of Justice in the Context of the Principle of Equality between Judicial Activism and Self-restraint' (2004) 5 *German Law Journal* 283.
Poole, KT and Rosenthal, H, 'The Enduring Nineteenth-Century Battle for Economic Regulation: The Interstate Commerce Act Revisited' (1993) 36 *Journal of Law and Economics* 837.
Radaelli, CM, 'Harmful Tax Competition in the EU: Policy Narratives and Advocacy Coalitions' (1999) 37 *Journal of Common Market Studies* 661.
——, 'The Puzzle of Regulatory Competition' (2004) 24 *Journal of Public Policy* 1.
Raz, J, 'Legal Principles and the Limits of Law Legal Principles and the Limits of Law' (1972) 81 *Yale Law Journal* 823.
Redfern, L, 'Rights in Land: Legal Status of the Spite Fence' (1948) 46 *Michigan Law Review* 701.
Reich, N, 'Union Citizenship – Metaphor or Source of Rights?' (2001) 7 *European Law Journal* 4.
Reid, E, 'Abuse of Rights in Scots Law' (1998) 2 *Edinburgh Law Review* 129.
——, 'The Doctrine of Abuse of Rights: Perspective from a Mixed Jurisdiction' (2004) 8 *Electronic Journal of Comparative Law* 1.
Ridsdale, M, 'Abuse of Rights, Fiscal Neutrality and VAT' (2005) 2 *EC Tax Review* 82.
Ringe, W-G, 'No Freedom of Emigration for Companies?' (2005) 16 *European Business Law Review* 621.
Ripert, G, 'Abus et relativité des droits' (1929) 49 *Revue Critique de Législation et Jurisprudence* 33.
Ritter, C, 'Purely Internal Situations, Reverse Discrimination, Guimont, Dzodzi and Article 234' (2006) 31 *European Law Review* 690.
Rivier, J-M, 'Rapport général: la résidence fiscale des sociétés' (1988) 73a *Cahiers de droit fiscal international* 44.
Robin-Olivier, S, 'Libre prestation de services, marchés publics et régulation sociale: le droit européen privilégie la concurrence fondée sur le coût du travail' (2008) 44 *Revue Trimestrielle de Droit Européen* 485.
Rodiere, P, 'Les arrêts Viking et Laval, le droit de grève et le droit de négociation collective' (2008) 44 *Revue Trimestrielle de Droit Européen* 47.
Roe, MJ, 'Delaware's Competition' (2003) 117 *Harvard Law Review* 588.
——, 'Delaware's Politics' (2005) 118 *Harvard Law Review* 2491.
Rogers, JR, 'State Tax Competition and Congressional Commerce Power: the Original Prudence of Concurrent Taxing Authority' (1996) 7 *Regent University Law Review* 103.
——, 'The Law and Policy of State Tax Competition: Much Ado About Nothing?' (2006) 4 *Georgetown Journal of Law & Public Policy* 101.
Romano, C, 'Using Tax Haven under European Law: Cadbury Schweppes and CFC Rules' (2006) 2 *International Tax Law Review* 127.
Romano, R, 'The State Competition Debate in Corporate Law' (1986–87) 8 *Cardozo Law Review* 709.
Ross, M, 'Beyond Francovich' (1993) 56 *The Modern Law Review* 55.
——, 'State Aids: Maturing into a Constitutional Problem' (1995) *Yearbook of European Law* 79.

Roth, W-H, 'Case C-212/97 Centros [1999] ECR I-1459' (2000) 37 *Common Market Law Review* 147.
——, 'From Centros to Ueberseering: Free Movement of Companies, Private International Law, and Community Law' (2003) 52 *The International and Comparative Law Quarterly* 177.
Rott, P, 'Minimum Harmonization for the Completion of the Internal Market? The Example of Consumer Sales Law' (2003) 40 *Common Market Law Review* 1107.
Roussos, A, 'Realising the Free Movement of Companies' (2001) 12 *European Business Law Review* 7.
Roxan, I, 'General Anti-avoidance in Action – News from Canada' (1998) 2 *British Tax Review* 140.
Ruiz Almendral, V, 'Tax Avoidance and the European Court of Justice: What is at Stake for European General Anti-Avoidance Rules?' (2005) 33 *Intertax* 562.
Ryan, PS, 'Case C-167/01 *Inspire Art* [2003] ECR I-10155' (2004) 11 *Columbia Journal of European Law* 187.
Sachdeva, AM, 'Regulatory Competition in European Company Law' (2010) 30 *European Journal of Law and Economics* 137.
Sauter, W, 'The Economic Constitution of the European Union' (1998) 4 *Columbia Journal of European Law* 27.
Saville, J, 'Sleeping Partnership and Limited Liability, 1850-1856' (1956) 8 *Economic History Review (NS)* 418.
Saydé, A, 'One Law, Two Competitions: An Enquiry into the Contradictions of Free Movement Law' (2010–11) 13 *Cambridge Yearbook of European Legal Studies* 365.
Schammo, P, 'Arbitrage and Abuse of Rights in the EC Legal System' (2008) 14 *European Law Journal* 351.
Scharpf, FW, 'The Joint-Decision Trap: Lessons from German Federalism and European Integration' (1988) 66 *Public Administration* 239.
——, 'The European Social Model: Coping with the Challenges of Diversity' (2002) 40 *Journal of Common Market Studies* 645.
——, 'The Joint Decision Trap Revisited' (2006) 44 *Journal of Common Market Studies* 845.
Schenk, DH, 'The Cuno Case: A Comparison of U.S. Subsidies and European State Aid' (2006) 3 *European State Aid Law Quaterly* 3.
Schiltz, C, 'Akrich: A Clear Delimitation Without Limits' (2005) 3 *Maastricht Journal of European and Comparative Law* 241.
Schlag, P, 'Rules and Standards' (1985–86) 33 *UCLA Law Review* 379.
Schmidt, SK, 'The Impact of Mutual Recognition – Inbuilt Limits and Domestic Responses to the Single Market' (2002) 9 *Journal of European Public Policy* 935.
——, 'Mutual Recognition as a New Mode of Governance' (2007) 14 *Journal of European Public Policy* 667.
Scholtens, JE, 'Abuse of Rights' (1958) 75 *South African Law Journal* 39.
Schön, W, 'Playing Different Games? Regulatory Competition in Tax and Company Law Compared' (2005) 42 *Common Market Law Review* 331.
——, 'The Mobility of Companies in Europe and the Organizational Freedom of Company Founders' (2006) 2 *European Company and Financial Law Review* 122.
Schütze, R, 'Supremacy without Pre-emption? The Very Slowly Emergent Doctrine of Community Pre-emption' (2006) 43 *Common Market Law Review* 1023.
Schwarzenberger, G, 'Uses and Abuses of the "Abuse of Rights" in International Law' (1956) 42 *Transactions of the Grotius Society* 147.

Sciarra, S, 'Integration through Coordination: The Employment Title in the Amsterdam Treaty' (2000) 6 *Columbia Journal of European Law* 209.
Seavey, WA, 'Principles of Torts' (1942) 56 *Harvard Law Review* 72.
Seer, R, 'The ECJ on the Verge of a Member State Friendly Judicature? Annotation to the Marks & Spencer Judgement' (2006) 3 *European Company and Financial Law Review* 237.
Sester, P and Cárdenas, JL, 'The Extra-Communitarian Effects of Centros, Überseering and Inspire Art with regard to Fourth Generation Association Agreements' (2005) 3 *European Company and Financial Law Review* 398.
Shilo, S, 'Kofin Al Midat S'Dom: Jewish Law's Concept of Abuse of Rights' (1980) 15 *Israel Law Review* 49.
Shouaib, M, 'Les origines coraniques de la théorie musulmane de l'abus de droit' (2001) 78 *Revue de Droit International et de Droit Comparé* 340.
Snell, J, 'The Notion of Market Access: A Concept or a Slogan?' (2010) 47 *Common Market Law Review* 437.
Sono, K and Fujioka, Y, 'The Role of the Abuse of Rights in Japan' (1975) 35 *Lousiana Law Review* 1057.
Sørensen, KE, 'Prospects for European Company Law after the Judgment of the ECJ in Centros Ltd' (1999) 2 *Cambridge Yearbook of European Legal Studies* 203.
——, 'Abuse of Rights in Community Law: a Principle of Substance or Merely Rhetoric?' (2006) 43 *Common Market Law Review* 423.
——, 'Dennis Weber, Tax Avoidance and the EC Treaty Freedoms: A Study of the Limitations under European Law to the Prevention of Tax Avoidance' (2007) 44 *Common Market Law Review* 212.
—— and Neville, M, 'Corporate Migration in the European Union' (2000) 6 *Columbia Journal of European Law* 181.
Sørensen, PB, 'Tax Coordination in the European Union: What are the Issues?' (2001) 8 *Swedish Economic Policy Review* 143.
Spaventa, E, 'From Gebhard to Carpenter: Towards a (non-)economic European Constitution' (2004) 41 *Common Market Law Review* 743.
——, 'Seeing the Wood despite the Trees? On the Scope of Union Citizenship and its Constitutional Effects' (2008) 45 *Common Market Law Review* 13.
Stadlmeier, S, 'Milestones on the Road to Keck' (2006) 2 *Croatian Yearbook of European Law and Policy* 51.
Stein, E, 'The European Coal and Steel Community: The Beginning of Its Judicial Process' (1955) 55 *Columbia Law Review* 985.
——, 'Assimilation of National Laws as a Function of European Integration' (1964) 58 *American Journal of International Law* 1.
——, 'Conflict-of-Laws Rules by Treaty: Recognition of Companies in a Regional Market' (1970) 68 *Michigan Law Review* 1327.
——, 'Harmonization of European Company Laws' (1972) 37 *Law and Contemporary Problems* 318.
——, 'Lawyers, Judges, and the Making of a Transnational Constitution' (1981) 75 *American Journal of International Law* 1.
——, 'International Integration and Democracy: No Love at First Sight' (2001) 95 *American Journal of International Law* 489.
Stone, FF, 'Touchstones of Tort Liability' (1950) 2 *Stanford Law Review* 259.
Streeck, W, 'On Suzanne Berger – How We Compete: What Companies Around the World Are Doing to Make it in Today's Global Economy' (2009) 7 *Socio-Economic Review* 505.

Strumia, F, 'Citizenship and Free Movement: European and American Features of a Judicial Formula for Increased Comity' (2006) 12 *Columbia Journal of European Law* 713.
Subiotto, R and Annacker, C, 'Free Movement of Goods and the Protection of Trademarks' (2005) 5 *The Journal of World Intellectual Property* 933.
Subramanian, G, 'The Influence of Antitakeover Statutes on Incorporation Choice: Evidence on the "Race" Debate and Antitakeover Overreaching' (2002) 150 *University of Pennsylvania Law Review* 1795.
——, 'The Disappearing Delaware Effect' (2004) 20 *Journal of Law, Economics, & Organization* 32.
Surrey, SS, 'Definitional Problems in Capital Gains Taxation' (1956) 69 *Harvard Law Review* 985.
Sussman, MJ, 'Countervailing Duties and the Specificity Test: an Alternative Approach to the Definition of Bounty or Grant' (1986) 18 *Law and Policy in International Business* 475.
Szladits, C, 'Foreign Law in English' (1983) 31 *The American Journal of Comparative Law* 158.
Szyszczak, E, 'European Community Law: New Remedies, New Directions? Joined Cases C-6/90 and C-9/90, Francovich and Bonafaci v Italy' (1992) 55 *The Modern Law Review* 690.
Taylor, GDS, 'The Content of the Rule against Abuse of Rights in International Law' (1972-73) 46 *British Yearbook of International Law* 324.
Tenore, M, 'Taxation of Cross-Border Dividends in the European Union from Past to Future' (2010) 19 *EC Tax Review* 74.
Tetley, W, 'Evasion/Fraude à la Loi and Avoidance of the Law' (1994) 39 *McGill Law Journal* 303.
Thompson, S, 'Was Ancient Rome A Dead Wives Society? What Did The Roman Paterfamilias Get Away With?' (2006) 31 *Journal Of Family History* 3.
Thym, D, 'United in Diversity: the Integration of Enhanced Cooperation into the European Constitutional Order' (2005) 6 *German Law Journal* 1731.
Tiebout, CM, 'A Pure Theory of Local Expenditure' (1956) 64 *Journal of Political Economy* 416.
Toner, H, 'Case C-192/99 *R* [2001] ECR I-1237' (2002) 39 *Common Market Law Review* 881.
Trachtman, JP, 'Regulatory Competition and Regulatory Jurisdiction' (2000) 3 *Journal of International Economic Law* 331.
——, 'Economic Analysis of Prescriptive Jurisdiction' (2001–02) 42 *Virginia Journal of International Law* 1.
——, 'Embedding Mutual Recognition at the WTO' (2007) 14 *Journal of European Public Policy* 780.
Triantafyllou, D, 'Case C-367/96 *Kefalas* [1998] ECR I-2843: Abuse of Rights *versus* Primacy?' (1999) 36 *Common Market Law Review* 157.
——, 'L'interdiction des abus de droit en tant que principe général du droit communautaire' (2002) 38 *Cahiers de droit Européen* 611.
Tridimas, T, 'Knocking on Heaven's Door: Fragmentation, Efficiency and Defiance in the Preliminary Reference Procedure' (2003) 40 *Common Market Law Review* 9.
Trubek, DM, 'Max Weber on Law and the Rise of Capitalism' (1972) *Wisconsin Law Review* 720.
Tryfonidou, A, 'Reverse Discrimination in Purely Internal Situations: An Incongruity in a Citizens' Europe' (2008) 35 *Legal Issues of Economic Integration* 43.

——, 'Family Reunification Rights of (Migrant) Union Citizens: Towards a More Liberal Approach' (2009) 15 *European Law Journal* 634.
Vaccaro, E, 'Transfer of Seat and Freedom of Establishment in European Company Law' (2005) 16 *European Business Law Review* 1348.
Vagts, DF, 'Extraterritoriality and the Corporate Governance Law' (2003) 97 *The American Journal of International Law* 289.
Van Gerven, W, 'Principe de Proportionnalité, Abus de Droit et Droits Fondamentaux' (1992) 5629 *Journal des Tribunaux* 305.
Van Ommeslaghe, P, 'Abus de Droit, Fraude aux Droits des Tiers et Fraude à la Loi' (1976) *Revue Critique de Jurisprudence Belge* 303.
Vanistendael, F, 'Halifax and Cadbury Schweppes: One Single European Rheory of Abuse in Tax Law?' (2006) 15 *EC Tax Review* 192.
Vaughan, D, 'Factortame and after: A Fishy Story' (2005) 16 *European Business Law Review* 511.
Vigneron, P and Steinfeld, P, 'Arrêt Fidium Finanz: un frein à l'effet erga omnes de la libre circulation des capitaux?' (2007) 43 *Cahiers de droit Européen* 239.
Viner, J, 'International Relations Between State-Controlled National Economies' (1944) 34 *The American Economic Review* 315.
Virgo, G, 'The Tax Avoidance Rollercoaster: Yet Another New Approach' (2001) 60 *Cambridge Law Journal* 259.
Wakefield, J, 'Fisheries: a Failure of Values' (2009) 46 *Common Market Law Review* 431.
Walton, FP, 'Motive as an Element in Torts in the Common and in the Civil Law' (1909) 22 *Harvard Law Review* 501.
Wathelet, M, 'Principe de proportionnalité: utilisation disproportionnée?' (2007) *Journal des Tribunaux* 313.
Watson, A, 'Roman Slave Law and Romanist Ideology' (1983) 37 *Phoenix* 53.
Watté, N, Nuyts, A and Boularbah, H, 'Droit international privé européen' (2006) 10 *Journal de droit européen* 293.
Wattel, P, 'Circumvention of National Law; Abuse of Community Law?' (1995) 32 *Common Market Law Review* 1257.
Weatherill, S, 'The Limits of Legislative Harmonization Ten Years after Tobacco Advertising: How the Court's Case Law has become a "Drafting Guide"' (2011) 12 *German Law Journal* 827.
Webb, MC, 'Defining the Boundaries of Legitimate State Practice: Norms, Transnational Actors and the OECD's Project on Harmful Tax Competition' (2004) 11 *Global Regulation* 787.
Weber, D, 'Abuse of Law – European Court of Justice, 14 December 2000, Case C-110/99, Emsland-Stärke' (2004) 31 *Legal Issues of Economic Integration* 43.
Weiler, JHH, 'The Transformation of Europe' (1991) 100 *Yale Law Journal* 2403.
Weisbach, DA, 'Formalism in the Tax Law' (1999) 66 *The University of Chicago Law Review* 860.
Wendel, WB, 'Civil Obedience' (2004) 104 *Columbia Law Review* 363.
Went, R, 'Game, Set, and Match for Mr. Ricardo? The Surprising Comeback of Protectionism in the Era of Globalizing Free Trade' (2000) 34 *Journal of Economic Issues* 655.
White, EL, 'In Search of the Limits to Article 30 of the EEC Treaty' (1989) 26 *Common Market Law Review* 235.
Wightman, J, 'Nuisance: the Environmental Tort? Hunter v Canary Wharf in the House of Lords' (1998) 61 *The Modern Law Review* 870.

Wilgus, HL, 'The Authority of Allen v Flood' (1902) 1 *Michigan Law Review* 28.
Winner, H, 'Has Tax Competition Emerged in OECD Countries? Evidence from Panel Data' (2005) 12 *International Tax and Public Finance* 667.
Wood, DP, 'Cuno v Daimler Chrysler, Inc.: State "Aids" from an American Perspective' (2007) 6 *European State Aid Law Quarterly* 3.
——, 'State Aid Management in the United States' (2013) *European State Aid Law Quarterly* 40.
Wouters, 'Private International Law and Companies' Freedom of Establishment' (2001) 2 *European Business Organization Law Review* 101.
Wymeersch, E, 'The Transfer of the Company's Seat in European Company Law' (2003) 40 *Common Market Law Review* 661.
Yntema, HE, 'Equity in the Civil Law and the Common Law' (1966-67) 15 *The American Journal of Comparative Law* 60.
Yu, ES-H and Scully, GW, 'Domestic Distortions and the Theory of Customs Unions' (1975) 42 *Southern Economic Journal* 218.
Zalasinski, A, 'Proportionality of Anti-Avoidance and Anti-Abuse Measures in the ECJ's Direct Tax Case Law' (2007) 35 *Intertax* 310.
Zalasinski, A, 'Some Basic Aspects of the Concept of Abuse in the Tax Case Law of the European Court of Justice' (2008) 36 *Intertax* 156.
Zatschler, C, 'Review of the Judgment in Case C-88/03, Portugal v Commission (Azores Tax Regime)' (2006) *European State Aid Law Quarterly* 779.
Zelinsky, EA, 'Symposium: Daimlerchrysler v Cuno and the Constitutionality of State Tax Incentives for Economic Development: The Property Tax Issue' (2006) 4 *Georgetown Journal of Law & Public Policy* 119.
Zielke, R, 'International Tax Planning with Comtax' (2009) 37 *Intertax* 197.

Working Papers

Becht, M, Mayer, C and Wagner, HF, 'Where Do Firms Incorporate? Deregulation and the Cost of Entry', ECGI Law Working Paper, no 70/2006 (August 2007), available at http://ssrn.com/abstract=906066.

Besselink, LFM, 'The Protection of Fundamental Rights post-Lisbon', General Report of the XXVth FIDE Congress, 30 May–2 June 2012, available at www.fide2012.eu.

Capobianco, A and Christiansen, H, 'Competitive Neutrality and State-Owned Enterprises: Challenges and Policy Options', OECD Corporate Governance Working Papers (2011), available at http://dx.doi.org/10.1787/5kg9xfgjdhg6-en.

de Mooij, RA and Nicodème, G, 'Corporate Tax Policy and Incorporation in the EU', DG TAXUD Taxation Papers, no 11/2007 (November 2007).

de Sousa, AF, 'Company's Cross-border Transfer of Seat in the EU after Cartesio', Jean Monnet Working Paper, no 07/09, available at www.JeanMonnetProgram.org.

de Witte, B, 'Setting the Scene: How did Services get to Bolkestein and Why?', EUI Working Papers, LAW 2007/20, available at http://hdl.handle.net/1814/6929.

Deakin, S, 'Regulatory Competition versus Harmonization in European Company Law', ESRC Centre for Business Research, Working Paper no 163 (March 2000), available at www.cbr.cam.ac.uk/pdf/WP163.pdf.

Genschel, P, 'Mutual Recognition in Regulation and Taxation', European Union Studies Association, 2005 Biennial Conference, available at aei.pitt.edu/3087/01/eusa-genschel-290305.pdf.

Kerber, W and Van den Bergh, R, 'Unmasking Mutual Recognition: Current Inconsistencies and Future Chances', Marburg Papers on Economics, no 2007/11 (19 April 2007), available at www.uni-marburg.de/fb02/makro/forschung/gelbereihe/artikel/2007-11_kerber.pdf.

Kowalczyk, C, 'Welfare And Customs Unions', NBER Working Paper, no 3476 (October 1990), available at www.nber.org/papers/w3476.pdf.

Majone, G, 'Mutual Recognition in Federal Type Systems', EUI Working Paper, SPS 1993/1, available at http://hdl.handle.net/1814/231.

Mance, J, 'Should the Law be Certain?', The Oxford Shrieval lecture, 11 October 2011, available at www.supremecourt.gov.uk/docs/speech_111011.pdf.

Michaels, R, 'EU Law as Private International Law? Re-Conceptualising the Country-of-Origin Principle as Vested Rights Theory', ZERP Diskussionspapier, 5/2006.

Ringe, W-G, 'Forum Shopping under the EU Insolvency Regulation', Oxford Legal Studies Research Paper, no 33/2008 (August 2008), available at http://ssrn.com/abstract=1209822.

——, 'Company Law and Free Movement of Capital: Nothing Escapes the ECJ?', Oxford Legal Studies Research Papers, no 42/2008 (November 2008), available at http://ssrn.com/abstract=1295905.

——, 'Sparking Regulatory Competition in European Company Law – The Impact of the Centros Line of Case-Law and its Concept of "Abuse of Law"', Oxford Legal Research Paper Series, no 2/2009 (January 2009), available at http://ssrn.com/abstract=1326964.

Sauve, J-M, 'L'abus de droit en matière fiscale', Les Entretiens du Palais-Royal (7 Mars 2007), available at www.conseil-etat.fr/cde/media/document/abus_de_droit_070307.pdf.

Spamann, H, 'Choice of Law in a Federal System and an Internal Market', Jean Monnet Working Paper, 8/01 (2001).

Suwa-Eisenmann, A and Verdier, T, 'Reciprocity and the Political Economy of Harmonization and Mutual Recognition of Regulatory Measures', Centre for Economic Policy Research, Discussion Paper, no 3147 (January 2002), available at www.cepr.org/pubs/dps/DP3147.asp.

UK Office of Fair Trading, 'Competition in Mixed Markets: Ensuring Competitive Neutrality', OFT Working Papers, OFT1242 (July 2010), available at www.oft.gov.uk/shared_oft/economic_research/oft1242.pdf.

Weisbach, DA, 'An Economic Analysis of Anti-Tax Avoidance Doctrines', John M Olin Law & Economics Working Paper, no 99 (17 May 2002), available at www.jstor.org/stable/1600430.

Policy Documents

Comite Intergouvernemental créé par la Conférence de Messine, 'Rapport des Chefs de Délégation aux Ministres des Affaires Étrangères' (Rapport Spaak), 21 April 1956, available at aei.pitt.edu/996/01/Spaak_report_french.pdf

Council (EC), 'General Programme for the abolition of restrictions on freedom of establishment' (Resolution), 18 December 1961, C2/36

——, 'General Programme for the abolition of restrictions on freedom to provide services' (Resolution), 18 December 1961, C2/32

Commission (EC), 'Proposal for a Council Directive on mutual recognition of diplomas, certificates and other qualifications of self-employed architects' COM (67) 155 final, 3 May 1967

Council (EC), 'General Programme for the elimination of technical barriers to trade which result from disparities between national legislations' (Resolution), 7 March 1968, C48/24

European Economic and Social Committee (EC), 'The General Programme for the elimination of technical barriers to trade which result from disparities between national legislations' (Opinion), 26 June 1968, C132/1

Parliament (EC), 'The Commission proposal on a General Programme for the elimination of technical barriers to trade which result from disparities between national legislations' (Report), 19 September 1968, Session 1968–1969, Document 114

Council (EC), 'Mutual recognition of checks' (Resolution), 28 May 1969, C76/7

——, 'General Programme for the elimination of technical barriers to trade which result from disparities between the provisions laid down by law, regulation or administrative action in Member States' (Resolution), 28 May 1969, C76/1

——, 'Programme for the elimination of technical barriers to trade in foodstuffs which result from disparities between the provisions laid down by law, regulation or administrative action in Member States' (Resolution), 28 May 1969, C76/5

——, 'Programme for the elimination of technical barriers to trade in industrial products which result from disparities between the provisions laid down by law, regulation or administrative action in Member States' (Resolution), 28 May 1969, C76/1

——, 'Supplementing the Resolution of 28 May 1969 establishing a programme for the elimination of technical obstacles to trade in industrial products, resulting from disparities between laws, regulations or administrative provisions in the Member States' (Resolution), 21 May 1973, C38/1

——, 'Measures to be taken by the Community in order to combat international tax evasion and avoidance' (Resolution), 10 February 1975, C35/1

Commission (EC), 'The scope for convergence of tax systems in the Community' (Report) COM (80) 139 final, 27 March 1980

——, 'The consequences of the judgment given by the Court of Justice on 20 February 1979 in case 120/78 (Cassis de Dijon)' (Communication), 3 October 1980, C256/2

——, 'Completing the internal market' (White Paper) COM (85) 310 final, 14 June 1985

European Economic and Social Committee (EC), 'The Proposal for a Council Regulation amending Regulation 1408/71 on the application of social security schemes to employed persons, to self-employed persons and to members of their families moving within the Community and Regulation 574/72 laying down the procedure for implementing Regulation 1408/71' (Opinion), 23 March 1988, C134/1

Commission (EC), 'Europe 1992: the overall challenge' (Summary of the Cecchini Report) SEC (88) 254 final, 13 April 1988
——, 'Second Survey on State Aids in the European Community in the manufacturing and certain other sectors' (Communication) SEC (90) 1165/3, 10 July 1990
——, 'Application of Articles 92 and 93 of the EEC Treaty and of Article 5 of Commission Directive 80/723/EEC of 25 June 1980 on the transparency of financial relations between Member States and public undertakings to public undertakings in the manufacturing sector' (Communication), 13 November 1993, C307/3
——, 'Management of the mutual recognition of national rules after 1992' (Communication) COM (93) 669 final, 15 December 1993
——, 'Proposal for a Council Regulation (EC, Euratom) on protection of the Community's financial interests' COM (94) 214 final, 7 July 1994
European Economic and Social Committee (EC), 'The regional structure of world trade' (Opinion), 15 September 1994, C393/30
Council (EC), 'Certain aspects for a European Union social policy: a contribution to economic and social convergence in the Union' (Resolution), 6 December 1994, C368/6
Essen European Council (EC), 'Presidency Conclusions', 9–10 December 1994, available at www.europarl.europa.eu/summits/
Council (EC), 'Debate on the Proposal for a Council Regulation (EC, Euratom) on protection of the Community's financial interests' (Legislative Procedure CNS/1994/0146), 20 March 1995
——, '1856th Meeting: ECOFIN' (Press Release) PRES/95/193, 19 June 1995
——, '1862nd Meeting: Labour and Social Affairs' (Press Release) PRES/95/199, 29 June 1995
Tax Law Reform Committee, 'Interim Report on Tax Legislation' (IFS Report), 23 November 1995, available at www.ifs.org.uk/publications/1913
Council (EC), 'Act adopted by Council after consultation of Parliament' (Legislative Procedure CNS/1994/0146), 18 December 1995
Commission (EC), 'The 1996 Single Market Review: background information for the Report to the Council and European Parliament' (Staff Working Paper) SEC (96) 2378, 16 December 1996
European Economic and Social Committee (EC), 'The Proposal for a European Parliament and Council Directive on the resale right for the benefit of the author of an original work of art' (Opinion), 18 December 1996, C75/17
Commission (EC), 'A European initiative in electronic commerce' (Communication) COM (97) 157 final, 16 April 1997
——, 'Freedom to provide services and the interest of the general good in the Second Banking Directive' (Interpretative Communication) SEC (97) 1193 final, 20 June 1997
Parliament (EC), 'Need for greater transparency in the Commission' (Written Question no 2392/97), 10 July 1997, C76/98
Commission (EC), 'Towards tax co-ordination in the European Union: a package to tackle harmful tax competition' (Communication) COM (97) 495 final, 1 October 1997
Council (EC), 'Concerning taxation policy' (Conclusions of the ECOFIN Council Meeting), 1 December 1997, C2/1
——, 'A code of conduct for business taxation' (Resolution), 1 December 1997, C2/2
OECD, 'Harmful Tax Competition: an Emerging Global Issue' (Report), 8 April 1998

Council (EC), 'Explanatory Report on the Convention on Jurisdiction and the Recognition and Enforcement of Judgments in Matrimonial Matters' (Borrás Report), 28 May 1998, C221/27

Parliament (EC), 'Indirect tax harmonization' (Written Question no 1898/98), 16 June 1998, C50/111

Commission (EC), 'Framework on training aid' (Communication), 11 November 1998, C343/10

——, 'Application of the State aid rules to measures relating to direct business taxation' (Notice), 10 December 1998, C384/ 3

——, 'Proposal for appropriate measures under Article 93(1) of the EC Treaty concerning Irish corporation tax' (State Aid E/2/98), 18 December 1998, C395/19

——, 'Proposal for appropriate measures under Article 93(1) of the EC Treaty concerning the International Financial Service Centre and Shannon customs-free airport zone' (State Aid E/1/98), 18 December 1998, C395/14

Parliament (EC), 'Proposal for a European Parliament and Council Directive on certain legal aspects of electronic commerce in the internal market' (Report) A4-0248/99, 23 April 1999

European Economic and Social Committee (EC), 'The Proposal for a European Parliament and Council Directive on certain legal aspects of electronic commerce in the internal market' (Opinion), 29 April 1999

Commission (EC), 'Mutual recognition in the context of the follow-up to the action plan for the single market' (Communication) COM (99) 299 final, 16 June 1999

Tampere European Council (EC), 'Presidency Conclusions', 15-16 October 1999, available at www.europarl.europa.eu/summits/

Council (EC), 'Mutual recognition' (Resolution), 28 October 1999, C141/5

——, 'Code of Conduct on Business Taxation' (Report from the Code of Conduct Group) SN 4901/99, 23 November 1999

Commission (EC), 'Regional Socio-Economic Studies on Employment and the Level of Dependency on Fishing' (Executive Summary), February 2000

——, 'Freedom to provide services and the general good in the insurance sector' (Interpretative Communication), 16 February 2000, C43/5

——, 'Proposal for a Directive of the European Parliament and of the Council amending Council Directive 95/21/EC concerning the enforcement, in respect of shipping using Community ports and sailing in the waters under the jurisdiction of the Member States, of international standards for ship safety, pollution prevention and shipboard living and working conditions (port State control)' COM (2000) 142 final, 21 March 2000

Lisbon European Council (EC), 'Presidency Conclusions', 23-24 March 2000, available at www.europarl.europa.eu/summits/

OECD, 'Towards Global Tax Co-operation: Progress in Identifying and Eliminating Harmful Tax Practices' (Report to the 2000 Ministerial Council Meeting and Recommendations by the Committee on Fiscal Affairs), June 2000

European Economic and Social Committee (EC), 'Mutual recognition in the single market' (Opinion), 29 November 2000, C116/14

Commission (EC), 'E-commerce and financial services' (Communication) COM (2001) 66 final, 7 February 2001

——, 'Towards an Internal Market without tax obstacles' (Communication) COM (2001) 582 final, 23 October 2001

——, 'Second biennial report on the application of the principle of mutual recognition in the single market' COM (2002) 419 final, 23 July 2002

——, 'The state of the internal market for services' (Report) COM (2002) 441 final, 30 July 2002

——, 'Action Plan to Counter the Social, Economic and Regional Consequences of the Restructuring of the EU Fishing Industry' (Communication) COM (2002) 600 final, 6 November 2002

Parliament (EC), 'Heavily fisheries-dependent regions, relative stability and access to fishery resources' (Written Question E-3187/02), 7 November 2002, 2003 C155E/106

——, 'Facilitating the access of products to the markets of other Member States: the practical application of mutual recognition' (Interpretative Communication), 4 November 2003, C265/02

——, 'First Report on the application of Directive 2000/31/EC of the European Parliament and of the Council of 8 June 2000 on certain legal aspects of information society services, in particular electronic commerce, in the Internal Market' COM (2003) 702 final, 21 November 2003

——, 'Extended impact assessment of Proposal for a Directive on services in the internal market' (Staff Working Paper) SEC (2004) 21, 13 January 2004

——, 'Community guidelines on State aid to maritime transport' (Communication) C (2004) 43, 17 January 2004

——, 'Implementation of the Commission Notice on the application of the State aid rules to measures relating to direct business taxation' (Report) COM (2004) 434, 9 February 2004

——, 'Proposal for a Directive of the European Parliament and of the Council on services in the internal market' COM (2004) 2 final/3, 5 March 2004

OECD, 'Guidance in Applying the 1998 Report to Preferential Tax Regimes' (Consolidated Application Note), 22 March 2004

Commission (EC), 'Guidelines on the effect on trade concept contained in Articles 81 and 82 of the Treaty' (Notice), 27 April 2004, C101/81

——, 'Approximation, mutual recognition and enforcement of criminal sanctions in the European Union' (Green Paper) COM (2004) 334 final, 30 April 2004

OECD, 'A Process for Achieving a Global Level Playing Field' (OECD Global Forum on Taxation), 3–4 June 2004

Commission (EC), 'The provisions of the proposal for a Directive on services in the internal market relating to the posting of workers with a particular emphasis on Article 24' (Commission Explanatory Note) 2004/0001 (COD), 5 July 2004

——, 'Preventing and combating corporate and financial malpractice' (Communication) COM (2004) 611 final, 27 September 2004

Committee of the Regions (EC), 'Proposal for a Directive of the European Parliament and of the Council on services in the internal market' (Opinion), 30 September 2004, C43/18

Commission (EC), 'Community guidelines on State aid for rescuing and restructuring firms in difficulty' (Communication), 1 October 2004, C244/2

European Economic and Social Committee (EC), 'What is the state of the enlarged Single Market? 25 Findings by the Single Market Observatory', 2004, available at www.eesc.europa.eu/.

Commission (EC), 'Mutual recognition of judicial decisions in criminal matters and the strengthening of mutual trust between Member States' (Communication) COM (2005) 195 final, 19 May 2005

——, 'State Aid Action Plan - Less and better targeted state aid: a roadmap for state aid reform 2005-2009' (Communication) COM (2005) 107 final, 7 June 2005
——, 'European Values in the Globalised World' (Communication) COM (2005) 525 final, 20 October 2005
——, 'Community guidelines on financing of airports and start-up aid to airlines departing from regional airports' (Communication), 9 December 2005, C312/1
——, 'Proposal for a Directive amending Council Directive 89/552/EEC on the coordination of certain provisions laid down by law, regulation or administrative action in Member States concerning the pursuit of television broadcasting activities' COM (2005) 646 final, 13 December 2005
Parliament (EC), 'Proposal for a Directive of the European Parliament and of the Council on services in the internal market' (Report) A6-0409/2005, 15 December 2005
Commission (EC), 'Tackling the corporation tax obstacles of small and medium-sized enterprises in the Internal Market – outline of a possible Home State Taxation pilot scheme' (Communication) COM (2005) 702 final, 23 December 2005
——, 'A citizens' agenda: delivering results for Europe' (Communication) COM (2006) 211 final, 10 May 2006
Council (EC), 'Code of conduct for the effective implementation of the Convention on the elimination of double taxation in connection with the adjustment of profits of associated enterprises', 28 July 2006, C176/8
European Economic and Social Committee (EC), 'Quality of working life, productivity and employment in the context of globalisation and demographic challenges' (Opinion), 13 September 2006, C318/157
Commission (EC), 'First progress report on the strategy for the simplification of the regulatory environment' (Working Document) COM (2006) 690 final, 14 November 2006
——, 'Modernising labour law to meet the challenges of the 21st century' (Green Paper) COM (2006) 708 final, 22 November 2006
——, 'Towards a more effective use of tax incentives in favour of R&D' (Communication) COM (2006) 728 final, 22 November 2006
——, 'Proposal for a Council Directive concerning indirect taxes on the raising of capital (recast version)' COM (2006) 760 final, 4 December 2006
——, 'Co-ordinating Member States' direct tax systems in the Internal Market' (Communication) COM (2006) 823 final, 19 December 2006
Parliament (EC), 'Application of Directive 96/71/EC on the posting of workers' (Resolution), 20 December 2006, C313E/452
Commission (EC), 'Directive 2005/36/EC: Everything you need to know about the recognition of professional qualifications' (User Guide), available at http://ec.europa.eu/internal_market/qualifications/docs/guide/users_guide_en.pdf
——, 'Relocation – Challenges and Opportunities' (EESC Special Reviews), 2006, available at www.eesc.europa.eu
Commission (EC), 'State Aid and Globalisation – the Competition Perspective' (Speech of Commissioner Neelie Kroes) SPEECH/07/259, 28 April 2007
European Economic and Social Committee (EC), 'The internal market in services – requirements as regards the labour market and consumer protection' (Opinion), 30 May 2007, C175/14
Commission (EC), 'Posting of workers in the framework of the provision of services: maximising its benefits and potential while guaranteeing the protection of workers' (Communication) COM (2007) 304 final, 13 June 2007
——, 'Sport' (White Paper) COM (2007) 391 final, 11 July 2007

——, 'The EU and sport: background and context' (Staff Working Document) SEC (2007) 935, 11 July 2007

——, 'Sector Inquiry under Article 17 of Regulation (EC) 1/2003 on business insurance (Final Report)' (Communication) COM (2007) 556 final, 25 September 2007

——, 'On a new strategy for the Community to prevent, deter and eliminate illegal, unreported and unregulated fishing' (Communication) COM (2007) 601 final, 17 October 2007

——, 'Impact assessment on cross-border transfer of registered offices' (Impact Assessment Board Opinion) D(2007) 9740, 8 November 2007

——, 'A single market for 21st century Europe' (Communication) COM (2007) 724 final, 20 November 2007

——, 'Proposal for a Council Directive amending Directive 2006/112/EC on the common system of value added tax, as regards the treatment of insurance and financial services' COM (2007) 747 final, 28 November 2007

Confédération Fiscale Européenne, 'The Concept of Abuse in European Law, based on the Judgments of the European Court of Justice Delivered in the Field of Tax Law' (Opinion Statement of the CFE ECJ Task Force), November 2007, available at www.cfe-eutax.org/node/87

Commission (EC), 'Mobility, an instrument for more and better jobs: The European Job Mobility Action Plan (2007-2010)' (Communication) COM (2007) 773 final, 6 December 2007

——, 'The application of anti-abuse measures in the area of direct taxation' (Communication) COM (2007) 785 final, 10 December 2007

——, 'Impact assessment on the Directive on the cross-border transfer of registered office' (Staff Working Document) SEC (2007) 1707, 12 December 2007

European Economic and Social Committee (EC), 'The Proposal for a Regulation of the European Parliament and of the Council on common rules for access to the international road haulage market (recast)' (Opinion), 12 March 2008, C204/31

Commission (EC), 'Anti-abuse rules' (CCCTB WG Working Document), 26 March 2008

——, 'Community guidelines on State aid for environmental protection' (Notice), 1 April 2008, C82/1

European Economic and Social Committee (EC), 'The new trade agreements negotiations' (Opinion), 22 April 2008, C211/82

Commission (EC), 'Geographic mobility in the European Union: Optimising its economic and social benefits' (Report) Contract VT/2006/042, April 2008, available at http://ec.europa.eu/social/BlobServlet?docId=512&langId=en

Lamassoure, A, 'The citizen and the application of Community law' (Report to the President of the French Republic), 8 June 2008

Commission (EC), '"Think Small First": A "Small Business Act" for Europe' (Communication) COM (2008) 394 final, 25 June 2008

——, 'Proposal for a Council Directive implementing the agreement concluded by the European community shipowners' associations (ECSA) and the European transport workers' federation (ETF) on the maritime labour convention, 2006 and amending Directive 1999/63/EC' COM (2008) 422 final, 2 July 2008

European Economic and Social Committee (EC), 'A new European Social Action Programme' (Opinion), 9 July 2008, C27/ 99

US Government Accountability Office, 'Cayman Islands: Business and Tax Advantages Attract U.S. Persons and Enforcement Challenges Exist' (Report to the Chairman and

Ranking Member, Committee on Finance, U.S. Senate) GAO-08-778, July 2008, available at www.gao.gov/cgi-bin/getrpt?GAO-08-778

Commission (EC), 'Community law on State aid' (Vademecum), 30 September 2008, available at http://ec.europa.eu/competition/state_aid/studies_reports/studies_reports.html

——, 'The Single Market Review: one year on' (Staff Working Document) SEC (2008) 3064, 16 December 2008

Australian Productivity Commission, 'Review of Mutual Recognition Schemes' (Research Report), January 2009

European Economic and Social Committee (EC), 'The social and environmental dimension of the internal market' (Opinion), 14 January 2009, C182/1

——, 'The European Economic Recovery Plan' (Additional Opinion), 24 March 2009, C228/149

Commission (EC), 'Reform of the Common Fisheries Policy' (Green Paper) COM (2009)163 final, 22 April 2009

——, 'Promoting Good Governance in Tax Matters' (Communication) COM (2009) 201 final, 28 April 2009

Tax Justice Network, 'Where on earth are you? Major corporations and tax havens', April 2009, available at www.taxresearch.org.uk/Documents/WoERevisedVersion.pdf

OECD, 'Countering Offshore Tax Evasion' (Questions and Answers), 28 September 2009

European Economic and Social Committee (EC), 'The Proposal for a Regulation of the European Parliament and of the Council laying down the obligations of operators who place timber and timber products on the market' (Opinion), 1 October 2009, C318/88

Commission (EC), 'Report on the implementation of the SBA' (Working Document) COM (2009) 680, 15 December 2009

——, 'Current stance of European Law in relation to quota-hopping' (Written answer of the DG Fisheries), 13 January 2010

US Federal Trade Commission, 'Competition, State Aids And Subsidies' (OECD Global Forum on Competition) DAF/COMP/GF/WD(2010)67, 12 February 2010

European Economic and Social Committee (EC), 'The Lisbon Agenda and the Internal Market' (Own-Initiative Opinion), 17 February 2010, C347/8

Commission (EC), 'EUROPE 2020: A strategy for smart, sustainable and inclusive growth' (Communication) COM (2010) 2020, 3 March 2010

European Council (EC), 'Conclusions' EUCO 7/10, 26 March 2010

Commission (EC), 'A new strategy for the single market: at the service of Europe's economy and society' (Monti Report), 9 May 2010

——, 'Smart Regulation in the European Union' (Communication) COM (2010) 543 final, 8 October 2010

——, 'Towards a Single Market Act: For a highly competitive social market economy' (Communication) COM (2010) 608 final, 27 October 2010

——, 'EURES Charter' C311/6, 16 November 2010

——, 'On the future of VAT: Towards a simpler, more robust and efficient VAT system' (Green Paper) COM (2010) 695 final, 1 December 2010

Council (EC), 'Conclusions on the Single Market Act' (3057th Competitiveness Council Meeting), 10 December 2010

Commission (EC), 'Proposal for a Council Decision concerning the conclusion of the European Convention on the legal protection of services based on, or consisting of, conditional access' COM (2010) 755 final, 15 December 2010

——, 'Proposal for a Regulation of the Parliament and the Council establishing a common organisation of agricultural markets and on specific provisions for certain agricultural products (Single CMO Regulation)' COM (2010) 799 final, 21 December 2010

Commission (EC), 'Impact Assessment: Proposal for a Council Directive on a Common Consolidated Corporate Tax Base' (Staff Working Document) SEC (2011) 315 final, 16 March 2011

——, 'Single Market Act: Twelve levers to boost growth and strengthen confidence' (Communication) COM (2011) 206 final, 13 April 2011

——, 'Proposal for a Council Regulation temporarily suspending autonomous Common Customs Tariff duties on imports of certain industrial products into the Canary Islands' COM (2011) 259 final, 18 May 2011

European Economic and Social Committee (EC), 'How EU policies have impacted on the job opportunities, the training needs and the working conditions of transport workers' (Explanatory Opinion), 15 June 2011, C248/22

Commission (EC), 'Proposal for a Council Directive on a Common Consolidated Corporate Tax Base (CCCTB)' COM (2011) 121 final/2, 3 October 2011

Murphy, RF, 'Closing the European Tax Gap' (Report for Group of the Progressive Alliance of Socialists & Democrats in the European Parliament), 29 February 2012

Commission (EC), 'Proposal for a Directive of the European Parliament and of the Council on the enforcement of Directive 96/71/EC concerning the posting of workers in the framework of the provision of services' COM (2012) 131 final, 21 March 2012

Parliament (EC), 'The proposal for a Council directive on a Common Consolidated Corporate Tax Base (CCCTB)' (Report) A7-0080/2012, 28 March 2012

European Economic and Social Committee (EC), 'Tax and financial havens: a threat to the EU's internal market' (Own-Initiative Opinion) C229/02, 24 May 2012

Council (EC), 'Debate on the Proposal for a Directive of the European Parliament and of the Council on the enforcement of Directive 96/71/EC concerning the posting of workers in the framework of the provision of services' (Legislative Procedure 2012/0061(COD)), 21 June 2012

Commission (EC), 'Concrete ways to reinforce the fight against tax fraud and tax evasion including in relation to third countries' (Communication) COM (2012) 351 final, 27 June 2012

——, 'Aggressive tax planning' (Recommendation) C (2012) 8806 final, 6 December 2012

——, 'Measures intended to encourage third countries to apply minimum standards of good governance in tax matters' (Recommendation) C (2012) 8805 final, 6 December 2012

——, 'An Action Plan to strengthen the fight against tax fraud and tax evasion' (Communication) COM (2012) 722 final, 6 December 2012

——, 'Impact Assessment accompanying inter alia Commission Recommendation on aggressive tax planning' (Staff Working Document) SWD (2012) 403 final, 6 December 2012

Council (EC), 'Debate on the Proposal for a Directive of the European Parliament and of the Council on the enforcement of Directive 96/71/EC concerning the posting of workers in the framework of the provision of services' (Legislative Procedure 2012/0061(COD)), 12 December 2012

Gravelle, JG, 'Tax Havens: International Tax Avoidance and Evasion' (CRS Report for US Congress), 23 January 2013

Parliament (EC), 'Fight against Tax Fraud, Tax Evasion and Tax Havens' (Report) A7-0162/2013, 2 May 2013
Council (EC), 'Council conclusions on tax evasion and tax fraud' 9549/13, 14 May 2013
European Council (EC), 'Conclusions' EUCO 75/1/13, 22 May 2013
G8 Summit, 'Lough Erne Declaration', 18 June 2013

Index

absolute advantage, principle *see under* economic integration paradigms
abuse terminology 11–16
  categories 13
  distribution of terminology 14 *Table*, 15–16, 15 *Fig*
  methodology 378 *Annex*
  official documents 11–13
  omnipresence 13
  sample categories 13
abuses of EU law
  analytical matrix 373–5, 373 *Fig*
  artificial practices 25–6
  debate fault-lines 3, 371–3, 377
  definition 371
  holistic approach 376–7, 376 *Table*
  private individuals 24, 25–6
  teleological tests 370–1
  topicality of concept 1–3
abuses of law/abuses of right, distinction
  artificiality requirement 30
  background 27
  context of abuse 30
  harmful intent/proportionality/ reasonableness 30–1
  joint treatment 27–8
  relation to legal environment 28–30
  sanction of 31
  summary 31
Adams, W 342
Agip Petroli case *see under* free movement
Almendral, R 191, 195–6, 307
Amand, C 30
Amato, G 362
Armstrong, KA 276
artificial practices
  abuses of law 25–6
  background 102–3
  centres of gravity *see* centres of gravity test
  choice of law 3
  factual settings 103–4
  incidental prevention *see* incidental prevention
  informal doctrines *see* informal doctrines
  key issues 103
  suspect periods *see* suspect periods
artificiality requirement
  definition of abuse concept 78, 83–93, 370–1
  legal certainty 193–4
Bacon, K 182, 319, 330
bank regulation 122–3
Barnard, C 281, 310
Beck, U 354–5, 375
Blackstone, W 172–3
border tax adjustments 267–8
Bratton, WW 292
broadcasting services
  identification of phenomenon 26
  incidental prevention 151–2
  real seat theory 124–6
Brock, J 342

Cadbury Schweppes see under direct taxation avoidance
capital duties 26
centres of gravity test
  bank regulation 122–3
  broadcasting services 124–6
  driving licences 138
  economic and social interpenetration 148
  effects doctrine 133–5
  in EU law 122–31
  financial services 123
  fixed/permanent establishment 129–30
  freedom of establishment 127–9
  frontier workers 144–5, 146–7
  genuine integration requirement 141–8
  habitual residence requirements 138–41
  insolvency proceedings 130–1
  intellectual property law 135–7
  key issues 120
  legal certainty 205–6, 208
  legal persons 121–2
  Member States hosting activities 120–1
  migrant citizens/workers 143–7
  natural persons 137
  output v input 131–7
  posted workers, national security schemes 126–7
  private international law 130, 141
  real seat theory, incorporation theory, distinction 121–2
  social benefits 140, 141–2, 147–8
  social security contributions 139–40
  student funding 142–3, 145–6
  VAT avoidance 122, 129
  vehicle imports 138–9
certainty *see* legal certainty
Chen, R 228

Cheyne, I 182
choice of law
  artificial practices 3
  direct taxation avoidance 95–6
  see also definition of concept, choice of law; free choice of law
common agricultural policy 26
common law/EU context *see under* economic constitution of EU
company incorporation 96–7
  free choice of law 155–6
  see also incorporation theory
company law 26
  freedom of establishment 105
competence disputes 16–17
corporate veil lifting 111–12
Costello, C 202, 210, 362
credit institutions, reorganisation 266–7
cross-border flows 266, 267
customs duties 26

Daniel, S 212
Deakin, S 376–7
definition of concept
  ambivalent terminology 92
  artificiality requirement 78, 83–93
  choice of law
    deliberate 83
    denial 98–101
    gain-seeking 78, 79–83
    validity 78, 93–8
  components 78
  cross-border abuses 79, 80
  economic irrationality 84–9
  economic reality 89–93
  exclusive intention 84–5
  expressive terminology 84
  frauds 87
  internal abuses 79, 80
  key definition 78
  legal cloaks 80, 81 *Table*, 90, 98
  legitimate motive, absence 85–6
  naked restraint 84
  national law circumvention 97–8
  objective element 93
  physical detours 86
  real-life costs/real-life value 86–7
  rights' abuses 82
  single legal regime 80, 82
  situations distinguished 78, 79 *Table*
  sound economic decisions 87–9
  teleological assessment 93–8
Delaware effect *see under* economic integration, paradigms
Di Bucci, V 325–6
differentials of regulation *see under* free movement
Digesta case 33–4

direct taxation avoidance
  appropriateness analysis 68, 71
  Cadbury Schweppes
    decision of court 66–9, 80, 84, 95, 100
    facts 64–6
  choice of law 95–6
  company structure 65–6
  controlled foreign companies (CFCs) 64–5
  exemption of dividends 69–70
  formal doctrine application 26, 63–72
  free movement scope 66–7, 71
  incidental prevention 153
  informal doctrines 106–9
  integration objective 67
  internal market regulation 257
  proportionality analysis 68–9, 71–2
  resident companies 71
  state aids 334–7, 339 *Table*
  suspect periods 119
  Thin Cap Group Litigation
    decision of court 70–2, 80, 84, 88–9, 90, 95–6, 100
    facts 69–70
distortions of competition *see under* free movement; state aids
dominant position abuses 19–20
driving licences
  habitual residence requirements 138
  incidental prevention 151
Dworkin, R 173

economic advantage to recipients *see under* state aids
economic constitution of EU
  abuse phenomenon, historical conditions for 348–54
  concept 341–8
  current EU law 346–8
  ECSC Treaty 345–6
  enlargement of EU 353–4
  European integration process 344–6
  freedoms of movement 346–7, 360–2
  harmonisation options 356–7
  initial movement to EU 350–1
  internal market regulation, conceptual timeline 350–2, 350 *Fig*
  key issues 340–1
  legal factors 349–50
  national laws' diversity 352–3
  new communications technologies 348–9, 353–4
  ordoliberal concept 341–8
  post-WWII 342–3
  pre-integration era 350
  private mobility power
    ambivalent appraisal 360–4
    historical precedents 358–9
    new form of 358–9

origins 354–60
socioeconomic costs 355–6
territorial unity/regulatory diversity 356
private power/public power fears 362–4, 369
public power
controlled deployment 343–4
mobility threat 354–5
socioeconomic perspective 348–9
state aids 347–8, 357–8
territorial unity /regulatory diversity
private mobility power 356–7
relationship 351–2
territorial unity reduction 358
US/common law context 342
Weimar economy 341–2
economic integration paradigms
absolute advantage, principle 229
Agip Petroli case *see under* free movement
area without internal frontiers 235–6
business competition 235–42
comparative advantage
as justification for integration 230–2
principle 229–30
corrective mechanisms 240–1
Delaware effect 245, 248
efficiency argument 239–40
European Coal and Steel Community (ECSC) 235, 240, 245–6
fairness argument 239
free movement 235, 241–2
jurisdictions, competition among 242–3
key issues 227–9
law market 242
level playing field 238
local laws' role 229–35
national laws' role 233–5
producer/regulatory arbitrage 244–5
regulatory competition 242–8
regulatory diversity/mobility 247–8
regulatory neutrality 235–42
state aids 319 *Fig*
state competition 242–8
undistorted business competition 235–9
economic irrationality *see under* definition of concept
economic reality *see under* definition of concept
economic and social interpenetration 148
effects doctrine 133–5
Eidenmüller, H 114, 208
Emsland-Stärke see under export refunds, formal doctrine application
enlargement of EU 353–4
Enrich, P 320–1
establishment *see* freedom of establishment
EU citizens
free movement 105–6
nationality, free choice of law 162–3
European Coal and Steel Community (ECSC) 235, 240, 245–6
economic constitution of EU 345–6
European integration process 344–6
export refunds, formal doctrine application 25–6, 49–53
additional evidence 50–1
constitutive elements 51
differentiated/non-differentiated 49
Emsland-Stärke 44, 48, 49, 50–1, 63, 80, 84, 85, 90, 99, 104, 183–7, 198–9
decision of court 50–1
facts 50
re-exportation 49, 53
re-importation 49
specific circumstances 51
Vonk Dairy Products 52–3, 80
decision of court 52–3
facts 52

factual situations' abuses 19
family reunification rights 160–2
Fawcett, JJ 38
financial services 123
fishing quotas 26, 165–6
flight cancellations/delays 178–80
foreign partnerships, free movement 300
formal doctrines
chronological order of judgments 47
definition of abuse 45
export refunds *see* export refunds, formal doctrine application
financial interests protection 44–6
free movement *see* free movement, formal doctrine application
internal/cross-border distinction 48
key issues 44
legislative origins 44–8
reticence 45–7
seminal cases 48
tax avoidance *see* direct taxation avoidance, formal doctrine application; VAT avoidance, formal doctrine application
see also informal doctrines
forum shopping 26
fraud/frauds
definition of concept 87
identification of phenomenon 24–5
fraus legis, *fraude à la loi* 32–3, 40, 41–2
free choice of law
company incorporation *see under* company incorporation
EU citizens' nationality 162–3
fishing quotas 165–6
key issues/summary 154–5, 166
legal certainty 209–10
migrant workers 157–8
road haulage services 156

shipping nationality 163–4
social allowances 159–60
social benefits 158
third country nationals, family reunification rights 160–2
unemployment benefits 160
welfare benefits 158
workers' free movement 156–8
free movement
Agip Petroli
decision of court 73–4, 80, 95, 100
economic integration, paradigms 232–3
facts 72–3
ambivalence 221–6, 296–301
capital duties 74–5, 76
competing paradigms 224–5
competitive advantage 297–9
differentials of regulation 296–301
direct taxation 66–7, 71
distortions of competition 296–7, 299
economic constitution of EU 346–7, 360–2
economic integration, paradigms 235, 241–2
fault lines 221
foreign partnerships 300
formal doctrine application 72–7
freedom of establishment 307–8
home regulation/host regulation 267
hospitable social jurisdiction 310–11
host equality/home equality 302–3, 311–13
inconsistent prohibition 304–8
ING AUER case
decision of court 76–7, 100
facts 74–6
internal market regulation 257–9
legal certainty 203–5
Member State's role 76–7
negative harmonisation conundrum 302
private business/member states, competition 224
public power 225
regulatory competition paradigm 306–7, 313–14
regulatory mobility 222
regulatory neutrality paradigm 305–6
reverse discrimination 301–4, 309–10
social dumping 309–14
socioeconomic mobility 222–3
state aids 316
tax avoidance 299–300
terminological variety 223–4
transactional structure 75–6
types of mobility 221, 222 *Table*
voyages in ballast 72–4
Freedman, J 96
freedom of establishment 127–9, 268–9
free movement 307–8
Freiburg school 341
Friedman, M 362
frontier workers 144–5, 146–7
fundamental rights' abuses 22

Gordley, J 363
Grauberg, T 90
Graveson, R 38
Greek undertakings 22, 27, 29
Gutteridge, HC 363

Halifax see under VAT avoidance
Hanson, J 228
harmonisation options 356–7
Holmes, OW 168, 212
home regulation/host regulation *see under* free movement; internal market regulation
host equality/home equality *see under* free movement; internal market regulation
human rights abuses 17, 22
see also rights' abuses

identification of phenomenon
distinctions *see* abuses of law/abuses of right, distinction
private individuals *see* private individuals
public authorities *see* public authorities
terminology *see* abuse terminology
immigration of third country nationals 26
incidental prevention
broadcasting services 151–2
direct taxation avoidance 153
driving licences 151
key issues/summary 149, 154
legal rules/interpretations 149–50
mutual recognition exceptions 150–1
professional ethics 150–1
re-import/re-export strategies 153–4
VAT avoidance 152–3
incorporation theory 121–2, 155
holistic approach 376–7, 376 *Table*
internal market regulation 283–5
see also company incorporation
indirect tax avoidance, informal doctrines 109–11
indirect taxes 26
informal doctrines
company law, freedom of establishment 105
corporate veil lifting 111–12
direct taxation avoidance 106–9
EU citizens, free movement 105–6
indirect tax avoidance 109–11
key issues/summary 104, 113
professional qualifications, mutual recognition 106
public procurement 112–13
re-importation of goods 104–5
rule of origins 104–5
social benefits, residence-changes for 106
see also formal doctrines

ING AUER case *see under* free movement
insolvency proceedings 130–1, 206, 208
  legal certainty 206, 208
intellectual property law
  centres of gravity test 135–7
  identification of phenomenon 23
internal market regulation
  alternative regulatory modes 283
  border tax adjustments 267–8
  conceptual timeline 350–2, 350 *Fig*
  concerned groups 249–50
  consumer/producer arbitrages 277–9
  credit institutions, reorganisation 266–7
  cross-border flows 266, 267
  direct taxation avoidance 257
  free movement 257–9, 267, 294–5
  freedom of establishment 268–9
  home law/host law treatment 255, 260
  home regulation/host regulation 264–72, 272–6, 283–6
  incorporation/real seat theories 283–5
  key issues 250
  migrant workers 268, 285–6
  multiple regulation 254–9
    definition 254–5
    mandatory requirements 258
  mutual recognition 264–6, 270–2
  negative harmonisation conundrum 272–6
  positive harmonisation 259–63
    meaning 259–60
    regulatory competition paradigm 261
    regulatory neutrality paradigm 260–3
  private power/public power fears 362–4, 369
  professional qualifications 269–70
  protectionism 250–4
    border taxes/border controls 251–2
    definition 250–2
    internal measures 252–3
    multilateral regulation, distinction 251
    regulatory neutrality/regulatory competition paradigms 253–4
  regulatory immobility 280–3
  regulatory mobility dilemma 279–80
  regulatory modes 293–4
  regulatory neutrality/regulatory competition
    controversial acts 365–6
    heuristic potential 291–2
    key issues 291
    multiple regulation 255–7
    negative harmonisation conundrum 276–9
    one law, two competitions 366, 367 *Table*
    paradigm changes 366–8
    paradigms 286–90
    practical consequences 292–3
    regulatory mobility dilemma 286–90
    trade-off 291–5
  state aids 315–21, 368–9
  welfare benefits 285–6
international double taxation 257
Islamic law (shari'a) 42
Israeli law 42

Japan 42
Jewish law 42
Josserand, L 30, 39, 85, 194–5
jurisdictions, competition among *see under* economic integration, paradigms

Kjellgren, A 192, 202

labour law *see under* state aids
Latin-American countries 42
legal certainty 197–8, 201
  artificiality requirement 193–4
  centres of gravity test 205–6, 208
  congruence gap 189–92
    graphic representation 190 *Fig*
    non-adaptability 189–90
  discretion 192
  export funds 183–7
  fight against abusive practices 192–3, 201, 210
  flexible legal norms 202–10
  flight cancellations/delays 178–80
  free choice of law 209–10
  free movement 176–8, 203–5
  illusion 211–13
  inherent legal uncertainty 193–201
  insolvency proceedings 206, 208
  institutional implications 213–16, 215 *Table*
  judicial role 216–17
  key issues 167
  legal cloaks 190–1
  legal congruence, trade-off
    conflict between virtues 169–70
    EU law 175–82
    general principles of EU law 178–80
    judicial discretion 168–9
    key issues/summary 167, 170 *Table*, 175–6, 182
    proportionality analysis 177–8
    universality of 168–75
  legal norms, rigid/flexible 170–2
  literal interpretation 172–3
  non-adaptability 183
  public force 212–13
  real seat theory 205–6
  rigid EU laws 183–9
  rigid legal norms 198–201
  source of abusive practices 183–9
  State aids 182
  statutory construction 202–3
  subjective tests 193–7
  suspect periods 206–8
  tax avoidance 191–2
  teleological interpretation 173–5, 180–2

VAT avoidance 187–9
waste definition 182
legal cloaks 80, 81 *Table*, 90, 98
legal certainty 190–1
legal congruence *see* legal certainty, legal congruence, trade-off
Lenaerts, A 32
level playing field 238
Lyons, T 15

Maduro, MP 227
market abuses 20
Member States' behaviour 18
migrant citizens, habitual residence 143–7
migrant workers
free choice of law 157–8
habitual residence 143–7
internal market regulation 268, 285–6
multiple regulation *see under* internal market regulation
mutual recognition
exceptions 150–1
see also under internal market regulation

negative harmonisation *see under* internal market regulation
Neuhaus, PH 213, 373
new communications technologies 348–9, 353–4

online gambling services 257
ordoliberal concept 341–8

Padoa-Schioppa, T 244
Part Service see under VAT avoidance
Pelkmans, J 243, 265
positive harmonisation *see under* internal market regulation
posted workers, national security schemes 126–7
posting of workers 26
power abuses 16, 17
private business/member states, competition 224
private individuals
abuses of law *see* abuses of Union law
communities of 23
consumers' abuses 20
dominant position abuses 19–20
factual situations' abuses 19
fraud/frauds 24–5
fundamental rights' abuses 22
intellectual property rights 23
key issues 19
market abuses 20
private-private abuses 19–23
private-public abuses 23–6
rights' abuses 21–2
workers' abuses 21
private international law
habitual residence requirements 141
real seat theory 130
private mobility 2–3
private mobility power *see under* economic constitution of EU
private operator test *see under* state aids
producer arbitrage 244–5
professional ethics, incidental prevention 150–1
professional qualifications
internal market regulation 269–70
mutual recognition
informal doctrines 106
suspect periods 117–19
professional requirements 26
protectionism *see under* internal market regulation
public authorities 16–18
competence disputes 16–17
human rights abuses 17
Member States' behaviour 18
power abuses 16, 17
public-private abuses 17–18
public-public abuses 16–17
public international law 42
public power
free movement 225
see also under economic constitution of EU
public procurement 112–13

re-import/re-export strategies, incidental prevention 153–4
re-importation of goods
identification of phenomenon 26
informal doctrines 104–5
real seat theory
internal market regulation 283–5
legal certainty 205–6
see also under centres of gravity test
regulatory arbitrage 244
regulatory competition *see under* economic integration, paradigms
regulatory immobility *see under* internal market regulation
regulatory mobility dilemma *see under* internal market regulation
regulatory modes *see under* internal market regulation
regulatory neutrality/regulatory competition paradigms *see under* free movement; internal market regulation; state aids
relocation of businesses 1
reverse discrimination *see under* free movement
Ricardo, D 229–30
rights' abuses
definition of concept 82
identification of phenomenon 21–2
see also human rights abuses

Ringe, W-G 376
road haulage services 156
Roman law 33–5
Roosevelt, President 359
Rotondi 34
rule of origins 104–5
Russian law 42

Schammo, P 306
Schmitt von Sydow, H 246–7
Schuman Declaration 245, 349–50
Schuman Plan 344–5
selectivity requirement *see under* state aids
Sherman Act (1890) (US) 359
shipping
  nationality 163–4
  regulation 333–4, 339 *Table*
  voyages in ballast 72–4
Smith, A 229
Snell, J 202–3
social allowances, free choice of law 159–60
social benefits
  free choice of law 158
  habitual residence requirements 140, 141–2, 147–8
  identification of phenomenon 26
  residence-changes for 106
social dumping 309–14
social security
  contributions 139–40
  state aids 337–8, 339 *Table*
socioeconomic mobility, free movement 222–3
Soviet law 42
Spaak Report 318, 325–6
state aids
  definitional conditions 322–31
  direct taxation 334–7, 339 *Table*
  distortion of competition 326–7
  economic advantage to recipients 322–4
  economic constitution of EU 347–8, 357–8
  economic integration 319 *Fig*
  freedoms of movement, comparison 316
  functional parallelism with abuses of law prohibition 331–9, 339 *Table*
  internal market regulation 315–21, 368–9
  key issues 315
  labour law 338, 339 *Table*
  mandatory/optional derogations 318
  permissive approach (US) 317–18, 319–20, 321
  private operator test 322–4
  prohibition 315–18, 321–2
  selectivity requirement 324–6, 333
  ship regulation 333–4, 339 *Table*
  social security 337–8, 339 *Table*
  transfer of state resources 327–30
state competition *see under* economic integration, paradigms
student funding 142–3, 145–6, 277–8
Sun, JM 243
suspect periods
  direct taxation avoidance 119
  European arrest warrant 117
  key issues/summary 114, 120
  professional qualifications, mutual recognition 117–19
  study grants 114–16
  trade marks 119–20
  unemployment benefits 116–17
  VAT avoidance, informal doctrine application 119

tax avoidance
  free movement 299–300
  French approach 40
  legal certainty 191–2
  UK approach 38–9
  universality of prohibition 41–2
  see also direct taxation avoidance; VAT avoidance, formal doctrine application
teleological assessment *see under* definition of concept
terminology *see* abuse terminology
territorial unity/regulatory diversity *see under* economic constitution of EU
Tetley, W 38
thin capitalisation *see* direct taxation avoidance, *Thin Cap Group Litigation*
third country nationals, family reunification rights 160–2
Tiebout, CM 243, 244
Titus-Livius 34
trade marks 119–20
Triantafyllou, D 15

unemployment benefits, free choice of law 160
union law abuses 27–31
universality of prohibition
  background 32
  civil law systems 33–5, 37–8
  conceptual diversity 32
  English law approach 35–9
  fraus legis, *fraude à la loi* 32–3, 40, 41–2
  French approach 32–3, 39–40
  international pervasiveness 42
  key issues 32, 43
  tax *see* tax avoidance
US/common law context *see under* economic constitution of EU

VAT avoidance
  alternative approach 62–3
  choice of law 94–5
  consequences of ruling 60
  constitutive elements 59–60, 63
  deductable proportion 56–7

formal doctrine application 26, 53–63
Halifax
decision of court 58–60, 84, 90, 92, 94, 99
facts 55–8
immovable property, leasing/letting 54
incidental prevention 152–3
informal doctrine application 109–11
input VAT recovery 53–4
legal certainty 187–9
objectivity 58–9
Part Service
decision of court 62–3, 92, 95
facts 60–1
real seat theory 122, 129
subjective test 194–5
taxable leasing services, artificial splitting 55
transactional structures 55–6, 60–1
VAT flows 57–8, 61
vehicle imports 138–9
von Quitzow, CM 260
Vonk Dairy Products see under export refunds, formal doctrine application
voyages in ballast 72–4

Watt, G 190, 212
Weatherill, S 91, 242, 258–9, 262, 279, 292
Weber, M 373
Weiler, JHH 265, 344–5
Weimar economy 341–2
Weisbach, DA 213–14
welfare benefits
free choice of law 158
internal market regulation 285–6
workers' abuses 21
workers' free movement 156–8

Ziegler, KS 23